Bikur Cholim-Machzikay
Hadath Congregation

ArtScroll Judaica Classics®

Rabbi Nosson Scherman / Rabbi Meir Zlotowitz

General Editors

פרקי אבות
עם פירוש מלוקט מספר שפת אמת
ועוד מגדולי החסידות

With Ideas and Insights of the

SFAS EMES

and other Chassidic masters

Anthologized and Adapted by

Rabbi Yosef Stern

A PROJECT OF THE

Mesorah
Heritage
Foundation

pirkei

Published by

Mesorah Publications, ltd

FIRST EDITION
First Impression ... February 1999

Published and Distributed by
MESORAH PUBLICATIONS, LTD.
4401 Second Avenue
Brooklyn, N.Y 11232

Distributed in Europe by
J. LEHMANN HEBREW BOOKSELLERS
20 Cambridge Terrace
Gateshead, Tyne and Wear
England NE8 1RP

Distributed in Israel by
SIFRIATI / A. GITLER
10 Hashomer Street
Bnei Brak 51361

Distributed in Australia and New Zealand by
GOLDS BOOK & GIFT SHOP
36 William Street
Balaclava 3183, Vic., Australia

Distributed in South Africa by
KOLLEL BOOKSHOP
Shop 8A Norwood Hypermarket
Norwood 2196, Johannesburg, South Africa

ARTSCROLL JUDAICA CLASSICS®
PIRKEI AVOS WITH IDEAS AND INSIGHTS OF THE SFAS EMES
© Copyright 1999 by MESORAH PUBLICATIONS, Ltd.
4401 Second Avenue / Brooklyn, N.Y. 11232 / (718) 921-9000

ISBN:
1-57819-144-0 (hard cover)
1-57819-145-9 (paperback)

Typography by CompuScribe at ArtScroll Studios, Ltd.
4401 Second Avenue / Brooklyn, N.Y. 11232 / (718) 921-9000

Printed in the United States of America by Moriah Offset
Bound by Sefercraft, Quality Bookbinders, Ltd., Brooklyn N.Y. 11232

ברכה לראש משביר

למע"כ האי גברא יקירא הנדיב הדגול והחשוב
איש האשכולות

הרה"ח **יחיאל בן ציון פישאהף** הי"ו

ומשפחתו שיחיו לאוי"ט
שתמכו בהוצאת הספר

לעילוי נשמת זוגתו אמם היקרה
האשה הדגולה והחשובה רודפת צדקה וחסד

מרת **מינדל** ע"ה

(למשפחת אורבך)

נפטרה ביום הרביעי כ"ד תשרי תשמ"ט

ולעילוי נשמות הוריהם
אביו הרבני רודף צדקה וחסד

הרה"ח מוהר"ר **דוב פישאהף** ז"ל

נכד הגה"צ חסידא ופרישא

מוה"ר **זאב נחום** זצ"ל

אבדק"ק ביאלה, מח"ס אגודת אזוב

אמו האשה החשובה

מרת **מירל** ע"ה

בניהם: **אהרן אשר ויעקב יצחק**
ובנותיהם: **רבקה, בריינדל ורחל**

כולם נהרגו על קדה"ש, ונקבע היאהרצייט כ"ה אדר ב'

חותנו הרבני הנעלה

מוה"ר **ישראל ניידר** ז"ל

נפטר י"ג תשרי תשל"ט

חמותו האשה החשובה

חיה זיסע ע"ה

נפטרה ז' שבט תשל"ה

ב״ה ה׳ שמות תשנ״ב לפ״ק

לכב׳ ידידי היקר והנכבד הרה״ג חו״ב נותן טעם לשבח הרב
דוד אלעווסקי שליט״א

שלום רב!

בנידון הספר המבאר את השפ״א לסוכות אשר חיבר הרב
יוסף שטערן שליט״א – הנה כידוע לך איניני נותן הסכמות
באופן עקרוני. ובפרט כאשר השפה האנגלית אינה שגורה בפי
לא שייך בכלל שאני אעבור ע״ז ואסכים עליו. אבל כפי
ששמעתי מכם שאנשים חשובים שבחו את הספר הנני מצרף גם
ברכתי להרב המחבר שליט״א שיצליח.

והנני בזה ידידך הדושו״ט

פנחס מנחם אלטר

מכתב ברכה מאת כ"ק האדמו"ר מנאוואמינסק שליט"א
לספרי הקודם על הגדה של פסח

(718) 436-1133

RABBI YAAKOV PERLOW
1569 - 47TH STREET
BROOKLYN, N.Y. 11219

יעקב פרלוב
ביחמ"ד עדת יעקב נאוואמינסק
ברוקלין, נ.י.

בס"ד יום ב' לסדר תזריע

נכבד נעלה וחביב, הרב הגאון וכו' הנעלה
מוה"ר יוסף שי' ווינער, שלום ורב טוב.

תשואת חן חן ע"ן על דבריו היקרים לכבוד פסח
האפורה, לענין רחבי הלכות את מנהגי הקדושה והבה
על הרגל הכתוב וחות גבד. נתעוררו על פ"ז רגלים
כך ונהירו נהת על הבר על פסח. הובא הובא והפלאת לתרגם
על הבנת את והמנהגו הלהדורים של קהלת ישראל התרגמו
לאחד ועל הרקים נתלו האחת בעל ון שהרך שואה
ועל הדין גופיה את הביבד ובבה לביהי גילה להוסף את
כדורית יעקב ובעל ינום אלהים. בצורית (פ' יהדו הדעת
אחרנו כיום לעולם ועד עור ועד.

יעקב פרלוב

Publisher's Preface

We are proud to publish yet another offering by **Rabbi Yosef Stern**, who has by now firmly established himself as an anthologizer and presenter of the thought of *Sfas Emes*. It is hard to think of works as rich and nuanced as *Sfas Emes*. For a hundred years, it has been an inexhaustible mine of profundity and penetrating insights on the Torah. Sprinkled throughout the work, and in a separate volume, are his comments on *Pirkei Avos / Ethics of the Fathers*. In this work, Rabbi Stern pulls together strands of thought on individual topics and weaves them together into a cohesive tapestry.

This he has done in his earlier works on *Sfas Emes*. Now he widens his horizons and includes the ideas of many other classic chassidic commentators. Most of them are from the "Polish tradition" of chassidic thought, which is renowned for its incisiveness, but there are many others, as well.

At the very least, this work will vastly enrich all who read it. At best, it will introduce many of its readers to the originals, so they, too, will become familiar with the *Sfas Emes* and the other sources assembled so skillfully by Rabbi Stern.

We are deeply grateful to our dear friend **Mr. Yechiel Benzion Fishoff**, who sponsored this work. Himself a respected scholar who grew up with the scholarship of *Sfas Emes* in his veins, he is making it possible for countless others to benefit from the scholarship contained between these covers. We are gratified that Mr. Fishoff deems our Schottenstein Talmud as a primary vehicle for Torah dissemination and has recruited others to join him in sponsoring its scholarship.

We are grateful, as well, to all those talented people who have joined to produce this work. They may all be proud to have made an important contribution to the Torah growth of countless people.

Rabbis Meir Zlotowitz/Nosson Scherman

Adar 5759
February 1999

Author's Preface

■ רַבִּי אֶלְעָזָר הַקַּפָּר אוֹמֵר: הַקִּנְאָה וְהַתַּאֲוָה וְהַכָּבוֹד מוֹצִיאִין אֶת הָאָדָם מִן הָעוֹלָם — *Rabbi Elazar HaKappar says: Jealousy, lust and glory remove a man from This World* (*Pirkei Avos* 5:28).

■ וּכְשֵׁם שֶׁהֵם מוֹצִיאִין הָרְשָׁעִים מִן הָעוֹלָם הָעֶלְיוֹן כָּךְ הַצַּדִּיקִים בְּתַאֲוָתָם וְקִנְאָתָם לִכְבוֹד ה׳ מוֹצִיא אוֹתָם מעוה״ז — *Just as the wicked are removed from the World to Come because of their infatuation with these traits, so too, the tzaddikim in the merit of their zealous devotion* (קִנְאָה) *and their single-minded desire* (תַּאֲוָה) *to enhance Hashem's glory are removed from This World* (**free translation adapted from** *Sfas Emes, Bamidbar* 5656).

בעזהי״ת, this volume, which is based on the *Sfas Emes'* teachings on *Pirkei Avos* as well as those of earlier chassidic leaders who inspired the *Sfas Emes,* and also on the teachings of the successors of the *Sfas Emes,* may, in some small measure, help remove the reader from the narrow confines of This World by infusing him with the unique קִנְאָה, תַּאֲוָה וְכָבוֹד that was espoused and practiced by these *tzaddikim.*

⊷§ The Scope of This Volume

The contents of this volume, consisting of almost a thousand *divrei Torah,* are derived from three sources. Firstly, the *Sfas Emes'* commentary on *Avos,* compiled by his grandson Rav Avraham Yissachar Binyamin Alter (for an appreciation of his life see *Days of Joy,* pp. xiv-xv) from an original manuscript of the *Sfas Emes* as well as the oral recollections of the *Sfas Emes'* family of the *shiurim* he gave them in *Pirkei Avos* every Shabbos afternoon during the summer. In addition, we have culled many of the teachings of *Sfas Emes* pertaining to *Avos* from the *Sfas Emes'* other works including his massive commentary on the Torah. In particular, much of the material in the fifth *perek* (especially that dealing with Korach's rebellion and the distinction between Avraham's and Bilaam's disciples) is derived from the *Sfas Emes'* commentary on *Sefer Bamidbar.* Finally, this *sefer* has been immeasurably enriched by the hundreds of *divrei Torah* that first appeared in the *Sefer Maggidei HaEmes* (Arad, 5756). This brilliant anthology, compiled by R' Shlomo Menachem Nadel, a distinguished member of the Gerrer Kollel in Arad, is the source for the numerous *divrei Torah* cited in the name of the *Sfas Emes'* predecessors and successors. In every instance, material culled from this *sefer* is cited by both the name of the original source and the *Maggidei HaEmes* itself. For example, a *dvar Torah* based on the *Bais Yisroel* would be cited as *Bais Yisroel, Maggidei HaEmes*.

Several caveats should be considered by the reader before commencing this volume.

* While we have provided the reader with Hebrew excerpts selected from virtually every segment of *Sfas Emes* (and other sources) discussed in this text, this work is *not* a translation of *Sfas Emes'* commentary on *Avos* (or of any of the other commentaries cited here). Instead, it is a free translation, often a paraphrase, with primary emphasis being placed on faithfully transmitting the broad theme that the *Sfas Emes* is imparting.

Despite the vast scope of this text, we do not maintain that this is an exhaustive treatment of the *Sfas Emes'* (and other luminaries') insights on *Avos*. Apart from considerations of space, the sheer volume and profundity of the *divrei Torah* related by these Torah giants make such a task impossible.

Perhaps most importantly, while we have done everything possible to present the thoughts of the *Sfas Emes* and other commentators in easily accessible form, we make no claim that this volume will make for light reading. As with most works dealing with the basic principles of Torah, it is best read in small portions, and requires time to absorb and assimilate. Over the course of time, however, it is hoped that such an approach will yield substantial cumulative effects. It is the author's fervent wish and prayer that the reader will pick up the book again and again, each time finding a new idea to be treasured and savored by a Jew thirsting to drink from the rich spiritual springs of *Pirkei Avos*.

Finally, many of the *Sfas Emes'* writings, by virtue of their profundity and obscurity, are subject to varying interpretations. While many people have assisted in the preparation of this volume for publication, the author alone assumes responsibility for the interpretations of this Torah classic, which are his own and most likely mirror his perceptions. May Hashem protect us from errors.

ᴇ§ Acknowledgments

To the sponsors:

Mr. and Mrs. Benzion Fishoff's generous support has made this volume possible. Mr. Fishoff, one of the great patrons of Torah causes, has not only supported the publication of this *sefer* but has also provided critical input in shaping the final form of this volume. While originally intended to be based solely on the writings of the *Sfas Emes,* this *sefer* was expanded to include the works of his mentors and successors on the basis of his advice. Mr. Fishoff also provided the author with a copy of the *sefer Maggidei HaEmes* (which he also sponsored).

May Hashem grant the Fishoffs the merit to support Torah endeavors. זְכוּת רַבֵּינוּ הַשָּׂפַת אֱמֶת יָגֵן עָלָיו וְעַל צֶאֱצָאָיו וְעַל כָּל יִשְׂרָאֵל לְאוֹרֶךְ יָמִים וְשָׁנִים.

To my family:

In memory of my dear father הֶחָבֵר ר׳ חַיִים בֶּן הֶחָבֵר ר׳ יוֹסֵף ז״ל whose *"eidele"* personality exemplified the sterling *middos,* the אַהֲבַת תּוֹרָה and יִרְאַת שָׁמַיִם elaborated upon in *Pirkei Avos.* May Hashem grant my mother שתחי׳ and my brother שליט״א the opportunity to perpetuate his דֶּרֶךְ הַחַיִּים for many years מִתּוֹךְ הַרְוָחָה. May they see many generations of descendants עוֹסְקִים בַּתּוֹרָה וּבְמִצְוֹת וּבְרִיאוּת.

The volume is being published after the first *yahrzeit* of my dear father-in-law הרה״ג ר׳ שְׁמוּאֵל שייַנבערג זצ״ל.

To his many *talmidim,* Rav Scheinberg epitomized מְסִירַת נֶפֶשׁ, complete self-sacrifice on behalf of Torah and *mitzvos.* This מְסִירַת נֶפֶשׁ manifested itself in every phase of his long and varied career. As a young man, shortly after his *bar mitzvah,* he traveled from America to Mir, Poland to learn at the feet of *gedolei Torah* such as Rav Eliezer Yehudah Finkel זצ״ל, Rav Yerucham Levovitz זצ״ל, and with R' Leib Malin זצ״ל. Subsequently, he and his עֵזֶר כְּנֶגְדּוֹ, Rebbetzin Scheinberg, שתחי׳, became one of this country's first *kollel* couples, helping Rav Aaron Kotler, זצ״ל, with great מְסִירַת נֶפֶשׁ, to establish the Lakewood Yeshivah. In fact, Rav Scheinberg, acting upon Rav Kotler's request, obtained the building which became the yeshivah's first home. For almost forty years, Rav Scheinberg was מַרְבִּיץ תּוֹרָה in Yeshivas Rabbi Yaakov Yosef and Rabbi Yitzchok Elchonon, inspiring countless *talmidim.* Many of his *talmidim* would attest years later to the life-long debt they owed their Rebbi. During the final phase of his life, he continued his pioneering efforts in Minneapolis and later in Eretz Yisrael by establishing Yeshivas Migdal Torah, now renamed *Nachlas Shmuel* in his memory. We are מִתְפַּלֵּל that Hashem grant Rebbetzin Scheinberg שתחי׳, her children, grandchildren, and great-grandchildren the opportunity to perpetrate his דֶּרֶךְ, לְאֹרֶךְ יָמִים וְשָׁנִים.

To his family, our father-in-law was the paragon of גְּמִילוּת חֲסָדִים and אַהֲבָה, and an outstanding מְחַנֵּךְ to each of his children and grandchildren. We are מִתְפַּלֵּל that Rav Scheinberg זצ״ל be a מֵלִיץ יוֹשֶׁר for his family and for all of *Klal Yisrael.*

To my *eishes chayil* who has encouraged me to complete this complex project and who has provided the environment and support so conducive to הַרְבָּצַת תּוֹרָה. May Hashem grant us the merit to witness together בָּנִים וּבְנֵי בָנִים עוֹסְקִים בַּתּוֹרָה וּבְמִצְוֹת.

To all those who contributed to this volume:

To my editor, Mrs. Ethel Gottlieb whose professional imprint can be found throughout this volume. Virtually every *dvar Torah* cited here benefited from her critique and workmanship. No detail was too insignificant for her attention. It is largely due to her efforts that this volume conforms to the high standards of the ArtScroll series.

A very special *yasher koach* is due to that young distinguished *talmid chacham* R' Shlomo Menachem Nadel שליט״א, for generously permitting us to extract material from his *sefer, Maggidei HaEmes,* a well-regarded anthology of chassidic sources on *Pirkei Avos.* In addition, this צוּרְבָּא מֵרַבָּנָן took time out from his busy schedule to review a substantial portion of an earlier draft of this *sefer.* I would also wish to express *Hakoras HaTov* to his father R' Nosson Nadel, widely renowned for his involvement in חֶסֶד שֶׁל אֱמֶת, for his efforts on behalf of the project. May Hashem grant them and their families אוֹרֶךְ יָמִים וְשָׁנִים לְהָגוֹת בַּתּוֹרָה וּלְקַיֵּם מִצְוֹתֶיהָ וְשֵׂכֶל וּבִינָה לְהָבִין וּלְהַשְׂכִּיל עִמְקֵי סוֹדוֹתֶיהָ.

To Rav David Olewski, שליט"א, *Menahel* of Mesivta Bais Yisroel, for his guidance and advice and for serving as an invaluable liaison to the Gerrer community.

To the staff of Mesorah Publications:

To Rabbi Nosson Scherman, a Torah educator, writer, and lecturer of great note who has championed this project through many vicissitudes. Were it not for his involvement and accessibility, in spite of his frenetic schedule, this book would never have seen the light of day.

To Rabbi Meir Zlotowitz for his painstaking attention to every detail of the project. The superb quality of all ArtScroll productions are a testament to his superior abilities.

My appreciation to R' Avrohom Biderman who helped coordinate the final production of this book and who was involved in every aspect of this project. Also to the typesetting department — Rifky Bruck, Mrs. Esther Feierstein, Toby Akerman, Toby Goldzweig, and Chumie Zaidman. To Toby Akerman for her painstaking care and aesthetic taste in paginating this volume. Thanks as well to R' Eli Kroen for his striking cover design. The beautiful design makes the book as pleasing to the eye as it is to the mind.

I am appreciative of Mrs. Faygie Weinbaum's reading and corrections, as well as that of Mrs. Mindy Stern.

To the members of Congregation Agudas Achim of Midwood, where I have been privileged to serve as their Rav, and to its president Mr. Arthur Pearlman.

I would like to thank Rabbi Moshe Kolodny, Archivist of Agudath Israel of America, for providing the source material for the Biography section of this book.

Above all, I must express my total gratitude to Hashem. No human effort could possibly reach fruition were it not for Hashem's unceasing help in every minute detail of the project.

Yosef Stern

Rosh Chodesh Adar 5759

February 1999

Introduction

Ten Generations From Baal Shem Tov to Sfas Emes[1]

The *Sfas Emes* occupies a pivotal role in the realm of chassidic thought (along with many other chassidic mentors). His contributions of Torah are important not only in their own right, but also as the culmination of ten generations commencing with the founder of the chassidic movement, the *Baal Shem Tov*.

This *Mesorah* is alluded to in the following *pasuk*, הָעֲשִׂירִי יִהְיֶה קֹדֶשׁ לַה׳, "*The tenth one shall be sacred to Hashem*" (*Vayikra* 27:32). Moreover, the letter ה׳ of הָעֲשִׂירִי which has the *gematria* (numerical value) of five may allude to the *Yahrzeit* of the *Sfas Emes*, the 5th of Shevat. (The author is indebted to Rav David Olewski of the Gerrer Mesivta Beis Yisrael for these insights.)

The following diagram illustrates the chain of chassidic tradition beginning with the *Baal Shem Tov* and culminating with the *Sfas Emes*.

1	Rabbi Yisrael Ben Eliezer	*Baal Shem Tov*	1698-1760
2	Rabbi Dov Ber	The Maggid of Mezritch	1704-1772
3	Rabbi Elimelech of Lyzhensk	*Noam Elimelech*	1717-1786
4	Rabbi Yisrael Hopstein of Koznitz	Koznitzer Maggid	1740-1814
5	Rabbi Yaakov Yitzchak Horowitz	The Chozeh of Lublin	1745-1815
6	Rabbi Yaakov Yitzchak	Yehudi of Peshis'cha	1766-1814
7	Rabbi Simcha Bunim Bernhardt	of Peshis'cha	1767-1827
8	Rabbi Menachem Mendel Morgenstern	of Kotzk	1787-1859
9	Rabbi Yitzchak Meir Alter of Ger	*Chiddushei HaRim*	1799-1866
10	Rabbi Yehuda Aryeh Leib Alter of Ger	*Sfas Emes*	1847-1905

Sfas Emes Descendants (Rabbis of Ger)

In the same manner that many generations of illustrious chassidic leaders preceded the *Sfas Emes*, so too this great Torah luminary was succeeded in his role as Rebbe of Ger by an outstanding son, and subsequently, by three outstanding grandchildren. The following diagram traces the lineage of the Gerrer dynasty from the *Sfas Emes* till today.

---

1. Much of the material for this section is based on biographies that first appeared in the *Jewish Observer* and *Dos Yiddishe Vort*.

Rabbi Avraham Mordechai Alter	*Imrei Emes*	1866-1948	served as Rebbe 1905-1948
Rabbi Yisrael Alter	*Beis Yisrael*	1895-1977	served as Rebbe 1948-1977
Rabbi Simcha Bunim Alter	*Lev Simcha*	1898-1992	served as Rebbe 1977-1992
Rabbi Pinchas Menachem Alter	*Pnei Menachem*	1926-1996	served as Rebbe 1992-1996
Rav Yaakov Aryeh Alter	Present Gerrer Rebbe		

In the following section, we will present a brief appreciation of some of the major personalities influencing the Gerrer approach to *chassidus*.

◄§ R' Simcha Bunim of Peshis'cha

R' Simcha Bunim Bernhardt of Peshis'cha, popularly known as the Rebbe R' Bunim, was truly a unique multifaceted individual. He was at different periods in his life a salesman for a lumber merchant, a licensed pharmacist, a linguist, but above all he was a Torah giant and a chassidic thinker whose *talmidim* became the founders of numerous dynasties. Virtually every branch of Polish *chassidus*, and especially the Rebbes of Ger, was profoundly influenced by R' Simcha Bunim.

Like many other early chassidic leaders, R' Simcha Bunim, was born into a distinguished rabbinic home that was staunchly opposed to the emergent chassidic movement. His father, R' Zvi, known as the Vadislaver Maggid, like so many other *maggidim* (itinerant preachers) of his time, traveled widely preaching to large and appreciative audiences throughout Poland, Bohemia, Moravia, Prussia and Saxony. R' Zvi possessed the great gift of being able to relate to various audiences at their own level. He utilized *meshalim* (parables) to attract the least learned of his listeners, philosophical concepts for the more sophisticated groups, and *lamdishe divrei Torah* for the *talmidei chachamim* in his audience. His son, R' Simcha Bunim, at various phases during his career would display the same talents. R' Zvi was also the author of noted *sefarim* including "*Asarah LeMeah*" and "*Eretz HaTzvi*." On his mother's side, R' Simcha Bunim was descended from the great halachic codifier, R' Yoel Sirkes (known as the *Bach*).

At an early age, R' Simcha Bunim was sent to study Torah at the Yeshiva of Rav Yirmiyahu of Mattersdorf, Hungary and subsequently to Rav Mordechai Benet of Nikolsburg.

Undoubtedly, Rav Benet, one of the great *gaonim* and *tzaddikim* of his time, profoundly influenced R' Simcha Bunim with his Torah and piety. It is possible that some of the future chassidic leader's familiarity with modern languages and philosophy may also have been derived from his *rosh yeshiva* who was conversant in many European languages and well versed in secular knowledge.

Despite his distinguished father's objections, R' Simcha Bunim began to turn to chassidic leaders for guidance, including R' Moshe Leib Sassover, who then resided in Apt, and subsequently to the founder of Polish *chassidus*, the Koznitzer Maggid. While it is not clear why the young scholar was attracted to *chassidus*, the mass defection from Torah and *mitzvos* that R' Simcha Bunim had observed in Germany and parts of Hungary may have influenced him. Despite the presence of many *gedolim* and *tzaddikim*, the broad masses, preoccupied with the struggle for physical survival, somehow were unable to relate to the Torah giants in their midst. R' Simcha Bunim felt that the fledgling chassidic movement would infuse *Yiddishkeit* with new life.

After several years of "*kest*" when he was supported by his father-in-law R' Moshe Berliner, R' Simcha Bunim was employed by R' Berek Bergson of Warsaw, who was a noted lumber merchant and philanthropist and whose wife Tamarel was a dedicated follower of the Maggid of Koznitz. In this capacity, R' Simcha Bunim's command of German (he was fluent in German, Latin and Polish) proved useful as he represented the Bergsons in Leipzig, Berlin, Dresden and Breslau. His travels provided him the opportunity to become acquainted with the Torah leaders of each of these communities. The bond between the Bergsons and R' Simcha Bunim continued well beyond his relatively short tenure as their employee. When R' Simcha Bunim succeeded the *Yid Hakadosh* as leading chassidic Rebbe of Poland, Tamarel Bergson almost single-handedly provided the financial support necessary for the fledgling movement to survive.

Despite his warm relationship with the Bergsons, R' Simcha Bunim regretted the disruption of his close relationship with *tzaddikim* that his travels to Germany necessitated. Seeking employment in Poland, he became a licensed pharmacist and opened a successful pharmacy in Peshis'cha. In fact, R' Simcha Bunim became a major supplier of medicine for Napoleon's army.

While it seemed that he was engrossed in his pursuit of *parnasah*, in reality, R' Simcha Bunim was actually preoccupied with his personal spiritual growth. His druggist counter was not only laden with medicines but also with *Sifrei Kodesh*, including *Shas*, *Zohar* and the sacred writings of the *Ari Hakadosh*. In fact, R' Simcha Bunim drew parallels between his vocation of healing the body (רְפוּאַת הַגּוּף) and his avocation of healing the soul (רְפוּאַת הַנֶּפֶשׁ). He reasoned, "Just as a few drops of the wrong medicine are lethal, so too a 'few drops' (an infinitesimal amount) of haughtiness can corrupt the soul." Moreover, just as a pharmacist must carefully tailor each prescription to meet every individual patient's need, so too a spiritual healer requires great sensitivity to deal with every one of his follower's concerns. One wrong move — erroneous advice or even an insincere motive — on the part of the individual dispensing spiritual relief can corrupt the soul. Despite his preoccupation with his pharmacy, R' Simcha Bunim maintained close personal contact with contemporary chassidic leaders including the Maggid of Koznitz, R' Dovid of Lelov, and especially the Chozeh of Lublin. Many of the Chozeh's *talmidim* could not appreciate that their mentor was so close to an individual who had a business relationship with Gentiles, had traveled to Germany, and who, on occasion, even wore Western dress when attending trade fairs. However, the Chozeh understood the true nature and the inner piety of his *talmid*.

A humorous, yet insightful story is related by *chassidim* concerning the association between R' Simcha Bunim's exterior clothing and his personality.

Once, R' Simcha Bunim traveled directly from a business appointment in Danzig to the Chozeh of Lublin without changing from his business attire. One of the more zealous *chassidim*, noticing one of his peers wearing Western garb, immediately took out a small pocketknife and ripped R' Simcha Bunim's jacket. R' Simcha Bunim was so immersed in the Chozeh's discourse that he did not even notice this affront, and he never made an issue of it even afterwards.

However, the Chozeh himself, upon hearing of this incident, demanded that the offender explain his bizarre behavior. Maintaining a straight face, the young man reminded the Chozeh of the advice that his *melamed* had given him many years ago. "If you experience difficulty with the *Chumash* text, don't hesitate to look at the '*teitsch*' (Yiddish translation)." Paraphrasing his teacher's suggestion the young *chassid* continued. "Since I had experienced difficulty in comprehending your *divrei Torah*, I decided to look in the '*Deitsch*' (i.e. R' Simcha Bunim who was dressed in Western-style "*Deitsch*" clothing) by tearing off his outer garb and becoming acquainted with his inner personality."

With a smile on his face, the Chozeh concluded, "You are correct. Henceforth, anyone who cannot understand our *divrei Torah* should seek the assistance of R' Simcha Bunim." The *Deitsch* was transformed to the *teitsch*! And indeed, R' Simcha Bunim now assumed the difficult but rewarding role of explaining the Chozeh's *divrei Torah* to the *chassidim*.

Subsequently, R' Simcha Bunim grew close to R' Yaakov Yitzchak Rabinowitz, the *Yid Hakadosh*. Unlike the Chozeh of Lublin who was constantly occupied with the many material concerns of the masses (i.e. *parnasah*, *shidduchim*, health) who came to seek his blessing, the *Yid Hakadosh* was primarily interested in transporting his *chassidim* from the confines of this material world into the overwhelming spirituality associated with *Olam Haba*. Whereas in the court of the Chozeh miracles occurred frequently, the *Yid Hakadosh* (and his followers along the chain of *Mesorah* culminating in the Ger dynasty) frowned upon miracles. Likewise, he would not grant his followers "*segulos*" (supernatural cures) for their illnesses. Instead, the *Yid Hakadosh* emphasized spiritual development and in-depth understanding of the *hashkafah* (ideology) of *chassidus*. It was also an environment where a great deal of emphasis was placed on *Yiras Shamayim*, fear of Hashem. The *Chiddushei HaRim* challenged the popular notion that the *Yid Hakadosh* had no teeth remaining in his mouth because of the ascetic life style in which he deprived himself of basic nutrition. "No," he insisted, "when the *Yid Hakadosh* simply recited a *berachah*, בָּרוּךְ אַתָּה ה׳, his teeth fell out of his mouth from the sheer veneration and fear of Hashem's Name that he had just enunciated!"

It was in such an atmosphere that R' Simcha Bunim thrived, until the passing of his mentor, the *Yid Hakadosh* (as well as of the Maggid of Koznitz and the Chozeh of Lublin), in 1815. After the *Yid's* passing, his followers turned to R' Simcha Bunim for advice regarding a possible successor. He responded with the following *mashal* (parable):

A devoted shepherd fell asleep while herding his sheep. Awakening from his deep slumber at midnight, he looks around and marvels at the idyllic scene unfolding before his eyes. The moon was shining, the sheep were sleeping contentedly in the meadow, the air was cool and there was clear drinking water before him. His heart surges with gratitude and joy, and he cries out, "Hashem, how can I thank You for all Your kindness to me? If You entrust me with Your sheep, I will guard them like the apple of my eye!" R' Simcha Bunim concluded, "If such a shepherd can be found, he should be our rebbe." Upon hearing the *mashal* and R' Simcha Bunim's incisive observation, the *chassidim*, including some who themselves were potential successors to the *Yid Hakadosh*, chose R' Simcha Bunim as the Rebbe.

During his twelve-year tenure, R' Simcha Bunim infused the chassidic movement with new strength. In many ways, he continued along the path of the *Yid Hakadosh*, placing primary emphasis on inner devotion (rather than overt displays of piety). Peshis'cha *chassidim* were noted for their long hours of preparation for *davening*, the many hours devoted to Torah study (as part of their הֲכָנָה) followed by relatively brief *tefillos*.[1] Following the approach of his mentor, the *Yid Hakadosh*, R' Simcha Bunim refrained from performing miracles, preferring to learn and disseminate Torah instead. In fact, there is a tradition that R' Simcha Bunim delivered a daily Gemara *shiur* and related many *chiddushei Torah* to his *talmidim*.

The Rebbe, R' Simcha Bunim, also emphasized the self-development of each of his *chassidim*. In particular, the *middah* of *emes*, complete fidelity to the truth, was emphasized. Not only should one not deceive others, but even fooling oneself to seek a spiritual level beyond one's capabilities was tantamount to *avodah zarah*. Everyone was expected to achieve his true potential — not beyond it. R' Simcha Bunim's *chassidim* were also imbued with all-encompassing יִרְאַת שָׁמַיִם, fear of Hashem, and יִרְאַת חֵטְא, fear of sinning. The Rebbe regretted that immediately after saying the *berachah* of *Shemoneh Esrei* pleading for Divine forgiveness (סְלַח לָנוּ), we immediately proceed to ask for healing (רְפָאֵנוּ) and *parnasah* (בָּרֵךְ עָלֵינוּ) without lingering on the significance of asking for forgiveness and doing *teshuvah*.

While preaching humility and self-negation, R' Simcha Bunim also emphasized the importance of realizing one's potential to rise above the petty concerns of this world and to become a truly spiritual person. He would tell his followers, "Everyone must have two pockets, one labeled בִּשְׁבִילִי נִבְרָא הָעוֹלָם, *the world*

---

1. In accordance with Peshis'cha *Chassidus*, it was their belief that preparation for a *mitzvah* is at least as important as the *mitzvah* itself.

was created on my behalf, and the other וְאָנֹכִי עָפָר וָאֵפֶר, *I am but dust and ashes."*

R' Simcha Bunim's teachings were imparted to his many *talmidim,* some of whom became the founders of the great chassidic dynasties that dominated Polish Jewry until the Holocaust. The chassidic courts of Kotzk (see the following essay), Sochatchov, Alexander, Sokolov, Worka, Amshinov, Radzymn, among others, were all followers of the great traditions first nurtured in Peshis'cha.

Even his opponents — those who felt Peshis'cha *Chassidus* deviated too far from the teachings of the *Baal Shem Tov* — were forced to acknowledge his wisdom and greatness. At the renowned wedding in Ostilla (refer to our essay on the *Chiddushei HaRim*) when many of R' Simcha Bunim's opponents sought to challenge and debate with his followers who were present (such as the *Chiddushei HaRim*), the sainted Galician chassidic leader, the *"Ohev Yisrael,"* adamantly refused to take part in any criticism of Peshis'cha *Chassidus.*

Towards the end of his life, R' Simcha Bunim lost his eyesight. Rather than complain, he accepted this handicap, maintaining that by losing his perception of this world he drew immeasurably closer to Hashem and the World to Come.

Even R' Simcha Bunim's last moments testified to the inherent greatness of this Torah personality. Noticing that his wife was crying, he soothed her, insisting that there was no reason to cry — "On the contrary, our entire life is merely a preparation for the final moment of delivering one's soul to the *Shechinah."*

◆§ The Kotzker Rebbe: Rabbi Menachem Mendel Morgenstern

When eulogizing the *Baal Shem Tov,* R' David Halpern, the Rav of Zaslov, commented that from time to time Hashem designates a very sacred soul, and dispatches it from Heaven to enter an equally special human body awaiting it on earth. This body and soul fuse together and have but one mission — to learn and teach others כִּי ה' הוּא הָאֱלֹקִים בַּשָּׁמַיִם מִמַּעַל וְעַל הָאָרֶץ מִתָּחַת, אֵין עוֹד, *that Hashem is the only God — in heaven above and on the earth below there is none other.* R' David concluded that such a unique soul was placed in the sainted body of the *Baal Shem Tov.*

It has been said that, several generations after the passing of the *Baal Shem Tov, Klal Yisrael* merited another such soul grafted onto an equally splendid body in the person of R' Menachem Mendel, later known as the Kotzker Rebbe.

Already as a young man, R' Menachem Mendel was known for his fiery personality and for his determination to always adhere to *emes,* the absolute truth, regardless of any possible repercussions. These character traits had already been brought to the attention of the Chozeh of Lublin, who requested that Menachem Mendel be brought to him. The following incident indicates how the Kotzker's complete candor and basic *hashkafah* (ideological approach) were already formed at this early stage in his career. Before coming to the

Chozeh's home, R' Menachem Mendel purchased a small pocketknife. The Chozeh (who was known for his ability to perceive through *ruach hakodesh*, as the name *Chozeh*, seer, indicates) greeted his young visitor by asking him, "Did you come to Lublin to purchase a knife?" R' Menachem Mendel's response, indicative of his sharp wit as well as his general opposition to the use of the supernatural (such as *ruach hakodesh*), was quite blunt. "You are not going to attract me with *ruach hakodesh*." Rather than taking this sharp retort as a personal affront, the Chozeh understood that such candor was simply a reflection of the love of *emes* that permeated every fiber of R' Menachem Mendel's being. Rapidly, the future Kotzker Rebbe became an intimate member of the Chozeh's inner circle. While it generally took years before a new arrival at the Chozeh's court was invited to join his private *minyan* (consisting of exactly ten individuals), R' Menachem Mendel was immediately invited to participate.

An interesting incident illustrates how already in those early years R' Menachem Mendel demonstrated unusually high standards in his deportment with his peers (בֵּין אָדָם לַחֲבֵירוֹ). For a long time, R' Menachem Mendel had sought to acquire a certain pair of *tefillin* that was renowned for its high quality and excellent workmanship. Finally, he was able to acquire such a pair at great cost, from the widow of R' Moshe of P'sheworsk. Rather than personally leave the Chozeh's court to obtain the *tefillin*, he arranged for someone else to bring them to him. Unable to control himself, the emissary wore the *tefillin* once prior to bringing them to R' Menachem Mendel. When the emissary confessed to his inappropriate behavior, the future Kotzker Rebbe responded, "I can no longer wear such *tefillin*. By using them without prior permission, you have violated the Biblical prohibition of לֹא תַחְמֹד, *do not covet*, as well as possibly of לֹא תִגְנֹב (cf. *Bava Metzia* 42b discussing whether borrowing without permission constitutes theft). *Tefillin* that somehow became a catalyst for such a grave sin are not for me. You keep them!"

However, R' Menachem Mendel, who focused on *individual* growth, felt that he could no longer remain in the Chozeh's court where primary emphasis was on the needs of the *masses* of *Klal Yisrael* who came to seek their Rebbe's advice and blessing. Instead, he followed the small group of elite individuals who followed the *Yid Hakadosh* (see the previous essay concerning the life of R' Simcha Bunim) to Peshis'cha where he established a chassidic court tailored to individual self-growth. It is noteworthy that contrary to popular practice (cf. *Berachos* 31a), the future Kotzker Rebbe, fearing that permission would not be granted, did not seek the Chozeh's permission or even bid him farewell before leaving, a practice which would be repeated more than 25 years later when some of R' Menachem Mendel's *talmidim* left him.

After the *Yid Hakadosh's* passing in 1815, the Kotzker remained in Peshis'cha, becoming a disciple of R' Simcha Bunim. It is hard to imagine the sheer poverty which R' Simcha Bunim's disciples endured. R' Feivel, one of R' Simcha Bunim's closest *talmidim*, noted that the wealthy philanthropist Tamarel Bergson (please refer to our essay on R' Simcha Bunim) would visit

Peshis'cha and distribute *gelt* (money) to the *chassidim*. R' Menachem Mendel gave his famous response, *"Gelt? What is money! Who needs, who wants money!"* R' Feivel recalled how he wasn't able to touch money for some six months after hearing the Kotzker's sharp and fervent reaction.

After R' Simcha Bunim's passing in 1827, the majority of his followers chose R' Menachem Mendel to become his successor. Rather than remain in Peshis'cha (where R' Simcha Bunim's only son, R' Avraham Moshe, resided and would establish a chassidic court of his own), R' Menachem Mendel — and most of R' Simcha's *talmidim* — moved to Tomashov, where rapidly a new movement, later known as Kotzker *Chassidus*, developed.

Already in those early years of his leadership, the Kotzker emphasized inner devotion rather than outward piety. Though his *chassidim* were known for their enthusiasm for the Rebbe and their fiery devotion to grasping his every word, R' Menachem Mendel would always remind them that the greatest significance should be attached to the *lasting* impact of all that they had experienced. At Sinai, *Klal Yisrael* witnessed thunder and lightning (קוֹלוֹת וּבְרָקִים) and yet, despite all their fervor (as it says, וַיָּנֻעוּ, *they shook*), ultimately they remained at a distance, as remote from Hashem as ever. As the *pasuk* concludes, וַיַּעַמְדוּ מֵרָחֹק, *they stood at a distance* (*Shemos* 20:15). The Kotzker would emphasize that our mission is best stated in the *pasuk* (ibid. 25:8), וְעָשׂוּ לִי מִקְדָּשׁ וְשָׁכַנְתִּי בְּתוֹכָם, *Build a Beis HaMikdash for Me* (Hashem) *so that I may reside in your midst* (not only in the *Beis HaMikdash*). He concluded, "The *Shechinah* resides wherever we permit him to penetrate our soul."

Kotzk was not simply a place to visit the Rebbe for a day or two. To capture the full flavor of this exalted experience, one had to remain weeks, if not months, by the Rebbe.

R' Menachem Mendel then moved his chassidic court to Kotzk, where he would remain the rest of his life and where his *chassidus* would acquire his unique character.

Let us consider some of the outstanding characteristics of Kotzk *Chassidus*:

Learning Torah — and learning in depth is primary. Following in the footsteps of his mentor R' Simcha Bunim, the Kotzker rejected anything that was superficial. He would place great emphasis on יְגִיעָה בַּתּוֹרָה, effort and exertion in learning Torah that is critical to attaining true comprehension of Torah.

Whereas Pharaoh, upon awakening from his dream, simply went back to sleep and dreamt again (cf. *Bereishis* 41:5, וַיִּישָׁן וַיַּחֲלֹם שֵׁנִית), Yaakov, in a similar situation, is aroused and proclaims, אָכֵן יֵשׁ ה' בַּמָּקוֹם הַזֶּה, *Indeed Hashem is present in this place* (cf. *Bereishis* 28:16). The Kotzker would exhort his followers not to "sleepwalk" through life but, on the contrary, to be eternally vigilant, seeking opportunities for further growth.

הַתְמָדָה, diligence, was a related attribute of Kotzker *chassidim*. It was not uncommon for followers of the Kotzker Rebbe to learn throughout the long Polish winter nights, sometimes studying Torah for as much as 15-16 hours without interruption.

A very important feature of Kotzk *Chassidus* is brevity and sharpness. The Kotzker's pronouncements were sometimes compared to the *Urim VeTumim* on the *Kohen Gadol's* breastplate, which provided the solution to *Klal Yisrael's* problem in just a few words. The Kotzker demanded a great deal from his *chassidim* and would often state what he expected of them in a pithy phrase which inspired them to great levels of devotion.

Kotzker *chassidim* claimed that the Heavenly Voice which emanates from Sinai (see *Perek* 6, *mishnah* 2 and our commentary), which is generally silenced by our preoccupation with material matters (גַּשְׁמִיּוּת), could still be heard in Kotzk. The Rebbe trained the sensitive ear to be attuned to that Heavenly Voice.

Despite all their spiritual achievements, a true Kotzker *chassid* was expected to conceal his accomplishments, in the spirit of הַצְנֵעַ לֶכֶת, "to walk humbly with Hashem" (cf. *Michah* 6:8). Kotzker *chassidim* would rejoice in public — their Rebbe was adamantly opposed to ever submitting to depression or any form of sadness — yet weep in private when they realized how far they were from attaining their full potential.

More than anything else, Kotzk was known for its complete embrace of the attribute of *emes*, the total truth. This attribute was reflected in the approach to learning adopted by the Rebbe's *chassidim*. As his son-in-law, the renowned R' Avraham of Sochatchov (known as the *Avnei Nezer*), writes in his introduction to *Eglei Tal* (his classic work on the 39 categories of work prohibited on Shabbos), his father-in-law frowned upon *pilpulim*, any approach to learning Torah that did not focus on the true *p'shat*.

This *middah* of *emes* was also reflected in the Kotzker's overall approach to life and his relationship with his *chassidim*. As a result, he was opposed to doing anything *beyond* one's capabilities, such as fasting frequently or denying oneself the basic amenities of life (see our commentary on *Perek* 6, *mishnah* 4, for an elaboration of this theme). He himself would never perform wonders (מוֹפְתִים), arguing that the primary function of a *tzaddik* was מְחַיֵּה הַחַיִּים, to invigorate the living, rather than מְחַיֵּה הַמֵּתִים, to resurrect the dead, which is Hashem's function.

Finally, in Kotzk, age and previous reputation mattered little. The Rebbe perceived an older *chassid* as a composite of two or three young *neshamos* contained in the body of an older person. In fact there were no *eltere chassidim* ("older *chassidim*"). Everyone was eternally young and brimming with youthful enthusiasm. The fact that one *had* learned or *had* accomplished much in the *past* mattered far less than one's *present* accomplishments.

Despite the Rebbe's many demands upon his *chassidim* — or perhaps because of these demands — his *chassidus* swelled. By the year 1840, his *beis hamedrash* could no longer contain the throngs that wanted to see him during the *Yamim Noraim*. The Rebbe, whose primary purpose was to develop a cadre of great *talmidim* rather than to cater to the masses seeking supernatural cures, at first contemplated asking many of his new followers to leave. Unable to do that, R' Menachem Mendel withdrew from his *chassidim*, living for the remaining 19 years of his life in semi-isolation. No longer would he receive visitors, no longer would he give a chassidic *tisch* (a festive meal in which *divrei Torah* are said and chassidic melodies are sung.) Only on rare occasions would the Rebbe make a brief appearance in the *beis hamedrash*, saying just a few words for the purpose of instilling *yiras Shamayim* in his followers.

Despite the Rebbe's withdrawal from his *chassidim*, the movement continued to thrive. Indeed, a group of *chassidim* led by R' Mordechai Yosef of Izbica (which would later emerge as a distinguished chassidic group featuring such leaders as the Rebbe of Radzin, R' Leibel Eger, and R' Tzadok HaCohen) departed without requesting his permission — just as the Kotzker had departed from the Chozeh many years before. However, the momentum and pace of Kotzker *chassidus* continued unabated. The Rebbe, now from the distance, remained the inspiration and the guiding force propelling his *chassidim* to ever greater heights. A דּוֹר דֵּעָה (the description given to the Wilderness Generation that experienced *Mattan Torah* and witnessed so many of the great miracles) developed in Kotzk, consisting of many of the great leaders of Poland, including the *Chiddushei HaRim*, R' Henoch Levin of Alexander, R' Menachem Mendel of Worka, the Rebbe's son-in-law R' Avraham Bornstein (later the Sochatchover Rebbe) and many others.

In 1859, the Rebbe was stricken with a heart ailment. The news of the Kotzker's illness and his gradual worsening condition served as a magnet, attracting hundreds of his *chassidim* to his *beis hamedrash*. When the Rebbe heard the cries of his devoted followers, he wondered, "Why? What do they want from me? It would be better if they continued learning Torah." As his strength abated he said, "I'm simply going from one room (This World) to another (The World to Come)." As the Kotzker's end drew near, he recited and explained the *pasuk* describing the uniqueness of Moshe's mission, לֹא כֵן עַבְדִּי *Not so is My servant Moshe; in My entire house he is the trusted one. Mouth to mouth do I speak to him, in a clear vision and not in riddles, at the image of Hashem does he gaze* . . . (*Bamidbar* 12:7,8). He explained that Moshe *Rabbeinu* received the unique gift of perceiving Hashem — and equally so, allowing the *Shechinah* to penetrate the hearts of *Klal Yisrael*.

Perhaps, we may conclude that this is the most fitting epitaph for the Kotzker: perceiving Hashem in his own manner (כִּבְיָכוֹל), ascending to the most rarefied level of *kedushah* and serving as a potent medium so that this *kedushah* should filter to all of *Klal Yisrael*.

◄§ The Chiddushei HaRim: Rabbi Yitzchak Meir Alter

A direct link can be drawn between the Maggid of Koznitz, the first chassidic leader of Poland, and the Rebbes of Ger. To a large extent, the *hashkafah* of Ger (and especially its emphasis on Torah study) was derived from the foundation laid by the Maggid of Koznitz which was later "filtered" through the prism of R' Simcha Bunim of Peshis'cha and the Kotzker Rebbe. In fact, the Maggid of Koznitz played an even more direct role in establishing the dynasty of Ger. He was the *shadchan* of the first Gerrer Rebbe's parents, bringing together Chaya Sarah, a poor orphan who nonetheless boasted a distinguished lineage[1] and R' Yisrael Rottenberg. The Maggid of Koznitz not only arranged the *shidduch* but actively participated in the wedding itself, to the extent that the *chasunah* was held in his residence. He also gave this couple a beautiful wedding gift: a blessing that their son would be a great Torah luminary. The bond between the *Chiddushei HaRim's* parents and the Maggid of Koznitz continued to grow. As soon as their son, Yitzchak Meir, was born, he was brought to the Maggid who actually played with him as if he were his own grandson. Chassidic tradition preserves the following dialogue between the 3-year-old Yitzchak Meir and the Maggid of Koznitz. The Maggid spoke first. "Yitzchak Meir, I will give you a *rendel* (a coin in circulation during that period) if you can show me where we can find Hashem." The precocious Yitzchak Meir responded immediately, "I will give you two *rendel* if you can show me anywhere Hashem *isn't*."

Yitzchak Meir continued to thrive in the best possible environment, the home of the Maggid of Koznitz. Here he could study with the Maggid's children and grandchildren, and even discuss complex Talmudic issues with the Maggid himself. Here this young *talmid chacham* was exposed to the many scholars and *tzaddikim* who traveled to see the Maggid.

Already before his *bar mitzvah* R' Yitzchak Meir was engaged to the daughter of R' Yitzchak Chalphan, a prominent chassidic Jew residing in Warsaw. (According to chassidic tradition the Chozeh of Lublin himself arranged this *shidduch*.) The marriage was delayed for three years, till R' Yitzchak Meir reached the age of 15. Meanwhile, his reputation as an outstanding scholar had spread, to the extent that he became an intimate of many of Warsaw's venerable *talmidei chachamim* at so tender an age.

Upon the passing of the Maggid of Koznitz in 1815, R' Yitzchak Meir at first continued traveling to Koznitz, this time to the Maggid's son, R' Moshe Briah. The following incident gives us some indication of the *hashkafos* of the *Chiddushei HaRim*, which were largely developed by the age of 17. Upon hearing a beautiful *dvar Torah* from R' Yitzchak Meir, R' Moshe Briah was so impressed that he kissed him on his forehead. The *Chiddushei HaRim*, who was constantly demanding more from himself, reacted by saying, "I need a Rebbe that makes demands of me rather than a Rebbe who kisses me."

A new era began in the life of the *Chiddushei HaRim*, this time as a loyal disciple of R' Simcha Bunim of Peshis'cha whose unrelenting search for *emes* and insistence upon שְׁלֵימוּת (constant self-development and striving for moral perfection) were exactly what he was seeking. R' Yitzchak Meir became an

---

1. Chaya Sarah was a descendant of the great Kabbalist, R' Nosson Nota Shapiro, known as the *Megaleh Amukos*, and R' Yonasan Eibeschutz, the author of many classic *sefarim*, e.g. *Urim VeTumim*.

integral member of those who were known as the "lions" of Peshis'cha — the young scholars whose fiery temperament and assiduous devotion to Torah left a permanent imprint on Polish Jewry. Such future Torah leaders as R' Menachem Mendel of Tomashov (the future Kotzker Rebbe), R' Yitzchak of Worka, R' Yaakov of Radzimin, R' Chanoch Henoch of Alexander and many others became intimate associates of R' Yitzchak Meir. In this rarefied atmosphere — where personal glory counted for nothing and *kavod Shamayim* was everything — the *Chiddushei HaRim* continued to develop spiritually.

However, the Peshis'cha movement was not without its detractors who felt that its emphasis on *internal* development and *limud haTorah* and de-emphasis of *external* piety somehow deviated from *chassidus'* original ideals, as espoused by the *Baal Shem Tov*. The opponents of Peshis'cha were determined to publicly demonstrate its errors and then, if necessary, place a ban (חֵרֶם) on the movement. They planned to confront R' Simcha Bunim at a wedding which was to be held in the forest of Ostilla. At the urging of his *talmidim*, R' Simcha Bunim did not attend himself; instead, he sent a delegation of five of his leading *talmidim*, spearheaded by R' Yitzchak Meir. Upon arriving at Ostilla, the *Chiddushei HaRim* quickly refuted the arguments of Peshis'cha's opponents. In fact, upon meeting the *Chiddushei HaRim*, the Apter Rebbe (R' Avraham Yehoshua Heschel), widely revered as the senior chassidic rebbe, dissociated himself from the opponents of Peshis'cha and lavished praise upon this young scholar and his peers.

During this entire period (from 1818 to 1827 when R' Simcha Bunim passed away) the *Chiddushei HaRim* actually resided in two places. His temporary residence (דִּירַת עֲרָאִי) was in Warsaw, where he was widely respected by all the *talmidei chachamim* who appreciated his greatness in Torah; and his permanent home (דִּירַת קֶבַע), in Peshis'cha, where he truly felt at home as merely another one of the intimate disciples of R' Simcha Bunim. His fealty to the movement is demonstrated by the *Chiddushei HaRim's* comment, "From Peshis'cha to Kotzk, *chassidus* is a commentary on the *Baal Shem Tov* (i.e. the first generations of chassidic scholars who sought to comprehend the teachings of the *Baal Shem Tov*). From Peshis'cha on, *chassidus* is a commentary on Peshis'cha." In fact, many of the leading movements of Polish *chassidus* were based upon the foundation established by R' Simcha Bunim of Peshis'cha.

Upon the passing of R' Simcha Bunim in 1827, R' Yitzchak Meir was considered by many to be his logical successor. However, he refused, instead proposing that his brother-in-law, R' Mendel of Tomashov (the future Kotzker Rebbe), assume the mantle of the movement. For over 30 years, the great *Chiddushei HaRim* subordinated himself to the Kotzker. Even after the Kotzker's self-imposed isolation (refer to our previous essay) which led some of his *talmidim* to leave him, R' Yitzchak Meir remained in Kotzk. Some indication of this *tzaddik* and *gadol's* capacity for self-negation to his Rebbe, the Kotzker, can be gleaned from the following incident. After compiling a massive commentary on *Choshen Mishpat* (the segment of *Shulchan Aruch* that deals with civil law) he showed his work to the Kotzker who expressed his fears that such an excellent work would displace the *Shach's* commentary on *Shulchan Aruch*. "If this *sefer* were mine," the Kotzker concluded, "I would burn it." As he was casting his prized manuscript into the flames, R' Yitzchak Meir with great fervor reiterated the teaching of *Chazal*, מִצְוָה לִשְׁמֹעַ דִּבְרֵי חֲכָמִים, "It is a *mitzvah* to listen to the advice of our wise men (i.e. his Rebbe, the Kotzker).

Throughout this era, the *Chiddushei HaRim* maintained a residence in Warsaw, where he became acquainted with many of the *gedolim* of his time who either lived in or were visiting that leading Polish city. In particular, the *Chiddushei HaRim* became acquainted with Rav Yisrael Salanter, Rav Shimon Sofer (the *Chasam Sofer's* son), Rav Isaac Charif of Slonim, and Rav Yosef Ber Soloveitchik of Brisk (known as the *Beis HaLevi*).

Upon the Kotzker's passing in 1859, it was widely presumed that the *Chiddushei HaRim* would be his successor. However, R' Yitzchak Meir himself steadfastly refused to assume the mantle of the Kotzker. In his eulogy for his Rebbi he interpreted the *pasuk*, הַצַּדִּיק אָבָד וְאֵין אִישׁ שָׂם עַל לֵב, *The righteous one perishes, and no man takes it to heart* (Yeshayahu 57:1) in the following manner: The *tzaddik* passed away and there is no one like him who can transmit Hashem's Torah so that it penetrates Jewish hearts. When eulogizing his mother, he addressed her *neshamah* in the following words: "Mamma, it is not my fault that people mistakenly think that I am a *gaon*. Now that you are entering the עוֹלָם הָאֱמֶת, the World of Truth, you will realize that I am nothing more than a simple Jew." He begged her forgiveness for having even given the impression that he was anything but אַ פָּשׁוּטְ׳עֶר אִיד (a simple Jew).

Despite his extreme reluctance to become the Kotzker's successor, the *Chiddushei HaRim* was literally coerced to do so. Large groups of *chassidim* — and even *misnagdim* (opponents of the chassidic movement) — surrounded his home in Warsaw and didn't let him rest until he yielded to pressure and reluctantly agreed to be designated as the Rebbe of the Kotzker's *chassidim*.

Upon assuming this position, the *Chiddushei HaRim* stated his approach to *chassidus* by comparing himself to his predecessors. "Reb Simcha Bunim led through his unbridled love (אַהֲבָה), the Kotzker by imposing fear of Hashem (יִרְאָה), and I will lead through Torah."

The *Chiddushei HaRim's* short term as Rebbe (from 1859-1866) is known among *chassidim* as the שֶׁבַע שְׁנֵי הַשָּׂבָע, *the seven years of plenty* (cf. *Bereishis* 41:29). And indeed they were years of unparalleled success and spiritual growth for Polish *chassidus*. As he stated at the outset, the *Chiddushei HaRim* emphasized *limud haTorah*. He explained why an individual who studies Torah is called a בֶּן תּוֹרָה, the "son" of Torah. Just as a son can't exist without his mother, so too a Jew should feel that he cannot live without Torah.

The *Chiddushei HaRim's* influence extended well beyond the confines of his own *chassidim*. Warsaw, from where he directed his followers, had emerged as the leading metropolis of Polish Jewry, and as a center of Torah-true activism (עַסְקָנוּת). There was no significant aspect of communal activity that Rav Yitzchak Meir was not involved in. Raising and distributing funds for *tzedakah*, ransoming prisoners from the Czar's prisons (פִּדְיוֹן שְׁבוּיִים) and above all, seeking to reverse many of the Czar's evil decrees which were intended to harass and eventually eliminate *Yiddishkeit*.[1]

The *Chiddushei HaRim* was also immersed in the struggle against the *maskilim* who often collaborated with the Czarist regime to close down yeshivos and to even prohibit Jews from wearing their distinctive garb. According to him, the struggle against *Haskalah* and their sympathizers in government circles was included in the category of יֵהָרֵג וְאַל יַעֲבוֹר, halachic issues of such significance that a Jew must die rather than violate these precepts. During the height of the struggle against *Haskalah*, the *Chiddushei HaRim* was forced to go into hiding and change his surname from Rottenberg to Alter (which is still used by his descendants today) in order to elude the Russian police who were seeking to arrest him.

Despite all the turmoil and challenges of those years, the *Chiddushei HaRim* nonetheless found the time to transcribe and publish his *chiddushei Torah* on *Shas* and *Shulchan Aruch*.

It was only in the last few years of his life that the chassidic movement, led by Rav Yitzchak Meir, became associated with the small Warsaw suburb of Ger (known in Polish as *Gora Kalwaria*). Seeking to escape the many pressures that resulted from the growth of his chassidic movement and from simply being located in metropolitan Warsaw, the *Chiddushei HaRim* accepted the offer of the town of Ger to be their Rav.[2]

In reality, the converse occurred. The small town of Ger became transformed from a sleepy suburb of Warsaw to a spiritual center of Polish Jewry. Warsaw, on the other hand, became known in Gerrer circles as וואַרְשָׁע הַסְּמוּכָה לְגוּר, *Warsaw which is adjacent to Ger*. The throngs coming to the home of the Gerrer Rebbe (as he was now known) were so great that a special railroad train was commissioned to bring *chassidim* from Warsaw to this small town (see the introduction to *Days of Joy* for a description of the pilgrimage and the train trip to Ger). Already during the *Chiddushei HaRim*'s lifetime, Ger — and Gerrer *Chassidus* — developed into a great center of Torah and *avodas Hashem* and as a focal point of Polish Jewry.

Explaining why the *tefillah* of אֱלֹקַי נְשָׁמָה, dealing with the daily restoration of the soul is recited immediately after *Bircas HaTorah*, the *Chiddushei HaRim* said simply, "Without Torah, what value is a *neshamah*?" This humble, unassuming individual, the *Chiddushei HaRim*, through his learning, his personality and writings, as well as his leadership of the chassidic movement, contributed immeasurably to the restoration of Torah to the *neshamah* of *Klal Yisrael*.

---

1. Eastern Poland was then ruled by Czarist Russia. This entire region was known as Congress Poland since it was allocated to Russia at the Congress of Vienna (1815).

2. The *Chiddushei HaRim* actually inherited this position from his father Rav Yisrael who had served as the town's Rav in his old age.

◄§ The Sfas Emes: R' Yehuda Aryeh Leib Alter

As a *bachur*, R' Yehuda Aryeh Leib Alter of Ger, better known as the *Sfas Emes*, would often stay up all night studying Torah. After one such session, he returned to his room for some much-needed rest when it was already day. A short while later, his grandfather, the revered *Chiddushei HaRim*, happened to notice his grandson apparently sleeping the day away. Quickly he roused the slumbering scholar and gently admonished him for wasting precious time that could be better used for Hashem's service. Throughout the benign dressing-down Yehuda Aryeh Leib remained firmly quiet, and when his grandfather finished, gave his solemn word to do better in the future.

News of this encounter reached one of Yehuda Aryeh Leib's comrades, who could not understand his friend's silence. "Why didn't you say anything when the Rebbe spoke to you?" he asked him. "Couldn't you have told him the truth, that you had learned through the night and had earned a short rest?"

"What? And miss such an opportunity?" was the response.

"What do you mean?"

"Every word a wise man speaks is precious. The Torah tells us that when Moshe scolded the tribes of Reuven and Gad for asking to settle on the east bank of the Jordan River, thinking that they wanted to get out of the battle to conquer *Eretz Yisrael*, they listened patiently. Only after he finished did they explain that they had no intention of abandoning the other tribes, and that their soldiers would lead the fight to take the Land.

"Why didn't they speak up to defend themselves at the beginning of Moshe's lecture? Because they were eager to hear every word that their leader Moshe had to say, even if it was misdirected chastisement.

"So when my holy grandfather told me how to improve myself, I considered it a great opportunity, not an insult. Not every day am I privileged to receive personal advice from such a sage, and I didn't want to miss it by interrupting with excuses."

This keen perceptiveness displayed by the *Sfas Emes* already in his youth continued to develop much more as he matured. His veneration of the Torah tradition and the living vessels who preserved it, as well as his unrelenting quest for new insights into Hashem's teachings, characterized his life and work until his last days.

Rabbi Yehuda Aryeh Leib Alter was the scion of a noble Rabbinic and chassidic family. His family tree included such Torah luminaries as Rabbi Meir of Rothenberg, Rabbi Yosel Sirkes (known as the *Bach*), and Rabbi Yonasan Eibeschutz. His grandfather, Rabbi Yitzchak Meir Alter of Ger, was known as the *Chiddushei HaRim*, after the title of the illustrious series of novellae he published. Rabbi Yitzchak Meir was a devoted disciple of such chassidic leaders as the Maggid of Koznitz, Rabbi Simcha Bunim of Peshis'cha, and Rabbi Menachem Mendel of Kotzk. It was he who founded the chassidic dynasty of Ger.

While publicly Rabbi Yitzchak Meir was an esteemed leader with a large and devoted following, his personal life was clouded with tragedy. He and his rebbetzin had thirteen children, all of whom died young. The last child, Rabbi Avraham Mordechai, was a sickly person, and by the age of 30 his condition had deteriorated to such an extent that the doctors expected the worst. When the end seemed inevitably at hand, his father came to his sickbed and urged him to cling to life. He said, "The Torah commands us, 'Choose life!' Hashem will reward you with additional years, and with a child to carry on your legacy."

These words boosted Rabbi Avraham Mordechai's spirits and his condition began to improve. Although his constitution remained weak, he lived on and within a year his prayers were answered. On the 29th of Nissan 5607 (1847), he and his wife were blessed with a son whom they named Yehuda, as an expression of thanks to Hashem for His compassion (cf. Bereishis 29:35). On this joyous occasion the Chiddushei HaRim wrote of his newborn grandson, "May the spirit of the Lord be upon him: the spirit of wisdom and understanding, of courage and purpose. And may all his endeavors in life be successful."

Because of Rabbi Avraham Mordechai's continuing weakness, it was agreed that the Chiddushei HaRim himself would supervise the child's upbringing. Thus a strong bond grew between the Rebbe and his grandson, especially after Rabbi Avraham Mordechai's tragic death when the child was only 8. Under the Rebbe's guidance, the boy received a thorough Torah education, benefiting from both the personal instruction and the powerful example of one of the greatest scholars and leaders of the time. The Chiddushei HaRim also secured the services of a highly competent and learned tutor for his grandson. In order to obtain this position, the tutor had to comply with three requests of the Sfas Emes' grandfather: to wake up his talmid every morning before dawn, to learn with him at least 18 hours every day, and to encourage the young disciple to deduce a new Torah thought every day. As demanding as these conditions may appear to us, they were met and exceeded by the Sfas Emes. No matter how early the melamed came, the young talmid was already awake and ready to learn. In a similar vein, when R' Chaim Halberstam, the author of Divrei Chaim and Rebbe of Sanz, met the Chiddushei HaRim's grandson, he exclaimed, "This young man is not simply a מְחַדֵּשׁ (someone who arrives at novel Torah insights), but rather he is himself a חִידוּשׁ (an unusual phenomenon) — an incredibly brilliant scholar at so young an age."[1]

---

1. This warm relationship between the Sfas Emes and the Divrei Chaim lasted until the latter's death. The Sfas Emes' father-in-law Rabbi Yidel Kaminer was a grandson of the Baruch Taam, the renowned gaon who was the father-in-law of Rav Chaim Halberstam. R' Yidel was consequently a nephew of the Sanzer Rav. After his wedding, the Sfas Emes resided for a short time at the Divrei Chaim's residence. Many years later, the two chassidic dynasties Ger and Sanz were again united — after the Sfas Emes' first wife passed away, he married the granddaughter of the Divrei Chaim.

The Rebbe took pains that his only grandson should grow up with a pure and honest character. This was accomplished through a careful upbringing that included a sagacious mixture of love and discipline. For example, once it happened that the boy was served barley for lunch. As children are wont to do, he shook his head and refused to eat until food more to his taste could be found. Recognizing that such arrogance could not be left unchecked, the Rebbe saw to it that the boy's lunches consisted of nothing but barley for the next *four weeks*. Eventually, Yehuda Aryeh Leib came to understand the point, never to be ungrateful to Hashem for the gifts He gives us.

At the age of 8, the boy went with his grandfather on a lengthy journey to visit the Kotzker Rebbe, who recognized in the youngster a wondrous prodigy. When asked why he had subjected the youngster to such long and arduous travel, the Gerrer Rebbe replied, "I wanted him to see and learn from a real Jew." From this visit, Yehuda Aryeh Leib developed a lifelong respect for the Kotzker Rebbe.

The *Sfas Emes* related an interesting incident that occurred while he was in Kotzk. The Rebbetzin mentioned that a theft had occurred in their home. When the Rebbe's *shamash* related the news to him, he reacted simply: "How is this possible? The Torah says לֹא תִגְנֹבוּ (*Do not steal*)." From this simple incident, the *Sfas Emes* learned a lifelong lesson in אֱמוּנָה פְּשׁוּטָה, simple faith in the Torah and *Chazal's* teachings.

As Yehuda Aryeh Leib approached the age of *bar mitzvah*, his enormous potential as a scholar became increasingly obvious. His grandfather, who by now had assumed the role of Rebbe of the chassidic court in the town of Ger near Warsaw, derived deep satisfaction from the boy's progress. When Yehuda was married at the age of 15 in 5622 (1862) to the daughter of Rabbi Yudel Kaminer, a highly respected *talmid chacham*, the Gerrer Rebbe told Rabbi Kaminer, "The Talmud teaches that someone who gives a gift should inform the recipient of its value. I can tell you with great pride that my grandson Leibele is a very valuable prize indeed!"

Before his passing, the *Chiddushei HaRim* made it clear that he wanted his gifted grandson, still barely out of his teens, to assume the mantle of leading his *chassidim* after he would no longer be able to do so. The young man, in his great modesty, expressed reservations about his fitness to assume this great responsibility at such a young age. In reply, the *Chiddushei HaRim* told him the following parable:

Once a mountain climber set himself the goal of climbing to a very high and difficult-to-reach peak. After long exertion, he finally arrived and was dismayed to find a group of small children playing there. "How on earth did you ever get here?" he asked them. "I struggled so long and hard to ascend to this peak, surely you are too young to achieve such a feat."

"Ah!" said one of the children. "You had to struggle because you started from the foot of the mountain. For us it was no problem. You see, we were born here."

With this parable, the *Chiddushei HaRim* intended to convey to his grandson that, in spite of his tender years, he had been born to greatness. Once he assumed the role of Rebbe, he would see that he was naturally suited for it.

Four years after his grandson's wedding, Rabbi Yitzchak Meir passed away. His last words were, "Leibele *Kaddish*," which his *chassidim* understood to mean that Yehuda Aryeh Leib should recite *Kaddish* for him, and take over as his successor. However, the retiring grandson felt that he was too young and inexperienced for such a weighty position and, despite the pleas of the *chassidim*, he refused.

Instead, he left Ger and found a mentor in Rabbi Chanoch Henoch HaKohen, who resided in Alexander. For four years he studied at his master's feet, preparing for the challenges he knew lay ahead. When Rabbi Chanoch Henoch died in 5630 (1870), Yehuda Aryeh Leib could no longer turn down the renewed requests from his grandfather's *chassidim*, and reluctantly agreed to serve as their Rebbe.

Once having accepted the position, however, he devoted himself wholeheartedly to his duties. The Gerrer *chassidim* quickly came to appreciate not only his sagacity but also the pure motives that governed all of his actions. He abolished the custom, prevalent in many chassidic circles, of accepting monetary gifts (*pidyonos*) from his *chassidim*, and relied instead for his livelihood on the meager proceeds of a tobacco shop run by his wife. Though he was not involved in the day-to-day operation of the business, he maintained careful supervision to ensure that it was run with scrupulous honesty. When he noticed that a wholesaler, who numbered among his *chassidim*, was selling his wares to the shop at a lower than normal price, he quickly put an end to the practice out of fear that the seller might, perhaps unconsciously, be inviting favoritism from the Rebbe.

Rabbi Yehuda Aryeh Leib and his family (including ten children, four of whom died in infancy) lived frugally, giving all of their income to charity apart from what they needed for the most basic necessities. He frowned on costly and extravagant celebrations and constantly reminded his *chassidim* that conspicuous consumption has no part in the lifestyle of Jews who wish to sanctify themselves. He and his family were sustained in their asceticism by their devotion to Torah study and community service. As much as he could, he tried to inculcate these values in his followers as well.

A *chassid* from a distant town once came to him complaining that he grew lonely because there were no other *chassidim* living near him.

Said the *Sfas Emes*, "If you have a Gemara with you, then you can never be lonely."

When people called on him to seek his advice (he usually received visitors between 9:30 and 11 o'clock in the morning), they invariably found him sitting before a volume of the *Shulchan Aruch*, which he studied every free moment. "How can one give advice without a *Shulchan Aruch* at hand?" he explained. The *Sfas Emes'* extraordinary proficiency in all aspects of Torah was acquired in large part by his insistence on not wasting a minute.

Somehow, the *Sfas Emes* found time to commit his own profound thoughts to writing, in commentaries on such holy books as Torah, Talmud, *Tehillim*, *Koheles*, *Mishlei*, *Esther*, and *Pirkei Avos*. Posthumously his writings were given the name *Sfas Emes* by his children, based on the verse (*Mishlei* 12:19): שְׂפַת אֱמֶת תִּכּוֹן לָעַד וְעַד אַרְגִּיעָה לְשׁוֹן שָׁקֶר, *The lips of truth will be established forever, but a lying tongue exists for only a moment.* This was the closing line in the last section he wrote in his commentary on the Torah and festivals (*Parashas VaYechi*, 5665), before he was stricken with his final illness. This title provided the Gerrer Rebbe with the name by which he is commonly known.

The following story helps us understand why the *Sfas Emes'* writings are characterized by such a cryptic and abbreviated style. Once he suggested to a certain *talmid chacham* that he write down his *chiddushei Torah*. The latter replied that he would like to but he simply did not have the time.

Said the *Sfas Emes*, "If you write tersely, as I do, it won't take so much of your time."

The *Sfas Emes* rarely agreed to leave his home, but on one occasion he had to travel to another city by train. When he arrived at his destination, he found a large crowd waiting to greet him. Reluctantly he accepted this honor but when one person in the crowd addressed him with the title "Rebbe," the *Sfas Emes* could not restrain himself.

"I'm not your rebbe!" he exclaimed. "I've never taught you anything."

The *Sfas Emes'* grandson, R' Yisrael Alter,[1] later remarked, this was the only time he knew of that his grandfather was in error. "He was the Rebbe of the whole Jewish people."

Despite near-total absorption with his studies, writings, and Rabbinic duties, the *Sfas Emes* also found time to take a deeply concerned interest in world events, especially those that affected the Jewish people. The suffering of Russian Jewry in the pogroms of the 1880s caused him deep anguish, as did the conscription of Jews to fight in the Russo-Japanese War of 1905. To those forced to fight in the Russian army he offered compassionate encouragement and heartfelt advice, urging them not to be tempted away from the tents of Judaism in their time of trial.

These cares took a tool on his health, however, and shortly after Russia's disastrous defeat by Japan he took ill. He passed away on the 5th of Shevat, 5665 (1905), at the age of 58. In retrospect, we can speculate that Hashem wished to spare this luminary and *tzaddik* the anguish of witnessing the suffering that the First World War was to have on European Jewry.

His years on earth were relatively short, but as his son, Rabbi Avraham Mordechai, noted on the way to the funeral, "He lived a full lifetime of complete days." In that lifetime, he helped build the town of Ger into the Jerusalem of Polish *chassidus*. Through his leadership, writings, and personal example, he gave powerful expression to the ideals of devotion to Torah and commitment to the Jewish people.

---

1. Author of the *sefer Beis Yisrael* and Gerrer Rebbe until 5738 (1978).

In order to give the reader some appreciation of the *Sfas Emes'* profundity, sagacity, *kedushah* and impact on his followers, we cite (and freely translate) an excerpt of a *kvitel* given to the *Sfas Emes'* son, the *Imrei Emes*, by a venerable *chassid* who remembered and attended the chassidic courts of the Kotzker, *Chiddushei HaRim* and R' Henoch of Alexander.

הייתי משמש בקודש שלשה קדשים האלה (דער קאצקער, דער חידושי הרי"ם און דער רבי"ן ר' הענוך פון אלעקסאנדער זצ"ל) כל השירים קודש ושיר השירים קודש הקדשים. הוא ניהו אביו מרן הקדוש ז"ל נבג"מ זי"ע ועכ"י אמן. הוא אשר היה מאיר בתורתו וקדושתו על כל פני תבל מקצהו ועד קצהו ועליו אמרו ז"ל אחד יש בינינו שראוי שתשרה עליו שכינה כמשה רבינו ע"ה אלא שאין שאין דורו ראוי לכך הוא אשר מסר נפשו על כלל ישראל כמרע"ה שנאמר עליו וירא בסבלותם ופירש"י ז"ל נתן עיניו ולבו להיות מיצר בצרת ישראל . . . יותר ממאה פעמים הייתי בגור במשך ל"ה שנים שעברו הרבה תורה למדתי ממנו ועפ"י רוב מה שהבנתי הבנתי בנקל ומה שלא הבנתי לא די שלא ירדתי לסוף דעתו אלא אף תחלת דעתו לא עמדתי. כי כל מי שהיו לו עינים לראות ולב להבין הי' רואה בעין שכלו שהשכינה מדברת מתוך גרונו של אותו צדיק.

I had the zechus of knowing intimately three sainted Rebbes (the Kotzker, the Chiddushei HaRim, and R' Henoch of Alexander). Rabbi Akiva's description of the unique role of Shir HaShirim may also be applied to your father זצ"ל, *'All the songs of Tanach (i.e. all the Rebbes prior to the Sfas Emes) are sacred but the Song of Songs (the Sfas Emes) was the most sacred of all.' The light of his Torah penetrated the entire universe, from end to end. Of him Chazal would say, 'There is an individual in our generation who deserves to perceive the Shechinah (Divine Presence) just as Moshe Rabbeinu did, but alas our generation was not worthy of this high honor.' Just as Moshe suffered along with the masses of Klal Yisrael in Egypt, so too did your father intensely perceive all of our generation's suffering.*

I was privileged to visit Ger over 100 times during the 35 years of your father's tenure and I learned a great deal of Torah from him. While I was able to comprehend much of what he taught me without much difficulty, there were other aspects of his profound teachings that I couldn't even begin to understand.[1] *Everyone who had eyes to see, and a heart to understand, would readily grasp that the Shechinah was speaking through the voice of that tzaddik.*

For a more complete appreciation of some fundamental aspects of the Sfas Emes' philosophy see The Three Festivals, pp. 23-29.

---

1. The writer of this *kvittel* is alluding to the renowned expression, לֹא יָרַדְתִּי לְסוֹף דַּעְתּוֹ, "I cannot fully comprehend what a particular gadol is saying." In the Sfas Emes' case, he couldn't even grasp the beginning — even an infinitesimal portion of his Torah.

◈ The Imrei Emes: R' Avraham Mordechai Alter

Gerrer chassidic tradition preserves the story of the *Sfas Emes'* Chanukah *gelt*. When the *Chiddushei HaRim* was distributing Chanukah *gelt* to his grandchildren, he asked his most beloved grandson, Yehuda Leib, the future *Sfas Emes*, what he desired. When the *Sfas Emes* replied that he didn't need anything, the *Chiddushei HaRim* promised him the best possible "Chanukah *gelt*," a son. And indeed, a few months before the *Chiddushei HaRim's* passing, on the 7th of Teves 5626, a son was born to the *Sfas Emes'* wife, Yocheved Rivkah. When the newborn infant was brought to his great-grandfather, the *Chiddushei HaRim* looked at him for quite some time and proclaimed proudly, "There was nothing more that I could have asked for."

R' Avraham Mordechai, growing up in the sacred environment of his father's chassidic court, already at an early age displayed great potential to follow in the footsteps of his ancestors and become an outstanding *gaon* and *tzaddik*. Upon the occasion of his son's *bar mitzvah*, the *Sfas Emes*, in a letter to his relative, the Piltzer Rebbe, described his son as a כְּלִי מוּכָן לְכָל הַשְּׁלֵימוּת, "a vessel that has the potential for perfection."

Already in his youth, the *Imrei Emes* was known as a *gaon* and as a *masmid* (diligent student of Torah). After the *Imrei Emes'* marriage to Chaya Radde the daughter of R' Noach Shachor of Biale, his father arranged for him to study with R' Ben Zion Ostrover, a venerable *chassid* of the Kotzker and the *Chiddushei HaRim*. An assiduous collector of *sefarim*, R' Avraham Mordechai studied the entire contents of every one (including the *cover* page) of the many thousands of volumes in his collection.

Upon the passing of the *Sfas Emes* on the 5th of Shevat 5666 (1905), the *Imrei Emes* was extremely reluctant to assume his father's mantle and become the Rebbe of thousands of *chassidim*. Eventually, he yielded to the importuning of many *chassidim* and gave his first *tisch* on Shavuos 5665 (1906).

Despite his extraordinary humility, the *Imrei Emes* made it apparent at the outset that he would not simply emulate his father. In fact, he argued, "I only resemble my father in one respect. He never merely imitated someone. I too, will never be content to simply emulate someone else without contemplating the consequences."

Indeed, as the new Rebbe of a rapidly growing movement, he instituted several innovations. Firstly, he insisted that the halachically preferred times for *davening* be vigorously observed. For example, *Shacharis*, which had commenced at a much later hour for many years going back to the era of Kotzk, would now begin punctually at 7:30 a.m., seven days a week. When some of the *chassidim* objected to this radical change in custom, R' Avraham of Parisov answered their objections with the following *mashal*. An individual was accustomed to being served a sumptuous meal by his wife, albeit only after a long wait. As long as the food was excellent, the wait was worthwhile. However, once the food deteriorated in quality, he saw no purpose in waiting that long. So too, if our *tefillos* were on the spiritual level of our ancestors in Kotzk, one could justify *davening* at a later hour. But, for our simple prayers, such lengthy preparations are no longer appropriate.

He also insisted that his *chassidim* spend many hours every day learning Torah, both on an individual basis and in the hundreds of Gerrer *shtieblach* that dotted Poland. Thus, he instituted a rule that an hour be devoted to communal study of Torah every Friday afternoon between *Minchah* and *Maariv* and on Shabbos morning before *"leining"* (reading of the *parashah*). The Rebbe not only demanded *hasmadah* from his *chassidim* but also displayed such diligence as well. Despite his enormous burdens as the leader of a chassidic group numbering over 100,000 followers (and some estimate as many as 250,000 followers) and as one of the foremost leaders of World Jewry, he found time to study 70 different topics (some for as little as a few minutes) every day. For the *Imrei Emes*, time was the most valuable commodity. Even when attending *simchos* or other community events, his mind was always absorbed in *limud haTorah* and his eyes were always looking at a *sefer*. When encountering an individual, he would always seek to "talk in learning" rather than simply converse with him. The *Imrei Emes* not only served as an abstract role model for his *chassidim*, but actually derived the great satisfaction of seeing thousands of *bnei Torah* and many hundreds of great *lamdanim*, young men who were conversant in the entire *Shas*, emerge from the ranks of his *chassidim*.

As immersed as he was in his learning, the Rebbe found time to be deeply involved in the challenges facing *Klal Yisrael* at large. He acutely felt the pain and poverty of much of Eastern European Jewry and was opposed to declaring another public fast day, fearing that this would further weaken our brethren who did not have enough to eat every day. He labored tirelessly to alleviate the plight of the thousands of people who pleaded for his blessings and for all those who sought help in earning a *parnasah*.

The following incident, related by the grandson of a young man who benefited from the *Imrei Emes' berachah*, demonstrates the Rebbe's concern for every Jew, his sagacity and insight and also his special concern for young people. A young boy, about 9 years old, realizing that his mother was gravely ill, traveled alone by horse and wagon from Warsaw to Ger to see the *Imrei Emes*. Upon arriving at the Rebbe's residence, he was told that the *Imrei Emes* was meeting with another chassidic leader. Moreover, it was highly unlikely that the Rebbe would listen to a child his age. The boy burst into tears. Upon hearing the commotion that ensued, the Rebbe opened the door to his private chambers and welcomed the youngster. Without even hearing the child's concerns, he assured him, "Go home, your mother is already well. However your father is worried about your whereabouts." And indeed his mother enjoyed a *refuah sheleimah*.

The *Imrei Emes* was deeply involved in many causes and had a particularly passionate interest in the future of *Klal Yisrael's* youth. Whereas in the past, contact with a chassidic Rebbe was limited to older people, he found time to speak to *bachurim* (unmarried young men). It was said in jest (and misinterpreted by an irreligious writer) that 10,000 of the *Imrei Emes'* *chassidim* ate on Yom Kippur. Of course this was referring to the children among his *chassidim* who were not yet *bar mitzvah*. The fruits of the *Imrei Emes'* intense efforts on behalf of young people manifested themselves in many respects — in the steadfast adherence of his *chassidim's* children to Torah and *mitzvos*, despite the many ill winds that buffeted Polish Jewry between the wars and most poignantly, in the *mesiras nefesh* of these young people in the crematoriums and slave labor camps. Gerrer *chassidim* acted defiantly, in full view of the Nazis ימ״ש, continuing to learn Torah, *daven* and, in many cases, even refusing to shave their *payos* and beards.

Agudath Israel was the most cherished of all the causes that the Rebbe was involved with. As busy as he was, he always had time for the Agudah. He was a founding member of the Agudah and attended the preliminary conference in Bad Nauheim, Germany in 1909 (along with *gedolim* such as Rav Chaim Soloveitchik, R' Eliezer Gordon of Telz, Rav Chaim Ozer Grodzenski of Vilna) and was a long-time participant in every aspect of the Agudah. He infused the movement with all of his energy, enthusiasm and *daas Torah* (opinions on worldly matters based on a Torah outlook) for almost 40 years.[1] In particular, the *Imrei Emes* was immersed in the decisions faced by Agudath Israel regarding building a Jewish *yishuv* in *Eretz Yisrael* and regarding its policy about accepting a partition of the land. The Rebbe not only urged his *chassidim*, wherever possible, to leave Poland where the future of Jewry was questionable and move to *Eretz Yisrael*, but he also visited *Eretz Yisrael* five times between the First and Second World Wars.[2]

Another cause close to the *Imrei Emes'* heart was the Beis Yaakov movement. His endorsement (and that of the Belzer Rebbe) lent a great deal of credence to the movement started by Sarah Schenirer and Dr. Leo Deutschlander. In particular, his support spurred *chassidim* to send their daughters to the Beis Yaakov movement's schools. Perhaps the best way to appreciate the contribution of the *Imrei Emes* — and the other *gedolim* supporting the Bais Yaakov movement — is to consider the alternative. One shudders to think of the consequences for *Klal Yisrael* had Sarah Schenirer's dream not been realized; an entire generation of women — whose parents and siblings were loyal *chassidim* of the *Imrei Emes* and other Rebbes — would have been lost to the cauldron of assimilation and *Haskalah*. Instead, these women became paragons of *tznius* (modesty) and

---

1. Students of the *Sfas Emes'* writings will appreciate that the dream of a unified Torah-true Jewry was already espoused by the *Sfas Emes*. See *The Three Festivals*, p. 126 for the *Sfas Emes'* novel approach to וְאָהַבְתָּ לְרֵעֲךָ כָּמוֹךָ.

2. During one of his visits, he played a major role in attempting to reconcile the two major factions of the Orthodox *yishuv*, those supporting Rav Yosef Chaim Sonnenfeld and those supporting Rav Avraham Yitzchak Kook.

middos tovos and led productive lives building Torah. During the Holocaust, many of these righteous women heroically and gallantly sanctified Hashem's Name.

Just as the *Imrei Emes* feared, the days of Eastern European Jewry were numbered. The heartrending suffering of German Jewry, commencing with the advent of Hitler ימ״ש in 1933, broke his heart and also strengthened his resolve to encourage his followers to migrate to Palestine. Unfortunately, the *Imrei Emes'* dream of a peaceful migration of Eastern European Jewry to *Eretz Yisrael* was not to be realized. The worst fears of the Rebbe came true — within a few years, the overwhelming majority of his *chassidim* and of Eastern European Jewry went up in the smokestacks. Thousands of *shtieblach* and their *sifrei Torah* were torched by the frenzied mobs. Even the last remains of Eastern European Jewry's ancestors were vandalized by an implacable foe determined to wipe the last vestiges of Hashem's people from the face of the earth.

The Rebbe himself shared in the ordeal of his brethren. Though he miraculously escaped (for an account of the many miracles involved in his release from the clutches of the Gestapo who had mounted an intensive effort to apprehend him, see *Dos Yiddishe Vort, Adar-Nissan 5758*, pp. 53-54) along with his children (who eventually succeeded him as the Rebbe of Ger), he lost over 50 grandchildren and great-grandchildren. In addition, his precious writings on all of Torah were permanently lost. Arriving in *Eretz Yisrael* in poor physical condition and brokenhearted over the tremendous losses that he had suffered along with *Klal Yisrael*, the *Imrei Emes* settled in Yeshiva *Sfas Emes* of Yerushalayim, which he had established during a previous visit to *Eretz Yisrael*. Due to his own infirmities as well as the manifold *tzaros* of the Jewish people, the *Imrei Emes* no longer assumed a public leadership role. He no longer held *tisch* and rarely spoke in public. However, behind the scenes, he was available to guide all those who sought his counsel.

The final years of the *tzaddik* brought joy and more suffering. He rejoiced at the wedding of his son (from his second marriage) R' Pinchas Menachem, later known as the *Pnei Menachem* (who served as Rebbe from 1992 to 1996; see the essay on him), and grieved at the outbreak of war in *Eretz Yisrael* in 1948. This *gaon* and *tzaddik*, the *Imrei Emes*, passed away on Shavuos 1948 during the intense fighting for control of Yerushalayim. Rav Isaac HaLevi Herzog stated so aptly, "The Torah was given on Shavuos and it returned to Heaven on Shavuos."

⋖§ The Beis Yisrael: Rav Yisrael Alter

Perhaps no Rebbe of Ger had a more difficult task than the *Beis Yisrael*. Whereas his predecessors could each build on the foundations laid by previous generations, Rav Yisrael Alter stood on ruins. His "foundation" was the crematoria of Auschwitz, the hundreds of Gerrer *shtieblach* razed to the ground and their tens of thousands of members whose eternal martyred *neshamos* ringed the כִּסֵּא הַכָּבוֹד (Divine Throne). Even those who survived the Holocaust and found their way to *Eretz Yisrael* were emaciated physically and spiritually despondent. And yet, somehow, in the 29 years of his reign (1948-1977), this Torah giant managed to rebuild not only Ger but also to magnetize the entire chassidic community in *Eretz Yisrael*. Just as Rabbi Akiva, mourning the loss of his 24,000 disciples, nonetheless managed to rebuild, beginning with a small nucleus of five sages, so too the *Beis Yisrael* somehow transformed a small and despairing base into a mighty Torah community.

To appreciate how the *Beis Yisrael* accomplished such a renaissance of Torah life, let us turn to his roots. He was, of course, the scion of great *gedolim*, the son of the *Imrei Emes*, the grandson of the *Sfas Emes*, and the great-great-grandson of the *Chiddushei HaRim*. Even as a child, he displayed tremendous potential, being dubbed by the *Sfas Emes* at the age of 5 as "Reb Yisrael." The great Rogatchover Gaon, who was known to never give undeserved compliments, said of him, "This young man knows *Shas.*" At age 15, he was engaged to the daughter of Reb Yaakov Meir Biderman, the son-in-law of the *Sfas Emes*.

One of the outstanding ingredients in the remarkable resurgence of Torah and *chassidus* in *Eretz Yisrael* was the steady return of young people to the Torah fold. Reb Yisrael possessed the ability to reach out and connect with young people. This special gift was already evident in pre-war Poland. While in most chassidic circles, *chassidus* and especially close contact with Rebbes was deemed to be the exclusive province of older people (or at least married *yungeleit*), in Ger, young people played a central role. The *Imrei Emes* assigned his son R' Yisrael to be his emissary to Gerrer youth, a mission which he performed spectacularly. No description of Poland between the wars would be complete without discussing the numerous *batei midrashim* that were established all over Poland, where Gerrer youth immersed themselves in Torah and *chassidus*. Additionally, no account of the Holocaust is complete without considering the tenacity and bravery of these same young people who continued learning Torah under the most adverse circumstances.

How did the *Beis Yisrael* rebuild Torah? Firstly, by picking up where he left off, with the young people. In three decades the Gerrer Rebbe built a network of Torah institutions where thousands of children were educated. His involvement in building Torah went beyond his own *chassidus*. The Gerrer Rebbe was one of the founders of *Chinuch Atzmai* (the Torah school network in Israel) and worked closely with his cousin Rabbi Pinchas Levin who was the head of the Beis Yaakov movement in *Eretz Yisrael*.

To the Gerrer Rebbe, *any ben Torah* (not necessarily one of his *chassidim*) was special. He felt a particular closeness to *talmidim* of Yeshivos Chevron, Kol Torah and Etz Chaim and, for a while, his *chavrusah* was someone who had studied in Chevron (the now-renowned Rav Moshe Sternbuch, author of *Moadim Uzmanim*, a classic compendium on the *moadim*).

How else did the Rebbe rebuild Torah? By turning to the same institutions that his father, the *Imrei Emes*, had supported in Europe, especially Agudath Israel. As a member of the *Moetzes Gedolei HaTorah* (Council of Torah Sages) he was involved in every major decision of that august body during the three decades of his tenure.

How did the Gerrer Rebbe rebuild? By not wasting time. Just as in Kotzk and in pre-war Ger, so too in *Eretz Yisrael*, time was considered the most valuable commodity. For example, the time for *davening* (refer to the previous essay concerning the *Imrei Emes'* innovations in this area) was scrupulously observed. He found time for everything: time to *daven*, to learn, to receive *chassidim*, to participate in communal affairs. His day began before dawn with a program of intense Torah study, and he expected the Gerrer *bachurim* to do the same. A familiar sight in Yerushalayim was when the soldiers from Schnellers Army Base jogged by the Gerrer Yeshiva and responded to his nod with "*Boker Tov*, Rebbe."

And finally, how did he rebuild Torah? By relating to tens of thousands of individuals and their problems as if each was unique. With a few brief well-chosen words, he would respond to economic, medical, spiritual or emotional problems, and the visitor would generally leave with a fresh new perspective on the situation and with the perception that his burden was somewhat alleviated. It is well known that many of his *chassidim* (and those of his successors, his brothers the *Lev Simcha* and the *Pnei Menachem*, to be discussed in the subsequent essays) did not descend from Polish, let alone Gerrer, backgrounds. In fact, some of his followers were from entirely non-chassidic backgrounds, propelled by the magnetism, sincerity and sheer greatness of this major builder and rebuilder of Torah.

◄§ The Lev Simcha: R' Simcha Bunim Alter

To the reader of our previous historical essays, the name Simcha Bunim evokes memories of the first personality whose life is described in detail, the famed R' Simcha Bunim of Peshis'cha. And in many respects, the life of the *Beis Yisrael's* brother and successor resembles that of his namesake.

Just as R' Simcha Bunim of Peshis'cha made every effort to conceal his greatness, operating under the guise of a lumber merchant and later a pharmacist, so too this Gerrer Rebbe ostensibly was for much of his life a highly successful international real estate entrepreneur. The resemblance continues. In the pursuit of his *parnasah*, R' Simcha Bunim of Peshis'cha traveled widely to Prussia, Hungary and Moravia. Wherever he went, he attempted to leave a positive impact. So too, Reb Simcha Bunim Alter in the guise of conducting business would attempt to improve the level of *Yiddishkeit* of his various host communities. For example, he anonymously contributed a large sum of money to repair the damaged *mikveh* in a British *kehillah*.

The exterior businesslike personality of both *gedolim* belied (and successfully masked) a very different interior. According to chassidic tradition, R' Simcha

Bunim of Peshis'cha was meditating about many of the most esoteric thoughts imaginable while supervising the transport of lumber along the Danube River. Likewise, R' Simcha Bunim Alter was once spotted gazing intently at an Antwerp show-window display. Upon closer inspection, and after noticing the perspiration running down his face, it became clear that the future Gerrer Rebbe was intensely concentrating on matters far beyond the contents of a Belgian store window. R' Simcha Bunim's effort to conceal his true greatness was carried to extraordinary lengths. Just as R' Simcha Bunim of Peshis'cha would *daven* relatively quickly, so too the Gerrer Rebbe. Afterwards, however, he would change his shirt which had become drenched with perspiration from the deep-seated emotions that would affect him every time he *davened*.

Another incident which illustrates to what lengths the *Lev Simcha* went to mask his greatness is told about the Klausenberger Rebbe's visit to him. The *Beis Yisrael* once took the Klausenberger Rebbe to visit Reb Simcha Bunim at his hotel room in the Galei Sanz hotel. Before knocking on the door, the *Beis Yisrael* told the Klausenberger Rebbe to peer through the keyhole, where he saw Reb Simcha Bunim engrossed in learning. By the time he opened the door for them the *sefarim* were gone, replaced by a copy of *Hamodia*, the Orthodox newspaper.

The resemblance is even more striking. Just as R' Simcha Bunim of Peshis'cha would at times don Western-style clothing (refer to the essay on his life), both for business purposes and to more effectively be *mekarev* (reach out to) his alienated brethren, so too, when assuming the title of Rebbe, Rav Simcha Bunim Alter eschewed the regal *levush* (clothing) often worn by Rebbes in favor of the simple clothing of an ordinary *chassid*.

Both R' Simcha Bunim of Peshis'cha and Rav Simcha Bunim Alter suffered greatly and accepted their personal suffering with complete faith. R' Simcha Bunim of Peshis'cha regarded his failing eyesight as a means of leaving This World and coming closer to Hashem. When the Rebbe's first daughter, born after 10 years of marriage, died half a year later, his wife was in the hospital recuperating from a serious operation. For a year he withheld the information from her, for fear that the tragedy would endanger her health. Moreover, R' Simcha Bunim would visit his wife every day in the hospital to tell her the antics of his daughter — who was no longer alive. Throughout his life he lived by the dictum of the *Chovos HaLevavos*, "A *chassid* has rejoicing on his face and keeps his sorrow in his heart."

R' Simcha Bunim of Peshis'cha was a true Torah giant and so too was his namesake. Rav Shlomo Zalman Auerbach who visited the Rebbe every *Chol HaMoed* commented, "Reb Simcha Bunim knows *Zevachim* and *Menachos* (tractates dealing with *korbanos*) as well as I know *Bava Kamma* (a more popular tractate dealing with damages and torts)." The Brisker Rav, Rav Yitzchak Zev Soloveitchik, told his children that Reb Simcha Bunim was a true *lamdan*, familiar with all of *Shas* and *Poskim*.

Perhaps, in the final analysis, both Torah leaders were remembered most for their innovations. Just as R' Simcha Bunim of Peshis'cha brought new life to the chassidic movement, so too the Gerrer Rebbe displayed his true genius by proposing and implementing a series of innovations that have left a permanent impact on the Torah world. At the sixth *Knessiah Gedolah* he instituted a *Daf Hayomi* for the Talmud *Yerushalmi* which previously had been studied only by great *talmidei chachamim*. In the decade and a half since this innovation, thousands of *bnei Torah* (not limited to the ranks of Gerrer *chassidim*) have adopted the practice of studying a page of *Yerushalmi* every day. New commentaries have been published to elucidate this relatively arcane area of Torah.

On the practical side, the Rebbe introduced a number of innovations which have significantly ameliorated the financial plight of *Eretz Yisrael's bnei Torah*, both within the Gerrer community and beyond.

It is not uncommon to hear complaints about the excessively high costs of lavish weddings and the virtual impossibility of purchasing an apartment in the Yerushalayim area. The Rebbe actually did something to remedy these problems, requiring his *chassidim* to drastically curtail the size and cost of weddings. Additionally, he spearheaded an extensive construction program of housing units in outlying areas of *Eretz Yisrael*. As a result, large Gerrer communities now exist in Ashdod, Arad, and Chatzor, boasting affordable housing designed to meet the needs of large families. In a sense, the newer *charedi* communities now dotting *Eretz Yisrael* (e.g. Kiryas Sefer, Beis Shemesh, Beitar) were all inspired by the initiative taken by the *Lev Simcha*. He also encouraged spiritual *chessed*, urging his *chassidim* to spend Shabbos in non-religious settlements to help bridge the gap between the Torah and the secular segments of Israeli society. When a spiritual threat to the Jewish people surfaced, the Rebbe was not afraid to lead the battle. He courageously led the struggle against the building of the Mormon Center of Brigham Young University on the Mount of Olives, and fought valiantly for *shemiras Shabbos* in Israel's many municipalities.

The *Chiddushei HaRim* once commented, "From the *Baal Shem Tov* to Peshis'cha is a commentary on the *Baal Shem Tov*; from Peshis'cha on is a commentary on Peshis'cha." One of the great commentaries on Peshis'cha, both through his teachings and his sainted lifestyle, was the great *Lev Simcha*. יהי זכרו ברוך

◆§ The Pnei Menachem: Rav Pinchas Menachem Alter

וְהָאִיכָּא וַרְדִּימַס? הַיְינוּ וַרְדִּימַע הַיְינוּ מְנַחֵם וְאַמַּאי קָרֵי לֵיהּ וַרְדִּימַס? שֶׁפָּנָיו דּוֹמִין לְוֶרֶד.

The Talmud relates that Rabbi Yose had five children. In response to the question that he had another child, Vardimus, the Talmud states that Vardimus is identical to Menachem, who was dubbed Vardimus because his face shone like a rose (*vered*).

This teaching of *Chazal* was utilized by Rav Dovid Olewski of Yeshivas Beis Yisrael in eulogizing the *Pnei Menachem*, Rav Pinchas Menachem Alter, at the Agudath Israel Convention in 5756 (1996).

In characterizing the previous Gerrer Rebbe, who returned his soul to his Maker suddenly on the 16th of Adar 5756, one is confronted with the problem as to which side of his multifaceted personality to emphasize: his greatness in Torah, his heartrending *tefillos* for *Klal Yisrael*, his sage advice given to thousands of petitioners, or his sensitive heart which suffered and empathized (not merely sympathized) with all of *Klal Yisrael's tzaros*. Perhaps, all these attributes are contained in Rav Olewski's description of the Rebbe's profile as similar to a rose. Anyone who merited to meet the Rebbe (as this writer did) will always remember his kindly face that exuded that rare combination of great *chachmah* and *ahavas Yisrael*.

Certainly, the Rebbe could be characterized as being brilliant. He admitted once that he completed *Shas* at an early age. His father, the *Imrei Emes*, and his mother, Feige Mintsha (whom the *Imrei Emes* married after his first wife passed away), had great aspirations for their son. As busy as he was with the burdens of *Klal Yisrael* and with his personal study sessions, the *Imrei Emes* found time to study with Pinchas Menachem every day. Miraculously escaping Nazi-occupied Warsaw with his father and two of his brothers, he learned in Ponovezh Yeshiva in Bnei Brak and later in Yeshivas Chayei Olam and Yeshiva Sfas Emes in Yerushalayim. At the time of his marriage (at age 20), the *Imrei Emes* characterized him as a בּוֹר סוּד שֶׁאֵינוֹ מְאַבֵּד טִפָּה, *a cemented cistern that does not lose a drop* (*Avos* 2:11). In 1957 he was appointed as the Rosh HaYeshiva of Yeshiva *Sfas Emes*. His *shiurim* dazzled the listeners with their scope and breadth. People who remembered pre-war Europe remarked that Rav Pinchas Menachem's *shiurim* reminded them of the classic Reb Menachem Ziemba. Rav Moshe Feinstein commented that Rav Pinchas Menachem reminded him of the Rogatchover Gaon, who had mastered the entirety of Torah.

The Rebbe was a great pleader and intercessor for *Klal Yisrael*. He never forgot the haunting memories of Nazi-occupied Warsaw and his miraculous rescue from the hands of the Gestapo. Braving a curfew to maintain a study session with his cousin, Pinchas Menachem was picked up by the Nazis and thrown into a truck that was headed to a slave labor camp (and probable death). Spurred on by an onlooker, he managed to jump off. But the anguished cries of his brothers who perished were never far away from him. His brief tenure as Rebbe (from 1992 — upon the passing of the *Lev Simcha* — till 1996) was marked by numerous tragedies in *Eretz Yisrael*. In particular, the terrorist attacks shortly before Purim 1996 tore at his heart. When he heard of the bomb at Dizengoff Square that exploded on *Taanis Esther* afternoon, he cried out, "I can bear it no longer." Witnesses report that he was crying incessantly at the grave of his father, the *Imrei Emes*, that was located near the Yeshiva Sfas Emes.

At his last *tisch* he spoke of the *mesiras nefesh* of Shaul *HaMelech* who went to battle against the Philistines knowing that he would not survive (having been informed by Shmuel that he would be killed by the foe). He spoke of David *HaMelech* who, in the 70 years of his life, completed his mission. Arriving home after the *tisch*, he said to the Rebbetzin the *pasuk*, וּמֹשֶׁה עָלָה אֶל הָאֱלֹקִים, *and Moshe went up to God [heaven]* (*Shemos* 19:3), explaining that sometimes *tzaddikim* have achieved all that they can for *Klal Yisrael* in this world, and feel that they can do more in heaven. Is it too much to assume that this *tzaddik* allowed himself to be the *korban* to avoid any future harsh decree?

PIRKEI AVOS

בָּל יִשְׂרָאֵל יֵשׁ לָהֶם חֵלֶק לָעוֹלָם הַבָּא, שֶׁנֶּאֱמַר: „וְעַמֵּךְ
כֻּלָּם צַדִּיקִים; לְעוֹלָם יִירְשׁוּ אָרֶץ, נֵצֶר מַטָּעַי,
מַעֲשֵׂה יָדַי לְהִתְפָּאֵר."

■ בָּל יִשְׂרָאֵל יֵשׁ לָהֶם חֵלֶק לָעוֹלָם הַבָּא — *All Israel has a share in the World to Come.*

⇜§ Setting Goals

אומרים זה מקודם לימוד המסכתא שלא ייאש עצמו שלא יוכל לקיים, ולאחריה
רבי חנניא בן עקשיא שלא יחשוב שהוא עול ואדרבא זכיה היא ויתעורר האדם
לעבודת בוראו כי המסכתא מלא מוסר ודברי תוכחות.

Both the prologue (*Kol Yisrael*) and the epilogue (*Rav Chananiah ben Akashya*) are significant. In the prologue, we emphasize that one should not despair. Even if one cannot achieve all the lofty ideals and high standards set in *Avos,* one still can anticipate enjoying a portion in the World to Come. In the epilogue, *Klal Yisrael* asserts that it is a privilege, rather than a burden, to observe Torah and *mitzvos.*

Bearing these two goals in mind — our eventual reward and our positive attitude towards the fulfillment of Hashem's will — we proceed to study the *Mesechta.*

⇜§ Enjoying the World to Come in This World

פי' גם בעולם הזה כל מעשיהם יש בהם חלק פנימיות מאור הצפון שנגנז במעשיו
גשמיי. ובמד' אחור קדם צרתני זכה זכה נוחל ב' עולמות כו' פי' שממשיך נחל וחיבור
משורש החיות אל ההסתר והעולם שיש בעוה"ז, כי מה שבח שנוחל עוה"ז, אך
מה שמחבר עוה"ז אל עולם העליון כנ"ל.
וזה הי' מכוון בריאת האדם בעולם הזה כדי לתקן כל הבריאה לברר שהכל מחיות
הש"י.

It is significant that the *mishnah* does not say בָּעוֹלָם הַבָּא, *in the World to Come,* which would refer to the eventual reward attained after our life on earth. Instead, it says לָעוֹלָם הַבָּא, literally *to the World to Come.* Even in This World, every action of the Jew is blessed with the aura of *Olam Haba.* This Divine gift is not always apparent. However, if one penetrates beneath the surface one detects a certain sanctity in every deed of the Torah-true Jew. This inner *kedushah* is derived from the sacred radiance of the World to Come that is enjoyed in some small measure in This World. In fact, the primary purpose of

*A*ll Israel has a share in the World to Come, as it is said (Yeshayahu 60:21): "And your people are all righteous; they shall inherit the land forever; a branch of My plantings, My handiwork, in which to take pride."

---

man's creation is that by virtue of his proper conduct he can elicit the latent Divine Spark that propels this material world. By doing so he can in some measure help to perfect the world.

In this light we may better appreciate a renowned Midrash stating that the Jewish people inherit This World as well as the World to Come (*Vayikra Rabbah* 14:1). While it may seem surprising that the Midrash extols the virtues of *Olam Hazeh* (especially the statement that we "inherit" This World), in reality the Midrash is referring to those aspects of *Olam Hazeh* which are closely linked to the spirituality of *Olam Haba*. In fact, the term נוֹחֲלִין used by the Midrash is related to נַחַל, *a stream*, implying that This World is nurtured by a constant stream of spirituality from *Olam Haba* evoked by our *mitzvos* and *maasim tovim* (good deeds).

∽§ Everyone — Even the Undeserving

ויש לומר שאין להם חלק פי' שאין להם חלק בפני עצמם אבל בכללות ישראל
יש להם חלק. וזהו שאמר כל ישראל היינו בכללות ישראל שנאמר ועמך כלם
צדיקים וכו' פי' שבכללות ישראל המה צדיקים.

---

*A*ccording to R' Simchah Bunim of Peshis'cha, the expression כָּל יִשְׂרָאֵל, *all Jews*, implies that even those individuals whose sins caused them to lose their personal portion in *Olam Haba* (e.g. Doeg, Geichazi, cf. *Sanhedrin* 90a) do share in the common *Olam Haba* enjoyed by all of *Klal Yisrael*. As the Mishnah emphasizes, כָּל יִשְׂרָאֵל יֵשׁ לָהֶם חֵלֶק לָעוֹלָם הַבָּא, *all* of Klal Yisrael (i.e. Klal Yisrael as a unified whole) *enjoys a portion in the World to Come* (*Maggidei HaEmes*).

∽§ Olam Haba in This World

דייקו על הלשון יש והיה צריך לומר יהיה כו'.
אולם אינו דומה מניעת הריוח העתיד להזיק הקרן, וכבר יש להם אז יהיה להם
חבל לאבד ח"ו וח"ו.

---

*T*he Mishnah does not state כָּל יִשְׂרָאֵל יִהְיֶה לָהֶם חֵלֶק לָעוֹלָם הַבָּא, *all of Klal Yisrael **will** merit a portion in the World to Come*, but rather it says יֵשׁ, they *presently* enjoy a portion in *Olam Haba*. *Olam Haba* is not merely relegated to the distant future but rather is something that very much exists in the present. Almost innately, *every Jew is assured* of a portion in *Olam Haba* which can only be forfeited as a result of committing certain grave sins.

The fact that *Olam Haba* is almost *an innate right* of every Jew is not only comforting but also helps us appreciate the gravity of those sins which could cause us (ח״ו) to forfeit our portion in the World to Come. By committing such heinous *aveiros*, we are not merely giving up a promised reward but are also yielding something that is already in our hands (*Bendiner Rav, Maggidei HaEmes*).

■ וְעַמֵּךְ כֻּלָּם צַדִּיקִים — *And your people are all righteous.* ■

⇜ The Merit of Milah

כל אחד מישראל נקרא צדיק על ידי שהקב״ה חתם בו חותם בעולם הזה, על בריתך שחתמת בבשרנו. שעל ידי זה יכולים להיות תמיד עם השי״ת.

According to the *Imrei Emes*, all Jews — no matter how estranged — are considered to be (to some extent) *tzaddikim* by virtue of being circumcised. We express our appreciation of this lifelong and indelible sign of our relationship with Hashem every time we recite *Bircas Hamazon*, by saying וְעַל בְּרִיתְךָ שֶׁחָתַמְתָּ בִּבְשָׂרֵנוּ, *for Your covenant which You sealed in our flesh* (*Maggidei HaEmes*).

⇜ Only When Klal Yisrael Is United

כשעמך כולם כשמתאספים כולם יחד אז כולם צדיקים, שכלם יכולים להיות צדיקים, לעולם יירשו ארץ שיכולים לירש גם את הארציות לעשות מהכל שמים.

The apparently superfluous term כֻּלָּם, *all*, implies that when we are united (i.e. we are all together), we merit the title righteous. A unified *Klal Yisrael* is not only able to attain significant spiritual goals but also to consecrate the physical world so that it can be used as a vehicle for spirituality. As the *pasuk* concludes, לְעוֹלָם יִירְשׁוּ אָרֶץ, *they shall inherit the land forever* — not only the heaven but even the earth can be converted into a base for spirituality (*Lev Simchah, Maggidei HaEmes*).

■ לְעוֹלָם יִירְשׁוּ אָרֶץ — *They shall inherit the land forever.* ■

קמפרש על עולם הבא. ופשוט הפי׳ על ארץ ישראל. וי״ל כי הכל אחד עולם הבא
וארץ ישראל.

והגם דפי׳ ארץ כפשוטו בא״י. מ״מ זה הוא הסימן שיש להם חלק לעוה״ב במה
שזוכין בעוה״ז להתדבק בארץ ישראל שהוא השורש של נפשות בנ״י וכתוב
ששם עלו שבטים כו׳ עדות לישראל שבעלייתן לביהמ״ק הי׳ עדות שיש להם
דביקות בשורשם. וזהו השם שמעיד עליהם ועל יחוסם עי״ז שיכולין לעלות
לביהמ״ק.

The simple interpretation of the phrase לְעוֹלָם יִירְשׁוּ אָרֶץ, *they shall inherit the land forever*, refers to the eternal right of *Klal Yisrael* to *Eretz Yisrael*. However, in this context, the *mishnah* is interpreting the term אָרֶץ, *the land*, as referring to *Olam Haba*, the eventual destiny of every Jew. This homiletical interpretation does not necessarily contradict the literal approach in which the term refers to the Promised Land, *Eretz Yisrael*. On the contrary, the Jew who successfully develops roots in *Eretz Yisrael* — not merely conquering the land but rather clinging to its intense spirituality — can be assured of his reward in the future world. As King David describes the Festival pilgrimages to Yerusha-layim: שֶׁשָּׁם עָלוּ שְׁבָטִים שִׁבְטֵי יָ-הּ עֵדוּת לְיִשְׂרָאֵל לְהוֹדוֹת לְשֵׁם ה׳, *For there the tribes ascended, the tribes of God, a testimony for Israel, to give thanks to the Name of* HASHEM (*Tehillim* 122:4). By successfully undertaking the annual pilgrimages, the Jew testifies to his heavenly roots and his ultimate reward, *Olam Haba*. Only someone whose roots emanated from heaven could success-fully present himself before Hashem on the Pilgrimage Festivals in *Eretz Yisrael*, as it is written, שָׁלוֹשׁ פְּעָמִים בַּשָּׁנָה יֵרָאֶה כָל זְכוּרְךָ אֶת פְּנֵי ה׳ אֱלֹהֶיךָ, *Three times a year all your males should appear before* HASHEM, *your God* (*Devarim* 16:16).

◆§ Every Jew's Portion in Eretz Yisrael

איתא ד׳ אמות בארץ ישראל מכפר. לפי זה הכוונה לעולם יירשו ארץ, ארץ
ישראל. ומזה הטעם ועמך כולם צדיקים כיון דמכפר.

According to the *Lev Simchah*, the term אָרֶץ refers to אֶרֶץ יִשְׂרָאֵל. Simply by virtue of possessing a portion of *Eretz Yisrael's* land (every Jew is entitled to four cubits of *Eretz Yisrael* soil) — a land whose ambiance is conducive to the forgiveness of our sins (cf. *Yalkut Mishlei* 17:11, ד׳ אמות בארץ ישראל מכפר), — we are assured of the distinction of being called *tzaddikim* (*Maggidei HaEmes*).

פרק ראשון

[א] מֹשֶׁה קִבֵּל תּוֹרָה מִסִּינַי, וּמְסָרָהּ לִיהוֹשֻׁעַ

1.

■ מֹשֶׁה קִבֵּל תּוֹרָה מִסִּינַי — *Moshe received the Torah from Sinai.*

◆§ Moshe Accepted the Torah

> ולכן הקדימו חכמים זאת המשנה באבות.
> לומר שאלה הדברים שהגידו אבות העולם לא יחשוב אדם להרהר בהם עפ״י
> אימוד דעתו כי זה בירושה מסיני.

It is tempting to view *Avos* as merely an anthology of the Sages' wisdom which could have been deduced through our own efforts. To refute this critical misconception, the *mishnah* at the very outset emphasizes that Moshe received the Torah — including *every* aspect of this *Mesechta* — at Sinai.

◆§ Human Effort or Divine Transmission?

> הגם שהתורה ניתנה לכל ישראל, אמנם יש ב׳ ענינים בתורה היגיעה שיכול כל
> איש ישראל למצוא ע״י יגיעה בתורה כ״א כפי השגתו אך יש עוד סגולה בתורה
> לחכמים ראשי הדורות להשיג מה שאינו עפ״י שכל אנושי והוא הירושה שניתן
> לנו כמ״ש תורה צוה כו׳ משה מורשה קהלת יעקב . . . ובגמ׳ אל תקרי מורשה
> אלא מאורסה, וזה ההפרש כי ירושה היא בלי יגיעה רק נחלה שאין לה הפסק
> אבל מאורסה היא התקרבות שבא ע״י פעולות האדם ויגיעתו בתורה וזה נאמר
> לכל פרט התקן עצמך ללמוד תורה שאינה ירושה לך דייקא. אבל לכללות
> ישראל נאמר מורשה קהלת יעקב, ולכן אמונת חכמים היא יסוד התורה.

While it is certainly true that every individual — not merely Moshe Rabbeinu — received the Torah at Sinai — a distinction should be made between an individual's capacity for great success in his Torah studies and the unique role of Moshe and his successors, the *Gedolei Torah* of every generation in comprehending the Divine Will and in transmitting Torah to *Klal Yisrael*.[1] This distinction is alluded to by the Gemara's interpretation of the renowned *pasuk,* מוֹרָשָׁה קְהִלַּת יַעֲקֹב, *the heritage of the congregation of Jacob* (*Devarim* 33:4). While the simple meaning of the *pasuk* indicates that Torah is an *inheritance,*

---

1. The Sages' capacity to understand and faithfully transmit Torah, a concept known as *Emunas Chachomim*, is a fundamental Torah belief; see *Sfas Emes* s.v. הכל משה.

Chapter One

[1] *Moshe received Torah from Sinai and transmitted it*

Chazal comment, אַל תִּקְרֵי מוֹרָשָׁה אֶלָּא מְאוֹרָשָׁה, *do not read as "an inheritance" but rather as a "betrothal."* Just as a betrothed couple can develop jointly the potential for a fruitful relationship, so too through our persistent efforts, we can reach our potential in Torah study. A later *mishnah* emphasizes that Torah is *not* an inheritance, שֶׁאֵינָה יְרֻשָּׁה לָךְ (2:17).

Both the simple *p'shat* and the Gemara's interpretation are correct. The Torah, transmitted by the *Gedolei Torah* of every generation to *Kehillas Yaakov*, the *community* of *Klal Yisrael*, is truly our inheritance. However, the *individual* scholar can only achieve his potential by exerting himself to understand all of Torah's intricacies. The *mishnah* cited previously, stating that Torah "is not an inheritance," refers to the individual, as it says, "It is not an inheritance *for you.*" On the other hand, *Klal Yisrael* is assured that Torah is its perpetual heritage.

◆§ Was Avos Said at Sinai?

בפי' הרע״ב אף אלו מסיני, הגם דלפי״ז מה הפי' הם אמרו כיון שכולם קבלו רק
בנ״ל דנקרא עתיד לחדש הגם שכבר ניתנה, עוי״ל הפי' שנתלה הכל בשכל עליון
שניתן דעת לבנ״י מדעת קונם לכוון ההלכה לתלות באסמכתא מה״ת . . . וי״ל
עוד אף אלו מסיני שנעשה מכל דבריהם אף של עצמם תורה ממש.

The *Bartenura* emphasizes that *Avos* was said by Hashem to Moshe at Sinai. He notes that שֶׁגַּם אֵלּוּ נֶאֶמְרוּ מִסִּינַי, "that these (the ethical teachings of *Avos*) were also said at Sinai." He interprets the term מִסִּינַי (from Sinai) to refer to Hashem Who revealed Himself at Sinai. This assertion seemingly contradicts the numerous instances in which the *mishnah* states, הֵם אָמְרוּ, *they* (the Sages) *said*, suggesting that the contents of this *Mesechta* were first said by *Chazal*.

This apparent contradiction may be resolved through a renowned saying of *Chazal*, כָּל מַה שֶׁתַּלְמִיד וָתִיק עָתִיד לְחַדֵּשׁ כְּבָר נֶאֶמְרָה בְּסִינַי, "Whatever novel Torah insights a diligent student may derive was already transmitted at Sinai" (cf. *Vayikra Rabbah* 22:1). Each of the scholars mentioned in *Avos* brought to light *Divrei Torah* originally given at Sinai.

The *mishnah* may also be referring to the *capacity* of *Chazal* to deduce on their own many of the most profound Divine thoughts originally given orally to Moshe at Sinai. This extraordinary gift (as well as their teachings) were given at Sinai. In this light, we can better understand the concept of "Asmachta" in which the Sages seemingly found an allusion to their teachings in the Torah itself. This refers to their capacity to go beyond elucidating the *Halachah* and to find references to their elucidations in the Torah itself.

Alternatively, the *Bartenura* may be suggesting that the sacred teachings of *Chazal* — even if deduced on their own — are considered *as if* they were given at Sinai.

❧ A Perfect Match

יש לדקדק דהו״ל ליה למימר בסיני ונראה לבאר דהנה כתיב והאיש משה עניו
מאד מכל האדם וכו' וכן במצרים אמר מי אנכי וכו' וכי אלך וכו' אוציא וכשאמר
לו הקב״ה שיתן התורה על ידו והוא היה רבן של כל ישראל לא סרב כלל והיכן
עוונותו . . . לזה אמר מסיני שלמד מסיני שניתן עליו התורה ולא על שאר
ההרים מפני שהוא נמוך מכל ההרים לכן גם הוא נתרצה מיד להנתן התורה על
ידו.

If the *mishnah* merely meant to inform us that Moshe received the Torah at Sinai, it would have stated, מֹשֶׁה קִבֵּל תּוֹרָה בְּסִינַי. The expression מִסִּינַי seems to be explaining why Moshe enthusiastically embraced his mission of receiving the Torah despite the unparalleled modesty that caused his initial reluctance to accept the challenge of leading *Klal Yisrael* out of Mitzrayim. Upon beholding the stark simplicity of Sinai, which was among the least imposing of all the mountains, Moshe understood why he was chosen to receive the Torah. The Torah which was to be given from the humblest of mountains could only be transmitted through the most modest person on earth (*Kedushas Levi, Maggidei HaEmes*).

■ וּמְסָרָהּ לִיהוֹשֻׁעַ — *And transmitted it to Yehoshua.* ■

❧ What Does Moshe Transmit to Yehoshua?

הכוונה על תושבע״פ . . . וק' הא כ' מהודך ולא כל הודך כו' . . . וק״ק לשון
ומסרה דהא אמרו שנשתכחו כמה הלכות בימי אבלו ש״מ כו' ובמ״ש ליהושע
יל״ד דהרי מסר לכל, רק י״ל על לוחות הראשונות שסודותיהם של ראשונות
מסר ליהושע . . . ויל״פ עוד פי' ומסרה על המסורות כי יש אם למקרא ויש נמי
אם למסורות וז״ש הלשון ומסרה ליהושע, ויש לבאר עוד כי הרי אנחנו יש לנו
התורה ואין יודעים מאומה רק אצלם נמסר ד״ת ממש.

This statement asserting that Moshe transmitted the Torah to Yehoshua requires clarification. Couldn't anyone have studied the Torah once it had been transmitted to *Klal Yisrael*? Evidently, the *mishnah* is referring to the Oral Law which requires diligent study and the tutelage of a great mentor, like Moshe.

Upon further examination, it seems that Moshe transmitted the entire Torah only to Yehoshua. This assertion is supported by the simple meaning of the *pasuk*, וַיִּסְמֹךְ אֶת יָדָיו עָלָיו, *he leaned his hands upon him* (*Bamidbar* 27:23), which implies that by placing his hands on Yehoshua, Moshe was transmitting all that he had received from Hashem to Yehoshua. The commentary *Tosafos Yom Tov* also agrees with this viewpoint.

This approach, however, seems to contradict *Rashi's* assertion that Moshe only bestowed *part* of his knowledge upon Yehoshua (cf. *Bamidbar* 27:20 s.v. מֵהוֹדְךָ). A related question also occurs. Didn't Moshe transmit the entire Torah to *all* of *Klal Yisrael*? A final question remains. While this *mishnah* implies that Yehoshua successfully retained Moshe's teachings, this seems to contradict a well-known *Chazal* (cf. *Temurah* 16a) that a great deal of Torah was forgotten during the thirty-day mourning period for Moshe, only to be restored through the prodigious efforts and skill of Osniel ben Kenaz.

These questions may be resolved if we assume that a unique aspect of Torah was exclusively transmitted to and successfully retained by Yehoshua, an aspect of Torah too rarefied for the rest of *Klal Yisrael*. The *mishnah* may be referring to the first *Luchos*. Although the "body" of the *Luchos* themselves were shattered when Israel worshiped the Golden Calf, Moshe retained and transmitted their spirit to Yehoshua — the secrets of Torah that they contained. This approach is supported by the term used to describe the process of transmitting the Torah, וְנָתַתָּ מֵהוֹדְךָ עָלָיו, *and you shall bestow from your majesty upon him* [Yehoshua] (*Bamidbar* 27:20). The term הוֹד, *glory*, alludes to the Divine crowns which were granted to *Klal Yisrael* upon saying *Na'aseh Ve-Nishma* and were removed when they worshiped the Golden Calf. However, Moshe retained these crowns — and the hidden treasures of Torah that they represented — and transmitted them exclusively to Yehoshua. (For a more comprehensive discussion of the significance of the Divine crowns see *The Three Festivals*, pp. 248-249.)

Furthermore, the term מְסָרָהּ may refer to Yehoshua's expertise in interpreting the *Mesorah* of Torah — the letters that comprise the words of the Torah — as well as his knowledge of the *Mikra* — the manner in which the words of the Torah are actually articulated. While all of *Klal Yisrael* was granted the capacity to interpret the Torah based on the authorized reading of its words, only Yehoshua could find meaning in the letters themselves. [For a more complete understanding of this concept and its halachic significance, cf. *Sanhedrin* 4a and the entire discussion of *Yesh Eim LaMikra* and *Yesh Eim LaMesores* in which the *Tannaim* debate whether the Torah should be interpreted on the basis of its articulation or on the basis of the letters themselves.]

Alternatively, we may distinguish between *receiving* the Torah — a characterization attained by all Jews — and truly *absorbing* its contents, a feat accomplished with unusual distinction by Yehoshua. Even in contemporary times there may exist individuals who have learned the entire Torah, but who among us can assert that they truly comprehend *all* of Torah, as Yehoshua did?

A major factor in Yehoshua's success was his selection by **Hashem** and

אֱ / א וִיהוֹשֻׁעַ לִזְקֵנִים, וּזְקֵנִים לִנְבִיאִים, וּנְבִיאִים מְסָרוּהָ לְאַנְשֵׁי כְנֶסֶת הַגְּדוֹלָה.

especially his fulfillment of the uniquely designed leadership mission with which he was entrusted. The following remarks address the nature of Torah leadership.

∾§ The Function of a Jewish Leader

כי באמת השי״ת רועה ישראל רק ע״י הצדיק אשר יצא לפניהם מכין מקום . . .
וע״י שיהי' איש על העדה כו' לא תהיה כו' וז״ש עדת ה' שבאמת השי״ת הוא
הרועה.

Contrary to popular misconception, the primary function of a Jewish leader is *not* to lead but rather to impress upon Israel that Hashem is their leader. This crucial distinction is demonstrated by Moshe's plea to Hashem: וְלֹא תִהְיֶה עֲדַת ה' כַּצֹּאן אֲשֶׁר אֵין לָהֶם רֹעֶה, *And let* HASHEM's *congregation not be like sheep without a shepherd* (Bamidbar 27:17). By mentioning Hashem's congregation (עֲדַת ה'), Moshe is emphasizing that we are Hashem's flock, not the leader's.

∾§ The Unique Status of Yehoshua

דיהושע דכתיב גביה ומשרתו יהושע כו' לא ימוש מתוך האוהל, כנראה שהיה
יושב כל הזמן ושומע גם מה שלימד לאהרן, ועל ידי זה היה יכול לקבל הכל.
ואפשר שאף שמע שמע מפי הגבורה ביחד עם מרע״ה. ויתכן שמשום כך זכה להיות
המנהיג אחר מרע״ה.
והלא לכל ישראל יש התורה, אולם ליהושע הוא מסר את הפנימיות.

While Yehoshua was by no means the only scholar capable of receiving the Torah transmitted by Moshe, he did enjoy the distinction of having been exposed to Moshe's teaching for a longer period than everyone else. The Gemara (*Eruvin* 54:2) relates that Moshe taught whatever he learned from Hashem to Aaron, then to the Elders (זְקֵנִים) and eventually to all of *Klal Yisrael* (see the Gemara there for further details of the process through which Torah was transmitted to *Klal Yisrael*). Seemingly, Yehoshua, described as being always in Moshe's presence (cf. *Shemos* 33:11), participated in every phase of the transmission of Torah to *Klal Yisrael*. It is even possible that Yehoshua may have been able to listen when Moshe received the Torah directly from Hashem. If the above assumption is correct, we can appreciate why Yehoshua was the logical successor to Moshe (*Beis Yisrael, Maggidei HaEmes*).

Alternatively, while others may have been capable of understanding the

to Yehoshua, and Yehoshua to the Elders and the Elders to the Prophets and the Prophets transmitted it to the Men of the Great Assembly.

many aspects of Torah, only Yehoshua could appreciate the inner depths (פְּנִימִיּוּת) of Torah (*Imrei Emes, Maggidei HaEmes*).

■ וִיהוֹשֻׁעַ לִזְקֵנִים — *and Yehoshua to the Elders.*

⊷§ The Elders and Judges

נראה שהם הע׳ זקנים שנא׳ אספה לי שבעים איש ויהושע מהם אך הם האריכו
ימים טפי, ולא הזכיר שופטים ויל״פ שהם בכלל זקנים ואפשר הם בכלל נביאים.

The Elders cited in the *mishnah* were both the contemporaries of Yehoshua and his successors. In response to Moshe's complaint that he cannot bear the burden of leading *Klal Yisrael* alone, Hashem appoints seventy elders, including Yehoshua (cf. *Bamidbar* 11:24-29). However, as stated in *Shoftim*, the Elders outlived Yehoshua.

It is noteworthy that the *mishnah* does not mention that the Torah was transmitted to the Judges (*Shoftim*). Apparently they are subsumed in one of the other categories, either as Elders or in the following category of Prophets.

■ וּנְבִיאִים מְסָרוּהָ לְאַנְשֵׁי כְנֶסֶת הַגְּדוֹלָה — *And the Prophets transmitted it to the Men of the Great Assembly.*

⊷§ The Men of the Great Assembly — Their Name

ויש להבין מאחר שגם מקודם היו אומרים הגדול הגבור והנורא א״כ מה
קראך אכנה״ג.
דשם כנה״ג אינו תואר שם רק הי׳ כנסי׳ גדולה ומפורסמת.
לולי דברי חז״ל הי׳ נראה כעין לשון סגי נהור כי בית שני הי׳ פחות במעלה מבית
ראשון ולכן נקראו אנשי כנה״ג.
. . . אבל מ״מ כיון שאין משמש אתנו במדת גבורה ונוראות אין זה שבח שנסדר
לפניו הואיל ואין עושה עמנו זה, ולזה השיבו אנשי כנסת הגדולה שאינו כן, רק
משמש גם עמנו במידתו שאל״כ איך אומה כזו יכולה להתקיים וכו׳ כנ״ל.

In order to appreciate the derivation of the name "Men of the Great Assembly," let us cite a passage of the Gemara (*Yoma* 69b). Rabbi Yehoshua ben Levi explained why they were called the "Men of the Great Assembly" — because they restored the crown (of Hashem's prominence) to its former glory. Moshe had said, הָאֵל הַגָּדוֹל וְהַנּוֹרָא, *the great, mighty, and awesome God.* Yirmiyahu came and said, "Gentiles are screaming in His Temple — where is mankind's awe of Hashem?" and thus deleted the term נוֹרָא (cf. *Yirmiyahu* 32:18, הָא-ל הַגָּדוֹל הַגִּבּוֹר). Subsequently, Daniel said, "Gentiles are subjugating Hashem's children — where is Hashem's might?" — and thus deleted the term גִּבּוֹר (cf. *Daniel* 9:4, הָא-ל הַגָּדוֹל וְהַנּוֹרָא). However, they (the members of the Great Assembly) reacted differently to the same events, reasoning that on the contrary, Hashem's Might is demonstrated by His patience to the wicked, curbing His Impulse to destroy evildoers. Likewise, His Awe is amply demonstrated by Israel's survival. Were it not for His Awe, how could one nation survive among seventy (hostile) nations? As a result of their restoring the mention of (and recognition of) Hashem's Attributes, the Men of the Great Assembly were honored and received the appelation, *great.*

Upon considering this passage, several questions arise. Would it not have been more appropriate to name this tribunal "Men of the Mighty Assembly" or "Men of the Awed Assembly" since they restored these attributes of Hashem? More profoundly, it seems difficult to believe that Yirmiyahu actually maintained that Hashem had "lost" his "awesomeness" and that Daniel doubted Hashem's "Might."

Responding to the first question, we may answer simply that the term "great" is an apt *description* of its accomplishments. In other words, it was known as a great and renowned conclave whose accomplishments included restoring the use of the terms גִּבּוֹר and נוֹרָא in the opening *berachah* of *Shemoneh Esrei.*

Alternatively, the term "great" should be interpreted as being euphemistic. Just as a blind person is called a סַגִּי נְהוֹר, *one with unusually powerful sight,* so too this conclave marked the beginning of the period of the Second *Beis HaMikdash,* a period that was in many respects inferior to that of its predecessor (cf. *Yoma* 21b enumerating the distinctions between the First and Second *Beis HaMikdash*).

Responding to the more fundamental question of the deletion of some of the words describing Hashem's praises by the Prophets before the *Anshei Knesses HaGedolah,* we note the Gemara's (cf. *Berachos* 25a) strenuous objection to *unlimited* praise of Hashem. Since it is impossible to enumerate all of Hashem's attributes, we simply limit ourselves to those stated explicitly in the Torah. Similarly, Yirmiyahu and later Daniel reasoned that Hashem's praise should be confined to those attributes that can be readily perceived during a particular period. For example, the term גִּבּוֹר used in the first *berachah* of *Shemoneh Esrei* refers to the mighty deeds that He is currently performing on behalf of *Klal*

They said three things: Be deliberate in judgment, and develop many disciples, and make a fence for the Torah.

Yisrael. Consequently, during a period of Divine Concealment, when it *appears* that Hashem's Attribute of Might has receded, it would be inappropriate to describe Hashem in such terms. On the other hand the *Anshei Knesses HaGedolah* disagreed, arguing that *Klal Yisrael's* survival proves that we still benefit from His Awe and His Might.

◆§ Uniqueness of Anshei Knesses HaGedolah

מסרה ליהושע ויהושע לזקנים וכו' פעל שיהי' הארה מכוחו של מרע''ה לכל הדורות. ואמר ונביאים מסרוה לאנשי כנה''ג הם אמרו פי' שהניחו הכח באלה המאמרים.

דבר גדול הוא שיכוונו כולם לומר ג' דברים הללו בשוה.

והקודמים להם לא מצינו שהוסיפו רק כאשר אמרו ועשו סייג לתורה אמר כ''א מה שנצרך לדורו.

The phrase הֵם אָמְרוּ, *they said*, and particularly the placement of this phrase just after the chain of Torah transmission which began with Moshe, implies that the *Anshei Knesses HaGedolah* were imbued with some measure of Moshe's unique capacity to teach and transmit Torah. Moreover, the phrase is a bit amazing. Unlike all the other teachings of *Avos* which were said by individuals or small groups of scholars, in this *mishnah* 120 scholars arrived (apparently independently) at the same conclusion. Additionally, by stating עֲשׂוּ סְיָג לַתּוֹרָה, *make a fence for the Torah*, the *Anshei Knesses HaGedolah* were setting a precedent through which each generation could clarify the ethical teachings that pertained to its unique needs. This explains why we find no mention of the teachings of previous generations.

■ הֱווּ מְתוּנִים בַּדִּין — *Be deliberate in judgment.*

◆§ Be Deliberate in Judgment

ובתרגום יונתן שצריך להיות זריז בדיני ממונות רק בד''נ צ''ל מתון, ופשוט ה''פ גם בד''מ דבד''נ גזה''כ להלין הדין דכ' צדק ילין בה . . . וצ''ל דבד''מ מפני שהוא בין בעלי בחירה צריך להזהר יותר מערמות הבעלי דינין . . . ואפשר משום דדיני ממונות כיון דתלוי בשיקול הדעת של הדיין, לכן צריך להיות יותר מתון מאיסור והיתר, . . . ואפשר דבאמת דיני ממונות יותר חמור משום שהוא לשמים ולבריות, וגם יי''ל להיפוך דהוראה פשיטא שצריך מתינות אלא אפי' דין דממונא בעלמא הוא ואיתא בחזרה מ''מ צריך ג''כ מתינות.

פשוט יי''ל שלפני הרגשות האדם ומעשה קטן או גדול אף מחשבה ותנועה קלה,

This general statement of the *mishnah* requires further clarification. Are we referring to civil cases, capital cases, or decisions rendered by a *posek* regarding matters of religious law?

The Aramaic interpretation of the Torah, *Targum Yonasan*, rules (*Parshas Emor*) that patience is only essential in capital cases where someone's life is at risk. On the contrary, a judge ruling on monetary matters should proceed as expeditiously as possible. The simple interpretation of the *mishnah*, however, seems to be referring to civil cases. The requirement to proceed cautiously in capital cases is derived from *pesukim* (cf. *Sanhedrin* 35a) and predates the teachings of the *Anshei Knesses HaGedolah*.

Let us consider several reasons for this *mishnah's* opinion that even דִּינֵי מָמוֹנוֹת require careful contemplation. This position may be based on the possibility of deceitful behavior on the part of the litigants (דִּין מְרוּמָה). Similarly, the judge is frequently required to render a subjective assessment of the various parties' claims. Such a process, described by *Chazal* as שׁוּדָא דְדַיָּינֵי (*Kesubos* 85b), requires a great deal of deliberation. The grave consequences of rendering a mistaken verdict — harming individuals as well as violating Hashem's Torah — also justifies the need for caution in concluding civil cases.

Would careful deliberation also be required for exclusively religious rulings? The justifications cited previously are seemingly unique to civil cases. On the other hand, one may argue that the *mishnah* is stating that *even* monetary affairs — which if judged incorrectly can always be reversed through the return of the money — requires extraordinary patience. It *certainly* follows, then, that all rulings necessitate prudent consideration.

This saying may also be interpreted homiletically as referring to every individual Jew, not necessarily a judge. The *mishnah* is urging us to evaluate carefully *every* decision — no matter how seemingly trivial. Every action and thought must be judged in the light of the Torah's requirements. This imposing requirement is alluded to in the first *pasuk* dealing with jurisprudence, וְאֵלֶּה הַמִּשְׁפָּטִים אֲשֶׁר תָּשִׂים לִפְנֵיהֶם, *And these are the ordinances that you shall place before them* (*Shemos* 21:1), which may be interpreted in the following manner: Place these statutes of the Torah before you in order that they be studied and their principles understood as they apply to every phase of life.

■ וְהַעֲמִידוּ תַלְמִידִים הַרְבֵּה — *And develop many disciples.*

◆§ Torah Education — Quality or Quantity?

קשה איך פליג ר"ג על אנשי כנסת הגדולה שהיו מהם נביאים. אלא שרבן גמליאל
ראה בזמנו שכל בית המדרש הוא בסכנה ולכן אמר שכל תלמיד שאין תוכו כברו
אל יכנס.

אף שיהי' תלמידי ב"ש וב"ה וכיוצא בזה מ"מ אל ימנעו מהתורה.
אדרבא עי"ז יתחזק אצל בנ"י התורה ובזה אתי שפיר דנקיט מסרוה לאבנה"ג.
עוד י"ל דר"ג לא פליג והכל א' כי ממאה יוצא עשרה לכן ר"ג לקח מיד אלו
העשרה אבל כאן העמידו תלמידים הרבה שיהי' לכולם העמדה וקיום ולדברי ר"ג
דבאין תוכו כברו אל יכנוס יש לפרש העמידו שיהי' תוכו כברו, וי"ל נמי שנקראו
כה"ג בשביל זה שחידשו אז העמידו תלמידים הרבה שיהי' כנופיא גדולה.

This statement of the *Anshei Knesses HaGedolah* seems to be emphasizing the quantity of their disciples rather than the quality of their teachings. Better to learn with many students, though one may lack sufficient time for each *talmid*, than to spend more time with a few choice students.

This approach to Torah education is in contradistinction to that of Rabban Gamliel who insisted that only those disciples whose "insides" were as good as their "outsides" (i.e. whose knowledge of Torah was not merely superficial and were sincere) would be admitted (cf. *Berachos* 28a), a point already noted by the *Bartenura*.

Since it is improbable that Rabban Gamliel would oppose the *Anshei Knesses HaGedolah*, let us consider several approaches to resolve their views.

Perhaps, a distinction may be drawn between standard procedure and measures adopted on an emergency basis. Rabban Gamliel, realizing the unique needs of his generation, only adopted his rigorous admission criteria as an emergency and would agree that ordinarily the approach of the *Anshei Knesses HaGedolah* would be proper. The reverse may also be true. Rabban Gamliel interpreted the policy stated in the *mishnah* — advocating teaching numerous *talmidim* — as an emergency measure and maintained that his approach was appropriate under ordinary circumstances.

Alternatively, our *mishnah* may be referring to the diversity of the *talmidim* rather than their quantity. The *Anshei Knesses HaGedolah*, foreseeing an age in which divergent opinions would arise, encouraged widespread Torah study despite the possibility of varying interpretations of Torah. On the contrary, they reasoned that mass Torah study would strengthen *Klal Yisrael's* commitment to Torah. This approach is supported by the placement of the *Anshei Knesses HaGedolah's* statement in the *mishnah* citing the transmission of the Torah. The *Anshei Knesses HaGedolah* are in effect saying, whereas until now the Torah had been passed from generation to generation in an atmosphere of unanimity, now divergent opinions would occur — and should be encouraged.

In truth, Rabban Gamliel and the *Anshei Knesses HaGedolah* may be relating the *same* message: Commence with a large body of *talmidim*. Not all of them, however, will remain immersed in Torah study. Subsequently, study intensively with the small cadre that remains. The *mishnah* is referring to the *initial*

[ב] שִׁמְעוֹן הַצַּדִּיק הָיָה מִשְׁיָרֵי כְנֶסֶת הַגְּדוֹלָה. הוּא הָיָה אוֹמֵר: עַל שְׁלֹשָׁה דְבָרִים הָעוֹלָם עוֹמֵד: עַל הַתּוֹרָה, וְעַל וְעַל הָעֲבוֹדָה, וְעַל גְּמִילוּת חֲסָדִים.

effort at disseminating Torah — teach everyone. Rabban Gamliel, however, insists that the final product — those students who *remain* immersed in learning — be of the highest caliber. In fact, the *Anshei Knesses HaGedolah* and Rabban Gamliel may have had differing interpretations of the term הַעֲמִידוּ, *develop*, *establish*. Whereas the *Anshei Knesses HaGedolah* emphasized that every *talmid* should be placed and supported in accordance with his efforts to learn, Rabban Gamliel emphasized the obligation of a rebbi to "make" a *talmid*. While his initial relationship to Torah may have been superficial, develop his capacity for scholarship so that his "insides may be as good as his outsides."

In conclusion, we note that the name *Anshei Knesses HaGedolah* (which can be rendered, the men of the *numerous* assembly) may have been derived from their recommendation of propagating Torah by teaching many students. As a result, the masses of *Klal Yisrael* would be exposed to Torah, leading to great multitudes of Torah-educated laymen.

■ וַעֲשׂוּ סְיָג לַתּוֹרָה — *And make a fence for the Torah.*

◆§ Limiting the Number of Talmidim

ועשו סייג לתורה היינו שאם יראו שהשעה צריכה לכך אז יאמרו שכל תלמיד וכו'.

This final segment of the *mishnah* may be modifying the previous statement of וְהַעֲמִידוּ תַלְמִידִים הַרְבֵּה. While under ordinary circumstances one should teach Torah to as many *talmidim* as possible, however, under extraordinary circumstances it may be appropriate to "erect a fence around the Torah" by circumscribing the number of *talmidim* (cf. *Berachos* 28a discussing Rabban Gamliel's interpretation of such a policy) (*Imrei Emes, Maggidei HaEmes*).

2.

■ הוּא הָיָה אוֹמֵר — *He used to say.*

◆§ To Whom Would He Say?

פירוש שאמר זאת לעצמו תמיד.

[2] *Shimon HaTzaddik was one of the remaining members of the Great Assembly. He used to say: The world depends on three things: on the Torah, on the service (of God) and on kind deeds.*

The expression הוּא הָיָה אוֹמֵר, *he used to say*, suggests a monologue, not a dialogue. Shimon HaTzaddik related to himself the basic thoughts stated in this *mishnah*.

■ עַל שְׁלשָׁה דְבָרִים הָעוֹלָם עוֹמֵד — *The world depends on three things.*

◆§ Are All Three Pillars Necessary?

הרע״ב פי׳ קרבנות ואם כן בגלות עומד העולם על ב׳ רגלים. אכן י״ל תפלה הוא
רגל הג׳, ולכן נקראת מעמדות, אנשי מעמד, שעליהם נסמך העולם. אבל נראה
דאו או קאמר . . . כמ״ש בשם הרבי ר׳ אלימלך ז״ל כי עד האר״י ז״ל תורה ועתה
גמ״ח כנ״ל.
פי׳ תורה מה שהאדם עושה בעצמו בעבודת ה׳ ועבודה היא המשכת כח וסיוע
מלמעלה וגמילת חסדים ליתן גם לאחרים משלו והן המה שלשה דרכים בעבודת
הבורא יתברך.

A simple reading of the *mishnah* seems to indicate that all three pillars are equally essential for the universe's continued existence. If so, the question arises, on what merit does this universe *currently* exist in the absence of the Divine Service in the *Beis HaMikdash* (עֲבוֹדָה)?[1]

Perhaps the term עֲבוֹדָה should be reinterpreted as any form of Divine Service — *davening* (תְּפִלָּה) as well as sacrifices (קָרְבָּנוֹת). In contemporary times, *tefillah* has replaced sacrifices as a vital pillar upholding the universe.

Alternatively, we may suggest that the universe can be supported by *any one* of these three pillars of our faith. Even after the abolishment of *korbanos*, the merit of Torah or *gemilus chasadim* was sufficient. Concurring with this view, the great Chassidic mentor Rav Elimelech of Lyzhensk maintained that in our times it is through acts of kindness that the world is primarily sustained.

It is significant that three distinct approaches to *avodas Hashem* are stated in the *mishnah*: firstly, Torah study which is initiated by the *individual*, followed by *avodah*, consisting of our pleas that Hashem bless *us*, and finally *gemilus chasadim*, in which the Jew shares his material and spiritual possessions with *others*. These three approaches — man's initiative enhanced by Hashem's bountiful blessings which are then shared with our less fortunate peers — are the pillars upon which the universe stands.

---

1. עֲבוֹדָה refers to the sacrificial service. The study of these laws and prayer replace the service in the absence of the *Beis HaMikdash*.

[ג] אַנְטִיגְנוֹס אִישׁ סוֹכוֹ קִבֵּל מִשִּׁמְעוֹן הַצַּדִּיק. הוּא
הָיָה אוֹמֵר: אַל תִּהְיוּ כַּעֲבָדִים הַמְשַׁמְּשִׁין אֶת הָרַב
עַל מְנָת לְקַבֵּל פְּרָס; אֶלָּא הֱווּ כַּעֲבָדִים הַמְשַׁמְּשִׁין אֶת

◆§ Whose Universe?

עולם עומד כל אדם עולם קטן עולמך תראה בחייך, תורה קבלת התורה ועבודה
עול מלכות שמים ובתורתך כתוב לאמר שמע ישראל כו' וגמ"ח הרמז על תמכין
דאורייתא עץ חיים היא למחזיקים בה.

The term עוֹלָם, the *universe*, may also refer to each individual Jew who is a
world in his or her own right.[1] According to this approach, Torah, *avodah*
and *gemilus chasadim* are not distinct entities but rather three different means
of infusing our life with the spirit of Torah. We can attain this specifically by
making a commitment to observe Torah and *mitzvos* (קַבָּלַת הַתּוֹרָה); by accepting Hashem's sovereignty over every aspect of our life, which is a form of
avodah known as קַבָּלַת עוֹל מַלְכוּת שָׁמַיִם; and through our acts of גְּמִילוּת חֶסֶד
whereby we are supporting Torah as the well-known verse in *Mishlei* (3:18)
teaches us: עֵץ חַיִּים הִיא לַמַּחֲזִיקִים בָּהּ, *it is a tree of life for those who grasp it*
(adapted from *Beis Yisrael, Maggidei HaEmes*).

3.

■ אַל תִּהְיוּ כַּעֲבָדִים הַמְשַׁמְּשִׁין אֶת הָרַב עַל מְנָת לְקַבֵּל פְּרָס — *Be not
like servants who serve the master for the sake of receiving a re-
ward.*

◆§ Do Not Perform Mitzvos Even to Uphold the Universe

י"ל כלפי מה שכתב מקודם דכל העולם עומד על שמירת התורה ומצות הרי זה
כמו קבלת פרס כי עובד ה' לקיים העולם בזכותו ולכן אמר אנטיגנוס שלא יהיה
הכוונה בעבודת ה' בשביל זה רק לעשות לשם שמים בלבד.

A clear relationship exists between Antigonus' statement and the
previous *mishnah* stating that the universe is sustained through Torah. Do
not perform *mitzvos* or study Torah for any ulterior motive — even for the
purpose of upholding the universe through your good deeds. Rather, perform
mitzvos because of your love and reverence of Hashem.

---

1. Cf. *Berachos* 17a, עולמך תראה בחייך, *you should realize your own world* (the fulfillment of your
dreams) *in your lifetime.*

[3] *Antignos, leader of Socho, received [the Torah] from
Shimon HaTzaddik. He used to say: Be not like servants who serve the master for the sake of receiving a reward; but rather be like servants who serve the master*

⋖§ When Reward Is Appropriate

ויל״ד דהול״ל בקיצור אל תשמשו עמלק״פ, וי״ל דמאריך בכוונה להודיענו דאם
א״א לו שלא עמל״פ אז יעשה ע״מ לקבל פרס בעין מתוך שלא לשמה כו׳ וע״ז
נאמר והוי מחשב הפסד מצוה וכו׳ דהיינו ע״מ לקבל פרס בעין מתוך שלא לשמה.

It is significant that the *mishnah* does not entirely eliminate the possibility of performing *mitzvos* in order to obtain a reward. It does not state, אַל תְּשַׁמְּשׁוּ עַל מְנָת לְקַבֵּל פְּרָס, *do not "serve" Hashem with the intention of receiving a reward*, but rather, ... אַל תִּהְיוּ כַּעֲבָדִים, *do not "act" as servants who seek a reward*. In other words, the *mishnah* is proposing an *ideal* form of עֲבוֹדָה, Divine Service for its own sake. However, it is perfectly acceptable, as an interim measure, to serve Hashem with the intention of receiving a reward. In fact, a subsequent *mishnah* (2:1) specifically states, וֶהֱוֵי מְחַשֵּׁב הֶפְסֵד מִצְוָה כְּנֶגֶד שְׂכָרָהּ, *calculate the cost of a mitzvah against its reward.*

■ הַמְשַׁמְּשִׁין ... שֶׁלֹּא עַל מְנָת לְקַבֵּל פְּרָס — *Who serve ... not for the sake of receiving a reward.*

⋖§ Fulfilling Hashem's Will

הול״ל אל תשמשו ע״מ לקבל פרס אך המכוון להיות כל מגמת האדם תמיד
לעשות רצון בוראו ...
וצריך איש ישראל לידע כי נברא רק לעשות רצון קונו.

Rather than merely stating, אַל תְּשַׁמְּשׁוּ עַל מְנָת לְקַבֵּל פְּרָס, *do not serve Hashem with the intention of receiving a reward*, it says, אַל תִּהְיוּ כַּעֲבָדִים, *do not act as servants who seek a reward*, implying that the *sole* justification for our existence — and our primary objective in life — is to serve Hashem. The *raison d'être* of the Jew is to fulfill Hashem's Will.

⋖§ Acquiring a Good Reputation

י״ל פר״ס בגימטריא ש״ם, והכוונה שלא יעבוד את השי״ת על מנת שיקבל שם
טוב, להגדיל את שמו. ואף ששנינו קנה שם טוב קנה לעצמו, וכן אמרו כתר שם

טוב עולה על גביהן כדכתיב טוב שם משמן טוב, מכל מקום את העבודה שעובד
ומשמש את השי"ת לא יעשה על מנת כן.

The mishnah may be alluding to the inappropriateness of serving Hashem in order to acquire a good reputation, for even this can be viewed as שֶׁלֹּא לִשְׁמָהּ. While subsequent mishnahs extol the virtue of acquiring a good name (see 2:8, קָנָה שֵׁם טוב קָנָה לְעַצְמוֹ, one who has gained a good reputation has gained it for his own benefit; also 4:17, כֶּתֶר שֵׁם טוב עוֹלֶה עַל גַּבֵּיהֶן, the crown of a good name surpasses all of them), this is intended to be the result, not the purpose, of Torah and mitzvos. Our motivation should always be to do רְצוֹן ה', the will of Hashem. This interpretation, it should be noted, is supported by the gematria of פְּרָס, reward (340), which is equivalent to שֵׁם, a [good] name (Lev Simchah, Maggidei HaEmes).

◆§ Don't Strive for Half a Loaf

גם י"ל פרס הוא מלשון מחצה, שלא יהיו כעבדים המשמשין על מנת לקבל
ולהשיג רק את המחצה בעבודתו ית"ש. אלא על מנת לקבל כולה, שיש לשאוף
להגיע לעבודת השי"ת בשלימות.

Frequently, the term פְּרָס refers to a portion of a whole loaf (cf. Berachos 39b, מברך על הפרוסה). Using this approach, the mishnah is exhorting us to seek nothing less than perfection — a complete, all-encompassing commitment to serve Hashem. The mishnah is urging us to be ambitious and raise our sights to seek the most exalted level of avodas Hashem (Lev Simchah, Maggidei HaEmes).

◆§ Clinging to Hashem

ואמרו ג"כ הוי מחשב הפסד מצווה כו', כי בוודאי שכר עוה"ב אינו ענין הגוף, רק
זה עצמו עוה"ב מה שזוכין להיות בטל להש"י כראוי, שהוא דבר שא"י להשיג
ולהיות ברור שאין להשיג להרוב ההעלם לכך נק' עולם כמו שעולם הזה נק' העלם
על שהחושך מכסה ומעלים כבודו ית', כמו כן עוה"ב הוא העלם של אמת על
שאין יכולין להשיג, ובעוה"ז ההעלם ע"י השקר, ובוודאי כן חשבון הפסד מצוה
מה שע"י המצוה מדבק האדם עצמו בהש"י שהוא שורש החיות, וכן וחי בהם
כנ"ל זה השכר הוא תכלית עשיות המצות, ולקבל פרס הוא לשון פרוסה שכוונתו
לעצמו ואינו דבק בשורש החיות כנ"ל היפוך וחי בהם כנ"ל.

Most profoundly, Antigonus is alluding to the true and ultimate reward of mitzvah observance — clinging to Hashem. We should not observe mitzvos with the intention of receiving anything in return. Instead, the ultimate reward of all that we accomplish in This World is complete self-negation to Hashem, a goal beyond man's reach in this world but the very essence of the World to Come, as we will elucidate.

While עוֹלָם הַבָּא is usually translated as the *World to Come*, and עוֹלָם הַזֶּה as *this world*, in reality, the word עוֹלָם is also derived from נֶעְלָם, *hidden*. Just as Hashem's Presence is often concealed from us in עוֹלָם הַזֶּה, so does His Presence totally dominate עוֹלָם הַבָּא to the extent that we cannot even begin to grasp the hidden (נֶעְלָם) treasures awaiting the soul in that realm. Thus, the *mishnah* is urging us — seek nothing for yourself[1] — perform *mitzvos* for the sole purpose of achieving total self-negation (לִהְיוֹת בָּטֵל לַה׳) to Hashem in that hidden realm of עוֹלָם הַבָּא.

Based on this approach, we can offer a novel interpretation to a subsequent *mishnah*: וֶהֱוֵי מְחַשֵּׁב הֶפְסֵד מִצְוָה כְּנֶגֶד שְׂכָרָהּ, *calculate the cost of a mitzvah against its reward* (2:1), which implies that one *is* rewarded for observing *mitzvos*. The *mishnah* is referring to the ultimate impact of *mitzvos* in *Olam Haba* — complete self-negation to Hashem. While such a rarefied existence may seem to indicate a loss of self in favor of the overwhelming Presence of Hashem (הֶפְסֵד מִצְוָה), contemplate the spiritual reward that such self-negation brings (כְּנֶגֶד שְׂכָרָהּ). The Torah's admonition וָחַי בָּהֶם, *live through them* [*mitzvos*] (*Vayikra* 18:5), may also refer to the Jew's only reward — clinging to the source of all life, Hashem! (adapted from *Sfas Emes*).

◄§ "As" Servants (כַּעֲבָדִים)

יש לדקדק דהל״ל למימר עבדים. ונראה כי בני ישראל באמת הם בחינת בנים רק הוו כעבדים פי׳ שניכר מזה ההפרש כי העובד שלא על מנת לקבל פרס יותר באמונה מעשהו.

The prefix כַּ, *like*, as in the word כַּעֲבָדִים (rather than עֲבָדִים, *servants*), reminds us that we are primarily Hashem's *children* (cf. *Devarim* 14:1, בָּנִים אַתֶּם). However, in order to impress upon us the importance of serving Hashem altruistically — and some of the *implications* of doing so — the *mishnah* uses the example of servants. The servant who continues to work despite not being compensated is displaying great faith in his master, realizing that just serving him is a worthy objective. In fact, this altruistically inclined servant will probably be more loyal to his master than someone who is regularly compensated. In this one respect we too should be like עֲבָדִים and conduct ourselves with steadfast loyalty to Hashem. Serving Hashem without any expectation of compensation implies not only a willingness to forego *immediate* reward but also demonstrates unquestioning faithfulness to Him.

---

1. According to this interpretation, the term פְּרָס is related to פְּרוּסָה, *a piece*, the intent being the total lack of physical reward for observance of *mitzvos*.

הָרַב שֶׁלֹּא עַל מְנָת לְקַבֵּל פְּרָס; שֶׁלֹּא עַל מְנָת לְקַבֵּל
פְּרָס; וִיהִי מוֹרָא שָׁמַיִם עֲלֵיכֶם.

⇒§ Do Such "Servants" Actually Exist?

לכאורה מי איכא עבדים כאלו . . .

וי״ל דב׳ דברים הם, הוו כעבדים וגם לשמש שלא עמל״פ, גם יי״ל דהיינו
המלאכים בשמים שלא מצינו שהי׳ להם קיבול שכר והם נק׳ עבדים כמו״ש במפ׳
הפי׳ משובח ומפואר בלשון חסידיו ועבדיו דעבדיו הם המלאכים.

אכן העליונים נק׳ עבדים שלא ע״מ לקבל פרס משרתיו עושי רצונו. והתחתונים
נטבע בהם להיות להם תאוה ורצון . . . אבל מי שעיניו פקוחות צריך לידע כי כל
מעשיו הם רצון המלך ולעתיד יתגלה זאת לעיני הכל וע״ז אומרים יכירו וידעו
כל יושבי תבל כי לך תכרע כל ברך תשבע כל לשון . . .

ומה שאסר להם מאכלות אסורות וביאות אסורות שבהם הקליפה דבוקה ולא
יוכלו לעשות עבודתם לשם שמים.

The *mishnah* seems to be demanding the impossible — to work without being compensated. Is there a precedent for any mortal working without receiving payment?

On a simple level, the *mishnah* may be stating two distinct thoughts. Serve Hashem (הֱוּ כַעֲבָדִים) with the same unyielding commitment that a servant displays to his master. However, it is imperative to go beyond that relationship. Unlike those servants who seek reward, do not seek benefit from your *avodas Hashem*.

More profoundly, the *mishnah* is urging the Jew to rise to the status of an angel. Just as angels serve Hashem without any expectation of reward, so too we should emulate their example and seek nothing for ourselves. A phrase recited in the daily *davening* supports this interpretation of the term עֲבָדִים — מְשֻׁבָּח וּמְפֹאָר בִּלְשׁוֹן חֲסִידָיו וַעֲבָדָיו, *praised and glorified by the tongue of His devout ones and His servants*. The liturgist perceives Hashem as being praised by the righteous (חֲסִידָיו) and by Hashem's servants (עֲבָדָיו), the angels.

By extension, the entire natural world serves Hashem without expecting compensation. All the celestial bodies (the sun, moon, etc.) have no concept of self-identity. They exist merely to serve Hashem. It is only man, beset with a יֵצֶר הָרַע, challenged by the temptation to do evil, who may desire to act contrary to Hashem's wishes. This then is the plea of our *mishnah* — emulate the natural world, remember that you exist for no other purpose than to fulfill the Divine Will.

Eventually, all men will realize that this is their *raison d'être*. As Yeshayahu (45:23) proclaims, כִּי לִי תִּכְרַע כָּל בֶּרֶךְ תִּשָּׁבַע כָּל לָשׁוֹן, *Every knee shall bend to Me, every tongue shall vow allegiance [to Me]*.

not for the receiving a reward.; and the fear of Heaven should be upon you.

The *mishnah*, however, implores us to arrive at this conclusion *now* by overcoming the many passions that may prevent us from achieving this noble mission.

In this light, we may glean additional comprehension of the many prohibitions of the Torah (מִצְוֹת לֹא תַעֲשֶׂה; e.g. the prohibition against eating non-kosher food). The Torah forbids us from partaking of those substances because they contain elements that suppress our innate desire to serve Hashem.

■ הַמְשַׁמְּשִׁין אֶת הָרַב — *Who serve the master.*

⋙ Serve Your Torah Teacher

י"ל הפי' הרב ממש, רבו שמלמדו תורה, והיינו שאף על פי שאין מרגישים שמקבלים מהרב טובה גם כן ישמשו אותו. וזו כוונת הגמ' גדולה שמושה של תורה יותר מלמודה.

Perhaps the *mishnah* is referring to the relationship between a student and his Torah teacher (רַב). Though you may not perceive yourself as receiving any benefit from your *rebbi*,[1] nonetheless attend to his needs — serve him. The famous Gemara (*Berachos* 7b), גְדוֹלָה שִׁמּוּשָׁהּ שֶׁל תּוֹרָה יוֹתֵר מִלְּמוּדָהּ, *attending to those who study Torah is greater than studying Torah under them*, may be reinterpreted in this light: Service of a Torah teacher is greater than study. In other words, serve your *rebbi* even though you may not think that you (to all external appearances) have learned anything from him (*Maggidei HaEmes, Imrei Emes*).

⋙ The Sadducees' Error

הגם שיהי' לו פרס מ"מ העבדות יהי' כמו העבודה של העובד שלעמל"פ ובזה לא הניחו מקום לרדות להמינים.

A gross error in interpreting this *mishnah* led to the formation of the heretical sect later known as Sadducees. Tzadok and Baisus, disciples of Antigonus, concluded erroneously from this *mishnah* that Hashem (ח"ו) does not and is unable to reward those who perform *mitzvos* (cf. *Rav* on *mishnah* 11). However, a careful reading of this *mishnah* supports the opposite conclusion. While

---

1. Cf. *Avodah Zarah* 5b which states that a person does not fully appreciate his *rebbi* until after 40 years!

[ד] יוֹסֵי בֶּן יוֹעֶזֶר אִישׁ צְרֵדָה וְיוֹסֵי בֶּן יוֹחָנָן אִישׁ
יְרוּשָׁלַיִם קִבְּלוּ מֵהֶם. יוֹסֵי בֶּן יוֹעֶזֶר אִישׁ צְרֵדָה
אוֹמֵר: יְהִי בֵיתְךָ בֵּית וַעַד לַחֲכָמִים, וֶהֱוֵי מִתְאַבֵּק

Hashem most certainly *does* compensate those who fulfill His *mitzvos*, our relationship to Him should be that of a servant who serves his master without anticipation of a reward.

■ וִיהִי מוֹרָא שָׁמַיִם עֲלֵיכֶם — *And the fear of Heaven should be upon you.*

◆§ Fear Hashem for Altruistic Reasons

כלומר כי גם המורא יהי' שלא עמל"פ דהיינו יראת העונש וכדומה רק יי"ש
לש"ש . . . הענין כי היר"ש ורואה גבהות ה' שאין לו חקר וגבול אזי ממילא בטל
אצלו החפץ לקבל פרס בשביל עשיות המצות, כי מעמיק ביראתו ית' אשר
עשיות המצות גובהן בשורש מאוד.
וז"פ ויהי מורא שמים עליכם כשלא תוכלו לעבוד שלא ע"מ לק"פ תחשבו ג"כ
על שכר.

This seemingly unrelated concluding passage may be actually expanding the parameters of serving Hashem altruistically. The *mishnah* is calling upon us not only to *love* Hashem without expecting any material reward (altruistically), but also to *fear* Hashem altruistically. Instead of being motivated by the less exalted form of יִרְאַת שָׁמַיִם, a fear of Divine retribution (יִרְאַת הָעוֹנֶשׁ), revere Hashem for no other reason (שֶׁלֹּא עַל מְנָת לְקַבֵּל פְּרָס) than that you are simply *awed* by Hashem's Majestic Presence (יִרְאַת הָרוֹמְמוּת).

On the other hand, the concluding passage of the *mishnah* may actually be suggesting the most effective means of serving Hashem altruistically — by contemplating His Awesome Presence and fearing Him. Anyone who delves into and begins to comprehend even a fraction of the Divine Presence will realize that no material reward can be sufficient for the performance of *mitzvos* which emanate from the source of all spiritualities, Hashem Himself.

Alternatively, the *mishnah* may be referring to the individual who is unable to serve Hashem altruistically (שֶׁלֹּא עַל מְנָת לְקַבֵּל פְּרָס). Such an individual needs to be motivated, at least *temporarily*, by the incentive of a reward (cf. 2:1, וֶהֱוֵי מְחַשֵּׁב הֶפְסֵד מִצְוָה כְּנֶגֶד שְׂכָרָהּ, *calculate the cost of a mitzvah against its reward*) in addition to the fear of punishment (מוֹרָא שָׁמַיִם).

◆§ Fear of Heaven

לא אמר מורא ה' אלא מורא שמים כמו שפירש רש"י על הפסוק ויאמר אלקים

[4] *Yose ben Yoezer, leader of Tz'redah, and Yose ben Yochanan, leader of Jerusalem, received (the Torah) from him. Yose ben Yoezer says: Let your house be a meeting place for sages; and sit in the dust of their feet*

יהי רקיע וגו' שנתהוו ונקרשו מגערתו ית"ש. וזהו ויהי מורא שמים עליכם, תהיה יראתכם כמו יראת השמים.

The phrase מוֹרָא שָׁמַיִם, *fear [awe] of Heaven* (rather than מוֹרָא ה', *fear [awe] of Hashem*), reminds us of *how* the heavens were created — on the basis of the Divine Statement יְהִי רָקִיעַ, *let there be a firmament* (*Bereishis* 1:6). As *Rashi* states (there), although the heavens were created on the first day, they were still in a moist, pliable form. It was only upon hearing the awesome Divine command יְהִי רָקִיעַ, *let there be a firmament*, that the heavens, awed by Hashem's "roar," assumed their present form (*congealed* and *stiffened*). Just as the heavens were created on the basis of Hashem's statement, so too the יְרֵא שָׁמַיִם (God-fearing person) emulates the heavens and seeks to fulfill Hashem's Will (Kotzker Rebbe, *Maggidei HaEmes*).

4.

■ יְהִי בֵיתְךָ בֵּית וַעַד לַחֲכָמִים — *Let your house be a meeting place for sages.*

⋖§ Make the Beis Hamedrash Your Home

היינו המקום שהוא בית ועד לחכמים שם יהיה ביתך. הא דלא פי' השפ"א כפשוטו משום שלא כל אחד יכול להגיע לזה שביתו יהיה בית ועד לחכמים, ולכן פי' שילך הוא למקום שהחכמים מצויים שם, והיינו בביהמ"ד.

While this phrase is usually interpreted that one's home should be designated as a meeting place for *talmidei chachamim* (scholars), this may not be a feasible goal for most people. Instead, the *mishnah* should be interpreted: You should designate a well-established meeting place for scholars as your "home." In particular, the focal point of a Jew's life, his true home, should be the *beis hamedrash*, the gathering place of *talmidei chachamim*[5] (*Lev Simchah, Maggidei HaEmes*).

⋖§ The Treasures of the Shas

פי' כל חכמי תנאים ואמוראים כאשר ילמוד לש"ס ויזכיר בשמם ההלכות כדאי'

בירושלמי שיהי' בעל השמועה עומד לפניך.

It is, however, possible to fulfill the spirit of this *mishnah* even within the privacy of one's own home — simply by availing oneself of the vast treasures of the Talmud (*Shas*). Whenever we study the pages of a Gemara and mention, by name, the sacred *Tannaim* (authors of the *mishnah*) and *Amoraim* (authors of the Gemara), we are inviting these Torah giants into our home. This interpretation is supported by the Yerushalmi suggestion (*Shekalim 2:5*) that we should perceive the sages of the Talmud as if they were in our presence while we are studying their teachings.

◈§ The Jewish Heart

יש לפרש על האדם עצמו שיעשה לבו בית ועד לחכמים.

Finally, the term בֵּיתְךָ, *your home*, may refer to the individual Jew himself. Let your heart — the home and seat of so many conflicting emotions — be a gathering for *talmidei chachamim*. Let your emotions by defined by Torah as interpreted by its scholars (*Lev Simchah, Maggidei HaEmes*).

■ וֶהֱוֵי מִתְאַבֵּק בַּעֲפַר רַגְלֵיהֶם — *Sit in the dust of their feet.* ■

◈§ Travel With Talmidei Chachamim

פי' הגם שביתך יהיה בית ועד ויבואו תמיד רק אצלך מכל מקום לפעמים אם ילכו
גם בדרך תלך עמהם ותתאבק בעפר רגליהם.

The *mishnah* is addressing the generous host who has already converted his home into a terminus for *talmidei chachamim*. Despite your unquestioned generosity, you would also benefit by traveling alongside Torah scholars, i.e. by sitting in the dust of their feet.

■ וֶהֱוֵי שׁוֹתֶה בַּצָּמָא אֶת דִּבְרֵיהֶם — *And you shall drink in their words thirstily.* ■

וכמו המשל לדגים שכל טפה רואין כאלו לא טעמו טעם מים והגם שתתאבק ותהי'
תמיד עם החכמים עכ"ז הוי שותה בצא"ד, גם י"ל והוי שותה היא הבטחה שלבסוף
יהי' כן ולא תירא שיתייבשן אצל.

מי שיש לו הרבה משי אז כיון שרגיל שאינו צמא אחרי . . .

Though one may constantly cling to *talmidei chachamim*, the *mishnah* exhorts us not to become so accustomed to their presence that we lose interest in their teachings. Just as fish drink the last drop of water as if it were their first, so too we should drink thirstily the teachings of *talmidei chachamim* despite our previous exposure to them.

In fact, the *mishnah* is assuring, as well as pleading with us, not to fear the effect of overexposure to Torah scholars because there is no such thing. In the merit of clinging to *talmidei chachamim*, be assured that you will never lose your appetite for their teachings. Whereas people who are accustomed to luxuries eventually derive less enjoyment from them, this is hardly the case with the ever vibrant and fresh teachings of the Torah (adapted from *Sfas Emes*).

⇜§ Just as You Would Not Forget to Eat

חסיד אחד התנצל בפני החידושי הרי"ם ז"ל שהוא סובל משכחה ושוכח תורתו. שאלו הרבי "ואת האוכל מגיש אתה בטעות אל האוזן"? לא. חזר ושאלו "ומדוע לא"? כי באכילה תלויים חיי. "דע, גם בתורתך תלויים חייך", הפטיר החידה"ר.

A follower of the *Chiddushei Harim* once complained to his Rebbe that he was constantly forgetting his learning. The Rebbe responded, "Did you ever, in a state of forgetfulness, place your food in your ear?" The startled *chassid* responded, "Certainly not!" The Rebbe questioned his *chassid* further, "Why not?" "Because my life depends on eating properly." "If so," the Rebbe concluded, "how can you forget your learning which is as vital to your life as food?"

5.

■ יְהִי בֵיתְךָ פָּתוּחַ לָרְוָחָה — *Let your house be open wide.* ■

⇜§ Open on All Four Sides

פי' הרע"ב כביתו של אאע"ה כו' י"ל שלבן נק' קרית ארבע שהוא אאע"ה האדם הגדול כו', ואולי זה מרומז במש"כ בפתח עינים שכל עינים כו'.

According to the *Bartenura*, the *mishnah* is urging us to open all four doors of our home to guests, just as Avraham did. This interpretation is supported

by the name with which the Torah refers to the city of Chevron — Kiryas
Arba. While this is generally translated as "the city of the four giants"
(cf. *Bamidbar* 13:22 enumerating four giants who lived in Chevron), in light
of our *mishnah*, the term may be understood as the city of Avraham whose
door was open on all four sides. The *Bartenura's* interpretation is also supported by *Rashi's* interpretation of the term פֶּתַח עֵינַיִם, *a crossroads* (*Bereishis*
38:14), where he comments, בְּפִתְחוֹ שֶׁל אַבְרָהָם אָבִינוּ שֶׁכָּל עֵינַיִם מְצַפּוֹת לִרְאוֹתוֹ,
*at the entrance to the tent of our father Avraham, at which all eyes looked
eagerly to see.* If we assume, as the *Bartenura* does, that every door of Avraham's home was open, *Rashi's* words may be interpreted literally: All eyes
were able to see, from every vantage point, the openings to Avraham's
house.

◆§ Let the Guest Leave!

היינו שלא לסגור את הדלתות בשעה שהאורח רוצה ללכת אלא למלאות רצונו.

By emphasizing the need for an open door, the *mishnah* may be subtly
reminding us that a guest is entitled to leave at will (make a graceful departure) in the same manner as he enters. Have an open door, allowing a guest to
arrive and leave when he desires. Do not pressure him to remain! (R' Yitzchak
of Vorka, *Maggidei HaEmes*).

■ וְיִהְיוּ עֲנִיִּים בְּנֵי בֵיתֶךָ — *Treat the poor as members of your household.*

◆§ Buy From the Poor

קשה דכתיב מהם תנו וכמ״ש רש״י שם א״ת ישמשני מי ישמני כו', ופשוט י״ל
על הנכנסין ויוצאין יהי' עניים כדי שתוכל ליתן להם להרוויח דאל״כ הרי חז״ל
היו להם עבדים כמו טבי כו'.

According to the *Bartenura*, the term בְּנֵי בֵיתֶךָ refers to domestic help. It is
preferable to hire the Jewish poor as domestic help rather than non-Jews
(especially not Canaanites who had been cursed by Noach). However, this
approach is seemingly contradicted by *Rashi* who explicitly states (in his commentary on *Vayikra* 25:44 s.v. ועבדך) that one may utilize non-Jews as servants
[except for members of the seven nations conquered by the Jewish people].

[5] *Yose ben Yochanan leader of Jerusalem says:*
Let your house be open wide; treat the poor as
members of your household; and do not converse

Furthermore, the Sages of the Talmud, such as Rabbi Gamliel, utilized non-Jewish servants (cf. *Berachos* 16b discussing Rabbi Gamliel mourning his servant Tovi's passing).

If, however, we interpret the term בְּנֵי בֵיתֶךָ to refer to the itinerant merchants (peddlers, salesmen) that frequent the house, we may resolve the above difficulties. While you may employ non-Jewish servants, be sure to conduct business with the Jewish poor, thus enabling them to earn an honorable living rather than depending upon charity.

◆§ The Full Extent of הַכְנָסַת אוֹרְחִים

השיב אדמו"ר מקאצק ז"ל "ראוי להראות לאורח את מקום לינתו לפני שמאכילים אותו, כדי שיאכל בשלוה". רבי הכניס אורחים הרבה ונתן להם נדבתו לפני שהאכילם.

הרה"ח ר' ברוך מרדכי טשארני מווארשא היה מופלג במצות הכנסת אורחים, והעניים הרגישו עצמם כבתוך ביתם עד שקשה היה להכיר מי הבעה"ב. פעם התארח אצלו עני שחשבו להיות עני אורח כמותו, התנצל בפניו "אני נמצא כאן זה כמה שבועות ואיני יודע אם יתנו לי להשאר כאן יותר". ענה לו רבי ברוך מרדכי "אף אני שוהה כאן תקופה ארוכה ואין פוצה פה חושבני איפה שגם אתה תוכל להשאר"...

יהודי אחד שהה יחד עם בני ביתו תקופה ממושכת בבית של מחשובי חסידי גור שבבורו פארק, כאשר נמשך שהותם זמן מה, תלה פתק על דלת ביתו עם שם משפחת האורחים בכדי שירגישו עצמם כאילו זה ביתם.

The following thoughts are based on the *literal* interpretation of the *mishnah*, referring to הַכְנָסַת אוֹרְחִים, *inviting guests*.

The term בְּנֵי בֵיתֶךָ implies that a guest is entitled to far more than a meal; in fact, he becomes an integral part of the family. The Kotzker Rebbe maintained that a guest should be shown his bed (his lodging) *before* being asked to partake of the meal. Thus, secure with the knowledge that he may stay for the night, he will heartily enjoy the meal. It is similarly told about Rabbi Eliezer, the Baal Shem Tov's father, who was widely known as a generous host, that he would insist upon granting his donation to the poor *before* inviting them to partake of his meal. He was aware that their primary mission was to collect funds and having successfully dispensed with that, they could then enjoy a meal.

The following two vignettes recounted about Chassidic *baalei batim* capture some of the meaning of בְּנֵי בֵיתֶךָ — making the poor feel at home.

שִׂיחָה עִם הָאִשָׁה. בְּאִשְׁתּוֹ אָמְרוּ, קַל וָחֹמֶר בְּאֵשֶׁת
חֲבֵרוֹ. מִכַּאן אָמְרוּ חֲכָמִים: כָּל הַמַּרְבֶּה שִׂיחָה עִם
הָאִשָׁה — גּוֹרֵם רָעָה לְעַצְמוֹ, וּבוֹטֵל מִדִּבְרֵי תוֹרָה,
וְסוֹפוֹ יוֹרֵשׁ גֵּיהִנֹּם.

[ו] יְהוֹשֻׁעַ בֶּן פְּרַחְיָה וְנִתַּאי הָאַרְבֵּלִי קִבְּלוּ מֵהֶם.
יְהוֹשֻׁעַ בֶּן פְּרַחְיָה אוֹמֵר: עֲשֵׂה לְךָ רַב, וּקְנֵה לְךָ
חָבֵר, וֶהֱוֵי דָן אֶת כָּל הָאָדָם לְכַף זְכוּת.

Rabbi Boruch Mordechai of Warsaw was so adept at disguising his role as
a host that many of his guests perceived him as just another poor man. Once,
one of the guests, believing that Rabbi Boruch Mordechai was another beggar,
wondered, "I've been here many weeks. I don't know if I will be permitted to
stay much longer." His host, maintaining his disguise, responded, "Let me
assure you I also have been here a long time and no one ever asked me to leave.
I trust that you too will be permitted to remain."

A similar story is related about a Gerrer *chassid* residing in Boro Park, who
in his own unique manner fulfilled the spirit of וְיִהְיוּ עֲנִיִּים בְּנֵי בֵיתֶךָ.

When a certain guest had remained for an extraordinarily long period, the
host simply added the guest's name to the family nameplate on the front
entrance. Thus, the guest was made to feel as though his host's home was,
indeed, his as well.

■ וְאַל תַּרְבֶּה שִׂיחָה עִם הָאִשָׁה — *And do not converse excessively with a
woman.*

◆§ **Between Speech and Prattle**

קול באשה ערוה ושם הוי דיבור בלבד וכאן כי רק א״ת שיחה.
דאיירי במקבל אורח ומצוה קעביד להרבות עמו שיחה וקמ״ל דאל ירבה כבאשה
מתארחת אצלו.

The juxtaposition of this segment to the previous statements of the *mishnah*
seems to discourage idle chatter (שִׂיחָה) with any woman, even a female
guest. Whereas it may be a *mitzvah* to converse with a male guest (so that he
feel at ease), one should not do so with a female guest. This approach (interpretation) resolves the seeming contradiction between this *mishnah* which only
prohibits שִׂיחָה, a significant conversation with a woman, and the Gemara
(*Kiddushin* 70b) which seems to forbid any kind of discussion (דִּיבּוּר) with a
woman. On the basis of this approach we distinguish between the guest to

excessively with a woman. They said this even about one's own wife; surely it applies to another's wife. Consequently, the Sages said: Anyone who converses excessively with a woman causes evil to himself, neglects Torah study and will ultimately inherit Gehinnom (perdition).

[6] *Yehoshua ben Perachyah and Nittai of Arbel received [the Torah] from them. Yehoshua ben Perachyah says: Appoint a Torah teacher for yourself; acquire a friend for yourself; and judge everyone favorably.*

---

whom one must speak briefly in order to ascertain her needs and any other woman with whom any talk is discouraged.

■ בְּאִשְׁתּוֹ אָמְרוּ, קַל וָחֹמֶר בְּאֵשֶׁת חֲבֵרוֹ — *They said this even about one's own wife; surely it applies to another's wife.*

◆§ Even About One's Own Wife

א״כ לא שבקת חיי, ולכן י״ל הפי׳ באשתו אמרו שאר הרחקות שצריכין לעשות,
ק״ו באשת חבירו לענין שיחה.

While a cursory reading of this *mishnah* seems to prohibit any prolonged conversation (שִׂיחָה) with one's wife, it seems improbable that *Chazal* would discourage a husband from conversing with his wife. Instead, the *mishnah* is referring to other restrictions that do exist, even between married couples (e.g. the laws of *niddah*). If husband and wife are subject to certain restrictions in their own relationships, it is reasonable to infer that one should certainly not converse excessively with a total stranger.

6.

■ עֲשֵׂה לְךָ רַב וּקְנֵה לְךָ חָבֵר — *Appoint a teacher for yourself; acquire a friend for yourself.*

◆§ Who Is More Important — A Rebbi or a Good Colleague?

מדמקדים עשיות רב שמע מינה שאין הפי׳ כהמפרשים שחבר יקר יותר רק שזה
רשאי ליקח ורב אסור משום שכר לימוד. ופי׳ הפשוט יתכן כי חבר צריך יותר לקנות
מרב כי מחבירו יכול לקבל יותר.

Many deduce from this *mishnah* that a trusted friend is even more valuable than a *rebbi*. Thus, we are told to *acquire* (קְנֵה) a friend, even if you must compensate (pay) him but regarding a teacher the *mishnah* simply states עֲשֵׂה, *make* (acquire) and designate a *rebbi* (teacher) for yourself. In fact, a close friend can often contribute more than a teacher.

However, this deduction may be unwarranted. On the contrary, a *rebbi* may be more valuable than a close friend, as evidenced from the *mishnah's* order, placing עֲשֵׂה לְךָ רַב *prior* to קְנֵה לְךָ חָבֵר. If so, why are we not instructed to compensate a *rebbi* just as we are a friend? Simply, it is because of the well-known *halachah* prohibiting compensation for teaching Torah (cf. *Shulchan Aruch*, *Yoreh Deah* for contemporary practice of compensating Torah teachers).

◂§ Learn From Everything in Life, Especially Yourself

נראה שיכול לעשות והאיך מכל דבר שרואה ומשיג.
לללמוד מענין זה ז׳׳הוע . . . דומלל מענין תוהגהנתהב וצומע ךוג וכמ זך לשמור
שפנה ,וכז הבקהפרדתו לע וירתשמ וכודמה שיכ לוכ סדאה דומלל מענינינ עצמו ריא
.עלבוד הבורא ב׳׳ה וב׳׳ש.

The phrase עֲשֵׂה לְךָ רַב may refer to our environment. Let the environment — your immediate surroundings — be your teacher. Everything in the material world carries a message. In particular, learn from *yourself*. Make yourself — עֲשֵׂה לְךָ — your own *rebbi*! Contemplate the love that you display for the material matters (creature comforts) of This World and then arrive at the following conclusion: If I demonstrate so much affection towards mundane material things, imagine how much I should love Hashem. Likewise, by contemplating the inordinate fear we experience sometimes regarding certain physical entities (people, wild animals), we can imagine the awe and fear that we should have for Hashem.

In a similar vein, learn from the attention and care you lavish on your body and extrapolate from there the respect and awe that your soul (נְשָׁמָה) so richly deserves. Just as you would spare no effort to ensure your physical health, so too expend the same energy on your soul's vitality and well-being.

One can even learn by observing the relationships people have with their employees. Just as an employer expects complete loyalty from his workers, so too demand no less from yourself when it comes to your service of Hashem.

◂§ Master Yourself

וגם יל׳׳פ לך ממש שהאדם יעשה א׳׳ע לרב על עצמו שלא לצאת מהגדר

Quite simply, the term רַב, which can also be defined as *master*, refers to oneself rather than to an external master. Master yourself! Control yourself so that your every action reflects the Torah and its values (adapted from *Sfas Emes*).

⋄§ Purchase a Friend as You Would Acquire Any Valuable

הדמיון הוא למשל אם תקנה איזה דבר באלף או אלפיים לירות, והיה אם תדמה
או תראה בזה איזה סדק ופרצה בל תנח ותשקוט עד שתביא מומחים ויחפש
עצות לתקן זאת ומכל שכן שלא יעלה על דעתך לעזוב ולהזניח בזאת. כן יהיה
אצלך מדת חבר טוב וצריכים לידע כמה כמה אוצר של יראת ואהבת השי"י מוטמן
בזה.

The term קְנֵה, *purchase, acquire*, implies that the same caution that is applied when procuring a valuable object (e.g. a home, car) also be reflected in your choice of acquiring a friend. Just as you would not finalize a contract for the acquisition of such a valuable item if you found even a minor flaw, so too, be cautious about accepting a friend whose character is flawed. If we contemplate how our own love and fear of Hashem (אַהֲבַת וְיִרְאַת ה׳) are immeasurably affected by our friends, then we should surely scrutinize them carefully (*Lev Simchah, Maggidei HaEmes*).

⋄§ The Advantage of a Friend Over a Rebbi

ויש לפרש הכוונה דברבי כתיב את ה"א תירא ואיתא לרבות תלמידי חכמים,
ואיתא בספרים הפי' שעל ידם יכול להגיע ליראת שמים. ואילו בחבר כתיב
ואהבת לרעך כמוך פועל יוצא ואהבת את ה"א. לכן יי"ל גדולה מעלת החבר
ממעלת הרבי, שאהבה גדולה יותר מיראה.

While a *rebbi* can encourage me to *fear* Hashem, only a trusted friend can lead me to *love* Hashem, an attribute even greater than fear (cf. *Ramban, Shemos* 20:8 s.v. זכור). This unique capacity of a friend is deduced from the renowned *pasuk* (*Vayikra* 19:18), וְאָהַבְתָּ לְרֵעֲךָ כָּמוֹךָ, which may be interpreted that through your relationship with your peers (וְאָהַבְתָּ לְרֵעֲךָ כָּמוֹךָ), you will love Hashem. On the other hand, when describing the respect due to Torah scholars, the *pasuk* in *Va'eschanan* (*Devarim* 6:13) says, אֶת ה׳ אֱלֹהֶיךָ תִּירָא, *fear Hashem your God.* [Cf. *Pesachim* 22b which interprets this *pasuk* as referring to the respect accorded to Torah scholars.] This implies that by associating with תַּלְמִידֵי חֲכָמִים you will learn to fear Hashem (adapted from *Lev Simchah, Maggidei HaEmes*).

■ וֶהֱוֵי דָן אֶת כָּל הָאָדָם לְכַף זְכוּת — *And judge everyone favorably.* ■

Evaluate the Overall Person

ונראה דהפי׳ דוודאי הגם שבדבר פרטי אינו עושה טוב מכל מקום את כל האדם
בכלל יש בו דברים ומדות אחרים של זכות המכריע זה הדבר ופי׳ כל האדם לפי
המצב בכלל.

The *mishnah* not only requires us to judge everyone's behavior favorably but also *assists* us in doing so. כָּל אֶת דָּן וֶהֱוֵי — Judge the *entire* person (כָּל הָאָדָם). Although specific character traits of an individual may be flawed, his overall character can certainly be distinguished. Instead of focusing on relatively minor flaws, concentrate on the more favorable and positive character traits.

The Heavenly Impact of Judging A Peer Favorably

עפירש״י ידונו אותך מן השמים לכף זכות, ואינו מובן דאיך שייך בשמים לומר
שידונו לכ״ז הלא קמי שמיא גליא, ואי הפי׳ דהמצוה שידין חבירו לכ״ז זה יכריע
אותו לכ״ז, א״כ גם כל מצוה כן ולמה נקיט דוקא זה וצריך לומר דמצוה זו יותר
חשובה בשמים, אולם אמר מו״ז ז״ל בשם הרבי מלובלין ז״ל דקשה הלשון והוי
דן דמי שמהו לדיין וכי תלוי בדינו ואמר דתלוי בזה דבאם אומר עליו זכות גם מן
השמים דנים כך דכך הגזירה שתלוי בתחתונים כפי מה שידברו. . . ולפי״ז ניחא
דשפיר מן השמים ג״כ ידונוהו עי״ז לזכות היינו שיזדמנו לו אנשים שילמדו עליו
ג״כ זכות וידונו אותו לזכות בשמים.

The Gemara (*Shabbos* 127b) relates that if we judge our peers favorably, Hashem, in turn, will judge us favorably. This saying of *Chazal*, at first sight, seems difficult to understand. While it is appropriate for mortals who do not possess complete information to judge a peer's questionable behavior in the best possible light, how can we say this about Hashem Who is fully aware of every possible rationale and motive for our behavior?

This statement may refer to the *merit* one deserves for judging one's peer favorably. In the merit of displaying this difficult character trait of being דָן לְכַף זְכוּת, Hashem will reciprocate by tilting the scales of justice in your favor. According to this approach, this attribute of judging one's peer favorably is appreciated by Hashem to such an extent that it alone can ensure a proper advantageous verdict.

The Chozeh of Lublin offered an ingenious approach not only to resolve this question but also to help us appreciate more fully the significance of judging people favorably.

He noted the surprising use of the term דָן, *judge*. It seems strange that an off-handed evaluation of a peer should be called a judgment. Yet, the literal meaning of the *mishnah* is correct. The Heavenly Tribunal bases its verdict of mortals on the evaluation of other mortals, their own friends and colleagues. If I evaluate an individual's behavior in the best possible light, Hashem too will judge that individual as favorably as possible.

In the merit of judging a peer favorably and thus sparing him from Divine Retribution, Hashem will enable my peers to judge me from a similar perspective (לְכַף זְכוּת) which, in turn, will ensure me a favorable judgment on Hashem's part.

◆§ Spare the Universe!

בעבודת ישראל כתב לפרש עפ"י אמרם ז"ל. חייב אדם לומר בשבילי נברא העולם. עוד אמרו שצריך לחשוב שכל העולם מחצה חייב ומחצה זכאי עד שהוא יכריע את כל העולם לכף זכות. וזה ביאור מתני' שע"י מעשיו הטובים יכריע את כל האדם לכף זכות.

A novel approach to this concept was suggested by the Koznitzer Maggid, based on the Talmud's assertion that every individual should assume that the universe's fate depends on his behavior (*Sanhedrin* 37a). In other words, the *mitzvos* he performs ensures the world's continued existence. If, ח"ו, he sins, the universe's continued existence is jeopardized.

In this light, the *mishnah* is then referring to our *personal* behavior (rather than our evaluation of peers). Through personal example, by performing that extra *mitzvah*, I can ensure that all mankind (כָּל הָאָדָם) — even the universe itself — be judged favorably (לְכַף זְכוּת) (*Maggidei HaEmes*).

◆§ Be a "Mensch"

הרה"ק ר' הערש בער מגרבוביץ ז"ל מגדולי חסידי קאצק ישב פעם עם בנו ולמד מסכת אבות כשהגיעו למתניתין שאלו בנו, דלכאורה הו"ל למימר בקיצור תדון כל אדם לכף זכות ולמה האריך התנא ואמר "הוי" דן את כל האדם לכף זכות אמר לו אביו "אם יגידו לך שאני חיללתי את השבת האם תאמין"? לא! "ואם יגידו לך שאני שיקרתי פעם אחת התאמין"? אולי כן, השיב הילד "ואתה יודע למה? מפני שאתה אינך מסוגל לחלל את השבת ואילו לשקר הנך מסוגל. וזה מה שאמרו הוי, זיי א מענטש (תהיה משהו, תהיה בן אדם) ואז כבר תדון כל אדם לכף זכות."

Perhaps, the best route to achieve this desirable but elusive character trait (מִדָּה) is to begin with oneself. If I insist that my own behavior be impeccable, not allowing for even a shadow of evil, I will thereby assume the best about others. This novel insight can be deduced from the seemingly superfluous term וֶהֱוֵי, *be*. The *mishnah* is urging us, "Be a *mensch*" — be a paragon of good *midos* yourself and by doing so you will be able to judge others favorably.

[ז] נִתַּאי הָאַרְבֵּלִי אוֹמֵר: הַרְחֵק מִשָּׁכֵן רָע, וְאַל
תִּתְחַבֵּר לָרָשָׁע, וְאַל תִּתְיָאֵשׁ מִן הַפֻּרְעָנוּת.

To illustrate the association between sterling *midos* and judging others favorably, we relate the dialogue that occurred between R' Hirsch Ber, a leading disciple of the Kotzker Rebbe, and his son, when learning this *mishnah*. R' Hirsch Ber asked his son, "If someone told you that I had desecrated Shabbos, would you believe him?"

"Absolutely not!"

"What would happen if someone told you that I had once lied?"

The son candidly replied, "I might believe that."

R' Hirsch Ber responded, "You wouldn't contemplate that I had desecrated the Shabbos simply because *you* wouldn't entertain committing such a grave sin. On the other hand, while you of course would never deliberately deceive someone, the notion of lying probably did enter your mind. If so, you could believe that I too had lied"[1] (*Maggidei Emes*).

⊷§ Must I Judge the Wicked Favorably?

בהרע"ב אדם שהוחזק ברשע מותר לדונו לחובה, ואינו מוכרח וי"ל אף ברשע
דבאינו רשע יש איסור לדון לכף חובה וראייתו מחושד בכשרים י"ל דכשר
באותו דבר מיקרי כשר כמובן.

According to the *Bartenura*, the requirement of judging one's peer favorably does not apply to a certified evildoer (רָשָׁע). This can be deduced from the renowned *Chazal* (*Shabbos* 97a), הַחוֹשֵׁד בִּכְשֵׁרִים לוֹקֶה בְּגוּפוֹ, *one who* (wrongly) *suspects the innocent* (of sinning) *will be punished*. This implies that it is only wrong to suspect the *innocent* — however, one may judge unfavorably the actions of the wicked.

The *Sfas Emes* differs, arguing that even the wicked should be judged as favorably as possible. Whereas it is prohibited to judge the innocent unfavorably it is meritorious to cast the best possible light even on the actions of the wicked. The Gemara cited by the *Bartenura* as proof for his assertion that one may judge the wicked unfavorably may actually prove the contrary — if we define the term כְּשֵׁרִים (innocent) as broadly as possible. Anyone who has not previously committed this sin, despite his (past) history of doing other transgressions, is assumed to be innocent and thus, must be judged favorably.

---

1. Editor's Note: We may conclude from this incident that people tend to evaluate others based on their personal value system. Therefore, we should make every effort to develop many fine *midos* so we can be דָן לְכַף זְכוּת.

[7] *Nittai of Arbel says: Distance yourself from a bad neighbor; do not associate with a wicked person and do not despair of retribution.*

◆§ Judge Hashem Favorably

אם אמרו כן באדם קל וחומר שצריך לדון את המקום ב״ה בכל דבר לכף זכות.

To conclude our commentary on this *mishnah* we would like to share the קַל וָחֹמֶר (*a fortiori*, an inference from minor to major) of Rabbi Yehoshua of Ostrov. If I am required to judge my peer favorably, then certainly I would be required to judge all of Hashem's actions favorably — whether or not I can immediately appreciate them (*Maggidei HaEmes*).

7.

■ הַרְחַק מִשָּׁכֵן רָע ■ — *Distance yourself from a bad neighbor.*

◆§ Who Is the Evil Neighbor?

אין כל אדם זוכה להיות לבו חלל בקרבו כי יש ב' נפשות יצה״ט ויצה״ר כמ״ש רש״י ז״ל ולזאת צריך להרחיק מהשכן באדם, ולרע ממש אין צורך הרחקה אעפ״י שהוא שכן, רק שמדובר מעניני הרשות שלא יתקרב אליו ע״י מעשה הרשות ע״י שיתקדש בדברים המותרים.

The *mishnah* may be alluding to our closest evil neighbor, the יֵצֶר הָרָע, *Evil Inclination*, that is embedded within virtually every Jew. While it is (hopefully) highly unlikely that we would succumb to the passionate importuning of the יֵצֶר הָרָע and commit actual transgressions (עֲבֵירוֹת), the *mishnah* is urging us to stay far away (הַרְחֵק) from even the permissible pleasures of the material world. By voluntarily renouncing physical pleasures — which though not Biblically prohibited retard our spiritual growth — we stifle the יֵצֶר הָרָע. *Chazal* stated this principle succinctly: קַדֵּשׁ עַצְמְךָ לְמוּתָּר לָךְ, *sanctify yourself by abstaining from what is permitted to you* (*Yevamos* 20a).

◆§ Daven in Shul!

פירוש שלא תהיה שכן רע למקום ברוך הוא, והיינו על מי שיש לו בית הכנסת בעירו ואין מתפלל בה.

The Maggid of Koznitz interpreted this *mishnah* homiletically on the basis of the Gemara's assertion (*Berachos* 8a) that one who *davens* alone rather than

[ח] יְהוּדָה בֶּן טַבַּאי וְשִׁמְעוֹן בֶּן שָׁטַח קִבְּלוּ מֵהֶם.
יְהוּדָה בֶּן טַבַּאי אוֹמֵר: אַל תַּעַשׂ עַצְמְךָ כְּעוֹרְכֵי
הַדַּיָּנִין; וּכְשֶׁיִּהְיוּ בַּעֲלֵי הַדִּין עוֹמְדִים לְפָנֶיךָ, יִהְיוּ בְעֵינֶיךָ
כִּרְשָׁעִים; וּכְשֶׁנִּפְטָרִים מִלְּפָנֶיךָ, יִהְיוּ בְעֵינֶיךָ כְּזַכָּאִין,
כְּשֶׁקִּבְּלוּ עֲלֵיהֶם אֶת הַדִּין.

[ט] שִׁמְעוֹן בֶּן שָׁטַח אוֹמֵר: הֱוֵי מַרְבֶּה לַחֲקוֹר אֶת

---

in shul is considered to be a bad neighbor of Hashem Who "resides" in the synagogue. The *mishnah* is urging you to distance yourself (הַרְחֵק) from being a bad neighbor (מְשָׁכֵן רָע) by joining with others and *davening* in shul (*Maggidei HaEmes*).

8.

■ אַל תַּעַשׂ עַצְמְךָ כְּעוֹרְכֵי הַדַּיָּנִין — *Do not act as a lawyer.*

◌§ Do Not Assist People in Justifying Their Sins

> ר"ל כמו שלומדין לאחד הטענות מה שיטעון נגד בעל דינו, כמו כן לא ילמוד האדם לההמון תשובות ותירוצים שיאמרו לפני הבורא יתברך לדין להתנצל לפניו, כי הוא יתברך יודע מחשבות והאמת, רק יוכיחם על דרך שאמרנו.

Perhaps, the *mishnah* is alluding to our relationship with the Supreme Judge, Hashem. Just as one should not furnish litigants with spurious arguments, so too we should not assist our fellow Jew in finding excuses for his deficiencies as he is being judged by Hashem. Standing in the presence of Hashem, Who is aware of the true motivations behind our actions, it would be far more prudent to encourage our peers to confess their errors than to attempt to rationalize them (*Avodas Yisroel, Maggidei HaEmes*).

■ יִהְיוּ בְעֵינֶיךָ כִּרְשָׁעִים — *Consider them both as guilty.*

◌§ Do Not Look at the Litigants

> עיין ספר חסידים, שלא יסתכל הדיין אז בפניהם. ויש לכוון זה בהלשון יהיו בעיניך כרשעים.

The term בְעֵינֶיךָ, "in your *eyes*," should be understood literally. Just as one should not gaze at an evil individual, so too it is advisable that a judge not

[8] *Yehudah ben Tabbai and Shimon ben Shatach received [the Torah] from them. Yehudah ben Tabbai says: [When serving as a judge,] do not act as a lawyer; while the litigants stand before you, consider them both as guilty; but when they are dismissed from you, consider them both as innocent, provided they have accepted the judgment upon themselves.*

[9] *Shimon ben Shatach says: Interrogate the witnesses*

---

look at litigants who may be guilty of committing evil (see *Shulchan Aruch, Choshen Mishpat* 17).

■ יִהְיוּ בְעֵינֶיךָ כְּזַכָּאִין — *Consider them both as innocent.*

◆§ "As" if They Were Innocent

הו״ל למימר זכאין שקבלו דין התורה. וי״ל הפירוש אף שעושה פשר אם כן לא קיים דין התורה ממש, עם כל זה יהיו בעיניך כזכאין. אי נמי גם כשקבלו באונס וכפיות בית דין.

The term כְּ, *as*, implies that even if the case was not settled according to the strict principles of *Halachah* (דין), but rather the parties themselves arrived at a *compromise* settlement (פְּשָׁרָה), nonetheless, they should be viewed as being innocent.

Alternatively, the *mishnah* is suggesting that as long as the litigants complied with the court's verdict — even if reluctantly or under the coercion of *beis din* — nonetheless, they are now deemed innocent.

9.

■ הֱוֵי מַרְבֶּה לַחֲקוֹר אֶת הָעֵדִים ■ — *Interrogate the witnesses extensively.*

◆§ Who Are These Witnesses?

קשה חקירות הוי רק ז' ולא שייך מרבה רק הפי' בדיקות שאין להם שיעור, ונראה לפרש דבד״ג משתעי דבד״מ הרי אדרבא אי' במס' סנהדרין דבטלו דו״ח מפני תקנת הלווין.

On a surface level, the *mishnah* seems to be urging a judge to thoroughly investigate witnesses. According to this approach, several caveats need

וֶהֱוֵי זָהִיר בִּדְבָרֶיךָ, שֶׁמָּא מִתּוֹכָם יִלְמְדוּ לְשַׁקֵּר.

[י] שְׁמַעְיָה וְאַבְטַלְיוֹן קִבְּלוּ מֵהֶם. שְׁמַעְיָה אוֹמֵר: אֱהַב
אֶת הַמְּלָאכָה, וּשְׂנָא אֶת הָרַבָּנוּת, וְאַל תִּתְוַדַּע
לָרָשׁוּת.

---

to be stated.

Firstly, the term חֲקִירוֹת cannot be interpreted in its usual sense, referring to the seven questions posed to witnesses (cf. *Sanhedrin* 40a). Those questions are finite — they can't be augmented or revised to fit the specific needs of a particular case. Instead, the *mishnah* must be referring to the בְּדִיקוֹת, the additional questions which a judge was authorized to pose to witnesses.

Moreover, the *mishnah* is only referring to capital cases (דִּינֵי נְפָשׁוֹת). It is well known that witnesses in civil cases (דִּינֵי מָמוֹנוֹת) are not investigated as thoroughly as in capital cases. In fact, they are not even required to respond to the seven basic questions — שֶׁבַע חֲקִירוֹת.

◆§ The Internal Witnesses

שיצ״ט ויצ״ר הם עדים שכל א׳ אומר שהאמת כדבריו, וכל מעשה שבא לפני
האדם צריך לשופטו ולהבחין האמת ע״י ישוב הדעת שמהפך כ״ד עד שנתברר
האמת, כי עדות ודעת הוא דבר א׳ שע״י הדעת מתברר עדות אמת, ע״י שאינו
ממהר לעשות מה שלבו חפץ, עד שנותן דעתו אל ההיפוך, כי שמא טוב להיפוך
עי״ז מתברר האמת.

Alternatively, the term עֵדִים, *witnesses*, may refer to the Good and Evil Inclinations (יֵצֶר טוֹב, יֵצֶר הָרָע) who each press their case with the same determination as witnesses. Just as witnesses insist they are stating the truth, so too, both the Good and Evil Inclinations insist that they are absolutely right. The Mishnah urges us to weigh carefully their "testimony," and contemplate prudently the course of action recommended by these internal witnesses.

It is significant that the terms עֵדוּת, *testimony*, and דַּעַת, *knowledge*, consist of the same root letters, דעת. Only by weighing and evaluating carefully, a concept known as יְשׁוּב הַדַּעַת, can one eventually overcome the importuning of the Evil Inclination. Often what appears to be the correct decision, based on an initial reaction, is the very opposite of the appropriate course to follow. Only by avoiding the natural tendency to yield to one's initial impulse and giving careful, deliberate thought to the issue at hand can proper decisions be made.

extensively; yet be cautious with your words, lest they learn from them to lie.

[10] Shemayah and Avtalyon received [the Torah] from them. Shemayah says: Love work; despise lordliness and do not be overly familiar with the government.

10.

■ אֱהַב אֶת הַמְּלָאכָה וּשְׂנָא אֶת הָרַבָּנוּת — *Love work; despise lordliness.*

◆§ Love the Effort, Hate the Glory

ואם יהיו כל העולם בעלי מלאכות מי יורה לנו שאלה. אלא אהוב את המלאכה היינו התורה שהיא המלאכה של הרבנות דהיינו שידע להורות, ושנא את הרבנות היינו הגיאות.

כי וודאי אדם זוכה על ידי העבודה ויגיעה לבוא אל השלימות ויכול לבוא לבחינת מנוחה אבל המכוון בעבודה אינו צריך להיות על זה שיגיע אל המנוחה רק להיות מרוצה מאד בגוף העבודה אף להיות כל ימיו, וזהו ושנא את הרבנות שזהו אחר השלימות הראוי.

The Kotzker Rebbe insisted that this *mishnah* cannot be interpreted literally — שְׂנָא אֶת הָרַבָּנוּת, *hate the Rabbinate.* How could *poskim* (experts on *Halachah*) develop if there is an atmosphere of animosity toward *Rabbanus*?

Rather, the *mishnah* is referring to the מְלָאכָה, the toil associated with the Rabbinate (רַבָּנוּת). Love the involved and intense Torah study and scholarship which is necessary for a Rav, but despise the glory and pompousness that may be associated with the Rabbinate (*Maggidei HaEmes*).

Alternatively, the terms מְלָאכָה and רַבָּנוּת may *both* refer to the high levels of scholarship (לִמוּד הַתּוֹרָה) which is a prerequisite for the successful pursuit of *Rabbanus*.

Love the effort (מְלָאכָה) itself, the total immersion, and the toil associated with Torah study, rather than the sense of satisfaction and accomplishment attained when successfully completing a segment of the Torah. On the contrary, the successful achievement should not be an end in itself. It is the יְגִיעָה associated with the process of Torah study that we must learn to appreciate even if we never achieve שְׁלֵמוּת (perfection). Know that the יְגִיעָה in Torah is a lifelong process and worthwhile in and of itself.

■ וְאַל תִּתְוַדַּע לָרָשׁוּת — *And do not become overly familiar with the government.*

[יא] אַבְטַלְיוֹן אוֹמֵר: חֲכָמִים, הִזָּהֲרוּ בְדִבְרֵיכֶם, שֶׁמָּא תָחוּבוּ חוֹבַת גָּלוּת וְתִגְלוּ לִמְקוֹם מַיִם הָרָעִים,

◆§ Abuse of Power

הרע"ב כמו שאירע לדואג ובי"ה ברמבי"ם. עי"ש שכ' אע"פ שהי' משיח' השם כו',
וקשה הראי' דשם הי' הוא הגורם, גם כל מלך ישראל ע"פ סנהדרין ואינו בכלל
רשות רק מה ששאול לא עלתה בידו הי' ע"י שנתחבר לדואג וזה גרם לו.

To illustrate the danger of coming too close to political authorities, the Bartenura cites the example of Doeg, whose downfall was precipitated by his association with Shaul, the first Jewish monarch (cf. *I Shmuel* Ch. 22 for the details of Doeg's involvement in the destruction of the city of Nov).

The analogy to Doeg seems difficult to understand. Firstly, it was Doeg who initiated his own downfall by conspiring to eliminate Nov. This does not necessarily lead to the conclusion that mere association with political authorities will be disastrous. Moreover, it is unlikely that the *mishnah* would use the term רְשׁוּת, generally associated with gentile despots, to refer to the noble monarch Shaul (cf. *Yoma* 22b stating that Shaul committed only one sin during his entire reign). רְשׁוּת refers to a tyrant who seized power and reigns by force, rather than the Jewish monarch who consulted with the *Sanhedrin* before taking any action.

On the contrary, it was Shaul who suffered because of his association with Doeg. By seeking counsel from Doeg, who was the head of the *Sanhedrin* (*Shocher Tov* 3:4), Shaul unwittingly paved the way for his own premature downfall. Doeg abused his position of authority — and therefore could be referred to by the word רְשׁוּת — when he wrongly counseled Shaul to annihilate Nov. [Cf. *I Shmuel* 15:26 which attributes Shaul's downfall to this refusal to eliminate Amalek. However, his association with the wicked Doeg may have contributed to his *final*, fatal error of tolerating Amalek.][1]

11.

■ אַבְטַלְיוֹן אוֹמֵר: חֲכָמִים הִזָּהֲרוּ בְדִבְרֵיכֶם — *Avtalyon says: Scholars, be cautious with your words.*

◆§ A Talmid Chacham Weighs His Words

דברי הצדיק הם במשקל ובמדה מדוייקת, כמו הרופא כשנותן רפואות הרי הוא
מדקדק מאוד על המשקל. יותר מזה הצדיק מדקדק בדברים היוצאים מהבל פיו

---

1. One may infer from the *Sfas Emes'* approach to the *mishnah* the prohibition of וְאַל תִּתְוַדַּע לָרָשׁוּת, *and do not become overly familiar with the government*, refers to gentile rulers.

[11] *Avtalyon says: Scholars, be cautious with your words, for you may incur the penalty of exile and be banished to a place of putrid water, and the students who*

הקדוש ועל זה יש משפט ודין בבית דין של מעלה שעל ידי צדיק פלוני ודיבוריו
דנים מי ומי יהיה להם רפואה. שכשיש עולם גדול בשבת קודש אזי קשה לו לומר
תורה, כי צריך תורה בשביל כל אחד ואחד ולכלול בתורה את כל אחד ואחד,
וכל אחד יקבל את שלו.

Rav Simchah Bunim[1] compared a scholar's words to a physician's medications. Just as a doctor meticulously weighs every medication he prescribes, so too the *tzaddik* weighs the impact of his every word on the physical and spiritual welfare of each of his followers. Moreover, the words of a *tzaddik* leave an impact not only on earth but also in heaven, where the Heavenly Tribunal determines the fate of individuals on the basis of the blessings of *tzaddikim* (צַדִּיק גּוֹזֵר וְהקב״ה מְקַיֵּים). Just as a physician cautiously adapts his prescriptions to suit the individual patient's need, so too the Torah scholar evaluates carefully the impact of his words on every one of his followers. In fact, Rav Simchah Bunim personally experienced difficulty in relating *Divrei Torah* to a large crowd, due to the necessity of adapting his thoughts to benefit *everyone* in the audience (*Maggidei HaEmes*).

■ הִזָּהֲרוּ בְדִבְרֵיכֶם שֶׁמָּא תָחוּבוּ חוֹבַת גָּלוּת — *Be cautious with your words, for you may incur the penalty of exile.*

◆§ Your Words Will Be Exiled

יל״פ דקאי על הדיבורים כלשון המובא בספרים שהי׳ הדבור בגלות.

While a simple reading implies that the *talmid chacham* will be exiled, it is also possible that the phrase שֶׁמָּא תָחוּבוּ חוֹבַת גָּלוּת (that you may incur the penalty of exile) refers to the immediately preceding antecedent דִבְרֵיכֶם, *your words.*

How can words be exiled? To appreciate this concept, we recall the renowned statement of the *Zohar* (*Vaeira* 25b) that the Divine Word (דְּבּוּר) went into exile during the period of Egyptian slavery and was not totally liberated until the Giving of the Torah when Hashem spoke directly to every Jew (וַיְדַבֵּר אֱלֹהִים). As long as the Jewish people were exiled, Hashem's most intimate form of speech, known as דְּבּוּר, was inaccessible to the vast majority of *Klal Yisrael*. Only in the rarefied atmosphere of Sinai, when Israel had achieved spiritual as

---

1. Rav Simchah Bunim of Peshis'cha was a pharmacist.

וְיִשְׁתּוּ הַתַּלְמִידִים הַבָּאִים אַחֲרֵיכֶם וְיָמוּתוּ, וְנִמְצָא שֵׁם שָׁמַיִם מִתְחַלֵּל.

[יב] הִלֵּל וְשַׁמַּאי קִבְּלוּ מֵהֶם. הִלֵּל אוֹמֵר: הֱוֵי מִתַּלְמִידָיו שֶׁל אַהֲרֹן, אוֹהֵב שָׁלוֹם, וְרוֹדֵף שָׁלוֹם, אוֹהֵב אֶת הַבְּרִיּוֹת וּמְקָרְבָן לַתּוֹרָה.

---

well as physical freedom, could Hashem speak again, with the intimacy and clarity of דִּבּוּר.

In the same vein, the *mishnah* is admonishing the *talmid chacham* to weigh carefully every word, since we may be again living in an era in which the words of Torah are in exile, i.e. easily misunderstood. While in previous generations a scholar could presume that his audience would appreciate and comprehend his words, that assumption is no longer necessarily true (adapted from *Sfas Emes*).

■ וְנִמְצָא שֵׁם שָׁמַיִם מִתְחַלֵּל — *And consequently the Name of Heaven will be desecrated.*

◆§ A Single Jew's Demise — A Source of חִלּוּל הַשֵּׁם

יש לדקדק דמתחלה הו״ל למימר ונמצא שם שמים מתחלל שזה עיקר הסיבה שיתחייבו גלות ויגלו למקום וכו׳.

וי״ל כי אנחנו עמו וצאן מרעיתו של הקב״ה נמצא שמי שגורם לאחד מישראל שימות ממעט כבודו יתב׳, שהרי חסר לו אחד מסכום עבדיו המשמשין אותו לעובדו. אם כן בזה שתתחייבו מיתה יתחלל שם שמים שיהיה חסר ח״ו משמו.

This phrase seemingly belongs at the *beginning* of the *mishnah* stating that as a result of the *talmid chacham's* teachings being misinterpreted, Hashem's Name might be desecrated. By placing this thought at the *mishnah's* conclusion, we are identifying another source of חִלּוּל הַשֵּׁם — the death of a single Jew. As the *mishnah* states, וְיִשְׁתּוּ הַתַּלְמִידִים הַבָּאִים אַחֲרֵיכֶם וְיָמוּתוּ, *the disciples who follow you there may drink and die.*

The Jewish people are described (*Tehillim* 100:3) as G-d's flock and His people (עַמּוֹ וְצֹאן מַרְעִיתוֹ). The death of even a single member of Hashem's flock, of any one of His servants, leads to an irreplaceable void and to a diminution of His glory (חִלּוּל הַשֵּׁם).[1] (Rav Simchah Bunim, *Maggidei HaEmes*).

12.

■ הִלֵּל וְשַׁמַּאי קִבְּלוּ מֵהֶם — *Hillel and Shammai received [the Torah] from them.*

come after you will drink and die, and consequently the Name of Heaven will be desecrated.

[12] *Hillel and Shammai received [the Torah] from them. Hillel says: Be the disciples of Aaron, loving peace and pursuing peace, loving and pursuing peace, loving people and bringing them closer to the Torah.*

◆§ Why Is Hillel's Name Mentioned First?

הול״ל שמאי והלל כדאי׳ בגמ׳ ולא עוד אלא שמקדימין דברי ב״ש ומסתמא בהם
גופייהו בוודאי כן והתי׳ עבור שהי׳ ענין וספר זה מדות טובות נאמרו בו לכן הקדים
הלל לשמאי, ולמ״ש הרע״ב לעיל דב׳ זוגות הראשון נשיא ושני אב״ד ואם כך
בהלל ושמאי הי׳ א״ש דמקדים הלל לשמאי דכאן הוכרח לזה.

Contrary to the usual practice of mentioning Shammai before Hillel — a practice which was adopted by Hillel's disciples (cf. *Eruvin* 13b) and was surely followed by Hillel himself — in this *mishnah*, Hillel is mentioned first.

This deviation from the usual practice may be based on Hillel's extraordinary humility (cf. *Shabbos* 31a relating many stories about Hillel's patience and humility). It is appropriate that in this tractate devoted to the development of fine character traits (מִדּוֹת טוֹבוֹת), the paragon of humility, Hillel, should be cited first.

The *Tanna's* desire for consistency with previous *mishnahs* may also have played a role in the priority given to Hillel's views. As the *Bartenura* already stated (*mishnah* 4), every *mishnah* in this *perek* consists of the teachings of a pair (זוּג) of scholars (e.g. יוֹסֵי בֶּן יוֹעֶזֶר, יוֹסֵי בֶּן יוֹחָנָן). In each instance, the first scholar mentioned was the Prince (known as the נָשִׂיא), a descendant of King David who served as the temporal leader of the Jewish people in *Eretz Yisrael*, and the second one was the presiding officer of the *Sanhedrin*. In order to remain consistent with the rest of the *perek*, Hillel the Prince is listed before Shammai, the President of the *Sanhedrin*.

■ הֱוֵי מִתַּלְמִידָיו שֶׁל אַהֲרֹן, אוֹהֵב שָׁלוֹם וְרוֹדֵף שָׁלוֹם — *Be among the disciples of Aaron, loving peace and pursuing peace.*

◆§ Become a Tzaddik's Talmid

לכאורה מיותר רק הול״ל הוי רודף שלום.

---

1. Editor's Note: חִלּוּל הַשֵּׁם is also related to the word חָלָל meaning hollow and void, hence the above interpretation of חִלּוּל הַשֵּׁם.

נראה כי אהרן פעל שיוכל האדם להיות כן ואל יחזיק טובה לעצמו בהיותו כן כי אינו
רק מתלמידיו של אהרן. הוי מתלמידיו של אהרן להיות מקושר ומחובר אליו, ואם
ההתקשרות לאהרן עצמו קצת קשה, מכל מקום הוי מתלמידיו, שאפשר להגיע
על ידי ההתקשרות לתלמידיו שאליהם בנקל יותר להתקשר ולהתחבר .. מה
שמברכים הכהנים אשר קדשנו בקדושתו של אהרן וכי יכול כל אחד להיות בקדושתו
של אהרן, אלא כדאי׳ הוי מתלמידיו של אהרן כו׳ ועל ידי זה אפשר להגיע לקדושתו
של אהרן.

Instead of merely saying, "Love peace and pursue peace," the *mishnah* prefaces with, "Be among the disciples of Aaron." Peacemaking is so difficult a pursuit that only by adopting Aaron as a *rebbi* can one hope to succeed. Any proficient peacemaker should not attribute his accomplishments to his own talents but rather to the precedent set by (and the merit of) Aaron (*Sfas Emes*).

The *mishnah* may also be emphasizing that the most effective means of developing a close relationship with a *tzaddik* is by becoming his *talmid*, or at least, the *talmid* of his *talmidim*. By relating to and becoming close to his disciples, one eventually develops a relationship to Aaron's teachings as well. The *berachah* recited by the *Kohanim* before the Priestly Blessing (בְּרְכַּת כֹּהֲנִים) — "that He sanctified with Aaron's holiness" (אֲשֶׁר קִדְשָׁנוּ בִּקְדֻשָׁתוֹ שֶׁל אַהֲרֹן) — should also be understood in this light. While it is presumptuous of any individual *Kohen* to claim to be as holy as Aaron, by professing to be Aaron's student and follower, he is saying that he can benefit from Aaron's *kedushah* (*Lev Simchah, Maggidei HaEmes*).

∾§ Teshuvah Achieved Through Shame

פ׳ הרע״ב שקירב אנשים ואמרו אילו ידע אהרן מעונותינו לא הי׳ מקרבנו ועי״ז שבו
בתשובה ואין רואין קירבות המקום ב״ה אותנו ויש לנו בודאי לשוב לפניו בתשובה
ע״י הבושה ובדרך הלצה ז״ש הוי מתלמידיו של אהרן כמו שתלמידיו למדו ממנו זה
הדרך תשובה על ידי הבושה.

Alternatively, the *mishnah* may be calling upon us to learn from Aaron's beneficiaries. The *Bartenura*, citing *Avos D'Rabbi Nosson*, relates how Aaron brought people closer to Torah. Upon seeing an individual commit a sin, rather than humiliate him, Aaron would befriend him. Almost immediately, the sinner felt gripped by a sense of shame. "How can I benefit from Aaron's warmth and friendship while continuing to sin?" the sinner would ask. Spurred by a sense of shame, he would repent.

We too, as Aaron's disciples, should react with an equal sense of shame. Having enjoyed the countless kindnesses of Hashem, we dare not transgress His Will.

◆§ The Secret of Aaron's Success

ולכאורה האידנא הוה להיפוך כי הרשע כשיש לו התחברות עם צדיק עוד מתגאה
כו, אך יי״ל כי ע״י שהי׳ כוונת אהרן לש״ש עי״ז הי׳ מגיע ההרהור יר״ש גם בזה
הרשע עד שנתקרב לתורה.

Aaron's approach of befriending evildoers is not appropriate for everyone.
Generally, this approach is fraught with pitfalls. Even if the *tzaddik* is not
influenced by the *rasha*, unfortunately instead of repenting the sinner will
oftentimes merely boast about his relationship with the *tzaddik* and remain a
rasha. Only Aaron, lacking any ulterior motive in his attempts at outreach, was
able to have a lasting impact on the sinners of his time. As a result of Aaron's
pure and noble intentions — the fact that he acted totally for Hashem's sake
— the sinner became possessed by a similar sense of fear of Hashem and was
willing to repent.

◆§ Peace in Theory, Peace in Practice

איתא ברבינו יונה הוי מתלמידיו של אהרן אוהב שלום ורודף שלום זכו׳ שיאהב בלבו
האמת והשלום וירדוף אחריו בפועל ידיו, כי יש בני אדם אוהבים אותו בלבם לא
שיטרחו עצמן לשום שלום בעולם וכו׳.
כל אחד חפץ להיות אוהב שלום ורודף שלום רעבטיגע איז דא וייניג, זהו לא דבר קל,
הדבר תלוי בכמה שמשקיעים בענין.

The *Pnei Menachem*, recalling *Rabbeinu Yonah's* interpretation, emphasized
the enormous challenge of truly pursuing peace. While anyone can love
peace, in theory, and may even desire to act as a peacemaker, few of us are able
to "pursue peace" by actively bringing enemies together as Aaron did. He
would reflect on the enormous effort necessary to be a true pursuer of peace
and act (*Maggidei HaEmes*).

◆§ The Peace of the Wicked

פי׳ שרדף שלום מהרשעים שאין מהראוי שהיה להם שלום ויתפרדו כל פועלי און
כתיב ולזה רדף מהם שלום.

Aaron pursued the *false* peace that the wicked were enjoying. By exposing
their evil deeds and removing the veneer of respectability that the wicked
enjoyed, Aaron forced them to yield their undeserved sense of peace and
security (Chozeh M'Lublin, *Maggidei HaEmes*).

[יג] הוּא הָיָה אוֹמֵר: נְגִיד שְׁמָא אֲבַד שְׁמֵהּ, וּדְלָא מוֹסִיף יָסֵף, וּדְלָא יַלִּיף קְטָלָא חַיָּב, וּדְאִשְׁתַּמַּשׁ בְּתָגָא חֲלָף.

■ אוֹהֵב אֶת הַבְּרִיּוֹת וּמְקָרְבָן לַתּוֹרָה — *Loving people, and bringing them closer to the Torah.*

◆§ The Relationship Between Loving People and Bringing Them Closer to Torah

מה השייכות מזה לזה, רק הענין שעל ידי שאוהב את הבריות יכול לקרבן לתורה, זה כלל גדול בתורה ואהבת לרעך כמוך, שעל ידי אהבה מגיע לתורה . . . גם בקבלת התורה היה כן שעל ידי שהיו כל ישראל כאיש אחד בלב אחד הגיעו לקבלת התורה, ה' עוז לעמו יתן וגו' . . . אין עוז אלא תורה שהשי"ת נותן התורה כאשר ה' יברך את עמו בשלום שעל ידי השלום יכולין לקבל התורה.

While it may appear that these are two distinct accomplishments of Aaron — loving people and bringing them closer to Torah — in reality, they are closely related. The most effective means of *kiruv* (bringing someone closer to Torah) is through *ahavas Yisrael* — sincere love of one's fellow Jew. As Rabbi Akiva related, וְאָהַבְתָּ לְרֵעֲךָ כָּמוֹךְ זֶה כְּלָל גָּדוֹל בַּתּוֹרָה, through fulfillment of the *mitzvah* of loving one's peers, we can create a great Torah nation. Similarly, Jewish unity was a crucial prerequisite for the Giving of the Torah. In *Parashas Yisro* the Torah describes the Jewish people's encampment as follows: וַיִּחַן שָׁם יִשְׂרָאֵל נֶגֶד הָהָר, *and Israel encamped there, opposite the mountain* (Shemos 19:2). Rashi comments that the use of the singular verb וַיִּחַן, *and he encamped*, teaches that they were as "one man with one heart." The renowned *pasuk,* ה' עֹז לְעַמּוֹ יִתֵּן ה' יְבָרֵךְ אֶת עַמּוֹ בַשָּׁלוֹם, *Hashem will give might to His nation, Hashem will bless His nation with peace* (Tehillim 29:11), illustrates the relationship between peace among Jews and the Giving of the Torah. Only when Hashem grants us the ability to live in peace, does He also grant us His strength, the Torah (*Beis Yisrael, Imrei Emes*).

◆§ Every Jew's Unique Contribution to Torah

היינו שמקרב כל אחד לחלק התורה שלו הנצרך לו.

It is well known that every Jew enjoys his unique portion in Torah. Certain aspects of Torah can only be discovered by this specific individual. (As we

[13] *He used to say: He who seeks renown loses his reputation; he who does not increase [his Torah learning] will come to an early demise; he who does not study Torah deserves death; and he who exploits the crown [of Torah] will pass away.*

---

request every Shabbos and *Yom Tov*, "Grant us our portion in Torah" [וְתֵן חֶלְקֵנוּ בְּתוֹרָתֶךְ].) Aaron was not content to merely bring the Jewish people closer to Torah. Instead, he insisted upon helping everyone achieve his unique potential for Torah scholarship (*Lev Simchah, Maggidei HaEmes*).

13.

■ נְגִיד שְׁמָא אֲבַד שְׁמֵהּ — *He who seeks renown loses his reputation.*

∾§ When Is It Wrong to Promote One's Name?

פי' מי שרוצה להמשיך שמו לשם גדולה ע"ז נאמר נגד כו' כענין הרודף אחר הכבוד הכ' בורח ממנו אבל לא באופן אחר.

This *mishnah* should not be understood as a complete prohibition against self-promotion. At times, it may be perfectly legitimate to develop one's reputation — especially if one's purpose in doing so is to sanctify Hashem's Name (קדוש הַשֵּם). Our *mishnah* is referring to those who promote their reputation purely for the purpose of obtaining glory, a theme similar to the well-known statement of *Chazal*, הָרוֹדֵף אַחַר הַכָּבוֹד בּוֹרֵחַ מִמֶּנּוּ, *One who seeks honor, honor will flee from him* (cf. *Midrash Tanchuma, Vayikra* 3).

■ וּדְלָא מוֹסִיף יָסֵף — *He who does not increase [his Torah learning] decreases it.*

∾§ Survival in Galus

איכא סבי בבבל אין זקן אלא שקנה חכמה לרמז אף שאי אפשר ללמוד כל היום רק דמקדמי ומחשבי גם כן יכול להקרא סבי וזה בבבל בגלות, ודלא מוסיף יסיף שממילא הולך ויורד היפך מזקנה וזה יסיף.

This *mishnah* may be referring to the secret of longevity in the Diaspora, despite the Torah's specific reference to long life in *Eretz Yisrael* (cf. *Devarim* 11:21, לְמַעַן יִרְבּוּ יְמֵיכֶם, *in order to prolong your days*). However, as the Gemara in *Berachos* (8a) relates, by *davening* and learning Torah in the *Beis*

א / יד] הוּא הָיָה אוֹמֵר: אִם אֵין אֲנִי לִי, מִי לִי? וּכְשֶׁאֲנִי
לְעַצְמִי, מָה אֲנִי? וְאִם לֹא עַכְשָׁו, אֵימָתַי?

HaK'nesses every morning and evening, those in galus can also merit long life. Such learning should only be viewed as *partial* fulfillment of one's obligation to study Torah. If one does not augment this minimal amount, then he is at risk of forfeiting this blessing of longevity (adapted from *Beis Yisrael*, *Maggidei HaEmes*).

14.

■ הוּא הָיָה אוֹמֵר: אִם אֵין אֲנִי לִי,מִי לִי — *He used to say: If I am not for myself, who will be for me?*

⇜ Hillel's Personal Credo

פי' כי הלל אמר כן לעצמו תמיד אם אין אני לי מי לי ושמעו אנשים אחרים
שאומר כן לעצמו לקחו מוסר.

The expression הוּא הָיָה אוֹמֵר, *He used to say*, suggests that Hillel said אִם אֵין אֲנִי לִי מִי לִי to himself. Others, hearing his compelling personal credo, adopted this approach to life for themselves as well.

■ אִם אֵין אֲנִי לִי . . . וּכְשֶׁאֲנִי לְעַצְמִי . . . וְאִם לֹא עַכְשָׁו — *If I am not for myself . . . if I am for myself . . . if not now . . .*

⇜ Our Three Greatest Challenges

וי"ל עוד כי ידוע כי בחי' עולם שנה נפש שהוא ענין נפש האדם וכל הבריאה
והזמן, והכל תלוי בתיקון נפש האדם הכל מתוקנים, וז"ש אם אין אני לי לתקן
נפשי, וכשאני לעצמי כו'. כי לא די בזה וצריך הוא לתקן כל הבריאה וגם הזמן
ניתקן ע"י, לכן אם לא עכשיו אימתי כי גם שעה זו צריך לתקן והיא עוברת, לכן
כשיחשוב האדם שכל ג' הדברים האלו הם תלוין בו לא יתרשל בעבודת הבורא
כנ"ל.

In order to appreciate the relationship between the various components of our *mishnah*, let us recall three fundamental concepts of Jewish thought — the universe (עוֹלָם), time (referred to as זְמַן or שָׁנָה), and the soul (נֶפֶשׁ). Each of these themes is voiced in the *mishnah*. By proclaiming אִם אֵין אֲנִי לִי מִי לִי, *If I am not for myself, who will be for me*, Hillel is urging us to exploit fully the innate potential of our soul (נֶפֶשׁ). However, Hillel insists that it is not enough to

[14] *He used to say: If I am not for myself, who will be for me? And if I am for myself, what am I? And if not now, when?*

---

perfect oneself. But rather, as he continues, וּכְשֶׁאֲנִי לְעַצְמִי מָה אֲנִי, *And if I am for myself, what am I?* I must also seek to perfect the entire universe (עוֹלָם). Moreover, every moment is immeasurably precious — we dare not waste time (זְמַן) — as the *mishnah* concludes, וְאִם לֹא עַכְשָׁיו אֵימָתָי. Upon contemplating the three great challenges that we all face — to perfect ourselves, to leave an impact on the entire universe, and to exploit every moment to its fullest — we rise to confront these challenges by rededicating ourselves to Torah and *mitzvos*. This is the most effective means through which these awesome objectives can be attained.

◄§ Are We Really Alone?

ודאי הקב״ה מסייע וכן. אחז״ל הבא לטהר מסייעין אותו, ופי׳ מסייע אינו דוקא רק על הקב״ה רק כל הנבראים וכל העולמות וגם הטבע מסייעין לעבוד השי״ת כנודע להעובדים, אך אם אם אין אני לי אין שום ברי׳ מסייע וז״ש וכשאני לעצמי מה אני פי׳ שאדם צריך לידע שע״י מעשיו אין שום ערך שיכול לעבוד כראוי רק ע״י שיודע שמסייעין וכו׳.

While a literal translation of the phrase אִם אֵין אֲנִי לִי, *If I am not for myself,* seems to suggest that we stand alone in our quest for spiritual growth, this interpretation is simply untenable. *Chazal* relate, הַבָּא לְטַהֵר מְסַיְיעִין אוֹתוֹ, one who seeks to purify himself is surely assisted by Hashem (cf. *Shabbos* 104a). The *mishnah* is merely emphasizing the importance of taking the *initiative*, as the foregoing *Chazal* stresses, הַבָּא לְטַהֵר, one who *seeks*, who comes (literally) to be purified. On the contrary, once we take the initiative, not only Hashem Himself (i.e. an act of direct Divine intervention), but also all of His creations, will in their own fashion assist those who seek to come close to Him.

It may be tempting for the individual now enjoying unparalleled success to forget the source of his new-found prowess. To prevent this misconception, the *mishnah* continues: וּכְשֶׁאֲנִי לְעַצְמִי, מָה אֲנִי, *and if I am for myself, what am I?* Remember that *your* deeds are not sufficient without the bountiful Divine assistance that you now enjoy.

◄§ The Kotzker's Concept of Self-Identity

אדמו״ר זצ״ל מקאצק אמר פעם ״אם אני הנני אני משום שאני הנני אני ואתה הנך אתה משום שאתה הנך אתה, הרי שאני הנני אני ואתה הנך אתה. אבל אם

אני הנני אני משום שאתה הנך אתה, ואתה הנך אתה משום שאני הנני אני, הרי
שאני אינני אני, ואתה אינך אתה."

A t this point, it might be appropriate to reflect on Judaism's concept of
self-identity (as well as our perception of others).

It should be stated in *positive* rather than *negative* terms. The Kotzker
Rebbe reflected profoundly: "If I am I because I am I and you are you because
you are you (i.e. my perception of others is based on a true understanding of
those individuals), then I truly am I and you truly are you. If, on the other
hand, I am I because you are you (i.e. my self-concept is based on denigra-
tion of others) and you are you because I am I (i.e. your self-concept is
based on denigrating me), then I am not I and you are not you" (*Maggidei
HaEmes*).

◂§ Never Lose Your Head

הרבי ר' העניך ז"ל מאלבסנדר הגיד מה בין חכם לטיפש, החכם עמל תמיד לפני
כל מעשה ובשעת מעשה ולאחריו, לדעת היכן הוא, היכן ראשו, לא כן הטיפש.
מעשה בכסיל אחד שגמר אומר להכניס סדר לחייו בל ישכח מהמוטל עליו, בלילה
הוא רשם על פתק את המלבושים תלה ליד ארונו ואת הנעלים שם ליד מטתו ואת
ראשו הוא מניח לתוך מטתו. בבקר מצא את מלבושיו ליד ארונו ואת נעליו ליד
מטתו התלבש במהירות והמשיך את הפתקא בידו. רשום היה כי ראשו מונח
במטתו. חיפש וחיפש ולא מצא שם את ראשו אמר "והיכן אני".
דאף שכל הדברים מסביבו על מכונם אבל הוא עצמו אינו במקומו.

R' Chanoch Henach of Alexander noted the distinction between a wise man
and a fool. Whereas the wise man always "keeps his head" — before, after
and during every initiative he contemplates its ramifications — the fool "loses
his head," he never thinks of the effects of his actions.

To illustrate the importance of keeping one's perspective and sense of self, he
related the following story.

A hopelessly disorganized fool determined to organize his life by recording
the whereabouts of all his belongings. Before going to sleep, he dutifully wrote:
"My clothing is hanging in the closet, my shoes are beside my bed and my
head is *in* my bed (under the covers)." Upon arising, he found his clothing and
shoes exactly where he had specified but his head was nowhere to be found —
not even in his bed! The moral (מוּסָר הַשָּׂכֵל) of the story: It is not sufficient for
peripheral matters to be in place, unless my head, the core of all my thoughts
and actions, is also in place (*Maggidei HaEmes*).

In this light, we may gain new insight into the *mishnah's* teaching אִם אֵין אֲנִי
לִי, מִי לִי. If I can't find myself (אִם אֵין אֲנִי לִי), how can I locate anything else (מִי
לִי)?

✑§ Homiletic Interpretations of אִם אֵין אֲנִי לִי מִי לִי

איתא בספרים אנ״י הוא אחד משמות השי״ת. לפי זה י״ל אם אין אני לי מי לי,
היינו אם אין השי״ת אתי אזי מי לי.

אם אין אני לי, אם אין, אם מחזיק עצמו לאין, אז אני לי שמו ית׳ שנק׳ אני הוא
לי, ואז מי לי, מי גדול כמוני. אבל כשאני לעצמי שאוחז את האני שלו לעצמיות,
שאוחז עצמו גדול אז מה אני.

זה הוא באלול כדאיתא דאני לדודי ודודי לי הוא ר״ת אלול, וכפי מה שאדם מכין
עצמו בפרט יש לו נגיעה בכלל בר״ה וזהו וכשאני לעצמי מה אני שבר״ה צריכים
להתבטל אל הכלל, ואם לא עכשיו אימתי זה עשרת ימי תשובה כדאיתא ביחיד
אימת וכו׳ אלו עשרה ימים וכו׳.

אולי הרמז על ימי הספירה כי איתא שהימים מסוגלים . . . ואם לא יכבשיו אימתי.
לא להזניח את העכשיו. הימים הטובים האלו זמן חשבון הנפש לכל אחד ואחד. וכל
יום ויום משלים ומתעלה האדם . . . כפי הרצון והשתוקות בימים אלו יכולים
להתקרב.

I
n addition to the foregoing approaches, this famous *mishnah* has been interpreted homiletically (דֶּרֶךְ דְּרוּשׁ). We will now present some of these approaches.

Perhaps, the term "I" refers to Hashem, Who is known by the Name אֲנִי (cf.
Succah 53a, *Tosafos* s.v. אם אני כאן). According to this approach, the *mishnah* is
stating: If Hashem does not bless my initiative, all my efforts will be in vain
(*Lev Simchah, Maggidei HaEmes*).

While it may appear that the *mishnah* is emphasizing the importance of
self-worth, the very opposite — the importance of self-negation — may actually be intended, if we interpret the term אֵין as אַיִן, *nothing*. In this sense, the
mishnah reads as follows: אִם אַיִן, If I perceive myself as nothing, then Hashem,
known as אֲנִי, will be beside me. Bolstered by Hashem's support, I can truly
exclaim, מִי לִי, Who is like me! (*Lev Simchah*).

Finally, the *mishnah* may be alluding to different phases of the Jewish year.
אִם אֵין אֲנִי לִי מִי לִי — if I do not prepare myself during the month of Elul, who
will assist me during the awesome judgment of Rosh Hashanah? On the other
hand, having prepared myself thoroughly during Elul, I need to submerge
myself into the broader community on Rosh Hashanah when *Klal Yisrael*
stands in judgment. Finally, אִם לֹא עַכְשָׁיו אֵימָתַי, if I do not repent during the
Ten Days of *Teshuvah*, when else can I enjoy such an opportunity? (*Imrei
Emes*).[1]

Alternatively, the *mishnah* may be referring to one of the most opportune
times of the year for personal growth — the weeks of *Sefirah*. A twofold mission faces us during those hallowed days: to perfect ourselves, evoking

---

1. It is well known that the term אלול is a mnemonic for אֲנִי לְדוֹדִי וְדוֹדִי לִי. I return to my friend
(Hashem) and my friend (Hashem) returns to me.

[טו] שַׁמַּאי אוֹמֵר: עֲשֵׂה תוֹרָתְךָ קֶבַע, אֱמֹר מְעַט
וַעֲשֵׂה הַרְבֵּה, וֶהֱוֵי מְקַבֵּל אֶת כָּל הָאָדָם בְּסֵבֶר
פָּנִים יָפוֹת.

---

the theme of the first phrase of the *mishnah* (אם אֵין אֲנִי לִי, מִי לִי), and subsequently, to become an integral part of the community, not as an individual
(כְּשֶׁאֲנִי לְעַצְמִי), but as part of כְּלַל יִשְׂרָאֵל as indicated by the plural form of
וּסְפַרְתֶּם לָכֶם referring to the *Omer*. Of course, as the *mishnah* concludes, it
would be a grave error not to take advantage of these extraordinary days — אם
לֹא עַכְשָׁו, אֵימָתַי, *if not now, when?* (adapted from *Beis Yisrael, Maggidei
HaEmes*).

15.

■ עֲשֵׂה תוֹרָתְךָ קֶבַע — *Make your Torah [study] a fixed practice.*

◆§ The Permanent Impact of Learning Torah

פי' עפ"י המשנה כל שמעשיו מרובין מחכמתו חכמתו מתקיימת, וזה נוהג אף
בכל פרט לימוד שיהי' בו מעשה יותר מחכמה, [פשוט שלא ילמוד דרך חקירה רק
לקבוע לימודו בלבו לקיים לימודיו ויותר אמור מעט מע' כו' להיות העיקר הקיום בלב
כמ"ש תורתך ודברך ישים על לבו, כתבם על לוח לבך כו' להביא לידי מעשה שזה
העיקר] וע"ז נאמר אמור מעט ועשה הרבה שיהי' בו תיקון הנפש בעסקו בתורה
יותר מגוף הלימוד וז"ש עשה תורתך קבע שבהביאו התורה לידי מעשה נק'
קבע כמ"ש שדומה לאילן ששרשיו מרובין כו' ואז נקרא תורתו כמ"ש רש"י
בתהלים משעמול בה נק' חורתו. וזהו פ' אשר דבר ה' נעשה להביא דברי תורה לבחי'
עשי'.

With these few words, the *mishnah* is defining the essence of studying
Torah, not as some kind of abstract speculation, but rather in such a
manner that it leaves a permanent impact. Torah study should spur the learner
to practice what he learned. Just as a later *mishnah* (3:12) defines the תַּלְמִיד חָכָם
as one whose deeds exceed his wisdom (שֶׁמַּעֲשָׂיו מְרֻבִּין מֵחָכְמָתוֹ), so too this
mishnah defines learning Torah itself as a process in which the lasting effect
is greater than the wisdom acquired through the actual learning. As Shlomo
eloquently writes, כָּתְבֵם עַל לוּחַ לִבֶּךָ, *Write the words of Torah on the tablet of
your heart (Mishlei 3:3).* When the Jewish people accepted the Torah they
proclaimed, כָּל הַדְּבָרִים אֲשֶׁר דִּבֶּר ה' נַעֲשֶׂה, *All the words that HASHEM has **spoken,** we will **do** (Shemos 24:3).* In other words, they enunciated at the very
beginning of their commitment to Torah that they were determined to practice

[15] *Shammai says: Make your Torah [study] a fixed practice; say little and do much; and receive everyone with a cheerful face.*

---

what they had heard at Sinai.

The term קֶבַע, *permanence* ("a fixed practice"), used to describe true Torah study may be further appreciated in light of a later *mishnah* (3:22) describing the genuine scholar as an individual who possesses many roots (שָׁרָשָׁיו מְרֻבִּין). Similarly, true learning is not a superficial act but rather leaves deep roots so firmly embedded in the heart of the *talmid chacham* that he no longer perceives Torah as Hashem's gift but rather as something very personal (cf. *Avodah Zarah* 19a). Once the scholar toils over a Torah discourse it is considered as if it is his own. This approach is supported by the term תּוֹרָתְךָ, *your Torah*.

We may also interpret the succeeding segment of this *mishnah* in a similar manner. אֱמֹר מְעַט וַעֲשֵׂה הַרְבֵּה, *say little and do much*. While this phrase is usually interpreted as a plea to accomplish more than we promise to do, the *mishnah* may be referring to the process of Torah study considered earlier. Rather than focus exclusively on the learning itself (i.e. the words of Torah), be concerned about the *practical* impact of your learning on your spiritual growth.

ובזמן שקשה לתת הראש לתורה, ביותר להזהר לתת תורה בהראש ולהרגיל המחשבה בתורה בכל זמן ומקום וממילא הכל טוב וגופא בתר רישא גרירא.

T he *Lev Simchah* aptly summarized the essence of this *mishnah* thus, "Even when it is difficult to immerse your head in Torah, at least you can immerse the Torah in your head." Gradually, the entire body, though accustomed to the material aspects of life, will follow the lead of the head and also become permeated with the teachings of Torah (*Maggidei HaEmes*).

■ וֶהֱוֵי מְקַבֵּל אֶת כָּל הָאָדָם בְּסֵבֶר פָּנִים יָפוֹת — *And receive everyone with a cheerful face.*

◆§ How Could Shammai Reject the Potential Convert?

ומה שרחק הגר שבא להתגייר, כי אמר רק את כל האדם אבל זה שבא להתגייר על מנת שתשימני כהן גדול וכדומה אינו בכלל אדם. אדמו"ר האמרי אמת ז"ל כשלמד פרקי אבות עם בניו ונכדיו והגיע למתני' אמר; "והוי מקבל את כל האדם בסבר פנים יפות" ... פעם אחת נכנס איש לחדרו באמצע אסיפת רבנים חשובים, קיבלו הרב מבנדין בכבוד מלכים, וצוה לרבנית

[טז] רַבָּן גַּמְלִיאֵל הָיָה אוֹמֵר: עֲשֵׂה לְךָ רַב, וְהִסְתַּלֵּק מִן הַסָּפֵק, וְאַל תַּרְבֶּה לְעַשֵּׂר אֳמָדוֹת.

להכין כיבוד באומרו "אורח יקר אצלינו". לאחר שהלך האורח לדרכו, שאלה הרבנית "מי הוא האורח"? השיב "איני יודע, אורח".

N ote the emphasis Shammai places on הָאָדָם, *the person,* implying that we are *not* required to treat someone whose personal conduct does not meet basic standards of human behavior in such a cheerful manner. With this caveat in mind, we can better appreciate his rejection of the gentile who offered to convert if he were appointed as *Kohen Gadol* (cf. *Shabbos* 31a). Such boorish conduct should not be countenanced by friendly words.

When learning this *mishnah* with his children and grandchildren, the *Imrei Emes* would suggest that his brother-in-law, the Bendiner Rav, was an example of the gracious treatment one should extend to those who seek your help. Once, a person walked in during a meeting between the Bendiner Rav and other distinguished *Rabbanim.* Instead of the man being evicted, he was treated royally. When his wife later asked him who the guest was, the Rav answered simply, "I don't know — just a guest" (*Maggidei HaEmes*).

◆§ Pretend That You Appreciate the Guest

וי"ל דבא לומר שאפילו חבירו רק סבור שמקבל אותו בסבר פנים יפות. אך הוא בלבו אינו מחבבו כלל ואינו סובל אותו וביקורו אצלו עליו לטורח, ובכל זאת מקבלו בסבר פנים יפות, גם זה מדה טובה.

A t times, it may be genuinely difficult to greet a peer warmly. If that be the case, suggests Rabbi Yitzchak of Vorka, at least pretend to welcome his arrival. The *mishnah* subtly suggests this with the word סֶבֶר, which can also mean *with the thought* (related to סְבָרָא, *a line of reasoning*). As long as by your conduct your peer believes that you welcome his arrival, then you have fulfilled this dictum.

16.

■ עֲשֵׂה לְךָ רַב וְהִסְתַּלֵּק מִן הַסָּפֵק — *Appoint a teacher for yourself, and remove yourself from uncertainty.*

◆§ The Importance of Having a Consistent Posek

[16] *Rabban Gamliel used to say: Appoint a Torah teacher for yourself and remove yourself from uncertainty; and do not give excess tithes by estimating [instead of measuring].*

כי על ידי זה לא יבא לעולם לידי ספק כי יוכל לשאל להרב.

The *mishnah* is pointing out one of the significant benefits of having a consistent *rebbi* and *posek* (competent halachic authority). It enables one to avoid unnecessary doubts. If questions arise as to the proper procedure, I simply consult with my *rebbi*.

■ וְאַל תַּרְבֶּה לְעַשֵּׂר אֲמָדוֹת — *And do not give excess tithes by estimating [instead of measuring].*

◈ Tithing of Income

תמוה דהא מדינא אסור ועתיו״ט, וי״ל קצת הפי׳ לפמ״ש בספה״ק שצריכין להפריש מעשר מכל מה שמרויח, ע״ז ג״כ הציווי להפריש מדה במדה לא באומד שמא יבוא לפעמים ליתן פחות.

It is unlikely that *Pirkei Avos*, whose objective is to relate sacred ethical teachings, would be relating to us a renowned *halachah* — that when allocating *maaser* (the tithe given to the *Levi*) it should be precisely one tenth rather than an approximation. Perhaps, the *mishnah* is referring to the virtuous practice of tithing one's income (cf. *Taanis* 9a). This too should be given as a precise amount rather than as an estimate.

◈ Yitzchak Estimated His Tithe

יש לדקדק מהא דכתיב גבי יצחק אבינו ע״ה וימצא יצחק בשנה ההוא מאה שערים, וברש״י שם ורבותינו אמרו אומד זה למעשר היה ע״ש. וי״ל דייצחק לא הספיק למדוד כי בכל רגע נתעשר יותר כמו שכתוב וילך הלוך וגדל וגו׳, על כן היה מוכרח לעשר על פי אומד.

This *mishnah* is seemingly contradicted by the practice of Yitzchak Avinu who estimated his tithe (cf. *Rashi* ד״ה מאה, *Bereishis* 26:12). Perhaps Yitzchak, blessed with ever increasing affluence, simply lacked the time to calculate and was forced to compute an estimate rather than a precise amount (*Imrei Emes, Maggidei HaEmes*).

[יז] שִׁמְעוֹן בְּנוֹ אוֹמֵר: כָּל יָמַי גָּדַלְתִּי בֵּין הַחֲכָמִים,
וְלֹא מָצָאתִי לַגּוּף טוֹב אֶלָּא שְׁתִיקָה. וְלֹא
הַמִּדְרָשׁ הוּא הָעִקָּר, אֶלָּא הַמַּעֲשֶׂה. וְכָל הַמַּרְבֶּה
דְבָרִים מֵבִיא חֵטְא.

17.

■ **כָּל יָמַי גָּדַלְתִּי בֵּין הַחֲכָמִים, וְלֹא מָצָאתִי לַגּוּף טוֹב אֶלָּא שְׁתִיקָה** — *All my days I have been raised among the scholars, and I have found nothing better for the body than silence.*

◆§ Growing Up Among Scholars

הרבי ר' בונם ז"ל פירש דהיינו שאני למדתי מהם והם למדו ממני.

The expression גָּדַלְתִּי בֵּין הַחֲכָמִים, "I have been raised among the scholars" (rather than "I was taught by scholars"), implies a symbiotic exchange. While Rabbi Shimon certainly benefited from his association with *talmidei chachamim*, they in turn benefited from him (Rabbi Henoch of Alexander, *Maggidei HaEmes*).

◆§ The Power of Silence

פעם ראיתי בספר ישן שמספר המילים שעל האדם לדבר עלי אדמות קצובות. האדם
לא יסתלק מהעולם עד שיגמור מלאכתו זאת. נמצא שאדם שחוסך במלים יאריך
ימים.

ע"ד מאמר העולם שטילע וואסרן גראבען טיעף. האדם נוצר עם שתי
אזנים לצורך אחד, לשמוע. שתי עינים לראות. ואילו הפה משמש לשני צרכים, לאכול
ולדבר. מכאן ראיה שהדיבור עצמו בלי מעשה אינו ראוי אפילו לאבר
מיוחד.

On a surface level, this *mishnah* is extolling the virtue of silence. Let us consider some of the reasons for this conclusion.

Reb Simchah Bunim related a venerable tradition stating that every individual is granted the capacity to speak a finite number of words during his life span in This World. By "rationing" words, we are promoting longevity (*Maggidei HaEmes*).

Silence — a refusal to engage in idle chatter and glib talk — is often indicative of personal depth. A celebrated aphorism, שטילע וואסרן גראבען טיעף, *still waters run deep*, captures the essence of this theme.

[17] *Shimon his son says: All my days I have been raised among the scholars, and I found nothing better for the body than silence; not study, but practice is the main thing; and one who talks excessively brings on sin.*

The Maggid of Mezeritch corroborated this thesis with an interesting observation. Whereas two ears were designated to listen, and two eyes to see, not a single organ was dedicated solely to speech. In fact, the mouth is utilized for eating as well as talking (*Maggidei HaEmes*).

◆§ The Subdued and Secondary Role of the Body

העניין שעיקר הטוב הוא כשהגוף שותק ואינו נוגע בשום דבר לטובת הנאתו והנשמה תנהיג הכל וכן בתורה ומצות אין לעשות בשום דבר לטובת עצמו הגוף וזה הפי׳ שהגוף שותק.

The term לַגּוּף, *the body*, implies that the *mishnah* is not merely advocating the virtues of silence but is also emphasizing that the body (i.e. all of its material needs) plays a secondary and muted role in the Jew's life. Often we are tempted to make decisions —even those affecting our observance of *mitzvos* and study of Torah — on the basis of our personal comfort and convenience. This approach is rejected by the *mishnah* which urges that the body be subordinate to the soul.

◆§ Silence Is in the Body's Best Interests

גדלתי בין החכמים וראיתי שאין לענות את הגוף בסיגופים, שבסופם חולשה המטמטמת הכל ובעקבותם גאוה ההורסת הכל. אבל השתיקה, לפעמים מענה מאד, כאשר רוצים להגיד דבר מה ומתגברים ושותקים. ומאידך אין השתיקה מביאה שום מחלה או חולשה אף לא לידי גאוה. הרי שאין טוב לענות לגוף אלא עם שתיקה.

The Kotzker Rebbe was generally opposed to depriving oneself of the basic amenities of life. For example, excessive fasting not only deprives the individual of the necessary strength required to serve Hashem, but also leads to haughtiness (boasting about his new-found piety). On the other hand, curbing one's impulse to talk foolishly can never have a negative effect on a person (*Maggidei HaEmes*).

The Beneficial Role of the Body

שתיקה מלשון תיק, כי טוב לגוף שהוא משמש תיק להנשמה.
שתיקה שמירת הלשון, כאשר שותקין אז גם הגוף ישתוק, גוף נקי, ברית הלשון
ברית המעור.

While the *mishnah* seems to relegate the body to a secondary role, careful examination of the text reveals a significant role for the body, as we shall now elucidate.

Firstly, as Rav Menachem Mendel of Vorka noted, the term שְׁתִיקָה, ordinarily interpreted as *silence*, may also be related to תִּיק, *a case*. Ideally, the body serves as the sacred casing for the Divine soul which, in This World, can only reach its potential within the confines of the body (*Maggidei HaEmes*).

Moreover, by remaining silent when appropriate, the body not only avoids many difficult situations and potential pitfalls but also helps us lead a more moral life, as the following remarks will clarify. To appreciate this relationship, it might be useful to recall two covenants (בְּרִיתוֹת) that are frequently cited in *Kabbalah*: the Covenant of Speech (בְּרִית הַלָּשׁוֹן), and the Covenant of Morality (בְּרִית הַמָּעוֹר). By observing the Covenant of Speech — often through the adroit use of silence — the body will merit to observe the Covenant of Morality, as well. This concept can be deduced from a careful reading of the Mishnah. לֹא מָצָאתִי לַגּוּף טוֹב אֶלָּא שְׁתִיקָה — I have found nothing better for curbing the sensual passions of the body than silence — observing the Covenant of Speech (cf. *Lev Simchah, Maggidei HaEmes*).

הרבי ר' העניך ז"ל מאלכסנדר הגיד דהיינו שכל זמן שעוד מוצאים גוף, גשם
וחומר אזי מוטב לשתוק. אבל כשאין מוצאין עוד מן הגוף אזי טוב לדבר (וזה כל
הנשמה וגו').

Finally, the *mishnah* never intended that we remain silent forever. As Rav Henoch of Alexander noted, silence is only appropriate as long as the body retains considerable influence and dictates our behavior. However, once our material passions have subsided — so that the body no longer determines our behavior — that silence is no longer necessary (*Maggidei HaEmes*).

Wine: The Personification of the Body
Incense: The Personification of the Soul

שזאת הוא תיקון הגוף ע"י השתיקה ורמז לזה יין דאיתא כשם שקול ודיבור יפה

לבשמים כן קשה ליין ע״ש במנחות במשנה שהי׳ הגיזבר מושך היין בשתיקה,
דאיתא חמרי וריחני פקחין, ונראה שהם ב׳ מיני חכמות, חכמה שבראש בחי׳
הנשמה והוא בחי׳ הריח כדאיתא איזהו דבר שהנשמה נהנית ולא הגוף זה הריח.
והוא בבחי׳ הקול והיין מפקח הגוף כדאיתא בפ׳ ותירוש ינובב בתולות והוא בכח
השתיקה כי תיקון הגוף ע״י הצמצום לעצור במילין שלא להגביר כח הגוף על
הנשמה, ואז זוכה לחכמה ונעשה כלי אל הנשמה, ובענין בשמים ויין מצינו דקול
יפה לבשמים ומ״מ בפנים הי׳ הקטורת בחשאי כדאיתא בגמ׳ קטורת בחשאי
מכפר על לשון הרע, ויין דקול רע ליין מ״מ בפנים הי׳ השירה על היין בשעת
הנסכים, והוא כענין דאיתא יין בשתיקה. ועתיד לארמא קלא לבסוף כשמפקח
הלב, וע״י בחי׳ גוף טוב דשתיקה מתדבק בו הארת הנשמה, ובבחי׳ העסק בתורה
ותפלה בעריכות שפתים וקול רם מתעלה אח״כ הנשמה בשורש העליון והוא
בחשאי לכן הקטורת לפנים ולפני ולפנים.

T he respective roles of the body (silence) and the soul (spiritual leadership)
are indicated in a beautiful comment of *Chazal* regarding the Divine Service in the *Beis HaMikdash*. Let us assume that wine, the source of so much
material pleasure, symbolizes the body, and incense — which is inhaled
but never consumed — symbolizes the soul. How appropriate then that the
wine (used for libations, נְסָכִים) was prepared in an atmosphere of total silence,
while the incense was formulated while the spice-makers spoke (cf. *Menachos*
87a).

In this light we can better appreciate a rather difficult *Chazal* and perhaps
also gain insight as to how wisdom may be acquired. We are told חמרי וריחני
פיקחין, "wine and spices lead to wisdom" (*Yoma* 76a). This may refer to different methods of acquiring wisdom — through the subordination and silencing
of the body, compared to wine, and by uplifting the soul, symbolized by
incense.

It is also noteworthy that the roles of wine and incense in the *Beis HaMikdash*
were reversed once the preparatory phase had been completed. At that point,
wine was poured alongside the Altar amidst the loud and joyous singing of the
Levites, while the incense (especially during the Yom Kippur *Avodah*) was
offered in the total silence and seclusion of the Holy of Holies (קֹדֶשׁ הַקֳּדָשִׁים). This
"role reversal" also conveys a compelling message. The material side of man
need not be dormant, but rather when properly channeled and successfully
restrained it can also play a significant and visible role. The soul, on the other
hand, which is the source of our most heartfelt prayers and most profound
Torah thoughts, not only is stimulated to grow in its present form, encased
within the body, but even its heavenly roots (שֹׁרֶשׁ הָעֶלְיוֹן) — so beyond our
comprehension that we must remain silent — are also stimulated (adapted from
Sfas Emes).

■ וְלֹא הַמִּדְרָשׁ הוּא הָעִקָּר, אֶלָּא הַמַּעֲשֶׂה — *Not study, but practice is the*
main thing.

[יח] רַבָּן שִׁמְעוֹן בֶּן גַּמְלִיאֵל אוֹמֵר: עַל שְׁלשָׁה דְבָרִים
הָעוֹלָם קַיָּם – עַל הַדִּין וְעַל הָאֱמֶת וְעַל הַשָּׁלוֹם,
שֶׁנֶּאֱמַר: ,,אֱמֶת וּמִשְׁפַּט שָׁלוֹם שִׁפְטוּ בְּשַׁעֲרֵיכֶם.''

🦋 🦋 🦋

✺§ What Did Shas Teach You?

מעשה באברך אחד שנכנס לפני האדמו״ר זצ״ל מקאצק, שאלו הרבי ״מה
למדת״? אמר לו ״למדתי את כל הש״ס״. הוסיף הרבי ושאל ״ומה לימד אותך
הש״ס״?

To illustrate this principle we relate the following story: When a certain
individual told the Kotzker Rebbe that he had completed *Shas*, the Rebbe
responded, "What did *Shas* teach you (in terms of your practical observance,
שְׁמִירַת הַמִּצְוֹת)?" True, the man had learned *Shas* (שֶׁהַמִּדְרָשׁ), but did it lead to
actual improvements in his actions (הַמַּעֲשֶׂה) and accomplishments? (*Maggidei
HaEmes*).

18.

■ עַל שְׁלשָׁה דְבָרִים הָעוֹלָם קַיָּם – עַל הַדִּין וְעַל הָאֱמֶת וְעַל הַשָּׁלוֹם — *The world
endures on three things — justice, truth and peace.*

✺§ A Mishnah for Our Times

אומר על ג' דברים כו', עי' בדברי החסיד ז״ל בפי' משנה זו והם ממש דברי הב״י
בחו״מ ריש סי' א'.

At first glance, it appears that this *mishnah* seems to contradict a previous
maxim in *mishnah* 2 which enumerates three other factors that sustain the
universe: Torah, the service (of God) and acts of loving-kindness. However, as
Rabbeinu Yonah (as elucidated by the *Beis Yosef*) notes, our *mishnah* conveys
a message of particular importance to the Jew suffering relentless poverty and
oppression — often associated with *Galus* — who may not be able to study
Torah in his accustomed depth, and is unable to be as generous as he wishes,
and certainly cannot perform the *avodah*. Despite these unquestionable set-
backs, some alternative is available, as our *mishnah* elucidates. Even if the
quality of Torah study has suffered in *Galus*, our loyalty to *mitzvah* observance
and to the requirements of *Halachah* certainly remain uncompromised (עַל הַדִּין).

[18] *Rabban Shimon ben Gamliel says: The world endures on three things — justice, truth and peace; as it is said (Zechariah 8:16): "You shall adjudicate the verdict of truth and peace at your gates."*

❧ ❧ ❧

For the truly sincere Jew, motivated by the highest standards of truth and religious integrity (עַל הָאֱמֶת), prayer is a partial substitute for sacrifice. And finally, the ultimate beneficial effect of *gemilus chasadim* — which is peace and stability (הַשָּׁלוֹם) — enabling the poor as well as the rich to sustain themselves, can also be achieved even in *Galus* (adapted from *Sfas Emes*).

⁍§ Can Truth Actually Exist

איתא במדרש בשעה שבא הקב"ה לברא את אדה"ר כו' אמת אומר אל יברא
שכולו שקר כו' שלום אומר אל יברא שכולו קטטה, ובכל זאת איתא במשנה על
שלשה דברים העולם עומד על הדין ועל האמת ועל השלום, הרי שיש אמת ושלום.
ומה הפירוש העולם עומד על האמת. אלא שהכונה היא לברר האמת, יש הסתרות
ובני ישראל מבררין האמת. כל דיין שדן דין אמת לאמתו וכו' כאילו נעשה שותף
להקב"ה במעשה בראשית . . . הסתכל בתורה וברא העולם, בתורה יש הכל, וכך
מבררין האמת.

Seemingly, our *mishnah*, emphasizing the role of truth in sustaining the universe, contradicts the renowned Midrash which states that the Attributes of Truth and Peace sought to convince Hashem not to create man. Subsequently, Hashem was compelled to cast away (i.e. deny any role to) these attributes before creating man (cf. *Bereishis Rabbah* 8:5).

Perhaps, the distinction may be made between a surface, easily discernible truth which does not exist in This World, and the in-depth truth, which can only be achieved through immersion in Torah study. While on the surface many phenomena may appear to be inequitable, and many occurrences appear to clash with our notions of truth and fairness, if we delve deeper — assisted by the Torah through which Hashem created the universe and its scholars who interpret its teaching — we are able to discern their true meaning (adapted from *Pnei Menachem, Maggidei HaEmes*).

⁍§ Truth vs. Peace

אמת, דין אותיותיהם בסדרן, לא כן אותיות שלום. ויש לפרש משום שאמת הוא
אמת ולכן אותיותיו בסדרן, מה שאין כן שלום, שהרי מותר לשנות מפני דרכי
שלום.

It is interesting that the letters comprising the word אֱמֶת (truth) are in the correct sequence of the *aleph beis*, whereas the term שָׁלוֹם is not in proper sequence. Perhaps, this alludes to the Talmud's ruling (cf. *Yevamos* 65b) that one may occasionally revise the truth (i. e. reverse the sequence of events) in order to preserve peace (Rabbi Menachem Mendel of Vorka, *Maggidei HaEmes*).

■ — רַבִּי חֲנַנְיָא בֶּן עֲקַשְׁיָא אוֹמֵר: רָצָה הַקָּדוֹשׁ בָּרוּךְ הוּא לְזַכּוֹת אֶת יִשְׂרָאֵל —
Rabbi Chananiah ben Akashia says: The Holy One, Blessed is He, wished to confer merit upon Israel.

⇒§ Mitzvos for Every Occasion

לכאורה קשה אם רצה לזכות היה לו ליתן פחות מצוות כדי שנוכל לקיימם
כהלכתם ומאידך פחות איסורים שלא נכשל בהם. אלא שרצה הקב"ה שנוכל
לקיים חוקיו ומצות ותורותיו גם באם יהיו טרודים בפרנסה וכדומה לפיכך הרבה
תורה ומצוות ומשכם לכל חלקי החיים כגון מעקה לבונה בית, כלאים לחורש
וזורע, מזוזה, סוכה, לקט שכחה ופאה וכדומיהן כדי שיוכל האדם לקיימם בכל מצב
שבו יהיה.

While it may seem at first sight that *Klal Yisrael* would benefit from being obligated to observe fewer *mitzvos* (which would lead to fewer transgressions if *mitzvos* were not properly observed), the *mishnah* is assuring us that we will encounter *mitzvos* in every situation. Even those of us who are immersed in the struggle for economic survival enjoy *mitzvos* that they are uniquely capable of performing. For example, a farmer is required to designate various parts of the harvest to the poor, and someone building a house enjoys the unique opportunity to observe the laws of *maakeh* (*Maggidei HaEmes*).

⇒§ Sharing Each Other's Mitzvos

יש לפרש דאם בעבירה איתא כל ישראל ערבין זה בזה, מדה טובה מרובה במצוה
בודאי, שעל ידי שעושה מצוה מזכה את כל ישראל. ולפי זה י"ל רצה הקב"ה
לזכות את ישראל היינו כללות ישראל, לפיכך הרבה להם תורה ומצות, שמכל
מצוה שיהודי עושה נעשה הרבה מצות לפי שכל ישראל זוכים במצוה זו. ואפילו
במצוות שלא כל אחד יכול לקיימן כגון יבום וכדומה גם כן זוכים בהם כולם על
ידי האחד שעושהו.

Ιn the spirit of כָּל יִשְׂרָאֵל עֲרֵבִין זֶה בָּזֶה (*Shavuos* 39a), that all Jews are guarantors of each other's observance of *mitzvos*, we suggest that if *any* Jew performs any of the 613 commandments, *every* Jew benefits. By transmitting to *Klal Yisrael* numerous *mitzvos* — including some that are rarely performed by most individuals — Hashem ensured that we would enjoy the merit of having performed *all* of the *mitzvos* of the Torah (*Lev Simchah, Maggidei HaEmes*).

◄§ Performing Mitzvos for Hashem's Sake

איתא בפירוש המשניות להרמב"ם שכשאדם עושה מצוה אחת כולה לשם שמים
זוכה על ידה לעולם הבא, רצה הקב"ה לזכות את ישראל לפיכך הרבה להם תורה
ומצות, אבל באם יחשוב על העולם הבא גם זה אינו לגמרי לשם שמים.

Αccording to the *Rambam*, this *mishnah* refers to those individuals who perform *mitzvos* — or even a single *mitzvah* — *LeShem Shamayim*, to enhance Hashem's glory without any consideration of material gain or even reward in *Olam Haba*. While Hashem "showered" us with *mitzvos* in order to give us ample opportunity to merit *Olam Haba*, we should perform *mitzvos* for their own sake.

◄§ Perfecting the Natural World

והענין הוא שעיקר התורה השייכה לישראל היא נשמת התורה ועשרת הדברות,
ורצה הקב"ה שבאמצעיות בנ"י יהי' תיקון לכל הברואים, ולכן המשיך כח התורה
לכל המעשים הגשמיים על ידי המצות מעשיות, והשי"ת עשה כן כדי להיות נתקן
גם הטבע.
פירוש לזכך האדם לפיכך הרבה להם תורה ומצות.

Τhere can be no greater source of merit than to consecrate the natural universe with the aura of Torah and *mitzvos*. While *Klal Yisrael* would have been able to attain its potential by simply having received and having plumbed the depths of the *Aseres HaDibros*, we were commanded many more *mitzvos* in the hope that the entire natural world would become infused with *kedushah* by serving as a vehicle for the performance of *mitzvos*. (For example, the field from which the various tithes and alms to the poor are given derives *kedushah* from being associated with these *mitzvos*. The doorposts upon which a *mezuzah* is mounted benefit from this sacred ambiance.) And there can be no greater

וּמִצְוֹת, שֶׁנֶּאֱמַר: „יהוה חָפֵץ לְמַעַן צִדְקוֹ, יַגְדִּיל תּוֹרָה
וְיַאְדִּיר."

---

zechus than bringing the spirit of Torah and *mitzvos* to the vast physical world
to purify *Klal Yisrael.*

Alternatively, the term לְזַכּוֹת may mean *to purify* (related to שֶׁמֶן זַיִת זַךְ).
Through Torah and *mitzvos, Klal Yisrael* is purged from all impurities.

■ יַגְדִּיל תּוֹרָה וְיַאְדִּיר — *That the Torah be made great and glorious.*

◆§ An Ongoing Process

קשה דהו״ל למימר הגדיל תורה, רק הפירוש על כח תורה שבעל פה שבני ישראל

1　　　therefore He gave them Torah and mitzvos in abundance, as it is said (Yeshayahu 42:21): "Hashem desired, for the sake of its [Israel's] righteousness, that the Torah be made great and glorious."

מוסיפין ומרחיבין כח התורה, ועל ידי המצות ממשיכין אור התורה לכל המעשים,
לכן הרבה להם דייקא תורה ומצות להודיען איך להגדיל ולהרחיב כח התורה
כנ״ל וזה יגדיל ויאדיר לשון עתיד כנ״ל.

Note that the *mishnah* does not say, הִגְדִּיל וְהָאְדִּיר (past tense), which would mean that Hashem *had* expanded the parameters of Torah by obligating us to observe many *mitzvos*. Rather, it says, יַגְדִּיל וְיַאְדִּיר (future tense), he *will* enhance. This implies that every time *Klal Yisrael* observes *mitzvos* we are continuously expanding the frontiers of Torah into new areas and spreading the light of Torah into the material world.

כָּל יִשְׂרָאֵל יֵשׁ לָהֶם חֵלֶק לָעוֹלָם הַבָּא, שֶׁנֶּאֱמַר: „וְעַמֵּךְ כֻּלָּם צַדִּיקִים, לְעוֹלָם יִירְשׁוּ אָרֶץ, נֵצֶר מַטָּעַי, מַעֲשֵׂה יָדַי לְהִתְפָּאֵר.‟

פרק שני

[א] רַבִּי אוֹמֵר: אֵיזוֹ הִיא דֶרֶךְ יְשָׁרָה שֶׁיָּבֹר לוֹ הָאָדָם? כָּל שֶׁהִיא תִפְאֶרֶת לְעוֹשֶׂיהָ וְתִפְאֶרֶת לוֹ

■ אֵיזוֹ הִיא דֶרֶךְ יְשָׁרָה שֶׁיָּבֹר לוֹ הָאָדָם — *Which is the proper path that a man should choose for himself?*

⋖§The Right Path of Life

דרך ישרה, כתיב בכל דרכיך דעהו והוא יישר אורחותיך, כל שהיא תפארת לעושיה ותפארת לו מן האדם.

By calling upon us to adopt the right path of life, the Mishnah is reflecting on Shlomo's plea: בְּכָל דְּרָכֶיךָ דָעֵהוּ וְהוּא יְיַשֵּׁר אֹרְחֹתֶיךָ, *know Him in all your ways and He will guide your path* (Mishlei 3:6). While Hashem actually guides us along the right path of life, it is *our* obligation to take the initiative (adapted from *Lev Simchah, Maggidei HaEmes*).

⋖§ Total Rejection of Pride

הרבי ר' בער ממעזריטש ז"ל הגיד שיבור כמו שדה בור, שצריך לעקור כל תפארת שיש לו מאחרים וכן תפארת שיש לאדם בעצמו. פי' הדרך הישר שיבור לו האדם, כל שהיא, להיות כל שהוא, להחזיק עצמו בכל שהוא, וזה תפארת לעושיה ותפארת לו מן האדם.

Perhaps the clue to our *mishnah* is the correct interpretation of the term שֶׁיָּבֹר, which also may be interpreted in the sense of "rejecting" [false pride] (cf. *Bava Basra* 29a, דמוברי באגי, *an uncultivated field*), or "selecting" the wholesome kernels from the chaff, related to בּוֹרֵר, *selecting* [adopting the proper path in life]. As the Maggid of Mezeritch interpreted this *mishnah*: "Only by *rejecting* any sense of self-pride (תִפְאֶרֶת לְעוֹשֶׂיהָ) and by casting away the accolades that others may bestow on me, can I achieve the proper path of life" (*Maggidei HaEmes*).

This approach may also be inferred from the term כָּל שֶׁהִיא, which is usually translated as "anything." Consider yourself to be a mere "anything" — as

All Israel has a share in the World to Come, as it is said (Yeshayahu 60:21): And your people are all righteous; they shall inherit the land forever; a branch of My plantings, My handiwork, in which to take pride."

Chapter Two

[1] *Rabbi says: Which is the proper path that a man should choose for himself? Whatever is a credit to himself and earns him the esteem of fellow men. Be as*

---

nothing special. Such humility will indeed be acclaimed by everyone (תִּפְאֶרֶת לוֹ מִן הָאָדָם) (*Maggidei HaEmes*).

■ **כָּל שֶׁהִיא תִפְאֶרֶת לְעוֹשֶׂיהָ וְתִפְאֶרֶת לוֹ מִן הָאָדָם** — *Whatever is a credit to himself and earns him the esteem of fellow men.*

◆§ How Would Someone Else React?

שיש לו כוונה בזה אבל אין ניכר לבני אדם זה לא טוב רק צ״ל גם תפארת לאדם
אחר ג״כ . . . וזהו דאי׳ בגמ׳ שפתח לו הנדר מה״ט וגם לאחרים יהיה נראה טוב
כי אל בינתך אל תשען, והאדם נוגע ואינו רואה חובה לעצמו והשוחד יעור ולזאת
צריך לראות לראות שיהיה נראה יפה גם בעיני אחרים.

The *mishnah* is urging us to consider how *others* would react to our behavior (תִּפְאֶרֶת לוֹ מִן הָאָדָם). The Gemara in *Nedarim* 22b cites our *mishnah* as a justification for annulling vows. While *you* may be perfectly comfortable in assuming vows of self-denial, think of how *others* may be discomfited by your behavior.

Another reason for determining the reaction of others before adopting a path of life, and the importance of being aware of the consequences of our behavior, is simply to avoid the innate biases to which we are all subject. It is virtually impossible for us to realize the flaws in our conduct. As *Chazal* teach (*Negaim* 2:5), "אֵין אָדָם רוֹאֶה נִגְעֵי עַצְמוֹ, a person is unable to recognize his own plagues" (i.e. weaknesses). This theme is conveyed more directly in a later *mishnah*: וְאַל בִּינָתְךָ אַל תִּשָּׁעֵן, *do not rely on your own understanding* (4:18).

◆§ How Would You React if Someone Else Behaved in This Fashion?

הוי״ל למימר ותפארת לאחרים. רק י״ל אם כשאדם אחר יעשהו יהיה יפה בעיניו,

If the *mishnah* merely meant to point out the importance of obtaining the approval of others before adopting a path of life, it should have said וְתִפְאֶרֶת לָאֲחֵרִים, that it meets the approval of *others*. The expression used here, מִן הָאָדָם, *of fellow men*, conveys another thought. In evaluating your own approach, consider how *you* would react if others behaved in a similar fashion. (For example, before condoning your own anger, consider how you would react if someone else became angry.)

✦ A Plea for Sincerity

פשוט כי יהי׳ כוונתו לטובה לאפוקי שיהי׳ תוכו לא טוב כמו שנראה מבחוץ ח״ו.

In previous interpretations of the *mishnah*, we emphasized the role player by *others* and how it should impact on our behavior (i.e. obtaining their approval; considering their reaction to your behavior). Additionally, we should be mindful that adopting a path of life entails far more than merely pleasing others in a superficial manner. On the contrary, any path chosen must be sincerely believed in by the individual (תִּפְאֶרֶת לְעֹשֶׂיהָ) as well as meet popular approval (תִּפְאֶרֶת לו מִן הָאָדָם). As *Chazal* stated (*Berachos* 28a) succinctly, שֶׁיְּהֵא תוכו כְּבָרו, a person's "insides" (i.e. his true personality, his inner makeup) should be identical with his "outside" (how he appears to others).

✦ Attribute Nothing to Yourself

היינו כל אשר נראה תפארת אצלו איזה מדה טובה ידע שהיא לעושיה ואינה שלו.

In a similar vein, Reb Yitzchak of Vorka suggested that we attribute every good character trait that we may possess as a gift from Hashem. We must be mindful of the fact that Hashem helped develop our personality, and we should not think it is solely the result of our own efforts (תִּפְאֶרֶת לְעֹשֶׂיהָ) (*Maggidei HaEmes*).

✦ Adopt Your Unique Path
Respect the Road Others Have Chosen

היינו שכל נשמה יש לה דרך אחר בעבודת השי״ת. שיש צדיק שמסגף עצמו, ויש צדיק שאוכל ושותה ואינו מסגף עצמו כלל. והוא גם כן צדיק גדול וקדוש מאוד. וכן בשאר ענינים יש חילוקים בין הצדיקים, וזהו מחמת שהולכים בדרך הישרה

ששייך לנשמתו באמת. על כן אינו תופס בדרך שאינה מיוחדת לו, ואף שמשבח
מאוד דרך הצדיק בעבודה ויפה בעיניו יותר מדרך שלו אעפי"כ אוחז צדיק דרכו.

R eb Simchah Bunim interpreted this *mishnah* in a unique and beautiful
    manner, emphasizing tolerance as well as diversity in *Avodas Hashem*.
Within the confines of *Torah* and *mitzvos*, much room for diversity exists. Some
tzaddikim deny themselves most material pleasures as they seek to come close
to Hashem. Others eat and drink heartily in order to gain sufficient strength
to serve Hashem. Our *mishnah* beseeches *Klal Yisrael's* leaders: Adopt — and
take pride in — your own unique path of *Avodas Hashem*, a path best suited
to your *neshamah* (תִּפְאֶרֶת לְעֹשֶׂיהָ). However, in your justified self-pride be
tolerant, do not forget that other approaches are *equally* valid (תִּפְאֶרֶת לוֹ מִן
הָאָדָם) (*Maggidei HaEmes*).

✥ Though You Are a Mere Mortal

להיות שמירת הקדושה במעשה אדם ותחבולותיו (מענטשליך הייליג) כדאיתא
בשם הרבי מקאצק ז"ל על הכתוב ואנשי קודש תהיון לי, וכאשר האדם עולה מכל
הטומאות הוא מתעלה ומגיע להשראת השכינה.
שהיא תפארת לעושי' היינו לבטל לגמרי רק להש"י שהוא עושה הכל, אמנם לא
הכל זוכין לזה רק לפחות מדריגה שני' הוא ותפארת לו מן האדם הוא התהפכות
החומר אל הצורה, שכן הי' רצון הש"י להיות האדם מוטבע בחומר ואעפ"כ
יתגבר הצורה ומצד זה בא תפארת להש"י מן האדם מצד שהוא אדם כנ"ל.

T o appreciate the *mishnah's* emphasis on our mortality — stating the term
    אָדָם, man, twice — we recall a theme often voiced by the Kotzker Rebbe:
"*Der heiliger mentsch*" (holy man). The Torah never expects us to transcend
our mortal limitations and become angels. Instead, we are called upon to be
אַנְשֵׁי קֹדֶשׁ, *sacred men*. Our greatest challenge is to live a hallowed life amidst
all the frailties and limitations that face us as mortals. In this respect,
the *mishnah* is urging us — as mortals — to choose a path (דֶּרֶךְ שֶׁיָּבֹר לוֹ הָאָדָם)
that will find favor in Hashem's eyes (תִּפְאֶרֶת לְעֹשֶׂיהָ) despite our very real
limitations as people (תִּפְאֶרֶת מִן הָאָדָם) (adapted from *Lev Simchah, Maggidei
HaEmes*).

In a similar vein, the *mishnah* may be proposing two alternative lifestyles.
Ideally, this would be a lifestyle of complete negation to Hashem, in which
our sole source of pride is the further glorification of our Creator's Name
(תִּפְאֶרֶת לְעֹשֶׂיהָ). However, such an idealistic lifestyle may be beyond most
individuals' capacities. Thus, this part of the *mishnah* concludes, תִּפְאֶרֶת לוֹ מִן
הָאָדָם — Hashem will also derive satisfaction from a person living a
sacred lifestyle acquired while living his life as a human being in this material
world.

מִן הָאָדָם. וֶהֱוֵי זָהִיר בְּמִצְוָה קַלָּה כְּבַחֲמוּרָה, שֶׁאֵין
אַתָּה יוֹדֵעַ מַתַּן שְׂכָרָן שֶׁל מִצְוֹת. וֶהֱוֵי מְחַשֵּׁב הֶפְסֵד

■ וֶהֱוֵי זָהִיר בְּמִצְוָה קַלָּה כְּבַחֲמוּרָה, שֶׁאֵין אַתָּה יוֹדֵעַ מַתַּן שְׂכָרָן שֶׁל מִצְוֹת —
*Be as scrupulous in performing a "minor" mitzvah as in a "major"
one, for you do not know the reward given for the [respective] mitzvos.*

◆§ Are All Mitzvos Rewarded Equally?

כלומר הא אין אתה צריך לידע כי אין עיסקך על זה לקבל פרס ואין אתה רוצה
לידע זה רק לעשות מצות ה' הן קל הן חמור, דלפי הפשוט קשה דמשמע דאילו היה
יודע מתן שכרן של מצוה היה בוחר בחמורה והוה ליה בעל מנת לקבל פרס.
לעניותי דעתי להמשיל משל המסדר חפצים זה על זה עד אלפים ורבבות כל של
מעלה יותר חשוב יותר, והנה כשרוצה להגביהם, לפעמים נוטל סולם ועולה
ומגביה מה שלמעלה שהוא עיקר החשיבות, ולפעמים על ידי שמניח מתחת דבר
מה ומגביה התחתון נמצא זה מגביה למה של מעלה ואחר כך יותר ויותר עד שגם
מה של מעלה מכולן מגביה עצמו, ומובן מזה איך כל המצות במקומם השייך לזה
על ידי זה מגביה זה יותר ויותר כו' עד של מעלה עליות גדולות כמו במצוה
הגדולה וגבוהה וזה פי' תרי"ג מצות התלוים בה, וזה פי' מצוה גוררת מצוה כו'
רק הפרש בעצם שחשוב וגבוה יותר אבל כולם אחת, והמשל הזה נוקב ויורד,
והמשכיל יבין לתרץ בזה כמה ענינים.
י"ל כיון שאי"ל סוף ושיעור למתן שכרן ובדבר שאי"ל סוף לא שייך חילוקים
וא"א למנות ולהכריע.
פי' הזהירות להמצוה שזה עיקר קיבול שכר וזה אין נפקא מינה בין קלה לחמורה
אבל מעצם המצוה לא איירי כי על זה נאמר לפום צערא אגרא.
עוד יש לפרש שאין אתה יודע מתן שכרן של מצוה כלומר כי הכל תלוי רק לפי
היגיעה לכן כשתתזהר במצוה קלה יעדוף שכרה ממצוה חמורה בלי יגיעה.
על מה שקראו חז"ל מצות שילוח הקן קלה כמ"ש בקלות אדמו"ר האמרי אמת ז"ל
לפי שאין לה הכנה, כמו שנאמר כי יקרא וארז"ל פרט למזומן. ועיקר המצוה הוא
ההכנה כי כל מה שנשאר בנפש האדם אחר עשיית המצוה הוא ההכנה והדביקות
שקנה בעשיית המצוה.
ולפעמים תלוי עשיית המצוה בשעת מוצלחת ובעת רצון ושכרה רב מאוד.

The *mishnah* urges us to be as diligent in observing "minor" (lighter) *mitzvos*
as in observing "major" (stringent) *mitzvos* since we do not know the
reward given for the respective *mitzvos*. May one then infer from here that all
mitzvos are rewarded in the same manner?

In truth we need not be overly concerned with this issue. As this passage

---

1. We prefer this approach to the literal translation, *you do not know the reward of mitzvos,* which
implies that if we did know which *mitzvos* are rewarded most generously, we would concentrate
on observing only those *mitzvos*. This would contradict our earlier assertion (שֶׁלֹּא עַל מְנָת לְקַבֵּל פְּרָס)
that we should not observe *mitzvos* for the purpose of obtaining a reward.

scrupulous in performing a "minor" mitzvah as in a "major" one, for you do not know the reward given for the [respective] mitzvos. Calculate the loss of a mitzvah

---

concludes, שֶׁאֵין אַתָּה יוֹדֵעַ מַתַּן שְׂכָרָן שֶׁל מִצְוֹת, "you do not *have to know* the reward granted for observing *mitzvos*."[1]

Moreover, it is impossible to truly evaluate the full impact of *mitzvos* on ourselves and on the universe. This — the ultimate effect of *mitzvos* — is the true שָׂכָר, *reward*, that the *mishnah* feels cannot be evaluated.

This theme may be elucidated with a beautiful מָשָׁל (parable). Suppose someone owned a warehouse in which thousands of items were piled one on top of another. Consider further that I wanted to lift the highest stacked item to an even higher position. One of two strategies could be followed to accomplish this objective: Either to climb on a ladder and reach the highest item, or simply place another item on the very bottom (in the space previously reserved for the lowest item). This action would compel all the other items — from the bottom to the very top — to be elevated one notch. So too, while performing what may *appear* to be a lighter *mitzvah*, one leaves an impact on all the other — more stringent — *mitzvos*, elevating them as well. This theme is reflected in the popular phrase recited prior to performing many *mitzvos*, תַּרְיַ"ג מִצְוֹת הַתְּלוּיִּים בָּהּ, that all other *mitzvos* are contingent (and elevated) on the performance of this *mitzvah*. [Refer also to our commentary on שֶׁמִּצְוָה גוֹרֶרֶת מִצְוָה, for the consequence of a mitzvah is a mitzvah (4:2).]

Actually, the reward for observing *mitzvos* is not only unfathomable but also infinite. As the Mishnah states, שֶׁאֵין אַתָּה יוֹדֵעַ, we cannot possibly comprehend the reward for observing *mitzvos*. It follows that is impossible to compare the reward accruing from various *mitzvos*. If I do not know the *total* sum — the infinite reward resulting from observing *mitzvos* — how can I possibly determine and compare the rewards associated with particular *mitzvos*?

Despite all of these caveats — that the reward associated with observance of *mitzvos* is beyond our comprehension and truly infinite — the opening passage, וֶהֱוֵי זָהִיר בְּמִצְוָה קַלָּה כְּבַחֲמוּרָה, gives us a clue as to perhaps the most critical factor that determines the reward granted for performing *mitzvos* — זְהִירוּת, *diligence*, and careful preparation *prior* to performing the *mitzvah*. Perhaps, your reward will be proportional to the eagerness and diligence demonstrated rather than the unfathomable reward of the *mitzvah* itself.

Not only the alacrity demonstrated in performing the *mitzvah*, but also the *effort* invested affect the *mitzvah's* reward. A "minor" *mitzvah* performed with great effort and with a great deal of diligence may deserve greater reward than a more stringent, "major" *mitzvah* performed lackadaisically.[1]

---

1. Based on this assumption, we can better appreciate why *chazal* described שִׁלּוּחַ הַקֵּן, the *mitzvah* of sending away the mother bird before taking the chicks or the eggs, as a "minor" mitzvah — since it can only be performed when one did not anticipate sighting birds.

In fact, the diligence and preparation (הֲכָנָה) associated with a *mitzvah* and the closer relationship with Hashem that ensues endures well beyond the performance of the *mitzvah* itself.

Even the timing of the *mitzvah* may affect its reward. *Chazal* refer to עֵת רָצוֹן, a time of Divine Goodwill when our *mitzvos* are particularly appreciated (cf. *Berachos* 8a). We also wish our peers בְּשָׁעָה טוֹבָה וּמוּצְלַחַת, that a particular undertaking (for the purpose of performing a *mitzvah*) be performed at a successful and auspicious time (adapted from *Sfas Emes*).

⇜ Everyone Perceives the Same Reward

כי אף של מצוה גדולה אפשר יש שכר יותר אבל בהבנת הענין כי אין הקב"ה
עושה קנאה ונמצא כל אחד כפי יגיעו נוטל וכל המצוה כפי היגיעה והשלימות רצון
העושה ואף כי עצם שכר המצוה גדול. אבל עדיין אין אדם שעושה המצוה קטנה
כ"כ בטוב משיג שכרה הגבוה ואחר השכר גבוה יש הפרש בין קטנות המצוה
וגדולות.

While performing a more "stringent" *mitzvah* may merit a greater reward than that of a "minor" one, the recipient of the reward for performing a מִצְוָה קַלָּה with all due effort (in This World or in the World to Come) does not perceive this disparity as long as he has not yet performed a מִצְוָה חֲמוּרָה. However, once he has performed a more "stringent" *mitzvah* (with equal effort) he realizes how much greater is the reward for a מִצְוָה חֲמוּרָה. This interpretation — emphasizing that each individual is rewarded according to his level of spiritual achievement — follows the principle of אֵין הקב"ה מַטִּיל קִנְאָה בְּמַעֲשֵׂה בְרֵאשִׁית, Hashem does not create a situation which would lead to jealousy among His creations (adapted from *Sfas Emes*).

⇜ Perform All Mitzvos for Their Own Sake

פי' כמו שבחמורה בודאי עושה לשם מצוה, כן מצוה שקלה לעשותה צריך להזהר
לעשותו לשם מצוה דייקא.

Reb Simchah Bunim interpreted the terms קַלָּה and חֲמוּרָה to refer to the difficulties encountered while performing the *mitzvah*. Just as one surely performs a more "difficult" *mitzvah* לִשְׁמָהּ, *for its own sake* (because the reward alone unquestionably would not be sufficient motivation to perform such a difficult undertaking), so too even a less difficult *mitzvah* should also be performed לְשֵׁם שָׁמַיִם for its own sake (adapted from *Maggidei HaEmes*).

⇜ Performance of Every Mitzvah Merits Olam Haba

פירוש על דרך שכתב הרמב"ם בפירוש המשניות רצה הקב"ה לזכות כו' כי

כשיקיים אדם מצוה כראוי וכהוגן ולא ישתף עמה כוונת העולם וכו' שיעשה
אותה לשמה מאהבה זכה בה לחיי העולם הבא כו' עיי"ש. זהו מצוה קלה כבחמורה
שכשיעשנה בשלימות יזכה על ידה לחיי העולם הבא.

The Lev Simchah, when interpreting this mishnah, recalled the renowned
comment of the Rambam (Makkos 3:16): כי כשיקיים אדם מצוה כראוי וכהוגן ולא
ישתף עמה כונה כוונת העולם וכו' שיעשה אותה לשמה מאהבה זכה בה לחיי העוה"ב,
"When a person appropriately performs any mitzvah of the 613 mitzvos, without any ulterior motive other than for the love of Hashem, he will merit a
portion in the World to Come on the basis of this one mitzvah alone."

⊷§ Beware of a "Lighter" Sin as You Would a More "Stringent" One

וכן בטח להיות נשמר ולשוב על עבירה קלה שמביא לחמורה . . .

As a logical corollary to this passage, the Beis Yisrael would remark that one
should beware of a "lighter" (minor) sin as one would a more "stringent"
(major) one (Maggidei HaEmes).

⊷§ Finding Mitzvos in Every Aspect of Life

לדבק גם דברים הרגילין ע"י שעושין הכל רק לרצונו, כי בכל דבר יש מצוה לה'
הן או לאו, וזה תכלית רצונו ית' להיות כל הנבראים מחוברין זה בזה עד שגם
הסוף ומדרגה התחתונה תהי' נמשכת אחר הראשית וההתחלה כנ"ל, ותכלית
הבריאה להיות הכל א' לכבודו ית' ומצוה לשון צותא וחיבור כמ"ש במ"א, ומצוה
קלה ממשיך הארה לדבר שפל יותר, וזהו בחי' יראת שמים להיות נמשך יראתו
ית' בכל מעשה קטן וגדול ונק' מצוה קלה.

Perhaps, the term קַלָּה may refer not only to "minor" mitzvos but to the
sacred challenge of "finding" opportunities to perform mitzvos in every
aspect of life, no matter how seemingly trivial and remote from kedushah
(sanctity) they may seem to be. Every one of Hashem's creations is somehow
associated with a mitzvah, either a positive commandment (מִצְוַת עֲשֵׂה) or a
negative commandment (לֹא תַעֲשֶׂה). The mishnah is alluding to the Divine
Blueprint for the universe, that every form of life — the lowest to the highest
— be linked together in an inexorable chain of כְּבוֹד שָׁמַיִם. In this context, the
term מִצְוָה may be interpreted as צַוְתָּא, an intimate relationship between each
and every rung of creation.

Based on this, we can derive additional insight into the term יִרְאַת שָׁמַיִם, fear
of heaven — that Hashem's presence should be derived from all of His creations
(adapted from Sfas Emes).

מִצְוָה כְּנֶגֶד שְׂכָרָהּ, וּשְׂכַר עֲבֵרָה כְּנֶגֶד הֶפְסֵדָהּ. הִסְתַּכֵּל בִּשְׁלֹשָׁה דְבָרִים, וְאֵין אַתָּה בָא לִידֵי עֲבֵרָה; דַּע מַה לְמַעְלָה מִמְּךָ – עַיִן רוֹאָה, וְאֹזֶן שׁוֹמַעַת, וְכָל מַעֲשֶׂיךָ בְּסֵפֶר נִכְתָּבִים.

■ וֶהֱוֵי מְחַשֵּׁב הֶפְסֵד מִצְוָה כְּנֶגֶד שְׂכָרָהּ — *Calculate the loss of a mitzvah against its reward.*

◈§ Cherish the "Loss" Resulting From a Mitzvah

והוי מחשב הפסד מצוה כנג"ש, כלומר כי ריבוי ההפסד הוא טוב יותר שעי"ז השכר בכפלים כי לפום צערא אגרא.

E ven the loss resulting from performance of a *mitzvah* (e.g. financial loss, the time involved) is beneficial since the loss associated with a *mitzvah* ensures a greater reward. As we read later (5:26), לְפוּם צַעֲרָא אַגְרָא, the greater the pain and exertion associated with a *mitzvah* the greater the reward.

◈§ Do Mitzvos With the Same "Joy" as One Would Do Aveiros

ואני רגיל לפרש הפסד מצוה לעשות חשבון בנפשו, אם יתנו לך מיליאהן רובל ושאר מחמדים כדי שתניח ולא להניח תפילין – בטח אל תחפוץ. והנה תשער בנפשך, כמה היה לך שמחה באם היה לך מיליאהן רובל, בזה השמחה ועוד יותר מזה – תצטרך להתמלאות בשמחה בהנחת תפילין ושמירת שבת ושמירת ברית קודש וכדומה לזה.

I n order to help us appreciate the concept of a *mitzvah's* loss, the *Imrei Emes* urged us to consider the following hypothetical (and unlikely) situation: Someone offers me a million dollars if I promise *not* to wear *tefillin*. What should I do? While we would, of course, utterly reject this request, this incentive to do an עֲבֵרָה (described by our *mishnah* as הֶפְסֵד מִצְוָה) can be of great assistance in performing the *mitzvah*. Wear *tefillin* with, at least, the same joy that you would have experienced had you accepted the million dollars.

■ דַּע מַה לְמַעְלָה מִמְּךָ — *Know what is above you.*

H owever, it is noteworthy that the *mishnah* says מַה, *"what is above you,"* rather than מִי, *Who,* which would clearly refer to Hashem. Let us consider some possible interpretations of the expression מַה לְמַעְלָה מִמְּךָ, *what is above you.*

against its reward and the reward of a sin against its cost. Consider three things and you will not come into the grip of sin: Know what is above you — a watchful Eye, an attentive Ear and all your deeds are recorded in a book.

⋸ Forces of Evil

פי׳ כי השגחת הקב״ה בעצמו על בנ״י, ונא׳ לא הביט און ביעקב כו׳ כי לא יגורך
רע כתיב א״כ כשאדם חוטא יש עין רואה מסט״א ונמצא בחטאו ח״ו נותן שליטה
והשגחה לאותן עינים המביטין ומשגיחין על החטאים, אבל כשאדם עושה טוב
משגיח עליו הקב״ה בעצמו, וזה ששיבח בלעם לא הביט און כו׳ פי׳ הקב״ה ששולט
על בנ״י אין משגיח ברעתם רק בעת רע ח״ו נפרדים מזאת המעלה ומ״מ עיקר
ההשגחה שעל בנ״י אין בו קטרוג לעולם.

Perhaps, the *mishnah* is referring to the phenomenon of הַסְתָּרַת פָּנִים, the *apparent* concealment of Hashem's הַשְׁגָּחָה (Providence), in response to our sins. The evil seer Balaam noted that Hashem Himself never perceives that the Jewish people are sinning — לֹא הִבִּיט אָוֶן בְּיַעֲקֹב, *He perceived no iniquity in Yaakov* (*Bamidbar* 23:21). Similarly, David exclaims, לֹא יְגֻרְךָ רָע, *no evil sojourns with You* (*Tehillim* 5:5). To resolve the seeming contradiction between the assurances that Hashem overlooks our sins and the harsh reality of Israel suffering in recompense for its sins, we resort to the notion of הַסְתָּרַת פָּנִים — that Hashem (כִּבְיָכוֹל) conceals His Presence and allows the forces of evil, known as סִטְרָא אַחֲרָא, to prevail.[1] (See *Devarim* 31:18, וְאָנֹכִי הַסְתֵּר אַסְתִּיר פָּנַי, *But I will surely have concealed My face*, and אַסְתִּירָה פָּנַי מֵהֶם, *I shall hide My face from them* (ibid. 32:20), where the Torah foresees a period of הַסְתָּרַת פָּנִים.) The term עַיִן רוֹאָה used in our *mishnah* may refer to the forces of evil (סִטְרָא אַחֲרָא) that look unfavorably upon *Klal Yisrael's* actions during periods of הַסְתָּרַת פָּנִים.

⋸ Your Actions Leave an Impact in Heaven

דע מה למעלה הוא ממך כי האדם מעלה במעשיו כל סדר עליות העולמות.

Homiletically, the *mishnah* may be interpreted in the following manner: דַּע, *know*, מַה לְּמַעְלָה, whatever occurs in Heaven is מִמְּךָ, is attributable to your behavior here on earth. The *mishnah* is urging us to never underestimate the enormous significance of our spiritual conduct here on earth which leaves an impact even in Heaven (adapted from *Sfas Emes*).

---

1. Editor's Note: An important fundamental truth to remember is that although Hashem may conceal His Presence (הַסְתָּרַת פָּנִים), He is *always present*.

✥ The Angels We Create

שמכל מצוה נברא מלאך סניגור ומכל עבירה נברא קטיגור, ובזה יש לפרש דע
מה למעלה, ר״ל שמה של מעלה הכל הוא ממך, ממעשיך כאן.

Chazal relate that when an individual performs a *mitzvah* he inspires the creation of an angel that will defend his actions. Likewise, every *aveirah* leads to the creation of a prosecuting angel (see 4:13; cf. *Zohar, Chadosh Rus* 75:2). This thought is alluded to in this mishnah: דַע, *know*, that מַה, *what* is created לְמַעְלָה, *above* (angels), results from your behavior (*Lev Simchah, Maggidei HaEmes*).

✥ Try to "Comprehend" Hashem (כביכול) From Your Own Reaction to Others

גם הפי׳ דע ממך מה של מעלה כמו״ש ומבשרי אחזה א׳ כי האדם השלם יוכל ליקח
דרך מוסר מעצם נפשו בראותו שחרה לו על המכעיס אותו מי שעשה לו טובה
ואיננו מכיר בטובו וכדומה הרבה כפי זה יבין הדרך להכיר טובות הבורא שגם
למעלה בוודאי כן הוא.

As unlikely as it may seem, at times we may better appreciate Hashem's management of the universe (Hashem is perceived as being לְמַעְלָה, *above*) from our *own* reaction to events (מִמְּךָ). For example, we would be justifiably indignant toward those who are ungrateful for past favors. Bearing this analogy in mind, we can begin to comprehend Hashem's goodness, as He lavishes us with His bounty despite our all-too frequent lack of gratitude. (Refer to our commentary on 1:6 for a similar theme.)

✥ When Is It Appropriate to Study Kabbalah?

גם הפי׳ כי הלימוד לידע סודות התורה אם הם בדרך חקירה בלבד אינו כלום אבל
אם בא ע״י עבודת האדם טוב שמביא לידי יר״ש.

*T*his phrase may also be alluding to the appropriate circumstances for the study of the mystical segment of the Torah known as *Kabbalah*. While it is certainly inappropriate to study *Kabbalah* merely as a speculative and philosophical exercise, it would be suitable — and perhaps even commendable — if study of this rarefied and esoteric segment of Torah fostered a closer relationship with the *Shechinah* and enhanced one's *Avodas Hashem*. According to this interpretation, the *mishnah* should be interpreted thus: דַע מַה לְמַעְלָה, study what is above (לְמַעְלָה) — the mystical components of Torah — but only מִמְּךָ,

if the desire for such knowledge stems from *you* — from a genuine search for your spiritual growth.

■ עַיִן רוֹאָה וְאֹזֶן שׁוֹמַעַת וְכָל מַעֲשֶׂיךָ בְּסֵפֶר נִכְתָּבִים — *A watchful Eye, an attentive Ear and all your deeds are recorded in a Book.*

◆§ Thoughts, Words and Deeds

עין רואה את המחשבות שבלב והם נגד ג' אופני העבודה מחשבה דיבור מעשה
כי אוזן שומעת הדיבורים וכל מעשיך כו', וצריכין להזהר בשלשתן. ומכל מקום
רק מעשיך בספר נכתבין.

The three expressions, עַיִן רוֹאָה, "a watchful Eye," אֹזֶן שׁוֹמַעַת, "an attentive Ear," and כָל מַעֲשֶׂיךָ בְּסֵפֶר נִכְתָּבִים "all your deeds are recorded in a Book," may allude to three distinct aspects of Hashem's הַשְׁגָחָה, His supervision of our behavior. His Eye perceives our innermost thoughts and His Ear listens to our speech. Yet, the *mishnah* assures us that it is primarily our deeds that are inscribed in the Divine Book.

◆§ We Are Accountable for the Actions of Our Eyes and Ears

עין שרואה מה שלא צריך, ואוזן ששומעת לדיבורים אסורים, נכתבים בספר אחד
עם כל מעשיך הלא טובים.

Reb Zvi Hersh of Rimanov found a direct link between the first two elements of this passage and the final reference to Hashem's Book. The eye that sees what it should not and the ear that listens to what it should not — their actions are recorded in the Divine Book (*Maggidei HaEmes*).

◆§ Three Eras of Jewish History

דע מה למעלה ממך, היינו בימים הקדמונים בבית ראשון היה עין רואה באורים
ותומים, וזהו עין רואה. ובבית שני לא היו משתמשין רק בבת קול, וזהו אוזן
שומעת. וכעת בגלות המר הזה כל מעשיך בספר נכתבים, יכול הצדיק לראות
הכל כעין נבואה במה שכתוב בספר ומסתכל בו.

The Maggid of Koznitz suggested that this short passage actually encompasses much of Jewish history. The *mishnah* is urging us, דַע מֵה לְמַעֲלָה מִמְּךָ, to know what occurred *before our times* (literally, *above*).

Remember the halcyon days of the first *Beis HaMikdash* when you actually perceived Hashem's Eye, His Divine Providence in the form of the *Urim*

ב] רַבָּן גַּמְלִיאֵל בְּנוֹ שֶׁל רַבִּי יְהוּדָה הַנָּשִׂיא אוֹמֵר: יָפֶה תַלְמוּד תּוֹרָה עִם דֶּרֶךְ אֶרֶץ, שֶׁיְּגִיעַת שְׁנֵיהֶם

V'Tumim. Also recall the period of the Second *Beis HaMikdash* when the *Shechinah* was "heard" through the *Bas Kol* (Divine Voice). In contemporary times, when we enjoy neither the presence of the *Urim V'Tumim* nor the *Bas Kol,* we can still perceive Hashem through His Book — the Torah[1] (*Maggidei HaEmes*).

◄§ The Lev Simchah's Sefer

> חסיד אחד נכנס פעם לקודש פנימה אצל אדמו״ר זצללה״ה הלב שמחה לבקש
> הסכמה עבור ספרו, אמר לו אדמו״ר זצ״ל ״גם אני הנני כותב ספר, ספר לא כל
> כך טוב, וכל מעשיך בספר נכתבים.״

When a scholar approached the *Lev Simchah* for an approbation (הַסְכָּמָה) for his forthcoming *sefer,* his response was, "I, too, am writing a *sefer,* though it is not that good a *sefer.* It is the book of my deeds, as it says, *and all your deeds are recorded in a Book*"[2] (*Maggidei HaEmes*).

◄§ Which Book?

> פירוש שמכל המעשים נעשו צירופין וצריך האדם לראות לגרום צירופין טובים
> באותיות התורה שהם חיות כל המעשים והמסתכל ויבין זאת לא יבוא לידי עבירה
> כנ״ל.

This phrase בְּסֵפֶר, *in a Book,* may refer to the Torah itself. Just as Hashem used the Torah as His blueprint for creating the universe, so too He sustains the world in direct proportion to our loyalty to the Torah. Through our actions, the sacred letters of the Torah — which according to tradition were used by Hashem as a means of maintaining the universe (cf. *Menachos* 29b, *Rashi* s.v. אחת) — are assisted in their mission of sustaining the universe. Upon realizing that our actions affect the very existence of the universe, we resolve not to sin (וְאֵין אַתָּה בָא לִידֵי עֲבֵרָה) (adapted from *Sfas Emes*).

2.

■ יָפֶה תַלְמוּד תּוֹרָה עִם דֶּרֶךְ אֶרֶץ — *Torah study is good together with an occupation.*

---

1. It is said of the Baal Shem Tov that he would always learn a passage of the Torah (while looking inside a *sefer*) before giving advice.
2. Editor's note: It can be said that each of us is writing a *sefer* — a record of our deeds.

[2] *Rabban Gamliel, the son of Rabbi Yehudah HaNasi says: Torah study is good together with an occupation, for exertion of them both makes sin forgotten.*

This *mishnah* has served as the basis for various approaches to living a Torah lifestyle while residing in a world permeated by values that are often inimical to Torah. This challenge is further complicated by the need to earn a livelihood. The renowned expression דֶּרֶךְ אֶרֶץ will be explored from the perspective of the *Sfas Emes* and other Chassidic commentators.

The term דֶּרֶךְ אֶרֶץ lends itself to various interpretations including the following: the necessity for an occupation to earn a livelihood; a proper social relationship with other people; and refined character traits. These variant interpretations often lead to differing treatments of this *mishnah*.

❖§ Not an Ideal State

אבל אם לא הי' חוטא כלל הי' מקבל עליו עול תורה וע"ז אי' לקמן שמעבירין עול ד"א . . .

והנה זה מבחי' עץ הדעת טוב ורע ונק' דרך ארץ . . . ות"ת הוא עץ החיים . . . וזהו עיקר התפארת להיות היראה ופחד הש"י גם כמו שהוא נסתר, וזה יר"ש בסתר ובגלוי וזה יפה ת"ת עם ד"א שיגיעת שניהם היינו יגיעת חיבור שניהם . . . משכחת עון כי הוא תיקון העוונות ובירור הקדושה.

In order to fully appreciate this *mishnah*, it is important to place it in the context of a later *mishnah* (3:6) which seemingly offers a totally different perspective on the issue of תּוֹרָה עִם דֶּרֶךְ אֶרֶץ. Instead of urging a symbiotic relationship between Torah and *Derech Eretz* as our *mishnah* seemingly does, we are assured, כָּל הַמְקַבֵּל עָלָיו עוֹל תּוֹרָה מַעֲבִירִין מִמֶּנּוּ . . . וְעוֹל דֶּרֶךְ אֶרֶץ, if we accept the challenge of a Torah life and all that this entails we need not worry about *"the yoke of worldly responsibilities,"* the pressures of everyday life.

We may reconcile this apparent contradiction by suggesting that the later *mishnah* is speaking about an ideal state that no longer exists while our *mishnah* pertains to the world in which we *presently* reside. Prior to Adam's sin, he enjoyed the ideal luxury of isolating himself from the outside world. He could completely commit himself to Torah (מְקַבֵּל עָלָיו עוֹל תּוֹרָה) without concerning himself about the necessity of earning a living (דֶּרֶךְ אֶרֶץ). However, after sinning, Adam and we, his descendants, were granted a new mission — which would help remedy his sin — to abide by the values of Torah while concurrently toiling for a living.

An analogy may be drawn between the contrasting approaches of these two *mishnahs* and the two trees planted in the middle of *Gan Eden*. The Tree of Life (עֵץ הַחַיִּים) symbolizes an ideal state in which we are fully immersed in the true source of life which is Torah. By partaking of the עֵץ הַדַּעַת טוֹב וָרָע, the *Tree of Knowledge of Good and Evil*, Adam regrettably opted for a lifestyle in which good and evil were intermingled. In such an environment, man's mission is no longer to completely isolate himself from his surroundings but rather to live a Torah life amidst the moral confusion of the world, and by doing so begin to remedy Adam's (and his descendants') sin of blurring the parameters of good and evil. In this light, we may derive additional insight from the following phrase: שֶׁיְּגִיעַת שְׁנֵיהֶם מַשְׁכַּחַת עָוֹן, the effort involved in harmoniously bringing *Derech Eretz* into Torah helps rectify Adam's sin (adapted from *Sfas Emes*).

✥ Practicing Torah While Engaging in Commerce

ששואלין אותו לעולם הבא שאלה ראשונה נשאת ונתת באמונה . . . ובמקום אחר אמרו חז"ל תחילת דינו של אדם על דברי תורה ונראה לבאר דשאלה אחת הוא דהא בהא תליא כיון דעסק במשא ומתן באמונה שפיר עסק בתורה דזוכר בפסוק לא תכחשו ונמצא לומד אז זה הפסוק . . . וזה כוונת המשנה יפה תלמוד תורה עם דרך ארץ, יפה דהיינו בשעה שעוסק בדרך ארץ דהיינו במשא ומתן ועוסק באמונה ונמצא לומד אז כמו שכתבנו, זה יפה וישר.

The famed Chassidic rebbe and scholar, R' Levi Yitzchak of Berditchev, interpreted this *mishnah* quite simply: While engaging in commerce, we enjoy numerous opportunities to practice the *dinim* (laws) of the Torah and to actually learn Torah. For example, when tempted to deceive a customer, we recall and *learn* the prohibition against lying, לֹא תְכַחֲשׁוּ וְלֹא תְשַׁקְּרוּ, *You shall not deny falsely, and you shall not lie* (*Vayikra* 19:11). Similarly, by avoiding defrauding a customer through the use of improper scales, we are remembering and studying the Torah's prohibition against such behavior (see *Devarim* 25:13-16, אֶבֶן שְׁלֵמָה וָצֶדֶק, *a perfect and honest weight*).

With this approach, we may resolve the renowned contradiction between Gemaras as to the first question that the soul is asked when standing in judgment before Hashem. In one instance, the Gemara relates that the soul is asked, "Did you deal honestly?" (*Shabbos* 31a). Elsewhere, the Gemara states that we are first called to account for the amount of time we dedicated to learn Torah (*Kiddushin* 40b). Based on our foregoing remarks, no contradictions exist between these two statements. The truly honest businessman will, of necessity, be constantly studying Torah in order to conduct his business affairs with halachic integrity. Of such a person, the *mishnah* can say, יָפֶה תַלְמוּד תּוֹרָה עִם דֶּרֶךְ אֶרֶץ, that an individual involved in both Torah and *Derech Eretz* simultaneously will be protected from sinning (*Maggidei HaEmes*).

✥ Leaving an Impact on the World

כי הלומד תורה ואינו עוסק בדרך ארץ הריהו דומה לארון מלא ספרים. דהארון

$\mathbb{R}$eb Simchah Bunim of Peshis'cha offered a parable to explain this *mishnah*. He compared someone involved in Torah but totally isolated from his peers to a bookcase that is laden with sacred volumes (סִפְרֵי קֹדֶשׁ). While this may seem admirable, obviously the full effect of the *sefarim* can only be experienced by *people* studying their contents, not by their mere lifeless presence in a bookcase. So too, studying Torah in complete isolation leaves almost little impact on the world beyond the immediate confines of the learner (adapted from *Maggidei HaEmes*).

◌§ The Primacy of Torah

הכוונה להרבה תורה עם מעט דרך ארץ, שהתורה תהיה העיקר, ולא לעשות את הטפל דהיינו המלאכה לעיקר ואת התורה לטפל.

$\mathbb{O}$ne should not misinterpret the mishnah as implying that there is equality between Torah and *Derech Eretz*. The preposition, עִם, *with*, seemingly connotes a secondary role to דֶּרֶךְ אֶרֶץ, which is, at best, a valued accessory to Torah[1] (*Beis Yisrael, Maggidei HaEmes*).

◌§ Changing Circumstances

כאשר בנו את ישיבת חכמי לובלין היה המצב הכספי קשה והופסקה העבודה, ורבי מאיר שפירא ז"ל רצה לנסוע לחו"ל לאסוף שם כסף עבור הישיבה. טרם נוסעו נכנס להפרד מרבו האדמו"ר מטשורטקוב ז"ל ונכנס גם לאאז"ל, אמר לו אאז"ל "איתא יפה תלמוד תורה עם דרך ארץ, לכאורה אם כן למה אצלנו בישיבות לא נוהגים כן, שילמדו וגם יעבדו, אלא משום שאיתא יפה ולא שמוכרח להיות כן, ובהיות והיום קשה לקיים זאת כמו שרואים ל"ע שמתקלקלים הרבה בחורי ישראל, אין צריכים לקיים זאת." ותשובה זו שמעה אחר כך בפי הר"מ שפירא ז"ל מענה לאותם שקינטרוהו בקושיא זו.

$\mathbb{P}$rior to embarking on a fund-raising trip to America, Rav Meir Shapiro visited the *Imrei Emes*. The latter, anticipating the frequently raised question, "Why don't *yeshivos* arrange for a dual program whereby *talmidim* would learn and simultaneously earn a livelihood as the *mishnah* recommends?" answered as follows: Our *mishnah* uses the term יָפֶה, implying that this is merely a commendable idea but not an absolute requirement. Though

---

1. Editor's Note: See also *Tosfos Yeshanim, Yoma* 85b s.v. תשובה and *Kovetz Maamarim* by Rav Elchonon Wasserman for a further discussion of this concept.

מַשְׁכַּחַת עָוֹן. וְכָל תּוֹרָה שֶׁאֵין עִמָּהּ מְלָאכָה, סוֹפָהּ ‎ב / ב
בְּטֵלָה וְגוֹרֶרֶת עָוֹן. וְכָל הָעוֹסְקִים עִם הַצִּבּוּר, יִהְיוּ
עוֹסְקִים עִמָּהֶם לְשֵׁם שָׁמַיִם, שֶׁזְּכוּת אֲבוֹתָם מְסַיַּעְתָּם,

the approach recommended by our *mishnah* may have been ideal at one time,
experience shows that in today's world combining the two is more difficult and
fraught with danger.

The *Pnei Menachem* reported that Rav Shapiro successfully utilized this
approach during his fund-raising trip (*Maggidei HaEmes*).

■ שֶׁיְּגִיעַת שְׁנֵיהֶם מַשְׁכַּחַת עָוֹן — *For the exertion of them both makes sin
forgotten.*

❧ Not Having Time to Sin

> אדמו"ר זצ"ל מקאצק אמר "איני רוצה חסידים שלא יחטאו רק מחמת האיסור
> לחטוא, אלא שלא יהיה להם פנאי לחטוא".

The *mishnah* is describing an idyllic state — (מַשְׁכַּחַת עָוֹן) not having enough
time to sin. The Kotzker would say, "I wish to have *chassidim* who not
only do not even desire to sin but who do not even have time to sin" (*Maggidei
HaEmes*).

> "יפה תלמוד תורה עם דרך ארץ" היינו שאברך לומד בכולל ועקרת הבית
> דואגת לפרנסת הבית, "שיגיעת שניהם משכחת עון."

❧ An Ideal Partnership

The *Lev Simchah* discerned from this *mishnah* an ideal partnership for young
couples. The husband would labor in Torah, studying in *kollel,* and his wife
would provide the wherewithal for his learning through her work (*Maggidei
HaEmes*).

■ וְכָל תּוֹרָה שֶׁאֵין עִמָּהּ מְלָאכָה — *All Torah study that is not joined with
work.*

❧ Bring the Torah Into Daily Life

> שאינו מכניס אור התורה בעניני מעשיו.

All Torah study that is not joined with work will cease in the end, and leads to sin. All who exert themselves for the community should exert themselves for the sake of Heaven, for then the merit of their forefathers aids them and their righteousness endures forever. Nevertheless, as

---

The term מְלָאכָה, *work,* refers to the difficult challenge of infusing our mundane activities (e.g. eating, sleeping, earning a livelihood) with the spirit of Torah. The most efficacious method of accomplishing this formidable goal is to perform *mitzvos* that relate to every aspect of our lives (e.g. *berachos* before eating). Alternatively, the *mishnah* may be encouraging us to work hard at learning Torah. It is only through in-depth study involving a great deal of effort that one can succeed in *Limud HaTorah.*

■ וְכָל הָעוֹסְקִים עִם הַצִּבּוּר יִהְיוּ עוֹסְקִים עִמָּהֶם לְשֵׁם שָׁמַיִם — *All who exert themselves for the community should exert themselves for the sake of Heaven.*

◄§ Neither Torah nor Derech Eretz

קאי אדלעיל כי העוסקי צבור אין להם פנאי לא לתורה ולא לדרך ארץ מכל מקום הוה ליה כתורה עם דרך ארץ.

The relationship between this concluding phrase and the rest of the *mishnah* may be as follows: Though you may be immersed in communal affairs (עוֹסְקִים בְּצָרְכֵי צִבּוּר), leaving no time for either Torah or *Derech Eretz,* I will consider your sacred endeavors as if you accomplished both Torah and *Derech Eretz.*

■ זְכוּת אֲבוֹתָם מְסַיַּעְתָּם. . . וְאַתֶּם, מַעֲלֶה אֲנִי עֲלֵיכֶם שָׂכָר הַרְבֵּה — *The merit of their forefathers aids them . . . Nevertheless, as for you, I [God] will bestow upon you a great reward.*

◄§ Your Ancestor's Merit: Your Reward

יש לפרש ואתם אך על פי שיש לכם הסיוע מזכות אבות, מעלה אני עליכם כאילו עשיתם.

The apparently redundant term וְאַתֶּם, *and you,* is intended to assure those who are immersed in communal activities: Although your success is prima-

וְצִדְקָתָם עוֹמֶדֶת לָעַד. וְאַתֶּם, מַעֲלֶה אֲנִי עֲלֵיכֶם שָׂכָר הַרְבֵּה כְּאִלּוּ עֲשִׂיתֶם.

[ג] הֱווּ זְהִירִין בָּרָשׁוּת, שֶׁאֵין מְקָרְבִין לוֹ לְאָדָם אֶלָּא לְצֹרֶךְ עַצְמָן; נִרְאִין כְּאוֹהֲבִין בִּשְׁעַת הֲנָאָתָן, וְאֵין עוֹמְדִין לוֹ לְאָדָם בִּשְׁעַת דָּחֳקוֹ.

---

rily in the merit of your ancestors (זְכוּת אֲבוֹתָם מְסַיַּעְתָּם), I will reward you as if you achieved everything in *your* own merit (*Maggidei HaEmes, Lev Simchah*).

3.

■ . . . *Beware of rulers* . . . — הֱווּ זְהִירִין בָּרָשׁוּת ■

◈§ Advice for the Communal Activist

אח״כ כ׳ היו זהירין ברשות כי העוסקי צבור צריכין הרבה פעמים להרשות ומלכות ולזה לא אמר הוא הי׳ אומר כדלקמן משום דענין דלהכן הוא עם הקודם.

This *mishnah* lacks the usual preface (הוּא הָיָה אוֹמֵר, *he used to say*), which would have implied that this is a new concept. This leads us to assume that the Tanna (author of the *mishnah*) is continuing his previous statement. He is exhorting the communal activists, mentioned in the previous *mishnah*, not to become needlessly close to the members of government.

◈§ More Than Mere Good Advice

לכאורה מה בכך ואטו עצה טוב קמ״ל להציל ממונו אידו דאפסיד אנפשי׳ ואולי כיון שלא יועיל שייך נמי לא תחנם.

The *mishnah* is not merely warning us to avoid an unnecessarily close relationship with the government; it may be *prohibiting* such a relationship. This is based on the *pasuk* of וְלֹא תְחָנֵּם, *nor shall you show them favor* (*Devarim* 7:2), which prohibits granting favors to gentiles. While such gratuities may be permitted under extraordinary circumstances when *Klal Yisrael's* interest are at stake, the *mishnah* warns us that involvement of this kind with the gentile world is rarely productive.

for you, I [God] will bestow upon you a great reward, as if you had accomplished it on your own.

[3] *Beware of rulers, for they befriend someone only for their own benefit; they act friendly when it benefits them, but they do not stand by someone in his time of need.*

◆§ Fact, Not a Criticism

דכאן אינו מדבר בגנותן רק כך דרך ונימוס מלכות ורשות חקור דבר לא להחניף.

This *mishnah* should not be interpreted as denigrating gentile rulers. Rather, it is merely warning Jewish leaders of the futility of any effort at ingratiating themselves with non-Jewish rulers. Despite their apparent interest in our overtures, in reality they are not susceptible to such influences.

■ הֱווּ זְהִירִין בָּרְשׁוּת . . . נִרְאִין כְּאוֹהֲבִין בְּשָׁעַת הֲנָאָתָן, וְאֵין עוֹמְדִין לוֹ לָאָדָם בְּשָׁעַת דָּחֳקוֹ — *Beware of rulers . . . they act friendly when it benefits them, but they do not stand by someone in his time of need.*

◆§ The Danger of Becoming Preoccupied With Mundane Matters

היינו דבר הרשות שזה צריך זהירות ושמירה גדולה כי היצר הרע מסתיר בתאוות דאדם אכילה שתיה כו' שיהיה נראה כמעורב תוך הקדושה ונראין כאוהבין היינו שמדובקין בהקדושה ובאמת אין מקרבין עצמן להקדושה רק לצורך עצמן לגנוב ושיתדבק האדם בהתאוות.

איתא בשפת אמת שהכוונה להיות נזהר בדברי הרשות, שאין מקרבין לו לאדם אלא בשעת הנאתן, ההנאה שיש לאדם היא רק רגע אחד, וכשעובר הרגע רואה שאין זה כלום, ואין עומדין לו לאדם בשעת דחקו, אלא עוד להיפך כדאיתא בגמ' יורד ומתעה ועולה ומרגיז נוטל רשות וכו' הוא נוטל הרשות, היצה"ר מפתהו שזה מצוה, והאדם אינו רואה שזה אינו כלום ושיבא לו רק היזק מזה.

The term רָשׁוּת may be interpreted as if it were read רְשׁוּת, *optional matters*. The *mishnah* warns us to be exceedingly careful not to become *immersed* in activities that are not required by the Torah. While it is undoubtedly necessary to eat, drink and sleep, and to engage in other mundane activities in order to sustain oneself, we are warned that the יֵצֶר הָרָע (Evil Inclination) seduces us to become *immersed* in such activities. The *mishnah* notes the insidious

[ד] הוּא הָיָה אוֹמֵר: עֲשֵׂה רְצוֹנוֹ כִּרְצוֹנֶךָ, כְּדֵי שֶׁיַּעֲשֶׂה רְצוֹנְךָ כִּרְצוֹנוֹ. בַּטֵּל רְצוֹנְךָ מִפְּנֵי רְצוֹנוֹ, כְּדֵי שֶׁיְּבַטֵּל רְצוֹן אֲחֵרִים מִפְּנֵי רְצוֹנֶךָ.

nature of the Evil Inclination as it seeks to subvert us, appearing as our friend (נִרְאִין כְּאוֹהֲבִין) at first — rationalizing that food and drink could be catalysts to attaining a higher level of Divine service.[1] However, in reality all this is merely a ploy to reach its own true objective which is inveigling us to become infatuated with materialism. Once the momentary pleasure derived from indulging our passions has passed, we realize how much spirituality we have sacrificed for a fleeting sensation. And now we are truly alone. As the *mishnah* concludes, in our time of need — when we are called to Judgment — instead of defending us, the יֵצֶר הָרָע abandons us (אֵין עוֹמְדִין לוֹ לָאָדָם בִּשְׁעַת דָּחֳקוֹ).

In a similar vein, the *Pnei Menachem* noted the wide discrepancy between the fleeting pleasures derived from succumbing to one's material urges and the lifelong consequences of sinning. He cited the Gemara (*Bava Basra* 16a) stating that the *Yetzer Hara* lures man and induces him to sin by persuading him that he is actually performing a *mitzvah* and then almost immediately seeks to incite Hashem's anger by denouncing the sinner, attempting to prosecute him for that very same sin (*Maggidei HaEmes*).

This approach, interpreting רָשׁוּת as *material concerns*, may be reconciled with the traditional interpretation of רָשׁוּת referring to government officials. This follows if we bear in mind that Hashem has delegated much of the administration of the secular world to "heavenly officials" or angels. [See *Ramban* (*Vayikra* 18:25 ד"ה ותמה) who expounds upon the theme that the Jew living in the Diaspora is subject, to an extent, to the control of שָׂרִים. A distinction may also be made between the six weekdays in which Hashem has empowered the angels to bestow His Blessings on *Klal Yisrael* and Shabbos when Hashem Himself showers His Blessing upon us.] By indulging unnecessarily in mundane pursuits and distancing ourselves, as it were, from the *Shechinah*, we become subject to the dominion of those Divine Forces. On the other hand, one who is immersed in Torah is virtually immune from the importuning of the *Yetzer Hara* and the control of Hashem's servitors (adapted from *Sfas Emes*).

4.

■ עֲשֵׂה רְצוֹנוֹ כִּרְצוֹנֶךָ כְּדֵי שֶׁיַּעֲשֶׂה רְצוֹנְךָ כִּרְצוֹנוֹ — *Treat His will as if it were your own will, so that He will treat your will as if it were His will.*

---

1. While it is theoretically possible to utilize food and drink as a means of Divine Service, such an approach is usually not successful and is, in fact, fraught with risks.

[4] *He used to say: Treat His will as if it were your own will, so that He will treat your will as if it were His will. Nulify your will in the face of His will, so that He will nullify the will of others in the face of your will.*

◆§ Make Hashem an Equal Partner

ודאי יש לאדם לעשות רצון הבורא ב״ה ביותר רצון וחשק ותשוקה מרצון עצמו,
אבל יש לפרש בעשיות רצונך תעשה רצונו כל כך כמו רצונך שישתתף רצון
המקום בכל דרכיו להיות לשם שמים ולא יהיה בהמעשה עבור רצונו יותר מעבור
רצון המקום שבזה המעשה עצמו ועל ידי זה לא יהיה לו רצון אחר כלל וזה
שכתוב שיעשה רצונך כרצונו כלומר שלא יהיה לך רצון רק לעשות רצונו
יתברך.

A simple reading of the *mishnah* seems to suggest that we fulfill Hashem's will with the same enthusiasm that we display in fulfilling our own desires. However, this approach seems difficult. Should we not fulfill Hashem's wishes with *greater* enthusiasm than our own wishes?

Upon further analysis, the *mishnah* is urging us that as we perform our own pursuits (רְצוֹנְךָ), Hashem should be viewed as an "equal" partner. We should consider Hashem's wishes (רְצוֹנוֹ) as much as our own even when we conduct our personal affairs. While this charge may seem unrealistic at first, the *mishnah* assures us that we will be rewarded for our efforts. כְּדֵי שֶׁיַּעֲשֶׂה רְצוֹנְךָ כִּרְצוֹנוֹ, eventually your wishes will converge with His. A time will come when every action of yours, no matter how mundane, will be undertaken to fulfill Hashem's will.

◆§ Perform Mitzvos as Swiftly as Possible

כמו שמרגיש האדם חמדה ורצון בלבו מיד עושה הדבר בלי ישוב לבד כשיש ס'
איסור בדבר כן צריך להיות כשמרגיש האדם שכן רצון הקב״ה.

Just as you would seek to satisfy your personal cravings almost instantaneously (assuming that no halachic problems were involved in their resolution), so too attempt to fulfill Hashem's desires as soon as possible.

◆§ Though You Lack Enthusiasm

ע״י שהאדם עושה רצון השי״ת במ״ע שהוא נגד רצונו היינו שעדיין אין רצון
האדם בשלימות להסכים לרצון השי״ת עכ״ז עושה רצון המקום ב״ה בחשק גדול

כמו שהי' עושה רצון של עצמו בחשק ותאוה ושמחה, כן עושה רצון השי"ת שאין
גוף רצונו מושך לזה עדיין, עי"ז מועיל שהשי"ת מכניע רצון האדם להיות שוה
ומוסכם לרצון השי"ת וז"ש שיעשה רצונך שיהי' כרצונו.

On occasion, we experience difficulty in mustering sufficient enthusiasm to
perform *mitzvos*. The *mishnah* encourages us to overcome this momentary
hurdle and nonetheless fulfill Hashem's will with the same enthusiasm that we
would display for our own needs. While such an effort may be difficult at first,
the *mishnah* assures us that in turn, Hashem will subdue our Evil Inclination
so that ultimately *we* will genuinely desire to perform His will.

◦§A Plea for Sincerity

ויש לפרש כרצונך כפשוטו שיהי' המעשה כפי הרצון לא בשקר, כי באמת נמצא
רצון טוב בלב כל איש ישראל, ומה שעושין יותר מהרצון אינו דבר של קיימא
דכתיב דובר שקרים לא יכון כו' אך אם באמת עושה ככל רצונו אף אם הוא מעט
יש בו ברכה וע"ז נאמר טוב מעט בכוונה . . . והשכר ע"ז שיעשה רצונך כרצונו
כלומר כמו שקשה להיות רצון האדם בשלימות כמו המעשה כמו כן קשה
לתחתונים לקבל השפעת השי"ת כפי רצונו ב"ה ולכן צריך ההשפעה להשתנות
אך הבר לבב שעושה כל מעשיו כפי רצונו ממש משלם לו הקב"ה שעושה לו כל
צרכו כרצונו ית' פי' בלי השתנות כנ"ל. וזה יי"ל ג"כ ויעש כן אהרן שלא שינה
פי' שלא נמצא במעשה אהרן שינוי והי' המעשה ממש כמו הרצון.

The opening phrase of our *mishnah* may actually be an eloquent plea for
complete sincerity in performing *mitzvos*. Fulfill Hashem's will (עֲשֵׂה רְצוֹנוֹ)
with all your desire (רְצוֹנֶךְ) — and *not beyond* the sincere desires of your heart.
Mitzvos performed insincerely are usually short lived and lack consistency. As
David states: דֹּבֵר שְׁקָרִים לֹא יִכּוֹן לְנֶגֶד עֵינָי, *one who speaks falsely* — or performs
mitzvos in an insincere manner — *shall not be established before my eyes,* cannot
stand in my presence (*Tehillim* 101:7). It is preferable to do less but with sincerity
than to perform more insincerely. (Of course we are merely referring to the
various חוּמְרוֹת, *stringencies*, that one may undertake. The *mitzvah* itself must
be performed regardless of our lack of inner desire to do so.)

The reward for such sincerity is clearly stated in the following phrase: שֶׁיַעֲשֶׂה
רְצוֹנֶךְ כִּרְצוֹנוֹ, *He will treat your will as if it were His will.* Just as we fulfilled His
will exactly, in accordance with the desires of our heart, so too will He bestow
His blessings upon us without change (in its pure form).[1] Frequently, Hashem
sees fit to "package" His blessings in a more material fashion (rather than with
spiritual *berachos*) for the benefit of mortals. However, someone on a high level
(מַדְרֵגָה), who only performs *mitzvos* with the purest motives, will merit to
receive Hashem's bounty in its absolute form.

---

1. For expansion of this theme see *The Three Festivals*, p. 377.

In this light, we may derive additional meaning from the comment of *Chazal* (*Bamidbar* 8:3, *Rashi* s.v. ויעש) that Aaron performed the *mitzvah* of kindling the Menorah without deviating from Hashem's wishes (שֶׁלֹּא שִׁנָּה). While Aaron would surely not have disobeyed or deviated in any way from Hashem's will regarding the performance of the *mitzvah*, *Chazal* are emphasizing that Aaron performed this *mitzvah* with complete sincerity. There was no inconsistency between his heart's desire and his performance of the *mitzvah*; they were in complete harmony.

■ בַּטֵּל רְצוֹנְךָ מִפְּנֵי רְצוֹנוֹ — *Nullify your will in the face of His will.* ■

◆§ Fulfilling the Divine Will

> וסיפא בטל רצונך מפני רצונו יש לפרש ג״כ להיפוך מפשוטו, כשעושה רצון
> המקום ב״ה לא יהי׳ מעורב רצון עצמו כלל אף לקבל פרס וכדומה, הגם שצריך
> להיות שמח בעשיות המצוה שזוכה לעשות רצון הקב״ה, מ״מ יהי׳ עיקר העשי׳
> כדי לעשות רצונו ב״ה בלבד, ורצון עצמותו יתבטל לעיקר המכוון לעשות רצון
> המקום ב״ה כנ״ל, וז״ש באהרן ויעש כן פרש״י שלא שינה ואיך בכח אנושי
> לעשות כל המצוה ממש כאשר צוה השי״ת והלא גבהו דרכיו כו׳ אך ע״י שמבטל
> באמת כל רצון עצמו ועושה רק כדי לעשות רצונו ית׳ בלבד כאשר צוה, נקרא
> בן שעשה.
> כי ע״ז אמרו ז״ל מחשבה טובה הקב״ה מצרפה למעשה רק שצריך להיות מוכן
> בכל רצונו לעשות רק רצון המקום ב״ה.

When performing Hashem's will, *negate* your own wishes. In an ideal state, personal pleasure that may be derived from performing a *mitzvah* (or any other consideration such as the reward anticipated for performing the *mitzvah*) should play no role. While this request seems impossible — how can anyone negate the personal pleasure derived from doing *mitzvos* — the goodwill and favor (רָצוֹן) engendered by performing *mitzvos* solely because of Hashem's will will eventually enable us to reach that lofty state. As *Chazal* say, מַחֲשָׁבָה טוֹבָה הקב״ה מְצָרְפָה לְמַעֲשֶׂה, Hashem considers the intention (*thought*) of performing a *mitzvah* without any ulterior motives to be as significant as if one actually performed the *mitzvah* (*Kiddushin* 40a).

Aaron served as a prime example of performing *mitzvos* — or at least seeking to perform *mitzvos* — altruistically. *Chazal* relate that when kindling the Menorah he never deviated from Hashem's wishes. It seems that *Chazal* are emphasizing the purity of his intention — Aaron did not deviate even for a moment to think of his personal stake in the *mitzvah*.

◆§ As You Would Nullify Prohibited Food

> פי׳ ביטול שאינו כלל כמו ביטול איסור שע״י שיש הרבה היתר בטל ונהפך איסור

להיות היתר כן יהי' בעיני האדם חשבון גודל רצון הקב"ה נגד רצונו שעי"ז
כשירגיש שכך רצון הקב"ה יהי' רצונו בטל ממש כעפר כאילו אינו כלל ועי"ז
זוכה להיות נהפך רצונו ממש לטוב.
וזה הענין דכתיב אשר יעשה אותם האדם בהם . . . ע"י שעושה רצון הקב"ה
בחשק עצום ס' פעמים ויותר וזהו ג"כ ענין בע"ת שהמרירות עצום יותר מ"ס
פעמים נגד תאות העבירה . . .

O ur *mishnah* judiciously uses the term בָּטֵל (nullify), which is usually associated with prohibited food, to demonstrate the most effective way of negating one's passion. When a small amount of non-kosher food is nullified in sixty
times as much kosher food, a radical transformation occurs. The small proportion of non-kosher is not merely nullified; it actually is transformed into kosher
food (cf. *Rosh, Chulin* 7:37 נהפך אסור להיות התר). So too, in the presence of the
Divine will, *our* wishes simply cease to exist. Every limb and organ of the body
previously dedicated to the fulfillment of material pleasures is now channeled
into the pursuit of spirituality.

The analogy between the nullification of non-kosher food and negating
physical passion may be drawn even further. By performing Hashem's will
with sixty times the enthusiasm that we display for fulfilling our personal
needs, we can be assured that our capacity for evil will become defunct. As the
Torah says, וָחַי בָּהֶם, *by which he shall live* (*Vayikra* 18:5) — by observing
mitzvos with enthusiasm, we merit renewed spiritual life in which every organ
of our body sheds its previous materialistic inclinations and becomes a vehicle
to fulfill Hashem's will. In fact, within the context of בְּטוּל חָמֵץ (nullification of
chametz) we find an allusion to the most effective method of nullifying the
Evil Inclination (בְּטוּל יֵצֶר הָרָע). This can be achieved if we consider everything
other than the Divine will as "mere dust."[1]

In this light, we can appreciate the special role of the *baal teshuvah* who not
only repents but also bitterly regrets his past transgressions with sixty times as
much passion as he had displayed when originally performing those transgressions. Such an exalted individual has indeed attained the state of בַּטֵל רְצוֹנְךָ, the
nullification of his past sins. This individual has not only repented but has
actually transformed his sins into sources of merit. (Cf. our commentary on the
Yamim Noraim in *Days of Awe*, pp. 243-251, 256-260 discussing the transformation of *aveiros* into *mitzvos* and the special role reserved for *baalei teshuvah*.)

In conclusion, we note that the term בְּטוּל אָסוּרִים, used to describe the nullification of non-kosher food, may also allude to the process through which the
passion to sin (רְצוֹנְךָ, *your desire*) is transformed into the desire to serve Hashem
(רְצוֹנוֹ, *His desire*).

---

1. Editor's Note: The expression "mere dust" refers to the declaration recited at the time of
completion of the search for *chametz* (בְּדִיקַת חָמֵץ). We state that all *chametz* is considered as עַפְרָא
דְאַרְעָא, *dust of the earth*. Please refer to ArtScroll's *The Pesach Haggadah with Ideas and Insights
of the Sfas Emes*, pp. 28-33, for a detailed discussion of this concept.

◆§ The Reward for Sincerely Performing Mitzvos

וי״ל עוד סיום המשנה בטל רצונך כו׳ שג״כ שכר אדם הנ״ל שעושה המעשים רק
כפי הרצון, . . . ולכן בשכל המעשים כפי הרצון ואין מתגברין עליו א״כ יכול
אח״כ לתקן הכל ע״י ביטול רצונו לרצון השי״ת.

Please refer to our earlier commentary emphasizing עֲשֵׂה רְצוֹנְךָ, stating
that *mitzvos* be performed at a level that is consistent with — and not
beyond — his inner desire. This passage describes the reward for such sincerity
— eventually his wishes will become identical with those of Hashem.

◆§ Positive and Negative Commandments

ביאור הענין שיש מ״ע ול״ת ע״י שהאדם עושה רצון השי״ת במ״ע שהוא נגד
רצונו היינו שעדיין אין רצון האדם בשלימות להסכים לרצון השי״ת עכ״ז עושה
רצון המקום ב״ה בחשק גדול כמו שהי׳ עושה רצון של עצמו בחשק ותאוה
ושימחה, כן עושה רצון השי״ת [אע״פ] שאין גוף רצונו מושך לזה עדיין, עי״ז
מועיל שהשי״ת מכניע רצון האדם להיות שוה ומוסכם לרצון השי״ת וז״ש
שיעשה רצונך שיהי׳ כרצונו
וכן להיפוך ע״י שהאדם שומר עצמו מעשות הרע נגד רצון המקום אף שרצונו
וחשקו מושכין אותו מ״מ דוחה רצונו בחשבו איך שתאותו . . . בטל באלף אלפים
נגד רצון השי״ת ועי״ז מבטל רצונו מפני רצון המקום.

The *mishnah* is emphasizing both phases of observing *mitzvos*. By performing מִצְוֹת עֲשֵׂה, *positive commandments*, with the same enthusiasm that we
ordinarily reserve for our mundane needs — despite our initial lack of eagerness — we are practicing עֲשֵׂה רְצוֹנוֹ כִּרְצוֹנְךָ, *treat His will as if it were your own
will*. Then by refraining from violating Hashem's commandments, realizing
that our wishes are null and void (בָּטֵל) compared to the Divine Will, we are
practicing בַּטֵּל רְצוֹנְךָ מִפְּנֵי רְצוֹנוֹ, *nullify your will before His will*.

◆§ Acknowledge Hashem's Role
in Your Spiritual Accomplishments

פי׳ שאחר תיקון המעשים צריכין לבטל הכל אליו ית׳, כי בכ״מ שיש יותר תיקון
שולט היצה״ר בענין מי שגדול מחבירו יצרו גדול ממנו, לכן העצה להתבטל אליו
ית׳ ועשה רצונו הוא בחי׳ תשוקה ואהבה ושולט ע״ז עה״ר, והעצה אח״כ
להתבטל רק אליו ית׳ ועי״ז יבטל רצון אחרים שלא יתערב באהבה זו אהבות
ורצונות זרים, וזה הגמר להתבטל אליו שע״ז זוכין לסיוע הבא מהשמים.

The *mishnah* may be referring to the individual who has made great strides
in his pursuit of *Avodas Hashem*. He has already attained the previous

objective of making his wishes identical with those of Hashem (עֲשֵׂה רְצוֹנוֹ כִּרְצוֹנֶךָ). Now, having achieved this lofty spiritual level, new challenges occur. The always creative *Yetzer Hara* devises new methods for causing him to sin. As *Chazal* relate, כָּל הַגָּדוֹל מֵחֲבֵרוֹ יִצְרוֹ גָדוֹל מִמֶּנּוּ, *the greater one is, the greater his temptation to sin* (*Succah* 52a).

The best manner of dealing with these new challenges is to identify those emotions that were instrumental in achieving our initial strides and dedicate them totally to Divine service. For example, if my initial spiritual accomplishments were inspired by an innate sense of אַהֲבַת ה׳, *love of Hashem*, then examine that innate sense of love to ensure that it has not become diluted with conflicting emotions (e. g. being passionate about values that conflict with Torah). As the *mishnah* continues: בַּטֵּל רְצוֹנְךָ מִפְּנֵי רְצוֹנוֹ — negate your innermost wishes, your emotions (רְצוֹנְךָ) and realize that all that you have accomplished with those emotions was achieved with Hashem's help. Subsequently, it is up to you to ensure that these emotions remain totally committed to serving Him (adapted from *Sfas Emes*).

⋖§ Let the "Pintele Yid" Surface

דהחוקרים מקשים איך שייך ציווי על אהבה שהיא תלוי׳ בטבע האוהב, ובוודאי להנטבעים בטבע היא קושיא אבל בנ״י הם מוכנים למסור נפשם למעלה מן הטבע, ובאמת כפי מציאת מסירת נפש באיש ישראל כך גדר האהבה אצלו ולכן אחר מס״נ באחד כתיב ואהבת וע״ז אמרו בטל רצונך מפני רצונו פי׳ כדי שיתגלה לך רצון האמת אליו ית״ש, וכן הפי׳ מסירת נפש, נפש הוא רצון, וע״י ביטול הרצונות שלא לה׳ המה, אז זוכה להתגלות רצון האמת.

Philosophers frequently experience difficulty with the Torah's commandment of וְאָהַבְתָּ אֵת ה׳ אֱלֹהֶיךָ, *You shall love Hashem your God* (*Devarim* 6:5), wondering how one can be *commanded* to love. After all, love is an emotion which is very much contingent upon one's unique personality.

This question is only valid from the perspective of one who is immersed in the natural world (טֶבַע) with all its limitations. However, every Jew is blessed with the capacity to live a "supernatural" existence and is even willing to give up his very life for Hashem's Torah when necessary. Such selfless dedication is not only based on the innate love that every Jew has for his Creator but also leads to an even more intense love of Hashem. This association between מְסִירַת נֶפֶשׁ (giving one's life for Hashem) and intensified *Ahavas Hashem* can be seen from the placement of וְאָהַבְתָּ, the commandment to love Hashem, **after** *Shema Yisrael*, from which we derive the obligation of *mesiras nefesh*.

In this light, we may interpret the phrase בַּטֵּל רְצוֹנְךָ in the following manner: Negate all other desires (בַּטֵּל) that may motivate your behavior in favor of *your innate desire* (רְצוֹנְךָ) to love Hashem, a concept frequently known as the "*pintele Yid*". In fact, the term מְסִירַת נֶפֶשׁ, literally translated as "yielding one's soul," may simply mean yielding one's desires (cf. *Bereishis* 23:8 where the term נֶפֶשׁ is interpreted by *Rashi* as *desire*).

❧ The Final Words of the Bendiner Rav

אחרי סעודת ליל שבת קודש ו' באדר שנת תרצ"ה, הגיעו רגעיו האחרונים של הרב מבנדין זצ"ל. שמעו אותו קורא ״אבא רחימא, אם זה רצונך, אנא שיהיה כמו שאתה רוצה,״ ויצאה נשמתו בטהרה.

The final words of the Bendiner Rav (son-in-law of the *Sfas Emes*) are a perfect example of the *mesiras nefesh* called for in our *mishnah*. After completing his Friday night meal and sensing that his end was near, he exclaimed, "Merciful Father, if this is Your wish (that I die), it is also my wish." With this powerful paraphrase of our *mishnah*, this great *tzaddik* expired (*Maggidei HaEmes*).

❧ Pesach and Shavuos

פסח הוא זמן חירותנו ואין בו שעבוד מלכיות והשאור שבעסה גם כן כלה ואז הזמן של מה דאיתא עשה רצונו כרצונך. בשבועות הוא הזמן של בטל רצונך מפני רצונו כדאיתא שאז הוא ביטול היצר הרע.

These two segments of the *mishnah*, עֲשֵׂה and בַּטֵּל, may allude to two *Yamim Tovim*. On Pesach, the time of our spiritual and physical freedom, עֲשֵׂה רְצוֹנוֹ כִּרְצוֹנֶךָ, we are *liberated* from the effects of the *Yetzer Hara* (which is compared to leavened dough, *chametz*). However, the task of *eliminating* the Yetzer Hara is left for Shavuos (בַּטֵּל רְצוֹנְךָ מִפְּנֵי רְצוֹנוֹ), as evil loses its viability on the occasion of the Giving of the Torah (cf. *The Three Festivals*, p. 230, for a discussion of this theme) (*Imrei Emes* in *Maggidei HaEmes*).

■ כְּדֵי שֶׁיְּבַטֵּל רְצוֹן אֲחֵרִים — *So that He will nullify the will of others.* ■

❧ Who Are the "Others"?

יפר עצת כל הקמים עליך לרעה ואני שמעתי שאין זה אלא דרך כבוד כלפי מעלה . . . (לשון הרע״ב)

דכיון שעושה רצון שמים למה ירצה שיבטל רצונו ית' וי״ל כי וודאי רצון אחרים הוא הפורענויות כי מאתו ית' לא תצא שום דבר רע רק טוב אך המקטרגים כו'. יבטל רצון אחרים היינו שרים סובבים.

יי״ל רצון אחרים היינו המחשבות הזרות של האדם יתבטלו ממנו על ידי שהוא יבטל רצונו להשי״ת.

[ה] הִלֵּל אוֹמֵר: אַל תִּפְרוֹשׁ מִן הַצִּבּוּר, וְאַל תַּאֲמִין
בְּעַצְמְךָ עַד יוֹם מוֹתְךָ, וְאַל תָּדִין אֶת חֲבֵרְךָ עַד
שֶׁתַּגִּיעַ לִמְקוֹמוֹ, וְאַל תֹּאמַר דָּבָר שֶׁאִי אֶפְשָׁר לִשְׁמוֹעַ,
שֶׁסּוֹפוֹ לְהִשָּׁמַע. וְאַל תֹּאמַר לִכְשֶׁאֶפָּנֶה אֶשְׁנֶה, שֶׁמָּא
לֹא תִפָּנֶה.

Our discussion of this segment of the *mishnah* concludes with an overview of the various interpretations of the phrase רְצוֹן אֲחֵרִים, *the will of others*. Who are these "others" whose will must be thwarted?

The *Bartenura* offers two explanations of this phrase. Firstly, this refers to all of *Klal Yisrael's* opponents whose evil designs will be foiled if we negate our will to that of Hashem. Then, the *Bartenura* suggests that the term "others" is actually a euphemism for Hashem Who will "negate" His will in favor of yours, if *Klal Yisrael* is found deserving. It seems difficult to comprehend that someone whose primary objective is to fulfill Hashem's will should simultaneously seek to nullify His wishes. Perhaps, the *Bartenura* is referring to those forces which seek to harm *Klal Yisrael* (i.e. Satan) and are alluded to by the term "others." All those elements, agents of Hashem whose objective is to punish an errant Jewish people, will be thwarted if we negate our wishes to Hashem's.

In a similar vein, the *Imrei Emes* explained that the term אֲחֵרִים, *others*, refers to the angels that represent the interests of the various gentile nations (e.g. the angel of Egypt), whose attempts to harm *Klal Yisrael* will not be realized.

However, the term אֲחֵרִים may refer to conflicting emotions within the Jewish soul (e. g. an affinity for values that are inimical to Torah). In the merit of negating your wishes to His, Hashem will ensure that those "impure" and baser instincts — often clashing with *Ahavas Hashem* —will be negated.

5.

■ אַל תִּפְרוֹשׁ מִן הַצִּבּוּר — *Do not separate yourself from the community.* ■

◆§ Even if You Can Accomplish More by Yourself

אף שבפני עצמו יש לו התרוממות מדריגה.

While the need to participate in one's community seems obvious, in reality, the *mishnah* is urging one to collaborate with the community even if you feel otherwise. You may believe that you would be far more successful if you carried out this particular mission alone, but אַל תִּפְרוֹשׁ, *do not separate yourself*.

[5] *Hillel says: Do not separate yourself from the community; do not believe in yourself until the day you die; do not judge your fellow until you have reached his place; do not make a statement that cannot be easily understood on the ground that it will be understood eventually; and do not say, "When I am free I will study," for perhaps you will not become free.*

■ וְאַל תַּאֲמִין בְּעַצְמְךָ עַד יוֹם מוֹתְךָ — *Do not believe in yourself until the day you die.*

◆§ Believing in Oneself on the Day of One's Death

שאז ביום המיתה גופא אינו בכלל זה כי היצה"ר פוסק ממנו (הגם דמצינו בספרים שרק אז מתעצם היצה"ר י"ל ברשע איירי שם וכאן בצדיק כמ"ש אין שלטון ביוה"מ ואפשר ז"ש ותשחק ליום אחרון ע"ש ברש"י שאז הצדיק שמח כי ביום זה אין לו להתיירא מיצה"ר, ואולי הפי' עד יו"מ ומכ"ש ביום המות עצמו ובס' מילי דאבות כ' ג"ז דעד ועד בכלל, ויל"פ יום מותך לשון השפלה . . . וא"כ כשרואה שעומד בצדקו גם בעת השפלה אז יוכל להאמין בעצמו.

The expression עַד יוֹם מוֹתְךָ, *until the day you die*, implies that we may be confident on the day of our death that we will no longer sin. As Shlomo HaMelech writes in the renowned *Eishes Chayil:* וַתִּשְׂחַק לְיוֹם אַחֲרוֹן, *she joyfully awaits the last day* (Mishlei 31:25) — "she" (the soul of the righteous) delights in its final day, secure in the knowledge that it will no longer be tempted to sin. While some commentators suggest that the *Yetzer Hara* redoubles its efforts on the day of a person's death, this is only true for the *rasha* who now succumbs to evil once again. The *tzaddik*, on the other hand, is spared that final trial. As Shlomo writes: וְאֵין שִׁלְטוֹן בְּיוֹם הַמָּוֶת, *nor is there authority over the day of death* (Koheles 8:8). The Evil Inclination has no sovereignty on the day of death.

Alternatively, the *mishnah* is urging us, don't be overconfident *prior* to the day of your death and *certainly* not on the day of your death when the *Yetzer Hara* is most powerful.

Perhaps, the term מוֹתְךָ, *your death*, may refer to the day of one's *downfall* (cf. כִּי בְּיוֹם אֲכָלְךָ מִמֶּנּוּ מוֹת תָּמוּת, *for on the day you eat of it, you shall surely die* [Bereishis 2:17], referring to Chavah's *downfall*, rather than her actual eath). According to this approach, the *mishnah* is imploring us, do not assume that you can no longer sin, unless you have successfully thwarted the *Yetzer Hara* on the day of your downfall. Anyone who resisted the very natural impulse to sin under adverse circumstances may rest assured that he can triumph over any other temptation.

■ וְאַל תָּדִין אֶת חֲבֵרְךָ עַד שֶׁתַּגִּיעַ לִמְקוֹמוֹ — *Do not judge your fellow until you have reached his place.*

◄§ You Will Never Reach His Place

כלומר ולמקום חבירך אי אפשר להגיע לעולם כי לא כל דעות בני אדם שוות ולכן אל תדין לחברך כלל.

While the *mishnah* suggests that we may judge our peers if we reach their place, this will never occur. In order to fairly judge a peer, I would have to share a similar perspective and outlook with him. Inasmuch as two people are never alike (cf. *Yerushalmi Berachos* 5:9, כְּשֵׁם שֶׁאֵין פַּרְצוּפֵיהֶם דּוֹמִין זֶה לָזֶה כָּךְ אֵין דֵּיעֹתָן דּוֹמֶה זֶה לָזֶה), this is impossible.

◄§ The Role of the Environment

למקומו ממש, כי לעתים המקום גורם לחטא, וכן לפעמים מדות רעות באות לאדם על ידי אב ואם, לכן אי אפשר לדון את חברך לכף חובה.

The term לִמְקוֹמוֹ may be interpreted literally, *his place*, the environment in which your peer was nurtured. It is well established that a person's surroundings (his immediate environment) as well as the home environment in which he is reared influence his behavior. Not having been exposed to those factors, you are incapable of evaluating his actions (Rabbi Yitzchak of Vorka, *Maggidei HaEmes*).

◄§ Consider His Spiritual Level

שלא ירד להתבונן בדבר שנראה גרוע ממנו כי א״י עניינו ואם הי' מסתירין לו כיוצא בזה אם הי' טוב ממנו.

The *mishnah* is not only urging us to refrain from prematurely judging a peer, but also *assists* us in avoiding that tragic error. When evaluating seemingly inappropriate behavior on the part of a peer, consider his *spiritual level*. Bear in mind that he may be exposed to spiritual trials well beyond anything that you have ever experienced. Perhaps if you had been subjected to those same trials, your behavior may have been no better (adapted from *Sfas Emes*).

⊸§ Evaluate a Person in Light of His Mission

הרי אי אפשר להגיע למקומו, שכל אחד יש לו מקום מיוחד ודבר מיוחד שלשם
כך נברא.

The *Imrei Emes* suggested that the term מְקוֹמוֹ, *his place*, may refer to his mission, his true "place" in life. While your peer's behavior may seem inexplicable in light of *your* objective in life, such behavior may be totally acceptable in the context of *his* mission (*Maggidei HaEmes*).

⊸§ Before Evaluating, Ask for an Explanation

פי׳ אם שמעת על אחד שעשה לך רעה או שדיבר עליך אל תדין אותו מיד, אלא
לך אליו ותשאלנו האם נכון הדבר ולמה עשה כן.

According to the *Imrei Emes*, the *mishnah* is saying quite simply, do not evaluate a peer's actions until you go to "his place" — and ask for an explanation of *his* apparently errant behavior (*Maggidei HaEmes*).

■ וְאַל תֹּאמַר לִכְשֶׁאֶפָּנֶה אֶשְׁנֶה, שֶׁמָּא לֹא תִפָּנֶה — *And do not say, "When I am free I will study," for perhaps you will not become free.*

⊸§ Learn Now — Even If You Will Have More Time Later

פי׳ אף אם כוונתו לשם שמים שיהיה לו אחר כך דעה מיושבת בלימוד יותר, מכל
מקום אם לא עכשיו אימתי.

Frequently people express sentiments with the purest of intentions. They may say, rather than study Torah *now* while I am preoccupied with many distractions, I will learn *later* with a clear mind. Despite the apparent sincerity of those sentiments, the *mishnah* urges us to learn *now*. As a previous *mishnah* states, וְאִם לֹא עַכְשָׁיו, אֵימָתַי, *if not now, when?* (1:14).

⊸§ A Self-Fulfilling Prophecy

פי׳ בשביל שתאמר כך לכן יענשו אותך שלא תוכל באמת להפנות.

The phrase לִכְשֶׁאֶפָּנֶה אֶשְׁנֶה, *when I am free I will study*, may actually be a self-fulfilling prophecy. If you proclaim that you do not intend to learn Torah until you have time, then you will be punished for such an attitude by being deprived of the leisure to learn Torah.

[ו] הוּא הָיָה אוֹמֵר: אֵין בּוּר יְרֵא חֵטְא, וְלֹא עַם הָאָרֶץ
חָסִיד, וְלֹא הַבַּיְשָׁן לָמֵד, וְלֹא הַקַּפְּדָן מְלַמֵּד, וְלֹא
כָּל הַמַּרְבֶּה בִסְחוֹרָה מַחְכִּים, וּבְמָקוֹם שֶׁאֵין אֲנָשִׁים

◄§ When I Have Done Teshuvah

אל תאמר לכשאפנה מן העבירות אשנה, שמא לא תפנה כל ימי חייך ומתי
תלמוד. על כן העצה לזה שקודם שילמוד או שיעשה מצוה יתחרט על כל מה
שעשה עד כה נגד רצון השי"ת. וזה יועיל שלא יוסיף כח בהקליפות.
אל תאמר לכשאפנה אשנה ר"ל לכשאפנה מן היצה"ר וממדותי הרעות אז
אשנה, שמא לא תפנה, כי אולי כל תפקידך בעולם הזה הוא רק לעמול ולעבוד
עבודת משא ולעמוד תמיד בקשרי מלחמה עם היצר.

According to Rabbi Zvi of Dinov the term לִכְשֶׁאֶפָּנֶה אֶשְׁנֶה refers to the
removal of *aveiros* (sins). Do not say you will delay learning Torah until such
time that you have purified yourself from all your sins since this may never
occur. Instead, it suffices to simply regret all past misdeeds *prior* to learning
Torah or performing a *mitzvah*.

In a similar vein, Rabbi Moshe of Kobrin suggested that שֶׁמָּא לֹא תִפָּנֶה means,
perhaps you are an individual whose mission in life is to never rest but instead
to be involved in a lifelong struggle against the *Yetzer Hara* (*Maggidei HaEmes*).

■ שֶׁמָּא לֹא תִפָּנֶה — *For perhaps you will not become free.*

◄§ Some People Never Have Time

פירוש שמא אתה איש של לא תפנה כי נשתלחת לזה העולם שתלמוד
הגם שלא תפנה.

According to the Kotzker Rebbe, the phrase שֶׁמָּא לֹא תִפָּנֶה may not be an
indication of what will occur but rather a description of the individual's
frenetic lifestyle. Some people never have time — neither now nor at a later date.
Since by virtue of your lifestyle you may never have time to learn Torah — an
intolerable situation — you be would well advised to commence learning Torah
now, and not put it off. In fact, your primary challenge in This World may be
to overcome all your temporary distractions and study Torah.

6.

■ אֵין בּוּר יְרֵא חֵטְא — *A boor cannot be fearful of sin.* ■

[6] *He used to say: A boor cannot be fearful of sin; an unlearned person cannot be scrupulously pious; the bashful person cannot learn, and the quick, impatient person cannot teach; anyone excessively occupied in business cannot become a scholar; and in a place where there*

ঙ Someone Who Fears Sin Will Not Remain Unlearned

אם היה ירא חטא לא היה נשאר בור אלא משתדל ללמוד ולדעת.

The Kotzker Rebbe pointed out that the *mishnah* may be interpreted "in reverse." Anyone who is truly afraid of sinning will not *remain* unlearned. Realizing that most transgressions result from ignorance, he will insist upon becoming more learned and immerse himself in Torah (*Maggidei HaEmes*).

ঙ Sin Thrives in a Spiritual Vacuum

פירוש שאינו מתקיים במקום בור וחלול.

The term בור may be related to בור, *a pit* or *hollowed area*. It is virtually impossible to become a G-d-fearing individual in a spiritual vacuum. *Yiras Shamayim* can only be nurtured in a supportive atmosphere (R' Henoch of Alexander, *Maggidei HaEmes*).

■ וְלֹא עַם הָאָרֶץ חָסִיד — *An unlearned person cannot be scrupulously pious.*

ঙ Materialism Is Not Conducive to Chassidus

ולא עם הארץ מי שמשותף בגוף ובלול בארציות, חסיד שחסיד הוא הכנעה שמטה ראשו לפנים משורת הדין. ואי אפשר לבוא לזה מי שמעורב בו לבושי העולם הזה. כמו שאמר הבעש״ט זצ״ל שישמח הנפש, אימתי כשהוא בלא לבוש התערובת.

The term עַם הָאָרֶץ, generally translated as an *unlearned, ignorant person*, may also be understood literally — "a man of the land," an individual who is immersed in material matters. Such a person cannot attain the exalted status of חָסִיד, *a scrupulously pious individual*, which implies a willingness to be very forgiving regarding material matters. As the Baal Shem Tov would say, the soul can only rejoice when it is liberated from the surface materialism of This World (ibid).

✑ The Techniques of Learning Gemara Lead to Chassidus

כי מדרך החסידות לבדוק את מעשיהם הטובים אולי לא היו בסדר ואחר כך
משתדלים לתקן את מעשיהם. ומי שאינו עושה כן אינו יכול להגיע לדרגת חסידות
מצינו בש״ס שלאחר אוקימתא חזרו ושאלו או אינו כן ולפעמים מתקיף עלה
אמוראי זה וזה ואחר כך מקשה תוספות.
מהרש״א וכדומה אולם עם הארץ שאינו למד ואינו יודע לבחון מעשיו ומחשבתו
פעמים הרבה ולדעת אם מעשיו ישרים באמת, לא יגיע לעולם למדריגת חסידות.

The עַם הָאָרֶץ (unlearned person) is not only lacking Torah knowledge which is vital to *Chassidus*, but also the *technique* of learning Torah, especially the dialectical method (logical argumentation) that is essential to the study of Gemara. The תַּלְמִיד חָכָם, accustomed to the give-and-take of the Gemara — and its commentators — learns to question *his own behavior*. The עַם הָאָרֶץ, on the other hand, not only acts improperly but is also unable to critically analyze the consequences of his behavior (*Chiddushei HaRim, Maggidei HaEmes*).

✑ Do Not Fault the Environment

עיקר כוונתו להזהיר בזה על אנשים האומרים כי המקום גורם הם להיות חסיד מה
שאין כן ב״כאן״, שזה ודאי אשר העיקר תלוי בלב ואם אין לבו נוטה לכך לא יועיל
המקום. וזה ולא עם הארץ, רצה לומר שהולך בבחינת ארציות בלבד, לא יוכל
להיות חסיד.

R' Menachem Mendel of Vorka offered an ingenious explanation of the term עַם הָאָרֶץ and its relevance to our *mishnah*. It is tempting to fault one's אֶרֶץ, *environment*, for one's lack of piety. Such an individual, who blames external factors rather than his own lack of internal self-development, will never become a חָסִיד (*Maggidei HaEmes*).

■ וְלֹא הַבַּיְשָׁן לָמֵד — *The bashful person cannot learn.*

✑ Moshe Was Not Ashamed to Admit that He Did Not Recall

איתא בגמ' ליבא מידי דלא רמיזא באורייתא. ואפשר דבפ' שמיני כתיב וישמע
משה וייטב בעיניו, וברש״י הודה ולא בוש לומר לא שמעתי אלא כך אמר שמעתי
ושכחתי. ואפשר דמכאן לקח התנא לומר לא הביישן למד.

Perhaps, the source for this statement, emphasizing the importance of admitting one's ignorance, may be derived from Moshe's confession that he had forgotten the reason why the goat offered as a חַטָּאת, *sin-offering*, on the day of the *Mishkan's* dedication was required to be burnt. As *Rashi* notes (cf. *Vayikra* 10:20, וייטב בעיניו) he confessed and wasn't ashamed to admit that he could not recall the *halachah* (*Beis Yisrael, Maggidei HaEmes*).

■ וְלֹא הַקַּפְּדָן מְלַמֵּד — *And the quick, impatient person cannot teach.* ■

⏤§ An Impatient Person Cannot Be a "Melamed"

בגור היה חסיד . . . והיה גם מלמד לבניו של השפת אמת, והיה כעס פעם כשישבו
הילדים של השפ"א ליד השולחן הקניטוהו מאחוריו כדרך הילדים, ובהיות ולא
ידע שילדי הרבי עשו לו כן התרגז על כך מאד. השפ"א כשראה זאת לא היה לו
נחת רוח מזה, ואמר לו "לא הקפדן מלמד", היינו שלמלמד אסור להתרגז כי אם
הוא יהיה רגזן אף אחד לא ירצה שילדיו לימדו אצלו. ובזה פי' מה שאמר יעקב
אבינו על שמעון ולוי, אחלקם ביעקב ואפיצם בישראל וברש"י שנתן לשמעון
להיות מלמדי תינוקות כו' שנתן להם פרנסתם בדרך שיפחדו לכעוס פן תילקח
מהם פרנסתם, ובזה שיבר קצת את רוגזם וכעסם. והוסיף שלכן קוראים לרבי
(אדמו"ר) "גיטע יוד" משום שהוא צריך להיות טוב, והצדיקים אף פעם לא
מתרגזים.

The small children of the *Sfas Emes* once provoked their private tutor (*melamed*) who, in turn, became very upset. Upon hearing of the tutor's reaction, the *Sfas Emes* reacted with a somewhat novel interpretation of our *mishnah*. He exclaimed, "לֹא הַקַּפְּדָן מְלַמֵּד, an overly sensitive person cannot serve as a *melamed*!"

Based on this interpretation, he offered a beautiful explanation of Yaakov's chastisement of Shimon and Levi, אֲחַלְּקֵם בְּיַעֲקֹב וַאֲפִיצֵם בְּיִשְׂרָאֵל, *I will separate them within Jacob, and I will disperse them in Israel* (*Bereishis* 49:7), which is interpreted by *Rashi* as their appointment as *melamdim* (teachers of children), who are generally dispersed because they travel from place to place to earn a living. By being assigned such a role, which requires unusual sensitivity and patience, Yaakov also ensures that the כַּעַס, *anger*, that had motivated his children to destroy the city of Shechem would eventually dissipate.

The great Chassidic rebbes were known as *gutte Yidden* (good Jews) because of their unique ability to never get angry (*Maggidei HaEmes*).

■ וְלֹא כָל הַמַּרְבֶּה בִסְחוֹרָה מַחְכִּים — *Anyone excessively occupied in business cannot become a scholar.* ■

⏤§ Some People Successfully Combine Torah With a Business Career

---

פי' דאי אמר לא המרבה בסחורה מחכים ה"א דכלל הוא שאין באפשרות

[ז] אַף הוּא רָאָה גֻלְגֹּלֶת אַחַת שֶׁצָּפָה עַל פְּנֵי הַמָּיִם.
אָמַר לָהּ: "עַל דְּאַטֵּפְתְּ אַטְּפוּךְ, וְסוֹף מְטַיְּפָיִךְ
יְטוּפוּן."

להתחכם כלל מי שמרבה בסחורה קמ"ל דרק לא כל כי לפעמים ימצא זה אבל
היא מילתא דל"ש וכ"ז הרע"ב אין התורה מצוי' בקביעות אבל לפעמים מתרמי
ואף כי יפה ת"ת עם ד"א מ"מ ד"א יהי' טפל לת"ת והריבוי יהי' בתורה היינו
רוב היום בתורה.

It is significant that the *mishnah* does not say, כָּל הַמַּרְבֶּה בִּסְחוֹרָה אֵינוֹ מַחְכִּים,
which would imply that it is impossible to combine intensive Torah study
and commerce; but rather, לֹא כָל הַמַּרְבֶּה בִּסְחוֹרָה מַחְכִּים, which means that not
everyone combining Torah and a business career succeeds. However, some
individuals can successfully combine both aspects of their lives. The *mishnah's*
de-emphasis of commerce does not necessarily conflict with the previous *mishnah* stating יָפֶה תַלְמוּד תּוֹרָה עִם דֶּרֶךְ אֶרֶץ, *Torah study is good together with an
occupation* (2:2). דֶּרֶךְ אֶרֶץ, a business activity, while commendable, should play
a secondary role, allowing us the time to be immersed in Torah study. (Refer
to our commentary on that *mishnah*.)

⇜ The "Commerce" of Torah

וי"ל מרבה בסחורה אף בתורה שרוצה להמשיך מרחוק כמ"ש ממרחק תביא
לחמה.

This *mishnah* may be interpreted homiletically as referring to the proper
approach to studying Torah (rather than as the relationship between Torah
and commerce). In the renowned final chapter of *Mishlei* (Ch. 31), *Eishes Chayil*,
widely assumed to be an ode to the Torah, Shlomo sings of the ability of the
Torah scholar to "bring bread from afar." This may allude to the *talmid
chacham's* capacity to elucidate a difficult Talmudic discussion by citing proofs
from remote and seemingly unrelated sources.[1] This approach is known as
commerce — "importing" proofs from a distant source, similar to a merchant
who travels to secure merchandise. The *mishnah* cautions, לֹא כָּל הַמַּרְבֶּה בִּסְחוֹרָה
מַחְכִּים; we should be aware that not everyone utilizing this advanced, often
esoteric approach to learning Torah will succeed. While this may be appro-

---

1. For example, a discussion about Shabbos might be clarified by drawing an analogy to a question
of *berachos*.

[7] *He also saw a skull floating on the water; he said to it, "Because you drowned others, they drowned you; and eventually those who drowned you will be drowned."*

---

priate for a select group of scholars, in general most people benefit more by focusing on the internal structure of the Gemara (adapted from *Sfas Emes*).

■ וּבְמָקוֹם שֶׁאֵין אֲנָשִׁים הִשְׁתַּדֵּל לִהְיוֹת אִישׁ — *And in a place where there are no leaders, strive to be a leader.*

◆§ Moshe: A Man Amidst Angels

והחלק איש שבו היה עניו מאד וחלק אלוקים נתעלה יותר מן המלאכים לכן כתיב עניו מכל וכו' אשר על פני האדמה אבל למעלה נתעלה מכל ורמז במקום שאין אנשים השתדל להיות איש היינו במרום.

This segment of the *mishnah* may be interpreted homiletically as referring to Moshe who while remaining humble on earth emerged as a truly powerful man in heaven, a place where no men (מְקוֹם שֶׁאֵין אֲנָשִׁים) — only angels — exist. *Chazal* (cf. *Shabbos* 88b) relate that this humblest of men was able to refute all of the angels' objections to Israel receiving the Torah. Moshe's exalted status can also be deduced from the *pasuk* (*Bamidbar* 12:3), וְהָאִישׁ מֹשֶׁה עָנָו מְאֹד מִכֹּל הָאָדָם אֲשֶׁר עַל פְּנֵי הָאֲדָמָה, describing him as being *the humblest man on earth*, thereby implying his superior status in Heaven (*Sfas Emes, Shevuos 5662*).

◆§ Even When No One Is Looking

אדמו"ר זצללה"ה הלב שמחה היה אומר לאברכים שנכנסהו לקו"פ לאחר חתונתם "במקום שאין אנשים (כלומר אפילו בחדרי חדרים), השתדל להיות איש, זיי א מענטש".

When advising young couples, the *Lev Simchah* would refer to this *mishnah* — בְּמָקוֹם שֶׁאֵין אֲנָשִׁים, (lit.) *in a place where there are no men*, maintain the same high standards of modesty that you adopted while under the *chuppah*. Even within the privacy of your home, conduct yourselves modestly although no one is observing your behavior (*Maggidei HaEmes*).

[ח] הוּא הָיָה אוֹמֵר: מַרְבֶּה בָשָׂר, מַרְבֶּה רִמָּה;
מַרְבֶּה נְכָסִים, מַרְבֶּה דְאָגָה; מַרְבֶּה נָשִׁים, מַרְבֶּה
כְשָׁפִים; מַרְבֶּה שְׁפָחוֹת, מַרְבֶּה זִמָּה; מַרְבֶּה עֲבָדִים,
מַרְבֶּה גָזֵל. מַרְבֶּה תוֹרָה, מַרְבֶּה חַיִּים; מַרְבֶּה

8.

■ מַרְבֶּה בָשָׂר מַרְבֶּה רִמָּה — *The more flesh, the more worms.*

◆§ Shabbos Meals Do Not Adversely Affect the Body

> ראיתי בספר שאכילת בשר בשבת לא מרבה, רמז בפרשת המן דבשבת כתיב
> ורמה לא היתה בו. ואיתא בגמ׳ טעם כל המינין טעמו במן, ומסתמא אף טעם
> בשר.

If we interpret the term בָשָׂר to refer to meat, the *mishnah* seems to be dis-couraging lavish meat meals. However, the Shabbos meal is compared to the manna[1] which, if desired, could taste like meat[2] — and should therefore include meat. The *Lev Simchah* pointed out that this is alluded to in the verse regarding the manna, וְרִמָּה לֹא הָיְתָה בּוֹ, *and there were no worms in it [the manna left for use on Shabbos].*

Just as the manna never spoiled and became rotten (if properly eaten), so too the Shabbos meal will never induce deterioration of the body (*Maggidei HaEmes*).

■ מַרְבֶּה נְכָסִים, מַרְבֶּה דְאָגָה — *The more possessions, the more worry.*

◆§ Your Livelihood May Be Behind You

> מספרים שפעם פגע הרה״ק רבי לוי יצחק מברדיטשוב ז״ל ביהודי מבוהל ברחוב
> ושאלו ״למה הנך נחפז כל כך״. השיב אותו היהודי ״רץ אני אחרי פרנסה״. ומנין
> לך, הוסיף רבי לוי יצחק לשאול, שפרנסתך בורחת מלפניך ועליך לרדוף אחריה,
> אולי היא מאחוריך גבך ועליך לעמוד במקומך ולהמתין עד שתשיגך.

R' Levi Yitzchak of Berditchev once encountered an individual who appeared to be quite depressed. When Reb Levi Yitzchak inquired as to the cause of this individual's distress, the man replied, "I am pursuing my

---

1. For further discussion of this concept please refer to *The Pesach Haggadah With Ideas and Insights of the Sfas Emes*, p. 123.

2. Cf. Yoma 75a stating that the manna contained the taste of every food.

[8] *He used to say: The more flesh , the more worms;
the more possessions, the more worry; the more
wives, the more witchcraft; the more maidservants, the
more lewdness; the more menservants, the more thievery.
[However,] the more Torah, the more life; the more*

livelihood." The Rebbe retorted, "How do you know that your *parnasah* is
running away and that you should be chasing it? Perhaps, you would be better
served by remaining stationary and waiting for your *parnasah*, which is right
behind you, to reach you" (*Maggidei HaEmes*).

■ מַרְבֶּה עֲבָדִים מַרְבֶּה גָזֵל — *The more menservants, the more thievery.*

◆§ Servants Stealing on Behalf of Their Master

פי׳ שיגזלו עבור הבעלים ובהמותיו כמו שכתוב בעבדי לוט.

While this phrase is usually interpreted to refer to servants stealing *from*
their master, in reality, it may equally well refer to servants stealing *on
behalf* of their master. One such example would be the servants of Lot who
permitted their master's sheep to graze in other people's fields (cf. *Bereishis* 13:7,
Rashi ויהי ריב).

■ מַרְבֶּה תוֹרָה מַרְבֶּה חַיִּים — *The more Torah, the more life.*

◆§ Every Letter of Torah Brings Life

איתא בעבודת ישראל שכאשר מרבים ודורשים בתורה מרבים חיות, בכל תיבה
ובכל אות מהתורה נמצא חיות וכפי מה שמעמיקים בתורה כך ממשיכים חיות.
התרי״ג מצות הם כנגד התרי״ג אברים וגידים והם החיות של האברים והגידים
וזהו דכתיב כי על כל מוצא פי ה׳ יחיה האדם.

In interpreting this phrase, the *Imrei Emes* cited the Maggid of Koznitz's
observation that every letter of Torah, as it is interpreted by *Chazal*, is a
source of life for those who exposit and study its profound teachings. It is well
known that the 613 *mitzvos* correspond to the 613 components of the body. By
delving into the teachings of every one of these *mitzvos*, we infuse each of these
organs with life. As the Torah itself says, כִּי עַל כָּל מוֹצָא פִּי ה׳ יִחְיֶה הָאָדָם, *rather
by everything that emanates from the mouth of God — the Torah — does man
live* (*Devarim*; 8:3) (*Maggidei HaEmes*).

ב / ח יְשִׁיבָה, מַרְבֶּה חָכְמָה; מַרְבֶּה עֵצָה, מַרְבֶּה תְבוּנָה;
מַרְבֶּה צְדָקָה, מַרְבֶּה שָׁלוֹם. קָנָה שֵׁם טוֹב, קָנָה לְעַצְמוֹ;
קָנָה לוֹ דִבְרֵי תוֹרָה, קָנָה לוֹ חַיֵּי הָעוֹלָם הַבָּא.

◆§ Teaching Others Torah

י״ל דמרבה הכוונה שמרבה תורה שגם אחרים יוכלו ללמוד. ומעשה בחסיד אחד
שנכנס אל כ״ק אדמו״ר זצלה״ה הל״ש והזכיר שבנו חולה במחלה קשה ואמר
לו ״מרבה תורה מרבה חיים״ ותיכף ומיד הלך הלה באמונת חכמים ופתח ישיבה
ונתוספו לבנו לחיות עוד כמה שנים.
בשם החידושי הרי״ם ז״ל פ׳ מי שכותב ספרי תורה מרבה חיים.

The *Lev Simchah* frequently quoted his father's (the *Imrei Emes*) interpretation of this passage — the true מַרְבֶּה תוֹרָה (one who increases Torah
study) is one who enables others to learn Torah. The *Lev Simcha* not only
interpreted the *mishnah* in this fashion but also utilized his interpretation to
prolong life. A *chassid* once came to him asking him to pray for his mortally
ill son. The Rebbe responded, מַרְבֶּה תוֹרָה מַרְבֶּה חַיִּים. The *chassid* immediately
went and opened a yeshivah. His son recovered and lived for many more years,
perhaps in this merit.

Similarly, the *Chiddushei HaRim* interpreted this passage to refer to one who
writes (or supports the writing of) *Sifrei Torah* (*Maggidei HaEmes*).

■ מַרְבֶּה יְשִׁיבָה, מַרְבֶּה חָכְמָה — *The more study, the more wisdom.* ■

◆§ Thinking About Hashem

ההיפוך מהמרבה בסחורה הנ״ל, רק שמיישב דעתו ומחשבתו תמיד בעבודת
הבורא יתברך, אז מרבה חכמה.

According to the Maggid of Koznitz, this expression may refer to the
concept known as יְשׁוּב הַדַּעַת, thoughtful contemplation about Hashem
which induces wisdom (*Maggidei HaEmes*).

■ מַרְבֶּה צְדָקָה, מַרְבֶּה שָׁלוֹם — *The more charity, the more peace.* ■

◆§ Giving Tzedakah to Atone for Giving
Too Much Tzedakah

הרב אליהו חיים מייזל אבדק״ק לודז׳ הרבה בצדקה עד למאד ופיזר נתן

study, the more wisdom; the more counsel , the more understanding; the more charity, the more peace. One who has gained a good reputation [good name] has gained it for his own benefit; one who has gained himself Torah knowledge has gained himself the life of the World to Come.

לאביונים כל פרוטה שאיקלע לידיו. ויהי כאשר לא יכלו בני ביתו לשאת את
המצב הקשה ששרר בביתם פנו אליו ואמרו לו "הרי אמרו המבזבז אל יבזבז
יותר מחומש". השיבם הרב בצדקותו ובפקחותו "הריני עברתי פעם על עבירה
זו של אל יבזבז, ובזבזתי יותר מחומש. על כן הריני נותן צדקה כתיקון על עון זה,
וככל שאני נכשל בעון זה, כן אלי להרבות בצדקת יותר"...

The famed Rav of Lodz, Rav Eliyahu Chaim Meisel, was renowned for his generosity, contributing so much charity that his own family lived in utter poverty. Eventually they objected to his extreme magnanimity, citing *Chazal* who opposed donating more than a fifth of one's income (*Kesubos* 50a). The Rav responded wisely, "Indeed, I erred by being too charitable. To rectify this sin, I must give even more *tzedakah*!" [*Tzedakah* is a *tikkun* for any עֲבֵרָה (see *Daniel* 4:24: וַחֲטָאָךְ בְּצִדְקָה פְרֻק, *Redeem your sin through righteousness*, i.e. giving *tzedakah*).] Therefore to "atone" for giving *too much tzedakah*, Rav Meisel said he had to give more! (*Maggidei HaEmes*).

◄§ Peace With Hashem

יש לפרש כלפי מעלה שלא יהרהר העני וכמו שכתוב או יחזק במעוזי יעשה שלום
לי.

By giving *tzedakah*, one not only enables the pauper to live peacefully with his peers but also causes his relationship with Hashem to be more harmonious. While suffering from abject poverty, the pauper may blame Hashem for his plight. Now that his material needs have been attended to, his relationship with Hashem improves as well.

■ קָנָה שֵׁם טוֹב, קָנָה לְעַצְמוֹ; קָנָה לוֹ דִבְרֵי תוֹרָה, קָנָה לוֹ חַיֵּי הָעוֹלָם הַבָּא — *One who has gained a good reputation [good name] has gained it for his own benefit; one who has gained himself Torah knowledge has gained himself the life of the World to Come.*

◄§ A Good Name or Torah — Which is Greater?

קשה דבש"ט עולה ע"ג כתר תורה (שפ"א).

רַבָּן יוֹחָנָן בֶּן זַכַּאי קִבֵּל מֵהִלֵּל וּמִשַּׁמַּאי. הוּא הָיָה [ט] ב / ט
אוֹמֵר: אִם לָמַדְתָּ תוֹרָה הַרְבֵּה, אַל תַּחֲזִיק טוֹבָה
לְעַצְמְךָ, כִּי לְכָךְ נוֹצָרְתָּ.

דקנה שם טוב קנה לעצמו, אבל קנה דברי תורה קנה לו חיי עולם הבא. וזה מה
דאיתא להלן ג' כתרים הם כתר תורה וכתר כהונה וכתר מלכות וכתר שם טוב
עולה על גביהן, דקנה שם טוב קנה לעצמו (לב שמחה).

The *Sfas Emes* notes the seeming contradiction between this *mishnah*
which implies that Torah is of greater significance than a good name and
the later *mishnah* (4:17) which states: וְכֶתֶר שֵׁם טוֹב עוֹלֶה עַל גַּבֵּיהֶן, *but the crown
of a good name surpasses them all*, it is even greater than Torah. We may resolve
the seeming contradiction in the following manner: While Torah is surely of
greatest significance, the *reward* for acquiring a good name can be enjoyed in
This World whereas that of Torah, as the *mishnah* concludes, awaits us in the
World to Come (adapted from *Lev Simchah, Maggidei HaEmes*).

⋖§ Acquiring Torah

זה ענין גדול יותר ממה שכתוב קודם מרבה תורה שיש לו קנין בהתורה וכמו
שכתוב לקמן במ"ח דברים התורה נקנית.

Whereas previously the *mishnah* spoke of the reward attained for
disseminating Torah (מַרְבֶּה תוֹרָה מַרְבֶּה חַיִּים), here we emphasize the attribute of קְנָה תוֹרָה — *acquiring* Torah — making the Torah an integral part of
one's personality. The means through which this lofty objective is reached is
discussed in detail later in the chapter known as קִנְיָן הַתּוֹרָה, the acquisition of
Torah (6:6).

9.

■ רַבָּן יוֹחָנָן בֶּן זַכַּאי קִבֵּל מֵהִלֵּל וּמִשַּׁמַּאי — *Rabban Yochanan ben Zakkai
received the tradition from Hillel and Shammai.*

⋖§ The "Least" of Hillel's Disciples

כי יונתן ב"ע שנשרף כל עוף שפרח עליו בשעה שעסק בתורה כדאי' אינו
בגדר מקבל ללמד לאחרים רק ריב"ז קבל כו'.

The Gemara relates that Hillel's greatest disciple was Yonasan ben Uziel
whose presence was so awesome that any bird flying above him would be

[9] *Rabban Yochanan ben Zakkai received the tradition from Hillel and Shammai. He used to say: If you have studied much Torah, do not take credit for yourself, because that is what you were created to do.*

---

instantaneously burnt (*Bava Basra* 134a). On the other hand, the "least great" of his disciples was Rabban Yochanan ben Zakkai who "only" knew all of *Chumash*, Mishnah, Gemara and 14 other areas of Torah, including such esoteric topics as understanding the speech of angels. It may seem surprising that the *mishnah* cites the tradition of Hillel's "least" accomplished *talmid* rather than his greatest. In response, we suggest that someone as awesome as Yonasan ben Uziel was simply too great to merely serve as a recipient (מְקַבֵּל) and transmitter of his Rebbi's teachings. Instead, he had to initiate his own *chiddushei Torah*. (Refer to the following commentary for another reason why Rabbi Yochanan ben Zakkai was the ideal transmitter of Hillel's traditions.)

■ אִם לָמַדְתָּ תּוֹרָה הַרְבֵּה, אַל תַּחֲזִיק טוֹבָה לְעַצְמְךָ — *If you have studied much Torah, do not take credit for yourself.*

⊷§ The Pitfalls of Learning a Little Torah

יש לפרש כי אם ילמוד תורה הרבה אז יזכה על ידי התורה שלא יחזיק טובה לעצמו מה שאין כן הלומד מעט אז מיד מחזיק טובה לעצמו. ורבי יוחנן בן זכאי אשר לא הניח לא מקרא ולא משנה הלכה ואגדה שלא למד זה כי כל מה שרואין ולומדין דברי תורה יודעים שלא להחזיק טובה.

The *mishnah* is not only urging us not to congratulate ourselves for having "studied much Torah" but is also *assuring* us that if indeed we learn a great quantity of Torah, then we will not become arrogant about our accomplishments. If, on the other hand, we only study a *little* Torah, we run the risk of erroneously priding ourselves on our limited (and often inconclusive) knowledge. Rabban Yochanan ben Zakkai, who had mastered every aspect of Torah — and never boasted of his accomplishments — was ideally suited to convey this message and serve as Hillel's transmitter.

■ אַל תַּחֲזִיק טוֹבָה לְעַצְמְךָ כִּי לְכָךְ נוֹצָרְתָּ — *Do not take credit for yourself, because that is what you were created to do.*

⊷§ Teach Others

שאל יחזיק הטובה הוא התורה שלמד לעצמו, רק ילמוד לאחרים גם כן.

[י] חֲמִשָּׁה תַלְמִידִים הָיוּ לוֹ לְרַבָּן יוֹחָנָן בֶּן זַכַּאי, וְאֵלּוּ
הֵן: רַבִּי אֱלִיעֶזֶר בֶּן הֻרְקָנוֹס, רַבִּי יְהוֹשֻׁעַ בֶּן חֲנַנְיָא,
רַבִּי יוֹסֵי הַכֹּהֵן, רַבִּי שִׁמְעוֹן בֶּן נְתַנְאֵל, וְרַבִּי אֶלְעָזָר בֶּן
עֲרָךְ.

The Maggid of Koznitz interpreted this *mishnah* quite simply: Don't keep
(אַל תַּחֲזִיק) the Torah to yourself (טוֹבָה לְעַצְמְךָ), but instead share your
knowledge with others — because that is what you were created to do (כִּי לְכַךְ
נוֹצָרְתָּ) (*Maggidei HaEmes*).

⋅§ Don't "Pick and Choose" Leniencies

אל תבחור לך את הקולות שנראות טובות בעיניך ותניח את החומרות.

The term טוֹבָה may also refer to "leniencies," halachic rulings which a person
believes are in his own interest (טוֹבָה). The *mishnah* urges us not to always
follow the more lenient ruling of a disputed halachic issue. (Cf. *Eruvin* 6b where
the Gemara discusses a person who always adopts the lenient halachic ruling
and states that he is considered to be a *rasha*.) (Kotzker Rebbe, *Maggidei
HaEmes*).

■ כִּי לְכַךְ נוֹצָרְתָּ — *Because that is what you were created to do.* ■

⋅§ You Were Created for the Purpose of
Not Taking Credit

כי לכך נוצרת שלא תחזיק טובה לעצמך כלומר אין רצון הקב״ה גוף הלימוד כי
יצירת האדם רק על זה שלא יחזיק טובה לעצמו כנ״ל.

Alternatively, the expression, כִּי לְכַךְ נוֹצָרְתָּ, *for this reason you were created,*
may refer back to the immediately preceding words, אַל תַּחֲזִיק טוֹבָה לְעַצְמְךָ,
do not credit yourself: It was worth creating man for the sole purpose that he
not take credit for his accomplishments. It is most gratifying to Hashem if man
does not take unwarranted pride in *his own* accomplishments (*Sfas Emes* in
Maggidei HaEmes).

⋅§ You Studied the Entire Torah in the Womb

יש לפרש עפ״י מה דאיתא כשהוולד במעי אמו מלמדים אותו כל התורה כולה,

[10] *Rabban Yochanan ben Zakkai had five [primary] disciples. They were: Rabbi Eliezer ben Hyrkanos, Rabbi Yehoshua ben Chanania, Rabbi Yose the Kohen, Rabbi Shimon ben Nesanel and Rabbi Elazar ben Arach.*

וזהו כי לכך נוצרת ... אדם השומר עצמו בקדושה מסוגל לזכור התורה שלמד אז
לכל ימי חייו.

The *Lev Simcha* suggested that the phrase, כִּי לְכָךְ נוֹצָרְתָּ, *because that is what you were created to do*, refers to the prenatal stage when the fetus is taught the entire Torah (cf. *Niddah* 30b). Do not take credit for your knowledge of Torah since you already studied the entire Torah in the womb. The *Lev Simcha* added that someone who lives a sacred life will eventually be able to recall, during his adult years, the Torah of the prenatal phase (*Maggidei HaEmes*).

◆§ Whatever You Learned Is but a Little

בעת שנכנס אברך אחד בן תורה מופלג בפעם הראשונה אל השפ"א ז"ל, שאלו
"האם הנך יודע ללמוד?" ענה על זה "א ביסל." אמר לו השפ"א "וער קען דען
מער ווי א ביסל?"

Perhaps, the simplest reason for the *mishnah's* advice that we not take credit for all the Torah that we have learned is quite simply because *all* our learning is merely a *fraction* of the entire Torah. The *Sfas Emes* once asked a young man renowned for his knowledge of Torah, "Do you know how to learn?" The young man replied, "A little," to which the *Sfas Emes* retorted, "Does anyone know how to learn more than a little?"

10.

■ חֲמִשָּׁה תַלְמִידִים הָיוּ לוֹ לְרַבָּן יוֹחָנָן בֶּן זַכַּאי — *Rabban Yochanan ben Zakkai had five [primary] disciples.*

◆§ The Hierarchy of the Sages

מסתמא מונה אותם בסדר זקנתן דא"א לומר שמונה אותם בסדר גדולתן דהא
אבא שאול אמר דר"א ב"ע גדול מכולן והוא נמנה באחרונה, וכסדר חשיבתן
א"א דר' יוסי הי' צריך להיות בראשונה דהי' כהן רק בסדר זקנתן, או אפשר
שמונה אותן מסדר שנעשו תלמידיו.

[יא] הוּא הָיָה מוֹנֶה שְׁבָחָן: (רַבִּי) אֱלִיעֶזֶר בֶּן הֻרְקָנוֹס, בּוֹר סוּד שֶׁאֵינוֹ מְאַבֵּד טִפָּה; (רַבִּי) יְהוֹשֻׁעַ בֶּן

Through a process of elimination we conclude that our *mishnah* is arranging these five sages according to their seniority (age). It is apparent that they are not listed on the basis of their greatness since Rabbi Elazar ben Arach, whom Abba Shaul considers to be the greatest of the sages, is listed last. It is also difficult to assume that the sages were listed according to their genealogical status (יחוס). If so, Rabbi Yose the Kohen should have been listed first.

Alternatively, these sages may have been arranged according to the order in which they became Rabban Yochanan ben Zakkai's *talmidim*.

■ הוּא הָיָה מוֹנֶה שְׁבָחָן — *He used to enumerate their praises.*

⋖§ Praise — How Much?

מכאן הוציא הוציא הסמ"ג דפני אוהביו מותר לספר בשבחו ש"ח ולא יבוא לידי גנותו
ובלא זה י"ל דהפי' שלא להרבות בכל השבחים אבל לספר שבח א' לא יבוא ליד
גנותו והרב חיד"א ז"ל מתרץ דרק שלא בפניו אל יספר והכא בפניהם הוי וכעין
מ"ש חכז"ל דפניו לית בי' משום לישנא בישא.

Rabban Yochanan ben Zakkai's practice of publicly extolling the virtues of his disciples seems to contradict a Gemara (*Arachin* 16a) that prohibits praising since such ostentatious praise is bound to invite criticism and lead to slander (גנות).

The distinction, in this instance, may be the audience. While it is meritorious to praise someone to a group of his friends and admirers, it would be inappropriate to do so to a neutral audience since this could precipitate criticism. The difference may also lie in the *degree* of praise offered. Whereas it is appropriate to offer *some* praise — and the accolades cited in our *mishnah* are only a fraction (מִקְצָת) of the virtues of these great scholars — one may not cite *all* of a peer's virtues. The *Chida* distinguishes between the inappropriate practice of praising "behind their back" and the acceptable practice of praising someone in their presence. (Cf. *Arachin* 15b in which Rabbah states that certain types of *lashon hara* are mitigated if they are spoken in the accused's presence.)

■ (רַבִּי) אֱלִיעֶזֶר בֶּן הֻרְקָנוֹס, בּוֹר סוּד שֶׁאֵינוֹ מְאַבֵּד טִפָּה — *(Rabbi) Eliezer ben Hyrkanos is like a cemented cistern that loses not a drop.*

[11] *He used to enumerate their praises: (Rabbi)[1] Eliezer ben Hyrkanos is like a cemented cistern that loses not a drop; (Rabbi) Yehoshua ben Chanania, praisewor-*

1. Some texts add the title to each name.

◆§ Rabbi Eliezer Was a Late Starter, but He Never Forgot a Word

והגם שלא היה לו גירסא דינקותא שהתחיל ללמוד בן כ״ח שנים כדאיתא בפרקי דרבי אליעזר, מכל מקום היה זכרן גדול על ידי שהיה חביב עליו ביותר כל דיבור של התורה היה מדבקו בגופו ממש ולא אבד טפה.

It is particularly remarkable that Rabbi Eliezer ben Hyrkanos, who did not begin studying Torah until he was twenty-eight years old, nonetheless, acquired complete mastery over every aspect of Torah to the extent that he never forgot anything he learned. His remarkable retentive powers are likened to a pit sealed with lime that does not lose a drop of water. His extraordinary memory may be attributed to his exceptional love of Torah. For him, Torah was not merely studied, but actually integrated into his very being, becoming a part of him.

◆§ Living a Sacred Life Leads to Retention

הגאון מדעננבורג רבי יוסף ראזין ז״ל זכר כל הש״ס, הוא היה פעם אצל השפת אמת ז״ל, וכאשר הלך אמר השפת אמת שמזכרונו ניכר שהיה שמור כולו בקדושה. לא עברתי ממצוותיך ולא שכחתי, אמנם כן כפי השמירה כן הזכרון, ובמשנה רבי אליעזר בור סוד כו'.

Rabbi Eliezer's phenomenal retention of Torah may be attributed to his sacred lifestyle. The *Lev Simcha* deduced a variant approach to the words שֶׁאֵינוֹ מְאַבֵּד טִפָּה based on Rabbi Eliezer's conduct.[1]

Upon meeting the Rogatchover Gaon, known for his extraordinary grasp of Torah — never forgetting a word — the *Sfas Emes* remarked that his visitor must have lived a life of unusual sanctity. The *Sfas Emes* found an allusion to the relationship between sanctity and retaining Torah from the *pasuk*, לֹא עָבַרְתִּי מִמִּצְוֹתֶיךָ וְלֹא שָׁכָחְתִּי, *I have not transgressed any of your commandments — and [therefore] I have not forgotten* (Devarim 26:13) (*Lev Simchah, Maggidei HaEmes*).

1. דהיינו שאינו מאבד אפילו טפה אחת של שכבת זרע

חֲנַנְיָא, אַשְׁרֵי יוֹלַדְתּוֹ; (רַבִּי) יוֹסֵי הַכֹּהֵן, חָסִיד; (רַבִּי)
שִׁמְעוֹן בֶּן נְתַנְאֵל, יְרֵא חֵטְא; וְ(רַבִּי) אֶלְעָזָר בֶּן עֲרָךְ,
כְּמַעְיָן הַמִּתְגַּבֵּר.

The expression בּוֹר סוּד, *a cemented cistern*, may also refer to Rabbi Eliezer's uncanny ability to conceal most of his vast knowledge. As the Gemara relates, Rabbi Eliezer never related to others anything that he had not heard from his own rebbi.

◆§ Preserved the "Pintele Yid"

פי׳ שיש נקודה [טובה] בכל איש ישראל רק אם שומר נפשו שלא יהיה בו חסרונות
ושיהי׳ כלי המחזיק ברכה שלימות הנפש ואז שורה בו ברכה כנ״ל.

The term בּוֹר סוּד may also refer to the *pintele Yid*, the Divine pure spark of goodness that every Jew is endowed with. Rabbi Eliezer, by attaining moral perfection, succeeded in preserving that spark from all the corrupting factors of the material world and became a source of blessing to others.

◆§ Concealed Most of His Learning

יי״ל הכוונה על מ״ש עליו שלא אמר דבר שלא שמע מפי רבו וכו׳, פי׳ שהחזיקו
בקרבו ולא אמר לאחר זהו בור סיד שאינו מאבד טיפה.

The expression בּוֹר סוּד, *a cemented cistern*, may also refer to Rabbi Eliezer's uncanny ability to conceal most of his vast knowledge. As the Gemara relates, Rabbi Eliezer never related to others anything that he had not heard from his own rebbi.

◆§ Preserved the "Pintele Yid"

פי׳ שיש נקודה [טובה] בכל איש ישראל רק אם שומר נפשו שלא יהיה בו חסרונות
ושיהי׳ כלי המחזיק ברכה שלימות הנפש ואז שורה בו ברכה כנ״ל.

The term בּוֹר סוּד may also refer to the *pintele Yid*, the Divine pure spark of goodness that every Jew is endowed with. Rabbi Eliezer, by attaining moral perfection, succeeded in preserving that spark from all the corrupting factors of the material world and became a source of blessing to others.

■ רַבִּי יְהוֹשֻׁעַ בֶּן חֲנַנְיָא, אַשְׁרֵי יוֹלַדְתּוֹ — *Rabbi Yehoshua ben Chanania, praiseworthy is she who bore him.*

thy is she who bore him; (Rabbi) Yose the Kohen is a scrupulously pious person; (Rabbi) Shimon ben Nesanel fears sin; and (Rabbi) Elazar ben Arach is like a spring flowing stronger and stronger.

❧ His Parents' Pride

שהיו בו מדות טובות והיו כולם משבחים אותו אשרי יולדתו אשר שזה גידל כו׳
כמ״ש חז״ל, ובאבות דר״ן פי״ד אי׳ שקרא עליו והחוט המשולש ע״ש שנדחקו
בפי׳ ונראה כי אביו ואמו היו צדיקים וגם הוא השלישי צדיק לכן נק׳ חוט המשולש
וזה ענין א׳ עם אשרי יולדתו.

T he term אַשְׁרֵי יוֹלַדְתּוֹ, *praiseworthy is she who bore him*, gives some indication of the *nachas* Rav Yehoshua ben Chanania's parents must have received from their son's sterling *middos*. In *Avos D' Rabbi Nosson* (a *Tosefta* based on *Pirkei Avos*) he is described as חוּט הַמְשֻׁלָשׁ, a *three-ply cord* (cf. *Koheles* 4:12, וְהַחוּט הַמְשֻׁלָשׁ בִּמְהֵרָה יִנָּתֵק, *a three-ply cord is not easily severed*), suggesting that he is the third link in a chain of *kedushah* which began with his father and mother.

■ רַבִּי שִׁמְעוֹן בֶּן נְתַנְאֵל, יְרֵא חֵטְא ■ — *Rabbi Shimon ben Nesanel fears sin.*

❧ Afraid of Sin — Not Its Consequences

רצה לומר כי יש בני אדם אשר יראים לחטוא מפני העונש המגיע להם, אבל הוא
לא היה ירא משום דבר בעולם, רק מן החטא בעצמו שיהיה מונעו מעבודת בוראו,
באמרו איך אוכל לחטוא נגד בוראי אשר מלא כל הארץ כבודו, ולית אתר פנוי
מיניה.

T he Maggid of Koznitz interpreted this segment of the *mishnah* quite simply: Rabbi Shimon ben Nesanel feared the sin itself — dreading the possibility that he might defy Hashem's will — rather than the punishment that he would receive as a result of sinning (*Maggidei HaEmes*).

❧ As Afraid of Sinning as of a Lion

שהי׳ מתפלל להינצל מחטא כמו המתירא מהארי מתפלל.

R abbi Shimon ben Nesanel's fear of sin was reflected in his *tefillah*. He would constantly pray that he should not commit *aveiros*. He would *daven*

[**יב**] הוּא הָיָה אוֹמֵר: אִם יִהְיוּ כָל חַכְמֵי יִשְׂרָאֵל בְּכַף
מֹאזְנַיִם, וֶאֱלִיעֶזֶר בֶּן הֻרְקָנוֹס בְּכַף שְׁנִיָּה, מַכְרִיעַ
מַכְרִיעַ אֶת כֻּלָּם. אַבָּא שָׁאוּל אוֹמֵר מִשְּׁמוֹ: אִם יִהְיוּ כָל
חַכְמֵי יִשְׂרָאֵל בְּכַף מֹאזְנַיִם, וְ(רַבִּי) אֱלִיעֶזֶר בֶּן הֻרְקָנוֹס
אַף עִמָּהֶם, וְ(רַבִּי) אֶלְעָזָר בֶּן עֲרָךְ בְּכַף שְׁנִיָּה, מַכְרִיעַ
אֶת כֻּלָּם.

with the same fervor that one would express when beseeching Hashem to be
spared from a rampaging lion.

12.

■ אִם יִהְיוּ כָל חַכְמֵי יִשְׂרָאֵל בְּכַף מֹאזְנַיִם — *If all the wise men of Israel were
on one pan of a balance-scale.*

⅏ Who Are the "Wise Men of Israel"?

> לבד מריב״ז הרב שלא הניח כו׳ וודאי הי׳ נמי בור סיד כו׳.

The term כָל חַכְמֵי יִשְׂרָאֵל, *all the wise men*, seemingly refers to all of Rabbi
Eliezer's contemporaries but not to their rebbi, Rabban Yochanan
ben Zakkai, who towered above his *talmidim*. Certainly Rabbi Eliezer's
outstanding retention of Torah was at least matched by Rabban Yochanan
ben Zakkai of whom the Gemara relates that he was expert in every aspect of
Torah.

■ וְ(רַבִּי) אֶלְעָזָר בֶּן עֲרָךְ בְּכַף שְׁנִיָּה מַכְרִיעַ אֶת כֻּלָּם — *And (Rabbi) Elazar ben
Arach were on the other pan, he would outweigh them all.*

⅏ Greater Than One or Greater Than All

> היה נראה כל אחד בפני עצמו עם רבי אליעזר אך מלשון אף עמהם משמע ממש
> נגד כל החכמים.

On the basis of this segment of the *mishnah*, one is likely to conclude that
Rabbi Elazar was greater than Rabbi Eliezer ben Hyrkanos and *any one* of
the wise men. However, the term אַף עִמָּהֶם, *even with them*, seems to imply that
Rabbi Elazar ben Arach was greater than *all* of them.

[12] He [Rabbi Yochanan ben Zakkai] used to say: If all the wise men of Israel were on one pan of a balance-scale, and Eliezer ben Hyrkanos were on the other pan, he would outweigh them all. Abba Shaul said in [Rabban Yochanan's name: If all the wise men of Israel, with even (Rabbi) Eliezer ben Hyrkanos among them, were on one pan of a balance-scale, and (Rabbi) Elazar ben Arach were on the other pan, he would outweigh them all.

◆§ Scope or Erudition

ובענין אי ראב״ה מכריע אי ראב״ע נראה שזה הפלוגתא דסיני ועוקר הרים הי מינייהו עדיף וקי״ל דסיני עדיף וכן כאן ואולי דלענין לב טוב לכ״ע קי״ע כראב״ע דזה תלוי בסברא והיינו עוקר הרים, עוד י״ל דשם מיירי בשצריכין לא׳ מהם להצילו או לשאר דבר אבל מ״מ יש לומר שיש עוקר הרים כל כך שיודע יותר מהסיני מחמת החריפות שלו.

Seemingly, the debate in our *mishnah* whether Rabbi Eliezer ben Hyrkanos, known for his phenomenal retention of Torah, or Rabbi Elazar ben Arach, known for his profundity (and thus described as a מַעְיָן הַמִּתְגַּבֵּר, a spring (well) that is self-replenishing), was greater is related to the famous dispute: Is greater honor due to the *talmid chacham* who possesses vast *scope* or to the scholar who is renowned for his *depth* of understanding?

On the one hand, the two issues may not be related. While one may dispute the relative merit of profundity and scope of knowledge, in the context of the next *mishnah* — which deals with desirable attributes and the proper path of life (דֶּרֶךְ יְשָׁרָה) — everyone agrees that the attribute advocated by Rabbi Elazar ben Arach, לֵב טוֹב, *a good heart* — which often arises from a profound and in-depth understanding of a situation — is preferable.

Alternatively, the Talmud's discussion of the virtues of depth versus breadth (*Horayos* 14a) is referring to a mutually exclusive situation where one scholar benefits at the expense of the other. For example, in the case of פִּדְיוֹן שְׁבוּיִים, where there are scarce resources to save both scholars' lives, we generally accord preferential treatment to the *talmid chacham* who displays greater scope of knowledge over the more profound analyst. However, in our *mishnah*, the attributes used to describe these sages are not necessarily mutually exclusive. Thus, Rabbi Elazar ben Arach, described as a "self-replenishing spring," was able to increase his knowledge of Torah through his analytical capacities, eventually emerging as a scholar simultaneously known for his breadth and depth of knowledge.

[יג] אָמַר לָהֶם: צְאוּ וּרְאוּ אֵיזוֹ הִיא דֶּרֶךְ טוֹבָה
שֶׁיִּדְבַּק בָּהּ הָאָדָם. רַבִּי אֱלִיעֶזֶר אוֹמֵר: עַיִן
טוֹבָה. רַבִּי יְהוֹשֻׁעַ אוֹמֵר: חָבֵר טוֹב. רַבִּי יוֹסֵי אוֹמֵר:

⦿§ Both Were "The Greatest"

י"ל דשניהם אמת ורבי אלעזר בן ערך נעשה תלמידו אחר כך וראיה דלא
אמר ורבי אלעזר בן ערך אף עמהם כמו שכתב ורבי אליעזר בן הורקנוס אף
עמהם.

In truth, no contradiction exists between the *mishnah's* conclusion stating that Rabbi Elazar ben Arach was the greatest *talmid* of Rabban Yochanan ben Zakkai and the previous statement that Rabbi Eliezer ben Hyrkanos enjoyed that distinction. The *mishnah* may simply have been referring to various eras during Rabban Yochanan's long tenure. At first, Rabbi Eliezer ben Hyrkanos was his greatest disciple. However, when Rabbi Elazar ben Arach joined the ranks of Rabban Yochanan's *talmidim*, he obtained that distinction. This approach is supported by the *mishnah* which when extolling Rabbi Eliezer ben Hyrkanos does not state, וְרַבִּי אֶלְעָזָר בֶּן עֲרָךְ אַף עִמָּהֶם, that Rabbi Elazar ben Arach was inferior to him, as it does when it speaks of Rabbi Elazar's greatness. This was, simply, because Rabbi Eliezer was being compared to other scholars *prior* to the arrival of Rabbi Elazar ben Arach.

⦿§ Great, but Not Necessarily Authoritative

וקצת קשה דלפי זה למה פסקו בתנור של עכנאי כרוב הלא הוא מכריע, ובאמת
מן השמים הסכימו כך מפני שמכריע. וי"ל דאחרי רבים להטות משמע אף שמטין
דאם לא כן מה הטיה שייך.

Despite the accolades reaped by Rabbi Elazar ben Arach, his halachic rulings are not necessarily authoritative, especially when his opinion conflicts with the majority of his contemporaries. This can be deduced from the famous Talmudic controversy known as תַּנּוּר שֶׁל עַכְנַאי, *the oven of Achana* (cf. *Bava Metzia* 59b), where, despite the presence of a heavenly voice (בַּת קוֹל) supporting Rabbi Elazar, the view of the majority of scholars prevailed. The Torah's preference for following the majority — regardless of any mitigating factors — may be deduced from the *pasuk*, אַחֲרֵי רַבִּים לְהַטֹּת (*Shemos* 23:2), which implies that we should we "lean" (follow) towards the majority view to the extent of ignoring any other factor.

[13] He [Rabban Yochanan ben Zakkai] said to them [the five disciples]: Go out and discern which is the good path to which a man should cling. Rabbi Eliezer says: A good eye. Rabbi Yehoshua says: A good friend.

13.

■ אֵיזוֹ הִיא דֶרֶךְ טוֹבָה שֶׁיִּדְבַּק בָּה הָאָדָם. רַבִּי אֱלִיעֶזֶר אוֹמֵר: עַיִן טוֹבָה ■
Which is the good path to which a man should cling. Rabbi Eliezer says: A good eye.

✦§ Good Eye

The term עַיִן טוֹבָה, *a good eye,* lends itself to various interpretations. Some of these draw a link to Rabbi Eliezer's phenomenal memory, discussed in the previous *mishnah,* and his advocacy of this attribute.

✦§ Do Not Be Jealous

שתהא טובה בשל חבירו ולא יהיה צר עין, כי זה יהי ח״ו מצד הכפירה, כי אם
יחשוב האדם שהכל מאתו יתברך לא יקנא לשום דבר בשל חבירו, כי ה׳ נתן לו
ודאי נכון הוא הדבר, רק אם לא יחשוב זאת ויחשוב שמהנכון הוא שיהא הכל
שלו, וכופר במה שהשי״ת נתן לו, ולזה אמר עין טובה.
כפי מה שכל אחד מסתכל בעין טובה על חבירו כך הקב״ה משגיח עליו בעין טובה
כדכתיב ה׳ צלך ואיתא כלה כו׳ שעיניה יפות אין כל .אופה צריכה בדיקה.

The *Maggid of Koznitz* interpreted this phrase as a plea against jealousy, noting that קִנְאָה, *jealousy,* is in actuality a subtle form of כְּפִירָה, *heresy.* One who truly believes that his entire fortune comes from Hashem will never envy another's fortune. On the contrary, he will be content knowing that Hashem has provided him with all of his needs.

The *Imrei Emes* pointed out the benefit of displaying a "good eye" toward one's peers. In the merit of עַיִן טוֹבָה, Hashem, in turn, will display a "good eye" to *Klal Yisrael,* seeking their merit, rather than their transgressions. This "reciprocal" and intimate relationship between us and our Creator was already voiced by David as he sings, ה׳ צִלְּךָ (*Tehillim* 121:5), *Hashem is your shadow* — His conduct towards us reflects our behavior towards Him.

Perhaps the famed *Chazal* (*Taanis* 24a) stating that a bride with beautiful eyes requires no further scrutiny may be interpreted allegorically as referring to the Jewish people, who are often depicted as Hashem's bride. If we display

A "Spiritual Good Eye"

> אין הכוונה דווקא ברכושו של חבירו, אלא אפילו בתורה שלא להיות צר עין במה
> שחבירו הוא יותר למדן ממנו, וכן ביראת שמים שלא להיות צר עין במה שחבירו
> הוא יותר חסיד וירא שמים ממנו.

The *Chiddushei HaRim* suggested that this attribute can be applied to spiritual as well as material matters. Just as we should not be envious of someone else's wealth, we also should not envy his knowledge of Torah or his righteousness (*Maggidei HaEmes*).

Looking at "Good Things"

> עין טובה יש לה ב' פירושים, עין טובה פארגינען יענעם, אחד לחבירו, ועין טובה
> לא להסתכל במקום שלא צריך, לא רק עבירה, הרהור, אלא אפילו הבטה גם לא
> במקום שלא צריך, העולם מפרש לא הביט און ביעקב אפילו לא הביט, הבטה
> שאינה טובה היא און ביעקב.

The *Pnei Menachem* emphasized the dual meaning of עַיִן טוֹבָה, *a good eye*. It refers, first of all, to the importance of *"farginnen"* — begrudging the good fortune of others. (Please refer to our tribute to the *Pnei Menachem*, in *Days of Awe*, page xxii, describing his lifelong advocacy of that trait.) Additionally, the term עַיִן טוֹבָה may refer to the eye that is discriminating and disciplined enough to only look at "good things" — only at what is appropriate for a Torah-true Jew. The *pasuk*, לֹא הִבִּיט אָוֶן בְּיַעֲקֹב, *He perceived no iniquity in Yaakov* (Bamidbar 23:21), may be reinterpreted in this light. Even *looking* at something that one should not be gazing at (לֹא הִבִּיט) is considered a grievous sin (אָוֶן) (*Maggidei HaEmes*).

Looking at the Good Aspects of Eretz Yisrael

> בחורף תרפ"א בקש אדמו"ר האמרי אמת ז"ל לנסוע לארץ ישראל. ניסה גיסו
> הרב מבנדין ז"ל לעכב בעדו, "וכאשר ישוב הרבי לפולין יצטרך לספר על
> מעשיהם הרעים וישנו חשש הוצאת דבת הארץ בבחינת מרגלים למה לו זאת"?
> השיבו האמרי אמת ז"ל "אז אפקח את העין הטובה ואראה רק טוב, אכרה את
> האוזן הטובה ואשמע אך טוב".
>
> איתא בספר הזכות: הטובה היא אם רעה (במדבר יג:יט) גם אם רעה, שתראה
> להם רעה, יראו הטובה היא כמו שהיא באמת ... שיכניסו עין טובה בארץ
> שהפנימיות היא טובה.

When the *Imrei Emes* sought to visit *Eretz Yisrael*, his brother-in-law, the Bendiner Rav, attempted to dissuade him. He argued that upon the Rebbe's return, he might feel compelled to describe the religious deficiencies of some of the Land's early settlers. This might be akin to criticizing the Land, which was the sin of the *meraglim*. The Rebbe responded by assuring his brother-in-law that he would "open his good eye" to see only good and "turn his good ear" to hear only good things." By doing so, he followed in the footsteps of his great-grandfather, the *Chiddushei HaRim*, who interpreted the *pasuk*, הֲטוֹבָה הוּא אִם רָעָה, *is it good or is it bad* (*Bamidbar* 13:19), to mean that even if the Land appears to be bad, we should attempt to perceive the underlying goodness that can be found beneath the surface problem (*Maggidei HaEmes*).

⋖ The Power of a Good Eye

קל וחומר הוא מה בעין רעה יכולין להזיק אפילו מי שאינו חייב בדבר, מכל שכן בעין טובה שיכולים לעשות טובה אף למי שאין לו שייכות שהרי מדה טובה מרובה וכו'.

The *Imrei Emes* reasoned as follows: If an עַיִן רָע, *an evil eye* — in the sense of viewing the world with mistrust and jealousy — can harm the innocent (cf. *Bava Metzia* 107b stating that most illnesses are generated by עַיִן רָע), then certainly displaying an עַיִן טוֹבָה, a good and generous eye, can help even those who are unknown and unrelated to us. For we know that the capacity to do good is far greater than the capacity to do evil.

⋖ The Association Between Rabbi Eliezer's Attributes

כלפי שהי' בור סיד שאמ"ט וע"י עין טובה שאינו רוצה של חבירו השכל נותן שזה מביא זכירה.

Whereas the previous *mishnah* highlighted Rabbi Eliezer's phenomenal memory, here his absolute lack of jealousy is emphasized. In truth, these attributes may be related. This most generous of men — who sought nothing that belonged to someone else and was totally self-reliant — richly deserved the gift of an outstanding memory, allowing him to draw upon, and thus maximize, his formidable intellectual resources. When a person is not jealous and is at peace with another individual having all that that person possesses, his own capacity for intellectual growth is increased (adapted from *Sfas Emes*).

■ רַבִּי יְהוֹשֻׁעַ אוֹמֵר: חָבֵר טוֹב — *Rabbi Yehoshua says: A good friend.*

שָׁכֵן טוֹב. רַבִּי שִׁמְעוֹן אוֹמֵר: הָרוֹאֶה אֶת הַנּוֹלָד.
רַבִּי אֶלְעָזָר אוֹמֵר: לֵב טוֹב. אָמַר לָהֶם: רוֹאֶה אֲנִי אֶת
דִּבְרֵי אֶלְעָזָר בֶּן עֲרָךְ מִדִּבְרֵיכֶם, שֶׁבִּכְלַל דְּבָרָיו
דִּבְרֵיכֶם.

◆§ A Good Friend

כל אדם צריך להיות לו חבר ואוהב נאמן שיוכל לספר לו את כל נקודות לבבו
אפילו בגנות מעשיו כמו שהיה יהודה חירה רעהו. לכל אחד יש משהו שאין
בחבירו ועל ידי שמתאספים יחד יכול כל אחד להושיע לחבירו.

While the simple meaning of this phrase refers to the need to befriend
another (as indeed the *Sfas Emes* interprets the *mishnah*), the *mishnah*
may also be alluding to the necessity of having a good friend to whom one can
relate confidential, often damaging information. For example, Yehudah felt free
to discuss his relationship with Tamar with his intimate friend Chirah (see
Bereishis Ch. 38) (R' Simcha Bunim, *Maggidei HaEmes*). The *Imrei Emes* also
noted that friends are able to pool their spiritual resources. Each individual is
endowed with a unique talent. By befriending each other, we can merge our
individual attributes, thereby enhancing our service of Hashem (*Maggidei
HaEmes*).

◆§ "Befriending" Hashem

הוא הבורא יתברך, שצריך האדם לדבק בהבורא יתברך שמו.

The Maggid of Koznitz interpreted this phrase as referring to Hashem.
Ideally, our relationship with Him should not merely be based on obedience,
but rather on clinging to Him, as one would to an intimate friend (*Maggidei
HaEmes*).

◆§ Through a Friend We Can Cling to Hashem *(Deveikus)*

גם על ידי חבר טוב יכולין להגיע, ואהבת לרעך כמוך אני ה'.

The *Lev Simchah* noted that חָבֵר טוֹב, a *good friend*, is valuable not only in his
own right but also as a means of coming closer to Hashem. The role played
by a good friend in inspiring one's *Avodas Hashem* can be deduced from the
pasuk, 'וְאָהַבְתָּ לְרֵעֲךָ כָּמוֹךָ, אֲנִי ה, *Love your neighbor as your self* (*Vayikra* 19:18),

2 / 13   *Rabbi Yose says: A good neighbor. Rabbi Shimon says: One who considers the outcome [of a deed]. Rabbi Elazar says: A good heart. He said to them: I prefer the words of Elazar ben Arach to your words, for your words are included in his words.*

---

whereby you will attain the exalted status of אֲנִי ה' — perceiving Hashem's Presence (*Lev Simchah, Maggidei HaEmes*).

◆§ Joining a Good Cause

גם יי"ל חבר טוב, חבר לדבר טוב.

Alternatively, the term חָבֵר טוֹב may be interpreted as טוֹב חָבֵר לְדָבָר, *a friend of a good cause*. By selecting carefully the cause with which one is involved, one fulfills the spirit of this *mishnah* (*Lev Simchah, Maggidei HaEmes*).

■ רַבִּי יוֹסֵי אוֹמֵר: שָׁכֵן טוֹב — *Rabbi Yose says: A good neighbor.* ■

◆§ Become a Good Neighbor

כן יש לפרש שכן טוב עד"ז דבלאו הכי קשה וכי ביד האדם לבחור שכניו שיהיו טובים.

The term *a good neighbor* may refer to our obligation to be a good neighbor. While it may be difficult to select our neighbors, we can certainly become a good influence on them (*Maggidei HaEmes*).

■ רַבִּי שִׁמְעוֹן אוֹמֵר: הָרוֹאֶה אֶת הַנּוֹלָד — *Rabbi Shimon says: One who considers the outcome [of a deed].*

◆§ Fearing Sin — Foreseeing The Future

פי בכל דבר מתיישב היטב מה יהיה תוכן הדבר והוא מכוון למדתו ושבחו דרבי שמעון היה ירא חטא.

A close relationship exists between Rabbi Shimon's trait of fearing sin and his advocacy of carefully anticipating the consequences of one's behavior. The person who fears sin always contemplates the future ramifications of his every action.

■ רַבִּי אֶלְעָזָר אוֹמֵר: לֵב טוֹב — *Rabbi Elazar says: A good heart.*

✥ Be Willing to Yield

להיות נכנע ורך כקנה להטות עצמו לכל צד.

Perhaps, the simplest interpretation of "a good heart" is a willingness to adapt oneself and yield to the needs and concerns of others. In fact, the Jewish people are compared to a supple reed (cf. *Taanis* 20a) because of our characteristic flexibility and willingness to yield on matters of personal pride rather than be needlessly rigid. (Of course this does not refer to halachic issues where frequently one may not yield.)

✥ Have a Heart

ישנם אנשים הסוברים שיש להם לב נשבר, אך עדיין אין להם לב כלל.
מבקשים לב טהור ברא לי אלקים וגו', וכי ישנו לב טמא. אלא כל מי שאינו מתפלל
על לב טהור וחושב שיש לו לב טהור, זהו טמא.

The term "a good heart" implies that we have a heart! This may seem obvious. Who doesn't have a heart? Yet, the *Imrei Emes* would remark that many individuals who think that they have a contrite heart are, in reality, totally lacking a true Jewish heart which is replete with sensitivity and feeling.

The Kotzker Rebbe interpreted the famous *pasuk*, לֵב טָהוֹר בְּרָא לִי אֱלֹקִים, *a pure heart create for me, O God (Tehillim* 51:12), in a similar vein, commenting that anyone who thinks that he already has a pure heart actually does not (*Maggidei HaEmes*).

✥ Everyone Has the Potential

כתיב ומצאת את לבבו נאמן לפניך, לכל אדם מישראל יש משהו מלב זה רק
שאינו יודע, וזה נקרא תעלומות לב.

Despite the difficulties in attaining the trait of *a good heart*, the *potential* for such an achievement is enjoyed by every Jew. As Nechemiah states: וּמָצָאתָ אֶת לְבָבוֹ נֶאֱמָן לְפָנֶיךָ, *You found his heart faithful before You (Nechemiah* 9:8) (i.e. the capacity of every Jewish heart to place its trust and faith in Hashem). Unfortunately, we are not always aware of our enormous potential. The liturgist (who composed the Yom Kippur Confession prayer) aptly describes this innate but often hidden capacity as תַּעֲלוּמוֹת לֵב, *the hidden heart.*

◆§ How to Attain This Trait

אמר שלב טוב אינו יכול להיות רק למי שאין לו נגיעה כלל בעולם הזה.

While we all enjoy the capacity for a לֵב טוֹב, often our preoccupation with the material pleasures of this world prevent us from fulfilling this potential. The *Chiddushei HaRim* maintained that only one who has removed himself from materialism could attain this highly desirable trait (*Maggidei HaEmes*).

◆§ The Power of a Good Heart

כתיב ולא ימס את לבב אחיו כלבבו מדה טובה מרובה ולב טוב של אחד יכול להגביה כל הלבבות כדאיתא בזוה״ק על הפסוק אודה ה׳ בכל לבב שדוד המלך היה משבח להקב״ה עם כל הלבבות של ישראל.

The Torah warns us that a timid and fainthearted soldier will "melt" the hearts of his comrades and cause them to flee. If this is the power that a "bad heart" possesses, imagine the capacity for good that a "good heart" has (bearing in mind that the capacity to do good is much greater than that of doing harm). One "good Jewish heart" can elevate many other hearts. As David proclaims, אוֹדֶה ה׳ בְּכָל לֵבָב, *I will thank Hashem with all hearts* (*Tehillim* 111:1) — I will move all hearts through the purity and enthusiasm of my own (*Imrei Emes*, *Maggidei HaEmes*).

◆§ The Impact of a Good Heart and a Good Eye

איתא עינא ולבא תרי סרסורי דעבירה ולהיפך לב טוב ועין טובה מסייע להתגלות מלכות שמים. וכן בכל דורות ובכל הסתרות כפי שהאדם מטה לבו ועיניו ומסתכלין כלפי מעלה ומכוונין לבם לאביהם שבשמים כן יש להם ההתגלות מלמעלה ונושעים מהגלות ומיצר הרע שזה עיקר הגלות.

The terms "a good eye" and "a good heart" may refer to our determination to channel the impulses of our heart and eyes for *mitzvos* rather than utilizing them as a means of doing *aveiros*. Just as an evil eye and an evil heart are precursors of sin (cf. *Bamidbar* 15:39, וְלֹא תָתוּרוּ אַחֲרֵי לְבַבְכֶם וְאַחֲרֵי עֵינֵיכֶם, *and not explore after your heart and after your eyes*), so too possessing a generous eye and heart — and the *mitzvos* that are engendered by those *middos tovos* — are the catalysts for the return of the visible presence of the *Shechinah* into our lives. Throughout the long *Galus* — no matter how distant we may feel from Hashem — by turning our heart and eyes to Hashem we can begin to extricate ourselves from the tight grip of the *Yetzer Hara* and slowly come closer to Him.

[יד] אָמַר לָהֶם: צְאוּ וּרְאוּ אֵיזוֹ הִיא דֶּרֶךְ רָעָה
שֶׁיִּתְרַחֵק מִמֶּנָּה הָאָדָם. רַבִּי אֱלִיעֶזֶר אוֹמֵר: עַיִן
רָעָה. רַבִּי יְהוֹשֻׁעַ אוֹמֵר: חָבֵר רָע. רַבִּי יוֹסֵי אוֹמֵר:

⧉ How to Survive Even Without a Good Friend

וכשאין לך שם עוד חבר טוב, תוכל לסמוך על רבי אליעזר בשעת הדחק עין
טובה, ומכל שכן רבי אלעזר בן ערך לב טוב, אשר בכלל דבריו דבריכם.

While ideally a good friend, as Rabbi Yehoshua notes, is essential for Torah
life, in the unfortunate absence of a good friend, one can survive on the
basis of the positive traits of *"a good eye"* and *"a good heart"* recommended by
Rabbi Eliezer ben Hyrkanos and Rabbi Elazar ben Arach respectively (*Lev
Simchah, Maggidei HaEmes*).

⧉ The Association Between the Virtues and the Values of Rabbi Yochanan ben Zakkai's Talmidim

ורבי אליעזר בן הורקנוס עין טובה לכן היה בור סוד שאינו מאבד טפה על ידי
שלא הביא קנאה בחבריו לא נתנו גם בו עין וזכר הכל ועל דרך טוב עין הוא יבורך
ניתן לו ברכה זו ורבי יוסי אומר חבר טוב על ידי שהיה מילדותו אצל חברים
וחכמים בבית המדרש. וכן הרואה את הנולד מביאו ליראת חטא שזה הי' מדת
יר"ש.

We may draw a parallel between the *values* espoused by Rabbi Yochanan
ben Zakkai's *talmidim* and their *virtues*. For example, Rabbi Eliezer ben
Hyrkanos who never was jealous of his peers (עַיִן טוֹבָה) was rewarded by their
total lack of envy of his phenomenal grasp of Torah. As a result, he was able
to retain everything that he had learned (בּוֹר סוּד שֶׁאֵינוֹ מְאַבֵּד טִפָּה). As stated in
Mishlei 22:9, טוֹב עַיִן הוּא יְבֹרָךְ, *the one with a generous eyes will be blessed.*

Similarly, having been associated with *talmidei chachamim* from birth (as
we read in the previous *mishnah*; refer to our commentary there regarding his
yichus), Rabbi Yehoshua ben Chanania could appreciate the significance of a
good colleague (חָבֵר טוֹב). Rabbi Shimon ben Nesanel known for his fear of
sinning (יְרֵא חֵטְא) could particularly appreciate the importance of contemplating the future impact of all our actions (הָרוֹאֶה אֶת הַנּוֹלָד).

14.

■ צְאוּ וּרְאוּ אֵיזוֹ הִיא דֶּרֶךְ רָעָה שֶׁיִּתְרַחֵק מִמֶּנָּה הָאָדָם. רַבִּי אֱלִיעֶזֶר אוֹמֵר: עַיִן ■

[14] *He said to them: Go out and discern which is the evil path from which a man should distance himself. Rabbi Eliezer says: An evil eye. Rabbi Yehoshua says: A wicked friend. Rabbi Yose says: A wicked*

רָעָה — *Go out and discern which is the evil path from which a man should distance himself. Rabbi Eliezer says: An evil eye.*

☙ Reaffirming Their Position

הגם ששמעו ששיבח דברי רבי אלעזר, מכל מקום הודו על האמת כפי מה שנראה לכל אחד ואחד.

Though Rabbi Yochanan had already indicated his preference for the approach of Rabbi Elazar who said that a *good heart* is the best way to conduct oneself and, by inference, that an evil eye is the greatest hazard, his *talmidim* were nonetheless justified in maintaining their previous positions, based on *their* interpretation of the Torah.

☙ How to Avoid an "Evil Eye"

אין צריכים לפחד מעין רעה, אבל צריכים להזהר בעין טובה.

According to R' Yechiel Meir of Gostynim, one the most efficacious means of avoiding "an evil eye" is to simply always be guided by the principle of "a local eye," a generous and compassionate outlook (*Maggidei HaEmes*).

☙ Begrudging Another's Success

להרה"ק רבי חיים מקרסנוביץ ז"ל מה טעם שאם האדם מפסיד ממונו על ידי סיבה טבעית משלים הוא עם מצבו, ואילו אם מפסיד הוא את ממונו בדין תורה אין הוא מרוצה מפסק הרב והרי הוא מלא תרעומת. והשיב, מפני שבדין תורה מרויח השני.

To explain the concept of "an evil eye," R' Chaim of Krasnowitz raised the following question: Why do people readily accept financial losses that occur in daily life, while they resist the verdict of a *Din Torah* requiring them to compensate a peer? He continued, "The answer is quite simple — and it gets to the essence of " 'an evil eye' ". Most financial difficulties only involve *losses*. However, whenever a party loses a *Din Torah*, the other party *gains*. While we are prepared to accept our loss, we absolutely cannot tolerate another's gain" (*Maggidei HaEmes*).

שֶׁכֵּן רָע. רַבִּי שִׁמְעוֹן אוֹמֵר: הַלֹּוֶה וְאֵינוֹ מְשַׁלֵּם. אֶחָד הַלּוֶה מִן הָאָדָם כְּלֹוֶה מִן הַמָּקוֹם, שֶׁנֶּאֱמַר: "לֹוֶה רָשָׁע וְלֹא יְשַׁלֵּם, וְצַדִּיק חוֹנֵן וְנוֹתֵן." רַבִּי אֶלְעָזָר אוֹמֵר: לֵב רָע. אָמַר לָהֶם: רוֹאֶה אֲנִי אֶת דִּבְרֵי אֶלְעָזָר בֶּן עֲרָךְ מִדִּבְרֵיכֶם, שֶׁבִּכְלַל דְּבָרָיו דִּבְרֵיכֶם.

[טו] הֵם אָמְרוּ שְׁלֹשָׁה דְבָרִים. רַבִּי אֱלִיעֶזֶר

שח הרה"ק רבי מאיר מפרמישלן ז"ל סוס נכנס לנהר בכדי לשתותו, פתאום החל לבעוט עד שנעשו המים מלאי רפש וטיט ורק אז התחיל לשתות בשלוה. יען שכאשר היו המים צלולים ראה צלו על פני המים חשב שבא סוס אחר לשתות מים כמותו, התחיל לבעוט עד שהעלה רפש וטיט ואז נתקררה דעתו והחל לשתות את מים העכורים.

R' Meir of Premishlan offered a beautiful *mashal* to illustrate this concept. When a horse is brought to a stream it kicks violently, refusing to drink until the water has become sufficiently roiled. The reason for this bizarre behavior is really quite simple. While wading in clear waters, the horse mistakes its own reflection for another horse. Only when a potential rival has been eliminated — when it can no longer see another horse in the turbulent water — will it drink, relaxed and assured that no one else is sharing his water (*Maggidei HaEmes*).

■ רַבִּי שִׁמְעוֹן אוֹמֵר: הַלֹּוֶה וְאֵינוֹ מְשַׁלֵּם — *Rabbi Shimon says: One who borrows and does not repay.*

◆§ A Form of Myopia

פ' שאינו רואה את הנולד . . .
ועי' בהרע"ב שפי' שלא ימצא מי שילונו ויל"פ נמי כפשוטו שאם יודע שלא יהי'
לו לשלם לא ילוה כלל.

Following the pattern of the other traits mentioned in this *mishnah*, which are the antithesis of the laudable traits mentioned in the previous *mishnah*, we may argue that not repaying debts is a form of myopia, the very opposite of *"considering the outcome of a deed"* (foreseeing the future). As the *Bartenura* notes, by not repaying *existing* debts I am almost ensuring that *future* creditors will be reluctant to lend, and this may ultimately lead to hunger. Having experienced the frustration of being rebuffed when I needed funds, I will be reluctant to ask others for help (adapted from *Sfas Emes*).

neighbor. *Rabbi Shimon says: One who borrows and does not repay; one who borrows from man is like one who borrows from the Omnipresent, as it is said (Tehillim 37:21): "The wicked one borrows and does not repay, while the Righteous One is gracious and gives." Rabbi Elazar says: A wicked heart.* He *[Rabban Yochanan ben Zakkai] said to them: I prefer the words of Elazar ben Arach to your words, for your words are included in his words.*

[15] *They each said three things.*

■ אֶחָד הַלֹּוֶה מִן הָאָדָם כְּלֹוֶה מִן הַמָּקוֹם — *One who borrows from man is like one who borrows from the Omnipresent.*

◆§ Hashem Guarantees

וזה כלוה מן המקום כי כיון שנגזר בשמים שיהי׳ לחבירו כסף זה רק הלוהו לזה
א״כ צריך הקב״ה לשלם לחבירו מה שמגיע לו גם י״ל כמ״ש אם כסף תלוה מצוה
להלוות והקב״ה ערב בעין על אמונתו הלוהו לשלם וזה צדיק חונן ונותן כמ״ש
צדיק ה׳ בכ״ד.

By comparing borrowing from a peer to borrowing from Hashem, the *mishnah* seems to be adding an additional dimension to the sin of not repaying debts. Inasmuch as Hashem had already determined that my creditor earn a certain annual income, but as a result of my delinquency in repaying my debt, I am "compelling" Hashem to act as my surrogate and compensate him. In turn, I now am indebted to Hashem, rather than to a mortal. In retrospect, not paying my initial debt was truly shortsighted. In fact, by not paying my debt, I am forcing Hashem to act in His role as the "guarantor" of all loans. The *mishnah* alludes to Hashem's role in ensuring payment of delinquent loans by citing the conclusion of the *pasuk* (לוֶֹה רָשָׁע וְלֹא יְשַׁלֵּם, *The wicked one borrowed and does not repay*), צַדִּיק חוֹנֵן וְנוֹתֵן, *but the Righteous one is gracious and gives* (Tehillim 37:21). The Righteous One, Hashem, known as the צַדִּיק שֶׁל עוֹלָם (cf. Tehillim 145:17, צַדִּיק ה׳ בְּכָל דְּרָכָיו), will graciously ensure payment.

15.

■ הֵם אָמְרוּ שְׁלֹשָׁה דְבָרִים — *They each said three things.*

◆§ Only Three Statements?

ע׳ ברע״ב ולפי׳ הראשון קשה דבר״א ודאי נמי אמרו טפי רק י״ל הפי׳ כל משך

אוֹמֵר: יְהִי כְבוֹד חֲבֵרְךָ חָבִיב עָלֶיךָ כְּשֶׁלָךְ, וְאַל תְּהִי
נוֹחַ לִכְעוֹס; וְשׁוּב יוֹם אֶחָד לִפְנֵי מִיתָתְךָ; וֶהֱוֵי

הזמן שהיו תלמידים לריב"ז.

It is unlikely that Rabbi Yochanan's five most prized *talmidim* only said three things of significance. Attempting to answer this question, the *Bartenura* suggests that these three statements were their only teachings that pertained to ethics. This also seems difficult — that five great scholars, whose teachings about ethics were the focal point of the previous *mishnahs*, would have no more than three ideas of their own to offer. It may be deduced from the context, in which we emphasized that they were disciples of Rabban Yochanan, that these were their only statements on ethics while they were his *talmidim*.

■ יְהִי כְבוֹד חֲבֵרְךָ חָבִיב עָלֶיךָ כְּשֶׁלָךְ וְאַל תְּהִי נוֹחַ לִכְעוֹס — *Let your peer's honor be as dear to you as your own and do not anger easily.*

◆§ Which Comes First — Honoring One's Peers or Controlling Anger?

ועל ידי זה אל תהי נוח לכעוס כמו שאינו כועס על עצמו והרע"ב כתב להיפך.

The juxtaposition of these two statements leads to an interesting and often practical question: What is the relationship between displaying respect for a peer and controlling anger? Whereas the *Bartenura* learns that anger control is a prerequisite for כְּבוֹד חֲבֵרִים, "honoring one's peers, " the reverse is also true. The most efficacious manner of controlling one's anger is to consider the identity of the person who is about to be the victim of your anger. As a practitioner of the rule that respect of a peer is as important as self-respect, one can only arrive at the following conclusion: Just as a person would not normally become angry at himself, so too one should not become angry at a peer.

◆§ React as if You Are Being Honored

רצה לומר אם מכבדין את חבירך, או יש לו שפע עושר ובנים, יהי חביב עליך כמו שעושין לך הכבוד העושר וכנ"ל.

According to the Maggid of Koznitz, the *mishnah* is urging us to appreciate the honor given to our friend (or the wealth of *nachas* that he enjoys) as if we ourselves were being honored (*Maggidei HaEmes*).

✌§ Do Not Take Too Seriously the Honor That You Receive

כאשר הגיע הרבי ר' שמעלקא ז"ל לניקלשבורג לכהן כרב, נסתגר בחדרו. שמעו אותו האנשים שעמדו בחוץ איך שמשבח את עצמו ואומר אל עצמו "ברוך הבא צדיק גאון וקדוש" וכדומה. כשיצא משם שאלוהו לפשר הדיבורים האלה, והשיבם: "ידעתי שעוד מעט יעשו לי קבלת פנים הדורה ויכבדו אותי וישבחו ויפארו בכבודי והנני מפרש לעצמי 'יהי כבוד חברך חביב עליך כשלך,' שידא בעיניך הכבוד שמחלקים לך חברך כמו הכבוד שאתה מחלק לעצמך, וכשם שאינך מתפעל מכבוד שלעצמך כך אל תתפעל בכבוד שמכבדים אותך חבריך."

When the renowned Rav Shmelke arrived in Nikolsburg, he remained secluded in his room. He was heard saying to himself, "Welcome to Nikolsburg, Righteous, brilliant and saintly individual." When asked to explain his "bizarre" behavior, he replied, "Knowing that I will soon receive a royal welcome during which all kinds of accolades will be lavished on me, I sought to 'inoculate' myself against the possibility that I might actually take seriously all the praise that I will hear. The most effective method of ensuring this objective is to simply tell myself everything that I will eventually be hearing from others. As the *mishnah* says, consider the honor that you will receive from *others* (יְהִי כְּבוֹד חֲבֵרְךָ) as if it came from you (כְּשֶׁלָּךְ). Just as you would not take too seriously the honor you accorded to yourself, so too do not take to heart what others say about you" (*Maggidei HaEmes*).

■ וְאַל תְּהִי נוֹחַ לִכְעוֹס; וְשׁוּב יוֹם אֶחָד לִפְנֵי מִיתָתְךָ — *And do not anger easily; repent one day before your death.*

✌§ Anger Is a Form of Death

דהנה איתא בזוהר הקדוש כשאדם הוא כועס אז הנשמה בורחת ממנו וזהו הענין מיתה על כן כשירצה האדם לכעוס אזי יחשוב תיכף שצריך לשוב בתשובה לפניו, כי זה הענין מיתה.

R' Levi Yitzchak explained the relationship between these two elements by noting the observation of the *Zohar* (*Korach* 179a) that when one becomes angry his soul (temporarily) leaves him. If anger is a form of death, it follows that one must repent before getting angry just as the *mishnah* requires us to repent a day before our death. Of course, as part of the process of *teshuvah*

מִתְחַמֵּם כְּנֶגֶד אוּרָן שֶׁל חֲכָמִים, וֶהֱוֵי זָהִיר בְּגַחַלְתָּן ב / טו
שֶׁלֹּא תִכָּוֶה – שֶׁנְּשִׁיכָתָן נְשִׁיכַת שׁוּעָל, וַעֲקִיצָתָן

we must learn how to control our anger (adapted from *Maggidei HaEmes*).

⊷§ Keep on Learning Until the Final Moment

בגמ' לעולם אל ימנע אדם עצמו מבית המדרש אפילו שעה אחת אולי הרמז על
מה דאיתא במשנה ושוב יום אחד לפני מיתתך, וזה שנזכר שם שלא ימנע עצמו
מבית המדרש וממדברי תורה אפילו בשעת מיתה.

A ccording to the *Beis Yisrael*, the best method of ensuring that our final
moments are spent in an atmosphere of *teshuvah* is to never cease learning
Torah. As the Gemara states, לְעוֹלָם אַל יִמְנַע אָדָם עַצְמוֹ מִבֵּית הַמִּדְרָשׁ אֲפִילוּ שָׁעָה
אַחַת, "A person should not be absent from the *beis hamidrash* even for a
moment" (*Shabbos* 83b). The expression "even for a moment" may refer to the
final moment of one's life (*Maggidei HaEmes*).

⊷§ The Final Blow

הרבי ר' בער ממעזריטש ז"ל אמר "כששני בני אדם נלחמים ומכים אחד את
השני אף שאחד מהם גבור ומנצח לחבירו, מכל מקום בתוך המריבה על כרחך
שאף החלש נותן לו מכה, והעיקר לתת המכה האחרונה "דעם לעצטין פאטש,"
כך בלי ספק היצר הרע מתגבר מדי פעם, אבל מה בכך, העיקר הוא ליתן לו
באחרונה ולנצחו." ואמרתי לפרש בזה שוב יום אחד לפני מיתתך, כי אינו יודע
איזה ה"פאטש" האחרון וצריך קיום וחיזוק לזה כי הוא מלחמה ואף שמנצח
במלחמה אחת עם כל זה היצר הרע לא ירף מלהלחם עוד ועוד.

T o appreciate the importance of doing *teshuvah* prior to death, R' Ber of
Mezeritch noted that when two individuals fight, each wants to strike the
final blow. Even the loser of the bout derives satisfaction from administering
the final punch. So too, the *Yetzer Hara* is determined to strike the final blow.
By constantly repenting, we may remain confident that whatever temporary
triumphs the *Yetzer Hara* may enjoy, we have the ability to render him powerless and the ultimate triumph will be ours to savor (*Maggidei HaEmes*).

⊷§ The Benefits of Constantly Doing Teshuvah

איתא אדם נידון בכל יום, וכן גבי תשובה אמרו שוב יום אחד לפני מיתתך וכו'
ונמצא כל ימיו בתשובה, וכיון שהוא נידון בכל יום ושב כל יום בתשובה בודאי
גם הקב"ה מכפר בכל יום.

sages, but beware of their glowing coal lest you be scorched — for their bite is the bite of a fox, their sting

T he *Lev Simchah* noted the benefits of constantly doing *teshuvah*. The Gemara (*Rosh Hashanah* 16a) relates that Hashem judges us every day. In response to our *teshuvah*, Hashem forgives our sins on a daily basis and thus, we help ensure a favorable verdict (*Maggidei HaEmes*).

∽§ The Day Before Your Spiritual Death

היא קודם הנפילה.

T he term לִפְנֵי מִיתָתְךָ, *before your death*, may also refer to spiritual death. By repenting just before the *Yetzer Hara* plans to attack me spiritually, I can help to foil his strategy (*Sfas Emes, Ki Savo* 5636)..

■ *Warm* — וֶהֱוֵי מִתְחַמֵּם כְּנֶגֶד אוּרָן שֶׁל חֲכָמִים וֶהֱוֵי זָהִיר בְּגַחַלְתָּן שֶׁלֹּא תִכָּוֶה *yourself by the fire of the sages, but beware of their glowing coal lest you be burnt.*

∽§ Warm Yourself — but Be Careful

ורק בתנאי והוי זהיר בגחלתן שלא תבוה כו'.

T hese two statements are closely related. While it is certainly meritori- ious to become intimate with scholars, as the *mishnah* states, הֱוֵי מִתְחַמֵּם כְּנֶגֶד אוּרָן שֶׁל חֲכָמִים, it is critical from the outset of our relationship that I be aware of my limitations and that I be careful not to be "burned" by their fire. Although it is acceptable to approach a great *talmid chacham* to benefit from his wisdom, do not forget the gap that still exists between you and him (adapted from *Sfas Emes*).

∽§ Warm — but Not Burnt

איתא משל לאמבטי רותחת שאין בריה יכולה לירד כו' אעפ״י שנכוה הקרה בפני אחרים, בני ישראל נקראים אמבטי רותחת שרצונם לעשות רצון שמים בהתלהבות . . . מי שבכוחו לקפוץ כנגד הבן בליעל במסירת נפש לעבודת ד' אז הוא לא נכוה רק להיפר מתעלה וגם מחמם אותם לפני אחרים שילכו גם כן בהתלהבות לעבודת ד', ואיתא הוי מתחמם באורן של תלמידי חכמים, והתלמיד חכם מעלה את האנשים הפשוטים.

עֲקִיצָתָן עַקְרָב, וּלְחִישָׁתָן לְחִישַׁת שָׂרָף, וְכָל דִּבְרֵיהֶם
כְּגַחֲלֵי אֵשׁ.

[טז] רַבִּי יְהוֹשֻׁעַ אוֹמֵר: עַיִן הָרָע, וְיֵצֶר הָרָע, וְשִׂנְאַת
הַבְּרִיּוֹת מוֹצִיאִין אֶת הָאָדָם מִן הָעוֹלָם.

[יז] רַבִּי יוֹסֵי אוֹמֵר: יְהִי מָמוֹן חֲבֵרְךָ חָבִיב עָלֶיךָ

To appreciate the metaphor הֱוֵי מִתְחַמֵּם, *warm yourself*, we recall the famous
Midrash (*Tanchuma Ki Seitzei* 9:1) describing Amalek's surprise attack on
the Jewish people. This attack was comparable to someone who jumped into a
scalding bath. Although he was badly burnt (i.e. Amalek was vanquished), he
cooled the waters sufficiently so that others could enter (i.e. other nations would
follow Amalek and attack *Klal Yisrael* with impunity).

The scalding bath alludes to the Jewish people who are full of enthusiasm to
serve Hashem. Amalek, who approached the cauldron with seething hatred,
was burnt. The *talmid chacham*, on the other hand, not only benefits from the
warmth and enthusiasm but is also able to impart his warmth to others (*Beis
Yisrael, Maggidei HaEmes*).

■ וּלְחִישָׁתָן לְחִישַׁת שָׂרָף — *Their hiss is the hiss of a serpent.*

✎§ No Personal Pleasure

חז״ל הגידו כל תלמיד חכם שאינו נוקם ונוטר כנחש אינו תלמיד חכם. ואולי י״ל
עפ״י מה דאיתא לעתיד לבוא מתקבצות ובאות כל החיות אצל הנחש ואומרים
לו כו׳. מה הנאה יש לך כו׳. וזה י״ל שאינו נוקם ונוטר כנחש פי׳ שלא נהנה בנקמתו
ואינו נקום ונוטר לכבוד עצמו אלא לכבוד תורתו.

The analogy of the *talmid chacham* to a serpent may be understood in light
of the well-known fact that a snake derives no pleasure when it bites its
victims (cf. *Taanis* 8a). So too, a *talmid chacham*, when he must rebuke those
who have humiliated him, does not do so out of personal pique, but rather to
restore the Torah's honor (*Maggidei HaEmes*).

16.

■ עַיִן הָרָע, וְיֵצֶר הָרָע, וְשִׂנְאַת הַבְּרִיּוֹת מוֹצִיאִין אֶת הָאָדָם מִן הָעוֹלָם — *An evil
eye, the evil inclination and hatred of other people remove a person
from the world.*

is the sting of a scorpion, their hiss is the hiss of a serpent, and all their words are like fiery coals.

[16] *Rabbi Yehoshua says: An evil eye, the evil inclination, and hatred of other people remove a person from the world.*

[17] *Rabbi Yose says: Let your peer's money be as*

⊷§ Three Causes of Premature Death

עין רעה קנאה יצה"ר נגד קנאה תאוה כבוד אשר נמי מוציאין את האדם מהעולם
תאווה שנאת הבריות כבוד.

A parallel may be drawn between this *mishnah* and a similar *mishnah* in a later *perek* which identifies הַקְּנָאָה, תַּאֲוָה וְכָבוד, *jealousy, lust and honor,* as three factors which lead to premature death (4:28). Our *mishnah* describes the *result* of the tragic flaws in character stated in a later *mishnah.* Thus, jealousy breeds an evil and jaundiced eye which begrudges another's success. Similarly, one who is driven by lust will ultimately fall into the clutches of the *Yetzer Hara.* And an insatiable appetite for *honor* will lead to a hatred for those who do not accord him enough honor (based on *Sfas Emes*).

⊷§ How Premature?

לא נתפרש אם הכוונה קודם זמן המיוחד לו מסתלק ע"י מדות הללו או כשיגיע
הזמן המיוחד והי' מוכן מצד איזה זכות לחיות עוד איזה זמן ורק ע"י שבא לו א'
ממדות הללו הם מוציאין אותו כו'.

The term "remove a person from the world" lends itself to two interpretations. While it may be understood literally — that those who suffer from these flaws will die before their designated time — it may also mean that those afflicted with these traits will live a normal life span. However, consider how their life span might have been prolonged beyond the actual allotted span by virtue of their merits, but because of these character flaws it was not.

17.

■ וְכָל ... רַבִּי יוֹסֵי אוֹמֵר: יְהִי מָמוֹן חֲבֵרְךָ חָבִיב ... וְהַתְקֵן עַצְמְךָ לִלְמוֹד תּוֹרָה
מַעֲשֶׂיךָ יִהְיוּ לְשֵׁם שָׁמַיִם — *Rabbi Yose says: Let your peer's money be as dear ... prepare yourself to study Torah ... let all your deeds be for the sake of Heaven.*

ב / יז כְּשֶׁלָּךְ; וְהַתְקֵן עַצְמְךָ לִלְמוֹד תּוֹרָה, שֶׁאֵינָהּ יְרֻשָּׁה לָךְ;
וְכָל מַעֲשֶׂיךָ יִהְיוּ לְשֵׁם שָׁמָיִם.

✌ Three Ways to Become a True "Chassid"

י״ל כי רבי יוסי חסיד וג׳ דברים הללו מכוונים למה שאמרו חז״ל מאן דבעי למהוי
חסידא יקיים מילי דאבות היינו התקן עצמך ללמוד תורה ולכן נקבע לימוד פרקי
אבות קודם חג השבועות שהוא הכנה לתלמוד תורה ואמרי לה מילי דנזיקין היינו
מה שכתוב ממון חבירך חביב עליך כשלך ואמרי לה מילי דברכות היינו מה
שכתוב וכל מעשיך יהיו לשם שמים.

Rabbi Yose who was identified previously as being a חָסִיד, *a scrupulously pious person*, is suggesting three practical means of attaining that singular distinction. His suggestions parallels those of the Gemara (*Bava Kamma 30a*) which recommends: (1) being exceedingly careful not to damage anyone, (2) studying and fulfilling the precepts of *Pirkei Avos*, and (3) always being careful to recite the appropriate *berachah*. Adopting Rabbi Yose's first recommendation, *Let your peer's money be as dear to you as your own*, almost certainly ensures that we will never cause damage to someone else. Rabbi Yose's suggestion, *prepare [apply] yourself to study Torah*, would certainly include in-depth study of *Avos* (which is read every year prior to Shavuos when the Torah was given). And by reciting *berachos* (which always include Hashem's Name) we are fulfilling the final recommendation of the *mishnah, let all your deeds be for the sake of Heaven.*

✌ Your Friend's Money: Your Own Torah

הרה״ק רבי אייזיק׳ל מזידיטשוב ז״ל ביאר בנוהג שבעולם אדם אומר חבירי
לומד גם עבורי, אבל כסף רוצה כל אחד שיהיה לו דוקא ואינו מסתפק בשל
חבירו. על זה משמיענו התנא דהסדר צריך להיות להיפר, יהי ממון חברך חביב
עליך כשלך, ר״ל שתשתמש עם ממון חברך כאילו יש לך ממון, והתקן עצמך
ללמוד תורה, ואל תסתפק במה שחברך לומד.

By juxtaposing the concepts of cherishing a peer's money and preparing yourself to study Torah, the *mishnah* is contrasting the role played by material and spiritual values: First, be content with your friend's money. This means that if he is wealthy, you should be as satisfied as if *you* were the wealthy one. On the other hand, regarding Torah study, do not subsist on someone else's Torah but rather *prepare yourself* to study Torah (R' Eizik of Zidichov, *Maggidei HaEmes*).

■ וְהַתְקֵן עַצְמְךָ לִלְמוֹד תּוֹרָה, שֶׁאֵינָהּ יְרֻשָּׁה לָךְ — *Prepare yourself to study*

*dear to you as your own; apply yourself to study Torah,
for it is not yours by inheritance, and let all your deeds
be for the sake of Heaven.*

Torah, for it is not yours by inheritance.

◅§ Do Not Reject the Support of Others to Study Torah

וז״ל יהי ממון כו׳ כלומר מה שחבריך נותנים לך להחזיקך על התורה יהא חביב
עליך כשלך ואל תבעט בהחזקה מאחרים, כדי ״והתקן עצמך ללמוד תורה כזו
שאינה ירושה לך,״ כלומר לחדש חידושים מעצמך, שאי אפשר לעסוק במו״מ
וללמוד בעיון לחדש הלכה, ובע״כ תקבל החזקה שיהא לך פנאי לזה ״וכל מעשיך
יהיו לש״ש.״

While *Pirkei Avos* generally emphasizes the virtues of תּוֹרָה שֶׁיֵּשׁ עִמָּהּ מְלָאכָה,
Torah and gainful employment or honest commerce, on occasion one
should readily accept the financial support of others. As the *Chiddushei HaRim*
interpreted our *mishnah:* Value the money you receive from others to study
Torah as if you had earned it by yourself. This is particularly true if you intend
to study Torah in depth and discover new Torah thoughts. As the *mishnah*
continues, such contributions to Torah scholarship that are genuinely original
and new — not an inheritance (שֶׁאֵינָהּ יְרֻשָׁה לָךְ) — frequently can only be
arrived at through immersion in Torah to the exclusion of any commercial
activity (*Maggidei HaEmes*).

◅§ How to Prepare to Study Torah

וזהו על ידי יראת שמים.
התקן עצמך היינו להיות כלי מוכן לקבל דברי תורה וההכנה הוא הביטול בלב
שלם שלא לרצות רק לידע מה רצונו ית׳ לעשות כן כמ״ש חז״ל שנמשלה תורה
במים שיורדין למקום נמוך מי שאין לו נגיעה בעצמותו ע״י הביטול לרצון השי״י.
היינו על ידי ענוה ושפלות כדכתיב מפי עוללים ויונקים יסדת עוז, להיות בקטן
שנולד.

One of the most important prerequisites for Torah is יִרְאַת שָׁמַיִם, *fear of
Hashem,* which is described by the Gemara (*Shabbos* 31b) as the "outer
keys" to the treasure, while Torah itself is described as the "inner keys" (*Beis
Yisrael, Maggidei HaEmes*).

Self-negation, desiring nothing else but to be a worthy receptacle of *Divrei
Torah,* is also an ideal form of preparation for Torah study. *Chazal,* noting the
comparison of Torah to water, הוֹי כָּל צָמֵא לְכוּ לַמַּיִם, *Ho, everyone who is thirsty,*

go to water (*Yeshayahu* 55:1), remark that Torah comes to rest in humble (low) people just as water seeks and descends to the lowest possible level. By preparing to study Torah, the scholar is actually undertaking a process of selfnegation in which his sole objective is to comprehend the Divine will (*Sefas Emes*).

It is in this spirit that King David wrote: מִפִּי עוֹלְלִים וְיוֹנְקִים יִסַּדְתָּ עֹז, *out of the mouths of babes and sucklings You have established strength* (the Torah) (*Tehillim* 8:3). The Torah scholar, when confronted with the immense treasures of Torah, feels no more knowledgeable than a small child (*Imrei Emes, Maggidei HaEmes*).

◈§ Is Torah an Inheritance?

קשה הא כתיב תורה צוה לנו משה מורשה קהלת יעקב, אלא לכל אחד מישראל יש חלק בתורה שצריך להתייגע להשיגו כדאיתא אם אין אני לי מי לי וכשמשיג כל אחד חלקו ומבטלו לתוך הכלל נעשה לו ירושה, כי בכלל ישראל התורה ירושה הוא דכתיב מורשה קהלת יעקב.

התקן עצמך ללמוד תורה כזו שאינה ירושה לך ובפסוק כ' מורשה ואיתא אל תקרי מורשה אלא מאורסה, אבל אית תורה ואית תורה, ויש תורה לגוף ויש תורה לנשמה . . . והתורה שקיבל מרע"ה בסיני מיוחדת היא לנשמת בנ"י והיא מורשה בכתיב אבל הקרי אמרו מאורסה שצריך האדם לתקן עצמו להוציא מכח אל הפועל רשימות אותיות התורה שנחקקו בנפשות בנ"י, ע"י תיקון הגוף להיות כלי שיאירו בו אותיות התורה, והוא עצמו הרמז התקן עצמך בפרוזדור שתכנס לטרקלין, כי הגוף הפרוזדור והנשמה הטקרלין.

כ"ק אאז"ל הגיד שאף דכתיב תורה צוה לנו משה מורשה וגו' עם כל זה ההתקן עצמך אינו ירושה. דאס וועלען דארף יעדער איינער אליין ארבעטען, צו גרייטען דאס הארץ, וועלען מקבל זיין. יעדער איינער דארף מקבל זיין אויף זער, מתחזק זיין.

This *mishnah* stating that Torah is "not an inheritance" seems to contradict a renowned *pasuk*, תּוֹרָה צִוָּה לָנוּ מֹשֶׁה מוֹרָשָׁה קְהִלַּת יַעֲקֹב, *The Torah that Moshe commanded us is the heritage of the congregation of Yaakov* (*Devarim* 33:4), which indicates that it *is* a יְרֻשָׁה, an inheritance. Perhaps, a distinction may be made between the community for whom Torah is an "heirloom" transmitted loyally from previous generations and the individual who must strive to reach his potential in Torah. The *mishnah* is urging us to attain our potential and especially to render our unique contribution to Torah. According to the *Chiddushei HaRim* this theme can be deduced from the words שֶׁאֵינָה יְרֻשָּׁה לָךְ — prepare yourself to study those portions that are not your inheritance but instead are derived through your efforts (*Maggidei HaEmes*).

However, the *talmid chacham* does not stop there. He is not content to "merely" arrive at new Torah thoughts. Instead, he makes his contribution to Torah, shares it with others and integrates it with the contributions of countless other scholars dating back to Sinai. When the *mishnah* is calling upon the Torah scholar to prepare to study Torah it is, in effect, asking him to become part of the larger Torah community through his unique contribution to Torah knowledge. Consider the metamorphosis that has taken place. The Torah, which was at first described as אֵינָה יְרֻשָּׁה, *not an inheritance*, now, as a result of the *talmid chacham's* scholarship and his generosity, becomes his inheritance.

In this light, we can better appreciate the Gemara's comment that the term מוֹרָשָׁה used to describe the Torah's inheritance should be read as מְאוֹרָשָׂה, *betrothed* (*Pesachim* 49b). Just as a betrothed couple realize that a great deal of effort is required to develop their relationship, so too the *talmid chacham's* relationship with Torah is strengthened through hard work and immersion in its sacred teachings (based on *Imrei Emes, Maggidei HaEmes; Sfas Emes, Succos* 5632, 5635, 5647).

The distinction may also be made between the impact of Torah on the soul and on the body. As the *pasuk* relates, תּוֹרָה צִוָּה לָנוּ מֹשֶׁה, Moshe bequeathed the Torah to *Klal Yisrael*, leaving a permanent impact on the innermost recesses of the Jewish soul. As a result of Moshe's legacy, every Jew enjoys the potential to study and contribute to Torah. However, our mission is to take that innate potential embedded in our soul and infuse our entire body and personality with the light of Torah. To attain that objective we cannot rely upon our legacy but instead we must work hard — as the *mishnah* reminds us: הַתְקֵן עַצְמְךָ, *prepare yourself*. The analogy between Torah and the betrothed bride (refer to the previous paragraph) assumes additional significance according to this approach. Just as the betrothed couple must gradually develop their relationship, so too by dint of hard work, the Torah, so deeply rooted in our *neshamah*, gradually permeates our body, as well.

During the last Shavuos of his life, the *Pnei Menachem*, quoting his father, the *Imrei Emes*, offered an additional — and innovative — approach to resolving the contradiction between the *mishnah* stating that Torah is not an inheritance and the *pasuk* which implies that it is. Torah itself may be an inheritance, however, the *preparations for Torah*, the הַתְקֵן, is not an inheritance. He concluded that every individual must prepare himself, in his own unique fashion, to receive the Torah (*Maggidei HaEmes*).

■ וְכָל מַעֲשֶׂיךָ יִהְיוּ לְשֵׁם שָׁמָיִם ■ — *And let all your deeds be for the sake of Heaven.*

◄§ A Lifelong Pursuit

פי' שבכל ימי חייו של האדם הוא צריך ליגע עצמו לדעת בלי רמאות ואונאה עצמית, מה הוא לשם שמים. ובכל זאת עליו לדעת שעדיין אינו עושה לשם שמים ממש.

The expression וְכָל מַעֲשֶׂיךָ, "all your deeds," implies that this is a lifelong pursuit. As long as we live, we must scrutinize our every activity and

determine whether our motives are purely for Hashem's sake or if we are
influenced by selfish personal considerations. Moreover, this pursuit is never
totally realized. It is important to remember that despite all our efforts, our deeds
are to some extent motivated by personal concerns. Realizing how much more
needs to be done before we can live our lives לְשֵׁם שָׁמַיִם, solely for Hashem's
Name, we strive even more to conduct our lives on such a lofty level (לְשֵׁם שָׁמַיִם)
(*Maggidei HaEmes*).

◄§A Part of Every Deed or All My Deeds?

סובל ב׳ פירושים להיות בכל מעשה רצון להש״י וגם להיות כל המעשה כולו רק
לשם שמים, וב׳ הפירושים אמת, כי אי אפשר להיות כל המעשים בלתי לה׳ לבדו,
אכן אם נמצא בכל מעשה רצון לה׳ על ידי זה יוכל לעשות גם כן מעשיהם מיוחדים
לה׳ בשלימות.

The phrase וְכָל מַעֲשֶׂיךָ, *all your deeds*, lends itself to two interpretations. It
may connote that our actions should be undertaken solely for Hashem's
sake. On the other hand, it may be merely stating that an element of לְשֵׁם שָׁמַיִם,
unselfish devotion to Hashem's wishes, should be an integral part of all of our
activities.

In truth, both approaches may be correct. While it is certainly impossible that
every aspect of every deed of ours be undertaken solely for Hashem's sake, it
is feasible that an *element* of לְשֵׁם שָׁמַיִם exists in all our behavior. In the merit
of preserving some "spiritual altruism" in *every aspect* of our behavior, we will
eventually merit that *some* of our activities will be conducted solely for
Hashem's sake.

◄§Reject Activities That Are Not "LeShem Shamayim"

היינו שאדם צריך לעשות כל מעשיו לשם שמים ולא לעשות שום דבר אם אינו
מוצא בו את הלשם שמים. וזה כוונת הפסוק בכל דרכיך דעהו וזה פי׳ שויתי ה׳
לנגדי תמיד.

The *Imrei Emes* emphasized the "negative" aspect of this statement: Do not
pursue activities in which no aspect of לְשֵׁם שָׁמַיִם can be found. Even the
most mundane activities should be undertaken, at least in part, for Hashem's
sake. As Shlomo states: בְּכָל דְּרָכֶיךָ דָעֵהוּ, *know Him in all your ways* (Mishlei 3:6).
The famous *pasuk:* שִׁוִּיתִי ה׳ לְנֶגְדִּי תָמִיד, *I have set Hashem before me always*

(*Tehillim* 16:8), bears the same message. Before embarking on any course of action, consider Hashem's "interests" — whether it would serve to enhance *Kvod Shamayim* (*Maggidei HaEmes*).

∽§ When Necessary, Disregard Public Opinion

אדמו״ר זצללה״ה הלב שמחה אמר פעם לאחד ממקורביו "מעודי לא עלה על
דעתי לחשוב מה יאמרו הבריות על מעשי. נוהג אני לשקול את מעשי על פי
אמיתותם, כך צריך לעשות או שמא כך. ועל פי שיקול זה הנני מחליט על צעדי.
מעולם לא עלה על לבי על לקחת בחשבון את מחשבות הזולת על פעולותי."

Another possible interpretation of the *mishnah* may be reflected by the following aspect of the *Lev Simcha's* conduct. He once remarked to a family member that he always made decisions based on their merits — as to whether they would enhance the glory of Hashem — rather than on the basis of public opinion (*Maggidei HaEmes*).

∽§ Even the "LeShem Shamayim" Should Be for Hashem's Sake

זקיני החידושי הרי״ם ז״ל הגיד שהלשם שמים יהיה גם כן לשם שמים, כעין שהגיד
הרבי מקאצק ז״ל צדק צדק תרדוף שאת הצדק עצמו יש לרדוף בצדק.

Contrary to the all-too-popular practice of achieving sacred goals through questionable means, the *Chiddushei HaRim* pointed out that the *means* as well as the ultimate objective must be pursued for the sake of Hashem. When discussing the need to pursue righteousness, the Torah states (*Devarim* 16:20): צֶדֶק צֶדֶק תִּרְדֹּף, just objectives (צֶדֶק) can only be attained through justifiable means (צֶדֶק) (*Maggidei HaEmes*).

18.

■ הֱוֵי זָהִיר בִּקְרִיאַת שְׁמַע וּבִתְפִלָּה — *Be meticulous in reading the Shema and in prayer.*

∽§ The Benefits of Diligently Reciting Shema

היא מסוגל ליראת חטא וזה פי׳ שויתי ה׳ לנגדי תמיד.

קֶבַע, אֶלָּא רַחֲמִים וְתַחֲנוּנִים לִפְנֵי הַמָּקוֹם, שֶׁנֶּאֱמַר:
„כִּי חַנּוּן וְרַחוּם הוּא אֶרֶךְ אַפַּיִם וְרַב חֶסֶד וְנִחָם עַל
הָרָעָה"; וְאַל תְּהִי רָשָׁע בִּפְנֵי עַצְמֶךָ.

אִיתָא בַּמִדְרָשׁ בְּשָׁלֹשׁ צָרִיךְ אָדָם לְטַהֵר לִבּוֹ קֹדֶם שֶׁיִּתְפַּלֵּל, הַכַּוָּנָה לִקְרִיאַת שְׁמַע
שֶׁמְּטַהֶרֶת אֶת הַלֵּב . . . וְעַל יְדֵי זֶה נִפְתָּח אַחַר כָּךְ פֶּתַח הַתְּפִלָּה.

The *Sfas Emes* noted that one of the benefits of diligently reciting *Shema* is
an enhanced sense of יִרְאַת חֵטְא, *fear of sin* (not merely fear of punishment).
His assertion may be based on the Gemara (*Berachos* 4b) which recommends
reciting *Shema* as an effective means of curbing the Evil Inclination.

Moreover, reciting *Shema* serves as the perfect prelude to *Shemoneh Esrei*.
Chazal note that having a pure heart (i.e. no ulterior motives) is an important
prerequisite for the success of our *tefillos*. There is no more effective means of
assuring the purity of our intentions than the recitation of *Shema* in which we
are called upon to sacrifice everything in order to fulfill Hashem's will (*Maggidei HaEmes*).

■ אַל תַּעַשׂ תְּפִלָּתְךָ קֶבַע — *Do not make your prayer a set routine.*

⋅ৡ Daven and Daven Again

אִיתָא אַל תַּעַשׂ תְּפִלָּתְךָ קֶבַע אֶלָּא רַחֲמִים וְתַחֲנוּנִים לִפְנֵי הַמָּקוֹם, מ'דַּאַרְף בֶּעֶטְעֶן
נָאךְ אַ מָאהְל אוּן נָאךְ אַ מָאהְל בִּיז מ'וֶועט אַדוּרְךְ הַאקְעֶן, פּוֹעֶל'ן אוּן אוֹיְס פּוֹעֶל'ן.

According to the *Pnei Menachem*, the term קֶבַע means a finite amount. Do
not simply *daven* once but rather continue *davening* until you believe that
you have accomplished something with your *tefillah* (cf. *Berachos* 32b).

In this light we may better appreciate the Gemara's ruling (*Berachos* 26a) that
תְּפִלַּת הָעֶרֶב אֵין לָהּ קֶבַע, "the evening prayer has no finite limits." Even in the
dark *galus*, where it often seems that our prayers are in vain, continue *davening*
and be assured that your *tefillos* accomplish a great deal (*Maggidei HaEmes*).

⋅ৡ Be Innovative

"הַפָּשׁוּט גַּם הַפֵּירוּשׁ לְהוֹסִיף כָּל פַּעַם וּלְחַדֵּשׁ בָּהּ דָּבָר בִּדְבָרִים שֶׁבַּלֵּב, לֹא כְּמִצְוַת
אֲנָשִׁים מְלוּמָדָה – אֲבָל כַּוָּנָתִי מְיוּחֶדֶת שֶׁתִּשְׁתַּדֵּל תִּתְבּוֹנֵן וְתִתְכּוֹנֵן לָבוֹא הַפַּעַם
לַתְּפִלָּה הַנְּכוֹנָה וְיַעֲזוֹר לְךָ תְּפִילָּה כָּזוֹ לִזְמַן, זְמַנָּם, זְמַנֵּיהֶם, וְיָרוּם וְיַגְבִּיהַ כָּל
הַתְּפִילּוֹת שֶׁלְּךָ אֲשֶׁר קָשֶׁה לְכַוֵּן בָּהֶם כָּרָאוּי וּמַעֲמִיד אֲנִי עָלַי שֶׁהִנְנִי מִתְחַזֵּק
לִפְעָמִים ע"י בִּתְפִלַּת שַׁחֲרִית שֶׁהִתְפַּלְלִי מָחֳרָת חֲתוּנוֹתַי."

pray, do not make your prayer a set routine, rather [an entreaty for] mercy and a supplication before the Omnipresent, as it is said (Yoel 2:13): "For He is gracious and compassionate, slow to anger, abounding in kindness and relentful of punishment"; and do not judge yourself to be a wicked person.

In one of his letters, the *Lev Simchah* interpreted this phrase as meaning always be innovative in your *tefillos*. Feel free to express the innermost emotions of your heart and your daily concerns as you *daven*.

While it may be impossible to reach such an exalted level every time we *daven*, if we can do so occasionally, we may rest assured that all our other more mundane *tefillos* will be received in the same spirit as that one extraordinary *davening*. In fact, the *Lev Simchah* would remark that he drew inspiration his entire life from the *Shacharis* that he *davened* the day after his wedding.

In this light we may interpret the Midrash that a person's prayers may be answered "once in seventy years" as meaning that certain prayers leave an impact for seventy years (*Maggidei HaEmes*).

■ וּכְשֶׁאַתָּה מִתְפַּלֵּל . . . אֶלָּא רַחֲמִים וְתַחֲנוּנִים לִפְנֵי הַמָּקוֹם — *When you pray . . . rather [an entreaty for] mercy and a supplication before the Omnipresent.*

◆§ Daven for the Shechinah's Revelation, Not Merely for Yourself

מרגלא בפומי' דאדמו״ר זצ״ל הלב שמחה; איתא בהגדת מטה משה מהרה״ק רבי משה מקאזניץ ז״ל בשם הרבי ר' בער ז״ל אל תעש תפלתך קבע שלא תהיה עיקר קביעות תפלתך לצרכיך הגופניים, אלא רחמים ותחנונים לפני המקום, היינו עבור צער וגלות השכינה, ומצפים לך לישועה. וי״ל וכשאתה מתפלל וכו' וען עם דאוונט זער אמאל יש לידע היאך להתפלל.

The expression לִפְנֵי הַמָּקוֹם, *before the Omnipresent*, is not merely indicating to **Whom** we *daven* but also for **what** we *daven*. The Maggid of Koznitz's son related the following in the name of the Maggid of Mezeritch — do not make **your** *tefillos* (and your needs) the primary focus of prayer. Instead, concentrate on the גָּלוּת שְׁכִינָה, the millennia-long exile of the Divine Presence which accompanies *Klal Yisrael*.

The Maggid of Koznitz also called attention to the peculiar phrase, וּכְשֶׁאַתָּה מִתְפַּלֵּל, *"when you pray."* Do we not all pray on a regular basis? The answer is that while it may be difficult to always keep in mind the lofty goals we have mentioned, when you *do* pray — on those occasions when you are able to pray

[יט] רַבִּי אֶלְעָזָר אוֹמֵר: הֱוֵי שָׁקוּד לִלְמוֹד תּוֹרָה,
וְדַע מַה שֶׁתָּשִׁיב לְאֶפִּיקוֹרוֹס; וְדַע לִפְנֵי מִי אַתָּה
עָמֵל; וְנֶאֱמָן הוּא בַּעַל מְלַאכְתְּךָ, שֶׁיְּשַׁלֵּם לְךָ שְׂכַר
פְּעֻלָּתֶךָ.

wholeheartedly — pray for the *Shechinah* rather than yourself (*Lev Simchah, Maggidei HaEmes*).

■ וְאַל תְּהִי רָשָׁע בִּפְנֵי עַצְמֶךָ — *And do not judge yourself to be a wicked person.*

While the simple meaning of the *mishnah* seems to emphasize the importance of spiritual self-esteem, admonishing us never to perceive ourselves as being evil, additional layers of meaning may be extracted as we will now elaborate.

◆§ Do Not Live in Isolation

כל אדם נשלח לעולם הזה בכדי לתקן דבר מה, ואם האדם מתבודד בד' אמותיו
ודבר אין לו עם אנשים לא יוכל לתקן כלום. וזה מה שאמר התנא ואל תהי רשע
בפני עצמך, ר"ל בהיותך בהתבודדות בינך לבין עצמך.

R' Baruch of Medzibozh interpreted this phrase quite simply. By living בִּפְנֵי עַצְמֶךָ, in isolation — and shunning contact with people — we can never *reach our potential.* Hashem placed us in This World in order to accomplish something unique and to somehow influence other people for good. It follows that by isolating ourselves from society we are committing a subtle but distinct act of רִשְׁעוּת, evil (*Maggidei HaEmes*).

◆§ Associate With the Righteous

רק תתחבר על כל פנים לצדיקים, ובתורתם ותפלתם יעלו גם כן את תפלתך, כמו
שמערבין החלבנה עם סממני הקטורת ונעשה כולו ריח ניחוח לה'.

In a similar vein, the Maggid of Koznitz interpreted this segment of the *mishnah* as being related to the previous part which emphasized the importance of proper *tefillah.* The most efficacious means of achieving that objective is not to be isolated from society but, on the contrary, to associate with the righteous. In their merit, your prayers will be accepted by Hashem. The importance of the wicked (or at least, the less righteous) subsuming their *tefillos* with

[19] *Rabbi Elazar says: a) Be diligent in the study of Torah, and know what to answer a heretic; know before Whom you toil; and [know] that your Employer can be relied upon to pay you the wage of your labor.*

those of the *tzaddikim* is underscored by the requirement that the foul-smelling spice, known as חֶלְבְּנָה, *galbanum*, not be offered alone but rather as an integral part of the collection of sweet-smelling spices. So too, our *davening*, which, to an extent, substitutes for the rituals of the *Beis HaMikdash*, is most efficacious if it is merged with the *tefillos* of Israel's righteous (*Maggidei HaEmes*).

◄§ Do Not Underestimate The Effect of Evil Behavior

שיחשוב האדם שכל העולם מחצה על מחצה והוא יכריע לכף זכות או להיפך ח״ו לכן אל תהי רשע בפני עצמך.

According to the Maggid of Koznitz, the *mishnah* is urging us to contemplate the *effect* of our evil behavior. Don't think that by conducting yourself improperly you are only hurting yourself (בִּפְנֵי עַצְמֶךָ). On the contrary, as the Gemara relates (*Kiddushin* 40b), we should always imagine that the entire universe is perched so precariously that one good deed sustains it and (ח״ו) one evil deed could be its undoing (*Maggidei HaEmes*).

◄§ Be Righteous Even in Private

אפילו כשאתה בפני עצמך אל תעשה עבירה רק יהי מורא שמים עליך.

The *mishnah* may be simply stating the importance of consistency in our observance of Torah and *mitzvos*. The same standards of religious and moral conduct that we set for ourselves in public must be adhered to in private. Don't be evil בִּפְנֵי עַצְמֶךָ, even when you are alone.

19.

■ וְדַע מַה שֶׁתָּשִׁיב לְאֶפִּיקוֹרוֹס — *And know what to answer a heretic.*

◄§ Do Not Start Up With a Heretic

מה שתאמר לא נאמר אלא מה שתשיב, כלומר אינך רשאי להתחיל עמו כדי להחזירו למוטב, אלא אם ירצה להדיחך דע מה שתשיבנו.

ב / כ-כא [כ] רַבִּי טַרְפוֹן אוֹמֵר: הַיּוֹם קָצֵר, וְהַמְּלָאכָה מְרֻבָּה,
וְהַפּוֹעֲלִים עֲצֵלִים, וְהַשָּׂכָר הַרְבֵּה, וּבַעַל הַבַּיִת
דּוֹחֵק.

[כא] הוּא הָיָה אוֹמֵר: לֹא עָלֶיךָ הַמְּלָאכָה לִגְמוֹר,
וְלֹא אַתָּה בֶן חוֹרִין לְהִבָּטֵל מִמֶּנָּה. אִם לָמַדְתָּ
תוֹרָה הַרְבֵּה, נוֹתְנִים לְךָ שָׂכָר הַרְבֵּה; וְנֶאֱמָן הוּא בַּעַל
מְלַאכְתֶּךָ, שֶׁיְּשַׁלֶּם לְךָ שְׂכַר פְּעֻלָּתֶךָ. וְדַע

The Maggid of Koznitz emphasized that the *mishnah* is not advocating
reaching out to a heretic, but, as the expression "respond" implies, we must
merely react to his attempts to sway us (*Maggidei HaEmes*).

20.

■ הַיּוֹם קָצֵר, וְהַמְּלָאכָה מְרֻבָּה — *The day is short, the task (work) is abundant.*

◆§ Every Day's Unique Challenge

כי באמת הזמן הוא בכלל הטבע אשר הוא בצמצום וקצבה, ועבודת הבורא ית'
הוא למעלה מכל זמן וקצבה, ומה העצה לזה, אך מי שמתקן בכל עת כפי היכולת
בידו, והתדבקות בשורש אי אפשר להיות רק כשהם תמימים, כי כל עוד שלא
מילא האדם הזמן כפי היכולת בטבע הימים חסרים לבוא להגיע אל השורש
כמובן, זולת בעלי תשובה שנאמר עליהם בשעתא חדא.

By stating הַיּוֹם קָצֵר, *the day is short*, the *mishnah* is referring not only to the
finite hours of the day but also to the infinite spiritual challenges that every
day brings. As the *Bartenura* notes, the following expression, וְהַמְּלָאכָה מְרֻבָּה,
the task is abundant, refers to the task of studying Torah with its *infinite*
treasures while living in This World with all of its *finite* limitation. These two
expressions juxtaposed in the *mishnah* are a study in contrasts: הַיּוֹם קָצֵר, the
very finite concept known as "the day," and מְלָאכָה מְרֻבָּה, the study of Torah
which transcends all natural limitations.

Indeed, the following *mishnah* (לֹא עָלֶיךָ הַמְּלָאכָה לִגְמוֹר, *you are not required
to complete the task*) assures us that we need not complete the task of studying
Torah. However, our inability to plumb the bottomless treasures of the entire
Torah does not absolve us from making every natural effort to use each
moment of every day to the fullest.

Generally, this process is incremental, utilizing every day to its maximum

[20] *Rabbi Tarfon says: The day is short, the task is abundant, the laborers are lazy, the reward is great and the Master of the house is insistent.*

[21] *He used to say: You are not required to complete the task, yet you are not free to withdraw from it. If you have studied much Torah, they give you great reward; and your Employer can be relied upon to pay you the wage of your labor, but be aware*

---

capacity. One can only attain perfection through the accumulated Torah study of an entire lifetime. However, one notable exception exists — the *Baal Teshuvah*, the returnee to Torah who is graced with the unique ability to surmount all time barriers and make huge strides in a short period (cf. *Zohar*).

■ הַיּוֹם קָצֵר, וְהַמְּלָאכָה מְרֻבָּה, וְהַפּוֹעֲלִים עֲצֵלִים — *The day is short, the task is abundant, the laborers are lazy.*

✥ The Reward Is Commensurate With the Task

הו״ל להקדים והשכר הרבה שמדבר במהות העבדות אך שזהו טעם לפי
שהפועלים עצלים לפי הטבע לכן השכר הרבה

The sequence of the various elements in the *mishnah* is also significant. It is precisely because the day is so short (הַיּוֹם קָצֵר), the task so immense (הַמְּלָאכָה מְרֻבָּה), and the "laborers" lazy (הַפּוֹעֲלִים עֲצֵלִים, which refers to the human body's natural tendency towards inertia), that the reward for leading a Torah-permeated life is so great.

21.

■ לֹא עָלֶיךָ הַמְּלָאכָה לִגְמוֹר, וְלֹא אַתָּה בֶן חוֹרִין לְהִבָּטֵל מִמֶּנָּה — *You are not required to complete the task, yet you are not free to withdraw from it.*

✥ The Task Can Be Accomplished

פי׳ לא עליך המלאכה שאתה תוכל לגמרה לכן אין אתה בן חורין להבטל ממנה.

The first two elements in the *mishnah* are closely related and they are placed in careful sequence. It is only because we do not have to single-handedly

❧ ❧ ❧

רַבִּי חֲנַנְיָא בֶּן עֲקַשְׁיָא אוֹמֵר: רָצָה הַקָּדוֹשׁ בָּרוּךְ הוּא
לְזַכּוֹת אֶת יִשְׂרָאֵל, לְפִיכָךְ הִרְבָּה לָהֶם תּוֹרָה וּמִצְוֹת,
שֶׁנֶּאֱמַר: "יהוה חָפֵץ לְמַעַן צִדְקוֹ, יַגְדִּיל תּוֹרָה וְיַאְדִּיר."

---

complete all of the spiritual challenges that we are not exempt from doing as
much as we can. If the task were beyond our capacity, Hashem would not
expect us to even try (*Chiddushei HaRim, Maggidei HaEmes*).

◈§ It Is Never Too Late to Begin

מכאן שלעולם לא מאוחר מדי ועליך רק להתחיל, כי מהתחלת העשיה אין כל
פטור, רק מגמר המעשה הנך פטור.

From this *mishnah* we can infer an extremely vital principle — that it is never
too late to change the moral course of one's life. If indeed we were obligated
to *complete* our mission, then one might rationalize that it is already too late.
But since we only need to *commence* it, then it is never too late in life to at least
begin.

■ וְדַע שֶׁמֵתַן שְׂכָרָן שֶׁל צַדִּיקִים לֶעָתִיד לָבֹא — *But be aware that the reward
of the righteous will be given in the World to Come.*

◈§ Only the Righteous Wait for Olam Haba

של צדיקים דוקא אבל רשעים כשיש להם איזה זכות משלמין להם בעולם הזה כמו
שכתוב ומשלם כו' ושל בינונים מעט בעולם הזה ומעט בעולם הבא.

that the reward of the righteous will be given in the World to Come.

❧ ❧ ❧

Rabbi Chanania ben Akashia says: The Holy One, Blessed is He, wished to confer merit upon Israel; therefore He gave them Torah and mitzvos in abundance, as it is said (Yeshayahu 42:21): "Hashem desired, for the sake of its [Israel's] righteousness, that the Torah be made great and glorious."

The *mishnah* is not only stating that the righteous are rewarded in *Olam Haba*, but also that *only* the righteous must wait until the World to Come to receive their just reward. By contrast, the wicked, as it is well known, receive their full compensation in This World. It follows that those individuals who are neither completely righteous nor completely wicked, known as בֵּינוֹנִים (the intermediate category), are rewarded partially in This World and the balance in the World to Come.

◆§ Enjoying Olam Haba in Olam Hazeh

הכוונה שעיקר שמחתן של צדיקים בעולם הזה הוא בעת שזוכרים שיהיה לה' המלוכה עד עולם ועולתה תקפץ פיה במהרה בימינו אמן.

The *Tiferes Shlomo* offered a beautiful rendition of this concluding passage of the *perek*. When the *tzaddik* reminds himself that eventually all mankind will accept Hashem's sovereignty, he feels amply rewarded even in This World. Realizing that eventually evil will disappear, the *tzaddik* experiences a taste of the World to Come while he is still in This World[1] (adapted from *Maggidei HaEmes*).

---

1. For a similar theme refer to our commentary on the Introduction to *Avos*, כָּל יִשְׂרָאֵל.

פרק שלישי

כָּל יִשְׂרָאֵל יֵשׁ לָהֶם חֵלֶק לָעוֹלָם הַבָּא, שֶׁנֶּאֱמַר: "וְעַמֵּךְ כֻּלָּם צַדִּיקִים, לְעוֹלָם יִירְשׁוּ אָרֶץ, נֵצֶר מַטָּעַי, מַעֲשֵׂה יָדַי לְהִתְפָּאֵר."

❧ ❧ ❧

[א] עֲקַבְיָא בֶּן מַהֲלַלְאֵל אוֹמֵר: הִסְתַּכֵּל בִּשְׁלֹשָׁה דְבָרִים וְאֵין אַתָּה בָא לִידֵי עֲבֵרָה: דַּע מֵאַיִן בָּאתָ, וּלְאָן אַתָּה הוֹלֵךְ, וְלִפְנֵי מִי אַתָּה עָתִיד לִתֵּן דִּין וְחֶשְׁבּוֹן. מֵאַיִן בָּאתָ? מִטִּפָּה סְרוּחָה. וּלְאָן אַתָּה הוֹלֵךְ? לִמְקוֹם עָפָר, רִמָּה וְתוֹלֵעָה.

1.

■ עֲקַבְיָא בֶּן מַהֲלַלְאֵל אוֹמֵר: הִסְתַּכֵּל בִּשְׁלֹשָׁה דְבָרִים וְאֵין אַתָּה בָא לִידֵי עֲבֵרָה: דַּע מֵאַיִן בָּאתָ, וּלְאָן אַתָּה הוֹלֵךְ, וְלִפְנֵי מִי אַתָּה עָתִיד לִתֵּן דִּין וְחֶשְׁבּוֹן
— *Akavia ben Mahalalel says: Consider three things and you will not come into the grip of sin: Know whence you came, whither you go, and before Whom you will give justification and reckoning.*

◆§ Constant Awareness, Not Merely Knowledge

פי' זה ההסתכלות צריך להיות בכל רגע שלא יהיה שום שכחה וממילא אי אפשר שיעשה שום מעשה נגד רצון השי"ת . . . ואין לנו לרמות עצמנו לצאת במה שיודעין זאת דרך כלל כי זה ההפרש בין ידיעה להסתכלות כי כל זמן שלא יתפעל האדם על ידי הידיעה זו אינו ידועה עצומה כי רק אחר הסתכלות יומם ולילה באה הידיעה האמיתית ולכן אמר התנא מקודם הסתכל ואחר כך דע.

From the sequence of the *mishnah* stating firstly הִסְתַּכֵּל, to be constantly aware of the basic truths enumerated in the *mishnah* (מֵאַיִן בָּאתָ, וּלְאָן אַתָּה הוֹלֵךְ, וְלִפְנֵי מִי), and only then דַּע, can we know, we may deduce that these beliefs are not easily arrived at, nor is general knowledge about their existence sufficient. It requires הִסְתַּכְּלוּת, day and night meditation about our humble origins and our ultimate destiny. Only by constantly probing into the very essence of our existence and through such a process arriving at the *Tanna's* conclusions can we be assured that וְאֵין אַתָּה בָא לִידֵי עֲבֵרָה, we will not come to sin. Anything less than total immersion into these vital questions — and their answers — is far too

Chapter Three

*All Israel has a share in the World to Come, as it is said
(Yeshayahu 60:21): "And your people are all righ-
teous; they shall inherit the land forever; a branch of
My plantings, My handiwork, in which to take pride."*

❧ ❧ ❧

*[1] Akavia ben Mahalalel says: Consider three
things and you will not come into the grip of sin:
Know whence you came, whither you go, and before
Whom you will give justification and reckoning.
"Whence you came?" — from a putrid drop; "whither
you go?" — to a place of dust, worms and maggots;*

superficial to leave much of an impact.

However, once we have attained — through constant reflection — a fuller
understanding of our origins and destiny, we can then proceed to the next phase,
knowing, by now almost intuitively, the three basic truths enumerated here (*Sfas
Emes, Michtav Avos*).

❧ Our Mission in Life

כשמסתכלים בשלשה דברים אלו מקיימים השליחות שבשבילה באו לעולם
הזה.

The *Imrei Emes* stated that by simply reflecting on these questions, we have
fulfilled our life's mission. Hashem dispatched man's soul from its sacred
heavenly origins into this mundane world knowing that we can maintain its
purity, even while it is encased in the body, by never losing sight of the fundamental beliefs stated in our *mishnah* (*Maggidei HaEmes*).

❧ Hashem Reciprocates

הסתכל רמז להסתבלות מלמעלה ה' משמים השקיף כו' . . . להסתכל בזה מאין
בא גורם הסתכלות מלמעלה שיהיה צדיק עיני ד' אל צדיקים.

The term הַסְתַּכֵּל has a dual meaning. It refers to our efforts to cast aside the
shackles of materialism and also merit His benevolent gaze upon us. As David
writes: ה' מִשָּׁמַיִם הִשְׁקִיף עַל בְּנֵי אָדָם לִרְאוֹת הֲיֵשׁ מַשְׂכִּיל דֹּרֵשׁ אֶת אֱלֹהִים, "Hashem gazed
down from heaven upon mankind, to see if there exists a reflective person who

seeks out God" (*Tehillim* 14:2). By reflecting upon life — and as a result turning to Hashem — we merit that He, in turn, will *gaze* upon us (*Beis Yisrael, Maggidei HaEmes*).

◆§ Remembering Hashem

ומי הביאך עד הלום רק הקב״ה.

The *mishnah* is urging us to contemplate that it was only through Hashem's guidance and kindness that we progressed from our lowly roots to our present position of prominence.

◆§ The Three Avos

הרמז לכח האבות, אברהם אבינו ע״ה, מאין באת, ואנכי עפר ואפר, אדם יסודו מעפר, ואצלו היו הבארות הראשונות, חפר בארות, הוציא את העפר. ולפני מי אתה עתיד ליתן דין וחשבון, הרמז ליצחק אבינו ע״ה. ויתכן לומר כדאיתא בגמ' לעתיד לבא יאמר לו הקב״ה וכו' ליצחק בניך חטאו וכו'. . . לימוד זכות שיוכלו להתקיים בדרך של יצחק, בדין. ולאן אתה הולך הרמז על יעקב אבינו ע״ה שהיה תמיד הולך, וישא יעקב רגליו וילך ארצה בני קדם, ויעקב הלך לדרכו.

These questions may also correspond to the three *Avos* who through their actions exemplified the issues raised in the *mishnah*. Avraham, describing himself as עָפָר וָאֵפֶר, "dust and ashes," exemplified man's humble origins, the טִפָּה סְרוּחָה. But Avraham was determined to rise — at least, in a spiritual sense — above his lowly beginnings. We find him digging wells and removing the earth from wells that had been sealed. By doing so, he demonstrated his determination to reach the wellsprings of his own *neshamah* by removing all the impediments to his growth.

וְלִפְנֵי מִי אַתָּה עָתִיד לִתֵּן דִּין וְחֶשְׁבּוֹן — the question reminding us of our ultimate Divine judgment corresponds to Yitzchak who will, more than any of the other *Avos*, defend *Klal Yisrael* in the final judgment in the World to Come (cf. *Shabbos* 89b). And the question reminding us to think of where we are going, לְאָן אַתָּה הוֹלֵךְ, recalls Yaakov who is described as "going" to meet new challenges (cf. *Bereishis* 29:1) (adapted from *Pnei Menachem, Maggidei HaEmes*).

◆§ The Yetzer Hara's Revised Version of the Mishnah

כתיב כי יפגשך עשו אחי ושאלך לאמר למי אתה ואן תלך ולמי אלה לפניך ואיתא בשל״ה שהיצר הרע שואל הג' שאלות שבמשנה דע מאין באת ולאן אתה הולך ולפני מי אתה עתיד ליתן דין וחשבון, היצר הרע רוצה על ידי זה לקלקל.

The *Imrei Emes*, citing the *Shelah*, notes that Yaakov anticipates — and warns his gift-bearing emissaries — that his brother Esav will ask similar questions to those of the *mishnah* (cf. *Bereishis* 32:18): לְמִי אַתָּה — "Whose are you" is a paraphrase of מֵאַיִן בָּאתָ. He continues: וְאָנָה תֵלֵךְ — "where are you going," which is virtually identical with וּלְמִי אַתָּה הוֹלֵךְ. And finally וּלְמִי אֵלֶּה לְפָנֶיךָ — "and whose are these that are before you" (i.e. what is its future) is similar to the question וְלִפְנֵי מִי אַתָּה עָתִיד לִתֵּן דִּין וְחֶשְׁבּוֹן. By extension, the *Yetzer Hara* asks the same questions that we should be considering our origins, our destiny. Of course the responses that the *Yetzer Hara* seeks to elicit are radically different from those of our *mishnah*.

⇜ A Passive Guarantee

אבל לעשות מ״ע לכאורה אינו בכלל.

It seems that the *mishnah* is assuring us that by recalling these basic truths we will never sin. The other equally critical aspect of Torah life, performing positive commandments (מִצְוֹת עֲשֵׂה), requires an active effort on our part (rather than mere passive recall of our origins and destiny).

⇜ Not Even the Thought of Sinning

און נישט נאר אן עבירה נאר אפילו ידי עבירה, א יד, א הרהור.

The term לִידֵי עֲבֵרָה (literally "the hands of sin") alludes to the full impact of meditating about the three fundamental thoughts of our *mishnah*. Not only will we be spared the possibility of sinning but even the very thought of committing an *aveirah* will not cross our mind[1] (*Pnei Menachem, Maggidei HaEmes*).

⇜ The Preferred Answers

פשוט מקודם לידע תמיד מאין בא ולאן הולך שאדם צריך להיות מהלך כנודע וזה הסתבלות שאמר מקודם ושיראה אם הליכתו כפי החשבון ואם אינו בכלל מהלך אז נאמר עליו שיראה מאין בא מט״ס כי האדם נברא מט״ס וזה לאות שצריך השלמת עצמו ולזאת אם אינו בכלל מהלך נק׳ תמיד כן שבא מט״ס וכן שהולך למקום עפר, אבל המהלך כבר נעשה שלם ועתה בא בכי״י מעבודת הקב״ה באופנים שונים ולא מט״ס, ואף שביאתו מט״ס אדרבא מעלה אליו שזכה להשלים עצמו וכן בהליכתו איך נאמר למקום עפר הרי הולך לג״ע ולהתדבק בחי החיים, ולזאת ו״ל שבפל התנא לשונו כנ״ל.

---

1. According to this interpretation, the term "יַד" may be related to יַד הַקַּרְדּוֹם (*Uktzin* 1:5), *the handle of an ax*. The evil thought is frequently the vehicle through which an *aveirah* is consummated. Also cf. *Shabbos* 64a where the term "יַד" is used in reference to evil thoughts.

The central theme of this *mishnah* is an earnest plea that we constantly strive to better ourselves in Torah and *Yiras Shamayim*. The true barometer of our progress in those areas is to evaluate the extent of advancement from our physical genesis to the rich spiritual life expected of every Jew. Remember where you came from and reflect whether you have progressed sufficiently from that point. Above all, ask yourself if you are you a מְהַלֵּךְ, an upwardly mobile individual who is constantly seeking new spiritual challenges. Such an individual is greatly influenced by the Divine Soul within him, not by his physical origins (טִפָּה סְרוּחָה). Similarly, his destiny is paradise, not the abyss (מָקוֹם עָפָר, רִמָּה). It is only when the answer to this overriding question is negative — when the individual is still mired in his lowly origins — that he need fear his ultimate end.

This approach, interpreting the *mishnah* as a plea for constant growth, is supported by the apparent redundancy in which we state twice these three questions, first without providing answers and only then answering each question. In light of the above approach, we suggest that the *unanswered* questions are addressed to the true מְהַלֵּךְ. To him we say simply, reflect on the distance that you have already traveled. Coming from lowly origins you are now imbued with the values of Torah. It is to the individual who unfortunately has not traveled that journey that we say, your end is as dismal as your physical beginnings.

◆§ The Body's Humble Origins

מאין באת מטיפה סרוחה, והלא נשמת האדם גבוה וכל אדם מישראל אומר בכל
יום אלקי נשמה כו' טהורה היא, אך כי כפי מה שיודע שגופו וגשמיות שלו הוא
טיפה סרוחה וממילא מבטל כל החיות להשי"ת שהרי יודע ומבין כי חיותו ממנו
שהרי איננו חי בלי נשמת ה' שנותנת חיים בכל רגע.
. . . ועי"ז לא בא לידי עבירה בשכל חיותו דבוק בראשית החיות שבא מהשי"ת.

The *mishnah* is surely not denigrating the pure soul implanted into us by Hashem. As we say every morning upon arising, נְשָׁמָה שֶׁנָּתַתָּ בִּי טְהוֹרָה הִיא, *the soul that You have given me is pure*. On the contrary, it is the body — and all the sensual desires that emanate from it — that is directly derived from the lowly putrid drop. By having us recall our humble origins, the *mishnah* is actually urging us to give priority to the soul and its latent spirituality and to de-emphasize the body and its physical demands. In fact, without the Divine soul, the body and all its sensual drives would never exist. Moreover, Hashem is constantly reinvigorating and renewing the soul so it may fulfill its Divine mission. Bearing all these thoughts in mind, the Torah Jew surely will not come to sin. As the *mishnah* states, וְאֵין אַתָּה בָא לִידֵי עֲבֵרָה.

◆§ Purity of Thought

שתסתכל ותתבונן בחשיבות של טיפה סרוחה, שממנה באת, וממילא תשמרנו

בקדושה וטהרה ותשמור עצמך מאוד שלא תקלקלן, ואז מבטיחה המשנה ואין
אתה בא לידי עבירה.

While it seems that the *mishnah* is denigrating the putrid drop from which the
human body is eventually formed, according to the *Lev Simchah*, it is also
urging us to think of the sanctity of our very origins. Consequently we will treat
the very private sphere of family life with utmost modesty (צְנִיעוּת) rather than
perceive it as a form of physical gratification. In the merit of such a sacred life style,
we may be assured that we will not sin (adapted from *Maggidei HaEmes*).

⧫§ The Three Partners

באמת מאלו הג' שותפין שיש באדם הן ג' הדברים מאין באת כח האב טיפה
סרוחה, ולאן אתה הולך הוא כח האשה, רמז לדבר שהמיתה באה לעולם ע"י
האשה . . . ולפני מי אתה עתיד ליתן דין וחשבון הוא כח הבורא שיש בו.

The three questions stated in the *mishnah* may correspond to the three partners
that participate in the creation of a person — male, female, and Hashem. The
putrid drop emanates from the male. The question dealing with death and the
decomposition of the body reminds us of Chavah, the first woman, who enticed
her husband to partake of the forbidden fruit, leading to his premature death.
Finally, the judgment faced by the soul is from Hashem.

■ לִמְקוֹם עָפָר, רִמָּה וְתוֹלֵעָה — *To a place of dust, worms and maggots.*

⧫§ The Place of Dust, Decomposition and Worms

הגם כי יש כמה צדיקים שלא נעשים רמה, מכל מקום הרי נאמר רק למקום עפר
למקום שיש שם עפר אבל יש באמת שלא נעשים עפר, אבל בני עלייה הללו
מועטים המה.
ועכ"פ מעורר זה לשפלות.

By utilizing the term מָקוֹם עָפָר וכו', *a place of dust . . .,* the *mishnah* is implying
that in rare instances the deceased will not decompose. Yet, the thought of
descending to a place where this happens — even if one does not personally
undergo such a fate — should be sufficient to deter anyone from sinning.[1]

---

1. The *Sfas Emes* then proceeds to describe actual incidents in his own era when bodies were found
to be totally intact. However, he concludes that in most instances, the decomposition of the body
is an act of Divine kindness, allowing the soul to reach its final resting place. One certainly should
not surmise that if the body decomposes in the customary fashion, it is due to the decedent's
shortcomings. To prove this point, he relates the story of Rabbi Eliezer the son of Rabbi Shimon
who experienced a small degree of decomposition. Refer also to Rabbi S. Y. Zevin's *Treasury of
Chassidic Tales* for a similar story about R' Elimelech of Lizhensk.

Hebrew text:

וְלִפְנֵי מִי אַתָּה עָתִיד לִתֵּן דִּין וְחֶשְׁבּוֹן? לִפְנֵי מֶלֶךְ מַלְכֵי הַמְּלָכִים, הַקָּדוֹשׁ בָּרוּךְ הוּא.

[ב] רַבִּי חֲנִינָא סְגַן הַכֹּהֲנִים אוֹמֵר: הֱוֵי מִתְפַּלֵּל בִּשְׁלוֹמָהּ שֶׁל מַלְכוּת, שֶׁאִלְמָלֵא מוֹרָאָהּ, אִישׁ אֶת רֵעֵהוּ חַיִּים בְּלָעוֹ.

■ וְלִפְנֵי מִי אַתָּה עָתִיד לִתֵּן דִּין וְחֶשְׁבּוֹן — *And before Whom you will give justification and reckoning.*

◆ Reaching One's Potential

וְאֵין כּוונת החשבון רק להפחיד האדם, רק שיבוש האדם באיזה חשבון יבא לפני המלך אם יהיה כדאי לחשוב המעשים טובים, כי דין קאי על עבירות וחשבון קאי על המצות.

דין אם חטא וקילקל וזה מקודם סור מרע וחשבון אם הוא בכלל עובד השי"ת ולא חטא מ"מ צריך לראות אם כך החשבון לפי כוחו איך יהי' החשבון.

דין הוא על החטאים שעשה וחשבון הוא על המצות שעשה שלא עשאם כראוי.

וכן הגוף הולך למקום עפר והנשמה למקום קדוש וטהור, וכן הגוף נידון בגיהנם ובקבר, והנשמה כפי חשבון עבודתה בקודש כך זוכית לעלות, וידוע שיש הרבה דינים בעולם העליון כי הזוכה למדרגה אחת חוזר ונידון במדרגה יותר עליונה ולעולם צריכה לתת חשבון הזכיות ופרשנו בזה המאמר לעולם ימוד אדם עצמו חצי' זכאי וכן העולם חצי' זכאי ופרשנו כי יש תמיד עולם א' ומדרגה א' אשר שם האדם והעולם חצי זכאי ובהוסיפם עולין יותר ושוב הם שם חצי' זכאי, ולכן אמת דבריהם כי החוטא גורם רעה לעולם ונגרשין ממדרגתם ושוב הם חצי' זכאי רק למטה ממקודם.

The apparently redundant phrase *justification and reckoning* may be understood in the following manner. One will not only have to be judged for the sins that he has committed but will also have to give a reckoning for the quality of his performance of the positive commandments and goood deeds that he should have performed. The *mishnah* is subtly admonishing us not to be content with simply refraining from sinning but rather to be constantly re-evaluating our performance of *mitzvos*.

In a similar vein, the *mishnah* is exhorting us not merely to distance ourselves from evil — thus avoiding Divine retribution for our sins — but also to constantly assess ourselves to determine if we are living up to our potential. One day we will be called upon to give a reckoning (חֶשְׁבּוֹן) whether we fully exploited our God-given potential.

Alternatively, the term דִּין refers to the punishment endured by the body in *Gehinnom* and its decomposition while in the grave. By contrast, חֶשְׁבּוֹן refers to the

"and before Whom will you give judgment and reckoning?" — before the King Who reigns over kings, the Holy One, Blessed is He.

[2] *Rabbi Chanina, the deputy Kohen Gadol Priest, says: Pray for the welfare of the government, because if people did not fear it, a person would swallow his fellow alive.*

---

constant reckoning that the soul faces as it ascends to the various spheres of *Gan Eden*. With each phase of its ascendancy to even loftier spiritual rewards, the soul is required to give a new reckoning to determine whether it deserves such a reward.

In this light, we can better appreciate the statement of *Chazal* that a person should always consider himself — and the universe — חֶצְיוֹ זַכַּאי וְחֶצְיוֹ חַיָּיב, "half innocent and half guilty" (*Kiddushin* 40b). The seemingly redundant term always alludes to the ongoing reckoning given by the soul as it ascends from one spiritual realm to another. While the *neshamah* may have merited one level of reward in *Gan Eden*, in a higher plane it may be judged to be no more than "half innocent."

2.

■ הֱוֵי מִתְפַּלֵּל בִּשְׁלוֹמָהּ שֶׁל מַלְכוּת, שֶׁאִלְמָלֵא מוֹרָאָהּ, אִישׁ אֶת רֵעֵהוּ חַיִּים בְּלָעוֹ — *Pray for the welfare of the government, because if people did not fear it, a person would swallow his fellow alive.*

⋙ Pray for the Welfare of a Gentile Monarch

קאי על האומות שטוב להיות להם מלך, דהא בישראל כתיב להיפוך דהי' חסרון מה שבקשו מלך, והרע"ב פי' אפי' מלכי אומות, וק' דבמלכי ישראל ל"ש כלל דעיקר מנהיגיהם דיינים וסנהדרין איש א"ר חיים בלעו.

It is unlikely that our *mishnah* is recommending that we pray for the welfare of a Jewish monarch, whose very appointment is frowned upon (cf. *I Shmuel* Chapter 8 for a full account of Hashem's scathing criticism of the Jewish people for requesting a king during Shmuel's lifetime). For *Klal Yisrael* it is the *Sanhedrin* and the *Dayanim* of the lower courts, not its political rulers, for whose welfare we pray.

This approach is in contradistinction to that of the *Bartenura* who comments that our *mishnah* refers *even* to a gentile monarch, implying that it certainly refers to a Jewish king.

[ג] רַבִּי חֲנִינָא בֶּן תְּרַדְיוֹן אוֹמֵר: שְׁנַיִם שֶׁיּוֹשְׁבִין
וְאֵין בֵּינֵיהֶם דִּבְרֵי תוֹרָה, הֲרֵי זֶה מוֹשַׁב לֵצִים,
שֶׁנֶּאֱמַר: ,,וּבְמוֹשַׁב לֵצִים לֹא יָשָׁב." אֲבָל שְׁנַיִם
שֶׁיּוֹשְׁבִין וְיֵשׁ בֵּינֵיהֶם דִּבְרֵי תוֹרָה, שְׁכִינָה שְׁרוּיָה

◄§ Fear as Well as Love of Hashem

כלומר שתתפלל לה' שיתן לכם שלימות של מלכות שמים, דהיינו האהבה וגם
היראה בעת שתמליכו אותו בתורה ותפלה ומעשים טובים, שאלמלא מוראה,
פירוש שלולא היראה, ותעבדו רק בבחינת האהבה, אז איש את רעהו חיים בלעו,
איש רומז להקב"ה, ורעהו זה האדם שעובדו בדביקות ותענוג . . . יהיו חיים בלעו,
כי מחמת התענוג והדביקות תתפרד הנפש מהגוף לגמרי.

According to the Maggid of Koznitz, the term בִּשְׁלוֹמָה is related to שְׁלֵמוּת,
perfection. Pray for a perfect and complete form of *Avodas Hashem*[1] consisting
of fear as well as love. As the *mishnah* continues, אֶלְמָלֵא מוֹרָאָהּ, *without fear* the
sense of undiluted love for Hashem, known as the Man (אִישׁ) (cf. *Shemos* 15:3 where
Hashem is referred to as *Man of War*, ה' אִישׁ מִלְחָמָה), would consume us mortals
who are known as רֵעֵהוּ, the beloved friends of Hashem. It is only the delicate blend
of love and fear of Hashem that sustains us (*Maggidei HaEmes*).

3.

■ **שְׁנַיִם שֶׁיּוֹשְׁבִין וְאֵין בֵּינֵיהֶם דִּבְרֵי תוֹרָה, הֲרֵי זֶה מוֹשַׁב לֵצִים . . . אֲבָל שְׁנַיִם
שֶׁיּוֹשְׁבִין וְיֵשׁ בֵּינֵיהֶם דִּבְרֵי תוֹרָה, שְׁכִינָה שְׁרוּיָה בֵּינֵיהֶם** — *If two sit together
and there are no words of Torah between them, it is a session of
scorners ... But if two sit together and there are words of Torah
between them, the Divine Presence rests between them.*

◄§ Convening a Meeting for the Wrong Purpose

מדקאמר מושב כו' ולא כ' עם לצים ל"י ש"מ שעל הישיבה עצמה הקפידא שעושין
קבע ועיכוב בלי ד"ת וכ' בסיפא כ"א בתורת ד' חפצו נשמע כי ברישא מיירי
בישיבה בלי תורה:

י"ל הראי' דשם קמוסיף והולך מקודם עצת רשעים ואח"כ אפי' דרך חטאים שוגגין
ואי"כ בע"י השלישית עוד קיל טפי ומ"מ כ' לצים וע"כ גם בישיבה בל שום דיבור
רק העדר מד"ת וזה נמי מושב לצים ולכן קיל הוי לגבי דרך חטאים. ואולי יש לומר
דאם יש ביניהם ד"ת שלא לשמה אז ג"כ שכינה שורה דמושב לצים ודאי לא הוי.

---

1. According to this approach, the term מַלְכוּת refers to the Sovereign Ruler, Hashem.

[3] *Rabbi Chanina ben Tradyon says: If two sit together and there are no words of Torah between them, it is a session of scorners, as it is said (Tehillim 1:1): "In the session of scorners he does not sit." But if two sit together and there are words of Torah between them, the*

By using the term בְּמוֹשַׁב לֵצִים, *in a session of scorners* (rather than simply עִם לֵצִים, *with scorners*), the *mishnah* seems to be emphasizing the sheer folly of convening a meeting that is totally bereft of Torah thoughts, even if no cynical individuals actually attend. This is corroborated by the *pasuk* immediately following the term מוֹשַׁב לֵצִים in *Tehillim* (1:1) which states כִּי אִם בְּתוֹרַת ה׳ חֶפְצוֹ, *his desire is only in the Torah of Hashem* — the antithesis of cynicism. This implies that the dearth of *Divrei Torah* alone is the ultimate contemptuous act.

Additional support for the *mishnah's* thesis that a convocation bereft of *Divrei Torah* is inherently the action of scorners (even if not a single cynical word is exchanged) may be derived from the sequence of the *pasuk* (ibid.) which first praises the individual who has not followed the path of the wicked nor the counsel of the sinner and finally never sat in a session of scorners. The progression of the *pasuk* from the wicked who deliberately commit *aveiros* to the unintentional sinner to the mere participant in a cynical gathering suggests that nothing inappropriate actually occurs at such a meeting — and yet its total lack of spiritual content precludes our participation.

On the other hand, we may deduce that any form of spirituality — even Torah that is *not* studied for its own sake — may be sufficient to remove the stigma of being deemed a gathering of cynics and scorners.

⋅§ The Ultimate Cynical Act

פי׳ כיון שיש לזכות להארה בזו להמשיך השראת השכינה א״כ הוא באמת מושב
לצים ומעין זה נמצא בתיו״ט אשר אם יכולים ליקח זהבים כו׳.

Nothing could be more cynical than squandering the opportunities for spiritual growth had this meeting been utilized for its proper purpose — discussing *Divrei Torah* which would have enabled the *Shechinah* to dwell in their midst — rather than to sit by idly. The *Tosfos Yom Tov* offers a beautiful *mashal* to illustrate this point. Imagine if an individual were given an opportunity to count gold coins for an entire hour and to keep them all, and yet this individual sits by idly rather than help himself to the gold coins. Could there be a more resounding rejection of gold — and all that it implies — than spurning such an opportunity? So too, we who are presented with the opportunity to study Torah (infinitely more precious than gold), *but* reject it in favor of idle chatter, are displaying the most scornful repudiation of Torah.

בֵּינֵיהֶם, שֶׁנֶּאֱמַר: „אָז נִדְבְּרוּ יִרְאֵי יהוה אִישׁ אֶל רֵעֵהוּ,
וַיַּקְשֵׁב יהוה וַיִּשְׁמָע, וַיִּכָּתֵב סֵפֶר זִכָּרוֹן לְפָנָיו, לְיִרְאֵי
יהוה וּלְחֹשְׁבֵי שְׁמוֹ." אֵין לִי אֶלָּא שְׁנַיִם; מִנַּיִן

⋄⧉ Cynics Were There First

אלא דמזה שיושבין בלא תורה הרי זה סימן שקודם שבאו לזה המקום היה כאן
מושב לצים והאויר מפריעם ללמוד תורה.
קיי״ל דכלי חרס נטמא בבית המנוגע באויר אף על פי שלא נגע בו המצורע כלל
או הנגע ומכאן רואים ההשפעה של אויר טמא.

The *Pnei Menachem* suggested that if somehow two Jews sat beside each other
and could not manage to speak even a few words of Torah — which would
be a perfectly natural act — this could only have occurred because this site
had previously been used by cynical individuals who had polluted the spiritual
environment of this location so that it would be virtually impossible to discuss
Divrei Torah.

The overriding importance of the environment is demonstrated by the law
stating that utensils become *tamei* merely by entering the airspace of a house that
is contaminated by *tzaraas* (*Maggidei HaEmes*).

⋄⧉ A Spirit of Humility

שני יהודים שיושבים בצוותא ואין ביניהם, שאין האחד מתנשא על חבירו, והאין
ביניהם ריי׳ל שהענוה מקשרת את שניהם, דברי תורה, קשר זה נחשב כדברי
תורה. לעומת זאת אם הם בבחינת הרי זה, שכל אחד מחשיב את ישות עצמו,
מושב לצים הוא מושבם.

According to the Kotzker Rebbe, the *mishnah* may actually be praising even
individuals who only sit beside one another, but do so with humility. The mere
fact that niether of these individuals considers himself to be greater than his fellow
— אֵין בֵּינֵיהֶם, *there is nothing between them* (i.e. neither one feels superior to the other)
— is regarded as if they were discussing Torah thoughts. On the other hand, if the
participants are imbued with a feeling of their self-worth, as the *mishnah* continues,
הֲרֵי זֶה, *behold this is* (i.e., behold how great and important I am) — then such a group
is considered to be a a gathering of cynics.

■ וְיֵשׁ בֵּינֵיהֶם דִּבְרֵי תוֹרָה שְׁכִינָה שְׁרוּיָה בֵּינֵיהֶם שֶׁנֶּאֱמַר: ״אָז נִדְבְּרוּ יִרְאֵי ה׳ אִישׁ
אֶל רֵעֵהוּ וַיַּקְשֵׁב ה׳ וַיִּשְׁמָע . . . וּלְחֹשְׁבֵי שְׁמוֹ״ — . . . *And there are words of
Torah between them, the Divine Presence rests between them, as it is
said: "Then those who fear Hashem spoke to one another, and Hashem*

Divine Presence rests between them, as it is said (Malachi 3:16): "Then those who fear Hashem spoke to one another, and Hashem listened and heard, and a book of remembrance was written before Him for those who fear Hashem and give thought to His Name." From this verse we would know this only about two people, how do we

---

listened and heard . . . and give thought to His Name."

◆§ Is There a Middle Road?

ולכאורה ק״ק שיהי׳ ההפרש כ״כ ברישא דמושב לצים ולא יהי׳ שום ממוצע
ביניהם וגם עינינו רואות שלומדים בעשרה מ״מ כו׳ רק י״ל בסיפא הפי׳ שאין
ביניהם רק ד״ת בדביקות דומיא דיראי ד׳ וגם רק אלעתיד נאמר רק מסתייע מה
שיוכל לבוא ע״י יש ביניהם ד״ת (אבל כשהמושב לצים א״א לבוא לעולם כי כת
לצים אין מקבלים כו׳), ויל״פ שע״י הלימוד יכולים לזכות למדרגה זו שש״ב דהפי׳
שיש מקום שישרה שכינה אם יהיו זכאין כי הרי הפ׳ מטיל עוד תנאים אחרים יראי
ד׳ וחושבי שמו א״נ יל״פ יש ביניהם ד״ת שכל עצמותם ד״ת וכל ישיבתם רק זאת
ותמיד כשהם יושבים יש ביניהם ד״ת וכמ״ש נדברו לא דברו ופי׳ נדברו – זייא
ווערין איבער גינימין מיט דיא רייד – אבל לא מאן דהוא שלומד דהא רואין אפי׳
עשרה שלומדין כו׳.
וישיבתן מיד לדבר ד״ת . . .

I t seems strange that the *mishnah* considers both extremes — the session of scorners and the totally righteous group of individuals who merit the Divine Presence — without considering the possibility of an intermediate state consisting of sincere people who study Torah without necessarily perceiving the *Shechinah* in their midst. Moreover, practical experience demonstrates that even multitudes of Jews often assemble to learn Torah without visibly perceiving the *Shechinah*.

Evidently, by stating that *the Divine Presence rests between them*, the *mishnah* is stating the ideal scenario and then relying upon us to draw the following conclusion. If under ideal conditions the *Shechinah* permeates a Torah gathering, then at the very least it behooves us — even under less favorable circumstances — to discuss some Torah at every gathering. On the other hand, once our session, by virtue of its total dearth of *Divrei Torah*, degenerates into a מוֹשַׁב לֵצִים, an assembly of cynics, then it is impossible that the *Shechinah* will grace this gathering. As *Chazal* state: "The Divine Presence never resides in a group of cynics" (*Sotah* 42a).

Let us consider the circumstances necessary for the *Shechinah* to truly grace a gathering of *talmidei chachemim*:

Firstly, the term "וְיֵשׁ בֵּינֵיהֶם," the *Divrei Torah* are "between them," implies an intense bond between these scholars that is forged solely through their Torah dis-

אֶלָּא שְׁנַיִם; מִנַּיִן שֶׁאֲפִילוּ אֶחָד שֶׁיּוֹשֵׁב וְעוֹסֵק בַּתּוֹרָה,
שֶׁהַקָּדוֹשׁ בָּרוּךְ הוּא קוֹבֵעַ לוֹ שָׂכָר? שֶׁנֶּאֱמַר: ״יֵשֵׁב
בָּדָד וְיִדֹּם, כִּי נָטַל עָלָיו.״

cussions. Similarly, the *pasuk* cited to support the *mishnah's* thesis that the *Shechinah* resides in an assembly of Torah scholars speaks of God-fearing individuals (יִרְאֵי ה׳). Moreover, this phrase also implies that their very essence and their entire existence is Torah. This interpretation is also supported by the term נִדְבְּרוּ, literally "they *were* spoken" (i.e. they were totally possessed by Torah), rather than they merely spoke *Divrei Torah*. Furthermore, the *pasuk* cited seemingly requires additional prerequisites for the manifestation of the *Shechinah*, namely that the two individuals be among *those who fear God and give thought to His Name*. In a similar vein, the phrase implies that the sole objective of this gathering is to discuss Torah and that as soon as these scholars convene they immediately discuss Torah. It is fair to assume that the above prerequisites for the visible perception of the Divine Presence rarely, if ever, occur. Beyond all these caveats, it is entirely possible that the blessed state described in our *mishnah* whereby *talmidei chachamim* are able to evoke the *Shechinah* through their communal learning may never occur in This World. The *pasuk* cited to support our contention begins with the term אָז, *then*, implying that only *then* — in the future world of *Mashiach* — will this lofty state be attained. Returning to our original question, indeed a middle road exists. Our own halting attempts to learn Torah, a far cry from the ideal state described in the *mishnah* but nonetheless a worthy step towards attainment of the ultimate objective of bringing the Divine Presence into our lives (adapted from *Sfas Emes*).

◆§ Listening Now; Recording Later

פי׳ אז קאי על ויכתב ס׳ זכרון, אבל ויקשב ה׳ וישמע מתקיים תמיד בחי׳ שכינה
שרוי׳.

Refer to our previous commentary in which we stated that the phrase in the *pasuk*, וַיַּקְשֵׁב ה׳ וַיִּשְׁמָע, *Hashem listened and heard*, will not be realized until the Messianic Era. Alternatively, it is possible that the first reward promised — that Hashem will listen to the sound of their learning and will grace the assembly of scholars with His Presence — will be immediately realized. It is only the second phase in which Hashem will record their deeds in perpetuity in His Book of Remembrances that will be deferred until the Messianic Era.

◆§ Thinking of Hashem's Name

יש לפרש דאיירי כשבאמת אינם מופנים רק צריכים לישב לאיזה צורך אך

know this only about two people; how do we know that if even one person sits and occupies himself with Torah, the Holy One, Blessed is He, determines a reward for him? For it is said (Eichah 3:28): "Let one sit in solitude and be still, for he will have received [a reward] for it."

חושבין כי הרי יהיה נקרא מושב לצים לכן הם עוסקים בתורה זהו שבח שלהם וזה נקרא ליראי ה' ולחושבי שמו.

חֹשְׁבֵי שְׁמוֹ, *give thought to His Name* — this expression of *thinking* of Hashem's Name may refer to those individuals who convene a meeting for purposes other than to discuss Torah. Yet, upon realizing that a convocation without Torah would be nothing more than a gathering devoid of the *Shechinah*, they think of Hashem's Name and by discussing Torah topics permit His Presence to reside in their midst.

■ מִנַּיִן שֶׁאֲפִילוּ אֶחָד שֶׁיּוֹשֵׁב וְעוֹסֵק בַּתּוֹרָה שֶׁהקב"ה קוֹבֵעַ לוֹ שָׂכָר? שֶׁנֶּאֱמַר: "יֵשֵׁב בָּדָד וְיִדֹּם כִּי נָטַל עָלָיו." — *How do we know that if even one person sits and occupies himself with Torah, the Holy One, Blessed is He, determines a reward for Him? For it is said: "Let one sit in solitude and be still, for he will have received [a reward] for it."*

⮜§ Those Who Study Torah Are Never Alone

י"ל הכוונה במ"ש ישב בדד היינו בלי השראת השכינה מטעם וידום מה שאינו מדבר בד"ת וממילא נשמע כי המדבר ד"ת אינו בדד רק שכינה שרוי' אצלו, ויל"פ מנין שאפי' א' כו' ישב בדד כו' דחוזר על שנים שיושבין וא' וא"י לעסוק בתורה והאחד לבדו עוסק בתורה כדי שלא יהי' נק' מושב לצים ולכן הקב"ה קובע לו שכר כמ"ש ישב בדד כו' היינו בדד כי השני כי נטל עליו נוטל שכר גם בעד השני.

Only those who are utterly silent and devoid of *Divrei Torah* (וִדֹּם) are truly alone (בָּדָד). However, those who study Torah, even if they reside in utter solitude, will enjoy the Presence of the *Shechinah*.

The *mishnah* may also be referring to an individual who is alone in a *spiritual* sense though he may *physically* be in the presence of another. Suppose two individuals meet and one of them realizes that his partner is unwilling to study Torah. Rather than join him in idle conversation, which would then render their group a מוֹשַׁב לֵצִים, he sits alone and studies Torah. As a result of his courageous decision to not follow his peer in the path of *bitul Torah*, he receives the reward that would ordinarily be allocated to his partner. As the *pasuk* concludes: כִּי נָטַל עָלָיו —

[ד] רַבִּי שִׁמְעוֹן אוֹמֵר: שְׁלֹשָׁה שֶׁאָכְלוּ עַל שֻׁלְחָן אֶחָד וְלֹא אָמְרוּ עָלָיו דִּבְרֵי תוֹרָה, כְּאִלּוּ אָכְלוּ מִזִּבְחֵי מֵתִים, שֶׁנֶּאֱמַר: "כִּי כָּל שֻׁלְחָנוֹת מָלְאוּ קִיא צוֹאָה, בְּלִי מָקוֹם." אֲבָל שְׁלֹשָׁה שֶׁאָכְלוּ עַל שֻׁלְחָן

---

he assumes upon himself the reward that would ordinarily have gone to his peer (adapted from *Sfas Emes*).

4.

■ שְׁלֹשָׁה שֶׁאָכְלוּ עַל שֻׁלְחָן אֶחָד וְלֹא אָמְרוּ עָלָיו דִּבְרֵי תוֹרָה כְּאִלּוּ אָכְלוּ מִזִּבְחֵי מֵתִים . . . אֲבָל שְׁלֹשָׁה שֶׁאָכְלוּ . . . וְאָמְרוּ עָלָיו דִּבְרֵי תוֹרָה כְּאִלּוּ אָכְלוּ מִשֻּׁלְחָנוֹ שֶׁל מָקוֹם — *If three have eaten at one table and have not spoken words of Torah there, it is as if they have eaten of offerings to the dead . . . But if three have eaten . . . and have spoken words of Torah there, it is as if they have eaten from God's table.*

◆§ The Significance of Discussing Divrei Torah While Eating

הענין הוא דכתיב לחם פנים לפני, דבאמת הקב"ה זן ומפרנס לכל הברואים, אבל יש כמה דברים וסיבות קרובות ורחוקות ויש מקבלין את פרנסותיהם בבחי' אחור כלאחר יד, ובנ"י רצה הקב"ה שיקבלו השפע בפנים דאיתא מאן דאכיל דלאו דילי' בהית לאסתכולי בי', והקב"ה נתן לבני"י תורה ומצוות שיזכו במעשיהם לקבל הצריך להם כמ"ש במ"א בשם מו"ז ז"ל בפי' הפסוק לחמי לאשי ריח ניחוחי תשמרו, שבנ"י יראו שהשפע פרנסה ירד מלמעלה בדרך ריח ניחוח כו', לכן המצוה לסדר הלחם, וכפי הסדר שבנ"י מעריכין כך הוא בא מלמעלה, ובנ"י זכו לזה בכח התורה דכתיב פנים בפנים דיבר ה' עמכם, פי' ההנהגה לבנ"י היא בבחי' פנים בפנים, ואפי' עתה שחרב בהמ"ק מ"מ ע"י התורה יכולין למשוך השפע בקדושה ובמשנה ג' שאכלו על שלחן א' ואמרו עליו ד"ת כאילו אכלו משלחנו של מקום דכתיב זה השלחן אשר לפני ה', א"כ ע"י התורה זוכין לבחי' לחם הפנים, שהוא פנימיות השפע להיפוך מזבחי מתים בלי מקום שאין ד"ת מקבלין שפע פנימיות.

In order to appreciate the significance of discussing *Divrei Torah* while eating, we should recall that *Klal Yisrael* is sustained in a very different manner than mankind at large. While it is certainly true that Hashem provides for all of His creations, the Jewish people are supported in a unique fashion as the following remarks will elucidate.

Mankind receives its daily bread from Hashem regardless of its merit. As we say in *Bircas Hamazon*, כִּי הוּא אֵ-ל זָן וּמְפַרְנֵס לַכֹּל, *Because He is God Who*

[4] *Rabbi Shimon says: If three have eaten at one table and have not spoken words of Torah there, it is as if they have eaten of offerings to the dead, as it is said (Yeshayahu 28:8): "For all tables are full of vomit and filth, without the Omnipresent." But if three have*

---

nourishes and sustains all. Klal Yisrael, however, is held to a higher standard, receiving their *parnasah* in direct proportion to their merit. They are sustained by Hashem only if deserving. The *pasuk* recited in the daily *davening* alludes to our unique means of deriving our *parnasah* in the following words: אֶת קָרְבָּנִי לַחְמִי לְאִשַּׁי רֵיחַ נִיחֹחִי תִּשְׁמְרוּ לְהַקְרִיב לִי בְּמוֹעֲדוֹ, *My offering, My food for My fires, My satisfying aroma, shall you be scrupulous to offer to Me in its appointed time (Bamidbar 28:2)*. What you perceive to be *your* bread — the product of your effort — is really My bread (לַחְמִי) to be enjoyed by you in direct proportion to the satisfaction (described by the Torah as a pleasant aroma) that I receive from your observance of Torah and *mitzvos*.

Being supported in a manner that is conditional upon our behavior may appear to place *Klal Yisrael* at a decided disadvantage vis-a-vis its gentile neighbors. In reality, there could be no greater privilege than to be sustained in such a fashion. As the *Zohar* notes: מַאן דְּאָכִיל דְּלָאו דִּילֵיהּ בָּהִית לְאִסְתַּכּוּלֵי בֵּיהּ, someone receiving a gift is ashamed to look directly at his benefactor. Thus, mankind-at-large, enjoying Hashem's munificence as an act of Divine charity, can do no better than develop an indirect relationship with its creator. *Klal Yisrael*, in the course of earning their daily bread, develops a far more intimate and direct relationship with Hashem known as פָּנִים בְּפָנִים, *face to face*. In this light, it is entirely appropriate that *Divrei Torah* — the true source of our daily bread — should grace our meals.

More profoundly, by requiring that we discuss *Divrei Torah* at every meal, the *mishnah* may be hinting that the relationship between our conduct and our allotment of *parnasah*, known as פָּנִים בְּפָנִים, actually began at the giving of the Torah. Recalling *Matan Torah*, Moshe *Rabbeinu* said to *Bnei Yisrael*, פָּנִים בְּפָנִים דִּבֶּר ה' עִמָּכֶם, *Face to face did Hashem speak with you (Devarim 5:4)*. Hashem commenced that intimate "face-to-face" relationship with us at Sinai. By reciting *Divrei Torah* while eating, we evoke this special relationship which began with the Giving of the Torah. (Cf. *The Three Festivals*, pp.222-223 and pp. 390-391, for further discussion of this concept.)

◆§ Is Bircas Hamazon Sufficient?

ועי' בהרע"ב לענין ברהמ"ז כו' פ' שיש בו פסוקים וענינים הרבה משא"כ ברכה שלפני', ובאם שהאדם לומד הדין של ברכת המזון הוא יוצא ידי חובת דברי תורה על השלחן ובברכת המזון עצמו לא יצא.

אֶחָד וְאָמְרוּ עָלָיו דִּבְרֵי תוֹרָה, כְּאִלּוּ אָכְלוּ מִשֻּׁלְחָנוֹ   ג / ד
שֶׁל מָקוֹם, שֶׁנֶּאֱמַר: ,,וַיְדַבֵּר אֵלַי, זֶה הַשֻּׁלְחָן אֲשֶׁר לִפְנֵי
יהוה.''

ולכאורה לפי"ז כשידברו בסוף ד"ת יהי' למפרע שלחנו ש"מ וגם השכינה אתיא
מעיקרא על סמך זה, . . . ועי' תוי"ט שדחה דברי הרע"ב דאטו איירי התנא במי
שאינו מברך כו' ומשום הא לא איריא דהתתנא אה"נ משבח בכל ישראל בזה, ויש
להכריע דודאי ע"י ברהמ"ז ושאר ברכות כבר יצא מידי זבחי מתים דאין לקראו
בלי מקום שהרי מקום הזכירו שמו של מקום וע"י ד"ת ממש הו"ל שלחנו של מקום.

According to the *Bartenura*, one has fulfilled the obligation of saying *Divrei Torah* at a meal simply by reciting *Bircas Hamazon*. While other commentaries (including the *Tosfos Yom Tov*) dispute this ruling, the *Chiddushei HaRim* defends the *Bartenura*, arguing that if someone does not merely recite the words of *"bentching"* but actually says them sincerely and with heartfelt gratitude (proper כַּוָּנָה) to Hashem for providing his sustenance, this is equivalent to — or even better than — saying *Divrei Torah* at the meal itself. If learning one of the many *halachos* of *Bircas Hamazon* suffices, then certainly saying *Bircas Hamazon* itself is enough! (*Maggidei HaEmes*).

In response to the *Tosfos Yom Tov's* question that since everyone recites *Bircas Hamazon*, the *mishnah's* criticism of those who do not say *Divrei Torah* while eating never applies, we may say the following: Indeed Rabbi Shimon, the author of this *mishnah*, is lauding *Klal Yisrael* for its distinction of enjoying *all* of its meals in the presence of the *Shechinah*.

A related question arises. If *Bircas Hamazon*, recited at the meal's conclusion, takes the place of the *Divrei Torah* said during the meal, it would appear that the *Shechinah* only arrives at the end of the meal. (True, other *berachos* are recited at the beginning of the meal, but only *Bircas Hamazon* contains sufficient *pesukim* and enough Torah thoughts to achieve the status of *Divrei Torah*.) We respond by suggesting that the *Shechinah* arrives at the commencement of the meal, on the totally reliable assumption that we will eventually recite *Bircas Hamazon*.

Perhaps we may resolve the dispute between the *Bartenura* and the other commentators whether *Bircas Hamazon* meets the criteria of *Divrei Torah* by suggesting that any meal in which we *bentch* (or even recite other *berachos*) no longer deserves to be called *offerings to the dead*, a pagan feast. On the other hand, to earn the status of being *Hashem's table*, one must recite *Divrei Torah* during the meal (*Maggidei HaEmes*).

◆§ Must One Say Divrei Torah at a Seudas Mitzvah?

ובסעודת מצוה נראה שאין צריכין כגון סעודת שבת וברית מילה והנה בהתורה

eaten at one table and have spoken words of Torah there, it is as if they have eaten from God's table, as it is said (Yehezkel 41:22): " 'And he said to me, 'This is the table that is before Hashem.' "

מצינו מצוה של אכילת מצה והחיוב לספר כמ״ש לחם שעונין עליו דברים שלא יהי׳ בלי ד״ת.

Seemingly at a meal associated with a *mitzvah* (*seudas mitzvah*), such as a *bris* or the Shabbos meal, it would not be necessary to say a *Dvar Torah*. The *mitzvah* alone should suffice and ensure that the *Shechinah* will grace this meal. However, the requirement that we discuss *Divrei Torah* at the *Seder* despite the many *mitzvos* associated with that meal seems to prove the contrary. In fact, matzoh is called לֶחֶם עוֹנִי because of the requirement that we recite *Divrei Torah* while eating. (Cf. *Pesachim* 115b; also *The Three Festivals*, pp. 59-60, and the *Sfas Emes Haggadah*, pp.50-51, for further discussion of this concept.)

◆§ The Primacy of Torah

ופי׳ אמרו עליו הוא להיות התורה עיקר ועולה על השלחן בענין שאמרו תורתן קבע ומלאכתן ארעי זו וזו נתקיימה בידן, שע״י שהתורה עיקר ממשיכין פנימיות גם בשפע הפרנסה כנ״ל.

The term עָלָיו, *over it*, implies the primacy of the Torah over material values as symbolized by the table. In fact, the best guarantor of *parnasah* is adhering to and learning Torah. As *Chazal* note: תּוֹרָתָן עִיקָר וּמְלַאכְתָּן עֲרַאי זוֹ וְזוֹ נִתְקַיְּימָה בְּיָדָן (*Berachos* 35b), those for whom Torah plays the central role in their lives while their occupation plays only a peripheral role will merit to retain their Torah learning as well as enjoy a secure *parnasah*.

■ זֶה הַשֻּׁלְחָן אֲשֶׁר לִפְנֵי ה׳ — *This is the table that is before Hashem.* ■

◆§ Hashem's Table

כלומר מאחר שיש שלחן שהוא לפני ד׳ בודאי הוא מהאומרים עליו ד״ת. א״כ ע״י התורה זוכין לבחי׳ להם הפנים, שהוא פנימיות השפע להיפוך מזבחי מתים בלי מקום שאין בו חיות פנימיות וע״י שאמרו עליו ד״ת מקבלין שפע פנימיות.

While the *pasuk* cited by the *mishnah* (Yechezkel 41:22) does not explicitly refer to the dining room table over which *Divrei Torah* are discussed (and

[ה] רַבִּי חֲנִינָא בֶּן חֲכִינַאי אוֹמֵר: הַנֵּעוֹר בַּלַּיְלָה,
וְהַמְהַלֵּךְ בַּדֶּרֶךְ יְחִידִי, וּמְפַנֶּה לִבּוֹ לְבַטָּלָה – הֲרֵי
זֶה מִתְחַיֵּב בְּנַפְשׁוֹ.

---

in fact, is referring to the Altar in the *Beis HaMikdash*), we may nonetheless deduce that it is referring to our home table for the following reasons. Firstly, on the basis of the *pasuk* cited in the *mishnah* describing a pagan feast as being devoid of the presence of Hashem (known as מָקוֹם — כִּי כָּל שֻׁלְחָנוֹת מָלְאוּ קִיא צוֹאָה בְּלִי מָקוֹם, *for all tables are full of vomit and filth, without the Omnipresent* (*Yeshayahu* 28:8). Therefore, a table which is the springboard for a discussion of *Divrei Torah* deserves the tribute of being called Hashem's Table. Moreover, if the *pasuk* were only referring to the Altar it would not have said זֶה הַשֻּׁלְחָן, *this is the table*, that is before Hashem's Presence. If there is a table on this earth which is Hashem's Table, it undoubtedly is the table graced with *Divrei Torah*.

Returning to the theme that we discussed in the opening commentary on this *mishnah*, that once the Jewish people accepted the Torah they were privileged to be sustained in direct proportion to their spiritual conduct, an approach known as being nurtured directly from Hashem's "Face," we can grasp the profundity of the *pasuk* cited by the *mishnah*. It is through Torah that the table — and every aspect of our *parnasah* — attains the status of being sustained from Hashem's Countenance. Just as the bread on the Table in the *Beis HaMikdash* was known as the לֶחֶם הַפָּנִים, literally "Bread of the Face," symbolizing that *Klal Yisrael's parnasah* flowed directly from Hashem, so too, by saying *Divrei Torah* at our more mundane tables our meals attain the similar status of being פָּנִים בְּפָנִים, nurtured directly from Hashem.

The term פָּנִים is also related to an inner dimension (פְּנִימִיּוּת). By contrast, the pagan feasts which were totally superficial and devoid of spiritual content (בְּלִי מָקוֹם) are appropriately known as זִבְחֵי מֵתִים, dead offerings barren of the *Shechinah*. Our meals that are permeated with *Divrei Torah* enjoy an inner dimension linking us with the *Shechinah*.

5.

■ הַנֵּעוֹר בַּלַּיְלָה . . . וּמְפַנֶּה לִבּוֹ לְבַטָּלָה – הֲרֵי זֶה מִתְחַיֵּב בְּנַפְשׁוֹ — *One who stays awake at night . . . but turns his heart to idleness — indeed, he bears guilt for his soul.*

⋖§ Why Is Bitul Torah Worse at Night?

יי"ל דרך בלילה קפדינן טפי אבטלה דהא לא איברי לילה אלא או לשינתא או לגירסא ואז הזמן פנוי ללמוד. [גם] יי"ל הנעור בלילה פירוש ניעור בעולם הזה

[5] *Rabbi Chanina ben Chachinai says: One who stays awake at night or who travels alone on the road, but turns his heart to idleness — indeed, he bears guilt for his soul.*

הדומה ללילה.
ונ״מ למשל א׳ מוכרח לבטל שעה נוח לו לבטל ביום מבלילה.

While wasting time and neglecting Torah study is always a grave sin, the consequences of remaining awake at night and not studying Torah are far more serious. As the Gemara notes: The night was created as a time for either sleeping or as an opportunity to study Torah (*Eruvin* 65a). To remain awake and not exploit that priceless opportunity is truly shameful. Consider the possible halachic ramifications of the *mishnah*: If for some reason we are compelled not to learn for a short time span — and we have the opportunity of determining when we will be *mevatel* — it is preferable to do so by day rather than at night.

Homiletically, the term בַּלַּיְלָה, *at night*, may refer to This World which is compared to the darkness of night (cf. *Pesachim* 2b). According to this approach, the *mishnah* is chastising those who during their relatively brief life span on this earth idle away their years rather than use their time wisely.

■ **[One]** — וְהַמְהַלֵּךְ בַּדֶּרֶךְ יְחִידִי וּמְפַנֶּה לִבּוֹ לְבַטָּלָה – הֲרֵי זֶה מִתְחַיֵּב בְּנַפְשׁוֹ ■ *who travels alone on the road, but turns his heart to idleness — indeed, he bears guilt for his soul.*

◆§ Why Is Bitul Torah Worse While Traveling?

עוי״ל דוקא מהלך בדרך כי התורה מצילתו מהמזיקין כי כל דרכים בחזקת סכנה
לכן ה״ז מתחייב בנפשו וכן במה נאה אילן זה.

Just as *bitul Torah* is a particularly grave *aveirah* at night, so too the traveler who insists upon wasting time rather than learning Torah is jeopardizing his own safety. Inasmuch as traveling is generally considered to be hazardous (cf. *Yerushalmi Berachos* 4:1 stating that all roads are considered to be dangerous), then it follows that the traveler is particularly in need of the additional protection that Torah affords. Consequently, it is foolish to be *mevatel* Torah under such circumstances.

■ וְהַמְהַלֵּךְ בַּדֶּרֶךְ יְחִידִי — *Who travels alone on the road.*

[ו] רַבִּי נְחוּנְיָא בֶּן הַקָּנָה אוֹמֵר: כָּל הַמְקַבֵּל עָלָיו עַל תּוֹרָה, מַעֲבִירִין מִמֶּנּוּ עַל מַלְכוּת וְעַל דֶּרֶךְ אֶרֶץ; וְכָל הַפּוֹרֵק מִמֶּנּוּ עַל תּוֹרָה, נוֹתְנִין עָלָיו עַל מַלְכוּת וְעַל דֶּרֶךְ אֶרֶץ.

⸗§ A Path Alone

פי' גם כשהולך בדרך הישר אלא שהוא יחידי שאינו דבוק בהשי"ת, ושונה ומפסיק ממשנתו ר"ל שמפסיק את עצמו מהשי"ת מחמת משנתו, דהיינו שבאה לו התגדלות והתפארות ממשנתו, שאומר על עצמו מה נאה מה אילן זה. ביאר הרה"ק רבי שמואל אליהו מזוואהלין ז"ל דהיינו בעל גאוה שחושב שאין כמוהו בעולם ויחידי הוא עושה דרכו, הריהו מתחייב בנפשו. אפילו האדם ההולך בדרך הישר, מכל מקום אם הוא יחידי, כלומר שדואג רק לעצמו ואינו טורח ליישר אף את הזולת לדרך הישר, הרי זה מתחייב בנפשו.

Perhaps we should emphasize the term *alone* (יְחִידִי). Even if one is traveling through life along the path of Torah, if he insists on taking his *own* road and attributes his vast knowledge to his *own* efforts — rather than crediting Hashem, the Giver of the Torah — he jeopardizes his very existence[1] (*Maggid of Zlotshoff, Maggidei HaEmes*).

In a somewhat similar vein, R' Shmuel Eliyahu of Zavollin understood the term יְחִידִי, *alone*, to be referring to that haughty individual who embarks on his own path, assuming that no one compares to him in wisdom. Such an egotistical and isolated existence is particularly fraught with danger.

The Bendiner Rav took a similar approach, suggesting that the mishnah is chastising those who are only concerned with their own personal spiritual progress without considering the need for others' spiritual growth (*Maggidei HaEmes*).

■ וּמְפַנֶּה לִבּוֹ לְבַטָּלָה — *But turns his heart to idleness.*

⸗§ Is This a Separate Case?

עתיו"ט דברי החסיד ז"ל וי"ל דהפי' דמצד לילה נמי מתחייב בנפשו ונ"מ למשל א' מוכרח לבטל שעה נוח לו לבטל ביום מבלילה וכדומה וכן הולך בדרך כו'.

The *Tosfos Yom Tov* strongly insists that this phrase is not referring to a separate case but rather explains the first two instances of the *mishnah* as

---

1. According to this interpretation, the expression וּמַפְסִיק מִמִּשְׁנָתוֹ should be interpreted in the following manner. He severs his link with Hashem *because* of his learning.

[6] *Rabbi Nechunia ben Hakanah says: If some-one accepts upon himself the yoke of Torah — the yoke of government and the yoke of worldly responsibilities are removed from him. But if someone throws off the yoke of Torah from himself — the yoke of government and the yoke of worldly responsibilities are placed upon him.*

---

follows: Merely remaining awake at night or traveling on a road is hardly a crime. It is only those individuals who idle away their precious time rather than study Torah who are jeopardizing their lives. According to this approach, the וְהַמְפַנֶּה לִבּוֹ.

However, in light of our previous assertion that it is worse to take time from Torah study by night than by day, we suggest that this segment of the *mishnah* may stand alone. It teaches us that *anyone* who wastes time (even by day) is liable for whatever may occur to him. Thus, the *mishnah* is citing three particularly dangerous practices: הַנֵּעוֹר בַּלַּיְלָה — staying awake at night without learning Torah; הַמְהַלֵּךְ בַּדֶּרֶךְ יְחִידִי — traveling alone and not learning Torah; and finally מְפַנֶּה לִבּוֹ לְבַטָּלָה — taking time from *Torah* study, even by day. According to this approach, the reading of וְהַמְפַנֶּה as one (anyone) who idles away time may be valid.

6.

■ כָּל הַמְקַבֵּל עָלָיו עֹל תּוֹרָה, מַעֲבִירִין מִמֶּנּוּ עֹל מַלְכוּת וְעֹל דֶּרֶךְ אֶרֶץ; וְכָל הַפּוֹרֵק מִמֶּנּוּ עֹל תּוֹרָה, נוֹתְנִין עָלָיו עֹל מַלְכוּת וְעֹל דֶּרֶךְ אֶרֶץ — *If someone accepts upon himself the yoke of Torah — the yoke of government and the yoke of worldly responsibilities are removed from him. But if someone throws off the yoke of Torah from himself — the yoke of government and the yoke of worldly responsibilities are placed upon him.*

⋖§ "Torah Only" Versus "Torah im Derech Eretz"

והא אמרו יפה ת״ת עם דרך ארץ, אך כי עול תורה הוא ביטול בלב שלם לרצון עליון, שזה עיקר יגיעה בתורה לבטל שכל האדם אל דעת התורה ורצון המקום ב״ה, ובשאין לאדם רצון אחר א״צ לעול ד״א, כי יש לימוד תורה כדי לידע איך להתנהג ולקיים מצות השי״י, וזה ת״ת עם ד״א כמ״ש במ״א ענין המצות לפמ״ש בזוה״ק תרומה דקיימא בעובדא צריך יגיעה רבה ע״י שהוא במעשה גשמיי וצריך להתהפך לטוב, וזה יגיעת שנידהם להיות אחד, אבל יש לימוד תורה כדי ליבטל לרצון השי״י כנ״ל והוא שאין חפץ להשיג ולידע, רק להיבטל תמיד למה שאינו משיג, ולהשיג יותר כדי שידע להיבטל יותר (על) [*אל] מה שאינו משיג וזהו עול תורה שהוא ביטול כל הרצון כנ״ל.

This *mishnah*, portraying the total negation of any obligation to the secular world (דֶּרֶךְ אֶרֶץ) as an ideal state, seemingly contradicts the renowned *mishnah* in the previous *perek* (2:2) advocating תּוֹרָה עִם דֶּרֶךְ אֶרֶץ, a unified and harmonious approach combining Torah and an association with the world of commerce. (Refer to our extensive commentary on that *mishnah*.)

Upon further contemplation, we realize that the two *mishnahs* are not dichotomous but simply reflect different life styles. While in many instances a lifestyle combining Torah and *Derech Eretz* would be appropriate, certain individuals enjoy even loftier spiritual ambitions. Their sole objective is to negate every wish and aspiration of their own in favor of fulfilling the Divine will, a concept known as *"bitul."* Such particularly enlightened individuals are rewarded with the fulfillment of their fondest wish, the removal of any impediment to their goal of serving Hashem.

These different approaches to *Avodas Hashem* come into sharp focus insofar as Torah study is concerned. The practitioner of *Torah im Derech Eretz* will study Torah with the objective of learning how to implement Hashem's will through the observance of *mitzvos* (which often can only be fulfilled in the physical ambiance of This World). We should, by no means, underestimate the daunting nature of this challenge — to integrate the spiritual content of Torah with the material entities, known as *Derech Eretz* — through which *mitzvos* are fulfilled. (For example, the *mitzvah* of *tzitzis* cannot be performed without a garment or the *mitzvah* of *mezuzah* without a door.) The previous *mishnah* describes this process as יְגִיעַת שְׁנֵיהֶם; the integration of Torah and *Derech Eretz* involves great *exertion*.

On the other hand, for those individuals whose sole objective is to negate their own desires to the Divine will, Torah study becomes a potent means of achieving this goal. For them, learning is not primarily intended to be *for* the purpose of determining the Divine will (though that objective is certainly important) but as a means through which they can *negate* themselves even more to Hashem's wishes. Such enlightened individuals view *limud Torah* as an ongoing dialectic of learning and self-negation. The more they learn, the more they realize their inadequacies and lack of knowledge, and consequently they seek to negate themselves to the *Shechinah*. All of the above discussion — our portrayal of this lifestyle — is subsumed in the pithy phrase עַל תּוֹרָה, the overriding and singular determination to fulfill the Divine will. While others need interaction with the secular world — with *Derech Eretz* — to fulfill their objective and reach their potential, those who embrace the Divine will to the exclusion of everything else merit that מַעֲבִירִין מִמֶּנּוּ עַל דֶּרֶךְ אֶרֶץ, all obstacles to his dream will be removed.

◆§ Even When Earning a Livelihood

אַף כִּי מָצִינוּ כַּמָּה תַנָּאִים שֶׁבּוֹדָאי קִבְּלוּ עֲלֵיהֶם עוֹל תּוֹרָה וְעִם כָּל זֹאת הָיָה עֲלֵיהֶם

עול דרך ארץ כמו רבי יצחק נפחא ורבי יוחנן הסנדלר וכיוצא. אכן לא היה להם
עול מזה בגלל עול התורה שהיה עליהם.

According to the Kotzker Rebbe, by committing oneself to Torah, we are not necessarily excluding the possibility of earning a livelihood. In fact, some of our greatest sages, such as Rabbi Yochanan and Rabbi Yitzchak, not only earned a livelihood but are even known by their profession — Rabbi Yochanan the shoemaker and Rabbi Yitzchak the blacksmith. However, their *parnasah* never became an obsession. Having accepted upon themselves the עול תורה, that all-embracing, commitment to Torah, nothing else — even the need to earn a livelihood — could approach that commitment.

◆§ Reentering Gan Eden Through Torah

אנשים משקיעים ראשם ורובם בעניני פרנסה ורוצים להרויח עוד ועוד, הרי הם
שוכחים שעצם העמל בעניני פרנסה הוא קללה כדכתיב בעת אפיך תאכל לחם.
שכאשר חטא אדם הראשון בחטא עץ הדעת גירשו הקב״ה מגן עדן, ובכדי שלא
יחזור לשם קללו שבזעת אפיך תאכל לחם וממילא יהיה טרוד בעניני פרנסה ולא
ילמוד תורה, ועי״ז ישאר מחוץ לגן עדן. ומכיון שהקב״ה חפץ להטיב לבריותיו,
לכן אפילו אחר הגזירה יכולים להתגבר על הנסיונות וללמוד תורה ואז יצליח גם
בעסקיו ויהיה פרנסה בריוח.

The *Pnei Menachem* would comment that people who are obsessed with the struggle to earn a *parnasah* forget that the need to work in order to earn a livelihood was the curse given to Adam: בְּזֵעַת אַפֶּיךָ תֹּאכַל לֶחֶם, *by the sweat of your brow shall you eat bread* (Bereishis 3:19). In order to ensure that Adam and his descendants would never return to *Gan Eden* — a distinct possibility had he immersed himself in Torah study — Hashem compelled him to struggle in his quest for *parnasah. Klal Yisrael*, on the other hand, enjoying the gift of Torah, can actually enter a spiritual *Gan Eden* by virtue of its learning. Instead of falling into the trap of adopting Adam's curse as our *raison d'être*, we would be better advised to immerse ourselves in the study of Torah. By choosing that approach we can be assured of *parnasah* as well as spiritual satisfaction (*Maggidei HaEmes*).

◆§ Hashem Will Provide Parnasah

אחד שהגיע לתור השאת ילדיו חשב לחפש לחפש הכנסה נוספת על עבודתו הקבועה.
שלח את בנו אל אדמו״ר זצ״ל הלב שמחה לשאול לחוות דעתו בכך. שאל
אדמו״ר זצ״ל ״מה עושה אביך באותן שעות שבהן מבקש הוא לעבוד העבודה
הנוספת״? ״לומד בבית המדרש״. ״אינני מבין הפטיר אדמו״ר זצ״ל, ״להמיר
את בית המדרש בעבודה?! עדיף שישב וילמוד, הקב״ה חפץ ביהודים שיושבים

A concerned parent about to marry off his children sent his son to ask the *Lev Simchah* whether he should take on another job. When informed that the young man's father was studying Torah in a *beis hamedrash* during the hours that he now proposed to work, the *Lev Simchah* immediately advised against such a trade-off. He said, "Hashem simply desires that you continue to study Torah. He, in turn, will provide sufficient *parnasah* to enable your father to marry off his children."

◆§ Geulah Amidst Galus

מעבירין משמע אפילו בהיותינו עבדים בגלות אע"פכ אין לך אדם שאין לו שעה שמתעורר לו קצת גאולה בנפש שיוכל לקבל עליו עול מלכות שמים, וכמו כן בכלל בודאי מי שמקבל עול תורה כראוי מסייע לגאולה, ומעבירין ממנו ומכחו עול מלכות, וכמו כן בעול דרך ארץ הגם מי שצריך לעבוד על פרנסתו מי"מ נתן לנו השי"ת מצות השבת שהוא יום מנוחה וכדאיתא שבת יעשה כולו תורה, וכל סוחר צריך להיות מקבל עול תורה ביום השבת ובכח זה מעבירין ממנו עול דרך ארץ בימי המעשה ולא אמרו מעבירין ממנו מלכות ודרך ארץ רק עול דרך ארץ אמרו שצריך האדם שלא יתערבב ע"י ולא יתקשר בכל העסקים אשר לא לה' המה, וכן בעול מלכות דאיתא מאן דכפית באחרא אי"א לו לקבל עול מלכות שמים, ומאן דכפית דייקא, אבל מי שזוכה הגם שהוא באיזה עבדות או בד"א, מי"מ אינו כפות ומשועבד לזה.

If we consider the full ramifications of our *mishnah's* statement, מַעֲבִירִין מִמֶּנּוּ עַל מַלְכוּת, that the burden of oppression is removed from anyone who accepts the challenge of Torah, we realize a significant fact. Even in the midst of the long *galus* that *Klal Yisrael* has experienced, it is still possible to experience a sense of *geulah* by immersing oneself in *limud Torah.* While this is always true, we obtain the greatest relief from the endless struggle for *parnasah* by immersing ourselves in Torah every Shabbos. As *Chazal* state, the Shabbos day should be totally devoted to Torah study (*Tanna D'Vei Eliyahu*, Ch. 1). But the rewards of *limud HaTorah* on Shabbos are by no means confined to that day. On the contrary, as the *mishnah* states, מְקַבֵּל עָלָיו עַל תּוֹרָה — by committing ourselves to learn Torah on Shabbos we are shielded from the "yoke of government and the yoke of worldly responsibilities" all week long. Of course, the need to relate to secular rulers remains. Likewise, the need to earn a *parnasah* still exists. However, by immersing ourselves in Torah every Shabbos we feel a palpable sense of relief during the week that follows. While the עַל מַלְכוּת (government) and עַל דֶּרֶךְ אֶרֶץ (the need to earn a livelihood) have not disappeared, the עַל, the sense of overriding commitment that these common situations usually possess, is greatly mitigated.

וְכָל הַפּוֹרֵק ■ — *But if someone throws off.*

◆§ Rejecting One's Innate Commitment to Torah

ונראה כי כל א׳ כשנברא יש עליו עול מלכות ועוד״א וגם עול תורה כמ״ש אדם
לעמל יולד אי׳ אם לעמלו ש״ת כו׳ לכן המקבל עליו מעצמו ג״כ עול תורה אז
מעבירין ממנו עו״מ ועוד״א והפורק ממנו עו״ת המוטל עליו אז מוסיפין לו עו״מ
יותר.

By stating פּוֹרֵק — which implies one who *rejects* — rather than אֵינוֹ מְקַבֵּל, *one who does not accept* (which would parallel the opening statement of the mishnah, הַמְקַבֵּל, *one who accepts*), the *mishnah* is alluding to an individual who rejects the innate sense of commitment to Torah that every Jew receives at birth along with an innate fear of sovereign power (עֹל מַלְכוּת) and a sense that eventually he will need to earn a livelihood (עֹל דֶּרֶךְ אֶרֶץ). By reaffirming his inborn commitment to Torah, the Jew is able to eventually minimize his innate fear of higher authorities and his obsession with *parnasah* as well. On the other hand, by rejecting even the minimal commitment to Torah, present at birth, he ensures that his other natural drives are greatly intensified.

◆§ Accepting and Rejecting Torah

פי׳ כשכבר העבירו ממנו העול מלכות ע״י שקבל עול תורה וחזר בו לכן עתה
נותנים כו׳ דשנה ופירש קשה טפי כמו שאמרו חז״ל. וברישא דמעבירין ממנו
וכשאינו מקבל לא נותנים ולא מעבירין רק כפי מזלו.

Perhaps the two instances mentioned in the *mishnah* — accepting and rejecting Torah — may refer to the same individual who first accepts the yoke of Torah (and enjoys the benefits of his decision) and then reverses his decision. This form of behavior is described by *Chazal* as שָׁנָה וּפֵירֵשׁ, one who has learned Torah and then renounced his learning (*Pesachim* 49b). Rejecting a previous commitment to Torah is considered by *Chazal* to be far worse than never accepting the yoke of Torah. This distinction is reflected in the fate that awaits them. Whereas the individual who has never committed himself to Torah is pretty much left to the mercies of the natural world, neither receiving additional burdens nor being relieved of his existing responsibilities, someone who has abandoned Torah is saddled with ever increasing burdens.

◆§ The Gift of Responsibility

נותנים הוא לשון מתנה, דכיון שאין עליו עול תורה תביא אותו הבטלה לידי
שעמום ודעות רעות, ולפיכך נותנים לו מן השמים עול מלכות שיטרידהו ללא

[ז] רַבִּי חֲלַפְתָּא בֶּן דּוֹסָא אִישׁ כְּפַר חֲנַנְיָא אוֹמֵר:
עֲשָׂרָה שֶׁיּוֹשְׁבִין וְעוֹסְקִין בַּתּוֹרָה, שְׁכִינָה שְׁרוּיָה
בֵינֵיהֶם, שֶׁנֶּאֱמַר: „אֱלֹהִים נִצָּב בַּעֲדַת אֵל." וּמִנַּיִן

הרף ולא יהיה פנוי לדברים ריקים ואסורים.

R′ Moshe of Kobrin emphasized that sometimes additional responsibilities are considered a gift. As the *mishnah* states: נוֹתְנִין עָלָיו עֹל מַלְכוּת, Hashem *gives him* (as a present) the burden of earning a livelihood. For an individual who is no longer committed to a regimen of intensive Torah study, and as a result faces the risk of being influenced by non-Torah ideals, there can be no greater Divine gift than to be burdened with ever increasing responsibilities which absorb so much of his time. In essence, because he is so busy there is less time for him to be exposed to inappropriate (non-Torah) beliefs (*Maggidei HaEmes*).

⤳ Throwing Nuts at a Chasan

נוהגים לזרוק על חתן העולה לתורה אגוזים ושקדים ומיני מתיקה, וזאת משום
שהנושא אשה מקבל עליו עול פרנסה כמו שאמרו חז״ל ריחיים בצוארו. ולכן
מראים לו בעת העלייה לתורה שאם יקבל על עצמו עול תורה יזמין לו הקב״ה
פרנסה בניקל כמו אגוזים ושקדים שגדלין מעצמם.

The *Chiddushei HaRim* offered a beautiful explanation for the time-honored *minhag* of throwing nuts at a *chasan* during his *aliyah*. This young man who is about to assume the additional burden of securing a *parnasah* upon his marriage is assured that if he commits himself to intensive Torah learning — מְקַבֵּל עָלָיו עֹל תּוֹרָה — his financial burdens will be eased. Just as nuts grow without extensive human effort (often growing in the wild), so too his livelihood will be provided for by Hashem, without undue effort on his part (*Maggidei HaEmes*).

7.

■ עֲשָׂרָה שֶׁיּוֹשְׁבִין . . . שְׁכִינָה שְׁרוּיָה בֵינֵיהֶם — *If ten people sit together . . . the Divine Presence rests among them.*

⤳ The Power of a Minyan

שבכל פעם שבני ישראל נאספים לעבודת ד' שכינה שורה בהם כדאיתא במשנה

[7] *Rabbi Chalafta ben Dosa of Kfar Chanania says: If ten people sit together and engage in Torah study, the Divine Presence rests among them, as it is said (Tehillim 82:1): "God stands in the assembly of God."*

עשרה שיושבין וכו' שכינה שרויה. ומעוררין הכח ממתן תורה קול גדול ולא יסף ולא פסק.

ורבותינו ז"ל נהגו להזכיר מש"כ בס' תניא (אגה"ק פכ"ג) וז"ל שמעתי מרבותי כי אילו נמצא מלאך אחד עומד במעמד עשרה מישראל ביחד אף שאינם מדברים בדברי תורה תפול עליו אימתה ופחד בלי גבול ותכלית משכינתא דשריא עלייהן עד שהיה מתבטל ממציאותו לגמרי.

The *Beis Yisrael* remarked that whenever Jews congregate for a sacred purpose (*Avodas Hashem*) they evoke the Divine Voice which was heard at Sinai. The "sound of *Matan Torah*," described as קוֹל גָּדוֹל וְלֹא יָסָף, *a great voice which never ceases* (*Devarim* 5:19), is experienced again whenever a *minyan* of Jews convene. In a similar vein, R' Schneur Zalman of Liadi commented that even an angel standing in the presence of a *minyan* of simple Jews would experience an overwhelming sense of awe from the Divine Presence (הַשְׁרָאַת שְׁכִינָה) which graces such a gathering (*Maggidei HaEmes*).

■ וּמִנַּיִן אֲפִילּוּ חֲמִשָּׁה — *How do we know this [is true] even of five?* ■

◈§ Different Levels of Kedushah

וצריך לומר כי יש תוספת מעלה בעשרה שהשכינה שרויה ביותר והכל בהדרגה. ולפי זה משמע בין חמשה לתשעה לא נפקא מינה מידי. וחז"ל הקשו מאחר דתרי, כל שכן עשרה. עשרה קדמה שכינה ואתיא וחמשה קדמה מעט ואתיא אבל לא כקדמה שבעשרה.

The *mishnah* seems to be distinguishing between an assembly of ten people in which the *Shechinah* is perceived most intensely and a group of five people. Although they also enjoy the Divine Presence, they do not perceive the *Shechinah* so acutely. Additionally, we may deduce that no distinction exists between a group of five and a group of nine; it is only in a *minyan* that the complete *presence* of the *Shechinah* may be enjoyed. On the other hand, both of these groups possess a distinction not enjoyed by smaller gatherings. The Gemara (*Berachos* 6a) relates that in the case of large groups the *Shechinah* arrives even *before* the gathering convenes. On the other hand, when two Jews meet to study Torah, the *Shechinah* also arrives — but only after the gathering has commenced.

וּמִנַּיִן אֲפִילוּ חֲמִשָּׁה? שֶׁנֶּאֱמַר: ,,וַאֲגֻדָּתוֹ עַל אֶרֶץ
יְסָדָהּ.'' וּמִנַּיִן אֲפִילוּ שְׁלֹשָׁה? שֶׁנֶּאֱמַר: ,,בְּקֶרֶב אֱלֹהִים
יִשְׁפֹּט.'' וּמִנַּיִן אֲפִילוּ שְׁנַיִם? שֶׁנֶּאֱמַר: ,,אָז נִדְבְּרוּ יִרְאֵי
יהוה אִישׁ אֶל רֵעֵהוּ וַיַּקְשֵׁב יהוה וַיִּשְׁמָע.'' וּמִנַּיִן אֲפִילוּ
אֶחָד? שֶׁנֶּאֱמַר: ,,בְּכָל הַמָּקוֹם אֲשֶׁר אַזְכִּיר אֶת שְׁמִי,
אָבוֹא אֵלֶיךָ וּבֵרַכְתִּיךָ.''

[ח] רַבִּי אֶלְעָזָר אִישׁ בַּרְתּוֹתָא אוֹמֵר: תֶּן לוֹ מִשֶּׁלּוֹ,
שֶׁאַתָּה וְשֶׁלְּךָ שֶׁלּוֹ; וְכֵן בְּדָוִד הוּא אוֹמֵר: ,,כִּי מִמְּךָ
הַכֹּל, וּמִיָּדְךָ נָתַנּוּ לָךְ.''

■ וּמִנַּיִן אֲפִילוּ שְׁנַיִם . . . וַיַּקְשֵׁב ה' וַיִּשְׁמָע — *How do we know this [is true]
even of two? . . . "and Hashem listened and heard."*

◄§ Hashem "Prepares" to Hear Our Divrei Torah

וקשה הראיה דגם בשמים שומע השי''ת ואם כן מהיכן הראיה כי שכינה שרויה
ביניהם דוקא. ונראה מדכתיב ויקשב כ' וישמע דלמה לי ויקשב רק הפי' שעושה
מעשה כדי לשמוע והיינו שכינה שרויה ביניהם.

The *mishnah* deduces that the *Shechinah* resides even in a gathering of two
Torah students from the apparent redundancy of the words וַיַּקְשֵׁב (listened)
and וַיִּשְׁמָע (heard). Both terms indicate that Hashem listens. In this context,
however, וַיַּקְשֵׁב refers to the *Shechinah's* preparation to "listen more closely" to
the *Divrei Torah* of *Klal Yisrael*. By "descending" to our lowly level and joining,
as it were, in our involved Torah discussion, the *Shechinah* is better able to
enjoy and hear (וַיִּשְׁמָע) our *Divrei Torah*.

■ ,,בְּכָל הַמָּקוֹם אֲשֶׁר אַזְכִּיר אֶת שְׁמִי'' — *"In every place where I will cause
My Name to be mentioned."*

◄§ Hashem Blesses Man's Efforts

ואין מובן פי' אזכיר דהו''ל למימר תזכיר. אך הפי' כי אין שום דבר ומעשה
בעולם שלא יהיה ממנו ית' ולכן על ידי עבודת האדם מסייע השי''י וזה שכתוב
אזכיר.

The Torah deliberately uses the term אַזְכִּיר אֶת שְׁמִי, "I will cause My Name
to be mentioned," rather than תַּזְכִּיר, "you will mention." The *pasuk* (Shemos

How do we know this [is true] even of five? For it is said (Amos 9:6): "He has established His bundle upon earth." How do we know this [is true] even of three? As it is said (Tehillim 82:1): "In the midst of judges He shall judge." How do we know this [is true] even of two? As it is said (Malachi 3:16): "Then those who fear Hashem spoke to one another and Hashem listened and heard." How do we know this [is true] even of one? As it is said (Shemos 20:21): "In every place where I will cause My Name to be mentioned, I will come to you and bless you."

[8] *Rabbi Elazar of Bartosa says: Give Him from His Own, for you and your possessions are His. And so has David said (Divrei HaYamim I 29:14): "For everything is from You, and from Your Own Hand we have given You."*

20:21) is emphasizing a vital concept: Man's efforts would never reach fruition without Hashem's blessings.

8.

■ תֵּן לוֹ מִשֶּׁלּוֹ שֶׁאַתָּה וְשֶׁלְּךָ שֶׁלּוֹ ■ — *Give Him from His Own, for you and your possessions are His.*

◄§ Tzedakah and Good Deeds Are Inspired by Hashem

הפי׳ בעת שנותן ידע שאינו נותן מעצמו כלום רק הכל נתינת הש״י כעין מה שכתוב אל תחזיק טובה לעצמך.

שאתה כשעושה מצוה בגופו, ושלך בממונו, הכל ממנו יתברך, ומידך נתנו לך כלומר אף כח הנתינה.

The *mishnah* is addressing those generous benefactors who not only contribute to charitable causes but also personally perform good deeds. Remember that your generosity is not only derived from your own nature but is also inspired by Hashem. Specifically, all the good deeds that you (שֶׁאַתָּה) personally perform and all the funds that you (וְשֶׁלְּךָ) have contributed to *tzedakah* emanate from Hashem. Even the personality traits that enable you to be so generous stem from Him. As the *mishnah* concludes: וּמִיָּדְךָ נָתַנּוּ לָךְ, from Your Hands we were given the capacity to be so giving (נָתַנּוּ).[1]

[ט] רַבִּי יַעֲקֹב אוֹמֵר: הַמְהַלֵּךְ בַּדֶּרֶךְ וְשׁוֹנֶה, וּמַפְסִיק
מִמִּשְׁנָתוֹ, וְאוֹמֵר: "מַה נָּאֶה אִילָן זֶה! וּמַה נָּאֶה נִיר

9.

■ הַמְהַלֵּךְ בַּדֶּרֶךְ וְשׁוֹנֶה, וּמַפְסִיק מִמִּשְׁנָתוֹ, וְאוֹמֵר: מַה נָּאֶה אִילָן זֶה . . . מַעֲלֶה
עָלָיו הַכָּתוּב כְּאִלּוּ מִתְחַיֵּב בְּנַפְשׁוֹ — *One who walks on the road while
reviewing [a Torah lesson] and interrupts his review, and exclaims,
"How beautiful is this tree! . . ." Scripture considers it as if he bears
guilt for his soul.*

◄§ An Outmoded Form of Avodas Hashem

והרע״ב פי׳ דאע״ג דעל ידי כן הוא מברך ברוך שככה לו בעולמו אף על פי כן
הרי זה מתחייב בנפשו. וקשה אמאי מתחייב בנפשו הלא מברך ברכה. וי״ל
שקודם מתן תורה השיג אברהם אבינו ע״ה את השי״ת על ידי חקירה, ומשנתן
השי״ת את התורה אסר לנו את החקירה וצריך להשיג את השי״ת רק על ידי
התורה, וזה הפי׳ שמפסיק ממשנתו ועוסק בחקירה וחוקר מהיכן יש כח לאילן זה
שיצמח הלא הוא מהשי״ת ורוצה להשיג את השי״ת ע״י חקירה [לבד שלא על
ידי התורה], בשביל זה מתחייב בנפשו.

It seems puzzling that simply interrupting one's learning to gaze at the wonders of nature should be considered a capital offense. To the contrary, it
would seem that an individual acting in such a manner should be commended
since he has now earned the opportunity to recite the *berachah*, שְׁכָכָה . . . בָּרוּךְ
לוֹ בְּעוֹלָמוֹ, *Blessed . . . Who has such in His universe*, which is said upon sighting
exceptionally beautiful trees (people or fields).

In response, the Kotzker Rebbe suggested that such behavior betrays a
serious misunderstanding of the proper approach towards *Avodas Hashem*.
Although it is certainly true that prior to the giving of the Torah great individuals such as Avraham Avinu were able to come close to Hashem by contemplating the manifold wonders of His universe, after *Matan Torah*, excessive
reliance upon such an approach is no longer valid. On the contrary, we are
required to seek out Hashem through intensive study of His Torah (*Maggidei
HaEmes*).

◄§ The Perils of the Road

1. In this vein, we may obtain additional insight into a previous *mishnah* (2:9): אַל תַּחֲזִיק טוֹבָה לְעַצְמְךָ
כִּי לְכָךְ נוֹצָרְתָּ — *Do not attribute* (אַל תַּחֲזִיק) all the good deeds (טוֹבָה) that you have achieved to
yourself (לְעַצְמְךָ). On the contrary, you have been created (and are continually assisted) by
Hashem for this purpose (כִּי לְכָךְ נוֹצָרְתָּ).

[9] *Rabbi Yaakov says: One who walks on the road while reviewing [a Torah lesson] and interrupts his review, and exclaims, "How beautiful is this tree! How beautiful is this plowed field!" — Script-*

כי דרך הוא סכנה וה' שומר וצריך על כל פנים שלא לעשות אז עבירה וביטול תורה היא עבירה לכן אין ה' שומרו אז.

While it is always wrong to interrupt learning to gaze at a tree, such behavior is far more risky while traveling. Beset by the many perils lurking along the road, one can ill afford the grave sin of *bitul Torah*. To interrupt one's learning under such circumstances can indeed be perilous.

◂§ Detaching Yourself From the Giver of the Torah

כתיב תמים תהיה עם ד' אלקיך וראיתי בתלמידי הבעש"ט שגם לומדי תורה כתיב תמים תהיה העיקר לדבוק בהשי"ת ופירש המשנה השונה ומפסיק ממשנתו, אף ללומדי תורה הוזהר לבל להנתק מעול מלכות שמים תמים תהיה תורת ד' תמימה גם כן רק עם ד' אלקיך.

According to the *Beis Yisrael,* the term וּמַפְסִיק מִמִּשְׁנָתוֹ (and interrupts his review) may refer to the unfortunate possibility that the Torah student detaches himself (מַפְסִיק) from the Giver of the Torah, Hashem, Who first taught Torah (מִשְׁנָתוֹ) to *Klal Yisrael.* He reminds us of the famous *pasuk,* תָּמִים תִּהְיֶה עִם ה' אֱלֹקֶיךָ, *You shall be wholehearted with Hashem, your God* (*Devarim* 18:13), which may be interpreted in the following manner: Even when you are immersed in studying Torah which is called תָּמִים (cf. *Tehillim* 19:8, תּוֹרַת ה' תְּמִימָה, *the Torah of Hashem is perfect*), remain עם ה' אֱלֹקֶיךָ and never forget the Divine Source of all your learning (*Maggidei HaEmes*).

◂§ How Can Praising Hashem Be Considered a Capital Offense?

בתוי"ט בשם ד"ח כי נלמד מרק השמר לך כו' יי"ל דמפרש מה דמסיים שם והודעתם לבניך יום כו' מה להלן באימה כו' קאי גם ארישא דשמור נפשך מאוד א"כ ש"מ דמעה"כ כאילו מתחייב בנפשו, ועי' בתוס' יו"ט מש"כ שסמוך אקרא דפן תשכח פי' דעי"ז בא לזה שישכח.

The Torah cautions us:
רַק הִשָּׁמֶר לְךָ וּשְׁמֹר נַפְשְׁךָ מְאֹד פֶּן־תִּשְׁכַּח אֶת־הַדְּבָרִים אֲשֶׁר־רָאוּ עֵינֶיךָ וּפֶן־יָסוּרוּ מִלְּבָבְךָ

זֶה!" — מַעֲלֶה עָלָיו הַכָּתוּב כְּאִלּוּ מִתְחַיֵּב בְּנַפְשׁוֹ.

[י] רַבִּי דוֹסְתַּאי בַּר יַנַּאי מִשּׁוּם רַבִּי מֵאִיר אוֹמֵר: כָּל הַשּׁוֹכֵחַ דָּבָר אֶחָד מִמִּשְׁנָתוֹ, מַעֲלֶה עָלָיו הַכָּתוּב

Only beware רַק הִשָּׁמֶר לְךָ וּשְׁמֹר נַפְשְׁךָ מְאֹד פֶּן תִּשְׁכַּח אֶת הַדְּבָרִים אֲשֶׁר רָאוּ עֵינֶיךָ וּפֶן יָסוּרוּ מִלְּבָבְךָ כֹּל יְמֵי חַיֶּיךָ וְהוֹדַעְתָּם לְבָנֶיךָ וְלִבְנֵי בָנֶיךָ. יוֹם אֲשֶׁר עָמַדְתָּ לִפְנֵי ה' אֱלֹקֶיךָ בְּחֹרֵב, *for yourself and greatly beware for your soul, lest you forget the things that your eyes have beheld and lest you remove them from your heart all the days of your life, and make them known to your children and your children's children — the day that you stood before Hashem, your God, at Horeb (Devarim 4:9).*

Chazal learn from this that one must study Torah with the same awe and reverence as was present at its transmittal at Sinai. Perhaps the *mishnah* understands that the interruption of Torah study to gaze at nature's beauty reflects an overly casual attitude towards Torah study — and thus falls under the category of "beware for yourself and greatly beware for your soul."

However, according to the *Tosfos Yom Tov*, the *mishnah's* condemnation of those who interrupt their learning to marvel at Hashem's handiwork is based on another element of this verse: *Only beware for yourself and greatly beware for your soul, lest you forget the things that your eyes have beheld.* By diverting his attention from the Torah that he is studying to the natural beauty of his immediate environment, the Torah student increases the likelihood that he will forget his learning. As the next *mishnah* tells us, such a person endangers his life.

■ וּמַה נָּאֶה נִיר זֶה — *How beautiful is this plowed field.* ■

◆§ Congratulating Yourself While Learning

פִּי' שֶׁבְּתוֹךְ יְגִיעָתוֹ מַרְגִּישׁ הַהִתְנַשְּׂאוּת בְּנַפְשׁוֹ לֵאמֹר מַה נָּאֶה מַה יָּגַעְתִּי זֹאת, וְזֶה הֶפְסֵק בְּלִימּוּדוֹ שֶׁעַ"ז זֶה אֵין מַעֲשָׂיו עוֹלִין וְעוֹד מוֹסִיף עָלָיו קִטְרוּג מוּתְחַיֵּיב בְּנַפְשׁוֹ כַּנַּ"ל. וּבְשֵׁם הָרַב הַקְ' מִפְּשִׁיסְחָא עַל מַה שֶּׁכָּתוּב בַּתַּנָּא דְּבֵי אֵלִיָּהוּ וְיוֹשֵׁב וְהוֹגֶה בַּתּוֹרָה כַּבְּהֵמָה הַחוֹרֶשֶׁת בַּשָּׂדֶה, פִּי' שֶׁאֵין הַבְּהֵמָה מַשְׁגַּחַת לִרְאוֹת אִם יָפֶה עָשְׂתָה רַק הוֹלֶכֶת וְעוֹשָׂה רָצוֹן בְּעָלֶיהָ כְּמוֹ כֵן צָרִיךְ לִהְיוֹת יְגִיעַת הָאָדָם בַּתּוֹרָה בִּתְמִימוּת לְשֵׁם הַשִּׁי"ת.

Allegorically, the term נִיר, *a plowed field,* may allude to the intellectual ground that has been broken by the intense learning of the Torah scholar. It is often tempting to pause while learning and congratulate oneself on the progress he has made thus far. However, just as plowing a field is merely the first step towards reaping a bountiful harvest, so too it would be premature to

[10] *Rabbi Dostai bar Yannai says in the name of Rabbi Meir: Whoever forgets anything of his Torah learning, Scripture considers it as if he bears guilt for his*

pride oneself on one's accomplishments while still plumbing the depths of Torah. In fact, such premature self-adulation invites much closer scrutiny of one's overall behavior and even the risk of losing one's life. As the *mishnah* concludes, כְּאִלּוּ מִתְחַיֵּב בְּנַפְשׁוֹ, *as if he bears guilt for his soul.*

In a similar vein R' Simcha Bunim of *Peshis'cha* offered a beautiful interpretation of the *Chazal* (*Tanna D'Vei Eliyahu*) stating that one should study Torah like an animal plows a field. Just as an ox never turns back to assess its progress but simply continues plowing as directed by its master, so too while learning we should never pause to congratulate ourselves. Rather, we should continue along the path of Torah as directed by Hashem.

10.

■ — כָּל הַשּׁוֹכֵחַ דָּבָר אֶחָד מִמִּשְׁנָתוֹ מַעֲלֶה, עָלָיו הַכָּתוּב כְּאִלּוּ מִתְחַיֵּב בְּנַפְשׁוֹ — *Whoever forgets anything of his Torah learning, Scripture considers it as if he bears guilt for his soul.*

⋐§ Achieving Total Recall of Torah

וקשה מאוד לקיים זה ורק ר"מ דנתקיים ביה ועפעפיך יישירו כו' כמו שכתוב בגמ' כי הותר לו לכתוב שלא מהכתב שסופר היה וכתב כל התורה מקודם גם בלבו כמו שכתוב כתבם על לוח לבך ולכן היה יכול לכתוב שלא מן הכתב. והעצה לזה על ידי הלימוד פעם שניה ושלישית כי דברי תורה משתכחים על ידי עסקים אחרים ובאם לומד תמיד אינו שוכח ולכן כשׁשׁוכח מהתורה התורה שוכחתו גם כן כמו שכתוב התעיף עיניך בו ואיננו.

The objective of our *mishnah*, attaining total recall of everything that one has learned, seems almost impossible to realize. Only scholars such as Rabbi Meir, who was blessed with a phenomenal memory, seem capable of fulfilling the *mishnah's* goal of never forgetting any aspect of Torah. In fact, Rabbi Meir, due to his unusual recall of Torah, enjoyed a privilege unlike any other scribe — that of being allowed to write a *Sefer Torah* from memory, rather than copying from a previously written *Sefer Torah*. This extraordinary scholar's grasp was so complete that it could be said about him that the Torah was actually inscribed on his heart (cf. *Mishlei* 3:3). However, for the less gifted among us, the goal of total recall seems well beyond reach.

Yet, through persistent review of the subject matter that has been studied, the hope exists that we will attain the *mishnah's* objective of total recall of Torah.

To appreciate the importance of constant review of one's learning, let us consider how we forget. Surely, we do not forget by *deliberately* attempting to erase *Divrei Torah* from our memory. It is simply because we are so preoccupied with other, more mundane matters (that take priority over *limud Torah*) and they take the place of our learning in our conscious memory. By assiduously reviewing our learning we ensure that the Torah we study will retain its rightful place in our memory.

✥ Worse Than Forgetting, Never Learning

ועי' בשו"ע הרב שלא תעלה על דעתך שתשב בטל ואינך מתחייב בנפשך
ועיי"ש שכתב באם אינו לומד הוא חייב בנפשו באמת ובשוכח רק מעלה עליו
הכתוב כו'.

R' Schneur Zalman of Liadi notes that while forgetting *Divrei Torah* is unfortunate, one should not assume that one could avoid the consequences of forgetting by simply not learning. Whereas our *mishnah* considers *forgetting* Torah as a sin similar to a capital offense, כְּאִלוּ מִתְחַיֵּב בְּנַפְשׁוֹ, *neglecting* Torah study is, indeed, a capital offense, מִתְחַיֵּב בְּנַפְשׁוֹ.

✥ Forgetting One's Own Unique Contribution to Torah (מִשְׁנָתוֹ)

אפשר לומר במה שידוע כי כל אחד קבל חלקו בתורה בסיני והחידוש ההוא אין
אחר יכול לחדשו כי הוא חלקו. וזה שכתוב כל השוכח דבר אחד ממשנתו דייקא
מהשייך לשרש נשמתו ושכחו מתחייב בנפשו.

According to the *Chida*, the term מִשְׁנָתוֹ, "his learning," refers to the individual who can no longer recall his own unique contribution to Torah. When the Torah was given to *Klal Yisrael*, every individual was granted the opportunity to make such an offering.[1]

This unique contribution to Torah knowledge is not only the product of assiduous effort on the part of every individual Jew, but it is also deeply rooted in the heavenly origins of every Jewish soul (נֶפֶשׁ). By forgetting one's unique *chiddushei Torah*, it jeopardizes not only his existence on earth but, equally so, he fails to fully utilize the heavenly roots — which nourish the soul. Thus, one is מִתְחַיֵּב בְּנַפְשׁוֹ.

---

1. This theme is reflected in our Shabbos prayers — וְתֵן חֶלְקֵנוּ בְּתוֹרָתֶךָ, "grant us *our* portion in Your Torah."

◆§ Forgetting the Giver of the Torah

> השוכח דבר אחד, י"ל ששכח ממשנתו את האחד יחידו של עולם, כדאיתא
> מהבעש"ט על מאמר וז"ל השונה פרק מאה פעמים בלי האחד, בלי האחד יחידו
> של עולם, שקראו הכתוב אשר לא עבדו. אולם מה שמתחייב בנפשו היינו במשכחו
> מלבו כלשון המשנה ופן יסורו מלבבך כו' עד שישב ויסירם מלבו.

According to the *Lev Simchah*, the term דָבָר אֶחָד alludes to Hashem Who is known as the יְחִידוֹ שֶׁל עוֹלָם, the Unique One of the universe. The Torah student should never forget that his Torah is not merely the advanced analysis of the writings of the *Tannaim* and *Amoraim* but rather stems directly from Hashem.

In a similar vein, the Baal Shem Tov explained the renowned *Chazal*: אֵינוֹ דוֹמֶה שׁוֹנֶה פִּרְקוֹ מֵאָה פְּעָמִים לְשׁוֹנֶה פִּרְקוֹ מֵאָה וְאֶחָד. One cannot compare someone who has reviewed his learning 100 times to someone who has reviewed his learning 101 times (*Chagigah* 9b). According to the Baal Shem Tov, we are not only referring to the additional time that the scholar reviewed his learning but also to the individual who, while learning, never forgot the "One," the Unique Source of all learning, Hashem. (Please refer to the previous *mishnah* for a similar thought.) (*Maggidei HaEmes*).

■ כְּאִלּוּ מִתְחַיֵּב בְּנַפְשׁוֹ — *As if he bears guilt for his soul.* ■

◆§ Protected by Previous Learning

> עי' ברע"ב הטעם שהי' משמרתו המשנה כו', וקשה דכן הוא גם בתקפה עליו
> משנתו וי"ל דהתורה שמאז משמרתו משא"כ בשיושב ומסיר מלבו.

The *Bartenura* explains that by forgetting one's learning, one no longer enjoys protection from the more threatening aspects of our environment that the Torah affords. The question arises: Wouldn't the same risk be faced by *anyone* who forgot his learning even if this occurred because of circumstances beyond his control (תָּקְפָה עָלָיו מִשְׁנָתוֹ)? In response, we suggest that such an individual is protected by his previous learning that he successfully retained. It is only those who demonstrate their disdain for Torah by deliberately forgetting what they are currently learning who do not enjoy such protection.

■ יָכוֹל אֲפִילוּ תָּקְפָה עָלָיו מִשְׁנָתוֹ — *Does this apply even if [he forgot because] his studies were too difficult for him?*

◆§ Learning Torah in Two Worlds

> פי' זה סימן שאין הדברים שייכים לו ושם כ' הדברים אשר ראו עיניך פ' שיש לו

כְּאִלּוּ מִתְחַיֵּב בְּנַפְשׁוֹ, שֶׁנֶּאֱמַר: „רַק הִשָּׁמֶר לְךָ, וּשְׁמֹר
נַפְשְׁךָ מְאֹד, פֶּן תִּשְׁכַּח אֶת הַדְּבָרִים אֲשֶׁר רָאוּ עֵינֶיךָ."
יָכוֹל אֲפִילוּ יָכוֹל אֲפִילוּ תָּקְפָה עָלָיו מִשְׁנָתוֹ? תַּלְמוּד
לוֹמַר: „וּפֶן יָסוּרוּ מִלְּבָבְךָ כֹּל יְמֵי חַיֶּיךָ." הָא אֵינוֹ
מִתְחַיֵּב בְּנַפְשׁוֹ עַד שֶׁיֵּשֵׁב וִיסִירֵם מִלִּבּוֹ.

[יא] רַבִּי חֲנִינָא בֶּן דּוֹסָא אוֹמֵר: כֹּל שֶׁיִּרְאַת חֶטְאוֹ
קוֹדֶמֶת לְחָכְמָתוֹ, חָכְמָתוֹ מִתְקַיֶּמֶת; וְכֹל
שֶׁחָכְמָתוֹ קוֹדֶמֶת לְיִרְאַת חֶטְאוֹ, אֵין חָכְמָתוֹ מִתְקַיֶּמֶת.

שייכות עד דברים אלו זה נק' ראו עיניך ויש לפרש על פי דברי האר"י ז"ל דכל
מה ששוכחין בעולם הזה מכח תקפו של משנתו של הקב"ה עתיד להזכירנו בעולם
הבא עיי"ש. וזה שכתוב פן יסורו מלבבך כל ימי חייך ואמרו חז"ל כל ימי חייך
להביא לימות המשיח והיינו רק כשלא תקפה משנתו רק שכח מעצמו על ידי
שמסיר מלבו וזה יסורו מלבבך תמיד ולא יזכור גם לעתיד על זה קפדה התורה
שמור נפשך כו' ומיקרי מתחייב בנפשו.

If someone, despite his best efforts, is unable to retain what he has studied, this indicates that this particular aspect of Torah is beyond his capacity. In fact, the *pasuk* cited in the *mishnah* (*Devarim* 4:9) specifically speaks of forgetting הַדְּבָרִים אֲשֶׁר רָאוּ עֵינֶיךָ, *the words [things] that your eyes have beheld* (i.e. the *Divrei Torah* that his soul grasped at Sinai). If, despite my best efforts to retain my learning, I still continue to forget, this alone indicates that my *neshamah* had never absorbed this aspect of Torah when it was given at Sinai.

Yet, hope exists even for those who are unable to retain much of their learning. According to the *Ari Hakadosh* (as cited by the *Shulchan Aruch HaRan, Hilchos Talmud Torah*), the Torah that we attempt to study in This World — though we may have forgotten it — will be recalled by us in the World to Come. In fact, Hashem Himself will review with us those aspects of Torah that we were unable to master during our life span in *Olam Hazeh*.

This relationship between our halting attempts to study and retain Torah in This World and the complete retention that we achieve in the World to Come may be deduced from the concluding segment of the *pasuk* cited in the *mishnah*, וּפֶן יָסוּרוּ מִלְּבָבְךָ כֹּל יְמֵי חַיֶּיךָ, *and lest you remove them from your heart all the days of your life* (*Devarim* 4:9).

The term כֹּל יְמֵי חַיֶּיךָ is traditionally interpreted us referring to the Messianic Era (יְמוֹת הַמָּשִׁיחַ) [as in the renowned statement cited in the *Haggadah*, כֹּל יְמֵי [וּפֶן חַיֶּיךָ לְהָבִיא לִימוֹת הַמָּשִׁיחַ]. Admonishing those who *deliberately* forget Torah (וּפֶן

soul, as it is said (Devarim 4:9): "Only beware for yourself and greatly beware for your soul, lest you forget the things that your eyes have beheld."

Does this apply even if [he forgot because] his studies were too difficult for him? [No, for] Scripture says (Devarim 4:9): "And lest you remove them from your heart all the days of your life." Thus, one is guilty of a capital offense only if he sits [idly] and removes them from his consciousness.

[11] *Rabbi Chanina ben Dosa says: Anyone whose fear of sin precedes his wisdom, his wisdom will endure; but anyone whose wisdom takes priority over his fear of sin, his wisdom will not endure.*

וְיָסוּרוּ מִלְּבָבְךָ), the Torah warns them that they will never again recall their learning even in the Messianic Era known as יְמֵי חַיֶּיךָ. We may deduce from this that those who assiduously attempted to retain their learning but nonetheless forgot will not suffer this fate but, on the contrary, will recall their Torah knowledge in the World to Come.

11.

■ כָּל שֶׁיִּרְאַת חֶטְאוֹ קוֹדֶמֶת לְחָכְמָתוֹ — *Anyone whose fear of sin precedes his wisdom.*

◆§ Fear Before Love

דהחכמה היא בחי' אהבת ה' ע"י שמבין ורואה בהשגתו אמיתות הבורא ית' שברא
הכל יש מאין בעניין שכ' אמור לחכמה אחותי את, אמנם כשמקדים האדם היראה
מקודם אף שאינו יודע ומאמין במצות הבורא ית', עי"ז אהבה והחכמה הבאה אח"כ
מתקיים לעד.

The *mishnah* is describing the proper sequence of two different approaches to *Avodas Hashem*: fear and love.

In order to fully appreciate Hashem's grandeur — and to love Him — one must first acquire a considerable amount of wisdom. The *mishnah* is encouraging us to commence our relationship with Hashem even prior to fully comprehending the many wonders of His Universe. On the contrary, the best assurance that we will eventually come to love Hashem (and understand His manifold wonders) is to first fear Him. If we follow the *mishnah*'s recommended sequence, fearing Hashem even without comprehending His management of the universe, we may rest assured that we will ultimately come to an even higher level of *Avodas Hashem* based on love. It is this potent combination — wisdom, an in-depth understanding of Hashem's ways, which is based on a foundation of simple fear of Hashem, that will — as the *mishnah* continues — endure.

◆§ Without Fear, Wisdom Can Be Harmful

שצריך האדם להקדים היראה פן יבוא לחטוא ע״י החכמה כמ״ש ברוב חכמה רב
כעס, מה רוב חכמה, הוא שלא להיות חכמתו מרובה ממעשיו, ובפסוק ארץ יראה
ושקטה שאמרה אדם הראשון על מצוה אחת נצטוה וחטא כו׳, דזה הוא הכנה קודם
קבלת התורה משמיעים השמעת דין יראה הארץ שלא יבואו ע״י החכמה לחטוא,
ולכן שקטה ונתקיים החכמה.

To appreciate the pitfalls of wisdom without fear of Hashem, we turn to the wisest of all men, Shlomo HaMelech who wrote: בְּרֹב חָכְמָה רָב כַּעַס, *for with much wisdom comes much grief* (*Koheles* 1:18). When an individual's fear of Hashem and his capacity for good deeds are exceeded by his wisdom then he is particularly prone to commit *aveiros* and consequently anger Hashem.

In this light, we can appreciate why the earth feared *Matan Torah* (cf. *Shabbos* 88a which interprets *Tehillim* 76:9, אֶרֶץ יָרְאָה וְשָׁקָטָה, *the earth feared and then became calm* (quiet), as referring to *Matan Torah*). While nature certainly welcomed the giving of the Torah, it feared that mankind would abuse the wisdom that it was about to receive.

According to the Midrash (*Yalkut Tehillim* 815), the earth reasoned as follows: If Adam who was commanded to perform one *mitzvah* nonetheless abused his relationship to Torah by partaking of the Tree of Knowledge, certainly the Jewish People exposed to the entire spectrum of Torah and *mitzvos* would be likely to sin. By expressing its fear that *Klal Yisrael* would not observe the Torah that it was about to receive, the earth not only articulated its concerns but also simultaneously helped to mitigate — as our *mishnah* assures us, *anyone whose fear of sin precedes his wisdom* — the effect of *Klal Yisrael* being exposed to Wisdom of Torah.

When fear of sinning (*as evidenced by the earth prior to Matan Torah*) *precedes* wisdom — the giving of the Torah itself — חָכְמָתוֹ מִתְקַיֶּמֶת, we can be assured that the wisdom will remain intact. (For a more complete discussion of the earth's reaction to *Matan Torah*, cf. *The Three Festivals*, pp. 286-290.)

◆§ Is Fear of Sin (יִרְאַת חֵטְא) a Prerequisite for Wisdom?

אין הפי׳ קדימה בזמן רק יותר חשוב וחביב וזה עיקר עבודתו ויגיעתו ואינו מבטל
היראה בשביל החכמה רק החכמה אגב אצלו.

While a literal translation of the term קוֹדֶמֶת, *prior to*, implies that one cannot attain wisdom without having achieved the status of being a God-fearing individual, it is possible that the *mishnah* actually means that we should place primary emphasis on fear of sinning rather than the acquisition of wisdom. From this perspective, if a conflict ever exists between what may appear to be intellectually correct (חָכְמָה) and the demands of one's fear of God (יִרְאַת חֵטְא), one's conscience should definitely prevail.

⋖§ The Potential Clash Between Fear and Wisdom

כאשר האדם מקיים מצוה מקבל הארה של יראה. ומי שחכמתו קודמת ליראתו, הארה זו של יראה מבלבלת את חכמתו ואינה מתקיימת. לא כן מי שיראת חטא קודמת לחכמתו, נמצא דהארה זו של יראה קודמת לחכמתו והארה זו ואף חכמתו מתקיימין.

The Kotzker Rebbe explained the importance of יִרְאַת חֵטְא preceding חָכְמָה in the following manner:

When performing a *mitzvah*, we receive an infusion of fear of Heaven. Those individuals whose perspective on life is defined solely by intellect, unseasoned by fear of Heaven, frequently experience a conflict with this incremental dose of fear of Heaven. As a result of this clash, the individual becomes confused and is unable to retain his wisdom. On the other hand, the individual whose fear of sin precedes his wisdom is able to integrate the fear of Heaven that he receives from performing *mitzvos* with his intellect (*Maggidei HaEmes*).

⋖§ How Can an Ignorant Person Fear Hashem?

בשפת אמת מביא קושיית המהר"ל, ומקשה כיצד יתכן שתהא יראת חטאו קודמת לחכמתו, ובכלל יש להבין הלא מפורש במשנה אין בור חטא ולא עם הארץ חסיד, שאפילו ליראת חטא אינו יכול להגיע. ומבאר השפת אמת שיש מפתחות החיצוניות, דאס גייט מיט אין יעדער טריט און טריט, און וואס מיין מ'לערנט דארף מען מער ויסען, מער פארשטיין, כדאיתא באיגרת הרמב"ן שאם אתה חכם ממנו אל תתגאה, כי אתה מזיד והוא שוגג, ובאמת מפורש כן בגמ' תלמידי חכמים שגגות נעשות להם כזדונות, ששגגת תלמוד עולה זדון וייל ער האט געדארפט מער לערנען.

It seems difficult to believe that one can fear Hashem *prior to* studying His Torah. As we learned previously, אֵין בּוּר יְרֵא חֵטְא, *a boor cannot be fearful of sin* (2:6). In response, the *Sfas Emes* noted that while it may be difficult to attain the optimal level of fear of Hashem without having some prior Torah knowledge, a certain basic level of fear may be attained and is a prerequisite so that any subsequent wisdom can be retained.[1] Of course, as one develops into a Torah scholar, one's obligations increase correspondingly. As we are taught below, שִׁגְגַת תַּלְמוּד עוֹלָה זָדוֹן, the *careless misinterpretation while studying is considered tantamount to willful transgression* (4:16). Since he has attained greater knowledge of Torah, it is expected that he perform *mitzvos* and fear Hashem in a superior fashion.

◆§ Shabbos Rosh Hashanah

שופר הוא חכמה ועל ידי שמקדימים יראת שמים הדבר מתקיים, ועל כן בשבת אין תוקעין בשופר גזירה שמא יעבירנו ד' אמות ברשות הרבים שזה הוא יראת חטא שיראים שלא יחטאו וזה עצמו נחשב כמו שופר.

The *Imrei Emes* finds an allusion in this *mishnah* to the Rabbinic decree that when Rosh Hashanah occurs on Shabbos, the *shofar* is not sounded. Though blowing the *shofar* is depicted by *Chazal* as an act involving great skill, חָכְמָה (cf. *Rosh Hashanah* 29b), we refrain from sounding the *shofar* on Shabbos, out of fear, יִרְאָה, that we may carry the *shofar* four cubits in a public thoroughfare [Cf. *Days of Awe*, pp. 191-196, for additional comments regarding the significance of not sounding the *shofar* on Shabbos Rosh Hashanah.] (*Maggidei HaEmes*).

◆§ Does Fear of Sinning Lead to Wisdom or Vice Versa?

אבן אמרו שם עוד וי למאן דלית לי' דרתא ותרעא לדרתא עביד, וזה צריך ביאור דלכאורה נראה דכל החכמה רק כדי לבוא ליראה א"כ מה חכמתו מתקיימת דמשמע דהעיקר החכמה, אך הפי' הוא דודאי תכלית האדם להיות ירא ה', והאלקים עשה שיראו מלפניו, אבן התורה מלמדת לאדם שערים הפנימים שיש ביראת ה', וכל הלימוד וחכמה להתחכם ביראת ה', כי יש הרבה מדריגות ביראת ה', והמקדים יראת חטא לחכמתו חכמתו מלמדתו להיות ירא ה' כי החכמה היא כולל הכל וכל אדם מתחכם במה שעוסק בו והירא מתחכם ביראתו וזהו העיקר.

While our *mishnah* suggests that fear of sin is a means of ensuring that wisdom will endure, the Gemara (*Shabbos* 31a) compares fear of Heaven to a house and Torah wisdom to a gate in the front of the house, implying that wisdom is a means of attaining, and maintaining, fear of Heaven.

· There is, however, no contradiction between these two sayings. Fear of Heaven is both a prerequisite to wisdom and a goal in itself. Initially, fear of sin

---

1. This thought is reflected in *Chazal's* (*Shabbos* 31b) description of fear of Hashem as מַפְתְּחוֹת הַחִיצוֹנִיוֹת, the *outer keys*, which are available to *everyone* (adapted from *Sfas Emes*).

inspires one to acquire Torah wisdom and thereby evolve to higher spiritual levels. This in turn leads to a more profound fear of Heaven, illustrated by the keys to the inner gates of the Talmud's imagery.

■ וְכֹל שֶׁחָכְמָתוֹ קוֹדֶמֶת לְיִרְאַת חֶטְאוֹ — *But anyone whose wisdom takes priority over his fear of sin.*

◆§ A Virtual Impossibility

תלמיד חכם מחמת שהוא קרוב צריך לזכור את השי"ת, ויגבה לבו בדרכי ה', צריך ליזהר יותר. ואם באמת אינו כן מוכח שאינו לומד תורת אמת. ואולי זה הפי' יראתו מרובה מחכמתו שאם יש לו יתור חכמה צריך להגיע על ידי שיהיה לו יותר יראה.

According to the *Pnei Menachem*, a *talmid chacham* who is immersed in learning should feel extremely close to Hashem. If, despite his study, his wisdom remains greater than his fear of sinning, this indicates that his *learning* is seriously flawed. Learning Torah properly brings the individual closer to Hashem and breeds fear of Heaven (*Maggidei HaEmes*).

■ אֵין חָכְמָתוֹ מִתְקַיֶּמֶת — *His wisdom will not endure.* ■

◆§ His Fear of Sinning Remains

משמע כי היראת חטא מקיימת רק הקנס שאובד החכמה וזה שכתוב יראת ה' טהורה עומדת לעד.

Though it criticizes those whose wisdom exceeds their fear of sinning, the *mishnah* also offers a subtle but significant and comforting message. The individual whose Torah wisdom takes priority over his fear of sinning may forget his learning. However, whatever semblance of fear of sin that he possesses will endure. As David sings, יִרְאַת ה' טְהוֹרָה עוֹמֶדֶת לָעַד, the *fear of Hashem is pure, enduring forever* (*Tehillim* 19:10). When our fear of Hashem is טְהוֹרָה, *pure* unsullied and unaffected by our excessive pre-occupation with obtaining wisdom, then, עוֹמֶדֶת לָעַד, *it remains forever.*

12.

■ כֹּל שֶׁמַּעֲשָׂיו מְרֻבִּין מֵחָכְמָתוֹ — *Anyone whose good deeds exceed his wisdom.*

[**יב**] הוּא הָיָה אוֹמֵר: כֹּל שֶׁמַּעֲשָׂיו מְרֻבִּין מֵחָכְמָתוֹ,
חָכְמָתוֹ מִתְקַיֶּמֶת; וְכֹל שֶׁחָכְמָתוֹ מְרֻבָּה מִמַּעֲשָׂיו,
אֵין חָכְמָתוֹ מִתְקַיֶּמֶת.

◄§ Doing Without Understanding

אינו מובן כיון שאינו יודע איך עושה. וי״ל אף שאינו יודע טעמו של דבר עם כל
זה עושה לשם שמים גם לבטל כל החכמות.
יי״ל המכוון בענין הקדמת נעשה לנשמע, ואז חכמתו מתקיימת.

It seems that the *mishnah* is setting an impossible standard for us to follow by
stating: מַּעֲשָׂיו מְרֻבִּין מֵחָכְמָתוֹ, *his good deeds exceed his wisdom* — that we
should observe *mitzvos* even if we are barely aware of their existence. Perhaps,
it is referring to the importance of observing *mitzvos* although we do not
comprehend the underlying rationale.

The *Lev Simcha* noted that a prime example of this trait — observing even
without understanding the purpose of a *mitzvah* — was *Klal Yisrael's* declaration at Sinai when they said, נַעֲשֶׂה וְנִשְׁמָע, we will perform *mitzvos* (נַעֲשֶׂה) and
only subsequently will we study their underlying rationale (*Maggidei HaEmes*).

■ חָכְמָתוֹ מִתְקַיֶּמֶת — *His wisdom will endure.*

◄§ The Role of Wisdom

יש להבין לכאורה מאחר שהחכמינו ז״ל אומרים שהמעשה עיקר אם כן מה אמרו
חכמתו מתקיימת ואין חכמתו מתקיימת מאחר שאין זה עיקר והול״ל למימר
שזה טוב יותר וכדומה נראה כי החכמה צורך גדול אל האדם ואפשר יותר מן
המעשה שנאמר החכמה תחיה בעליה והיינו שעל ידי החכמה שבו סר מדרך רע
ומבין להבדיל בין הרע ובין הטוב שלא לטעות אמנם לעבודת השי״ת אשר על
זה נברא האדם וודאי עיקר המעשה.

Far from denigrating the importance of wisdom, the *mishnah* seems to be
emphasizing its significance and noting that we are blessed with wisdom in
direct proportion to the number of our good deeds.

Does our *mishnah's* emphasis on wisdom contradict the previous *mishnah*,
which stated לֹא הַמִּדְרָשׁ הוּא הָעִקָּר אֶלָּא הַמַּעֲשֶׂה, *not study, but practice is the main
thing* (1:17)?

In order to resolve this question, we must distinguish between the needs of
every individual and the prime purpose of Torah life, Divine service.

As far as the individual is concerned, acquiring wisdom — the ability to

[12] *He used to say: Anyone whose good deeds exceed his wisdom, his good wisdom will endure; but anyone whose wisdom exceeds his deeds, his wisdom will not endure.*

---

discern between right and wrong — is of paramount importance. As *Koheles* says, הַחָכְמָה תְּחַיֶּה בְעָלֶיהָ, *wisdom preserves the life of its possessors* (7:12); it is only through wisdom that one can truly live. On the other hand, in the realm of Divine service, nothing is as important as a simple desire to follow the Divine will, despite our lack of a sophisticated understanding of the reason for His commandments.

■ וְכֹל שֶׁחָכְמָתוֹ מְרֻבָּה מִמַּעֲשָׂיו — *But anyone whose wisdom exceeds his good deeds.*

⋖§ Wisdom for the Purpose of Performing Good Deeds

כי מי שמעשיו מרובין מחכמתו פי' מתוך חכמתו שע״ז סובב עיקר חכמתו לרבות המעשה להיות ביתר שאת וכוונה רצוי' לבוראו חכמתו מתקיימת וממילא גורמת לו מעשים יותר כנ״ל שהמעשה גורמת חכמה יותר והחכמה שנתרבה לו ג״כ מתקיים ותביאנו למעשים יותר ומי שחכמתו מרובה ממעשיו שעיקר מעשיו להרבות חכמתו אין חכמתו זאת מתקיימת והכלל כי החכמה גדולה להאדם אבל צריכה להתבטל להמעשה שעבודת האדם להבורא ב״ה וב״ש יהי' הצורך אצלו יותר מחכמתו שהוא תיקן עצמותו כנ״ל.

In light of our previous remarks emphasizing the role of *maasim tovim* in serving Hashem, we suggest a novel approach to the relationship developed in our *mishnah*. Let us assume that the prefix מ means "because of" rather than "greater than." According to this approach, the *mishnah* is praising the individual who is able to perform numerous good deeds (מַעֲשָׂיו מְרֻבִּין) *because of* his determination to utilize his wisdom (מֵחָכְמָתוֹ) for the primary purpose of doing Hashem's will. Such an individual will merit to retain his wisdom. On the other hand, an individual who performs good deeds for the sole purpose that he merit increased wisdom will *not* retain such wisdom. This individual is suffering from confused priorities, perceiving wisdom as an objective in itself, whereas, in reality, it is only valuable as a means of serving Hashem.

⋖§ Appreciating Hashem's Wonders

מעשיו הכוונה על הבינה להתבונן בדרכי ד' ובדרכיו ועל ידי זה מתקיים החכמה יהיב חכמה לחכימין כתיב ד' בחכמה יסד ארץ כונן שמים בתבונה ראשית

[יג] הוּא הָיָה אוֹמֵר: כֹּל שֶׁרוּחַ הַבְּרִיּוֹת נוֹחָה הֵימֶנּוּ,
רוּחַ הַמָּקוֹם נוֹחָה הֵימֶנּוּ; וְכֹל שֶׁאֵין רוּחַ הַבְּרִיּוֹת
נוֹחָה הֵימֶנּוּ, אֵין רוּחַ הַמָּקוֹם נוֹחָה הֵימֶנּוּ.

הבריאה היתה בחכמה ואחר כך כונן שמים לעתיד על ידי תבונה שמתבונן האדם.
ועל ידי זה יכול להגיע גם לחכמה על ידי הבינה.

According to the *Beis Yisrael*, the term חָכְמָתוֹ מְרֻבָּה מִמַּעֲשָׂיו refers to the proper utilization of one's innate wisdom for the purpose of appreciating Hashem's numerous wonders. Whereas the term חָכְמָה, *wisdom*, refers to the knowledge that we accumulate, מַעֲשָׂיו, *his deeds*, alludes to the *results* and the true purpose of our wisdom, which is acquiring greater insight in the manifold wonders of Hashem's Universe. This concept is often described by *Chazal* as בִּינָה, using one's wisdom to deduce significant conclusions. As Shlomo writes, ה' בְּחָכְמָה יָסַד אָרֶץ כּוֹנֵן שָׁמַיִם בִּתְבוּנָה, *Hashem founded the earth with wisdom; He supported the heavens with understanding* (Mishlei 3:19).

While Hashem created the universe in His wisdom, its continued existence is supported upon our in-depth appreciation of His wonders (*Maggidei HaEmes*).

◆§ Does This Mishnah Apply to All Men?

לכאורה מה יעשה והוא חכם גדול כגון שלמה שנתן לו ה' בינה יתירה. וצריך
לומר דמכל מקום בכחו לרבות לרבות יותר מעשים ויראה מאת השי"י.

At first sight, one would assume that our *mishnah*, insisting that our deeds exceed our wisdom, does not apply to Shlomo HaMelech who was endowed by Hashem with virtually limitless wisdom. On the other hand, we may argue that *no one* is exempt from the high standard espoused by the *mishnah*. While Shlomo was undoubtedly wiser than any other man, it is fair to assume that his capacity for performing good deeds increased commensurately with his wisdom.

■ אֵין חָכְמָתוֹ מִתְקַיֶּמֶת — *His wisdom will not endure.* ■

◆§ Forgetting Superfluous Wisdom

היינו התוספת ממעשיו.

The *mishnah* is not necessarily suggesting that someone whose wisdom exceeds his deeds will forfeit all of his accumulated wisdom. In all probabil-

[13] *He used to say: If the spirit of one's fellows is pleased with him, the spirit of the Omnipresent is pleased with him; but if the spirit of one's fellows is not pleased with him, the spirit of the Omnipresent is not pleased with him.*

ity, he simply loses that portion of his wisdom that cannot be used productively to perform good deeds.

◄§ Learning or Deeds

אף שהתלמוד גדול יי׳׳ל דלא קאי על לימוד אלא על חקירות ושכלות. ואולי יי׳׳ל דנהי דהתלמוד גדול עם כל זה העיקר הוא המעשה כדאיתא לא המדרש עיקר אלא המעשה שמעשה המצות יותר מקשרים הגוף.

O**ur** *mishnah* valuing deeds more than wisdom seems to corroborate an earlier *mishnah* stating: לֹא הַמִּדְרָשׁ הוּא הָעִקָּר אֶלָּא הַמַּעֲשֶׂה, *not study, but practice is the main thing* (1:17). On the other hand, *Chazal* elsewhere seemingly place primary emphasis on learning — וְתַלְמוּד תּוֹרָה כְּנֶגֶד כּוּלָם, *and Torah study is equivalent to all the mitzvos* (*Shabbos* 127a).

We may reconcile this apparent contradiction by distinguishing between simple intellectual speculation — חָכְמָה, *wisdom* — which is definitely inferior to the performance of good deeds, and in-depth study of Torah — למוד, *study* — which motivates the fulfillment of *maasim tovim*.

Alternatively, we suggest that Torah study is primary. However, by performing the actual *mitzvah*, one affects and elevates his *physical* body — a dimension we do not find with regard to the study of Torah.

13.

■ כָּל שֶׁרוּחַ הַבְּרִיּוֹת נוֹחָה הֵימֶנּוּ, רוּחַ הַמָּקוֹם נוֹחָה הֵימֶנּוּ — *If the spirit of one's fellows is pleased with him, the spirit of the Omnipresent is pleased with him.*

◄§ Indication (סימן) or Cause (סיבה)

נראה דאין הפי׳ שהוא סימן דאם כן הו׳׳ל למימר להיפוך כל שרוח המקום נוחה הימנו רוח הבריות נוחה הימנו. אולם התנא משמיענו להשתדל לעשות כן שיהיה רוח הבריות נוחה הימנו.

ולכאורה נדמה שכ׳׳א יכול לקרב לכל הבריות שינוחו הימנו כי הש׳׳י ממציא לירואיו חן בעיני הבריות אבל מכאן משמע שאינו תלוי ביד האדם רק בצדקותיו.

[יד] רַבִּי דוֹסָא בֶּן הָרְכִּינַס אוֹמֵר: שֵׁנָה שֶׁל שַׁחֲרִית,
וְיֵין שֶׁל צָהֳרַיִם, וְשִׂיחַת הַיְלָדִים, וִישִׁיבַת בָּתֵּי
כְנֵסִיּוֹת שֶׁל עַמֵּי הָאָרֶץ מוֹצִיאִין אֶת הָאָדָם מִן הָעוֹלָם.

[טו] רַבִּי אֶלְעָזָר הַמּוֹדָעִי אוֹמֵר: הַמְחַלֵּל אֶת
הַקֳּדָשִׁים, וְהַמְבַזֶּה אֶת הַמּוֹעֲדוֹת, וְהַמַּלְבִּין פְּנֵי חֲבֵרוֹ

The *mishnah* is not stating that if people are pleased with an individual, then Hashem is also pleased with the person. If this were the case, the *mishnah* should have been written in reverse order: כָּל שֶׁרוּחַ הַמָּקוֹם נוֹחָה הֵימֶנּוּ רוּחַ הַבְּרִיּוֹת נוֹחָה הֵימֶנּוּ, *If Hashem is pleased with an individual, then people too will appreciate that person.*

By first specifying people's reaction to our behavior (רוּחַ הַבְּרִיּוֹת), the *mishnah* is exhorting us to act in a manner pleasing to our peers, so that Hashem, too, will be able to derive satisfaction from us. This is no mean feat. While it may appear relatively easy to find favor in people's eyes, it actually requires a great deal of Divine assistance rendered only to those who fear Hashem.

■ נוֹחָה הֵימֶנּוּ — *Is pleased with him.*

◆§ Enjoy Him, Not His Assets

נראה הפי' מגוף האדם ולא מסבת דברים אחרים כגון שהוא עושר ומטיב עם
אחרים ובסבה זו הוא אהוב דזה אינו בכלל נוחה הימנו.

By using the term הֵימֶנּוּ, *with him,* the *mishnah* is emphasizing that one is pleased with the conduct of the person who is loved because of the person's own merits and exemplary behavior and not due to external factors such as his wealth.

■ וְכֹל שֶׁאֵין רוּחַ הַבְּרִיּוֹת נוֹחָה הֵימֶנּוּ, אֵין רוּחַ הַמָּקוֹם נוֹחָה הֵימֶנּוּ — *But if the spirit of one's fellows is not pleased with him, the spirit of the Omnipresent is not pleased with him.*

◆§ To Be Liked, Do Teshuvah

וכל שאין רוה''ב נוחה הימנו יעשה תשובה ועי''ז יהי' נוחה הימנו.

We may deduce from our *mishnah* that popularity is not related to our ability to influence people but rather is contingent upon Divine assistance which is provided to those who observe the Torah.

[14] *Rabbi Dosa ben Harkinas says: Late morning sleep, midday wine, children's chatter, and sitting in the assemblies of the ignorant remove a person from the world.*

[15] *Rabbi Elazar the Moda'ite says: One who desecrates sacred things, who disgraces the festivals, who humiliates*

If so, the best remedy for unpopularity is doing *teshuvah*. By doing *teshuvah*, one can be assured of securing Divine assistance in order to win popular acclaim.

14.

■ שֵׁנָה שֶׁל שַׁחֲרִית, וְיַיִן שֶׁל צָהֳרַיִם, וְשִׂיחַת הַיְלָדִים, וִישִׁיבַת בָּתֵי כְנֵסִיּוֹת שֶׁל עַמֵּי הָאָרֶץ מוֹצִיאִין אֶת הָאָדָם מִן הָעוֹלָם — *Late morning sleep, midday wine, children's chatter, and sitting in the assemblies of the ignorant remove a man from the world.*

◆§ A Wasted Day

לא נאמרו דברי המשנה אלא כלפי סדר יומו של אדם. מי שמתעצל לקום ממשכבו וממשיך בשינה של שחרית, יהיה להוט אחר יין של צהרים, והאיש אשר אלה לו, ימשיך ויבלה את זמנו לאחר מכן בשיחת הילדים. ולעת ערב כאשר ילך לביהי"כ ישלים את יומו בישיבת בתי כנסיות של עמי הארץ. ואדם כזה מוציא את עצמו מן העולם פשוטו כמשמעו.

According to the *Lev Simchah*, our *mishnah* is referring to a particularly bad sequence of events. An individual who sleeps late in the morning (שֵׁנָה שֶׁל שַׁחֲרִית) will be inclined to imbibe wine in the afternoon (יַיִן שֶׁל צָהֳרַיִם). He will then tend to engage in idle chatter (שִׂיחַת הַיְלָדִים). Even when he attends *shul* in the evening, he will spend his time in the company of ignorant people (וִישִׁיבַת בָּתֵי כְנֵסִיּוֹת שֶׁל עַמֵּי הָאָרֶץ). One who wastes time in this manner is simply functioning in the most self-destructive ways (*Maggidei HaEmes*).

15.

■ וְהַמְבַזֶּה אֶת הַמּוֹעֲדוֹת . . . אֵין לוֹ חֵלֶק לָעוֹלָם הַבָּא — *[One] who disgraces the festivals . . . he has no share in the World to Come.*

◆§ Minimizing the Impact of the Festival

גבי שאול כתיב ובני בליעל אמרו מה יושיענו זה ויבזהו. ונראה מזה פי' מבזה את

ג / טו־טז בָּרַבִּים, וְהַמֵּפֵר בְּרִיתוֹ שֶׁל אַבְרָהָם אָבִינוּ, וְהַמְגַלֶּה פָנִים בַּתּוֹרָה שֶׁלֹּא כַהֲלָכָה, אַף עַל פִּי שֶׁיֵּשׁ בְּיָדוֹ תּוֹרָה וּמַעֲשִׂים טוֹבִים — אֵין לוֹ חֵלֶק לָעוֹלָם הַבָּא.

[טז] רַבִּי יִשְׁמָעֵאל אוֹמֵר: הֱוֵי קַל לְרֹאשׁ, וְנוֹחַ לְתִשְׁחֹרֶת, וֶהֱוֵי מְקַבֵּל אֶת כָּל הָאָדָם בְּשִׂמְחָה.

המועדות שאומר על הזמנים המקודשים ''מה יושיענו זה''. צריכים להאמין שהימים טובים נותנים כח על כל ימות השנה.

To appreciate the term מְבַזֶּה, to *shame* or *disgrace*, we recall the reaction (as described in *I Shmuel* 10:27) of Saul's opponents to him, וּבְנֵי בְלִיַּעַל אָמְרוּ מַה יֹשִׁעֵנוּ זֶה וַיִּבְזֻהוּ, *But base men said, "How can this person save us," and they ridiculed him.* They demonstrated their contempt for him by doubting his capacity to help them or defend their interests. Similarly, the one who disgraces the festivals maintains that the *Yom Tov* does not influence him. We must know and understand that each festival leaves a permanent impact which sustains us for the rest of the year.

⊷§ The Reward for Appreciating Yom Tov

ממשמע שהמבזה אין לו חלק אף אנו נאמר כי המשתוקק כל הימים אל המועדות אפילו אין בידו תורה ומעשים טובים יש לו חלק לעולם הבא.

We may deduce the following קַל וָחֹמֶר: If those who disparage the festivals are denied a portion in *Olam Haba*, it follows that those who appreciate and learn from the *Yamim Tovim* will enjoy a portion in the World to Come.[1]

■ וְהַמַּלְבִּין פְּנֵי חֲבֵרוֹ בָּרַבִּים — *One who humiliates his fellow in public.*

⊷§ Three Is a Crowd

אולי לעניין זה שלשה נקראו רבים.

According to the *Sfas Emes*, humiliating a person in front of a gathering consisting of as few as three people is considered to be בָּרַבִּים, a *public* affront.

---

1. This is based on the general principle that Hashem's Attribute of Goodness is far more generous than His Attribute of Punishment (cf. *Makkos* 5b).

his fellow in public, who nullifies the covenant of our forefather Avraham, or who perverts the meaning of the Torah contrary to the halachah — though he may have Torah and good deeds, he has no share in the World to Come.

[16] *Rabbi Yishmael says: Be yielding to a superior, pleasant to the young, and receive every person cheerfully.*

■ אֵין לוֹ חֵלֶק לָעוֹלָם הַבָּא — *He has no share in the World to Come.* ■

◈§ Doesn't Every Jew Already Have a Portion in the World to Come?

גם דכל ישראל יש להם חלק לעולם הבא אבל זה יצא מכלל כל ישראל

While it is certainly true that every Jew enjoys a portion in the World to Come, by engaging in these egregious practices, this person has, in effect, removed himself from the ranks of *Klal Yisrael*, and has thus forfeited the portion he once had.

16.

■ וֶהֲוֵי מְקַבֵּל אֶת כָּל הָאָדָם בְּשִׂמְחָה — *And receive every person cheerfully.* ■

◈§ Accepting Yourself With Joy

כל אדם ואדם גם את האדם בעצמו עצמותו הכל על ידי שמחה.

The term כָּל הָאָדָם, *every person*, suggests that just as we are obligated to accept others joyously, so too, we must learn to accept *ourselves* joyously (despite all our foibles and idiosyncrasies) (*Bendiner Rav, Maggidei HaEmes*).

17.

■ שְׂחוֹק וְקַלּוּת רֹאשׁ מַרְגִּילִין אֶת הָאָדָם לְעֶרְוָה — *Mockery and levity accustom a man to immorality.* ■

◈§ The Power of Good Habits

על ידי הרגל לתורה ולמצות אינו בא לידי עבירה, היפך משחוק וקלות ראש

[יז] רַבִּי עֲקִיבָא אוֹמֵר: שְׂחוֹק וְקַלּוּת רֹאשׁ מַרְגִּילִין אֶת הָאָדָם לְעֶרְוָה. מַסּוֹרֶת סְיָג לַתּוֹרָה; מַעְשְׂרוֹת סְיָג לָעשֶׁר; נְדָרִים סְיָג לַפְּרִישׁוּת; סְיָג לַחָכְמָה שְׁתִיקָה.

שמרגילין לעבירה.

The *Beis Yisrael* reasoned that if practices contrary to the Torah, such as mockery and levity, induce us to sin, then certainly becoming accustomed to following the will of Hashem will prevent us from sinning (*Maggidei HaEmes*).

■ קַלּוּת רֹאשׁ — *Levity.*

◆§ The Head Without Tefillin

איתא וקלות ראש שאין מניחים תפילין על הראש, והנה איתא בגמ' דחזיה דבדח טובא א"ל אנא תפילין מנחנא. וזה דאיתא וראו כל עמי הארץ וכו' אלו תפילין שבראש ויראו ממך וזה תפילין שבראש מביא יראת שמים כל שכן לעצמו, ולזה עם תפילין לא הוי שחוק שיזיק אבל על ידי קלות ראש כנ"ל מזיק השחוק רח"ל.

The Bendiner Rav homiletically interpreted the term קַלּוּת רֹאשׁ to mean a head is unusually light because it lacks *tefillin*. An individual who is wearing *tefillin* is less likely to be influenced by the evil effects of mockery and levity. The Gemara relates (*Berachos* 30b) that R' Zeira defended his habit of laughing wholeheartedly by stating, "I am wearing tefillin," *and thus I am not affected by the potentially evil effect of laughter.*

Our Sages (*Berachos* 6a) explain the verse, "And the nations of the earth will see the Name of God called upon you and they will fear you" (*Devarim* 28:10), to mean that the gentile world will be gripped by a sense of fear when gazing at the head-*tefillin* worn by every Jew. This supports the above contention: If gentiles develop fear by simply seeing *tefillin*, surely *Klal Yisrael* who regularly wear *tefillin* will certainly be filled with awe and will thus be prevented from sinning.

■ מַסּוֹרֶת סְיָג לַתּוֹרָה — *The transmitted Oral Torah is a [protective] fence around the Torah.*

◆§ Retention of Torah

פי' שתתקיים התורה בידו או שעל ידי זה יזכה לתורה.

[17] *Rabbi Akiva says: Mockery and levity accustom a man to immorality. The transmitted Oral Torah is a [protective] fence around the Torah; tithes are a [protective] fence for wealth; vows are a [protective] fence for abstinence; a [protective] fence for wisdom is silence.*

The expression מַסוֹרֶת סְיָג לַתּוֹרָה may be understood to mean that it is easier to *retain* Torah that is not the product of our own efforts but rather is transmitted from generation to generation. Alternatively, it may be interpreted that those who enjoy a מְסוֹרָה — are fortunate to learn Torah from dedicated teachers who transmit the traditions of previous generations — will merit to learn and comprehend Torah.

■ מַעֲשְׂרוֹת סְיָג לָעשֶׁר — *Tithes are a [protective] fence for wealth.*

◆§ Tithing Leads to Wealth

סיפר כ״ק מרן אדמו״ר זצללה״ה הפני מנחם ״פעם שאלו לאאז״ל (האמרי אמת)
אם יש שורש בתורה למעשר כספים. והשיב: הפוסקים נחלקו אם מעשר כספים
דאורייתא אם לא, אבל אין ספק שהנוהג להפריש מעשר כספים נותן צדקה בלב
שמח ובעין טובה, ביודעו שהכסף כבר אינו שלו. נמצא שמתוך הפרשתו מקיים
מש״כ ולא ירע לבבך בתתך לו. וזוכה לסיומא דקרא כי בגלל הדבר הזה יברכך
ה׳א׳. ע״כ. ובזה יתפרש מתני׳ בטוב כי ע״י מעשרות בא לידי עושר כדכתיב
כי בגלל הדבר הזה יברך כו׳.

The association between tithing and accumulating wealth was developed beautifully by the *Pnei Menachem*. When asked whether a Biblical obligation exists to tithe one's income (a concept known as *ma'aser kesafim*) he noted that *Poskim* (halachic authorities) differ regarding whether such a Biblical obligation exists. However, by arranging in advance that a predetermined tithe be set aside for *tzedakah* purposes (and then simply allocating charity from that fund), we recognize that the money is not truly ours and thus we merit to fulfill the *mitzvah* of *tzedakah* in the best possible manner — with joy. The relationship between giving *tzedakah* joyously and one's own success is stated quite explicitly: נָתוֹן תִּתֵּן לוֹ וְלֹא יֵרַע לְבָבְךָ בְּתִתְּךָ לוֹ כִּי בִּגְלַל הַדָּבָר הַזֶּה יְבָרֶכְךָ ה׳ אֱלֹקֶיךָ בְּכָל מַעֲשֶׂךָ וּבְכֹל מִשְׁלַח יָדֶךָ, *You shall surely give him, and let your heart not feel bad when you give him, for in return for this matter, Hashem, your God, will bless you in all your deeds and in your every undertaking* (Devarim 15:10) (*Maggidei HaEmes*).

◆§ Insulating Us From the Hazards of Wealth

> ובשפ״א איתא לפרש שהסייג שלא יגיע לו קלקול על ידי העשירות שיכול להזיק
> בעבודת ד׳. ואולי י״ל עפ״י הידוע בסה״ק שענין המעשרות הוא למען נדע שהכל
> ממנו ית׳, כי על ידי שמפריש מכל אשר לו לה׳ זוכר שהוא הנותן כח לעשות חיל,
> ולא יטעה לומר כחי ועוצם ידי כו׳ את כל החיל הזה.

According to the *Sfas Emes*, giving *maaser* insulates us from any of the possible harmful effects of becoming wealthy. The Torah warns of the adverse consequences of becoming wealthy by stating: וְרָם . . . פֶּן תֹּאכַל וְשָׂבָעְתָּ, *Lest you eat and be satisfied . . . and your heart will become haughty and you will forget Hashem, Your God* (*Devarim* 8:12, 14). In particular, the Torah was concerned that we would forget the source of our wealth and attribute our success to our own prowess and efforts. As the Torah states: וְאָמַרְתָּ בִּלְבָבֶךָ כֹּחִי וְעֹצֶם יָדִי עָשָׂה לִי אֶת הַחַיִל הַזֶּה, *And you may say in your heart, "My strength and the might of my hand made me all this wealth"* (ibid. 8:17). By tithing — returning a portion of our new-found wealth to Hashem — we ensure that we will never forget the true source of our wealth.

■ נְדָרִים סְיָג לַפְּרִישׁוּת — *Vows are a [protective] fence for abstinence.*

◆§ Becoming or Remaining a "Porush"

> שמביאתו לידי זה או ששומרתו שלא ינטל ממנו כנ״ל.

As mentioned above, in our discussion of the מַסּוֹרֶת סְיָג לַתּוֹרָה, the term סְיָג can have several connotations. Thus, the expression נְדָרִים סְיָג לַפְּרִישׁוּת may be interpreted in two ways: First, by using vows properly[1] we are able to *attain the status of* פְּרִישׁוּת, *perishus*, abstinence from the physical pleasures of this world. Alternatively, the *mishnah* may be offering advice how best to *maintain* an already existing regimen of פְּרִישׁוּת: In order to remain vigilant against the passions of *Olam Hazeh*, take vows upon yourself. By upgrading your previous commitments to the status of a vow you greatly facilitate the likelihood of maintaining your sacred life style.

◆§ Yaakov's Vows

> כתיב וידור יעקב נדר, גם זה רמז על מה דאיתא נדרים סייג לפרישות, ואיתא

---

1. Although it is generally inadvisable to take a vow [טוֹב אֲשֶׁר לֹא תִדֹּר מִשֶּׁתִּדּוֹר וְלֹא תְשַׁלֵּם, *better that you do not vow at all than that you vow and not pay* (*Koheles* 5:4)], nonetheless, there are circumstances when *Chazal* do encourage the taking of a vow. A classic example is Yaakov Avinu; refer to our next essay.

במדרש לאמר להיות נודרים בעת צרה, הרמז בעת שצר לאדם בעבודת השם.
יכול לידור ולקבל עליו ואחר כך בוודאי מכח הנדר יכול לקיים ולמצוא המקום
שאין לך אדם שאין לו מקום.

A classic example of vows that led to *perishus* are the vows assumed by Yaakov Avinu (cf. *Bereishis* 28:22) in which the Patriarch vows to build a house for Hashem and to tithe all that Hashem gives him in exchange for the fulfillment of Hashem's promises to him. While *Chazal* usually frown upon those who assume vows, they justify Yaakov's vow on the basis of נוֹדְרִין בְּעֵת צָרָה, one may take a vow upon oneself (of abstinence or commitment) during times of distress (cf. *Chullin* 2b and *Tosfos* s.v. אבל). In a larger sense, the term צָרָה may refer not only to physical suffering but also to a feeling of being spiritually confined [the term צָרָה being related to צַר *narrow,* i.e. מִן הַמֵּצַר קָרָאתִי יָּ-הּ, *From the straits did I call upon God* (*Tehillim* 118:5)]. This is often a sense that one has not yet found his unique niche in *Avodas Hashem.* By vowing — and faithfully fulfilling our vow — we gradually begin to find "our place," our path and purpose in life.

◆§ Abstinence (פְּרִישׁוּת) — Prerequisite for Torah

כפי שאדם מפריש את עצמו מעניני עולם הזה יכול להתקרב אל השי"ת ולקבל
עול תורה . . . אי אפשר להגיע לתורה ולירat שמים אם אינו מסתייג מהבלי
עולם הזה כדאיתא. וכן אצל מתן תורה איתא בארבעה עביד פרישה. לרמז להם
שנצרך פרישה מקודם ועי"ז יוכלו לקבל תורה . . . וזה ענין הפרישה לא להניח
מקום ליצה"ר לשלוט עליו. ולזכור תמיד מזה אף שהולך בדרך התורה היצר אורב
לו. וגם לא לפול אם רואה הסתרות.

The *Beis Yisrael* emphasized the vital role played by the attribute of abstinence from the material pleasures of This World as a prerequisite for accepting Torah and attaining fear of Heaven. Indeed, the Giving of the Torah at Sinai was preceded by three days of abstinence (cf. *Shabbos* 86a). While Torah study is certainly potent, it is not enough to totally deflect the lures of the *Yetzer Hara.* Only by abstaining from worldly pleasures while immersing oneself in Torah can one be assured of respite from the Evil Inclination (*Maggidei HaEmes*).

■ סְיָג לַחָכְמָה שְׁתִיקָה — *A [protective] fence for wisdom is silence.*

◆§ One of the Many Virtues of Silence

לא אמר שתיקה סייג לחכמה כמו שכתוב באינך מסורת סייג לתורה כו'. יש לפרש
לפי ששתיקה מביאה לכמה מעלות לבד החכמה כמו שכתוב לא מצאתי לגוף טוב
משתיקה. ואילו אמר שתיקה סייג לחכמה היה משמע שרק זאת מעלת השתיקה.

ג / יח

[יח] הוּא הָיָה אוֹמֵר: חָבִיב אָדָם שֶׁנִּבְרָא בְּצֶלֶם;
חִבָּה יְתֵרָה נוֹדַעַת לוֹ שֶׁנִּבְרָא בְּצֶלֶם, שֶׁנֶּאֱמַר:
„כִּי בְּצֶלֶם אֱלֹהִים עָשָׂה אֶת הָאָדָם." חֲבִיבִין יִשְׂרָאֵל
שֶׁנִּקְרְאוּ בָנִים לַמָּקוֹם; חִבָּה יְתֵרָה נוֹדַעַת לָהֶם

In the interests of consistency, the *mishnah* should have said, סְיָג לַחָכְמָה שְׁתִיקָה
(as it says, מַסּוֹרֶת סְיָג לַתּוֹרָה וכו׳). However, that would have implied that the
primary virtue of silence is that it leads to wisdom. On the contrary, silence
enjoys many more virtues, including that which we learned previously
(1:17): וְלֹא מָצָאתִי לַגּוּף טוֹב אֶלָּא שְׁתִיקָה, *and I found nothing better for oneself than
silence.*

◄§ Speech or Silence — Which Is Preferred?

פעם שאל אדמו״ר זצ״ל הלב שמחה לאחד „הרי אמרו מלה בסלע משתוקא
בתרין, אם כן מה עדיף, לשתוק או לדבר"? השיב הלה, „לשתוק". אמר
לו אדמו״ר זצ״ל „אתה אינך סוחר. עבור שתיקה במשך כל היום כולו לא
תקבל כי אם שתי סלעים, ותמורת כל מלה שתתדבר תקבל סלע, נמצא
שבמשך היום כולו תוכל לרכוש סלעים מרובים"... ותוך כדי דיבור הפטיר
הרבי ז״ל ואמר „אבער שווייגען איז פארט בעסער" (אבל בכל זאת עדיף
השתיקה).

A *chassid*, recalling the Gemara (*Megillah* 18a) stating that "speech is worth
one *sela* (a common coin of Talmudic times) while silence is worth
two *selaim*," asked the *Lev Simchah* whether it would be preferable to
remain silent all day or to talk as appropriate. In response, the *Lev Simchah*
noted, "From your question, I can detect that you are not a business person.
Any entrepreneur will realize that while a day's silence may be worth two
selaim, an entire day's speech — at the rate of one *sela* per word — is worth
many *selaim*."

But after a short pause the *Lev Simchah* concluded, "אבער שווייגען איז פארט
בעסער, *but silence is still better*" (*Maggidei HaEmes*).

◄§ The Difference Between a Wise Man and a Fool

הרבי ר׳ בונם ז״ל מפשיסחא ביאר החילוק שבין החכם לשוטה, כי השוטה אומר
כל מה שהוא יודע, ואילו החכם יודע את מה שהוא אומר.

According to R' Simchah Bunim of Peshis'cha, the difference between a wise
man and a fool is quite simple. Whereas a fool says whatever he knows, a

[18] *He [R' Akiva] used to say: Beloved is man, for he was created in [God's] image; it is indicative of greater love that it was made known to him that he was created in [God's] image, as it is said (Bereishis 9:6): "For in the image of God He made man." Beloved are the peole of Israel, for they are described as children of the Omnipresent; it is indicative of a greater love that it was made known to them that they are described as*

---

wise man knows whatever he says (i.e. he does not venture an opinion about matters beyond his competence) (*Maggidei HaEmes*).

18.

■ *Beloved* — חָבִיב אָדָם שֶׁנִּבְרָא בְצֶלֶם . . . ''כִּי בְּצֶלֶם אֱלֹקִים עָשָׂה אֶת הָאָדָם'' ■ *is man, for he was created in God's image. . ."For in the image of God He made man."*

◆§ Why Not Cite a Previous Pasuk?

It seems surprising that the *mishnah* cites the *pasuk*, כִּי בְּצֶלֶם אֱלֹקִים עָשָׂה אֶת הָאָדָם, *for in the image of God He made man* (Bereishis 9:6), rather than the earlier *pasuk*, וַיִּבְרָא אֱלֹקִים אֶת הָאָדָם בְּצַלְמוֹ בְּצֶלֶם אֱלֹקִים בָּרָא אֹתוֹ, *So God created Man in His image, in the image of God He created him* (ibid. 1:27), describing man's creation. In the following remarks, we will consider several approaches to resolve this problem.

◆§ The Body as Well as the Soul

וקשה דמביא זה הפסוק והלא בתחלה כתיב בצלמנו, ויברא את האדם בצלמו, אכן פי' המשנה כי ודאי עיקר הבריאה בצלם אלקים הוא הנפש והנשמה כמ''ש חז''ל וייצר ב' יצירות כו', אכן גם בצלם הגוף נמצא לבנ''י התקשרות ודביקות בציור הפנימי והוא באמת ע''י המילה שנתן הקב''ה.
וזה שהוכיח מדכתיב שופך דם האדם וכו', כי בצלם אלקים עשה מוכח כי בגוף נמצא ג''כ זה הצלם.

Whereas the first *pasuk* demonstrates that the soul was created in Hashem's image, the *pasuk* cited above condemning murder demonstrates that the *body* too was created in this image. While the Divine spark may not be visible to the casual observer, it is certainly subsumed in the human body. *Klal Yisrael*, by participating in the rite of *bris milah*, symbolic of the curtailment

שֶׁנִּקְרְאוּ בָנִים לַמָּקוֹם, שֶׁנֶּאֱמַר: "בָּנִים אַתֶּם לַיהוה
אֱלֹהֵיכֶם." חֲבִיבִין יִשְׂרָאֵל, שֶׁנִּתַּן לָהֶם כְּלִי חֶמְדָּה;
חִבָּה יְתֵרָה נוֹדַעַת לָהֶם, שֶׁנִּתַּן לָהֶם כְּלִי חֶמְדָּה,
שֶׁנֶּאֱמַר: "כִּי לֶקַח טוֹב נָתַתִּי לָכֶם, תּוֹרָתִי אַל
תַּעֲזֹבוּ."

of physical passion, is able to elicit and exploit the Divine imprint latent in all
of us.

◆§ Remaining in God's Image

וי"ל דסד"א כשנגסרה חוה ניטל ונשתנה הצלם קמ"ל דלא כן הי' דהרי זה הפסוק
הוא טעם איסור שפיכת דם.

כי קודם החטא הי' נגלה הצלם אלקי, רק אחר דכתיב משנה פניו ותשלחהו
ונשתנה הציור ונתלבש בכתנות עור על זה מביא המשנה שאעפ"כ חבה יתירה
נודעת והוא כמו"ש וברית לו להודיעם, כי סוד ה' ליראיו הוא הפנימיות בחי' עץ
החיים.

ואח"כ שאכל מעל הדעת טוב ורע הי' התיקון על ידי המצות וברייתות שנתן לכן
הקב"ה ובכח זה נוכל לחזור להתדבק בעץ החיים שהיא התורה . . . ולכן הביאו
הפסוק בצלם אלקים עשה את האדם שנאמר אחר החטא.

The *pasuk* cited by our *mishnah* demonstrates that man was not only
originally created in Hashem's image but that he also continued to retain
this image despite various events that had occurred since his creation. For
example, one might assume that when Chavah was created (formed from a rib
that had been separated from Adam), man's profile would be permanently
altered. Furthermore, one could maintain that after Adam had partaken of the
fruit of the Tree of Knowledge — which led to certain changes in his physical
appearance such as his wearing clothes — his Divine likeness would also be
tarnished. To counter this misconception, the *mishnah* says: חִבָּה יְתֵרָה נוֹדַעַת לוֹ
[שֶׁנִּבְרָא בְּצֶלֶם [אֱלֹקִים, *it is indicative of a greater love that it was made known to*
him that he was created in [God's] image.

Hashem displayed extraordinary love to us by assuring us that we continue
to remain in His image even after sinning. Whereas we originally were created
in Hashem's likeness, which involved a purely passive role on our part, now
mankind and especially *Klal Yisrael* enjoy a far greater challenge — to *return*
to its original Divine image through the observance of Torah and *mitzvos*. By
eating the fruit of the Tree of Knowledge of Good and Bad, Adam blurred
the distinction between good and bad. Only by partaking of the fruit of the
Tree of Life, Torah and *mitzvos*, can Adam's descendants reverse their forefa-

children of the Omnipresent, as it is said (Devarim 14:1): "You are children of Hashem, your God." Beloved are the people Israel, for a cherished utensil was given to them; it is indicative of a greater love that it was made known to them that they were given a cherished utensil, as it is said (Mishlei 4:2): "For I have given you a good teaching; do not forsake My Torah."

ther's tragic error and retrieve their original Divine image.

As David sings, סוֹד ה׳ לִירֵאָיו וּבְרִיתוֹ לְהוֹדִיעָם, *The secret of Hashem is to those who fear Him, and His covenant to inform them (Tehillim 25:14).* "Hashem's secrets" — the inner depths of Torah — were originally given to the first man, living under ideal conditions in Eden. However, his descendants banned from Paradise are informed (לְהוֹדִיעָם) that through Hashem's covenant (בְּרִיתוֹ) — the Torah — they may regain the same exalted spiritual level that they once enjoyed in Eden.

ﹳﻜ The Lev Simcha's Dream

הראו לי בחלום דמשנה זו ראיה לדברי האור החיים שכתב על הפסוק ויברא אלקים את האדם בצלמו בצלם אלקים ברא אותו, כי בצלמו זה צלם הניכר בכל אדם ואפילו בבני אדם הריקנים מקדושה, ויש ענין צלם אלוקים רוחני נעלם עכ״ד. דחביב אדם כו׳ קאי על צלם הניכר בכל אדם, חבה יתרה כו׳ זה על הצלם אלוקים רוחני נעלם.

The *Or HaChayim* noted the apparent redundancy in the *pasuk* describing man's creation: וַיִּבְרָא אֱלֹקִים אֶת הָאָדָם בְּצַלְמוֹ בְּצֶלֶם אֱלֹקִים בָּרָא אֹתוֹ, *So God created man in His image, in the image of God He created him (Bereishis 1:27).* He suggests that while all of Hashem's creations were created in His image (בְּצַלְמוֹ), only *tzaddikim* are able to evoke some small measure of the צֶלֶם אֱלֹקִים רוּחָנִי נֶעֱלָם — the hidden spiritual image of Hashem that is embedded within each of us.

The *Lev Simchah* was shown in a dream that the text of our Mishnah corroborates the *Or HaChayim's* thought. Whereas ... חָבִיב אָדָם, *beloved is man ...* refers to the basic "Image of God" enjoyed by all mankind, but *a greater love* refers to the *tzaddikim* who enjoy the more sublime level of this hidden, spiritual dimension (adapted from *Lev Simchah, Maggidei Ha-Emes*).

■ חָבִיב אָדָם שֶׁנִּבְרָא בְּצֶלֶם [אֱלֹקִים] — *Beloved is man, for he was created in [God's] image.*

The Extra Dimension

ולכן הביאו הפסוק בצלם אלקים עשה שנאמר אחד החטא וזה נקרא חבה יתירה
כענין שכתבתי במ''א פי יפה שעה אחת בתשובה ומעשים טובים בעוה''ז כו'
ודו''ק.

הידיעה שהאדם נברא בצלם אלקים, הרי היא יתירה, כי באמצעות ידיעה זו יוכל
האדם לבוא לגיאות.

■ חִבָּה יְתֵרָה — *A greater love.*

Sfas Emes suggests that the *mishnah* chooses to cite the verse which follows Adam's sin of his penitence because the term extra (or *greater*), may refer to the extra dimension of love enjoyed by the *baal teshuvah*. As *Chazal* say, מָקוֹם שֶׁבַּעֲלֵי תְשׁוּבָה עוֹמְדִין צַדִּיקִים גְּמוּרִים אֵינָם עוֹמְדִין, *in the place where the baal teshuvah stands, [even] the totally righteous do not stand* (Berachos 34b) (*Sfas Emes*).

Alternatively, the term יְתֵרָה, *extra*, may contain an implicit warning of the dangers of excessive pride. As the Chozeh of Lublin would say, at times merely realizing that he was created in G-d's likeness (שֶׁנִּבְרָא בְּצֶלֶם) may lead a man to become arrogant (*Maggidei HaEmes*).

■ חָבִיב אָדָם שֶׁנִּבְרָא בְּצֶלֶם [אֱלֹקִים] ... חֲבִיבִין יִשְׂרָאֵל, שֶׁנִּתַּן לָהֶם כְּלִי חֶמְדָּה — *Beloved is man, for he was created in [God's] image ... Beloved are the people of Israel, for a cherished utensil was given to them.*

In Hashem's Likeness (צֶלֶם אֱלֹקִים)

על ידי התורה יכולים להגיע לצלם אלקים דכתיב תורה צוה לנו משה ר''ת צל''ם,
ולהיפר מעביר פרמא מפניו. כפי מה ששומרים תורה ומצות כך נשמרים.

By juxtaposing these two concepts, the *mishnah* teaches us that only through Torah can we reach our potential implicit in being created in Hashem's image. Indeed, the first letter of each word in the phrase תּוֹרָה צִוָּה לָנוּ מֹשֶׁה, *Moshe commanded to us the Torah* (Devarim 33:4), spell צֶלֶם, image (*Imrei Emes, Maggidei HaEmes*).

■ כְּלִי חֶמְדָּה — *A cherished utensil.*

Attraction to Torah

יש לפרש שהעליונים ותחתונים חמדוה אז בקבלת התורה זולת האומות שלא

The term בְּלִי חֶמְדָּה, *kli chemdah*, lends itself to various interpretations. It may refer to the Torah itself which was coveted by *Klal Yisrael* (though rejected by mankind) and even by the angels who fought strenuously to keep the Torah for themselves.

On the other hand, the term *chemdah* is not only an apt description of the Torah's appeal, but also a subtle reminder of our need to remain attracted to Torah. It may be difficult at first to appreciate the Torah that we study; as *Chazal* say, *all beginnings are difficult* (*Rashi, Shemos* 19:5 s.v. ועתה). However, by assiduously studying Torah despite our lack of initial attraction, we will eventually merit to fully appreciate and enjoy what we study.

In fact, the term בְּלִי חֶמְדָּה may refer to the attraction that we will eventually develop towards Torah. As the Gemara relates, הַנּוֹתֵן בְּעַיִן יָפָה נוֹתֵן, *a gift is given generously* (cf. *Bava Basra* 65a). By giving us the Torah, Hashem granted us the passionate desire to come closer to Him which is an integral part of Torah study. There is no greater indication of Hashem's love for us than the intense love for Torah that He granted to the Jewish people.

⊷§ The Inner Secret of the Torah

The term יְתֵרָה implies something beyond human comprehension — just as the נְשָׁמָה יְתֵרָה which man is granted each Shabbos defies comprehension. The חַבָּה יְתֵרָה referred to here is referring to the Giving of the Torah when the Revelation was experienced by *Klal Yisrael*. Never before did the Jewish people enjoy a moment of such intimacy with their creator. It is of that moment that Shlomo wrote: כִּי ה׳ יִתֵּן חָכְמָה מִפִּיו דַּעַת וּתְבוּנָה, *For Hashem grants wisdom; from His mouth [come] knowledge and understanding* (*Mishlei* 2:6). While all wisdom emanates from Him, at Sinai we were exposed to the most sublime secrets of the Torah emanating directly from Hashem's mouth (מִפִּיו דַּעַת וּתְבוּנָה), as it were. Shlomo speaks of this hallowed moment with the words, יִשָּׁקֵנִי מִנְּשִׁיקוֹת פִּיהוּ, *He will kiss me from the kisses of His mouth* (*Shir HaShirim* 1:2). We would like Hashem to kiss us from the "kisses of His mouth" as He did at Sinai (cf. *The Three Festivals*, pp. 85,86).

[יט] הַכֹּל צָפוּי, וְהָרְשׁוּת נְתוּנָה. וּבְטוֹב הָעוֹלָם נִדּוֹן, וְהַכֹּל לְפִי רֹב הַמַּעֲשֶׂה.

[כ] הוּא הָיָה אוֹמֵר: הַכֹּל נָתוּן בָּעֵרָבוֹן, וּמְצוּדָה פְרוּסָה עַל כָּל הַחַיִּים. הֶחָנוּת פְּתוּחָה, וְהַחֶנְוָנִי מַקִּיף, וְהַפִּנְקָס פָּתוּחַ, וְהַיָּד כּוֹתֶבֶת, וְכָל הָרוֹצֶה לִלְוֹת יָבֹא וְיִלְוֶה. וְהַגַּבָּאִים מַחֲזִירִין תָּדִיר בְּכָל יוֹם וְנִפְרָעִין מִן הָאָדָם, מִדַּעְתּוֹ וְשֶׁלֹּא מִדַּעְתּוֹ, וְיֵשׁ לָהֶם עַל מַה שֶׁיִּסְמְכוּ. וְהַדִּין דִּין אֱמֶת, וְהַכֹּל מְתֻקָּן לִסְעוּדָה.

⇜ Three Festivals

וי״ל הרמז נודעת להם הוא המועד של חג השבועות שעשה זכר למתן תורה ביום זה לעולם כמ״ש זכר עשה לנפלאותיו, ובימים הטובים מתעורר דביקות ודעת בלבות בנ״י להשי״ת, וי״ל כי כן הג׳ חיבות שנזכרו במשנה רמוז על הג׳ מועדות, חביבין ישראל שנקראו בנים למקום ונודעת להם הוא מועד של פסח שנגאלנו מבית עבדים וכ׳ בני בכורי ישראל, וחביב אדם שנברא בצלם ונודעת להם הוא חג הסוכות, שהוא הצל והגנה שיש לאדם בכח שנברא בצלם אלקים וזה עיקר ההגנה, ולכן רמזו ונקטו כאן אדם ולא ישראל, כי יש אחיזה לכל הע׳ אומות בקרבנות החג.

In conclusion, the entire *mishnah* may be interpreted as being an allusion to the Three Festivals, Pesach, Shavuos and Succos.

Specifically, the first segment of the *mishnah* stating that all mankind was created in the image of God alludes to the *succah* which *Chazal* describe as a source of protection. Just as the *succah* shelters us from the inclement outside environment, so too man's Divine image shields him from being swayed by improper influences. To emphasize the universal nature of Succos — when offerings were brought on behalf of all the nations of the world — the *mishnah* states, *beloved is man*, referring to *all* of mankind, and not just Israel.

The second segment, חֲבִיבִין יִשְׂרָאֵל שֶׁנִּקְרְאוּ בָנִים לַמָּקוֹם, *beloved are the people Israel, for they are described as children of the Omnipresent*, refers to the Exodus from Egypt when we became Hashem's children. In fact, Hashem's first summons to Pharaoh to release the Jews was based on our status as Hashem's children — בְּנִי בְכֹרִי יִשְׂרָאֵל, *My firstborn son is Israel* (*Shemos* 4:22).

Finally, the phrase שֶׁנִּתַּן לָהֶם כְּלִי חֶמְדָּה, *for a cherished utensil was given to them*, refers to the festival of Shavuos when we received the Torah. Each festival, *Klal Yisrael's* intimate ties to Hashem, חִבָּה יְתֵרָה, are renewed.

[19] *Everything is foreseen, yet the freedom of choice is given.*

The world is judged with goodness, and everything depends on the abundance of good deeds.

[20] *He used to say: Everything is given on collateral, and a net is spread over all the living. The shop is open; the Merchant extends credit; the ledger is open; the hand writes; and whoever wishes to borrow, let him come and borrow. The collectors make their rounds constantly, every day, and collect payment from the person, whether he realizes it or not. They have proof to rely upon; the judgment is a truthful judgment; and everything is prepared for the [final festive] banquet.*

19.

■ הַכֹּל צָפוּי וְהָרְשׁוּת נְתוּנָה — *Everything is foreseen, yet the freedom of choice is given.*

⋙ Predestination or Free Will?

היינו שידיעה ובחירה אין סתירה.

According to the Bendiner Rav, this phrase addresses the seeming conflict between יְדִיעָה, Hashem's *Omniscience* (whereby He is aware of all of our actions), and בְּחִירָה, *free will*. The *mishnah* simply reassures us that while הַכֹּל צָפוּי, Hashem is aware of all our future actions, הָרְשׁוּת נְתוּנָה, man is still free to act as he pleases. יְדִיעָה, Hashem's knowledge of what we will, in no way influences our בְּחִירָה, choice to act as we please (*Maggidei Ha-Emes*).

■ וּבְטוּב הָעוֹלָם נָדוֹן ■ — *The world is judged with goodness.*

⋙ Judging the World

רש״י ז״ל פירש במדת הרחמים בחינת טוב. ופשוט יש לומר כפי התנהגות העולם
וטובה כך היא נידונת.

Rashi interprets the term טוב, *goodness*, as referring to Hashem's Attribute of Mercy. However, the term may also be applied to man's good deeds. The

[כא] רַבִּי אֶלְעָזָר בֶּן עֲזַרְיָה אוֹמֵר: אִם אֵין תּוֹרָה,
אֵין דֶּרֶךְ אֶרֶץ; אִם אֵין דֶּרֶךְ אֶרֶץ, אֵין תּוֹרָה. אִם
אֵין חׇכְמָה, אֵין יִרְאָה; אִם אֵין יִרְאָה, אֵין חׇכְמָה. אִם
אֵין דַּעַת, אֵין בִּינָה; אִם אֵין בִּינָה, אֵין דַּעַת. אִם אֵין
קֶמַח, אֵין תּוֹרָה; אִם אֵין תּוֹרָה, אֵין קֶמַח.

world is not judged capriciously, but rather on the basis of its moral behavior. This thought is reflected in the closing phrase of this *mishnah* — וְהַכֹּל לְפִי רוֹב הַמַּעֲשֶׂה, *and everything depends on the abundance of deeds.* (adapted from *Sfas Emes*).

21.

■ אִם אֵין תּוֹרָה, אֵין דֶּרֶךְ אֶרֶץ; אִם אֵין דֶּרֶךְ אֶרֶץ, אֵין תּוֹרָה — *If there is no Torah, there is no worldly occupation; if there is no worldly occupation, there is no Torah.*

◄§ Two Eras

פירשנו כי קודם החטא הי' מוכן להיות תורה קדמה לד"א, שהיו בנ"י מיוחדים
לקבל התורה כמו שהיא למעלה אש דת שהי' ניתקן כל העשי' לגמרי, כמ"ש כל
אשר דיבר ה' נעשה, פי' שקיבלו בנ"י ע"י לתקן כל המעשים ע"פ הנהגת מלכותו
ית', ואם אין ד"א אין תורה בענין אמרם ז"ל קדמה לתורה, והוא ענין עבודת
האדם להש"י מתוך השכל והכרת האמת שמכירין טובת הבורא ית' על כל
ברואיו וחסדיו המרובין, ואח"כ זוכין לתורה שהיא עבודה עליונה כפי רצון הש"י
באמת, והמשל, הכל עובדין אותו ע"פ קיום שליהותו ורצונו, וזה ענין ואתם תהיו
לי ממלכת כהנים.
סוף דבר במעמד הר סיני ניתקן העשי' וכמ"ש העשוי' בהר סיני כו', ורק אחר
החטא בעגל ירדנו ממדרגה זו וניתקן אח"כ בדר"א קדמה לתורה שכיון שנשאר
פסולת בעולם צריכין מקודם לתקן המעשה והגוף ע"י מדות והכנעות כנ"ל ואח"כ
זוכין לתורה ובתד"א איתא . . . לשמור את דרך עה"ח מכאן שד"א קדמה
לתורה.

These two seemingly contradictory statements may refer to two distinct eras within the history of *Klal Yisrael*. The first statement, אִם אֵין תּוֹרָה אֵין דֶּרֶךְ אֶרֶץ, placing primary emphasis on Torah study, alludes to the high standing that *Klal Yisrael* enjoyed prior to worshiping the Golden Calf. This was a time of lofty spiritual aspirations, in which our forefathers dared to dream that through their acceptance of the Torah they could shape and influence the entire natural world. These compelling dreams were implied in the statement (*Shemos* 19:8), כֹּל אֲשֶׁר דִּבֶּר ה' נַעֲשֶׂה, which may be interpreted as "whatever Hashem created through

[21] R' Elazar ben Azaryah says: If there is no Torah, there is no worldly occupation; if there is no worldly occupation there is no Torah.

If there is no widsom, there is no fear of God; if there is no fear of God, there is no wisdom.

If there is no knowledge, there is no understanding; if there is no understanding, there is no knowledge.

If there is no flour, there is no Torah; if there is no Torah, there is no flour.

His Word, we will shape and recast in the spirit of Torah." While this goal may seem to be beyond our reach, bear in mind that *Klal Yisrael* originally received the Torah in a supernatural form (and totally unlike any entity that we can now imagine). As Moshe writes, אֵשׁ דָּת (*Devarim* 33:2), the Torah was presented to us in the form of a "fiery law code," a concept that defies description in natural terms. Had we not sinned by venerating the Golden Calf, we would have retained the same supernatural Torah originally enjoyed by the angels. In such a blessed ambiance, it would have been possible to perfect the entire natural world so that it serves as the ideal environment for Torah. As we say every day, עוֹלַת תָּמִיד הָעֲשׂוּיָה בְּהַר סִינַי, *it is the continual elevation-offering that was done at Mount Sinai*. At Mount Sinai, the entire natural world — the עוֹלָם הַמַּעֲשֶׂה, *the World of Action* — would have been nurtured and molded in the image of Torah.

The following statement, אִם אֵין דֶּרֶךְ אֶרֶץ אֵין תּוֹרָה, offers hope for us living in the present-day world, a universe which is very much governed by the laws of nature. Though we no longer enjoy the option of designing the natural world to conform with Torah, we can learn to appreciate Hashem through the many wonders of His universe. As a result of coming closer to Hashem by appreciating His management of the universe (דֶּרֶךְ אֶרֶץ), we eventually merit to perceive the Divine Presence through Torah study as well.

The distinction between appreciating Hashem through nature and perceiving Him through Torah may be understood from the following parable concerning a mortal monarch. While all of his subjects are compelled to obey his edicts, only his most intimate courtiers are privileged to hear the monarch's innermost desires. So too, while all of nature reflects, and in its own inimitable fashion harmoniously fulfills the Divine will, only *Klal Yisrael*, immersed in Torah, is able to hear the Divine Voice instructing us how to fulfill His will.

Our unique status is hinted at in the verse, *And you shall be to Me a kingdom of ministers* (*Shemos* 19:6). As a nation of ministers (see *Rashi*), we are privileged to communicate directly with Hashem.

This approach in interpreting the *mishnah* is corroborated by the comment of *Tanna D'Vei Eliyahu* regarding the verse (*Bereishis* 3:24) describing the function of the Cherubim and the fiery sword that were posted outside of *Gan Eden* to prevent Adam's return, "to guard the path of the Tree of Life." The *Tanna D'Vei Eliyahu* remarks, "From here we see that *Derech Eretz* precedes Torah."

Whereas Adam, while in Eden, undertook the mission of shaping the universe so that it conformed to the lofty spiritual level that he then enjoyed, once he was expelled from there he undertook another, even more daunting challenge. He hoped to first find the *Shechinah* in the natural world outside of Eden through *Derech Eretz*, and only then ascend to the level where he could perceive the *Shechinah* through Torah. [For a more in-depth discussion of these concepts see *The Three Festivals*, pp. 234-236.] (adapted from *Sfas Emes*).

■ אִם אֵין חָכְמָה, אֵין יִרְאָה; אִם אֵין יִרְאָה, אֵין חָכְמָה — *If there is no wisdom, there is no fear of God; if there is no fear of God, there is no wisdom.*

⊷§ Prerequisite or Result of Wisdom

> יש יראה קודם חכמה כדכתיב ראשית חכמה יראת ה' ויש יראה אחר חכמה וזו
> יראה דנפקת מגו תורה. וזהו שאיתא אם אין חכמה אין יראה אם אין יראה אין
> חכמה.

Here the *mishnah* is discussing two levels of fear of Hashem. First, there is an initial sense of fear that is a prerequisite for attaining wisdom. As David writes, רֵאשִׁית חָכְמָה יִרְאַת ה', *the beginning* (foundation) *of wisdom is the fear of Hashem* (*Tehillim* 111:10). On the other hand, a far more sophisticated form of יִרְאַת ה' *results* from studying Torah. It is about this advanced level of fear of Hashem that the *mishnah* writes, אִם אֵין חָכְמָה אֵין יִרְאָה (*Imrei Emes, Maggidei HaEmes*).

■ אִם אֵין קֶמַח, אֵין תּוֹרָה; אִם אֵין תּוֹרָה, אֵין קֶמַח — *If there is no flour, there is no Torah; if there is no Torah, there is no flour.*

⊷§ Heavenly Bread vs. Bread of the Earth
(לחם הארץ) (לחם מן השמים)

> רמז לענין המן שהמן היה קמח שקודם התורה לחם מן השמים הוא שורש המזון
> קודם שבא לעולם הזה, והכניסה לארץ ישראל ואכלת ושבעת כו', בחינה לחם מן
> הארץ, היה הקמח שאחר התורה.

The *mishnah* may be alluding to two different methods through which Hashem sustained *Klal Yisrael*.

Prior to the Giving of the Torah, Hashem sustained *Klal Yisrael* by providing them with heavenly bread known as the manna — *Behold! I shall rain down for you bread from heaven* (*Shemos* 16:4). The Torah itself describes the manna as being "bread from heaven," because of its intense spirituality.

On the other hand, upon entering *Eretz Yisrael*, *Klal Yisrael* could no longer subsist on the manna. Instead, they tilled the sacred soil of the land, never forgetting that it was only in the merit of Torah that they enjoyed their material (*if there is no Torah, there is no flour*). Indeed, the Torah reminds us, וְאָכַלְתָּ וְשָׂבָעְתָּ וּבֵרַכְתָּ אֶת ה' אֱלֹקֶיךָ, *you will eat and you will be satisfied, and bless Hashem your God* (*Devarim* 8:10). Thank Hashem for the food that you enjoy and remember that it is only through His largess that your material needs are provided. [For further discussion of this concept see *The Three Festivals*, pp. 221-223.]

⊷§ Good Deeds and Mitzvos

אם אין קמח אין תורה,יל"פ קמח על מעשים טובים ומצות כי תורה בעצמה ג"כ
לא די כי רק בצירוף שניהם.

Just as flour is a necessary ingredient for baking bread, so too Torah, good deeds and observing Hashem's *mitzvos* are vital ingredients in achieving the fulfillment afforded by Torah.

⊷§ The Impact of Torah on Its Students

פי' שתכלית התורה להוציא ממנה קמח ומזון, ושמעתי מאמור"ז ז"ל שלכן יש
בתורה ברכה לפני' ולאחרי' כמו במזון כשהוא רעב מברך על שהזמין לו השי"ת
הלחם, וכשהוא שבע יש ברהמ"ז על השביעה מה שהלחם מתעכל במעיו ומשביעו
ולכן שיעור ברהמ"ז כל זמן עיכול, וכמו כן יש לברך לאחרי' על קבלת חיות ומזון
מהתורה שיהי' נבלע בדמיו ודפח"ח, וכ' הטריפני לחם חקי ואין לחם אלא תורה
שיזמין השי"ת לאדם דברי תורה שיעשו בו רושם ויקח חיות ומזון מהדברים שזה
תכלית התורה ומה"ט נקראת התורה לחם שנותן מזון וקיום.

The term flour may refer to not only the physical sustenance necessary for Torah study but also to the sense of satiation that one derives from studying Torah. Just as one feels satisfied after partaking of food, so too the Torah students feel satiated after partaking of its treasures. Similarly, in the same way that one recites a blessing *before* eating to thank Hashem for providing nourishment and *after* eating to express appreciation for the food that He has provided, so too we recite a blessing before and after studying Torah.

First we thank Hashem for giving us the Torah, and after reading the Torah (in public) we express our appreciation of the impact that Torah has left upon us.

In light of this, Shlomo's plea, הַטְרִיפֵנִי לֶחֶם חֻקִּי, *but allot me my daily bread* (*Mishlei* 30:8), may also be understood as an appeal that he be granted his portion in Torah, the force which spiritually influences and sustains man.

◆§ Flour Not Wheat

> קמח היינו עיקר שורש התורה והרגשת הטעם תלויה כפי ערך לימוד התורה של
> האדם. יש מי שלומד כמו שאוכל חטים בלי טעם ויש מי שלומד ומרגיש טעם, וזהו
> יגלה לן טעמי דבתריסר נהמי שנרגיש הטעם.

According to the *Imrei Emes*, by using the term flour rather than wheat, the mishnah is alluding to the satisfaction derived when one makes a serious effort to study Torah. Without "flour" — an intensive effort (similar to that used to make wheat into flour) to plumb the depths of whatever segment of Torah one is studying — one is left without a sense of achievement in learning (אֵין תּוֹרָה), one has consumed but not "tasted" it. As it says before *Kiddush* Shabbos morning, יְגַלֶּה לָן טַעֲמֵי דִּבְתְרֵיסַר נַהֲמֵי, *May He reveal to us the purpose of the twelve loaves*, referring not only to the twelve loaves placed on the Table in the *Mishkan* but also to the inner depths of Torah that we yearn to enjoy (*Maggidei HaEmes*).

■ אִם אֵין תּוֹרָה אֵין קֶמַח — *If there is no Torah, there is no flour.* ■

◆§ The Prosperous Rasha, the Poor Tzaddik

> אם אין תורה אין קמח פי' בכלל העולם אם יש הרבה עוסקים ברורה יש נמי
> פרנסה בעולם, וע"י בפי' החסיד ז"ל עמ"ש אם אין תורה א"ק כי מציאותה בטל
> לגמרי והוי כעפרא דארעא ופי' דבריו כי רואין רשעים ממלאים כרסם עד לשבעה
> ובלי תורה נמצא להם קמח לרוב ע"ז ב' כי אוכלים עפר ולא קמח כי נק' קמח ע"ש
> שהוא דבר המזין ורוחני קצת והיינו כשבא לאיזה צורך שיוכל ללמוד כראוי
> וכדומה והוי המזון סועד ללבו שפיר נק' קמח משא"כ בשאינו יוצא הקמח לידי
> שום פעולה והיינו בלי תורה אינו נק' קמח אינו נק' קמח רק עפרא דארעא.
> וכן להיפוך יש צדיקים שאין להם פרנסה . . .
> ופירש האריז"ל שחיות מאמרו ית' שיש במאכל הוא חיות אל הנפש
> והגשמיות אל הגוף . . . שע"י ד"ת זוכין למצוא פנימיות המזון שבקדושה וע"ז
> רמזו חז"ל אם אין קמח אין תורה הוא פנימיות הקמח שמזין אל הנפש וג' ב"כ אם
> אין תורה אין קמח שבלי כח התורה אין פנימיות המזון מתגלה. ולכן אמרו בגמ'
> שצריכין להזכיר בברכת המזון ברית ותורה שע"י בריתו שחתם בבשרנו וע"י
> התורה יכולין אנו למצוא מזון הפנימיות.

It appears that our *mishnah* is contradicted by empirical experience. Frequently, the wicked — totally devoid of Torah learning — prosper. Likewise, we are all acquainted with righteous people who lack material wealth.

The fact may be, however, that our *mishnah* should be understood in a communal context: If (ח״ו) Torah study would cease, everyone's livelihood would also be jeopardized.

Another possible resolution to this apparent difficult question lies in the term קֶמַח, *flour*. While it is certainly true that everyone needs to eat, the *rasha* who is eating merely to enjoy himself — who lives in an environment devoid of Torah — is actually partaking of lifeless, sterile *dust* rather than life-giving flour. It is only the student of Torah who partakes of "flour," which sustains the soul as well as the body.

We can expand upon this approach by drawing upon the teaching of the sainted *Arizal*, who distinguished between the exterior physical appearance of food which nurtures the body and its inner spiritual content. He derives this distinction through a unique interpretation of the verse, כִּי לֹא עַל הַלֶּחֶם לְבַדּוֹ יִחְיֶה הָאָדָם כִּי עַל כָּל מוֹצָא פִּי ה׳ יִחְיֶה הָאָדָם, *that not by bread alone does man live, rather by everything that emanates from the mouth of God does man live (Devarim 8:3).* Man lives from the word of Hashem that lies beneath the exterior of the bread.

In this light, we may interpret the *mishnah* in the following manner: אִם אֵין קֶמַח אֵין תּוֹרָה — without the spiritual sustenance of the soul provided by the spiritual component of food, it would be virtually impossible to study Torah. But the converse is also true: אִם אֵין תּוֹרָה אֵין קֶמַח — it is only through immersion in Torah that one is able to extract the spiritual power that lies within the food we eat.

The requirement that we refer to Torah study in *Bircas Hamazon* by saying וְעַל תּוֹרָתְךָ שֶׁלִּמַּדְתָּנוּ *(for Your Torah which You taught us)* may be explained in a similar manner. It is only through the Torah that we study that we are able to elicit that inner spiritual substance contained within food that nurtures our soul.

On the basis of this insight of the *Arizal*, we may derive additional meaning from a previous *mishnah* in the *perek* (*mishnah* 4). שְׁלֹשָׁה שֶׁאָכְלוּ עַל שֻׁלְחָן אֶחָד וְאָמְרוּ עָלָיו דִּבְרֵי תוֹרָה כְּאִלּוּ אָכְלוּ מִשֻּׁלְחָנוֹ שֶׁל מָקוֹם, *If three have eaten at one table and have spoken words of Torah there, it is as is they have eaten from the table of the Omnipresent.* The *Divrei Torah* spoken at the table and enjoying the capacity to bring forth the inner spiritual core of food transform our ordinary table to one that has the lofty status of being Hashem's Table. It becomes a place where we experience inspiring spiritual growth as well as physical satiation (*Sfas Emes Eikev 5649*).

◆§ Worrying About Parnasah

הרמז שאם אין קמח מחמת שאין תורה. ואם האדם מקבל עול תורה מעבירין

ממנו העול מפרנסה. וכן מפורש וברך את לחמך כו׳ והסירותי מחלה מקרבך זהו
המחלה דאגת פרנסה.

One who is struggling financially despite his efforts at earning a livelihood may incorrectly assume that this is because he is not investing enough effort in his quest for *parnasah*. This *mishnah* teaches us that, in reality, the converse is true: If there is a scarcity of food — אֵין קֶמַח — it is because of a deficiency in attitude towards Torah study, אֵין תּוֹרָה. This interpretation of our *mishnah* corroborates the theme voiced in a previous *mishnah*: כָּל הַמְקַבֵּל עָלָיו עֹל תּוֹרָה ... מַעֲבִירִין מִמֶּנּוּ עֹל דֶּרֶךְ אֶרֶץ —, *If someone takes upon himself the yoke of Torah ... the yoke of worldly responsibilities are removed from him* (3:6).

The *Beis Yisrael* offered a novel, truly beautiful interpretation of the Torah's assurance, וַהֲסִרֹתִי מַחֲלָה מִקִּרְבֶּךָ, *and I shall remove illness from your midst* (*Shemos* 23:25). According to him, this refers not primarily to physical illness but rather to the incessant obsession about *parnasah* that often plagues a person. We are assured that in the merit of studying Torah, Hashem will remove that totally unwarranted fear (*Maggidei HaEmes*).

⇥§ Eating — Without Becoming Materialistic

נצרך שמירה יתירה שלא יתגשם האדם, וזה הרמז אם אין תורה אין קמח,
שאכילת האדם יהיה בדרך התורה ... וזאת הסמיכות אם בחקותי כו׳ ונתתי
גשמיכם בעתם ... שאינו מזיק לו ועוד מעלה את העניינים הגשמיים ... לעשות
מזה גם מן תורה.
מקודם איתא אם אין קמח אין תורה ואח״כ אם אין תורה אין קמח, י״ל דהכוונה
שיאכל כדי שיהיה לו כח ללמוד תורה.

By eating in a manner appropriate for a Torah Jew, we ensure that we will never become affected by the food that we eat. The Torah frequently warns us of the danger of becoming materialistic as a result of eating excessively (cf. *Devarim* 8:12). To counter this ever present danger, the *mishnah* counsels us, אִם אֵין תּוֹרָה אֵין קֶמַח. Only partake of קֶמַח — of every aspect of the physical world — in the spirit of Torah. The relationship between living a Torah life and not becoming excessively materialistic is spelled out at the very beginning of the Torah's most sublime blessings: אִם בְּחֻקֹּתַי תֵּלֵכוּ ... וְנָתַתִּי גִשְׁמֵיכֶם בְּעִתָּם, *If you will follow My decrees ... then I will provide your rains in their time* (*Vayikra* 26:3,4). If you walk in My ways I will provide rain (which is symbolic of material possessions) בְּעִתָּם, in their proper time — in such a manner that you will not be hurt by your exposure to material things (*Beis Yisrael, Maggidei HaEmes*).

[22] He [R' Elazar ben Azariah] used to say: Anyone whose wisdom exceeds his deeds, to what is he

In a very similar vein, the *Lev Simcha* interpreted אִם אֵין קֶמַח, אֵין תּוֹרָה, אִם אֵין תּוֹרָה אֵין קֶמַח, implying a close association between flour and Torah — the sole justification for eating is for the purpose of obtaining the strength to study Torah (*Maggidei HaEmes*).

◆§ Simchas Torah

ובשמחת תורה אחרי שגומרין את התורה וקודם שמתחילים ללמוד את התורה מקבלים על עצמינו ללמוד במשך השנה הבאה עושין סעודה, לרמוז אם אין קמח אין תורה ואם אין תורה אין קמח.

According to the *Beis Yisrael*, our *mishnah* may be alluding to the *seudah* that is traditionally held upon completing the Torah every Simchas Torah. This festive meal (קֶמַח) is justified by the completion of the Torah. On the other hand, the joy experienced at the *seudah* provides a powerful incentive to continue learning Torah in the following year. As the *mishnah* concludes, אִם אֵין קֶמַח אֵין תּוֹרָה, without the support provided by this meal we would not be able to achieve the strides that we expect to attain in the coming year (*Maggidei HaEmes*).

◆§ The Importance of Eating

יש לדקדק למה לא עשו הגבלה קודם מתן תורה גם על אכילה ושתיה. אלא שאם אין קמח אין תורה.

We conclude this anthology of interpretation by referring to the observation of the *Pnei Menachem*. While *Klal Yisrael* was required to separate from their wives for three days prior to *Matan Torah*, they were certainly not required to abstain from food and drink for a similar period. Besides the obvious hazard to life in depriving oneself for so long a period, the reason why such a drastic measure was not taken may be to underscore the importance of eating properly as a prerequisite for Torah study (*Maggidei HaEmes*).

22.

■ כָּל שֶׁמַּעֲשָׂיו מְרֻבִּין מֵחָכְמָתוֹ, לְמָה הוּא דוֹמֶה? – לְאִילָן שֶׁעֲנָפָיו מוּעָטִין וְשָׁרָשָׁיו מְרֻבִּין – *One whose good deeds exceed his wisdom, to what is he likened? — to a tree whose branches are few but whose roots are numerous.*

לְמָה הוּא דוֹמֶה? לְאִילָן שֶׁעֲנָפָיו מְרֻבִּין וְשָׁרָשָׁיו
מוּעָטִין, וְהָרוּחַ בָּאָה וְעוֹקַרְתּוֹ וְהוֹפַכְתּוֹ עַל פָּנָיו,
שֶׁנֶּאֱמַר: "וְהָיָה כְּעַרְעָר בָּעֲרָבָה, וְלֹא יִרְאֶה כִּי יָבוֹא
טוֹב, וְשָׁכַן חֲרֵרִים בַּמִּדְבָּר, אֶרֶץ מְלֵחָה וְלֹא תֵשֵׁב."
אֲבָל כָּל שֶׁמַּעֲשָׂיו מְרֻבִּין מֵחָכְמָתוֹ, לְמָה הוּא דוֹמֶה?
לְאִילָן שֶׁעֲנָפָיו מוּעָטִין וְשָׁרָשָׁיו מְרֻבִּין, שֶׁאֲפִילוּ כָּל
הָרוּחוֹת שֶׁבָּעוֹלָם בָּאוֹת וְנוֹשְׁבוֹת בּוֹ, אֵין מְזִיזִין
אוֹתוֹ מִמְּקוֹמוֹ, שֶׁנֶּאֱמַר: "וְהָיָה כְּעֵץ שָׁתוּל עַל מָיִם,
וְעַל יוּבַל יְשַׁלַּח שָׁרָשָׁיו, וְלֹא יִרְאֶה כִּי יָבֹא חֹם, וְהָיָה
עָלֵהוּ רַעֲנָן, וּבִשְׁנַת בַּצֹּרֶת לֹא יִדְאָג, וְלֹא יָמִישׁ
מֵעֲשׂוֹת פֶּרִי."

⊷§ A Tree of Many Roots

נראה דאף שיש בהאילן שרשים הרבה מכל מקום אם יש ענפים עוד יותר אין
האילן טוב דצריך להיות שרשים יותר מענפים.

The *mishnah* teaches us that although a tree may have many roots, it — and
by extension the *talmid chacham* — needs to have more roots than branches
to be firmly entrenched and to thrive.

⊷§ Good Deeds: Deeply Rooted Wisdom:
Up in the Air

כי מצות מעשיות נדבקים בהאדם בעצם אבל החכמה אין לו דביקות בעצם
והחכמה רק כמו באויר ולכן מזיק לזה הרוחות שבעולם.

By comparing good deeds to the root of a tree and wisdom to its branches, the
mishnah is speaking eloquently about the relationship between *mitzvos*
that we actually performed and theoretical wisdom. Whereas the former are
deeply rooted and become an integral part of an individual, the latter is "positioned up in the air" — useful but never becoming truly absorbed by the
individual.

Just as branches sway with every wind, so too wisdom alone does not
necessarily lead to belief in Hashem. On the contrary, wisdom can be influenced and diverted by every "ill wind," every ideology that is contrary to

likened? — to a tree whose branches are numerous but whose roots are few; then the wind comes and uproots it and turns it upside down, as it is said (Yirmiyahu 17:6): "And he shall be like an isolated tree in an arid land and shall not see when good comes; he shall dwell on parched soil in the wilderness, on a salted and uninhabited land.

But one whose good deeds exceed his wisdom, to what is he likened? — to a tree whose branches are few but whose roots are numerous; even if all the winds in the world were to come and blow against it, they could not budge it from its place, as it says (Yirmiyahu 17:8): "And he shall be like a tree planted by water, spreading its roots toward the stream, and it shall not notice the heat's arrival, and its foliage shall be fresh; in the year of drought it shall not worry, nor shall it cease from yielding fruit.

Torah. On the other hand, *mitzvos* and *maasim tovim*, deeply rooted in the individual, help protect the individual from being affected by the "ill winds" (the non-Torah ideologies) that may buffet him.

■ וּבִשְׁנַת בַּצֹּרֶת לֹא יִדְאָג ■ — *In the year of drought it shall not worry.*

⋦ Why Would a Tree Worry?

יי״ל דקאי על הנמשל ועוד נראה על גוף האילן שכל דבר שאינו לעשות פעולתו דואג וכדאיתא הדרכים מבקשין תפקידם ומכש״כ האדם שהוא יסוד הנבראים.

It seems odd to make reference to a tree having "worry." Thus, this expression would seem to refer to the individual whose deeds exceed his wisdom, rather than to the subject of the verse, the tree.

On the other hand, if we interpret the term דְּאָגָה, *worry*, in its broader sense as referring to the frustration that every living entity — animate or inanimate — suffers when it cannot realize its full potential, we could argue that a tree which sheds its fruit does indeed worry. It assuredly follows, then, that man, who is the apex of Hashem's creation, should worry if he does not live up to his God-given potential.

[כג] רַבִּי אֶלְעָזָר (בֶּן) חִסְמָא אוֹמֵר: קִנִּין וּפִתְחֵי נִדָּה הֵן הֵן גּוּפֵי הֲלָכוֹת; תְּקוּפוֹת וְגִמַטְרִיָאוֹת — פַּרְפְּרָאוֹת לַחָכְמָה.

❧ ❧ ❧

רַבִּי חֲנַנְיָא בֶּן עֲקַשְׁיָא אוֹמֵר: רָצָה הַקָּדוֹשׁ בָּרוּךְ הוּא לְזַכּוֹת אֶת יִשְׂרָאֵל, לְפִיכָךְ הִרְבָּה לָהֶם תּוֹרָה וּמִצְוֹת, שֶׁנֶּאֱמַר: ״יהוה חָפֵץ לְמַעַן צִדְקוֹ, יַגְדִּיל תּוֹרָה וְיַאְדִּיר.״

[23] *Rabbi Elazar ben Chisma says: The laws of bird offerings and the laws regarding the beginning of menstrual periods — these are essential laws; astronomy and mathematics are like seasonings to wisdom.*

❧ ❧ ❧

Rabbi Chanania ben Akashia says: The Holy One, Blessed is He, wished to confer merit upon Israel; therefore He gave them Torah and mitzvos in abundance, as it is said (Yeshayahu 42:21): "Hashem desired, for the sake of its [Israel's] righteousness, that the Torah be made great and glorious."

פרק רביעי

כָּל יִשְׂרָאֵל יֵשׁ לָהֶם חֵלֶק לָעוֹלָם הַבָּא, שֶׁנֶּאֱמַר: ,,וְעַמֵּךְ
כֻּלָּם צַדִּיקִים, לְעוֹלָם יִירְשׁוּ אָרֶץ, נֵצֶר מַטָּעַי,
מַעֲשֵׂה יָדַי לְהִתְפָּאֵר.״

❦ ❦ ❦

[א] בֶּן זוֹמָא אוֹמֵר: אֵיזֶהוּ חָכָם? הַלּוֹמֵד מִכָּל אָדָם,
שֶׁנֶּאֱמַר: ,,מִכָּל מְלַמְּדַי הִשְׂכַּלְתִּי.״ אֵיזֶהוּ גִבּוֹר?

1.

■ בֶּן זוֹמָא אוֹמֵר: אֵיזֶהוּ חָכָם? הַלּוֹמֵד מִכָּל אָדָם, שֶׁנֶּאֱמַר: ,,מִכָּל מְלַמְּדַי הִשְׂכַּלְתִּי״
— Ben Zoma says: Who is wise? He who learns from every person, as
it is said: "From all my teachers I grew wise."

⋲§ Always a Talmid

דהקב״ה הטביע במע״ב בכל אדם שיהי׳ בו משהו להתלמד ממנו ואם אין ביכולתו
ללמוד מכל אדם נמצא שלא נגמר חכמה שבו וי״ל דמה״ט בא כ״פ בלשון חז״ל
תלמיד חכם שבל כחו של חכם ע״י שהוא תלמיד.
פירוש ״תלמיד חכם״, כי הלומד מכל אדם הוא החכם, וזהו תלמיד, מי שהוא תמיד
בבחינת תלמיד, הוא חכם . . . שהחכם צריך להרגיש בעצמו שהוא רק ״תלמיד״
חכם וטרם הגיע למדריגת חכמה. ורגיל היה על לשונו של אדמו״ר מקאצק ז״ל
לומר על עצמו שהוא תלמיד חכם, שרבו הרה״ק רבי ר׳ בונם ז״ל היה חכם,
וכשהוא תלמידו על כן הוא תלמיד חכם (שיח שרפי קודש).

While others may have attained *some* wisdom, only one who has the ability
to learn from *everyone* is a truly wise person. The rationale for this rather
surprising definition of a *chacham* is quite simple: When Hashem created the
universe, he endowed each individual with something unique, which he, in
turn, could teach others. Our wisdom is only complete if we have made full use
of the opportunity to learn from everyone's unique contribution. In this light
we can appreciate why scholars are known as *talmidei chachamim*, literally "the
disciples of scholars," rather than as *chachamim*, wise men, in their own right.
It is only because of their willingness to continue to learn from others that they
deserve the title "wise."

In fact, the Kotzker Rebbe would always emphasize that he was a *talmid
chacham* because he was — i.e. he remained — a *disciple* of his mentor, R'
Simchah Bunim (*Maggidei HaEmes*).

Chapter Four

All Israel has a share in the World to Come, as it is said (Yeshayahu 60:21): "And your people are all righteous; they shall inherit the land forever; a branch of My plantings, My handiwork, in which to take pride."

❦ ❦ ❦

[1] Ben Zoma says: Who is wise? He who learns from every person, as it is said (Tehillim 119:99): "From all my teachers I grew wise." Who is strong?

⇜ Never Stop Learning

רע״ב כ׳ שיתהלל וזה עצמו פ׳ המשנה. איזהו חכם הלומד מכל אדם . . . אף
מפחות ע״י שיודע שהכל רק מהש״י.

Yirmiyahu admonished: אַל יִתְהַלֵּל חָכָם בְּחָכְמָתוֹ וְאַל יִתְהַלֵּל הַגִּבּוֹר בִּגְבוּרָתוֹ אַל
יִתְהַלֵּל עָשִׁיר בְּעָשְׁרוֹ. כִּי אִם בְּזֹאת יִתְהַלֵּל הַמִּתְהַלֵּל הַשְׂכֵּל וְיָדֹעַ אוֹתִי . . . , Let not the
wise man glorify himself with his wisdom, and let not the strong man glorify
himself with his strength, let not the rich man glorify himself with his wealth. For
only with this may one glorify himself — contemplating and knowing Me . . . (9:22,
23). The prophet makes it abundantly clear that wisdom (or strength or wealth)
is not a worthy objective in its own right. This virtue is only admirable if it is
utilized as a means of attaining the ultimate objective — knowing Hashem.

In this regard, the mishnah is asking who is the true wise man, that would
earn Yirmiyahu's accolade — the one whose wisdom serves as a stepping stone
towards the ultimate objective of knowing Hashem. Only the wise man who
despite all the wisdom that he has already amassed continues to learn, even from
those whose wisdom is inferior to his, can be considered a true חָכָם.
By learning from those who are less knowledgeable — because he believes
that as Hashem's subjects they have something to teach him — he demonstrates
his belief that wisdom emanates from Hashem, rather than one's own efforts.

⇜ Learning From One's Enemies

ואף מן לא טוב יוכל ללמוד איך בא הטעות וכ״ז מובן וע״ז הראי׳ שנא׳ מכל מלמדי
השכלתי אף שהי׳ לו ג׳״כ מלמדים רשעים כאחיתופל והוא נקרא חכם כי אתו החכמה
שאף מן ההיפוך הוא מכיר בחכמתו ללמוד שלא לעשות כן א״כ החכמה אצלו.

Unlike most scholars whose mentors were all individuals of exemplary character, David studied at the feet of Achitophel (cf. *Avos* 6:3 where Achitophel is identified as David's *rebbi*, teacher) who eventually joined Avshalom's rebellion and who is identified by *Chazal* as one of the few individuals who does not enjoy a portion in *Olam Haba*.

By citing this *pasuk*, the *mishnah* is defining the essence of wisdom — being *intuitively* wise, rather than absorbing wisdom from a wise mentor. Only a true חָכָם — such as David — could learn from the likes of an Achitophel and yet retain his piety.

What could David learn from Achitophel? What can *we* learn from our foes? In all probability, we can learn from their *errors*. If we contemplate how so great a scholar as Achitophel could commit such an egregious error as to rebel against King David — and then determine *not* to do as he did — we have indeed learned a great deal.

✑ The Mirror Image

שמעתי בשם מורי (הבעש״ט) זלה״ה ביאור משנה איזהו חכם הלומד מכל אדם, על פי משל המסתכל במראה יודע חסרונו, כך ברואה חסרון זולתו יודע שיש בו שמץ מנהו (בו עצמו) ודפח״ח.

יש ללמוד מכל מעשה שרואין ואף עבירה מרשע שנזדמן לאדם לראות יש לו ללמוד שגם הוא צריך לתקן דבר זה.

The author of the first collection of chassidic literature, the *Toldos Yaakov Yosef*, R' Yaakov Yosef of Polonia, explained that a peer acts as the mirror image of oneself. While it may be difficult to recognize *our* own deficiencies, we can easily see someone else's shortcomings. Just as we use a mirror to evaluate our own physical appearance, so too by analyzing a peer's behavior — and learning from him — we can see our own faults as well[1] (*Maggidei HaEmes*).

✑ How Much "Sociability" Is Appropriate?

השפ״א כתב במכתב לבנו האמרי אמת ״ואשר אמרת שתלך לבית החסידים, אם כי אינך מרגיש תועלת, טוב מאד להיות מעורב עם החסידים, ולקבל הטוב, וכמאמר התנא 'איזהו חכם הלומד מכל אדם'. רק שלא לבטל הרבה. וירא שמים יצא את כולם.״

It seems that the *mishnah's* recommendation of learning from *everyone* requires a great deal of sociability and intermingling with people, despite the

---

1. This approach is based on the well-known principle that we are only exposed to those events (or people) that have relevance to us. If we, despite our seeming righteousness, were exposed to evil people, this indicates that, to some extent, we share their deficiencies.

obvious problems associated with such an approach — i.e., that the time could be more profitably used for Torah study as well as the numerous advantages of *hisbodedus*, developing a relationship with Hashem by being immersed in Torah and *Avodas Hashem* solitarily. The *Sfas Emes* cautioned his son (later known as the *Imrei Emes*) to balance these conflicting needs, and to spend some time mingling with *chassidim* (who were themselves individuals steeped in learning and *Yiras Shamayim*), and to learn from their virtues, while not to spend too much time associating with other people because of the time it takes from learning (*Maggidei HaEmes*).

⇥ David's Wisdom

מכל מלמדי השכלתי ומצינו כי דהע״ה נק׳ חכם שכ׳ ואדוני חכם כמלאך אלקים או דדייק מזה עצמו דכ׳ השכלתי.

The *mishnah* implies that David became a wise man as a result of learning from everyone. That David was wise is corroborated by the *pasuk* וַאדֹנִי חָכָם כְּחָכְמַת מַלְאַךְ הָאֱלֹהִים, *And my master is wise like the wisdom of an angel of God* (II Shmuel 14:20). Indeed, David himself implies that he was wise — מִכָּל מְלַמְּדַי הִשְׂכַּלְתִּי, *from all my teachers I grew wise* (Tehillim 119:99).

⇥ David's Conversations

איתא באלשיך דכי עדותיך שיחה לי היינו שדוד המלך ע״ה כשהיה מדבר עם אדם היה מדבר עם חלק התורה שנמצא באדם. בדוד המלך כתיב (ש״א טז, יב) וטוב רואי ואיתא במדרש (ויק״ר כ,א) כל הרואהו נזכר לתלמודו היינו שהיה פותח ומגלה הדברי תורה שנמצאים באדם ועל ידי כך היה האדם עצמו גם כן נזכר לתלמודו.

The final segment of the *pasuk* cited, כִּי עֵדְוֹתֶיךָ שִׂיחָה לִי, is seemingly unrelated to the *mishnah's* major thesis that David learned from everyone. Yet, upon further analysis, we deduce that the *pasuk* is demonstrating *how* David learned from everyone. The wise monarch sensed that every Jew enjoyed his own unique "niche," his own potential contribution to Torah scholarship. However, to elicit this spark, ordinary conversation (שִׂיחָה) would not be sufficient. Instead, David managed to talk to people (שִׂיחָה) in such a manner that their innate Torah potential, their personal testimonial (עֵדוּת) to Hashem, would surface[1] (*Imrei Emes, Maggidei HaEmes*).

---

1. *Chazal* succinctly summarized David's talent for eliciting every individual's portion in Torah by stating (Vayikra Rabbah 20:1), כל הרואהו נזכר לתלמודו, "everyone who would see [David] would recall his learning" (*Maggidei HaEmes*).

■ אֵיזֶהוּ גִבּוֹר? הַכּוֹבֵשׁ אֶת יִצְרוֹ — *Who is strong? He who subdues his personal inclination.*

◈ Who Becomes Mighty

> כלומר דבוודאי אלו יש להם ענין ושייכות רק כובש יצרו הוא גבורה בנפש וגבור
> כפשטי׳ הוא גבור בהגוף.

The *mishnah* is not necessarily denying that those who are physically strong may deserve the title גִבּוֹר, but rather it is emphasizing that even those who are strong in a *physical* sense can *become* strong spiritually by controlling their Evil Inclination.

◈ His Own Yetzer Hara

> רצה לומר יצרו המיוחד לו, שלכל אחד יש יצר מיוחד לדבר אחד, ולזה צריך כל
> אחד לעשות לעצמו גדרים וסייגים בדברים שרואה שיצרו תוקף עליו להכשילו
> בו, כי כל אחד גלל כן נברא, וזהו שמעינו בגמרא (שבת קח, ב) שכל אחד
> מהאמוראים היה זהיר טפי בדבר אחד.
>
> איתא בספרים שלכל אחד יש לו יצר הרע המיוחד לו. וכן מצינו אצל דוד המלך
> ע״ה (תהלים יא, כד) ואשתמר מעוני, היינו עון שלי.

The Maggid of Koznitz emphasized the uniqueness of each individual's Yetzer Hara. As the *mishnah* states, הַכּוֹבֵשׁ אֶת יִצְרוֹ, he who conquers *his* Evil Inclination. Once we become aware of our own very personal temptations, we are uniquely positioned to take corrective measures to curb this impulse to sin. The Gemara (*Shabbos* 118b) relates that each of the Amoraim (sages of the Talmud) were particularly diligent in performing a certain *mitzvah* or displaying a particular character trait. The *Imrei Emes* corroborated this approach by noting that David did not merely guard himself from sinning but rather, as he says, וָאֶשְׁתַּמֵּר מֵעֲוֹנִי, *I was vigilant against my sin* (*Tehillim* 18:24). David guarded himself from *his* sin — his particular weakness (*Maggidei HaEmes*).

◈ Channeling the Evil Inclination to Serve a Higher Purpose

> כבר נודע מה שכתבו רבותינו הקדושים ועי׳ בס׳ רמזי תורה כי פי׳ כובש שלא
> לדחותו רק לכבשו להיות נכנע ומבוטל להקדושה וזה גבורה גדולה. אדמו״ר

זצוק״ל הלב שמחה ביאר בדברות קדשו בפ׳ פינחס (תשל״ז) על הפסוק (במדבר כח, ד) את הכבש אחד תעשה בבקר ואת הכבש השני תעשה בין הערבים, כי איש ישראל צריך שיקריב לפני ה׳ קרבנות תמיד, שנים בכל יום, קרבן אחד בשחרית וקרבן אחד בין הערבים.

By using the expression כּוֹבֵשׁ, *to subordinate* (rather than דּוֹחֶה, *push away*), the *mishnah* is hinting at the most efficacious method of dealing with the *Yetzer Hara* — not destroying it, but rather *subordinating* it, to serve our better impulses (to our *Yetzer Hara*).

In a homiletical sense, we may reinterpret the phrase אֶת הַכֶּבֶשׂ הָאֶחָד תַּעֲשֶׂה בַבֹּקֶר וְאֵת הַכֶּבֶשׂ הַשֵּׁנִי תַּעֲשֶׂה בֵּין הָעַרְבָּיִם, *You shall offer the one sheep in the morning, and the second sheep shall you offer in the afternoon* (*Shemos* 29:39), to refer to the daily "sacrifice" of the *Yetzer Hara*. Every morning and every afternoon we recapture (related to כּוֹבֵשׁ אֶת יִצְרוֹ) and regain control of our Evil Inclination (*Lev Simchah, Maggidei HaEmes*).

◆§ Permanently Subdue the Evil Inclination

לשון הכובש כי יש שאדם מתגבר על היצר ואחר כך שוב מתגבר היצר, . . . ולכן נזכר לשון כיבוש לכבוש את היצר שלא יכול שוב להתגבר עליו.

Just as a warrior who captures his foe *permanently* suppresses him, so too by *capturing* (כּוֹבֵשׁ) the *Yetzer Hara*, we ensure that it will never again pose a threat to us (*Beis Yisrael, Maggidei HaEmes*).

■ טוֹב אֶרֶךְ אַפַּיִם מִגִּבּוֹר — *He who is slow to anger is better than the strong man.*

כי הגבור ללחום וכדומה אף שעושה מה שלבו חפץ בגבורתו שהוא גבור מאחר שרצון לבו אינו ברשותו נמצא כי אינו עושה כרצונו כלל רק ברוח שטות שבא לו במהירות ואין זה רצונו שהרי אח״כ מתחרט אח״כ נמצא כי הגבורה הוא רק כשלבו ברשותו שיכול להטותו כרצונו א״כ יש לו ענין הגבורה.

Perhaps, we can best appreciate the superiority of moral strength over physical might if we realize that only the morally strong are in control of themselves. While the mighty often act impulsively — and often later regret what they have done — the morally strong individual is in complete control of his actions. What greater manifestation of strength is there than the ability to control one's behavior!

◆§ Moral Strength Resulting from Confronting the Yetzer Hara

בהרע״ב ארך אפים הבא מצד הגבורה של כבוש היצר. לא מצד רכות הטבע כו׳.
קשה נהי דלהאדם טוב יותר כשבא מצד גבורה אבל אינו משבח את האדם רק
את המדה של אריכות אפים וזה ודאי טוב יותר כשבטבעו מאריך אף. ואפשר
לומר כשבא מצד גבורה מאריך אף תמיד ומצד הטבע הוא רק כשבטבעו מסכים
לזה.

A ccording to the *Bartenura*, the *pasuk* טוֹב אֶרֶךְ אַפַּיִם מִגִּבּוֹר refers to patience
that derives from strength, i.e. successfully conquering the *Yetzer Hara*.
In contrast to those individuals who are blessed with a patient personality —
but whose patience sometimes suffers during difficult times — someone who
attains the virtue of patience by taming his *Yetzer Hara* will remain patient,
even when his natural inclinations dictate otherwise.

■ וּמֹשֵׁל בְּרוּחוֹ מִלֹּכֵד עִיר — *And a master of his passions is better than
a conqueror of a city.*

◆§ Conquering the World, Not a Mere City

האדם נקרא עולם קטן (תנחומא פקודי ג, א) ועיר רק חלק קטן מעולם לכן
מושל ברוחו עדיף מלוכד עיר ומי שלבו ברשותו ומושל ברוחו נקרא גבור הכובש
עולם.

W hereas the hero conquers a city, the spiritual giant who tames his *Yetzer
Hara* has conquered an entire world — himself! (Cf. *Midrash Tanchuma
Pekudei* 3:1 which describes the human being as a "small world.")

■ אֵיזֶהוּ עָשִׁיר? הַשָּׂמֵחַ בְּחֶלְקוֹ — *Who is rich? He who is happy with his
lot.*

◆§ Our Attitude Towards Wisdom vs. Our Attitude Towards Wealth

איזהו חכם הלומד מכל אדם . . . אבל עשיר ההיפוך מזה להיצמצם שמח בחלקו
כי הם מהיפוך להיפוך.

It is significant that the *mishnah* advocates a totally different position regarding acquisition of wealth than it does towards acquiring wisdom. While we are encouraged to acquire as much wisdom as possible, even to the extent of learning from others, regarding wealth we are urged to *limit* our ambitions (be content with our lot).

≈§ His Portion

עוד פי' השמח בחלקו שעיקר שמחתו בעשרו שיודע שהעושר מיוחד לו שבוודאי שייך העשירות אליו כי פועל אדם ישולם לו וממילא אינו חומר יותר שהרי אין עיקר שמחתו בעשרו רק בחלקו מצד זה שהעשירות חלקו הוא שהשי"ת חלק זה אליו בפרט, ועל זה הראיה יגיע כפיך כי תאכל כו' שזה שבא מגיע כפו שייך אליו בפרט.

ובזה נבין לשון תד"א שאמר הקב"ה עשיר ושמח בחלקו הפי' שאין לומר ששמח בחלקו מצד הריבוי שהרי הכל שלו רק הלשון שמח שנאמר עליו מצד שחלקו הוא בכאן והחיות ממנו ית' א"כ שהוא חלק מעצמותו עי"ז השמחה וחלקו הוא בנ"י.

True wealth is attained by the individual who recognizes that Hashem has allocated him *his* proper portion (חֶלְקוֹ) — no more and no less. Such a wholesome attitude is based on the unshakable belief that Hashem compensates every individual equitably for his efforts.

The relationship between feeling amply compensated and the joy derived from true wealth is designated by the verse cited by the *mishnah*, יְגִיעַ כַּפֶּיךָ כִּי תֹאכֵל, *When you eat of the labor of your hands* (*Tehillim* 128:2). When you enjoy the fruit of *your* labor, recognizing that what you have is provided by Hashem to meet *your* needs, Hashem will make you happy.

In this light, we can comprehend an otherwise inscrutable *Tanna D'Vei Eliyahu* which describes Hashem as "wealthy and satisfied with His portion." It would certainly be inappropriate to depict Hashem as being "content" with the *quantity* of His wealth inasmuch as the entire universe is His. Rather, *Chazal* are emphasizing that Hashem is "justifiably" proud of His universe and especially of *Klal Yisrael* who are created and sustained by Him.

≈§ More Than I Deserve

כבר נודע אשר הריבוי בא מברכת ה' כמו שכתוב (משלי י, כב) ברכת ד'. היא תעשיר, אולם כשיש לו בחינת השמח בחלקו שמודה להשי"ת על מעט שיש לו שיודע ומבין שגם זה אינו כפי מעשיו אם כן שורה על זה ברכת ד'.

בְּחֶלְקוֹ, שֶׁנֶּאֱמַר: "יְגִיעַ כַּפֶּיךָ כִּי תֹאכֵל אַשְׁרֶיךָ וְטוֹב
לָךְ." "אַשְׁרֶיךָ" — בָּעוֹלָם הַזֶּה, "וְטוֹב לָךְ" — לָעוֹלָם
הַבָּא.

While it may seem difficult to achieve the state of being content with one's portion, this objective can be realized if we recall that all that we have is far more than we deserve. If we adopt this wholesome attitude — of appreciating that all our material wealth is an unrequited Divine gift — Hashem will, in turn, bless all our efforts.

⊷§ Who Becomes Rich

איזהו עשיר שנעשה עי"ז עשיר.

While other individuals may already *be* wealthy, only one person can *become wealthy* — even without having a lot of money — he who is content with his lot (הַשָּׂמֵחַ בְּחֶלְקוֹ).[1]

⊷§ Two Criteria for True Wealth

פירוש מי שהוא עשיר והוא שמח בחלקו הוא עשיר וראיה ממה שכתוב אשריך
בעולם הזה הרי שיש לו עשירות.

This *mishnah* may be understood as referring to a person who is already materially wealthy. While he may perceive that he is wealthy, in reality, material possessions alone are not enough to attaining true wealth. It is only by integrating wealth and satisfaction with one's lot that we can be truly wealthy. This approach is supported by the closing words of the verse quoted from *Tehillim*, אַשְׁרֶיךָ וְטוֹב לָךְ, *You are praiseworthy and all is well with you* (128:2). This seemingly applies to the individual who is blessed with material possessions, as the *mishnah* explains: "You are praiseworthy, in This World."

■ יְגִיעַ כַּפֶּיךָ כִּי תֹאכֵל אַשְׁרֶיךָ וְטוֹב לָךְ — *When you eat of the labor of your hands, you are praiseworthy and all is well with you.*

⊷§ A Happy Person Lacks Nothing

---

1. We may interpret the previous segments of the *mishnah* similarly. אֵיזֶהוּ חָכָם? הַלּוֹמֵד מִכָּל אָדָם, Who *becomes* a wise man? He who learns from every person. אֵיזֶהוּ גִבּוֹר? הַכּוֹבֵשׁ אֶת יִצְרוֹ, Who *becomes* mighty? He who subdues his personal inclination.

with his lot, as it is said (Tehillim 128:2): "When you eat of the labor of your hands, you are praiseworthy and all is well with you." "You are praiseworthy" — in This World; "and all is well with you" — in the World to Come.

אשריך בעוה"ז דע"י ששמח על כל דבר א"כ מה חסר לו בעוה"ז.

A person who rejoices over whatever he receives feels that he lacks nothing. Thus, he will always be happy in This World.

◆§ The Perils of Overspending

אבל האוכל יותר ממה שמרויח אין זה עשירות רק כעין גזל, ויש לפרש דכשנהנה מיגיעו אז הוא שמח בחלקו מה שאין כן כשבא להון שלא ביגיעה אז מי שיש לו מנה רוצה מאתים.

By citing the *pasuk* יְגִיעַ כַּפֶּיךָ כִּי תֹאכֵל, the *mishnah* is expanding the definition of wealth to include the determination to consume only that which we legitimately earned. Consuming beyond one's means resembles theft, since invariably one may be forced to resort to illicit means of obtaining money. Moreover, true contentment can only be obtained by enjoying the *legitimate* fruits of one's labor. Someone who acquires wealth that he did not earn will often lust for more wealth, as *Chazal* state, מִי שֶׁיֵּשׁ לוֹ מָנֶה רוֹצֶה מָאתַיִם, "one who possesses a *manah* desires two *manah*."

◆§ Rejoice in This World — Rejoice in the World to Come

כפיך כ"ת כו' פי' כשיהי' אשריך בעוה"ז ותשמח כשתאכל יגיע כפיך אז וטוב לך, וזהו הראי' שמביא מהפסוק דכיון ששכר ירא ה' הוא אשריך בעוה"ז וטוב לך כלומר שיהי' לו שמחה מזה שאשריך כו' ש"מ ששבח גדול הוא השמח בחלקו.

The *mishnah's* statement, *"You are praiseworthy"* — in This World; *"and all is well with you"* — in the World to Come, is not merely stating two unrelated concepts but is rather drawing a link between happiness in This World and happiness in the World to Come. By rejoicing in the fruits of your hard-earned labor in This World, and not coveting another's wealth, you will merit to enjoy the bountiful "good" of the World to Come.

By citing this *pasuk* and interpreting it as referring to This World and the World to Come, the *mishnah* is demonstrating the significance of one's rejoicing in his lot. By rewarding those who fear Hashem (see the *pasuk* which precedes that cited, אַשְׁרֵי כָּל יְרֵא ה' הַהֹלֵךְ בִּדְרָכָיו, *Praiseworthy is each person who fears Hashem, who walks in His paths*) with the blessing of enjoying the fruit of their labor, we may deduce that this is indeed a great privilege.

◄§ The Sweat of Your Hands, Not Your Head

הרבי מקאצק ז"ל אמר אימרא חריפא על פסוק זה כי כאשר רק הידים עובדות מבלי שהראש והמוח יהיו שותפים בעסקים, והיינו כפיך יגיע בלבד תאכל, אזי אשריך וטוב לך, משום שאם כשעובדים עם הידים משתתפים גם את הראש לפרנסה אזי כבר לא לומדים ולא מתפללים.

The Kotzker Rebbe noted that only hands (כַּפֶּיךָ) should be involved in the struggle to earn a livelihood.[1] If one becomes so immersed that his entire intellect is absorbed in the pursuit of wealth, then invariably the spiritual aspect of life — Torah study and prayer — are bound to suffer (*Maggidei HaEmes*).

■ — אֵיזֶהוּ מְכֻבָּד? הַמְכַבֵּד אֶת הַבְּרִיּוֹת, שֶׁנֶּאֱמַר: ,,כִּי מְכַבְּדַי אֲכַבֵּד, וּבֹזַי יֵקָלוּ." *Who is honored? He who honors others, as it is said: "For those who honor Me I will honor, and those who scorn Me shall be degraded."*

◄§ Honoring Hashem by Honoring People

קשה דהולי"ל המכבד את הקב"ה כמ"ש כי מכבדי אכבד ואולי שאין שייך כלפי מעלה אך הלא מצינו כבד את ה' מהונך ווי"ל דמכבד לבריות מטעם כי הם בראוי השי"ת ורצונו ית' לכבדם הרי זה מכבד להקב"ה . . .
השי"ת מלך הכבוד וחולק כבוד ליראיו כמו שאמרו חכמינו ז"ל (ברכות נח, א) בלשון הברכה של ראיית המלך שחלק מכבודו לבשר ודם וכמו בן מה שמצאנו כבוד בעולם מצד כי כל מה שברא הכל לכבודו ולפי מה שאדם נכבד במעשיו יותר יש פאר וכבוד למי שבראו.
ולכך המכבד את הבריות ואינו מקפיד כ"כ על טוב רק האיש מצד שהם מצד בריותיו של הקב"ה . . . הוא מורה בזה שכל הכבוד מצד הבורא ית"ש והוא מרבה כבוד

1. Please refer to our commentary on *Perek* 2, *mishnah* 2, citing the *Kedushas Levi's* emphasis on applying practical *Halachah* in the workplace: Even when one's hands are immersed in the struggle for a livelihood, one's mind should be preoccupied with Torah.

Who is honored? He who honors others, as it is said (I Shmuel 2:30): "For those who honor Me I will honor, and those who scorn Me shall be degraded."

שמים מאד. מייירי כשאין לו שום מעלה מ׳׳מ יוכל להיות מכובד כשיכבד ברידות.

It seems somewhat surprising that we prove the significance of honoring people by citing a *pasuk* that speaks about honoring Hashem.

One might suggest that the term מְכַבֵּד הַבְּרִיּוֹת, honoring Hashem's creatures, is a mere euphemism; rather than implying that mortals can truly honor Hashem, the *Tanna* merely hints at the honor due Him by speaking of the honor that we should accord to our peers. This explanation presents a difficulty, however, since we find explicit references in *Tanach* to honoring Hashem (e.g. *Mishlei* 3:9, כַּבֵּד אֶת ה׳ מֵהוֹנֶךָ, *Honor Hashem with your wealth*).

Perhaps, by citing "For those who honor Me I will honor," the *mishnah* is stating the underlying reason for honoring people — we do so because they are Hashem's creations. The relationship between honoring Hashem and honoring people is reflected in the *berachah* recited upon seeing a monarch — שֶׁחָלַק מִכְּבוֹדוֹ לְבָשָׂר וָדָם, *Who has apportioned of His glory to a mortal*. While we are paying our respects to a mortal, we recognize that we are in fact giving praise and honor to Hashem.

One of the most important ramifications of this "revised" definition of honor is that we should pay little attention to the *nature* of the individual being honored. *Everyone* was created by Hashem and thus deserves our respect. In fact, by honoring someone because they are Hashem's creation, we are, in effect, honoring Hashem.

Whereas the *mishnah* previously spoke of wisdom, wealth and strength, we now focus on the individual who *lacks* all those virtues. Despite being poor, unintelligent and weak, this individual eminently deserves to be honored simply by virtue of being created by Hashem.

◆§ Only Hashem Can Dispense Honor

דעיקר כבוד משמים ולא מבשר ודם. ועל ידי שמכבד ברידותיו של הקב׳׳ה זוכה
לכבוד משמים כמש׳׳כ כי מכבדי אכבד כו׳.

It is significant that the reward for honoring other human beings is to be honored by Hashem (rather than by those particular individuals). This is based on the fact that true honor can only come from Hashem. By honoring mortals, Hashem's creations, we merit to be honored by Hashem (*Yecha'hein Pe'er, Maggidei HaEmes*).

[ב] בֶּן עַזַּאי אוֹמֵר: הֱוֵי רָץ לְמִצְוָה קַלָּה, וּבוֹרֵחַ מִן הָעֲבֵרָה; שֶׁמִּצְוָה גוֹרֶרֶת מִצְוָה, וַעֲבֵרָה גוֹרֶרֶת עֲבֵרָה, שֶׁשְּׂכַר מִצְוָה מִצְוָה, וּשְׂכַר עֲבֵרָה עֲבֵרָה.

2.

■ בֶּן עַזַּאי אוֹמֵר: הֱוֵי רָץ לְמִצְוָה קַלָּה — *Ben Azzai said: Run to [perform even] a "minor" mitzvah.*

✦§ Should One Prefer to Do a "Minor" Mitzvah?

שׂשכר מצוה כו'. כי עיקר עשיית מצוה לעשות ציווי הקב"ה ואין הפרש בין קלה לחמורה אף כי גורם נחת רוח יותר בחמורה, אבל כשבאה מצוה זו לפניו הרי היא כאילו הציווי עתה כי אין המשנה מדברת לדחות החמורה מפני הקלה רק שהרצון לקלה יהיה ממש באותו חשק ורצון כמו לחמורה.
וזה טעם ברכת אשר קדשנו במצותיו וצונו מצד זה באין לקיים המצוה. אולי דוקא למצוה קלה שהיא לשם שמים ביותר. או הפי' אף למ"ק כבחמורה.

The *mishnah* is urging us to have an enthusiastic response towards performing a "minor" *mitzvah*. Indeed, if one could only perform one of two *mitzvos*, one being more stringent than the other, certainly the more stringent *mitzvah* would enjoy priority. The *mishnah* here is recommending that when performing a *mitzvah* we focus entirely on the *mitzvah* that we are *presently* performing — regardless of its status compared to other *mitzvos*. If we recall that we are primarily observing *mitzvos* because of our desire to perform Hashem's will — rather than because of the reward awaiting us (which may be commensurate with the significance of the *mitzvos*) — we would make no distinction between *mitzvos*. To emphasize the ultimate equality of all *mitzvos*, *Chazal* instituted that in every *berachah* recited prior to performing a *mitzvah*, we recite the word (אֲשֶׁר קִדְּשָׁנוּ בְּמִצְוֹתָיו וְצִוָּנוּ), that we are performing the *mitzvos* to fulfill Hashem's command.

In fact, one may argue that performing a "minor" *mitzvah* assumes greater significance because it is done *solely* to fulfill Hashem's will, whereas one who performs a "greater" *mitzvah* may be motivated by the potential reward.

✦§ Run to Perform a Mitzvah

פעם בקש הגאון רבי עקיבא אייגר לתהות על קנקנו של נכדו של הרה"ק רבי אייגר שהצטרף לחבריא הקדושה בקאצק, ושאלו אודות שיטת בן עזאי במס' שבת (ה, ב) הסובר דמהלך כעומד דמי והקשו בתוס' (בד"ה בשלמא לבן עזראי) בשם

[2] *Ben Azzai says: Run to [perform even] a "minor" mitzvah, and flee from sin; for one mitzvah leads to another mitzvah, and one sin leads to another sin; for the reward of a mitzvah is a mitzvah, and the reward of a sin is a sin.*

הירושלמי על דעתיה דבן עזאי אין אדם מתחייב על ד׳ אמות ברה״ר לעולם דיעשה כמי שהונחה על כל אמה ואמה ויפטר ומשני משכחת לה בקופץ. ותמה הגרע״א וכי גזר רבה (בשופר לולב ומגילה) שמא יעבירנו ה׳ אמות ברה״ר רק בענין שקופץ ד״א (והא מילתא דלא שכיחא הוא). ור׳ לייבל אייגר ענה בדרך שאלה ״איננו מבין, הלא כאשר בא מצוה לידי יהודי הרייהו קופץ״! והוסיף מרן אדמו״ר זצוקללה״ה שיש לסייע לדבריו ממתני׳ דהכא, דבן עזאי לשיטתו דקאמר לעולם הוי רץ למצוה קלה כבחמורה, א״כ חזינן דסבירא ליה שעל האדם לרוץ בעשיית המצוות.

In order to illustrate the importance of running to perform a *mitzvah* with enthusiasm and alacrity, we cite a halachic discussion between Rabbi Akiva Eiger and his grandson, Rabbi Leibele Eiger, who had become a follower of the Kotzker Rebbe. (While some of the halachic points may be a bit involved, the overall message is well worth the effort.) It is well known that *Chazal* prohibited sounding the *shofar* when Rosh Hashanah occurs on Shabbos because they were concerned that someone might carry the *shofar* four cubits in a public thoroughfare, an activity prohibited on Shabbos. Rabbi Akiva Eiger asked: Ben Azzai maintains that one is only liable for carrying four cubits if he jumps that distance while carrying (see *Shabbos* 5b, *Tosafos* s.v. בשלמא). According to Ben Azzai: Why would the Sages prohibit the observance of so vital a precept as *shofar* because of the unlikely event that someone would jump so great a distance while carrying the *shofar*?

His grandson, already steeped in chassidic thought, responded, "Doesn't every Jew jump while performing *mitzvos*?" The *Pnei Menachem* cited this *mishnah* to corroborate R' Leibele Eiger's answer, noting that Ben Azzai states in our *mishnah*, הֱוֵי רָץ לְמִצְוָה, always *run* to a *mitzvah* — and when one runs he takes broad strides.

⸗§ Leading to Greater Things

ויש לפרש עוד שהיא עצה איך לבוא לחמורה שעל ידי הקלה לעשות יבוא לחמורה.

Through performing a "minor" *mitzvah*, which may be easier to observe, we merit the opportunity to perform a more stringent *mitzvah*.

⋑§ Flee From "the" Sin

וכן ובורח מן העבירה ה' הידועה, פי' העבירה הקלה וכמו מקודם במצוה.
ואמר הרבי מאלכסנדר זצ"ל על דרך דאיתא (נזיר כג, ב) גדולה עבירה לשמה
והכוונה שהגם שזו העבירה בעצמה היא לשמה, עם כל זה תברח ממנה משום
עבירה גוררת עבירה ויבוא לעשות עבירה פשוטה גם כן וזה העבירה עבירה
הידועה לשמה.
ולפי זה הפירוש קלה היינו שלא לשמה.

The term מִן הָעֲבֵרָה, "from *the* sin" (implying a specific sin), may be continuing the thought which preceded it, which discussed observing minor
mitzvos. Just as we begin by observing "minor" *mitzvos* (see commentary
above), which in turn will lead us to observe more stringent *mitzvos*, so too,
we commence our regimen of staying away from *aveiros* by fleeing from
even the "lighter" *aveiros*. This will lead us to eventually abstain from the
more "difficult" *aveiros* (those which we are more tempted to violate) as
well.

Alternatively, R' Henoch of Alexander explained that the term "from *the*
sin" refers to a sin committed for "Hashem's sake." The Gemara (e.g. *Nazir* 23b)
relates that on occasion one may be justified in performing an *aveirah* in the
interest of Hashem and *Klal Yisrael*.[1] However, such a "Divinely sanctioned
sin" should rarely be committed — and certainly not without the sanction of
Klal Yisrael's greatest authorities. Thus, the *mishnah* is warning us: No matter
how pure your intention, flee from sin! Do not justify transgressing Hashem's
will in order to save *Klal Yisrael*. To prove the long-term damage caused by
committing this initial sin, the *mishnah* continues, "*one sin leads to another sin,*"
committing such a "rarefied" sin invariably leads to other, less "noble" violations. In this context, we may reinterpret the term מִצְוָה קַלָּה as referring to a
mitzvah performed שֶׁלֹּא לִשְׁמָהּ, not necessarily for Hashem's sake but simply
because of personal benefit (glory, prestige). Nonetheless, perform this "minor"
mitzvah. In that merit you will eventually perform *mitzvos* for their own sake.
As the *mishnah* says, מִצְוָה גּוֹרֶרֶת מִצְוָה, *one mitzvah leads to another mitzvah.*

⋑§ First Flee From Sin, Then Run to Perform Mitzvos

יי"ל הוי רץ למצוה קלה כשאתה בורח מן העבירה, שלא תרוץ למצוה
כשהעבירה בידך.

---

1. The Gemara cites Yael's relationship with Sisra prior to her heroic slaying of him as an example
of that seldom-used principle. It is universally accepted that this principle is not applied in
contemporary times.

The juxtaposition of running to *mitzvos* and fleeing from *aveiros* may be significant. As the *Lev Simchah* pointed out, it is senseless to actively pursue *mitzvos* while at the same time still "clutching" *aveiros*. Only after fleeing sin can one truly seek out *mitzvos* (*Lev Simchah, Maggidei HaEmes*).

■ שֶׁמִּצְוָה גוֹרֶרֶת מִצְוָה — *For one mitzvah leads to another mitzvah.*

◂§ By Performing One Mitzvah, I Am Performing All Mitzvos

ויש להבין למה הוצרך התנא לטעם שמצוה גוררת מצוה הרי המצוה עצמה מצד הציווי יש לרוץ אחרי' לקיימה אך כי בא לומר שיש באמת בקיום המצוה קלה ג''כ עשיות כל המצות בכח ולא בפועל כי אנו אומרים על מצוה א' תרי''ג מצות התלויים בה ופי' זה שהמצות מסודרים זה על זה ותלוין זב''ז וכשאדם מקיים מצוה א' נעשה פעולת כל המצות בכח מצוה זו שתלוין זה בזה למשל דברים המקושרים זע''ז שבהגבהת אחת יגבה הכל וזה עצמו הפי' מצוה גוררת מצוה שגוררת ממש שאר המצוות.

It seems as if the *mishnah* is explaining why we should pursue *mitzvos:* because one *mitzvah* leads to another *mitzvah.* Such justification, however, seems unnecessary since *mitzvos* are observed for their own sake and not because of their potential to lead to another *mitzvah.*

Upon closer analysis, the *mishnah* is implicitly questioning the *existence* of a "minor" *mitzvah,* rather than *justifying* its performance. While some *mitzvos* may *appear* to be of lesser significance, in reality by performing those commandments one is performing *all* of the 613 *mitzvos.* This theme is reflected in the supplication recited before donning *tallis* and *tefillin,* where it states וְתַרְיַ''ג מִצְוֹת הַתְּלוּיִם בָּהּ, *and the 613 mitzvos which are connected to it.* This can best be appreciated by contemplating a heavy load consisting of many items that are tied together. By lifting up any *one* of the items in the bundle, I am in fact lifting up *all* of the items. So too, by performing one *mitzvah* — which is intricately bound with and emanates from the same source, Hashem, as all other *mitzvos* — I am performing all *mitzvos.* In fact, the term מִצְוָה גוֹרֶרֶת מִצְוָה literally means *[one] mitzvah drags along another mitzvah.* (Refer to our commentary on שֶׁשְּׂכַר מִצְוָה מִצְוָה for further insight on the relationship between רָץ לְמִצְוָה קַלָּה and the balance of the *mishnah.*)

◂§ One Level of a Mitzvah Leads to Another

כי המצות הם רמזים תלוין באורות עליונים וע'' המצוה במעשה גשמיי יכול לעלות מדרגה אחר מדרגה עד שיהי' לו התקשרות לשורש המצוה. וע''ז איתא מצוה גוררת מצוה פ' בכל מצוה יש מדרגות רבות עד מצות ה' ממש.

To appreciate the full significance of this statement, מִצְוָה גוֹרֶרֶת מִצְוָה, it is useful to recall that David describes a *mitzvah* as מִצְוַת ה', *Hashem's commandment* (*Tehillim* 19:9). As is stated in Kabbalistic literature, the true — and most rarefied — form of *mitzvos* is beyond our understanding. The spiritual root of all *mitzvos* are only fully perceived by Hashem Himself. However, מִצְוָה גוֹרֶרֶת מִצְוָה, as we commence to observe *mitzvos* at the level of our comprehension — often in the physical form through which we perform *mitzvos* (e.g. wearing *tefillin*, taking the *lulav*) — we attain a more complete understanding of their deeper significance and eventually draw closer to Hashem the source of all *mitzvos* (adapted from *Sfas Emes*).

◈§ Even a Delayed Mitzvah

שעה ארוכה עמד פעם הרה"ק רבי יצחק מווארקא ז"ל כשסביבו חסידים רבים וחיכה ללבנה שהסתתרה מאחורי עננים, עמד בסבלנות המתין ואמר; "איתא מצוה גוררת מצוה, פי' מצוה אף על פי שהיא נגררת 'א מצוה וואס שלעפט זאך', גם היא מצוה, גם זמן ההמתנה וההכנה למצוה יחשב."

The term מִצְוָה גוֹרֶרֶת may also allude to a delayed *mitzvah* (related to גָּרַר, *drag*). Though a *mitzvah* may have been delayed, it is still a *mitzvah*, and the delay itself is its preparation.

Once, R' Yitzchak of Worka was waiting with his *chassidim* for the moon to appear from behind the clouds in order to be מְקַדֵּשׁ לְבָנָה (recite the blessing on the New Moon). He urged his followers not to become unduly frustrated by the excessive delay. After all, he reasoned, even the delay involved in a *mitzvah* — the time that is spent waiting for the moon to appear — is considered to be a *mitzvah*. As our *mishnah* reads, מִצְוָה גוֹרֶרֶת, a "schlepped" (delayed) *mitzvah*, is itself a *mitzvah* (*Maggidei HaEmes*).

■ שְׂכַר מִצְוָה מִצְוָה — *For the reward of a mitzvah is a mitzvah.*

◈§ The Same Reward for All Mitzvos

עיקר השכר הוא קיום המצוה.

Above, we suggested that the phrase מִצְוָה גוֹרֶרֶת מִצְוָה explains why we should perform the "minor" *mitzvos* as enthusiastically as — if not more than — more stringent *mitzvos*. In the same vein, "The reward of a *mitzvah* is a *mitzvah*" may also serve to justify treating "minor" *mitzvos* with the same deference as more stringent *mitzvos*. As the *mishnah* relates, שְׂכַר מִצְוָה מִצְוָה, the primary reward for performing *mitzvos* is the opportunity to fulfill Hashem's will (rather than actual compensation), which remains the same regardless of the *mitzvah's* stringency.

◆§ There Can Be No Greater Reward

> פי׳ כיון דיפה שעה א׳ בתומע״ט בעוה״ז מכ״ח עוה״ז א״כ אין לזה שכר שלם בעוה״ז רק שכר מצוה מצוה.

Perhaps the simplest reason for our *mishnah's* assertion that the reward for *mitzvos* is the opportunity to perform more *mitzvos* is that no other reward could possibly compare to a *mitzvah* itself. In fact, according to a later *mishnah* (4:22), all of the World to Come pales in comparison to a moment in This World where one can be immersed in Torah and *mitzvos*.

◆§ Accepting Hashem's Reward Is Also a Mitzvah

> שמה לי שרצונו בעשיות המצות או במה שרצונו ית׳ להשביעינו מטובו הלא אדרבא זה תכלית רצונו ית׳ . . . וזה ענין אמרם ז״ל הוו כעבדים המשמשין שלא ע״מ לקבל פרס, כי השכר עצמו צריכין לקבל לשמו ית׳ ולהתענג ביותר מזה שנעשה רצונו שהוא להטיב לכל שזה רצונו.

The term שְׂכַר מִצְוָה may refer to the reward I receive from Hashem for performing His *mitzvos*. That too — the satisfaction that Hashem receives upon bestowing His blessings upon us when we perform *mitzvos* — is considered to be a *mitzvah*. If we recall that our *raison d'être* is to be a source of "nachas" to Hashem, then it matters little whether His satisfaction is derived from our performance of His *mitzvos* or from our acceptance of His bounty as a result of performing His will.

In this light, we may redefine the laudable trait, of "Serving Hashem not for the purpose of receiving a reward" as applying to the proud acceptance of the reward for observing *mitzvos*. This person is not motivated by selfish considerations but the desire that Hashem derive "satisfaction" from showering His people with blessings.

3.

■ אַל תְּהִי בָז לְכָל אָדָם ... שֶׁאֵין לְךָ אָדָם שֶׁאֵין לוֹ שָׁעָה — *Do not be scornful of any person ... for you have no person without his hour.*

מַפְלִיג לְכָל דָּבָר, שֶׁאֵין לְךָ אָדָם שֶׁאֵין לוֹ שָׁעָה, וְאֵין ד / ג
לְךָ דָבָר שֶׁאֵין לוֹ מָקוֹם.

◆§ Everyone Was Created for a Purpose

בשם החסיד ז״ל כי ודאי לא לחנם בראו הבורא ית׳ ובוודאי שיש לו כוונה
מיוחדת והוא פי׳ אמיתי ופשוט נראה שא״י שעה כי השעות שחוזרין בכ״י כפי
הליכות וקביעות המזלות בהגלגל לכן מגיע לכ״א שעה פי׳ מזל הנ״ל.

Never disparage the importance of any one of Hashem's creations. While we may not understand why a particular individual exists, Hashem undoubtedly had a purpose for his creation. Perhaps, that individual's most significant moment has not yet arrived but it will, for every person has a time when he can and will utilize his potential (adapted from *Sfas Emes*).

The term שָׁעָה may also be understood literally as *hour*. Though the Jewish people, at times, may be able to overcome the natural forces that are empowered by Hashem and control the universe on a daily basis, we generally are affected by those forces known as מַזָּלוֹת (cf. *Shabbos* 156a and *Tosfos* ibid. s.v. אין). (For that reason אֲדָר is widely believed to be a fortuitous month and אָב is a difficult period.) Each individual, no matter how insignificant his impact thus far, will eventually enjoy a moment when his מַזָּל will "smile upon him."

◆§ Even the Wicked Enjoy Their Moments

כי כל מה שברא הקב״ה לכבודו ברא אם כן אף הרשעים גורמים כבוד שמים
בטובתם ושלא בטובתם ואם כן המבזה האדם ממעט כבוד שמים ומכל מקום אין
התנא מדבר ברשע גמור שמצוה לבזותו והרי זהו כבוד שמים ויש לבזות מעשיו
אבל לא שם אדם שבו שהרי יוכל להיתקן עוד ולכל אדם יש עכ״פ תיקון כנודע
ופי׳ שעה כתבו בספרים הקדושים מלשון רצון כמו שכתוב (בראשית ד,ד) וישע
ד׳ אל הבל כו׳ שהוא מלשון ריצוי לקונו ופי׳ שלכל אדם יש איזה דבר טוב
שיהיה מרוצה לקונו שעל זה נברא זה כנ״ל.

The *mishnah* cautions us not to be scornful of any person because the wicked, in their own strange way — often against their will — contribute to the sanctification of Hashem's Name. Often, the destruction of evil and the elimination of evildoers enhances glory of Hashem as much as the good deeds of the righteous,[1] and by disparaging the wicked, then we may be, unintentionally,

---

1. Cf. *Shemos* 14:4, *Rashi* s.v. ואכבדה discussing how Hashem's glory was enhanced when Pharaoh was destroyed.

and do not be disdainful of anything, for you have no person without his hour, and you have no thing without its place.

---

diminishing the glory of Hashem. In fact, the term שָׁעָה may be interpreted in this light to mean a saving grace (related to וַיִּשַׁע ה' אֶל הֶבֶל וְאֶל מִנְחָתוֹ, *Hashem turned to Hevel and to his offering, Bereishis 4:4*). Everyone, even the wicked ones, enjoy some saving grace which may be pleasing in Hashem's eyes.

It is important, however, to note that our *mishnah* is not referring to individuals who are totally wicked. By condemning the behavior of these people, we are honoring Hashem. On the other hand, the wicked *individuals* themselves, despite their present transgressions, should not be condemned since they enjoy the potential for improvement.

◆§ Why Ben Azzai Authored This Mishnah

ירצה שבן עזאי תמיד היה הולך וגדול עד כי גדל מאד, שהציץ במעשה מרכבה
ומת (חגיגה יד, ב) כנ"ל. ולא ח"ו שנענש, אלא שנדבק מרוב תשוקה כנ"ל. וכדי
שלא יעלה על לבו שום התפארות, לזה אמר תמיד אל תהי בז לכל אדם.

The Maggid of Koznitz noted, it is particularly appropriate that Ben Azzai — who plumbed the depths of the Torah's most esoteric secrets including מַעֲשֵׂה מֶרְכָּבָה, Yechezkel's vision of the Divine Presence,[1] should state, *do not be scornful of any person*. Despite the extraordinary spiritual heights to which he ascended, he reminded himself — and us — of the need to appreciate everyone, even the simplest Jew (*Maggidei HaEmes*).

◆§ Treasure the Good Moments

כשמקבלים פעם קצת רצון אמיתי כדאיתא שאין לך אדם שאין לו שעה צריכים
לאחוז בזה כדכתיב אחזתיו ולא ארפנו ולהשגיח שזה לא ילך לאיבוד, צריכים
לבקש שתשאר רשימה, קיסטא דחיותא, גם לזמן שנופלים וזהו שאיתא בגמ'
(ברכות ח, א) לעת מצא זו לעת מיתה היינו נפילה.
כל הכחות מהשבעים שנה הם הכנה למצוא בזה השעה.

The *Imrei Emes* interpreted this passage as a plea to treasure — and preserve — the good moments in life (i.e. those rare moments of spiritual bliss). If one

---

1. Cf. *Chagigah* 14b, that Ben Zoma's soul expired while he was contemplating some of the most esoteric secrets of the Torah. His premature death was not a punishment for studying these topics but rather the natural result of his soul attaining the level that it could no longer bear living in this material world.

can somehow hold on to these all too rare moments, one can be sustained spiritually for an entire lifetime. As Shlomo writes (*Shir HaShirim* 3:4): אֲחַזְתִּיו וְלֹא אַרְפֶּנּוּ, *I will grasp* those blissful moments, *and I will not loose my hold*, even in the more difficult phases of life (*Maggidei HaEmes*).

In another context, the *Imrei Emes* wrote that all of our spiritual efforts for an entire lifetime are directed at enjoying that one moment of spiritual growth and bliss.

■ וְאַל תְּהִי מַפְלִיג לְכָל דָּבָר ... וְאֵין לְךָ דָבָר שֶׁאֵין לוֹ מָקוֹם — *And do not be disdainful of anything ... and you have no thing without its place.*

כלומר שבכל דבר יש לו חיות מהשי"ת וזה החיות נקרא מקום ועל שם זה אמרו חז"ל שהקב"ה מקומו של עולם ואין עולמו מקומו והקב"ה נקרא בלשון חכז"ל מקום ב"ה ובו"ש והכלל שהנקודה חיות שבכל דבר נקרא מקום. וז"ש שלא יאמר על שום דבר שהוא מרוחק לגמרי מהקדושה אף שהוא דבר רע שמ"ל לו מקום והוא ניצוץ קדוש המחי' אותו ולשון מפליג הוא ניתוק וכריתה ממקום דביקתו שלא יאמר זה מקדושה ואדרבה ע"י שיודע שכל החיות בא מהקדושה יוכל לבטלו בשורשו.

The Omnipresent — known as מָקוֹם since His Presence fills the entire universe (cf. הקב"ה מְקוֹמוֹ שֶׁל עוֹלָם; *Bereishis Rabbah* 68:10) — is everywhere. While we may not perceive the *Shechinah* everywhere, do not commit the cardinal error of assuming that anything (לְכָל דָּבָר) is detached (מַפְלִיג) from Hashem's Presence. As the *mishnah* concludes, וְאֵין לְךָ דָבָר שֶׁאֵין לוֹ מָקוֹם, *and you have no thing without its place* (i.e. everything is sustained by the Presence of Hashem, known as מָקוֹם).

In fact, Chassidic tradition (dating back to the *Baal Shem Tov* and the *Maggid of Mezeritch*) asserts that a residue of the Divine Presence (known as נְקוּדָה הַפְּנִימִית, an inner Divine spark) is embedded in each of us, even in the evildoers, which allows one to persevere. Were it not for the presence of that Heavenly spark — and the potential for evildoers to utilize that spark as a means of returning to Hashem — evil would cease immediately. The presence of that Divine spark is also a portent of great hope. Even the evildoer, since he is never fully detached from Hashem, can build on his inner spiritual core and eventually find his way back to Hashem (adapted from *Sfas Emes*).

◆§ Everything Can Be Found in the Torah

דאמרי חז"ל בחקותו תלכו שתהיו עמלים בתורה למצוא בכל דבר אור התורה ... שיש בכל דבר חלק בתורה וע"ז אמרו א"ת מפליג לכל דבר להפרידו משורש התורה שאין לך דבר שאין לו מקום פ' בתורה.

על דרך שאמר דוד המלך ע"ה עד אמצא מקום לה' משכנות לאביר יעקב. דבר

הוא השכינה, כדאיתא במדרש בדבר ה' שמים נעשו היא המלוכה, אם כן דבר
מורה על המלוכה, אף שעתה בחורבן אין לה מקום בודאי עתיד להיות לה מקום,
וצריך כל אדם לשום אל לבו לקדש איבריו ולבו ומוחו ולברר כל גופו, למען יהיה
מקום פנוי לשכינה למלך מלכי המלכים הקב"ה, וישים תמיד מחשבתו לזאת
שיהא מחנהו קדוש שיוכל המלך לשכון בו, ותמיד יהיה מוכן ומזומן לזאת, ועל
ידי זה נזכה שהבורא יתברך יגאלינו בקרוב ויחזיר עבודת בית המקדש למקומ"ו
במהרה בימינו אמן.

We might also interpret the term מָקוֹם, *place*, to refer to the Torah's capacity to contain *everything*. The *mishnah* urges us, "Do not assume that anything — no matter how mundane — is 'detached' " (i.e. not included) in the Torah. The comment of *Chazal* that *"One should toil in the Torah,"* may refer to our obligation to search for the spiritual antecedents of *everything* in the Torah.

In fact, even those temporary measures instituted by *Chazal*, are derived from the Torah, which empowered *Chazal* to establish these practices. We can thus understand our *mishnah* as saying: In extraordinary times (שָׁעָה) or circumstances (מָקוֹם), *Chazal* were empowered to take unusual measures.

The Maggid of Koznitz interpreted this passage to refer to the *Shechinah's* "quest" for a resting place. Hashem's Presence is also known as דָּבָר, since the universe was created through Hashem's word — בִּדְבַר ה' שָׁמַיִם נַעֲשׂוּ, *by the word of Hashem the heavens were made* (*Tehillim* 33:6). His Presence was (and to an extent, still is) "seated" at the site of the *Beis HaMikdash*. It can also find a resting place (מָקוֹם) in the heart and soul of every Jew. It is our sacred obligation to attain that level of purity that we may indeed merit to be a repository for the *Shechinah*. Through our becoming a home for the דָּבָר, Divine word, the Divine Presence, we merit that it will return to Its proper abode, the rebuilt *Beis HaMikdash* (*Maggidei HaEmes*).

⋑ In the Right Hour You Can Find Your Place

הרמז על כל אדם שיכול למצוא את השעה, וגם את המקום וזה הרמז בשבת אל
יצא איש ממקומו ביום השביעי ... אין לך אדם שאין לו שעה אם שעה יודע ועושה
בשעה הזאת שרמזו חז"ל יפה שעה אחת בתשובה כו', אז אין לך דבר שאין לו
מקום הוא מוצא את המקום שיכול לעמוד בתשובתו.

In conclusion, let us consider the relationship between שָׁעָה, a fleeting *moment*, which is of course a *temporary* phenomenon, and מָקוֹם, *place*, which conveys a sense of permanence.

Through fully exploiting and properly utilizing the occasional good moment (אֵין לְךָ אָדָם שֶׁאֵין לוֹ שָׁעָה), we will not only enjoy that most prized moment of *teshuvah* and good deeds (cf. *mishnah* 22) but we will be able to maintain the

ד / ד

[ד] רַבִּי לְוִיטַס אִישׁ יַבְנֶה אוֹמֵר: מְאֹד מְאֹד הֱוֵי שְׁפַל רוּחַ, שֶׁתִּקְוַת אֱנוֹשׁ רִמָּה.

progress we make and ultimately find our permanent spiritual niche (מָקוֹם) in life, as well.

Perhaps the most opportune moment (שָׁעָה) for finding one's "niche" (מָקוֹם) is Shabbos, the day about which Moshe admonishes the Jewish people, אַל יֵצֵא אִישׁ מִמְּקֹמוֹ בַּיּוֹם הַשְּׁבִיעִי, *let no man leave his place on Shabbos* (*Shemos* 16:29). Do not leave; maintain a firm grip on the ideal time of the week. Preserve the spiritual gains that you make every Shabbos, as you find your place in life (*Beis Yisrael, Maggidei HaEmes*).

4.

■ — רַבִּי לְוִיטַס אִישׁ יַבְנֶה אוֹמֵר: מְאֹד מְאֹד הֱוֵי שְׁפַל רוּחַ, שֶׁתִּקְוַת אֱנוֹשׁ רִמָּה
Rabbi Levitas of Yavneh said: Be exceedingly humble in spirit, for the anticipated end of mortal man is worms.

⤳§ Always Remain Humble

> אין הפירוש להיות שפל מאוד דאם כן הו"ל מימר הוי שפל רוח מאוד רק הפירוש לראות היטב איך להיות תמיד שפל רוח וקאי מאוד על רוב הזהירות שצריך להיות בזה.
>
> הוי לשון הווה הי' שפל רוח . . . להיות שפל רוח – תמיד הזמן.

Seemingly, the *mishnah* is urging us to be very humble. However, if that were the *mishnah's* intent it should have said הֱוֵי שְׁפַל רוּחַ מְאֹד מְאֹד. By placing מְאֹד first, Rabbi Levitas is emphasizing the importance of exerting every effort (מְאֹד מְאֹד) to *remain* humble (*Sfas Emes*).

In a similar vein, R' Elimelech of Lyzhensk emphasized the use of the present tense הֱוֵי. Humility is a virtue that is commendable for all times and all seasons (*Maggidei HaEmes*).

⤳§ Feel Humble About Your Lack of Humility

> מה שכפל הלשון מאד מאד, היינו שגם זה אל יעצבוך מה שאין אתה שפל רוח.

By repeating the term מְאֹד, the *mishnah* is emphasizing not only the overriding importance of humility but the need to be humble if we seem unable to attain the prized virtue of humility. Some individuals are unable to feel

[4] *Rabbi Levitas of Yavneh says: Be exceedingly humble in spirit, for the anticipated end of mortal man is worms.*

---

humble, despite their many efforts (they decline all honors, and yet feel possessed by a feeling of haughtiness and superiority). Rather than becoming depressed and frustrated which, after all, is itself a subtle form of haughtiness (how could someone as distinguished as myself lack the *middah* of humility?), the *mishnah* is encouraging us to accept with humility and grace our inability to attain this prized virtue.

◆§ The Truly Humble Do Not Look Back

איתא כל הבורח מן הכבוד הכבוד רודף אחריו. ולכאורה למה מגיע לו העונש הזה הלא הוא בורח. ונראה משום שבשעה שהוא בורח הריהו מפנה ראשו ובוחן לדעת אם הכבוד רודף אחריו.

The Gemara (*Eruvin* 13b) relates that honor pursues those who flee from it. The question then arises: If this individual is sincerely avoiding honor, why should he be burdened with the undesirable attribute of honor? The *Chiddushei HaRim* responded: Indeed, one who truly flees will not be burdened with honors. However, the Gemara is referring to someone who, while running away from honor, turns around frequently to ensure that the honor that he "rejected" is still pursuing him (*Maggidei HaEmes*).

◆§ Acquiring Humility in Eretz Yisrael

בפ' שלח כתיב שאמר כלב טובה הארץ מאד מאד. ואיתא בספרים הרמז למאד מאד הוי שפל רוח. כי בארץ ישראל תמיד עיני ה״א בה, והרי איתא במקום גדולתו של הקב״ה שם אתה מוצא ענוותנותו לכן בארץ ישראל יכול האדם לסגל לעצמו מדת הענוה.

The *Lev Simchah* noted the parallel between the expression מְאֹד מְאֹד used in our *mishnah* and Calev's response to the Spies who maligned *Eretz Yisrael*. He said, טוֹבָה הָאָרֶץ מְאֹד מְאֹד, *the land is very, very good* (*Bamidbar* 14:7). Rabbi Levitas' choice of this expression indicates that the most propitious place to acquire humility is in *Eretz Yisrael*. As the Gemara (*Megillah* 31a) relates: כָּל מָקוֹם שֶׁאַתָּה מוֹצֵא גְבוּרָתוֹ שֶׁל הַקב״ה אַתָּה מוֹצֵא עַנְוְתָנוּתוֹ, which may be homiletically rendered: *The place where Hashem's greatness is most acutely felt [Eretz Yisrael] is also the place which is most conducive to acquire humility* (*Maggidei HaEmes*).

◆§ A Mortal's Final Wish

> וי"ל על פי מה שנודע כי אין מנוח להנשמה זולת כשהגוף נבלה ונאבד ונעשה רמה
> זולת צדיקים גדולים ולכן כתיב כאן אנוש שם הפחות שמקוה לזה שיעלה למקומו
> לכן טוב לו שבחייו יהיה שפל רוח בטל במציאות, ובעל המאמר רבי לויטס איש
> יבנה לשון חשיבות ולכן הזהיר על השפלות.

While the post-mortem deterioration of the body is usually not something we aspire to, the *mishnah's* choice of the term תִּקְוָה, *hope*, casts an entirely new perspective on this process. With the rare exception of some *tzaddikim* whose bodies never deteriorate, the *neshamah* of most individuals cannot rest in peace until the body's decomposition is complete. In this vein, Rabbi Levitas, despite his exalted status as a leading dignitary of Yavneh, especially urges us to adopt a humble lifestyle. Never forget that you are but a mere mortal (as indicated by the term אֱנוֹשׁ rather than the more prestigious אִישׁ) whose ultimate repose can only be achieved by adopting a humble life style.

◆§ An Antidote Against Decomposition

> י"ל כי זה עצה למעט הרמה על ידי שפלות כי קנאה וגאוה אחת היא ומי שאין
> בו קנאה אין עצמותיו מרקיבין כמו שאמרו חז"ל.

On the other hand, we may adopt the perspective that the body's decomposition, while a natural occurrence, is hardly ideal. It would certainly be far better if the body were to remain intact. To minimize the deterioration, it would be conducive to adopt a humble approach to life.

This interpretation, suggesting that humility prevents excessive decomposition, may be supported by a similar statement of the Gemara (*Shabbos* 152b) that anyone who lives a life free of jealousy will merit that his bones will not rot after his passing. Similarly, we may conclude that one who studiously avoids גַּאֲוָה, *haughtiness*, will be spared any indignities to their remains after death.

◆§ Humility and Resurrection (תְּחִיַת הַמֵּתִים)

> ויל"ק עפמ"ש חז"ל פ"ק דסוטה הקיצו ורננו ש"ע מי שנעשה שכן לעפר בחייו
> ורש"י פי' שאינו קם לתחה"מ לכן י"ל כי איש לשון חשיבות ואנוש פי' שחשוב
> גם בעיני עצמו ומתגאה לכן תקותו רמה שישאר רמה בקבר ולא יקום בתחה"מ.

We may also interpret the *mishnah* as impressing upon us the finality of the punishment inflicted upon the haughty: decomposition and nothing more, with no opportunity to participate in the ultimate Resurrection.

This interpretation is supported by the Gemara (Sotah 5a) defining the essential criterion for eligibility for resurrection: הָקִיצוּ וְרַנְּנוּ שֹׁכְנֵי עָפָר, *Arise and rejoice all those who have dwelt in the dust* (Yeshayahu 26:19). מִי שֶׁנַּעֲשָׂה שָׁכֵן לְעָפָר בְּחַיָּיו — This applies only to "those who have been neighbors (i.e. close) to the dust (acting as humble as earth) during their lifetime."

While virtually all Jews will participate in the Resurrection, only the truly humble will merit to rejoice (רַנְּנוּ) and burst into song at the moment of the Resurrection.

◄§ Our Greatest Hope: Remembering Our Mortality

שעיקר התקוה היא הבטול לאן אתה הולך ואם כן העיקר השפלות.

Alternatively, the *mishnah* may be emphasizing that the very thought of our mortality and the eventual decomposition of the body is our greatest source of salvation (תִּקְוָה). It is well known that one of the most effective antidotes against sinning is the thought of death (cf. Berachos 5a) (adapted from Sfas Emes).

■ מְאֹד מְאֹד הֱוֵי שְׁפַל רוּחַ — *Be exceedingly humble in spirit.* ■

◄§ Won't Others Suffer the Same Fate?

ומקשין הלא גם חבירו יהי' רמה וי"ל לפי שיש כמה מדרגות באדם, אדם גבר איש אנוש, ואנוש הפחות מכולם לכן אמר שתהי' שפי"ר אולי אתה אנוש. ואל יקשה כלל כל מה שמקשין העולם הלא בכל אדם תקותו רמה אם כן למה ישפיל בפני כל אדם כי אין זה טעם על השפלות רק טעם על מידת השפלות שזה עיקר התקוה כנ"ל.

The *mishnah* urges us to be humble in the presence of others because of our mortality and eventual decomposition. But will that other person not suffer a similar fate? If he is as mortal as I am, why subordinate myself to him? The resolution to this question may lie in the term אֱנוֹש, which always connotes the lowest spiritual level man can achieve. Never lose sight of the possibility that your friend may be on a much more exalted level than you. He may have attained the status of אָדָם, אִישׁ, or גֶּבֶר — terms that connote a more exalted spiritual life than the lowly אֱנוֹש. As an אֱנוֹש, who transgresses in This World and will suffer the consequences in the World to Come, you would do well to humble yourself before one on a higher level.

This question may also be resolved on the basis of our previous comment that the thought of eventual death is our greatest salvation, preventing us from

[ה] רַבִּי יוֹחָנָן בֶּן בְּרוֹקָא אוֹמֵר: כָּל הַמְחַלֵּל שֵׁם שָׁמַיִם בַּסֵּתֶר, נִפְרָעִין מִמֶּנּוּ בַּגָּלוּי. אֶחָד שׁוֹגֵג וְאֶחָד מֵזִיד בְּחִלּוּל הַשֵּׁם.

sinning. If so, the possibility that someone else may also suffer the same fate is irrelevant (adapted from *Sfas Emes*).

◈§ A Measure of Man Is His Recognition of His Mortality

תקות אנוש, אימתי, בזמן שמחזיק עצמו לרמה.

The *Imrei Emes* inserted a comma between the phrase תִּקְוַת אֱנוֹשׁ and the term רִמָּה, interpreting it in the following manner: If in the course of our lifetime we are so humble that we perceive ourselves to be nothing more than רִמָּה (decomposed flesh), then there is hope (תִּקְוַת אֱנוֹשׁ) (*Maggidei HaEmes*).

◈§ A Measure for Measure

איתא בגמ' קשה רמה למת כמחט בבשר החי ר"ל שכמה שאדם עקץ ודקר לחבירו במדקרות לשונו, כך ייענש אחרי מותו ליעקץ מן הרימה. וזהו אומרו שתקות אנוש רמה, תקות מלשון קו המדה, מדה כנגד מדה.

The Bendiner Rav noted that the term תִּקְוַת is related to קַו, *measuring rod.* The *mishnah* may be alluding to one of the major causes of the body's decomposition — hurting a peer's feelings. Just as one stung a peer with his caustic and insensitive remarks, so too, in direct proportion (תִּקְוָה), he will undergo the painful process of decomposition.

This approach is supported by the analogy drawn between the pain suffered from the insertion of a needle into live flesh and the decomposition of the body (cf. *Berachos* 18b). This analogy refers not only to the physical pain but also — and especially so — to the underlying cause, the sharp "needlelike" pricks and insensitive barbs directed at a peer by one's thoughtless remarks. This is the suffering associated with the decomposition of the body (*Maggidei HaEmes*).

◈§ Do Not Be Overly Concerned About Your Body

פעם שאל אחד את חוות דעתו של האדמו"ר מקאצק אם לעלות לארץ ישראל שאלו הרבי מקאצק "למה תרצה לעלות לשם?" השיב הלה "כדי שלא להצטער בצער גלגול מחילות לאחר פטירתי מן העולם" גער בו הרב מקאצק "וכי עד כדי

[5] *Rabbi Yochanan ben Beroka says: Whoever desecrates the Name of Heaven in secret, they will exact punishment from him in public; unintentional or intentional, both are alike regarding desecration of the Name.*

כָּךְ חָבִיב עָלֶיךָ גּוּפְךָ – עַד שֶׁאַתָּה דּוֹאֵג לְגוּפְךָ לְאַחַר פְּטִירָתְךָ?"

An individual once approached the Kotzker Rebbe about the possibility of moving to *Eretz Yisrael* because *Chazal* (*Kesubos* 112a) teach that those who are buried in the Diaspora will experience difficulties at the time of the Resurrection, a concept known as צַעַר גִּלְגּוּל מְחִילוֹת. The Kotzker Rebbe responded, "Do you cherish your body so much that you are concerned about what will occur to it after your passing?"[1]

5.

■ רַבִּי יוֹחָנָן בֶּן בְּרוֹקָא אוֹמֵר: כָּל הַמְחַלֵּל שֵׁם שָׁמַיִם בַּסֵּתֶר, נִפְרָעִין מִמֶּנּוּ בַּגָּלוּי — *Rabbi Yochanan ben Beroka says: Whoever desecrates the Name of Heaven in secret, they will exact punishment from him in public.*

◆§ How Is It Possible to Privately Desecrate Hashem's Name?

מִלַּת בַּסֵּתֶר תְּמוּהַ, כִּי אִם הָיָה בַּסֵּתֶר מַה חִלּוּל ה' אִיכָּא. אַךְ דְּנוֹדַע כִּי הִנֵּה הַבּוֹרֵא יתב"ש מְלֹא כָל הָאָרֶץ כְּבוֹדוֹ וְלֵית אֲתַר פָּנוּי מִינֵיהּ כְּלָל, וְהוּא הַנּוֹתֵן כֹּחַ גַּם בְּהוֹלְכִים לַחֲטוֹא, אִם כֵּן כַּאֲשֶׁר יַחֲשׁוֹב הָאָדָם זֹאת בְּוַדַּאי לֹא יֶחֱטָא, אַךְ כְּשֶׁחוֹטֵא הוּא מְבַקֵּשׁ לְהַסְתִּיר עַצְמוֹ מֵהַשְׁגָּחַת הַבּוֹרֵא יתב"ש לֵית אֲתַר פָּנוּי מִינֵיהּ כְּלָל וּכְלָל בְּשׁוּם אוֹפֶן, רַק שֶׁהוּא חוֹשֵׁב בְּדַעְתּוֹ שֶׁמַּסְתִּיר עַצְמוֹ מֵהַשְׁגָּחָתוֹ, נִמְצָא בָּזֶה שֶׁמַּסְתִּיר עַצְמוֹ מְחַלֵּל שֵׁם שָׁמַיִם, שֶׁעוֹשֶׂה פְּגָם וְהֶפְסֵק בִּמְצִיאוּת הַבּוֹרֵא. וְזֶה הַמְחַלֵּ"ל שֵׁם שָׁמַיִם, שֶׁעוֹשֶׂה זֶה הַמָּקוֹם חָלָל מֵאֵת הַבּוֹרֵא יִתְבָּרֵךְ, וְזֶהוּ פִּי' וְנוֹקֵב שֵׁם ה' שֶׁעוֹשֶׂה נֶקֶב וְחָלָל בְּשֵׁם ה', אַף כִּי בְוַדַּאי אִי אֶפְשָׁר לְהַסְתִּיר מִמֶּנּוּ יתב"ש בְּשׁוּם אוֹפֶן, כִּי הוּא מְמַלֵּא כָל עָלְמִין וּבְגוֹ כָל עָלְמִין.

The very concept of desecrating Hashem's Name in *private* seems to be an oxymoron. If no one knows about an individual's inappropriate behavior, how could Hashem's Name be profaned?

---

1. While burial in *Eretz Yisrael* is a time-honored tradition dating back to Yaakov Avinu (cf. *Kesubos* 111a), there are many reasons for this practice, especially the atonement associated with *Eretz Yisrael*, and it is not solely to prevent the body from suffering.

To resolve this question, we need to define carefully the concept of חִלּוּל הַשֵּׁם, which is usually translated as *desecration of Hashem's Name*. However, this term may also be related to חָלָל, which means *to create a vacuum*. Whenever one commits an act that would profane Hashem's Name — despite his awareness of Hashem's objections to such behavior — he is, in effect, trying to hide from the *Shechinah*. Worse yet, he is attempting to create a vacuum in which Hashem's Presence is not felt. While, of course, such blatant attempts at removing Hashem from our daily lives are bound to fail,[1] the sheer audacity of such an attempt creates, as it were, a certain "diminishment" in the perceptible Presence of the *Shechinah* on earth. If mortals act in blatant disregard of the Divine will, in some measure, the *Shechinah* is less palpable. When describing the ultimate act of desecration of Hashem's Name — blasphemy — the Torah uses a similar expression וְנֹקֵב שֵׁם ה', one who pronounces blasphemously (*Vayikra* 24:16). He is like someone who נֶקֶב, *pierces*, i.e. creates a hole in, Hashem's Name. By cursing Hashem, we are in a sense creating a vacuum in which His Presence is not felt (*Maggid of Koznitz, Maggidei HaEmes*).

◈§ His "Cover Is Blown"

ברש"י שלא יאמרו כו', הגם שיש באמת צדיק ורע לו זהו רצון הקב"ה בכדי שיהי' הבחירה חפשית והקב"ה מוותר בזה הגם שיש גם מזה ח"ו אבל מה שהאדם מוסיף ח"ו ודאי אסור לכן נפרעין ממנו בגלוי שיתגלה זה עצמו שבעל עבירה הוא.

The term נִפְרָעִין, generally interpreted as "punish," may also mean *to uncover, expose* (cf. *Shemos* 32:25 כִּי פְרָעֹה אַהֲרֹן, *for Aharon had exposed them*). If a person dares to desecrate Hashem's Name in private, while maintaining a very righteous public front (allowing others to deem him a *tzaddik*), his "cover" will be blown and eventually everyone will realize that his piety was merely a false front.

Rashi (*Yoma* 86) explains that Hashem felt compelled to "blow" the so-called *tzaddik's* cover in order to avoid the possibility that people will say that a truly righteous individual is suffering.

In truth, the concept of truly righteous suffering is found throughout the Talmud and Midrash. Yet, Hashem in His Infinite Wisdom tolerates the possible desecration of His Name that results from the suffering of the righteous. If anything, the phenomenon serves the purpose of reinforcing our sense of free will. If all the righteous were *immediately* rewarded (and all of the wicked immediately punished), no one would ever be tempted to sin.

---

1. Of course, the entire universe is suffused with Hashem's Presence. Even the capacity of the wicked to sin emanates from Hashem. Under ideal circumstances, a would-be sinner should desist from committing the misdeed by realizing that it is Hashem Who grants him the capacity to sin --- and to Whom he is ultimately accountable.

On the other hand, Hashem cannot condone the *chilul Hashem* caused by our own action. Thus, wicked individuals masking as the righteous not only are eventually punished, but their true identity is also revealed. This makes it abundantly clear that they deserved their fate and that they are not among the ranks of the suffering *tzaddikim*.

◄§ An Intuitive Grasp — Recognizing the Rasha

רצה לומר שהבורא יתב״ש מגלה ומפרסם חטאו לרבים, שבת קול יוצאת בכל יום דין פלניא דמריד במאריה ואף שאין שומע אותו, אף על פי כן מזלייהו חזו, ובא הכח הזה בלבות ומחשבות בני אדם.

The *Zohar* (*Nasso* 126b) relates that a Heavenly voice emanates daily proclaiming, דֵין פְּלַנְיָא דְמָרִיד בְּמָארֵיה, "This is the individual who rebelled against his Master (Hashem)." Anyone who desecrated Hashem's Name is exposed by this Heavenly voice. While most people will not actually *hear* this voice, Hashem provides some people with an *intuitive* grasp for recognizing those who have desecrated His Name (*Maggid of Koznitz, Maggidei HaEmes*).

◄§ Your Own Worst Enemy

או יאמר נפרעין ממנו בגלוי שהוא מודיע עצמו חטאו בדבריו ובתנועותיו בדברים אחרים, ואינו מבחין כלל, מכל מקום הצדיק יבחין וישמע דברים פנימיים מהחיצונים, וכמו שהיה מעשים רבים משים בפני צדיקים ואנשי מעשה מספרים מהבעש״ט ז״ל שאמר לתלמידיו שכל אדם העובר עבירה בלילה מודיעו בפיו ביום, ופעם אמר על בעל עגלה פלוני שלא הקפיד על טהרה בביתו, בדקו אחריו וראו איך שותה מכלי חדש וכשאמרו לו שצריכים לטובלו, השיבם "כן טבל, לא טבל, הכל שוה".

Alternatively, someone who profaned Hashem's Name is often his own worst enemy. While he adopts a pious front, at least in public, such an individual is unable to be *consistently* righteous. Eventually, the inconsistencies in his behavior will become apparent to those who are discerning enough. His entire bearing, his speech, his overall deportment, will eventually reveal his true identity (ibid.).

The Baal Shem Tov would tell his disciples that someone who commits a sin at night will unwittingly, the following day, reveal what he had done.

A certain wagon driver was known to be lax in his observance of the laws of ritual purity. One day, someone noticed him drinking from a new utensil which had not been immersed in a *mikveh*. When confronted with his apparent error, the wagon driver responded, "To immerse or not to immerse, it's all

[ו] רַבִּי יִשְׁמָעֵאל בַּר רַבִּי יוֹסֵי אוֹמֵר: הַלּוֹמֵד עַל מְנָת
לְלַמֵּד, מַסְפִּיקִין בְּיָדוֹ לִלְמוֹד וּלְלַמֵּד; וְהַלּוֹמֵד עַל
מְנָת לַעֲשׂוֹת, מַסְפִּיקִין בְּיָדוֹ לִלְמוֹד וּלְלַמֵּד, לִשְׁמוֹר
וְלַעֲשׂוֹת.

the same." This response reflected his indifference towards every aspect of
taharah (*Maggidei HaEmes*).

◄§ Sanctifying Hashem's Name in Private

א"כ יש ללמוד ק"ו מדה טובה המרובה שע"י קידוש שמו בסתר זוכין ג"כ
לבוא להקדושה בהתגלות ובסתר הוא בלב וצריך כל איש הישראלי לייגע
עצמו להכין א"ע למסי"נ בעבור קדושת שמו ית' ובכל מצוה כשמוכן לזה
זוכה לקדושה ומי שיירא מאד מח"ה ושומר כל מעשיו לבל יתחלל שמו
ית' ע"י גרמתו שכרו שיזכה לקדש שמו ית' ושאם יבא לידי נסיון יעמוד
בנסיונו.

שכאשר יש לאדם מחשבות זרות נפרעין ממנו בגלוי שבזמן שהוא בא לעבודת
ה' עם מסירות נפש אין הוא יכול למצוא עצה לעצמו.

By applying the principle that Hashem's reward for good deeds exceeds the
punishment for bad ones (*Makkos* 5b, *Rashi s.v.* על), we may deduce that
someone who sanctifies Hashem's Name in private will certainly be rewarded
with the opportunity to sanctify His Name in public. Contrary to popular
misconception, it is possible to sanctify Hashem's Name in utter privacy, even
within the innermost recesses of one's heart — simply *by determining* that
when the opportunity occurs, we will perform a public sanctification of
Hashem's Name. In the merit of determining *privately* to always sanctify
Hashem's Name and of carefully monitoring one's behavior that we never
cause (even indirectly) a *chilul Hashem*, we will enjoy the opportunity to
publicly sanctify Hashem's Name. In a similar vein, the *Imrei Emes* learned that
one who desecrates Hashem's Name in his heart (i.e. entertaining the *thought*
of violating Hashem's will) will find it difficult to properly sanctify Hashem's
Name in public when necessary.

■ אֶחָד שׁוֹגֵג וְאֶחָד מֵזִיד בְּחִלּוּל הַשֵּׁם — *Unintentional or intentional, both
are alike regarding desecration of the Name.*

◄§ The Severity of an "Unintentional" Chilul Hashem

בתוס' כתבו כמה פעמים דבכל מקום נקט התנא הפשוט תחילה, ואם כן לכאורה
הו"ל למימר אחד מזיד ואחד שוגג. ואולי חילול השם הוא כל כך חמור ששוגג

[6] *Rabbi Yishmael bar Rabbi Yose says: One who studies [Torah] in order to teach is given the means to study and to teach; and one who studies [Torah] in order to practice is given the means to study and to teach, to observe and to practice.*

ומזיד הם אותו דבר פשוט לגביו, וזה קמ"ל התנא במה דנקט השוגג תחילה, כי
יש לו להיזהר שלא לבא ח"ו בשוגג לידי חילול השם. ואולי באמת נקט הפשוט
תחילה, על דרך דאיתא ומשלם לשונאיו של רשעים נפרעין בעולם הבא, לכן
פשוט הוא של שוגג נפרעין בעולם הזה [ועי' קידושין מ,א בתוד"ה אין מקיפין,
ועי' בחא"ג מהרש"א קידושין שם].

While one who sins unintentionally is generally punished less severely, in reference to the cardinal sin of *chilul Hashem* no such distinction is made. In fact, our *mishnah* cites the sin of *unintentional chilul Hashem* first, giving the impression that it is obvious that unintentional desecration of Hashem's Name is punished the same as a deliberate desecration of Hashem's Name (cf. *Tosafos Shabbos* 20b stating that the obvious case is always mentioned first). In fact, the primary purpose of this segment of the *mishnah* may be to warn us to be exceedingly careful so that we not come to an unintentional *chilul Hashem*.

If we assume that the *mishnah* is referring to punishment in This World, we can better appreciate why the case of the *unintentional chilul Hashem* is stated first. While it is apparent that those who cause an *unintentional chilul Hashem* will be punished in This World, the fate of those who *deliberately* desecrate Hashem's Name is not quite so clear. Perhaps, so heinous a sin can only be expiated in the World to Come (*Pnei Menachem, Maggidei HaEmes*).

ובעבודת ישראל כתב ליישב כי יש שני מיני אנשים, יש שעושה עבירה וסובר
במחשבתו שאין הקב"ה רואה אותו, ויש ששכח שהקב"ה מלא כל הארץ כבודו,
ואילו היה מי שיזכירנו שהקב"ה רואה מעשיו היה פורש מן העבירה, אלא
שבשעת העבירה נסתלקה ממנו הנשמה הקדושה ולא נשאר בו כי אם החומר
ונעשה כמו בהמה, וזה אחד שוגג ואחד מזיד בחילול השם, ר"ל ששניהם הם
שוים, אלא שזה שוגג בחילול השם מחמת ששכח שהשם יתברך רואה אותו, וזה
מזיד בחילול השם.

The Maggid of Koznitz suggested that the term שוֹגֵג does not refer to a purely unintentional act that somehow generated a *chilul Hashem* and perhaps would not be punished as severely. Instead, we are referring to an individual who, motivated by his *yetzer hara*, conveniently forgets that Hashem is observing him (*hashgachah pratis*) and consequently sins deliberately. Had someone been available to remind him of the Divine Presence which fills the entire

[ז] רַבִּי צָדוֹק אוֹמֵר: אַל תִּפְרוֹשׁ מִן הַצִּבּוּר; וְאַל תַּעַשׂ
עַצְמְךָ כְּעוֹרְכֵי הַדַּיָּנִין; וְאַל תַּעֲשֶׂהָ עֲטָרָה לְהִתְגַּדֵּל
בָּהּ, וְלֹא קַרְדֹּם לַחְפָּר בָּהּ. וְכָךְ הָיָה הִלֵּל אוֹמֵר:
וְדְאִשְׁתַּמַּשׁ בְּתָגָא חֲלָף. הָא לָמַדְתָּ: כָּל הַנֶּהֱנֶה מִדִּבְרֵי
תוֹרָה, נוֹטֵל חַיָּיו מִן הָעוֹלָם.

universe, he surely would not have sinned. On the other hand, the intentional
sinner is totally oblivious to Hashem's sovereignty over the world (and not
merely His awareness of our actions). Such a person is considered an intentional
sinner (*Maggidei HaEmes*).

6.

■ רַבִּי יִשְׁמָעֵאל בַּר רַבִּי יוֹסֵי אוֹמֵר: הַלּוֹמֵד עַל מְנָת לְלַמֵּד, מַסְפִּיקִין בְּיָדוֹ לִלְמוֹד
וּלְלַמֵּד — *Rabbi Yishmael bar Rabbi Yose says: One who studies
[Torah] in order to teach is given the means to study and to teach.*

◄§ Learning With the Intention of Teaching

פי' הרע"ב לא לגמול חסדים כו' ויותר יל"פ שבשעת הלימוד אינו מכוון שידע
איך לעשות.

According to the *Bartenura*, this passage is addressed to great individuals
(such as Rabba, cf. *Rosh Hashanah* 18a) whose primary objective was to
learn and teach Torah rather than perform acts of kindness.

However, the contrast between one who studies in order to teach and one
who studies in order to practice also suggests a more basic approach: In the first
instance, one is learning Torah without thinking about the *practical* applica-
tions of his learning and especially how it pertains to performing *mitzvos*. By
contrast, one who studies in order to practice is always thinking of the appli-
cability of his learning to the performance of *mitzvos*.

■ וְהַלּוֹמֵד עַל מְנָת לַעֲשׂוֹת מַסְפִּיקִין בְּיָדוֹ לִלְמוֹד וּלְלַמֵּד, לִשְׁמוֹר וְלַעֲשׂוֹת —*And
one who studies [the Torah] in order to practice is given the means to
study and to teach, to observe and to practice.*

◄§ Learning to "Remake" the Universe

וְעִיקַר הַתְּשׁוּבָה בְּכֹחַ הַתּוֹרָה . . . מְתַקְּנִים כָּל הַפְּגָמִים ע"י תּוֹרָה . . . וְזֶהוּ הַלּוֹמֵד
ע"מ לַעֲשׂוֹת לְתַקֵּן הַכֹּל ע"י הַתּוֹרָה.

[7] *Rabbi Tzadok says: Do not separate yourself from the community; [when serving as a judge] do not act as as lawyer; do not make [the Torah] a crown for self-glorification, nor a spade with which to dig. So too, Hillel used to say: He who exploits the crown [of Torah for personal benefit] shall fade away. From this you derive that whoever seeks personal benefit from the words of Torah removes his life from the world.*

The term לַעֲשׂוֹת may also be taken literally, *to create*. The *mishnah* is extolling the virtues of someone who studies with the intention of rectifying the spiritual damage that the universe has suffered as a result of our numerous transgressions. Just as a Jew's deviation from Torah causes untold harm to the universe itself, so too his return to his heritage repairs the breach that he had created (*Sfas Emes, Shabbos Shuvah 5653*)

7.

■ רַבִּי צָדוֹק אוֹמֵר . . . וְאַל תַּעֲשֶׂהָ עֲטָרָה לְהִתְגַּדֶּל בָּהּ — *Rabbi Tzadok says: . . . do not make [Torah] a crown for self-glorification.*

⊷§ Teaching Torah Without Seeking Fame

אַף עַל פִּי שֶׁאָמַר הַתַּנָּא לְעֵיל שֶׁצָּרִיךְ לְלַמּוֹד לַאֲחֵרִים, אַף עַל פִּי כֵן לֹא תְּהֵא כַּוָּנָתוֹ לְהִתְגַּדֵל בָּהֶם וְלִהְיוֹת נִקְרָא רַב, אֶלָּא תְּהֵא עִקָּר כַּוָּנָתְךָ לְשֵׁם שָׁמַיִם.

The Maggid of Koznitz explained that this *mishnah* should be understood in the context of the previous *mishnah* which extolled the virtues of learning Torah for the sake of teaching. Usually, a certain degree of fame is associated with having disciples. Nonetheless, our primary purpose should be simply to disseminate Torah, and not for the purpose of enhancing our reputation and attaining fame (*Maggidei HaEmes*).

■ וְלֹא קַרְדֹּם לַחְפֹּר בָּהּ — *Nor a spade with which to dig.*

⊷§ A Spade to "Dig Out" Torah's Treasures

אִיתָא אֲפִילוּ בְּעִנְיְנֵי יַהֲדוּת לְהִתְגַּדֵל בְּמַדְרֵיגוֹת גְּדוֹלוֹת, צָרִיךְ לְכַוֵּן רַק לְשֵׁם שָׁמַיִם וְלֹא לִרְצוֹת לְהִתְגַּדֵל. וְלֹא קַרְדֹּם לַחְפּוֹר בָּהֶם הַיְינוּ אֲפִילוּ לִפְתּוֹחַ הַסְּתָרוֹת

[ח] רַבִּי יוֹסֵי אוֹמֵר: כָּל הַמְכַבֵּד אֶת הַתּוֹרָה, גּוּפוֹ
מְכֻבָּד עַל הַבְּרִיּוֹת; וְכָל הַמְחַלֵּל אֶת הַתּוֹרָה, גּוּפוֹ
מְחֻלָּל עַל הַבְּרִיּוֹת.

[ט] רַבִּי יִשְׁמָעֵאל בְּנוֹ אוֹמֵר: הַחוֹשֵׂךְ עַצְמוֹ מִן הַדִּין,
פּוֹרֵק מִמֶּנּוּ אֵיבָה וְגָזֵל וּשְׁבוּעַת שָׁוְא. וְהַגַּס לִבּוֹ
בְּהוֹרָאָה, שׁוֹטֶה רָשָׁע וְגַס רוּחַ.

הַגְּנוּזוֹת, זֶה גַם צָרִיךְ לִהְיוֹת לְשֵׁם שָׁמַיִם. אָסוּר לֵהָנוֹת מֵהַקְּדוּשָׁה וְעַל זֶה נֶאֱמַר וְלֹא
יָבוֹאוּ לִרְאוֹת כְּבַלַּע אֶת הַקֹּדֶשׁ וּמֵתוּ וְאִיתָא שֶׁהָיָה הָאָרוֹן מְכַלֶּה בָּהֶם הַיְנוּ שֶׁהָיוּ
אָז אוֹרוֹת וְעֵת רָצוֹן וְעַל יְדֵי שֶׁהָיָה לְהִתְגַּדֵּל בָּהֶם הָיָה הָאָרוֹן מְכַלֶּה בָּהֶם. אִיתָא
בַּגְּמָ' מַעֲשֶׂה בְּכֹהֵן אֶחָד וְכוּ' וְרָאָה רִצְפָּה מְשׁוּנָּה מֵחֲבֵרוֹתֶיהָ וְכוּ' וְלֹא הִסְפִּיק לִגְמוֹר
אֶת הַדָּבָר וְכוּ' וְיָדְעוּ בְּיִחוּד שֶׁשָּׁם אָרוֹן גָּנוּז וְכוּ' מִתְעַסֵּק בְּקַרְדּוּמוֹ הָיָה הַיְנוּ בְּעִנְיַן
קַרְדּוֹם לַחְפּוֹר בָּהֶם.

Whereas the first phrase עֲטָרָה לְהִתְגַּדֵּל בָּהּ refers to personal profit attained
from studying Torah, this passage alludes to the potential dangers resulting from studying for the lofty purpose of comprehending the hidden treasures
of Hashem's wisdom. As the *Imrei Emes* points out, even spiritual objectives
must be undertaken for Hashem's sake (refer to our discussion to *mishnah* 2:17),
not for the spiritual pleasure derived from plumbing the depths of Torah. Torah
study should never be exploited as one would use a spade to unearth hidden
treasures. The Tribe of Levi, bearers of the *Aron*, the repository of Judaism's
most sacred treasures, were explicitly warned not to gaze upon the *Aron* while
it was being covered by the *Kohanim* (Bamidbar 4:20). In fact, many Levites perished because they benefited in a *spiritual sense* from the *Aron*. In a similar vein,
the Gemara (Yoma 54a) relates that a certain *Kohen* was *digging with his spade*
when he noticed that a part of the Temple floor was raised. Unwittingly, he had
discovered the area in which the *Aron* had been buried by King Yoshiyahu.
However, the *Kohen* expired before he could relate his discovery. One wonders:
Why would this seemingly sincere individual perish simply because he chanced
upon the site of the *Aron*? The answer, suggests the *Imrei Emes*, lies in the
misguided objectives of the *Kohen* who discovered the site of the *Aron*. He was
digging with his spade, seeking to reach unprecedented and unauthorized
spiritual heights through his discovery of the *Aron* (*Maggidei HaEmes*).[1]

■ הָיָה הִלֵּל אוֹמֵר: וּדְאִשְׁתַּמֵּשׁ בְּתָגָא חֲלָף — *Hillel used to say: He
who exploits the crown [of Torah for personal benefit] shall fade away.*

---

1. The *Imrei Emes* offers a homiletic interpretation of this episode. This *Kohen,* attempting to reach

[8] *Rabbi Yose says: Whoever honors the Torah is himself honored by people; and whoever disgraces the Torah is himself disgraced by people.*

[9] *Rabbi Yishmael his son says: One who withdraws from judgment removes from himself hatred, robbery, and [the responsibility for] an unnecessary oath, but one who is too self-confident in issuing legal decisions is a fool, wicked, and arrogant of spirit.*

◈§ Not Even to Be Spared Punishment

בילדותו נוהג היה המגיד מקאזניץ להתמיד בלימודו במשך כל הלילה בבית המדרש. פעם בימי חנוכה סירב אביו להרשו להשאר שם כל הלילה בחששו שמא ישחק עם יתר הנערים כפי שנהגו הם בלילות חנוכה, על כן הזהירו שלא ישאר בביהמ"ד אלא עד זמן שיכבה נרו. כאשר התיישב ללמוד הילד הקדוש אתרחש ליה ניסא ודלק הנר הקטן שעות מרובות. כאשר חזר הביתה מלימודו קידמו אביו בכעס על שהמר את דברו והכהו מכות נאמנות. כאשר נשאל למה לא גילה לאביו שלמד כל אותה העת, השיב "אמנם הייתי יכול לתרץ את עצמי, ואבי היה מאמין לי יען שאף פעם אינני משקר. אכן, כלום מותר לאדם להשתמש בכבוד התורה לצורך עצמו."

Already as a child, R' Yisrael, the future Maggid of Koznitz, would study Torah all night in the *Beis Hamedrash*. While his father generally accepted this arrangement, he was reluctant to allow his son to remain there during Chanukah fearing that Yisrael would associate with other children who were playing cards or other such practices customary on Chanukah. Rather than prohibit Yisrael from learning in the *Beis Hamedrash* altogether, he simply insisted that his son leave once his candle would be extinguished. Chassidic tradition relates that miraculously this future Torah leader's candle remained lit much longer than anyone had anticipated. Upon arriving home in the wee hours of the morning, he was severely punished by his father for disobeying his express instruction to return home when his light burned out. The child stoically accepted his father's criticism rather than explain that indeed his candle had miraculously burned bright all night. when asked to justify his reticence, he simply said: "I do not seek to ever benefit from torah" (*Maggidei HaEmes*).

9.

■ ■ שׁוֹטֶה, רָשָׁע וְגַס רוּחַ — *Is a fool, wicked, and arrogant of spirit.*

unprecedented spiritual heights, was deterred because of his self-centered objectives. The reference to the discovery of the *Aron* is an allusion to the spiritual level that the *Kohen* sought to attain.

[י] הוּא הָיָה אוֹמֵר: אַל תְּהִי דָן יְחִידִי, שֶׁאֵין דָן יְחִידִי אֶלָּא אֶחָד. וְאַל תֹּאמַר: „קַבְּלוּ דַעְתִּי!" שֶׁהֵן רַשָּׁאִין וְלֹא אָתָּה.

[יא] רַבִּי יוֹנָתָן אוֹמֵר: כָּל הַמְקַיֵּם אֶת הַתּוֹרָה מֵעֹנִי, סוֹפוֹ לְקַיְּמָהּ מֵעֹשֶׁר; וְכָל הַמְבַטֵּל אֶת הַתּוֹרָה מֵעֹשֶׁר, סוֹפוֹ לְבַטְּלָהּ מֵעֹנִי.

◦§ Any One of These Justifications

נראה הפי' אחד מאלו או שהוא שוטה ואינו יודע אשר פורק ממנו איבה כו' או שהוא רשע או גס רוח.

The *mishnah* is offering three *alternative* explanations for the overeagerness of some individuals to render halachic verdicts (*pasken*). Either they are *foolish*, forgetting the virtues stated earlier in the *mishnah* of *not paskening* (avoiding needless hatred, staying away from theft, eliminating the possibility of swearing falsely). On the other hand, such behavior on the part of knowledgeable individuals (who are aware of the perils of *paskening* hastily) can only be attributed to their wicked nature or *haughtiness*.

10.

■ הוּא הָיָה אוֹמֵר: אַל תְּהִי דָן יְחִידִי — *He used to say: Do not act as a judge alone.*

◦§ Even if You *Must* Judge, Do Not Do It Alone

דלעיל אמר החושך עצמו מה"ד כו' ועתה מוסיף הגם כי לפעמים תדין עכ"ז תצרף עמך אחרים דלמטי' שיבא כו'.

This *mishnah* should be understood in the context of the previous *mishnah* which recommended that, if possible, we totally avoid judging disputes. If, however, due to unavoidable circumstances we must render a verdict, at least we should seek the participation of others.

■ שֶׁאֵין דָן יְחִידִי אֶלָּא אֶחָד — *For none judges alone except One.*

4/ 10-11　**[10]** *He used to say: Do not act as a judge alone, for none judges alone except One; and do not say, "Accept my view," for they are permitted to, but not you.*

[11] *Rabbi Yonasan says: Whoever fulfills the [study of] Torah despite poverty will ultimately fulfill it in wealth; but whoever neglects the [study of] Torah because of wealth will ultimately neglect it in poverty.*

◆§ Hashem's Beis Din

הגם דאי׳ דכביכול מצרף עמו ב״ד י״ל דהקב״ה ראוי לדון יחידי רק שאינו רוצה ונמלך בפמליא ש״מ, עוד י״ל דלעולם דן ביחידות ואח״כ נמלך בהם ומסכימים גם י״ל שלגבי השי״ת אף שיש כולם מ״מ נק׳ דן יחידי כמובן, גם הפי׳ כי בעונש מצרף שהם ידונו בלבדם הפורעניות אבל בלבדו הוא דן רק טוב.

Although we find that Hashem consults, as it were, with His "Court" (cf. *Rashi, Bereishis* 19:24 s.v. וה׳, which states that whenever the expression וַה׳, *and Hashem*, is used, it refers to Hashem's *Beis Din*), perhaps the *mishnah* is referring to Hashem's *capacity* for judging alone. No one but the Almighty can judge alone — yet even He chooses to consult with His Heavenly Tribunal before pronouncing judgment. Alternatively, the initial judgment is rendered by Hashem, while the final verdict is presented to the Heavenly Tribunal for its concurrence. A distinction may also be made between a verdict to reward mankind, which is decided by Hashem Himself, and the decision to punish, which usually involves the participation of the Heavenly Tribunal. Finally, we may understand the *mishnah* to be saying that any celestial body empowered by Hashem to participate in His deliberations is by necessity so inferior to Him that we can state categorically that Hashem judges alone.

◆§ Only Hashem Can Judge With Pinpoint Precision

שופט שבא לדון דיני נפשות עליו לדון גם הנפשות העתידות לצאת מן האדם הנדון וגם לרבות ממונו שעתיד הוא להוריש לצאצאיו. שופט בשר ודם אינו יכול לעשות כן כדאיתא, לא כן הקב״ה שדן יחידי, באופן שלא יסבול מן הדין זולת הנידון בעצמו. אפילו נוטל מן הנידון את ממונו להחזירו בידו ליורשיו.

Rabbi Yaakov David of Amshinov offered a novel interpretation of the phrase שֶׁאֵין דָּן יְחִידִי אֶלָּא אֶחָד: Only Hashem (Who is One) is able to judge an individual in such a manner that no one else is undeservedly affected. When a mortal imposes the death penalty, not only is the accused affected but also all his future descendants and anything the condemned would have bequeathed to them had he lived longer. On the other hand, Hashem enjoys several advantages over a mortal judge. He is able to simultaneously appraise the defendant and also determine whether any worthy descendants are in his future, thereby meriting that the accused be spared. Moreover, while a mortal judge who, by capriciously sentencing the defendant to death, affects his descendants' financial well being by denying them any future inheritance that he would have bequeathed to them had the defendant been exonerated, Hashem can compensate them for their financial loss (*Maggidei HaEmes*).

⇜ Only Hashem Can Judge a Jew

פעם נכנס משמשו של האוהב ישראל ז"ל לחדרו מחייך, שאלו הרבי "צחוק זה מה טיבו." השיב המשמש "הרבנית לומדת פרקי אבות, ובמקום להגיד אל תהי דן יחידי כו', אמרה אל תהי דן יהודי." נענה הרבי ואמר, "היא צודקת, רק השי"ת רשאי לדון יהודי."

Once the *Ohev Yisrael's* aide reported that the Rebbetzin had misread the *mishnah* as שֶׁאֵין דָּן יְהוּדִי אֶלָּא אֶחָד, *Only Hashem can judge a Jew*. The Rebbe responded, "The Rebbetzin is correct; no mortals — only Hashem (Who is אֶחָד) — can truly pass judgment on a Jew" (*Maggidei HaEmes*)

■ וְאַל תֹּאמַר קַבְּלוּ דַעְתִּי. — *And do not say, "Accept my view."* ■

⇜ Do Not Be Obstinate

פירוש שלא להתעצם כל כך עד שיודו לו לדבריו.

The *mishnah* is referring not only to efforts of one judge to impose his ruling on his peers through coercion, but also to the equally insidious attempt to impose one's will by simply restating one's opinion rather than giving serious consideration to the opinion of others. Stubbornly pressing one's point, in the hope that through persistence and tenacity your opponent will eventually succumb, violates the spirit of our *mishnah*.

11.

■ רַבִּי יוֹנָתָן אוֹמֵר: כָּל הַמְקַיֵּם אֶת הַתּוֹרָה מֵעֹנִי סוֹפוֹ לְקַיְּמָהּ מֵעשֶׁר; וְכָל הַמְבַטֵּל ■ אֶת הַתּוֹרָה מֵעשֶׁר סוֹפוֹ לְבַטְּלָהּ מֵעֹנִי — *Rabbi Yonasan says: Whoever fulfills the [study of] Torah despite poverty will ultimately fulfill it in wealth; but whoever neglects the [study of] Torah because of wealth will ultimately neglect it in poverty.*

The basic premise of the *mishnah* seems very difficult, since we know that many poor people remain poor despite their diligent study of Torah. Similarly, many wealthy people remain affluent despite their lack of Torah study. We will offer a wide variety of approaches to resolve the apparent conflict between the *mishnah* and reality.

◆§ Even if He Were Wealthy

אין הפי׳ שסופו להיות עשיר דאנו רואין איפכא רק הפי׳ שגם אם הי׳ עושר ג״כ
לא הי׳ נמנע מלקיים וכן להיפוך במבטל כו׳.
קשה דיש כמה עשירים מתים רשעים. וי״ל דאלו היו מבטלים בלא זה נמי והתנא
מדבר רק באלו שהעשירות מונעם מן התורה אבל לא ברשעים בלא זה.

The expression *will ultimately fulfill it in wealth* can be interpreted as an indication of our high esteem for the individual who fulfills the Torah in poverty, rather then a *guarantee* of eventual wealth. Someone who learns, amidst all the deprivations of poverty, *would* surely continue to do so even if he were "burdened" with the many challenges that accompany wealth. Likewise, it is safe to assume that someone who did not study Torah while enjoying wealth would continue his unfortunate behavior even if afflicted with poverty.

If Hashem at times causes the wealthy to suddenly become poor, it may be to enable them to resume learning Torah now that they are "relieved" of the burden of managing their wealth. However, Hashem only intervenes when the hope exists that such a drastic change in fortune will serve a purpose. If the wealthy individual would continue to ignore his heritage of Torah and *mitzvos* even as a pauper, then nothing is accomplished by impoverishing him. Instead, Hashem permits him to die with his wealth intact, dispensing punishment in the World to Come.

◆§ Rejoicing in One's Lot

ויל״פ עוד עושר השמח בחלקו כדלעיל כי זוכה להיות שמח בחלקו.

Perhaps, the assurance of eventual wealth implied by the *mishnah* does not refer to monetary riches (which frequently are never enjoyed by the righteous), but rather to wealth as defined by the first *mishnah* of this chapter: אֵיזֶהוּ עָשִׁיר הַשָּׂמֵחַ בְּחֶלְקוֹ, *Who is wealthy? He who is happy with his lot.* The true wealth is rejoicing in one's portion. The *mishnah* assures us that in the merit of studying Torah, despite our dissatisfaction with our status (מְקַיֵּם אֶת הַתּוֹרָה מֵעֹנִי), we will eventually be able to enjoy a measure of contentment, regardless of our material means.

⧽ The Perils of Smugness

> וזה ענין יקר להיות שמח בכל מחמת שהוא רצון הבוב״ה וב״ש . . . ואמרו חז״ל כשם שמברך על הטובה כך מברך עה״ר פי׳ להבריך ולהרכיב הרעה תוך השורש להיות שמח ביסורין כדי להבין כוונת מוסר הש״י ונמצא מוציא יקר מזולל . . . וז״ש אם ב״ת ונתתי גשמיכם כו׳, לשון עבר .. שלמפרע הי׳ הכל טוב . . . גם שאחז״ל אין עשיר אלא בדעת שאחז״ל כל המבטל התורה מעושר, שלאחר כל העשירות בדעת וגם שמח בחלקו כנ״ל, עכ״ז צריך שמירה שמא יבוא ח״ו מתוך עשירות הזה לביטול תורה.

In our previous remarks, we defined wealth as a sense of contentment with one's lot. Let us elaborate on some of the characteristics associated with that blissful feeling. We will also examine a possible drawback that may result from being overly content with one's current status.

Firstly, the individual who is blessed with the gift of being content with his lot perceives *everything* as being Hashem's will. While he would be prepared to accept Divine Judgment — regardless of the degree of suffering that he endures — such an individual is able to discern the Divine hand in everything that occurs. For him, all the suffering that he experiences is merely an expedient means of coming closer to Hashem. As such, he perceives that nothing truly evil occurs. All that may appear to be unjust is really a means of accelerating his return to Torah, the source of all good. Through his sterling personality, he epitomizes the lofty goal set by *Chazal* (*Berachos* 54a), חַיָּב אָדָם לְבָרֵךְ עַל הָרָעָה, כְּשֵׁם שֶׁמְּבָרֵךְ עַל הַטּוֹבָה, that a person is required not only to bless (the traditional interpretation of לְבָרֵךְ) Hashem for the bad that occurs (as well as the good), but also to *integrate* (the term לְבָרֵךְ being derived from מַבְרִיךְ, *grafting*) the apparent bad with the inner core of good that lies beneath all that occurs in life.

This individual also benefits from the gift of extraordinary hindsight, enjoying a retrospective vision of the universe shared by only a few. This unique view is alluded to by the Torah when it states, אִם בְּחֻקֹּתַי תֵּלֵכוּ . . . וְנָתַתִּי גִשְׁמֵיכֶם בְּעִתָּם, *If you will follow My decrees . . . then I will provide your rains in their time* (*Vayikra* 26:3,4). Homiletically, this may be understood as: If you observe My *mitzvos*, you will come to realize that I *had given* your rain (and all material blessings) in the proper time (and proportion).

Yet, a certain danger is inherent in such smugness — forgetting Hashem. Just as material wealth can be a catalyst to spiritual doom, so too *excess* spiritual satisfaction may breed a sense of smugness that may stifle one's growth. As the *mishnah* continues, וְכָל הַמְבַטֵּל אֶת הַתּוֹרָה מֵעֹשֶׁר, one who does not learn Torah while enjoying spiritual wealth may (ח״ו) be deprived of this "ethereal" sense of satisfaction. Consigned to spiritual poverty, he will continue along that downward trajectory, and *will ultimately neglect it in poverty.*

✦§ A Plea for Sustenance

ויש לפרש שהתנא אמר זאת בדרך תפלה להשי״ת, כל המקיים את התורה מעוני סופו לקיימה מעושר, אף שנסיון של עשירות גדול הוא מכל מקום בוודאי יקיים את התורה, ולזאת יכול השי״ת להשפיע לו עשירות כי בין כך ובין כך יקיים את התורה. וכן המבטל את התורה מעושר סופו לבטלה מעוני, היינו שאם הקב״ה יעשה אותו עני גם כן יבטל את התורה, אם כן מוטב שישאר לו עושרו.

According to R' Yechezkel of Kozmir, this *mishnah* should be interpreted as a plea for continued sustenance, regardless of our spiritual shortcomings. The pauper — who still maintains his regular routine of Torah study — even if granted affluence, will continue to study Torah. Likewise, the wealthy individual, realizing that he has perhaps not fully discharged his spiritual obligations, still pleads for continued material success, arguing that, if impoverished, he would suffer from the same failings. If so, the tragedy of sudden, impoverishment would accomplish little (*Maggidei HaEmes*).

✦§ Lack of Comprehension

פירוש הגם שלומד בתחילה ואינו מרגיש טעם בלימודו סופו להרגיש טעם, וזהו המקיים מעוני טעם בלי סופו לקיים מעושר בטעם.
כשיודע שהוא עני ומבטל עצמו סופו להגיע להבנה יותר... וזה הדרך לעבדות השם.

According to the Kotzker Rebbe, the term עָנִי refers to the lack of comprehension which often occurs when commencing to study Torah. Though one's initial efforts at learning may be poor in understanding indeed, if he persists and continues learning, he will eventually merit to comprehend the rich treasures of Torah (*Maggidei HaEmes*).

The *Beis Yisrael* expanded upon this thought by emphasizing the benefits one can have from *not* fully comprehending Torah. Such an individual, painfully aware of his spiritual deficiencies, negates himself to the awesome Presence of Hashem. It is this sense of self-negation and humility that enables him to make huge strides in Torah study (סוֹפוֹ לְקַיְּמָה מֵעֹשֶׁר) (*Maggidei HaEmes*).

✦§ The Cycle Will Not Repeat Itself

יי״ל דאילו כתב סופו להיות עני, הייתי אומר דעכשיו יקיים את התורה

[יב] רַבִּי מֵאִיר אוֹמֵר: הֱוֵי מְמַעֵט בְּעֵסֶק, וַעֲסֹק בַּתּוֹרָה; וֶהֱוֵי שְׁפַל רוּחַ בִּפְנֵי כָל אָדָם; וְאִם בָּטַלְתָּ מִן הַתּוֹרָה, יֶשׁ לְךָ בְּטֵלִים הַרְבֵּה כְּנֶגְדֶּךָ; וְאִם עָמַלְתָּ בַּתּוֹרָה, יֶשׁ לוֹ שָׂכָר הַרְבֵּה לִתֶּן לָךְ.

מעוני וממילא סופו להיות עשיר, להכי כתב סופו לבטלה מעוני, ר"ל שאין מספיקים בידו לקיים את התורה מעושר אלא מעתה ישאר מבטל את התורה מעוני.

The Baal Shem Tov noted that the *mishnah* does not state סוֹפוֹ לִהְיוֹת עָנִי, *will ultimately become a pauper*, but rather סוֹפוֹ לְבַטְּלָה מֵעֲנִי, *will ultimately neglect it in poverty* — as a pauper he will not learn from his sudden downfall and resume learning Torah. Instead, he will continue his previous behavior. As a result, the cycle of "riches to rags" will not be reversed. Rather, he will remain poor, both materially and spiritually (*Maggidei HaEmes*).

◆§ Not Learning From Tragedy

משל לתינוק היושב לפני רבו ומסיר לבו משמוע לדברי רבו מאיזה שחוק שמשחק עצמו באיזה דבר, וקם רבו ונוטל מידו, והוסיף לבכות ביותר על שנטל ממנו זה הדבר ולא היה לומד ודו"ק.

Perhaps the greatest tragedy of all is *not comprehending* why tragic events occur. The Maggid of Koznitz, when explaining this *mishnah*, draws the analogy to the child whose toy was confiscated by his teacher, because of his inattention to the lesson. Rather than learn from this event and pay closer attention, the child cried for the loss of his toy. So too, when tragedies occur, Heaven forefend, we may commit the cardinal error of crying only because of the tragic events rather than for their underlying cause (*Maggidei HaEmes*).

12.

■ רַבִּי מֵאִיר אוֹמֵר: הֱוֵי מְמַעֵט בְּעֵסֶק וַעֲסֹק בַּתּוֹרָה — *Rabbi Meir says: Reduce your business activities and engage in Torah study.*

◆§ Reduce Your Working Hours

והגם שבל"ז יש לו עתים לתורה מ"מ דרך למעט מהעסק לשם ה'.

[12] *Rabbi Meir says: Reduce your business activities and engage in Torah study. Be humble of spirit before every person. If you should neglect the [study of] Torah, you will come upon many excuses to neglect it; but if you labor in the Torah, God has ample reward to give you.*

The *mishnah* is referring to someone who *already* reserves time every day for Torah study, a concept known as קְבִיעוּת עִתִּים לַתּוֹרָה. It is to such an individual that the *mishnah* speaks — though you are already studying Torah, and maintaining a rigorous work schedule, at the same time diminish your working hours to allow more time for *limud haTorah*.

✑ Always Be Hungry for Torah Study

שאלו הרבי מקאצק ״אומרים למדן הוא זה שמילא כריסו בש״ס ופוסקים, למה כריסו ולא ראשו״? המשיך הרבי ובאר ״מה כרס זה בכל זה בכל יום הוא מחדש רעבונו, כך צריך להיות הלמדן. רעב כל יום לתורה.״

The Kotzker Rebbe noted the popular expression that one is considered to be truly knowledgeable only if he has filled his belly (מִילָא כְּרֵיסוֹ) with knowledge of the Talmud and Halachic literature (cf. *Rama, Yoreh De'ah* 246:4). While it would seem more appropriate to define such a person as one whose *head* is filled with Torah knowledge, the metaphor ″belly″ conveys the sense of incessant intellectual hunger and thirst that is the hallmark of a true scholar (*Maggidei HaEmes*).

✑ Do Not Get Bogged Down in Preparations

פעם פנה אדמו״ר הלב שמחה ז״ל לאחד ואמר לו בלשון המשנה ״הוי ממעט בעסק ועסוק בתורה – אל תרבה בעסק ובהכנות לקראת לימוד התורה, רק קח גמרא והתיישב ללמוד.״

According to the *Lev Simchah*, the *mishnah* is urging us not to spend excessive time *preparing* ourselves to learn Torah.[1] It would be more profitable to simply open a Gemara and start learning (*Maggidei HaEmes*).

---

1. The *mishnah* is referring to excessive *physical* preparations prior to learning Torah (i.e. finding an appropriate chair or table, searching for the best possible location). On the other hand, it is certainly commendable to prepare oneself *spiritually*. The *Lev Simchah* himself would prepare with great devotion, before learning Torah (*Maggidei HaEmes*).

ד / יג

[יג] רַבִּי אֱלִיעֶזֶר בֶּן יַעֲקֹב אוֹמֵר: הָעוֹשֶׂה מִצְוָה אַחַת קוֹנֶה לוֹ פְּרַקְלִיט אֶחָד; וְהָעוֹבֵר עֲבֵרָה אַחַת, קוֹנֶה לוֹ קַטֵּיגוֹר אֶחָד. תְּשׁוּבָה וּמַעֲשִׂים טוֹבִים כִּתְרִיס בִּפְנֵי הַפֻּרְעָנוּת.

■ וְאִם בָּטַלְתָּ מִן הַתּוֹרָה, יֶשׁ לְךָ בְּטֵלִים הַרְבֵּה כְּנֶגְדֶּךְ — *If you should neglect the [study of] Torah, you will come upon many excuses to neglect it.*

◆§ A Possible Cause of Business Failure

ואם בטלת מה"ת כו' כלומר לא תעלה על דעתך כשתתרבה בעסק ותבטל מתורה תרוייח דיהי' הרבה בטלים כנגדך ולא יגמור מחשבתך במסחרך ולא תרויח ואדרבה אם עמלת בתורה ותמעיט בעסק יש לו שכר הרבה ליתן לך בעוה"ז למלאות החסרון של מיעוטך בעסק כנ"ל ההמשך.

The expression יֶשׁ לְךָ בְּטֵלִים הַרְבֵּה כְּנֶגְדֶּךָ is referring to the first segment of the *mishnah* emphasizing the need to curtail one's business activities in favor of Torah study. If we disregard this advice and nonetheless engage in commerce during time allocated for Torah study, we are bound to suffer the consequences. The most meticulously planned business deal will unravel not because of its inherent flaws but because Hashem will unleash the many forces at His command (בְּטֵלִים הַרְבֵּה) to foil such a plan.

If, on the other hand, you find time for learning at the expense of your business schedule, as originally advocated, then, as the *mishnah* concludes, יֶשׁ לוֹ שָׂכָר הַרְבֵּה לִתֵּן לָךְ, Hashem will amply reward you even in This World — to compensate for your apparent business losses.

■ וְאִם עָמַלְתָּ בַּתּוֹרָה, יֶשׁ לוֹ שָׂכָר הַרְבֵּה לִתֵּן לָךְ — *But if you labor in the Torah, God has ample reward to give you.*

◆§ You Are Your Worst Enemy

ונראה לפרש על דרך שאמרו שאין הקב"ה מייחס שמו על הרע, כמו שנאמר ויקרא אלקים לאור יום ובחושך לא כתיב רק ולחשך קרא לילה . . . ולכך בעונש אמר יש לך בטלים הרבה, כמאמר הכתוב תמותת רשע רעה, הרעה עצמה ממית את הרשע, אבל בשכר אמר יש לו שכר הרבה שהוא בעצמו נותן השכר לעושי רצונו.

It is significant, as the Maggid of Koznitz pointed out, that when describing the frustration experienced by those who do not engage in Torah, the *mish-*

[13] *Rabbi Eliezer ben Yaakov says: He who fulfills a single mitzvah gains himself a single advocate, and he who commits [even] a single transgression gains himself a single accuser. Repentance and good deeds are like a shield against retribution.*

---

nah includes the term לְךָ, *you*, whereas while describing the reward bestowed upon those who learn Torah, emphasis is placed on the role of Hashem, לֹ, *He has ample reward*. This subtle but important distinction is also reflected in the Torah's description of the creation of light and darkness. Hashem's Name is *explicitly* mentioned during the creation of light — symbol of good — וַיִּקְרָא אֱלֹהִים לָאוֹר יוֹם — *God called to the light: "Day,"* but it is only *implied* as the Torah describes darkness — which symbolizes evil — וְלַחֹשֶׁךְ קָרָא לָיְלָה — *and to the darkness He called: "Night"* (*Bereishis* 1:5).

From these two instances, we can derive an important principle: Hashem rewards, but does not punish, directly. Instead, He exposes the evildoer to the very fickle fortunes of the natural world. No longer shielded by Divine Presence, the *rasha* quickly suffers the consequences of his behavior. David also voices this theme: תְּמוֹתֵת רָשָׁע רָעָה (*Tehillim* 34:22) — The evil (רָעָה) generated by the wicked (רָשָׁע) — not by Hashem — will kill him (תְּמוֹתֵת) (adapted from *Maggidei HaEmes*).

◄§ Extra Reward (שָׂכָר הַרְבֵּה)

> מלשונם שאמרו שכר הרבה משמע שניתן לו שכר הרבה יותר מן המגיעו עבור הלימוד עצמו, כי השכר הוא גם על מה שבכל עיסוקיו ופעולותיו הוא עוסק ופועל תורה׳דיג, וגם על מה שפועל ועוסק להביא ולהכניס תורה באחרים.

The *mishnah* describes the reward received for Torah study as being *ample;* (הַרְבֵּה). This suggests that one who is immersed in Torah is compensated not only for studying but also for the positive impact the Torah now has on his life and on all those that he has influenced (*Lev Simchah, Maggidei HaEmes*).

13.

■ רַבִּי אֱלִיעֶזֶר בֶּן יַעֲקֹב אוֹמֵר: הָעוֹשֶׂה מִצְוָה אַחַת קוֹנֶה לוֹ פְּרַקְלִיט אֶחָד, וְהָעוֹבֵר עֲבֵרָה אַחַת, קוֹנֶה לוֹ קַטֵּיגוֹר אֶחָד. — *Rabbi Eliezer ben Yaakov says: He who fulfills a single mitzvah gains himself a single advocate, and he who commits [even] a single transgression gains himself a single accuser.*

✑§ Are All Angels Equal?

קשה הא מדה טובה מרובה ה׳ מאות כו׳ וי״ל הפרקליט יש לו כח להמליץ טוב
ה׳ מאות פעמים.
והפי׳ שע״י תשובה חוזר ונעשה מהקטיגור פרקליט.

This *mishnah* implies that the defending angel created by a *mitzvah* is equal to the prosecuting angel that emerges from a sin. This seems to contradict the principle that Hashem's attribute of rewarding good deeds is 500-fold that of His attribute of punishing (מִדַּת פֻּרְעָנוּת). It may be, however that they are equal only in a *quantitative* sense — each *mitzvah* creates a defending angel just as each *aveirah* creates a prosecuting angel. This is hardly true in a *qualitative* sense. On the contrary, each angel speaking in *Klal Yisrael's* merit is 500 times as effective as each prosecuting angel.

Moreover, the *mishnah* may be alluding to the radical transformation that occurs as the very angel that sought to prosecute metamorphoses into a defending angel through true repentance.

✑§ Isn't One Defending Angel Sufficient?

מקשים א״כ הרי אמרו אם יש מלאך מליץ כו׳ אפילו א׳ מתתקצ״ט כו׳ וא״כ הרי
גם הרשעים מלאים מצות כו׳ ולעולם לא יענשו כיון שיש תמיד מליצי יושר נגד
המגיד פשע, וע״ד הלצה יש לפרש מ״ש אחד מני אלף לשון אאלפך חכמה שיהי׳
בקי ומלומד אותו המליץ ולא מליץ בעלמא.

In describing the deliberations of the heavenly tribunal, Iyov said: אִם יֵשׁ עָלָיו מַלְאָךְ מֵלִיץ אֶחָד מִנִּי אָלֶף, *even if there is only one defending angel among a thousand* (33:23), this would prove sufficient to save Israel from the ravages of *Gehinnom*. This being the case, why should one be concerned about the myriads of prosecuting angels that could (ח״ו) harm him — isn't a *single* defender of *Klal Yisrael* sufficient to outweigh them? Indeed, if any virtue suffices to save a soul, why are the wicked — who undoubtedly have their saving graces — punished for their sins? Does the Talmud (*Eruvin* 19b) teach that even the least worthy Jew is as full of *mitzvos* as a pomegranate is full of seeds?

Careful examination of the *pasuk* cited previously reveals a possible resolution to this question. The one in a thousand angel who rallies to our defense is described as מֵלִיץ אֶחָד מִנִּי אָלֶף, which may be interpreted not only in the traditional sense of "one out of a thousand," but also as a *well-rehearsed* defender [the term אָלֶף related to אֲאַלֶּפְךָ חָכְמָה, *I will teach you wisdom* (Iyov 33:33)]. To assume the burden of defense in an environment overwhelmingly populated by prosecuting angels requires a highly articulate angel whose daunting task is eased by the Torah and *mitzvos* performed by his clients. The totally wicked, while possibly enjoying a "stray angel" to take up their defense, are unable to provide their defender the wherewithal to mount a successful defense as a consequence of their terrible behavior.

■ תְּשׁוּבָה וּמַעֲשִׂים טוֹבִים כִּתְרִיס בִּפְנֵי הַפֻּרְעָנוּת — *Repentance and good deeds are like a shield against retribution.*

◆§ A Shield (כִּתְרִיס) Versus a Defender (פְּרַקְלִיט)

וצ"ע אם כן הוא גם בל"ת . . . ואולי דהיינו דמסיק כתריס.
נראה דב' מילי נינהו מצוה ופרקליט דבריש אינו מגין כתריס והחילוק דמצוה
היינו טוב לשמים בלחוד אבל מעש"ט פי' טוב לשמים ולבריות לכן חביב ביותר
וכן כחה של תשובה גדול.

Whereas the first segment of this *mishnah* depicted *mitzvos* as the progenitor of *defending* angels, here repentance and good deeds are described as a *shield*.

Perhaps, the concept of a shield alludes to those angels created as a result of our tenacious refusal to yield to temptation and violate negative commandments. Whereas the angels created as a result of our *positive* commandments *aggressively defend* us from prosecution, those nurtured by our observance of *negative* commandments *shield* us from ever being prosecuted.

In a somewhat similar vein, we may distinguish between performance of *mitzvos* which are a great source of satisfaction to Hashem and good deeds which are beneficial to one's peers as well as pleasing to Hashem. In the latter case, no prosecutor even stands a chance of casting aspersions. Good deeds act as a shield against would-be antagonists. Similarly, the power of heartfelt *teshuvah* is so immense that *Klal Yisrael* needs no defense attorney. Their heartfelt repentance effectively shields them from punishment (adapted from *Sfas Emes*).

◆§ Teshuvah and Good Deeds

וי"ל בגווני דתשובה בלבד אינו מכפר מ"מ עם המעש"ט היינו מצוות אז מגינים
מן הפורענית.

The question arises: Why are both *teshuvah* and good deeds necessary to shield us from suffering? Wouldn't either of these potent spiritual weapons suffice? Perhaps, the *mishnah* is assuring us that even if one has violated the most serious transgression for which *teshuvah* alone does not atone (such as sins which bear the penalty of *kares*, banishment of the soul), the *combined* effect of repentance with good deeds will shield the individual from retribution.

[יד] רַבִּי יוֹחָנָן הַסַּנְדְלָר אוֹמֵר: כָּל כְּנֵסִיָּה שֶׁהִיא לְשֵׁם שָׁמַיִם, סוֹפָהּ לְהִתְקַיֵּם; וְשֶׁאֵינָהּ לְשֵׁם שָׁמַיִם, אֵין סוֹפָהּ לְהִתְקַיֵּם.

14.

■ רַבִּי יוֹחָנָן הַסַּנְדְלָר אוֹמֵר: כָּל כְּנֵסִיָּה שֶׁהִיא לְשֵׁם שָׁמַיִם, סוֹפָהּ לְהִתְקַיֵּם; וְשֶׁאֵינָהּ לְשֵׁם שָׁמַיִם, אֵין סוֹפָהּ לְהִתְקַיֵּם — *Rabbi Yochanan the Sandler says: Every assembly that is dedicated to the sake of Heaven will endure to the end, but one that is not for the sake of Heaven will not endure to the end.*

◄§ An Element of Spirituality in Every Conclave

פי' אף בכנסי' לצורכי עוה"ז עב"ז הכוונה יהי' לש"ש בכ"ד דעתו.

The expression כָּל, *every*, suggests that any assembly, even the most mundane gathering convened to resolve temporal issues, should nonetheless include a spiritual element, a hint of Hashem's Presence.

◄§ Even Spiritual Gatherings Should Be for Hashem's Sake

גם הכנסיה שהיא לשם שמים צריכה שתהיה לשם שמים.

Alternatively, the inclusive term כָּל reminds us that even gatherings that are specifically convened for spiritual purposes — those that deserve the label *a gathering for the sake of Heaven* — must live up to their stated objectives. These events should never be plagued with bickering, factionalism and petty jealousy (Kotzker Rebbe, *Maggidei HaEmes*).

◄§ An Internal Gathering

פירוש באדם עצמו גם כן, לאסוף ולכנוס כל המחשבות והכוחות לשם שמים.

The term כְּנֵסִיָּה does not necessarily refer to an *external* gathering. It may be a call for us to muster all our own abilities and talents for the purpose of sanctifying Hashem's Name (*Chiddushei HaRim, Maggidei HaEmes*).

[14] *Rabbi Yochanan the Sandler says: Every assembly that is dedicated to the sake of Heaven will endure to the end, but one that is not for the sake of Heaven will not endure to the end.*

◄§ Gathering for Hashem's Sake Versus Dispute for Hashem's Sake

והגם ששנינו גם כן מחלוקת לשם שמים סופה להתקיים, אולם שם במחלוקת לשם שמים שואל התנא איזה מחלוקת שהיא לשם שמים, ומשיב כגון מחלוקת הלל ושמאי, ללמדנו דעת כי לנהוג מחלוקת לשם שמים צריך שיהיו אנשים גדולים כאלו. אולם בכנסיה שלשם שמים אין התנא שואל איזה כנסיה וכו'.

In the following chapter we read of a somewhat similar concept, מַחֲלֹקֶת לְשֵׁם שָׁמַיִם, *dispute for the sake of Heaven* (5:20). It is significant that the *mishnah* discussing a dispute for Hashem's sake gives an example of this concept, namely the Talmudic disputes of Hillel and Shammai. Our *mishnah*, on the other hand, does not present an example of a gathering for the sake of Heaven. This distinction between the two *mishnahs* is not merely semantic but rather bears a crucial message: While only great Torah personalities such as Shammai and Hillel can argue for Hashem's sake, gathering *leShem Shamayim* is much easier. Any sincere group of Torah-committed Jews can come together for the purpose of sanctifying Hashem's Name (adapted from *Imrei Emes, Maggidei HaEmes*).

◄§ Historical Example of Gatherings not for Hashem's Sake: Those Who Complained About the Manna

... הָאסַפְסֻף ... לשון אסיפה ולפי שלא הי' לשם שמים בשלימות נתוסף בו אתוי"ן.

In *Parashas Beha'aloscha* we read about a gathering of Jews (identified by *Chazal* as the *Erev Rav*, Egyptian converts) who complained about the manna. Whatever their ultimate motives may have been (cf. *Sfas Emes*, ibid. 5655), the Torah indicates this gathering was not totally for Hashem's sake by using the diminutive word אֲסַפְסֻף rather than the traditional אֲסֵיפָה (*Sfas Emes Beha'aloscha* 5655).

◄§ Korach's Assembly

ויקהלו על משה ועל אהרן אבל לא היה כנסיה לשם שמים ולא נתקיים כי כח

[טו] רַבִּי אֶלְעָזָר בֶּן שַׁמּוּעַ אוֹמֵר: יְהִי כְבוֹד תַּלְמִידְךָ
חָבִיב עָלֶיךָ כְּשֶׁלָּךְ; וּכְבוֹד חֲבֵרְךָ כְּמוֹרָא רַבָּךְ;
וּמוֹרָא רַבָּךְ כְּמוֹרָא שָׁמָיִם.

[טז] רַבִּי יְהוּדָה אוֹמֵר: הֱוֵי זָהִיר בְּתַלְמוּד, שֶׁשִּׁגְגַת
תַּלְמוּד עוֹלָה זָדוֹן.

האסיפה לבוא לאחדות ולעורר השורש של יעקב אבינו . . . אבל בקהלם אל תחד
ולא באו להאחדות.

Korach sought to unite *Klal Yisrael* for the purpose of rebelling against Moshe
and Aharon. However, such a gathering, not for Hashem's sake, was
doomed since it lacked a critical catalyst, the attribute of true אַחְדוּת, *unity*, that
was instilled in us by Yaakov Avinu. When blessing his children, Yaakov
insists that they remain united (cf. *Bereishis* 49:1, הֵאָסְפוּ וְאַגִּידָה). However, when
blessing Levi — and upon foreseeing the insurrection of Levi's descendant,
Korach — he specifically excluded himself from any form of participation in
their gathering by saying, בִּקְהָלָם אַל תֵּחַד כְּבֹדִי (*Bereishis* 49:6), *With their congregation, do not join, O my honor!* Of course, any convocation, condemned by the
strongest advocate of *Klal Yisrael's* unity, is doomed to failure (*Sfas Emes,
Korach* 5643).

15.

■ רַבִּי אֶלְעָזָר בֶּן שַׁמּוּעַ אוֹמֵר: יְהִי כְבוֹד תַּלְמִידְךָ חָבִיב עָלֶיךָ כְּשֶׁלָּךְ — *Rabbi
Elazar ben Shamua says: Let the honor of your student be as dear to
you as your own.*

⋅§ Reciprocal Rebbi-Talmid Relationship

יהי כבוד תלמידך חביב עליך כשלך. ויהי מורא רבך כמורא שמים.

According to the *Lev Simchah*, we may deduce from the *mishnah's* sequence
that a reciprocal relationship exists between a *rebbi* (mentor, Torah teacher)
and his *talmid* (disciple). In an atmosphere in which the *rebbi* respects his *talmid*
as much as he esteems himself, the student, in turn, will appreciate the need for
kavod haTorah and will fear his *rebbi* as much as he venerates Hashem (*Maggidei HaEmes*).

[15] *Rabbi Elazar ben Shamua says: Let the honor of your student be as dear to you as your own; the honor of your colleague as the reverence for your teacher; and the reverence for your teacher as the reverence of Heaven.*

[16] *Rabbi Yehudah says: Be meticulous in study, for a careless misinterpretation is considered tantamount to willful transgression.*

⧉ Why Respect a Talmid?

אולי י״ל כי המלמד צריך לחשוב שעל ידי תלמידו נעשה לרב ובלעדו לא היה לו למי ללמד, נמצא דכמו שצריך תלמידו לכבדו כן צריך הוא לכבד לתלמידו כי הרי כל מה שמתכבד הוא, בא לו ע״י תלמידו. גם י״י עפ״י מה דאיתא ומתלמידי יותר מכולם.

Rebbeim and *talmidim* enjoy a symbiotic relationship. Of course, *talmidim* owe much of their knowledge to their *rebbi's* teaching. But, equally so, the *rebbi* owes his role as a disseminator of Torah to his students. By honoring his *talmidim*, a Torah teacher is displaying respect to the primary source of his own respect. Moreover, much of the *rebbi's* knowledge is derived from interacting and studying Torah with his students. As Rabbi Chanina said, וּמִתַּלְמִידַי יוֹתֵר מִכּוּלָם, "I learned more from my *talmidim* than from anyone else" (*Taanis* 7a) (*Maggidei HaEmes*).

■ וּמוֹרָא רַבָּךְ כְּמוֹרָא שָׁמָיִם ■ — *And the reverence for your teacher as the reverence of Heaven.*

⧉ Only if the Rebbi Fears Hashem

היינו כמה שהרבי הוא ירא שמים כך יש לתלמידו מורא מרבו.

According to Rabbi Yitzchak of Worka, this statement implies that a direct relationship exists between the degree of fear of Hashem possessed by a *rebbi* and the commensurate respect that he will earn from his *talmidim*: מוֹרָא רַבָּךְ, the fear of your *rebbi* will be, כְּמוֹרָא שָׁמָיִם, like the *rebbi's* fear of Heaven (*Maggidei HaEmes*).

16.

■ *Rabbi* — רַבִּי יְהוּדָה אוֹמֵר: הֱוֵי זָהִיר בְּתַלְמוּד, שֶׁשִּׁגְגַת תַּלְמוּד עוֹלָה זָדוֹן ■

[יז] רַבִּי שִׁמְעוֹן אוֹמֵר: שְׁלֹשָׁה כְתָרִים הֵם: כֶּתֶר תּוֹרָה, וְכֶתֶר כְּהֻנָּה, וְכֶתֶר מַלְכוּת; וְכֶתֶר שֵׁם טוֹב עוֹלֶה עַל גַּבֵּיהֶן.

Yehudah says: Be meticulous in study, for a careless misinterpretation is considered tantamount to willful transgression.

◦§ Wrong Learning Is Worse Than No Learning

ומ"ש הפוסקים לענין אומר מותר באיסור והיתר כגון מבטל איסור לכתחלה י"ל דכאן הפי' שלמד בפי' טעות ושם כשלא למד כלל.

This *mishnah* warns us of the perils of misinterpreting Torah, even unintentionally, noting that an erroneous theory can lead to deliberate violations of Halachah.

While *Chazal* do on occasion treat an act arising from ignorance of Halachah less severely than a deliberate violation (cf. *Taz, Yoreh De'ah* 99:9), this distinction only holds true in a case of total ignorance of proper procedure. On the other hand, misinterpretation of Torah, no matter how innocuous the intent, is bound to lead to deliberate violations.

◦§ Tzaddik's Mistakes Contribute to Rasha's Transgressions

יש לבאר הענין על פי מאמרם ז"ל זכה נוטל חלקו וחלק חבירו בגן עדן וכן הרשע נוטל חלק הצדיק בגיהנום. ופי' הענין כי זדון הרשע מביא הצדיק לשגגות. וגם שגגת הצדיק מביא הרשע לזדונות ואולי זה שאמרו שגגת תלמוד עולה זדון כי כל ישראל ערבין זה בזה. ומצד זה נוטל זה חלקו זה כנ"ל.

It is difficult to assume that the unintentional error of the righteous scholar will lead *him* to sin. Perhaps, the *mishnah* is suggesting an *indirect* link between the *tzaddik's* misinterpretations and the *rasha's deliberate* actions.

To appreciate this relationship, it would be useful to recall the intimate relationship that exists between all Jews. This link is articulated in the renowned *Chazal*, כָּל יִשְׂרָאֵל עֲרֵבִים זֶה בָּזֶה, *all Jews are responsible for each other* (*Shevuos* 39a). We are not only responsible for our peers' spiritual behavior, we are also *rewarded* (or punished) for their deeds. As *Chazal* state (*Chagigah* 15a), זָכָה צַדִּיק נָטַל חֶלְקוֹ וְחֵלֶק חַבֵרוֹ בְּגַן עֵדֶן, the *tzaddik* may merit to receive the reward that a wicked person would have received in *Gan Eden* (cf. *The Three Festivals*,

[17] *Rabbi Shimon says: There are three crowns —
the crown of Torah, the crown of priesthood, and the
crown of kingship; but the crown of a good name surpasses them all.*

---

p. 330). When the souls of all Jews are inexorably united, we can appreciate that
the errors of the righteous may lead to the willful violations of the wicked[1] (*Sfas
Emes, Nitzavim 5635*).

17.

■ רַבִּי שִׁמְעוֹן אוֹמֵר: שְׁלֹשָׁה כְתָרִים הֵם – כֶּתֶר תּוֹרָה, וְכֶתֶר כְּהֻנָּה, וְכֶתֶר
מַלְכוּת; וְכֶתֶר שֵׁם טוֹב עוֹלֶה עַל גַּבֵּיהֶן — *Rabbi Shimon says: There are
three crowns — the crown of Torah, the crown of priesthood, and the
crown of kingship; but the crown of a good name surpasses them all.*

◄§ Three Crowns or Four Crowns?

יש לדקדק הלא עם כתר שם טוב יש ארבעה כתרים ולמה אמר שלשה. אולי יש
ליישב דכתר שם טוב הכוונה שיש לו כל הג׳ האחרים וכוללם יחד ולכן עולה על
גביהם.
דהקשה השפ״א מהכא דכתר שם טוב עולה על גבי כתר תורה וא״כ איך משמע
התם דקנה לו ד״ת גדול מקנה שם טוב ולהנ״ל א״ש דכתר שם טוב כולל כל הג׳
אף תורה והתם איירי בשכר עצם קניית ש״ט ושכר קניית ד״ת.

The obvious question occurs: The *mishnah* commences by stating that these
are *three* crowns and yet enumerates *four* crowns — Torah, priesthood,
kingship and the crown of a good name.

Perhaps, the term וְכֶתֶר שֵׁם טוֹב, *crown of a good name*, should not be perceived
as a separate entity but rather as the crown that emerges from fusing together
the other three crowns. With this approach, we can now resolve the apparent
contradiction (pointed out by the *Sfas Emes*, refer to our commentary on 2:8)
between this *mishnah* which elevates the crown of a good name to a preemi-
nent position and a previous *mishnah* (2:8) which implies that a שֵׁם טוֹב, *good
name* (reputation), while important, is inferior to the Torah itself. Undoubtedly,
Torah is superior to any single attribute. However, the crown of a good name
emerging from the synthesizing of Torah, Divine service and royalty is
even more significant than any one of the three crowns alone (*Maggidei
HaEmes*).

---

1. Conversely, the willful violation of the wicked may lead to the errors of the righteous
(ibid.).

[יח] רַבִּי נְהוֹרַאי אוֹמֵר: הֱוֵי גּוֹלֶה לִמְקוֹם תּוֹרָה, וְאַל
תּאמַר שֶׁהִיא תָבוֹא אַחֲרֶיךָ, שֶׁחֲבֵרֶיךָ יְקַיְּמוּהָ
בְיָדֶךָ. וְאֶל בִּינָתְךָ אַל תִּשָּׁעֵן.

⪧ The Crown of Hashem's Good Name

לכאורה יפלא דמה שייך יותר גדול מתורה. אלא י"ל כתר שם טוב הכוונה לשם
שמים, שבכתר שם טוב עולה על גביהן, ר"ל שמכניס ומעלה את שם השם על
גביהן על גבי התורה, הכהונה והמלכות. הכוונה ששם שמים יהיה על גביהן
בתורה כהונה ומלכות ואז הן ג' כתרים.

. . . אינו דומה שונה פרקו מאה פעמים למאה ואחד הכוונה מאה פעמים עם האחד
יחידו של עולם.

The apparent inconsistency between the statement that three crowns exist
while the actual enumeration is four crowns may be resolved by reinterpret-
ing the term שֵׁם טוֹב. We may say that it refers not to the good name acquired
by humans but rather to the sacred Good Name of Hashem.[1]

By emphasizing the supremacy of the "crown of the good name," the *mishnah* is reminding us never to forget the *Origin* of the other three crowns. The
Torah itself, the honor bestowed upon Aharon's priestly family, as well as the
royal prerogatives of kings all emanate from — and owe their continued
existence — to Hashem.

In a similar vein, the statement of *Chazal* (*Chagigah* 9a) valuing someone
who reviewed his learning 101 times more than one who studied it "merely"
100 times may be rendered as referring to one who studied one hundred times
with One — Hashem, Who is known as the יְחִידוֹ שֶׁל עוֹלָם, "the One and
Unique Master of the universe" — recognizing the Source of the Torah (*Lev
Simchah, Maggidei HaEmes*).

18.

רַבִּי נְהוֹרַאי אוֹמֵר: הֱוֵי גּוֹלֶה לִמְקוֹם תּוֹרָה, וְאַל תּאמַר שֶׁהִיא תָבוֹא ■
Rabbi — אַחֲרֶיךָ, שֶׁחֲבֵרֶיךָ יְקַיְּמוּהָ בְיָדֶךָ, "וְאֶל בִּינָתְךָ אַל תִּשָּׁעֵן"
*Nehorai says: Exile yourself to a place of Torah, and do not assume
that it will come after you, for it is your colleagues who will cause
it to remain with you; "and do not rely on your own understanding."*

---

1. For this reason, many of the greatest Kabbalists who performed miracles utilizing Hashem's
Name were known as בַּעַל שֵׁם טוֹב ("the master of the Good Name").

[18] *Rabbi Nehorai says: Exile yourself to a place of Torah, and do not assume that it will come after you, for it is your colleagues who will cause it to remain with you; "and do not rely on your own understanding"* (Mishlei 3:5).

◆§ Better a Lesser Position Among Scholars Than a Preeminent Role Elsewhere

מה לשון גולה הלא אין בן חורין אלא העוסק תורה, ובגמ׳ לא ר״נ שמו רק
ראב״ע שהלך למקום מים היפים כו׳ ושכח למודו חזר ואמר הוי גולה למקום
תורה ע״ש במס׳ שבת . . . שליתרו נקרא בן כשהי׳ תוך הרשעים הי׳ נחשב
כצדיק ושם שם אין נחשב לכלום כמ״ש גבי הצרפית באת אלי להזכיר עוני . . . וודאי
במקומות אשר אינם בני תורה וודאי הת״ח שיש שם בניקל לו לסגל מצות
ומעש״ט כי נחשבים הם לפניו ית׳ שם יותר, אבל במקום בני תורה צריך יגיעה
יתירה, עכ״ז אמר הוי גולה למקום תורה שכדאי להיות נק׳ שם גולה מלהיות
אנשי המקום כענין הוי זנב לאריות כו׳.

To appreciate the importance and spiritual impact of being exiled to a Torah center we recall the reaction of the woman who hosted Eliyahu HaNavi, who complained, בָּאתָ אֵלַי לְהַזְכִּיר אֶת עֲוֹנִי, *you have come to me to call attention to my sins* (I Melachim 17:18). Her remarks indicated that she normally felt herself to be a comparatively righteous individual, but now that Eliyahu arrived, her level of observance paled in comparison to his exalted spirituality.

Yisro, too, sacrificed his spiritual preeminence in the pagan environment of Midian for an inferior role among the Jewish people. In general, it is often easier to attain *initial* spiritual growth in a veritable wilderness. Spiritual strides achieved in an atmosphere of total alienation from Torah and *mitzvos* are greatly valued by Hashem.

Yet, the *mishnah* calls upon us to forgo the fleeting progress achieved by being alone, in favor of the more permanent gains achieved in a Torah environment.

Our *mishnah* is urging us to exile ourselves to a place of Torah, and yield the sense of spiritual superiority attained in a veritable Torah wasteland in favor of the "exile." The relative inferiority that one may feel when residing in a Torah-saturated environment is surpassed by its many benefits.

In this light, we can gain insight into an otherwise puzzling incident. The Gemara (*Shabbos* 147b) relates that Rabbi Elazar ben Arach who was highly praised by his mentor, Rabban Yochanan ben Zakkai (refer to our commentary 2:11), forsook his yeshivah for an extended vacation at the spas of Diumsus. Upon returning, and realizing how much of his learning he had forgotten

[יט] רַבִּי יַנַּאי אוֹמֵר: אֵין בְּיָדֵינוּ לֹא מִשַּׁלְוַת הָרְשָׁעִים וְאַף לֹא מִיִּסּוּרֵי הַצַּדִּיקִים.

[כ] רַבִּי מַתְיָא בֶן חָרָשׁ אוֹמֵר: הֱוֵי מַקְדִּים בִּשְׁלוֹם כָּל אָדָם, וֶהֱוֵי זָנָב לָאֲרָיוֹת, וְאַל תְּהִי רֹאשׁ לְשׁוּעָלִים.

[כא] רַבִּי יַעֲקֹב אוֹמֵר: הָעוֹלָם הַזֶּה דּוֹמֶה לִפְרוֹזְדוֹר בִּפְנֵי הָעוֹלָם הַבָּא; הַתְקֵן עַצְמְךָ בַּפְּרוֹזְדוֹר כְּדֵי שֶׁתִּכָּנֵס לַטְּרַקְלִין.

[refer to the Gemara (ibid.) for details of Rabbi Elazar's first *Aliyah* to the Torah; also refer to *Sfas Emes'* commentary on *Parashas HaChodesh*], he acknowledged the wisdom of this *mishnah*. It is difficult to believe that the sainted Rabbi Elazar sought an extended vacation from yeshivah. He certainly would never have forsaken the "four cubits of Halachah" for the hedonistic pleasures of a spa. Rather, Rabbi Elazar felt he could enhance his spiritual growth by becoming the "resident" scholar of Diumsus, trusting that his piety would shine by comparison to the crass hedonism of the resort's townspeople. Upon realizing the pitfalls of such an approach and the effect of being away so long from yeshivah, he proclaimed, הֱוֵי גוֹלֶה לִמְקוֹם תּוֹרָה. It is better to be an exile in a *place of Torah* than to be a "star" in a wasteland. This theme is restated forcefully in a subsequent *mishnah* (4:20): הֱוֵי זָנָב לָאֲרָיוֹת; וְאַל תְּהִי רֹאשׁ לְשׁוּעָלִים, it is better to be a *tail* (i.e. an insignificant presence) among spiritual lions than to be the *head* (the leading spirit) among foxes.

20.

רַבִּי מַתְיָא בֶן חָרָשׁ אוֹמֵר: הֱוֵי מַקְדִּים בִּשְׁלוֹם כָּל אָדָם, וֶהֱוֵי זָנָב לָאֲרָיוֹת, וְאַל ■ תְּהִי רֹאשׁ לְשׁוּעָלִים — *Rabbi Masya ben Charash says: Initiate a greeting to every person; and be a tail to lions; and do not be a head to foxes.*

◆§ A Plea Against Mediocrity

ק״ק דהרי יש עוד חיות קטנות משועל ובדידהו הו״ל למינקט וי״ל דקמ״ל אפי׳
שועלים שגדולים קצת וגם מחוכמים מ״מ ארי חשיב יותר.

By choosing the metaphor of a fox (an animal of modest size and bearing) rather than that of an even smaller animal, the *mishnah* is insisting that we not even content ourselves with becoming the head of a mediocre group of

[19] *Rabbi Yannai says: It is not in our power [to explain] either the tranquility of the wicked or the suffering of the righteous.*

[20] *Rabbi Masya ben Charash says: Initiate a greeting to every person; and be a tail to lions; and do not be a head to foxes.*

[21] *Rabbi Yaakov says: This World is like a lobby before the World to Come; prepare yourself in the lobby so that you may enter the banquet hall.*

people symbolized by the fox which, although not as regal as a lion, is clever enough and enjoys a middling presence of its own (adapted from *Sfas Emes*).

21.

■ **רַבִּי יַעֲקֹב אוֹמֵר: הָעוֹלָם הַזֶּה דוֹמֶה לִפְרוֹזְדוֹר בִּפְנֵי הָעוֹלָם הַבָּא; הַתְקֵן עַצְמְךָ בַּפְּרוֹזְדוֹר כְּדֵי שֶׁתִּכָּנֵס לַטְּרַקְלִין** — *Rabbi Yaakov says: This World is like a lobby before the World to Come; prepare yourself in the lobby so that you may enter the banquet hall.*

◄§ This World Is *Not* the Palace

מפני שרוב בני אדם סוברים שעולם הזה הוא כמו דירה פתוחה בחמדת כל, ועל ידי זה העולם הזה פתוח לפניהם ועולם הבא נסתר מאתם, והוא כשחוק בעיניהם ומעט מזעיר אשר הם נכנסים בהיכל מלך פנימי.

Contrary to the all-too-popular (and tragic) misconception, This World is *not* a palace laden with treasures which we can retrieve at will. Instead, This World is merely the corridor leading to the true treasures of the World to Come.

The Maggid of Koznitz pointed out the consequences of the all-too-common confusion of the nature of *Olam Hazeh* and *Olam Haba*. As a result of harboring this misconception, many people are so absorbed with amassing the so-called "treasures" of This World that the true treasure, the banquet hall of the King's palace — *Olam Haba* — is never realized (*Maggidei HaEmes*).

◄§ The True Corridor: Fear of Heaven (יִרְאַת שָׁמַיִם)

הפרוזדור הוא יראת שמים שהיא מפתחות החיצוניות.

A lobby is used not only as a reception area but also as a means of entry into the building itself. By using the metaphor of a lobby or corridor, the *mishnah* is emphasizing that This World is not merely a place to *await* one's future destiny but also the means of *entry* into the World to Come. The true objective of every Jew is to prepare ourselves for the transition from the corridor to the banquet hall of the palace.

There is one potent weapon in Hashem's arsenal that we can deploy to ease the passage from This World to the World to Come — fear of Hashem, which is described by the Gemara (*Shabbos* 31b) as the "outer keys" (by comparison to the inner depths of the Torah itself). [Refer to *The Three Festivals*, p. 240, for a more comprehensive explanation of this concept.] In This World, which is the *outer* entrance to the *inner* palace, it is entirely appropriate that we emphasize the virtue of יִרְאַת שָׁמַיִם because it will ease our transition from here to the Hereafter (*Imrei Emes, Maggidei HaEmes*).

❧ Shabbos, the Corridor to Olam Haba

שֶׁבִּפְנֵי שֶׁהָאָדָם מֵכִין עַצְמוֹ בָּעוֹלָם הַזֶּה בְּשַׁבָּת מֵכִין הַדֶּרֶךְ לְשַׁבָּת לֶעָתִיד.

According to the *Beis Yisrael*, our *mishnah* is referring to the Shabbos which most closely resembles *Olam Haba* in This World. Prepare yourself in the corridor — on Shabbos (cf. *Berachos* 57b), in *Olam Hazeh* — so that you will eventually reap the reward of that future world described by *Chazal* as יוֹם שֶׁכּוּלוֹ שַׁבָּת וּמְנוּחָה לְחַיֵּי הָעוֹלָמִים, *to the day that will be entirely Shabbos and contentment for the eternal life* (*Maggidei HaEmes*).

❧ The True Corridor: Fear of Heaven (יִרְאַת שָׁמַיִם)

הַפְּרוֹזְדוֹר הוּא יִרְאַת שָׁמַיִם שֶׁהִיא מַפְתְּחוֹת הַחִיצוֹנִיּוֹת.

A lobby is used not only as a reception area but also as a means of entry into the building itself. By using the metaphor of a lobby or corridor, the *mishnah* is emphasizing that This World is not merely a place to *await* one's future destiny but also the means of *entry* into the World to Come. The true objective of every Jew is to prepare ourselves for the transition from the corridor to the banquet hall of the palace.

There is one potent weapon in Hashem's arsenal that we can deploy to ease the passage from This World to the World to Come — fear of Hashem, which is described by the Gemara (*Shabbos* 31b) as the "outer keys" (by comparison to the inner depths of the Torah itself). [Refer to *The Three Festivals*, p. 240, for a more comprehensive explanation of this concept.] In This World, which is the *outer* entrance to the *inner* palace, it is entirely appropriate that we emphasize the virtue of יִרְאַת שָׁמַיִם because it will ease our transition from here to the Hereafter (*Imrei Emes, Maggidei HaEmes*).

ᴥ Shabbos, the Corridor to Olam Haba

שכפי שהאדם מכין עצמו בעולם הזה בשבת מכין הדרך לשבת לעתיד.

According to the *Beis Yisrael*, our *mishnah* is referring to the Shabbos which most closely resembles *Olam Haba* in This World. Prepare yourself in the corridor — on Shabbos (cf. *Berachos* 57b), in *Olam Hazeh* — so that you will eventually reap the reward of that future world described by *Chazal* as יום שֶׁכּוּלוֹ שַׁבָּת וּמְנוּחָה לְחַיֵּי הָעוֹלָמִים, *to the day that will be entirely Shabbos and contentment for the eternal life* (*Maggidei HaEmes*).

ᴥ The Corridor and Palace Are Both in This World

אַף שאיתא גם כן יפה כן יפה שעה אחת בתשובה ומעשים טובים מחיי עולם הבא, אך גם בעניני עולם הזה נמצא הארה גנוזה והוא מעין עולם הבא כמו שכתוב עולמך תראה בחייך, רק שמלובש בעולם הזה והלבוש פרוזדור, פי׳ כפי מה שאדם עובד בלבוש הזה שלא להתדבק בו, כפי עבודתו ופרישתו מהגשמיות נפתח לו אור הגנוז בו, והוא הטרקלין.

The *Sfas Emes* proposes an ingenious interpretation which emphasizes more than ever the important role played by *Olam Hazeh*. He maintains that *both* the lobby — the superficial veneer of materialism that pervades daily life — and the banquet hall of the palace — the true spiritual life — can be found in This World. By stating הַתְקֵן עַצְמְךָ בַּפְּרוֹזְדוֹר כְּדֵי שֶׁתִּכָּנֵס לַטְּרַקְלִין, *prepare yourself in the lobby so that you may enter the banquet hall*, the *mishnah* is urging us to peer beyond the surface materialism (lobby) that often permeates *Olam Hazeh* and find the inner spiritual beauty — the light of Torah and *mitzvos* — that lies beneath the surface. *Chazal* alluded to this concept with that pithy, yet beautiful blessing: עוֹלָמְךָ תִּרְאֶה בְּחַיֶּיךָ, *you should merit your true world* — the palace — *in your life span*, in This World (*Berachos* 17a). Of course, the path leading to inner spirituality (the palace) in *Olam Hazeh* is by no means an easy one. Our daunting but eminently worthwhile challenge is to somehow not succumb to the allure of the material pleasure beckoning to us in the "corridor,"

ד / כב וּמַעֲשִׂים טוֹבִים בָּעוֹלָם הַזֶּה מִכָּל חַיֵּי הָעוֹלָם הַבָּא;
וְיָפָה שָׁעָה אַחַת שֶׁל קוֹרַת רוּחַ בָּעוֹלָם הַבָּא מִכָּל חַיֵּי
הָעוֹלָם הַזֶּה.

so that we can reap the rich spiritual harvest of the "palace," while yet alive in *Olam Hazeh*. On the basis of this approach, we are also able to resolve the apparent contradiction between this *mishnah*, which seems to reduce *Olam Hazeh* to the status of a corridor, and the following *mishnah* which extols the infinite value of even a *moment* in *Olam Hazeh*. However, according to this interpretation of our *mishnah*, we are not denigrating This World but, on the contrary, urging every Jew to find true meaning even in *Olam Hazeh*.

22.

■ **הוּא הָיָה אוֹמֵר: יָפָה שָׁעָה אַחַת בִּתְשׁוּבָה וּמַעֲשִׂים טוֹבִים בָּעוֹלָם הַזֶּה מִכָּל חַיֵּי הָעוֹלָם הַבָּא** — *He used to say: Better one hour of repentance and good deeds in This World than the entire life of the World to Come.*

∽§ "An Hour"

מה פי' שעה אי א' מכ"ד ביום או על רגע.

כי עוה"ז הוה רק שעה קטנה כמו שמקדים להמשיל לפרוזדור שעובר בו רק
בשעה קלה כצל ימינו.

The *precise* meaning of the term שָׁעָה in this context is unclear. Should it be interpreted in its traditional sense, "an hour," or perhaps שָׁעָה refers to the smallest measure of time? If so, even a fleeting, well-spent moment in This World is equivalent to all of *Olam Haba*.

Perhaps, most ingeniously, the term שָׁעָה אַחַת should not be understood as referring to a specific length of time on This World, but rather as an apt description of *Olam Hazeh*. Our *entire* life span in This World is nothing but a fleeting moment compared to the eternity of the World to Come; as David writes, יָמָיו כְּצֵל עוֹבֵר, *his days are like a passing shadow* (*Tehillim* 144:4). According-ing to this approach, our *mishnah* parallels the previous *mishnah* which com-pared This World to a corridor opening to the palace of *Olam Haba*.

∽§ Which Hour?

י"ל שעה לשון רצון כשהאדם יש לו תמיד תשוקה ורצון אחד להתדבק בו ית'
[כמאמר רשב"י ז"ל אני לדודי בכל יומא בחד קטורא אתקטרנא בי' בקב"ה ...

*good deeds in This World than the entire life of the World
to Come; and better one hour of spiritual bliss in the World
to Come than the entire life of This World.*

ובאמת הרצון והתשוקה הוא הדבר שאין להשיגו בעוה"ב כ"כ כמו בעוה"ז,
כמשל בן המלך שמגעגע לחזור לבית אביו כאשר חכמים הגידו כי זה הי' כל
המבוקש בשליחות נשמת האדם לעוה"ז כדי להתרבות התשוקה בלב האדם
להתדבק בשורשו וזה אומרו יפה שעה אחת כו'.

Clearly, the simplest meaning of שָׁעָה אַחַת is any hour in which we genuinely
aspire to come closer to Hashem, a concept known as עֵת רָצוֹן, *a time of good
will.* Any moment of *Olam Hazeh,* in which mortals are somehow able to
escape the clutches of the material world and "reach out" to Hashem, is far
more precious than all of *Olam Haba.*

To better appreciate the soul's inner yearning to "reconnect" with its Creator,
think of a prince who has been banished from the royal court. Just as he longs
to return to the king's palace, so too the soul — while still in This World —
avidly seeks to return to Hashem. In fact, the sole purpose for the soul's
"descent" from its heavenly origins to This World is to inspire man to seek his
Creator.

✑ A Moment of Tranquility

פירוש יפה שעה אחת בתשובה ומעשים טובים בעולם הזה, היינו מתוך טרדות
עולם הזה מכל חיי העולם הבא, היינו מיושב אהל במנוחה ואין לו שום טירדה.
ודי"ל.

The *mishnah's* use of בָּעוֹלָם הַזֶּה, "in This World," rather than שֶׁל עוֹלָם הַזֶּה, "of
This World," conveys an additional message — how beautiful is a moment
of tranquility amidst all the turbulence of *Olam Hazeh* (R' Yechezkel of Kozmir,
Maggidei HaEmes).

✑ Serving Hashem While Still Striving

הרבי זושא ז"ל אמר על כך, שלו לא יהיה עולם הבא על זה שעבד את השי"ת
לאחר שהגיע להכרה, כי העבודות לאחר ההכרה זהו עצמו הגן עדן הגדול ביותר,
הוא יכול לצפות לעוה"ב על העבודות שעבד עד שהגיע להכרה, מה שעבד מתוך
אמונה.

In a similar vein, R' Zusha would say that he will merit *Olam Haba* not on the
basis of his Divine service accomplished *after* he had begun to appreciate

Hashem's greatness. In that case, the opportunity to serve Hashem was itself sufficient reward. As our *mishnah* implies, no greater reward exists than living a life of *teshuvah* and good deeds in This World. It is by fulfilling Hashem's will faithfully, *prior* to understanding His nature, that he will merit *Olam Haba* (*Maggidei HaEmes*).

◆§ Why Not Mitzvos?

ובזה יתפרש נמי מ״ש לקמן יפה שעה א׳ בתשובה ומעש״ט בעוה״ז מכ״ח עוה״ב אבל מצות לא זכר כי מצות הם גם בעוה״ב כמו שמצינו מלאכי השרת בשמים עושין שליחות ומצוות אבל מעש״ט שהפי׳ בין אדם לחבירו וכן תשובה ב׳ אלו לא שייך בעוה״ב,

It is significant that the *mishnah* describes the beauty of an hour spent in an ambiance of repentance and good deeds, but does not specifically mention the performance of *mitzvos*. Unlike *teshuvah* and good deeds which can *only* be performed in This World, *mitzvos* can, to a certain extent, be performed in *Olam Haba*. For example, angels who exist primarily in the spiritual realm of *Olam Haba* are constantly fulfilling Hashem's commandments, as they perform their sacred missions. By contrast, good deeds refer to those things we do to assist others. It is no longer possible to assist a peer in the ethereal realm of the World to Come. Similarly, once the soul has departed for *Olam Haba*, it is too late to repent for its misdeeds.

◆§ Entering the Palace (טְרַקְלִין) Through Teshuvah and Maasim Tovim

והוא עצמו תשובה ששב לפנימיות החיות שבדברי עוה״ז להתדבק בשורש הדבר, ועי״ז מעלה הכל לשורשו והיא תשובה, וכן מעשים טובים הפי׳ שעושה כל דבר בדביקות אור כי טוב הגנוז בו, כמ״ש חז״ל שהקב״ה גנז אור כו׳ לצדיקים, וכל גניזה היא במקום החושך והסתר, והוא כנ״ל למצוא הארה הגנוזה ע״י עבודה מבחוץ כנ״ל, רק העיקר שיהי׳ כל עוה״ז בעיני האדם בפרוזדור כו׳, וכפי הביטול להפנימיות מתגלה לו כנ״ל.

While we generally translate תְּשׁוּבָה as repentance, in reality, it involves much more. In its most literal — and fundamental — sense, *teshuvah* means to *return* (לָשׁוּב) to one's roots by scraping away the outer veneer of This World that so attracts the physical body in favor of the spirituality favored by the soul. Similarly, the popular expression מַעֲשִׂים טוֹבִים suggests much more than "good deeds." Rather, it implies a return to the pure spirituality of the world's beginning, to the primeval light of Creation which is described as the "good light" [וַיַּרְא אֱלֹהִים אֶת הָאוֹר כִּי טוֹב, *God saw that the light was good* (*Bereishis* 1:4)]. While Hashem hid that light and preserved it for the righteous, nevertheless it is possible to elicit some rays of that luminescence through our good deeds. Hence, the term מַעֲשִׂים טוֹבִים, aimed at eliciting that original luminescence, are deeds that enable us to arrive at the palace while still living in the corridor, This World (adapted from *Sfas Emes*).

✺ "Peace of Mind"

איתא בזוהר בעל תשובה בשעתא חדא ברגעא חדא. רגע אחד להתיישבות
בעבודת השם.

A ccording to the *Beis Yisrael*, the term תְּשׁוּבָה is related to יִשּׁוּב הַדַּעַת, *peace of mind*. One moment of genuine peace of mind in This World — a moment in which we can set aside all our mundane concerns and focus on our relationship with Hashem — is equivalent to all of the World to Come. The comment of the *Zohar* (*Parashas Vayeira* 129:1, בַּעַל תְּשׁוּבָה בְּשַׁעְתָּא חֲדָא בְּרִגְעָא חֲדָא), that a *baal teshuvah* can accomplish in one hour, or even one moment, what others require an eternity to do, may be interpreted in a similar light. Someone who enjoys that rare gift of יִשּׁוּב הַדַּעַת, true *peace of mind*, may accomplish what others, lacking this gift of tranquility, can never achieve (*Maggidei HaEmes*).

■ וְיָפָה שָׁעָה אַחַת שֶׁל קוֹרַת רוּחַ בָּעוֹלָם הַבָּא מִכֹּל חַיֵּי הָעוֹלָם הַזֶּה — *And better one hour of spiritual bliss in the World to Come than the entire life of This World.*

✺ A Timeless World

הנה מהלך ת"ק אמה בגשמיות, אבל במחשבה שהוא למעלה מזמניות, והתענוג
גם כן שם למעלה מהזמן, מה שבגשמיות אלפיים שנה שם הוא ברגע אחד.

T hough *Chazal* describe the distance between heaven and earth in finite terms (cf. *Chagigah* 13a), this is solely from the perspective of the physical world in which we now live. In the realm of esoteric Torah thought, no temporal barriers exist. When describing the majestic and supernatural pleasure of the World to Come we seek to transcend the physical limitations of daily life and adopt the perspective of rarefied Torah thought so that we can begin to grasp a scintilla of the great spiritual treasures that await the righteous. As our *mishnah* emphasizes, a moment of the bliss of the World to Come is as enjoyable as all the pleasure to be derived from millennia of This World. In that timeless universe, a fleeting moment is as valuable as centuries in This World

[כג] רַבִּי שִׁמְעוֹן בֶּן אֶלְעָזָר אוֹמֵר: אַל תְּרַצֶּה אֶת חֲבֵרְךָ בִּשְׁעַת כַּעֲסוֹ; וְאַל תְּנַחֲמֵהוּ בְּשָׁעָה שֶׁמֵּתוֹ מֻטָּל לְפָנָיו; וְאַל תִּשְׁאַל לוֹ בִּשְׁעַת נִדְרוֹ; וְאַל תִּשְׁתַּדֵּל לִרְאוֹתוֹ בִּשְׁעַת קַלְקָלָתוֹ.

(Maggid of Mezeritch, Maggidei HaEmes).

⋖§ Delayed Compensation

הקשה אחד מגדולי הדור לאדמו״ר זצ״ל מקאצק הלא מצינו בוצינא טבא מקרא והשיב לו הרבי מקאצק גם זה הוא רק בעולם הזה ודו״ק.

In response to the question posed by a great sage that the pleasures of *Olam Haba*, however sublime, are *delayed* while the physical rewards of This World are far more *immediate*, the Kotzker Rebbe made this observation: This question is only valid from the temporal perspective of *Olam Hazeh* where we can only grasp what is immediately obvious. From the timeless perspective of the World to Come, no distinction exists between delayed reward and the promise of immediate payment (*Maggidei HaEmes*).

⋖§ Which Is Better — a Moment in Olam Hazeh or in Olam Haba

מקשים דלכאורה סתראי נינהו. וי״ל דהואיל ותשובה ומעש״ט כתריס בפני הפורענות, נמצא שע״י שעה אחת של תשובה ומעש״ט בעוה״ז יכול לקנות שעה אחת של קורת רוח בעוה״ב ... נמצא ששניהם אחד וכנ״ל.

Seemingly, the latter part of the *mishnah*, emphasizing the esoteric pleasures of *Olam Haba*, contradicts the first phrase which prefers a moment of *teshuvah* to all of *Olam Haba*. However, upon further contemplation we realize both themes of our *mishnah* are closely related. It is only through the repentance and good deeds of This World that we merit the hour of spiritual bliss awaiting us in *Olam Haba* (*Maggidei HaEmes*).

והרה״ק רבי משה ליב מסאסוב ז״ל פירש עפ״י מאמרם ז״ל מקום שבעלי תשובה עומדים צדיקים גמורים אינם עומדים. והטעם שאמר עומדים ולא אמר הולכים, לפי שבעל תשובה שנכשל בחטא מבקש מהשי״ת שישלול ממנו הבחירה כדי שלא ישוב לכסלה אף שעי״ז יפסיד שכרו בעוה״ב. ולכן בעל תשובה הריהו עומד, לא כן הצדיק שיש לו בחירה הוא הולך. ולזה מקום שבע״ת עומדים צדיקים

[23] *Rabbi Shimon ben Elazar says: Do not appease your fellow at the time of his anger; do not console him while his dead lies before him; do not question him about his vow at the time he makes it; and do not attempt to see him at the time of his degradation.*

גמורים אינם עומדים. ולכן לבעלי תשובה יפה שעה אחת של תשובה בעוה"ז מכל חיי העוה"ב, לא כן צדיקים גמורים שאצליהם יפה שעה אחת של קורת רוח בעוה"ב מכל חיי העוה"ז ודפח"ח.

According to R' Moshe Leib of Sassov, the first phrase of the *mishnah* extolling the virtues of *Olam Haba* refers to the *baal teshuvah* who, having returned from the abyss, is assured that he will not be tempted again. *Chazal* (Berachos 34b) refer to the level which two penitents reach as מָקוֹם שֶׁבַּעֲלֵי תְשׁוּבָה עוֹמְדִים, "the place where *baalei teshuvah stand*" — they stand in place, confident that they will not sin again. For them every moment spent in the rarefied ambiance of *teshuvah* in This World exceeds any reward in This World.

On the other hand, the righteous man enjoys no such assurance, and, on the contrary, thrives amidst the challenge of adversity. Although capable of dealing with the temptations of This World, he awaits his moment of spiritual bliss in The World to Come (*Maggidei HaEmes*).

23.

■ וְאַל תִּשְׁתַּדֵּל לִרְאוֹתוֹ בִּשְׁעַת קַלְקָלָתוֹ — *And do not attempt to see him at the time of his degradation.*

◆§ Do Not Look for the Worst Possible Interpretation

דקדק פעם מה פירוש הלשון אל תשתדל. ואולי י"ל הכוונה שלא יהא לו שנאה כבושה בלב על חבירו, ועי"ז יראה תמיד קלקלתו, אף אם לאמיתו של דבר לא קלקל או שהיה לו סיבה טובה וכדומה.

If the *mishnah* merely meant that one should not watch while a friend is being embarrassed, it would have simply said, אַל תִּרְאֶה בִּשְׁעַת קַלְקָלָתוֹ. The apparently superfluous term, תִּשְׁתַּדֵּל, *attempt* implies much more. Do not harbor a sense of lingering resentment against your peer which would invariably lead you to look for — תִּשְׁתַּדֵּל לִרְאוֹתוֹ — the worst possible explanation for his behavior (קַלְקָלָתוֹ) (*Imrei Emes, Maggidei HaEmes*).

ד/כד-כה [כד] שְׁמוּאֵל הַקָּטָן אוֹמֵר: ,,בִּנְפֹל אוֹיִבְךָ אַל תִּשְׂמָח,
וּבִכָּשְׁלוֹ אַל יָגֵל לִבֶּךָ. פֶּן יִרְאֶה יהוה וְרַע בְּעֵינָיו,
וְהֵשִׁיב מֵעָלָיו אַפּוֹ."

[כה] אֱלִישָׁע בֶּן אֲבוּיָה אוֹמֵר: הַלּוֹמֵד יֶלֶד, לְמָה הוּא
דוֹמֶה? לִדְיוֹ כְתוּבָה עַל נְיָר חָדָשׁ. וְהַלּוֹמֵד זָקֵן,
לְמָה הוּא דוֹמֶה? לִדְיוֹ כְתוּבָה עַל נְיָר מָחוּק.

<hr>

24.

■ שְׁמוּאֵל הַקָּטָן אוֹמֵר: ,,בִּנְפֹל אוֹיִבְךָ אַל תִּשְׂמָח, וּבִכָּשְׁלוֹ אַל יָגֵל לִבֶּךָ. פֶּן יִרְאֶה
ה' וְרַע בְּעֵינָיו, וְהֵשִׁיב מֵעָלָיו אַפּוֹ." — *Shmuel HaKattan says: "When your
enemy falls do not be glad, and when he stumbles let your heart not
be joyous. Lest Hashem see and it displease Him, and He turn His
wrath from him [to you]."*

◄§ Constant Struggle Against the Yetzer Hara

וכי יש תמיד שונא לאדם. ובשם המפרשים שקאי על היצר הרע שאין שונא גדול
ממנו, והפי' שגם שנעזר לפעמים להתגבר עליו לא ישמח ויבטח שכבר נצחו
שיוכל לחזור כמקדם.

The term אוֹיִבְךָ, *your enemy* (suggesting a certain constant foe), refers to the
yetzer hara who constantly pursues us. The *mishnah* warns us never to rest
content, assuming smugly that the *yetzer hara* has been vanquished. Such
rejoicing is premature and may lead to the *yetzer hara's* resurgence.

◄§ Even When Hatred Is Warranted

קשה הלא פסוק הוא. אולם איתא בתוס' שאף שיש לשנא לעוברי עבירה מכל
מקום מזהיר הכתוב מפני השנאה שבאה מחמת כמים הפנים לפנים וגו'. ושמעתי
מאחד דשמואל הקטן הוא שתיקן ברכת המינים, היינו להתפלל שיאבדו, לכן היה
מזהיר על השנאה הבאה מחמת כמים הפנים לפנים ואמר בנפול אויבך אל
תשמח, כי צריכים להבחין בין שנאה לשנאה.

While it appears that Shmuel HaKattan is merely citing a *pasuk* in *Mishlei*
(24:17-18), upon closer examination we realize that he is carefully defining
the parameters of hatred. Even when hatred is warranted — i.e. towards the

[24] *Shmuel HaKattan says (Mishlei 24:17-18): When your enemy falls do not be glad, and when he stumbles let your heart not be joyous, lest Hashem see and it displease Him, and He turn His wrath from him [to you].*

[25] *Elisha ben Avuyah says: One who studies [Torah] while [he is still] a child, to what can he be likened? — to ink written on fresh [clean] paper. And one who studies [Torah] as an old man, to what can he be likened? — to ink written on smudged [erased] paper.*

Jew who sins intentionally and habitually (cf. *Pesachim* 113b *Tosafos s.v.* שראה) — it is important to distinguish between the hatred due such an inveterate sinner and the personal animosity that results from your assumption that this individual hates you. While the former type of hatred is a *mitzvah*, the latter is prohibited.

It is appropriate that Shmuel who composed וְלַמַּלְשִׁינִים, *And for slanderers*, the blessing in the *Shemoneh Esrei* calling for the downfall of the hated heretics and non-believers, simultaneously warns against displaying *personal* antipathy towards sinners (*Imrei Emes, Maggidei HaEmes*).

25.

■ אֱלִישָׁע בֶּן אֲבוּיָה אוֹמֵר: הַלּוֹמֵד יֶלֶד, לְמָה הוּא דוֹמֶה? – לִדְיוֹ כְּתוּבָה עַל נְיָר חָדָשׁ. וְהַלּוֹמֵד זָקֵן, לְמָה הוּא דוֹמֶה? – לִדְיוֹ כְּתוּבָה עַל נְיָר מָחוּק — *Elisha ben Avuyah says: One who studies [Torah] while [he is still] a child, to what can he be likened? — to ink written on fresh [clean] paper. And one who studies [Torah] as an old man, to what can he be likened? — to ink written on smudged [erased] paper.*

◁§ A Microcosm of Elisha's Life

נראה דאלישע כיון דבילדותו למד היה סופו להיות ניתקן גם כן.

Elisha ben Avuyah is not only offering sound advice but is also reflecting on his own life. It is well known (cf. *Chagigah* 15a) that this great sage and mentor of Rabbi Meir eventually abandoned Torah practice, even to the extent that he desecrated Shabbos in public. Whereas according to the *Talmud Bavli*, Elisha never repented, the *Talmud Yerushalmi* (cited by *Tosafos Chagigah* 15a, *s.v.,* שובו) maintains that Elisha recanted on his deathbed and consequently merited *Olam Haba*.

[כו] רַבִּי יוֹסֵי בַּר יְהוּדָה אִישׁ כְּפַר הַבַּבְלִי אוֹמֵר: הַלּוֹמֵד מִן הַקְּטַנִּים, לְמָה הוּא דוֹמֶה? לְאוֹכֵל עֲנָבִים קֵהוֹת, וְשׁוֹתֶה יַיִן מִגִּתּוֹ. וְהַלּוֹמֵד מִן הַזְּקֵנִים, לְמָה הוּא דוֹמֶה? לְאוֹכֵל עֲנָבִים בְּשׁוּלוֹת, וְשׁוֹתֶה יַיִן יָשָׁן.

Reflecting on the many phases of his checkered life, Elisha attributes his capacity to eventually repent to the Torah that he had learned as a child (הַלּוֹמֵד יֶלֶד) (cf. *Tosafos* ibid. discussing his father's resolution to teach him Torah) (adapted from *Sfas Emes*).

∞§ Who Is a Youth?

ושיעור ילד הוא עוד בו נשמתו מיקרי עוד ילד ליום שלאח״כ שנעשה זקן יותר ממקודם.

שיהיה חדש כל פעם ברצון חדש בתנועה והרגש חדש. ולאו דוקא ילד אלא שיהיה בכל פעם נולד וחדש.

דר״ל שצריך לשוב בתשובה ויהיה לו מוחין חדשים ויהיה בקטן שנולד. איתא באבות דרבי נתן הלומד תורה בילדותו דברי תורה נבלעין בדמיו. פי׳ שבח הראשון הוא כח חזק מפני שלא נבלע בו שום דבר אחר ומפני זה נתקשר מאד בתוה״ק עד שיקרה אצלו יותר מכל חמדת עולם הזה.

ולכאורה דבריו סותרים אהדדי. ונראה בביאור דבריו דעד ששים שנה יכול להתחיל ללמוד כבימי הילדות אף שלא למד עד אז. ולא הוי כדיו כתובה על נייר מחוק. אבל לאחר ששים שנה קשה מאד להתחיל ללמוד כמו בימי הילדות, ואף שלומד לא הוי אלא כמו נייר מחוק. אלא שזהו דוקא אם לא למד עד אז, אבל זה שלומד כל ימיו בהתחדשות בלימוד התורה, אצלו גם לאחר ששים שנה עוד בו נשמתו בו מיקרי ילד ליום שלאחר כך, דהוי כדיו כתובה על נייר חדש.

Certainly our *mishnah* is not discouraging elderly people from studying Torah. In fact, the term יֶלֶד may even apply to an adult.

For example, if we assume as Yehudah ben Tema does (in *Avos* 5:25) that the age of sixty marks the beginning of זִקְנָה, *old age* (seniority), anyone under that age would be considered a יֶלֶד and remains a prime candidate for Torah study. Even more optimistically, the *Sfas Emes* argues that one remains a "youth" for one's entire life span. By encouraging us to learn while we are still young, the *mishnah* is motivating us to learn every day of our life. Learn today — when you are a comparative youth — rather than wait till tomorrow when you are a day older. Moreover, as the *Chiddushei HaRim* pointed out, the *mishnah* may be referring to intellectual agility and freshness rather than chronological age.

[26] *Rabbi Yose bar Yehudah of Kfar HaBavli says: One who learns [Torah] from the young, to what can he be likened? — to one who eats unripe grapes or drinks [unfermented] wine from his vat. But one who learns [Torah] from the old, to what can he be likened? — to one who eats ripe grapes or drinks aged wine.*

In a similar vein, the Maggid of Koznitz interpreted this *mishnah* as being a plea to repent. Just as a convert is considered halachically a newly born individual (*Yevamos* 22a), so too every time we do *teshuvah* we are rejuvenated (*Maggidei HaEmes*).

On the other hand, the *mishnah* may be interpreted in its simplest sense as a plan to study Torah while young. While certainly no cut-off point exists beyond which one experiences difficulty in absorbing Torah, the earlier one studies the better. To support his contention, the *Chiddushei HaRim* cites *Avos DeRav Nassan* (a *Baraisa* patterned on *Pirkei Avos*) which lauds one who studies Torah בְּיַלְדוּתוֹ, while young. Though it may be possible to *intellectually* absorb Torah at a later stage in life, the all-important *emotional* connection to Torah, a bond described as דִּבְרֵי תוֹרָה נִבְלָעִין בְּדָמָיו, *the words of Torah are absorbed into his bloodstream*, is best formed at an early stage before one is exposed to any competing influences.

In conclusion, we mention the *Lev Simchah's* resolution to the apparently contradictory statements of the *Sfas Emes* (cited previously) regarding the optimal age for Torah study. Whereas, in one instance the *Sfas Emes* suggested that the prime time for *limud Torah* is prior to age sixty, elsewhere he maintained that one is never too old to enjoy the status of a יֶלֶד, a child. Perhaps, the distinction is as follows: If one commences Torah study prior to age sixty, then one can *always* enjoy the vitality of youth. Thus, Elisha ben Avuyah, who had studied Torah while young (and later drifted away), was able to return to the fold (refer to our previous remarks). On the other hand, it is difficult to *begin* learning if one has not studied prior to age sixty (*Maggidei HaEmes*).

◆§ Erased Paper: The Human Body

כי הגוף כמו נייר והעבירות מקלקלין הנייר בחקיקיות וטעיות הכתב.

The metaphor *smudged [erased] paper* may refer to the human body which is fresh and impressionable during one's youth, but over time becomes tainted by the numerous scars and misleading impressions left by *aveiros*.

[כז] רַבִּי מֵאִיר אוֹמֵר: אַל תִּסְתַּכֵּל בַּקַּנְקַן, אֶלָּא בְּמַה שֶׁיֶּשׁ בּוֹ; יֵשׁ קַנְקַן חָדָשׁ מָלֵא יָשָׁן, וְיָשָׁן שֶׁאֲפִילוּ חָדָשׁ אֵין בּוֹ.

[כח] רַבִּי אֶלְעָזָר הַקַּפָּר אוֹמֵר: הַקִּנְאָה וְהַתַּאֲוָה וְהַכָּבוֹד מוֹצִיאִין אֶת הָאָדָם מִן הָעוֹלָם.

☙ Is There a Middle Case?

הנה הדיוקים סותרים דהול"ל או חדש וישן או יפה ומחוק גם התחיל גם ילד ומסיים זקן ובינוני מה תהא עליו לבן י"ל שיש אמצעי נייר ישן אבל אינו מחוק.

The *mishnah* cites both extremes — studying Torah as a child, which is compared to writing on a new piece of paper, and learning as an older person, compared to writing on erased paper. However, we may infer that a middle (third) case exists — studying Torah during middle age, which following the *mishnah*'s pattern, is comparable to writing on old but not necessarily erased paper (adapted from *Sfas Emes*).

26.

■ רַבִּי יוֹסֵי בַּר יְהוּדָה אִישׁ כְּפַר הַבַּבְלִי אוֹמֵר . . . וְהַלּוֹמֵד מִן הַזְּקֵנִים, לְמָה הוּא דּוֹמֶה? — לְאוֹכֵל עֲנָבִים בְּשׁוּלוֹת וְשׁוֹתֶה יַיִן יָשָׁן. — *Rabbi Yose bar Yehudah of Kfar HaBavli says: . . . But one who learns [Torah] from the old, to what can he be likened? — to one who eats ripe grapes or drinks aged wine.*

☙ Learning From Judaism's Elders

אלישע משבח הנערים ורבי יוסי בר יהודה משבח הזקנים. יש לומר דהלומד מדברי חכמים שמצותן נקראים מצות זקנים, וכן כתיב זקניך ויאמרו לך, גם כן הוי בכלל לומד מן הזקנים. ולפי זה כל הלומד מהגמ' רש"י ותוס' ומשאר דברי חכמים גם כן נקרא לומד מן הזקנים. והעיקר שילמוד מהם איך ללמוד, ואת המעשה אשר יעשה.

By contrast to Elisha ben Avuyah who extols the virtues of youth, Rabbi Yose bar Yehudah finds merit in age, preferring to study Torah at the feet of elders. We may assume that he is not only referring to the contemporary elders of his generation but also to *Klal Yisrael's* historical elders, the great Torah scholars

[27] *Rabbi Meir says: Do not look at the vessel, but at what is in it; there is a new vessel filled with old wine, and an old [vessel] that does not even contain new wine.*

[28] *Rabbi Elazar HaKappar says: Jealousy, lust and glory remove a man from the world.*

---

of all time. As Moshe reminds us, שְׁאַל ... זְקֵנֶיךָ וְיֹאמְרוּ לָךְ, *ask ... your elders and they will tell you* (*Devarim* 32:7). Whenever we study Gemara with commentaries of *Rashi* and *Tosafos* and other noted scholars, who are not only interpreting the Talmud but are also imparting to us their approach to *Avodas Hashem*, we are fulfilling the *mishnah's* advice, to learn from our elders (*Lev Simchah, Maggidei HaEmes*).

27.

■ רַבִּי מֵאִיר אוֹמֵר: אַל תִּסְתַּכֵּל בַּקַנְקַן, אֶלָּא בְּמַה שֶׁיֵּשׁ בּוֹ; יֵשׁ קַנְקַן חָדָשׁ מָלֵא יָשָׁן, וְיָשָׁן שֶׁאֲפִלּוּ חָדָשׁ אֵין בּוֹ — *Rabbi Meir says: Do not look at the vessel, but at what is in it; there is a new vessel filled with old wine, and an old [vessel] that does not even contain new wine.*

✑§ A Third Approach

> פליג אתרווי' אלישע משבח הנערים וריב"י משבח הזקנים ורבי מפשר ביניהם יש
> חדש כו' ולא תליא כלל בהאדם.
> ויש איש ילד עם נשמה זקנה מלאה מצות ויש ישן שאפי' חדש אין בו.

In contrast to Elisha ben Avuyah who emphasizes the importance of youth and Rabbi Yose bar Yehudah who places primary emphasis on having an

---

1. Whereas in the standard *Mishnayos* text (utilized by the *Sfas Emes*) this statement is attributed to Rebbi, the standard *Pirkei Avos* text cites Rabbi Meir.

older mentor, Rebbi (Rabbi Meir)[1] proposes a third approach, favoring neither youth nor age. Instead, he urges us to focus on the "age" and maturity of the soul rather than the chronological age. Do not look at the vessel — the body — but rather seek to understand what it contains. Upon opening a new vessel, you will at times find old wine — a young man with an advanced (mature) soul. At other times, you will find an old vessel lacking even new wine — an elderly person with an immature soul.

28.

■ רַבִּי אֶלְעָזָר הַקַפָּר אוֹמֵר: הַקִנְאָה וְהַתַּאֲוָה וְהַכָּבוֹד מוֹצִיאִין אֶת הָאָדָם מִן הָעוֹלָם ■

— *Rabbi Elazar HaKappar says: Jealousy, lust and glory remove a man from the world.*

⋈ Historical Antecedents

אמו״ז ז״ל הגיד בשם הרב המגיד מקאזניץ ע״ה כי נכתבו פרשת קין ודור המבול
והפלגה כי כל אדם יש בו מאלה הדורות, וצריך לתקן עצמו, והם בחי׳ קנאה תאוה
וכבוד, קין קנאה, דור המבול תאוה, דור הפלגה כבוד, קין והבל כל העולם כולו
שלהם היתה לכל אחד מהם הי׳ חצי העולם ומלואה ובכל זאת הקנאה היתה אצלם
כל כך גדולה.

By citing these three primary causes of man's downfall, our *mishnah* is draw-ing upon ample historical precedent both from the universe's earliest years and from the behavior of the Jewish people in the Wilderness.

At the beginning of history, Kayin's jealousy of his brother Hevel led to his downfall. The *Beis Yisrael* points out the sheer folly of Kayin's jealousy. While a certain degree of jealousy might be rationalized (if not justified) on the part of someone who is struggling, Kayin, along with his brother, was destined to inherit half of the entire universe! Yet, the insatiable, often irrational vice of jealousy drove Kayin to quarrel and eventually kill his brother.

Similarly, the generation of the Flood was destroyed because of its insatiable lust and finally the builders of the Tower of Bavel motivated by the desire for glory, proclaimed, וְנַעֲשֶׂה לָּנוּ שֵׁם, *let us make a name for ourselves* (*Bereishis* 11:4). They too were quickly dispersed and driven from power.

When the Jewish people traveled in the Wilderness, they too were beset and gravely damaged by these three vices: the jealousy of Korach seeking out Aharon's prerogatives; the lust of the *erev rav* who craved meat and choked on the quail; and finally, the spies who slandered *Eretz Yisrael* mainly because of their concern that they would have to forfeit their coveted positions upon entering the Promised Land.

⋈ All Three or Any One?

נראה הפי׳ על א׳ מאלו הג׳
וכמ״ש רש״י ז״ל הראיה מקרח גחזי וירבעם.

Rashi (in his commentary to *Pirkei Avos*) gives an example of a Biblical character who was tragically flawed in respect to each of these vices. Specif-ically, Korach's jealousy led to his undoing; Geichazi (Elisha's disciple) was motivated by his greed and lust to seek gifts from Naaman (*II Melachim* 5:20 ff.), and consequently was banished from Elisha's inner circle and from *Olam Haba*; and finally, Yeravam whose rebellion against the Davidic monarchy was spurred by his thirst for glory (cf. *Sanhedrin* 102b). We may deduce from *Rashi* that any one of these three vices is sufficient to *remove a man from the world.*

◄§ The Three Facets of the Divine Image (צֶלֶם אֱלֹהִים)

פ' שמאבדין ע"י דברים אלו הצלם אדם

וידוע שזה הצלם הוא בנפש רוח ונשמה ובג' דברים הנ"ל פוגמים הדמות אדם ...

The term הָאָדָם, *the man*, alludes to the Divine Image imprinted in man. As a result of the three vices of jealousy, lust and glory, the three segments of the soul — נֶפֶשׁ, רוּחַ נְשָׁמָה, — all implanted by Hashem, are corrupted. (For further discussion of this concept see *The Three Festivals*, p 370.) (Adapted from *Sfas Emes.*)

◄§ Antidotes to the Three Vices

In this section we will consider some effective antidotes to the lethal character traits of *jealousy, lust* and a craving for *glory* (קִנְאָה, תַּאֲוָה, כָּבוֹד).

◄§ Consider the Objective

חסיד אחד בא לפני הרבי ר' העניך ז"ל והתנצל על הקנאה והתאוה והכבוד שיש

בו. אמר לו "קנאה נאך וואס, תאוה צו וואס, כבוד פאר וואס''.

According to R' Henoch of Alexander, the most efficacious way of combating these three vices is to consider one's ultimate objective. In his words, קנאה נאך וואס, תאוה צו וואס, כבוד פאר וואס, *"Jealous at what? Lust after what? Glory for what?"* Consider what you are jealous of. Is that momentary, often trivial objective worth arousing jealousy? Ask yourself, after what are you lusting? And finally, for what purpose are you seeking glory? If we contemplate the sheer insignificance of the objectives that we are pursuing, we would never succumb to them (*Maggidei HaEmes*).

◄§ "The Bottom Line" — Only Jealousy

בעצם לא נשאר לאדם לבסוף כי אם הקנאה בלבד, לפי שהאדם נמנע מלמלאות

תאותו מפני הכבוד, והכבוד עצמו אינו מקבל כי הרי יש לו גם תאוה, כך שלבסוף

הוא נשאר רק בהקנאה.

R' Henoch of Alexander emphasized the futility of the vain chase after jealousy, lust and glory (honor). Any individual possessing a modicum of self-honor will be too ashamed to publicly satiate his vilest lust. Consequently neither his desire for honor nor his passion will be satisfied. Instead, he is left with nothing but lingering jealousy towards those who are *truly* successful (*Maggidei HaEmes*).

⦿§ Embrace the Opposite Virtue — A Good Eye (עַיִן טוֹבָה)

וכשזה להיפך רואים שהכל מהשי״ת, על ידי עין טובה, מ׳זעט גוט ביי יענעם, מ׳פארגינט יענעם.

The *Pnei Menachem* (known for his constant advocacy of the virtue of עַיִן טוֹבָה; cf. Introduction to *Days of Awe*, p. XXII) recommended a simple antidote to the triple plague of jealousy, lust and glory — displaying an עַיִן טוֹבָה, *a good eye*, to all. If we genuinely believe that everything we possess emanates from Hashem — and that passion or jealousy *will not change anything* — it follows that we should always act compassionately and with great generosity to our peers. A person motivated by a good eye will always genuinely wish others the best possible outcome and always be happy with another's success (*Maggidei HaEmes*).

⦿§ The Torah Itself Is the Best Antidote

אאז״ל אמר הקנאה והתאוה והכבוד מוציאין את האדם מן העולם, והתורה היא ההיפך מזה שהיא נותנת חיים כמו שכתוב וחיי עולם נטע בתוכנו ... קבלת התורה בכדי לתקן הנ״ל, שמצות הגבלה היתה לכל אחד ואחד מקום מיוחד בכדי שלא תהיה קנאה, אחר כך מצות פרישה כנגד תאוה, ולאחר זה ויתיצבו בתחתית ההר שזה הכנעה וענוה כנגד כבוד.

The *Imrei Emes* noted that the Torah itself is the best antidote for the three sins of jealousy, lust and pursuing glory. Each of the events occurring prior to the Giving of the Torah was intended to rid *Klal Yisrael* of one of these negative traits. For example, the fence erected around Mt. Sinai was intended to ensure that every member of *Klal Yisrael* enjoyed his own place at the Giving of the Torah, thereby minimizing the possibility of jealousy. By separating from their spouses prior to *Matan Torah*, the Jewish people's sense of lust was curtailed. Finally, by standing *below* Har Sinai (rather than *ascending* the mountain), *Klal Yisrael* became inured to the plague of seeking glory (*Maggidei HaEmes*).

■ מוֹצִיאִין אֶת הָאָדָם מִן הָעוֹלָם — *Remove a man from the world.*

⦿§ Plaguing Us Throughout Life

שח מרן אדמו״ר מקאצק ז״ל ״בשלש אבסניות מבקר כל אדם בדרך הילוכו על

האדמה. באכסניה של קנאה, באכסניה של תאוה ובאכסניה של כבוד. האדם
נברא עם הקנאה, התאוה באה עם הרגלו בה וכניעתו לה והכבוד משרך דרכו
אחריו כצל. בשתי האכסניות של קנאה ושל תאוה עברתי מהר, נפטרתי מהן
בדהירה אבל באכסניה השלישית, של כבוד נאלצתי להתאבק קשה עד כי דמיתי
בנפשי שגידי יתפוצצו. . . כאשר הייתי עול ימים ובקרתי בראשונה אצל החוזה
מלובלין ז"ל, כבדני להתפלל בבוקר במנינו הפרטי שבו השתתפו רק החבריא
הקדושה שלו ושנים רבות עמלתי לעקור מבין שיני את הכבוד הזה".

The Kotzker Rebbe interpreted this *mishnah* from the perspective of his long and diversified life. He perceived life as a long journey, each phase along the way being comparable to an inn. The first two "inns," those of jealousy and lust, were brief stopovers, which he was able to easily bypass (surmount). However, the final detour — the lure of glory and honor — was the most difficult to overcome, especially honor resulting from proximity to great Torah personalities. He recalled how as a young man, he had been honored to *daven* in the private *minyan* of the sainted Chozeh of Lublin. It took years till the Kotzker Rebbe was able to totally eradicate the lasting impact of this honor (*Maggidei HaEmes*).

⌾ Living in the Capital and Not Knowing the King

שח הרה"ק רבי אברהם מסלונים ז"ל כלום יתכן שאדם יהיה בעיר המלוכה ולא
ידע מן המלך, וכמו כן כאשר אדם שרוי בתוכו של עולם איך זה אפשרי שאינו
יודע ממלכו של עולם. אכן הקנאה והתאוה והכבוד מוציאין את האדם מן העולם,
לכן אינו יודע.

According to R' Avraham of Slonim, the "world" in the *mishnah* does not only refer to the World to Come but also to This World. As a result of displaying jealously, lust, and glory, we in effect detach ourselves from Hashem, Who governs This World. Imagine living in the capital city of a monarchy and not knowing who is the king! (*Maggidei HaEmes*).

⌾ To Live in This World, Be Small

כי האדם נקרא עולם קטן, ואם הוא קטן אז נקרא עולם, אבל אם אינו קטן אינו
נקרא עולם, כי מי שיש בו קנאה אינו בקטנות, כי אם היה שפל רוח בפני כל אדם
לא היה מתקנא בחבירו, וכן מי שהוא בקטנות אינו מתאוה לשום דבר ופשיטא
שאינו רודף אחר הכבוד, ואם כן מי שיש בו שלשה דברים הללו הוא בבחינת
גדלות, מוציאין אותו מן העולם שאינו נקרא עולם.

Man is called an עוֹלָם קָטָן, *a miniature world*. Not only is man a microcosm of the world, but he can exist in the universe as long as he lives up to

[כט] הוּא הָיָה אוֹמֵר: הַיְלוֹדִים לָמוּת, וְהַמֵּתִים לְחִיוֹת,
וְהַחַיִּים לִדּוֹן – לֵידַע לְהוֹדִיעַ וּלְהִוָּדַע שֶׁהוּא
אֵל, הוּא הַיּוֹצֵר, הוּא הַבּוֹרֵא, הוּא הַמֵּבִין, הוּא הַדַּיָּן,
הוּא עֵד, הוּא בַּעַל דִּין, הוּא עָתִיד לָדוּן. בָּרוּךְ הוּא,
שֶׁאֵין לְפָנָיו לֹא עַוְלָה, וְלֹא שִׁכְחָה, וְלֹא מַשּׂוֹא פָנִים,
וְלֹא מִקַּח שֹׁחַד; שֶׁהַכֹּל שֶׁלּוֹ. וְדַע, שֶׁהַכֹּל לְפִי הַחֶשְׁבּוֹן.

---

the aspect of being קָטָן, *small*. He can achieve this by being humble, curbing his passions and fleeing from honor. Any manifestation of jealousy, lust and craving for glory deprive man of the distinction of being a humble member of the universe, an עוֹלָם קָטָן (*Maggid of Mezeritch, Maggidei Ha-Emes*).

⇜§ Any Kind of Honor Kills

פעם ביקר אדמו"ר האמרי אמת ז"ל בביתו של הגאון רבי יוסף חיים זוננפלד ז"ל,
כיבדו רבי יוסף חיים לשבת על כסא גבוה ומרופד, סירב אדמו"ר זצ"ל לשבת
עליו. שאל רבי יוסף חיים "הרי אמרו כל מה שיאמר לך בעל הבית עשה חוץ
מצא." השיבו "היא הנותנת, דכבוד הוא בכלל "צא," שהוא משלשה דברים
ה'מוציאין' את האדם מן העולם."

When the *Imrei Emes* visited Rav Yosef Chaim Sonnenfeld, the Rav of Yerushalayim honored him by offering him a seat on an elegant and lavishly appointed chair. The Gerrer Rebbe demurred. When Rav Yosef protested that one is required to honor all of a host's requests other than to leave, the Rebbe responded, "Honor is a form of יְצִיאָה (leave-taking), leading to premature departure from This World" (*Maggidei HaEmes*).

⇜§ Survival Amidst Mystery

פי' שלא יוכל להתקיים בתוך העלם שהעצה שהתדבק בנקודה הנעלמת
שבעוה"ז נסתרת כנ"ל.

The term עוֹלָם is related to הֶעְלֵם, *concealment*. In fact, This World is known as עוֹלָם הַזֶּה because of the *hidden* sparks of sanctity which can be found amidst the outer atmosphere of materialism (cf. *Sfas Emes, Beshalach* 5633 for a detailed exposition of this concept). It is only by refraining from jealousy, lust and glory that we can successfully elicit the few sparks of *kedushah* in This World.

[29] *He used to say: Those born will die; the dead will come to life; and the living will be judged — in order that one should know, teach and make aware that He is God, He is the Fashioner, He is the Creator, He is the Discerner, He is the Judge, He is the Witness, He is the Plaintiff, He will judge. Blessed is He before Whom there is no iniquity, no forgetfulness, no favoritism, and no acceptance of bribery, for everything is His. Know that everything is according to the reckoning.*

29.

■ הַיִלוֹדִים לָמוּת — *Those born will die.*

❧ Born to Die

> אולי יש לפרש עפ״י מה שמספרים מהרר״ב ז״ל מפשיסחא שסמוך לפטירתו
> שמע את זוגתו הרבנית בוכה עמוקות, אמר לה: "מדוע את בוכיה? הלא זה כל
> חיי האדם בעולם הזה, ללמוד כיצד להחזיר נשמתו ליוצרה – אם כן למה לך
> לבכות"? ובזה יל״פ הילודים למות, כלומר שלא נולד האדם אלא כדי ללמוד
> כיצד למות.

When R' Simchah Bunim of Peshis'cha was about to pass away, he heard his wife crying bitterly. He comforted her by responding, "Why cry? Isn't that the purpose of all life — to learn how to die — to ultimately restore one's soul to Hashem with the same purity that He had originally implanted it in us?" This thought can be deduced from our *mishnah*: From the moment of our birth, we are destined to die (*Maggidei HaEmes*).

■ הַיִלוֹדִים לָמוּת . . . לֵידַע לְהוֹדִיעַ וּלְהִוָּדַע שֶׁהוּא אֵל — *Those born will die . . . in order that one should know, teach and make aware that He is God.*

❧ All of Life Is a Testament to Hashem

> והכל כדי לידע להודיע שהוא היוצר הבורא הדיין כו'.

From the sequence of our *mishnah*, we can attain a degree of comprehension about the purpose of the various phases of life. All that occurs — birth, death Resurrection of the Dead — happens for the purpose of making it known that Hashem is the Creator and Perfect Judge of Man.

וְאַל יַבְטִיחֲךָ יִצְרְךָ שֶׁהַשְּׁאוֹל בֵּית מָנוֹס לָךְ — שֶׁעַל
כָּרְחֲךָ אַתָּה נוֹצָר; וְעַל כָּרְחֲךָ אַתָּה נוֹלָד; וְעַל כָּרְחֲךָ
אַתָּה חַי; וְעַל כָּרְחֲךָ אַתָּה מֵת; וְעַל כָּרְחֲךָ אַתָּה עָתִיד
לִתֵּן דִּין וְחֶשְׁבּוֹן לִפְנֵי מֶלֶךְ מַלְכֵי הַמְּלָכִים, הַקָּדוֹשׁ
בָּרוּךְ הוּא.

❀ ❀ ❀

רַבִּי חֲנַנְיָא בֶּן עֲקַשְׁיָא אוֹמֵר: רָצָה הַקָּדוֹשׁ בָּרוּךְ הוּא
לְזַכּוֹת אֶת יִשְׂרָאֵל, לְפִיכָךְ הִרְבָּה לָהֶם תּוֹרָה וּמִצְווֹת,
שֶׁנֶּאֱמַר: "יהוה חָפֵץ לְמַעַן צִדְקוֹ, יַגְדִּיל תּוֹרָה וְיַאְדִּיר."

◆§ Great Personalities

> הילודים למות על ידי אדם וחוה והמתים להחיות על ידי אברהם ושרה . . . החיים
> לידון בח״י יצחק . . . לידע להודיע ולהוודע זה תכלית האחרון בח״י יעקב וישראל
> וישורון שאז יתברר דעת שלימה כמ״ש ומלאה הארץ דעה.

Each phrase mentioned in the *mishnah* is exemplified through the lives of great Biblical personalities. Thus, *those born will die*, as a result of the sin of Adam and Chavah. The following phrase, *and the dead will be resurrected*, refers to Avraham and Sarah. Hashem promised the *Avos* that they personally would witness the Resurrection of the Dead.[1]

The following phrase, *the living will be judged*, referring to the final judgment occurring after *Techiyas HaMeisim*, corresponds to Yitzchak who exemplified the Attribute of Justice. And finally, the *mishnah's* "climax" — the *raison d'être* of all Jewish life — *in order that one should know, teach and make aware*, proclaims Hashem's Sovereignty to all mankind. This was epitomized by the life of Yaakov Avinu whose name was changed to Yisrael upon triumphing over Esav's evil angel. Likewise, the Jewish people, Yaakov's descendants, when they will have finally vanquished Esav during the Messianic era, will bear permanent witness to Hashem. As Yeshayahu says, כִּי מָלְאָה הָאָרֶץ דֵּעָה אֶת ה' כַּמַּיִם לַיָּם מְכַסִּים, *For the earth will be as filled with knowledge of Hashem as water covering the sea bed* (11:9).

■ וְאַל יַבְטִיחֲךָ יִצְרְךָ שֶׁהַשְּׁאוֹל בֵּית מָנוֹס לָךְ — *And let not your evil inclination promise you that the grave will be an escape for you.*

---

1. The Gemara (*Sanhedrin* 90b) deduces this from the *pasuk* (*Devarim* 11:21), לָתֵת לָהֶם כִּימֵי הַשָּׁמַיִם עַל הָאָרֶץ, to give *them* (the Avos) Eretz Yisrael, so they too may enjoy the Holy Land.

And let not your evil inclination promise you that the grave will be an escape for you — for against your will you were created; against your will you were born; against your will you live; against your will you die; and against your will you are destined to give an account before the King Who rules over kings, the Holy One, Blessed is He.

❧ ❧ ❧

Rabbi Chanania ben Akashia says: The Holy One, Blessed is He, wished to confer merit upon Israel; therefore He gave them Torah and mitzvos in abundance, as it is said (Yeshayahu 42:21): "Hashem desired, for the sake of its [Israel's] righteousness, that the Torah be made great and glorious."

◆§ Eventually You Will Fulfill Your Mission

דלפעמים אדם משתלח לעולם הזה לתקן איזה דבר והיצר הרע מתאמץ על זה
ביותר למונעו ומסיתו שהגם שיהיה לו יסורי גיהנם מטעים לו האיסור יותר, על
זה אמר התנא שעל כרחך אתה מת ונוצר כו׳ להתגלגל כמה פעמים עד שיתקן
הדבר המוטל עליו אם כן למה לו להמתין.

With these words, the *mishnah* is refuting one of the *yetzer hara's* most frequent, though misleading, arguments. We are all innately aware that we have been placed in This World to fulfill a sacred mission. While this mission may vary according to each individual's capacities, we all share that sense of purpose. To seduce us to fail in our lifelong destiny, the *yetzer hara* argues that the momentary pleasure to be derived from committing an *aveirah* far exceeds *anything* — any punishment that may be inflicted in *Gehinnom* for failing to fulfill our potential. While this tortured rationale is, of course, not true, the *mishnah* offers another response: *Against your will you live; against your will you die.* Even after death you will live again; despite the rantings of the *yetzer hara* you will eventually return to the world to complete your mission.[1] So why fight the inevitable and at the same time, bring upon yourself the inevitable retribution of *Gehinnom*? Instead, achieve your destiny during your present sojourn in This World.

---

1. This approach is based on the Kabbalistic concept of גִּלְגּוּלִים — that a soul is returned to earth several times if necessary, to fulfill its mission (cf. *Ramban's* commentary to *Iyov*).

כָּל יִשְׂרָאֵל יֵשׁ לָהֶם חֵלֶק לָעוֹלָם הַבָּא, שֶׁנֶּאֱמַר: ה / א

"וְעַמֵּךְ כֻּלָּם צַדִּיקִים, לְעוֹלָם יִירְשׁוּ אָרֶץ, נֵצֶר מַטָּעַי, מַעֲשֵׂה יָדַי לְהִתְפָּאֵר."

פרק חמישי

[א] בַּעֲשָׂרָה מַאֲמָרוֹת נִבְרָא הָעוֹלָם. וּמַה תַּלְמוּד לוֹמַר? וַהֲלֹא בְמַאֲמָר אֶחָד יָכוֹל לְהִבָּרְאוֹת? אֶלָּא

1.

■ בַּעֲשָׂרָה מַאֲמָרוֹת נִבְרָא הָעוֹלָם. וּמַה תַּלְמוּד לוֹמַר? וַהֲלֹא בְמַאֲמָר אֶחָד יָכוֹל לְהִבָּרְאוֹת? — *With ten statements the world was created. What does this come to teach us? Indeed, could it not have been created with one statement?*

⇥ Levels of Understanding

> היה צריך לומר מאמרים ואמרו מאמרות. הרמז למ' אורות, על הים חמישים, על הים כבר היו להם כל הנ' אורות.

Rather than utilize the grammatically appropriate term מַאֲמָרִים (masculine gender; which would be consistent with מַאֲמָר אֶחָד written later in the mishnah), we speak of עֲשָׂרָה מַאֲמָרוֹת. According to the *Pnei Menachem*, the term מַאֲמָרוֹת may allude to מ' אורות (literally "forty lights"). Hashem created the universe in such a fashion that man, the apex of His Creation, could benefit from 40 levels of insights into His wisdom. Many generations later, when *Klal Yisrael* witnessed the fifty מַכּוֹת at the *Yam Suf* (as we say in the *Pesach Haggadah*), they attained an even greater awareness of the Creator, ascending to the 50th level of understanding (נ' שַׁעֲרֵי בִינָה) (adapted from *Pnei Menachem, Maggidei HaEmes*).

⇥ Bereishis: The First Divine Statement

> לכאורה ראי' מכאן להמפרשים בראשית ברא ממש שנבראו מקודם בכלל דאלו לפירש"י בראשית ברוא כו' ויהי אור כו' לא יתכן כאן בראשית נמי מאמר וקשה דהרי כבר נחשב מאמר יהי רקיע והגם דרש"י פי' יחזק הרקיע, הרי נאמר ג"ב ויעש א' את הרקיע וה"פ כמ"ש חז"ל את השמים ואת כו', לרבות צבאותי' זה הי' טפל וזהו עצמו מאמר גם י"ל כי יש כמה עניני שמים וכן שמי השמים.

All Israel has a share in the World to Come, as it is said (Yeshayahu 60:21): "And your people are all righteous; they shall inherit the land forever; a branch of My plantings, My handiwork, in which to take pride."

Chapter Five

[1] With ten statements the world was created. What does this come to teach us? Indeed, could it not have been created with one statement? This was to exact

---

The apparent discrepancy between the *mishnah's* contention that Hashem created the universe utilizing *ten* statements and the actual description of the Creation in *Bereishis* (Ch. 1 and 2:18) which contains only *nine* Divine statements (i.e. nine instances in which the term וַיֹּאמֶר אֱלֹהִים, *God said*, is used) is resolved by the Gemara's (*Rosh Hashanah* 32a) suggestion that the act of Creation itself (בְּרֵאשִׁית בָּרָא אֱלֹהִים), though not prefaced by the term וַיֹּאמֶר, is counted as the *first* Divine statement.

This terse remark of *Chazal* supports the *Ramban's* (cf. *Bereishis* 1:1) contention that the term בְּרֵאשִׁית should be interpreted as "in the beginning" (as if it said בָּרִאשׁוֹנָה). According to this approach, Hashem first created heaven and earth. However, if we maintain as *Rashi* does that the first *pasuk* of the Torah is not referring to an actual creation event, but is rather stating that "in the beginning *of* creation (בְּרֵאשִׁית בְּרוֹא) Hashem said, 'Let there be light,' " it seems difficult to maintain that *Bereishis* should be considered as a Divine statement in its own right.

Another question arises. Even according to the *Ramban's* approach that *Bereishis* is an independent Divine statement, exactly what was created through this statement? It is unlikely that *Bereishis* is enumerated as one of the ten Divine statements because the creation of the heavens mentioned in the *pasuk* is counted as a Divine statement in *pasuk* 6 where it states וַיֹּאמֶר אֱלֹהִים יְהִי רָקִיעַ, *God said, "Let there be a firmament,"* and in *pasuk* 8 it states that the firmament (רָקִיעַ) is called שָׁמָיִם, *"Heaven."*

Perhaps, our *mishnah* is referring not to the creation of heaven and earth itself but rather to the creation of all the "hosts" (e.g., the stars) of heaven and earth [later (2:1) described as וְכָל צְבָאָם]. According to the Midrash, their creation is alluded to by the term אֵת הַשָּׁמַיִם וְאֵת הָאָרֶץ, which includes the auxiliaries of heaven and earth (e.g., the stars).

Alternatively, the apparent contradiction between the *mishnah's* reckoning of ten Divine statements and the actual count of nine may be resolved by recalling that the term שָׁמָיִם may refer to various celestial bodies. In fact, the Gemara (*Chagigah* 12b) relates that there are several firmaments. בְּרֵאשִׁית בָּרָא אֱלֹהִים and יְהִי רָקִיעַ are counted as distinct statements since they allude to

לְהִפָּרַע מִן הָרְשָׁעִים, שֶׁמְּאַבְּדִין אֶת הָעוֹלָם שֶׁנִּבְרָא
בַּעֲשָׂרָה מַאֲמָרוֹת, וְלִתֵּן שָׂכָר טוֹב לַצַּדִּיקִים, שֶׁמְּקַיְּמִין
אֶת הָעוֹלָם שֶׁנִּבְרָא בַּעֲשָׂרָה מַאֲמָרוֹת.

different entities known as "Heaven."

◆§ Which Single Statement? (מַאֲמָר אֶחָד)

> והלא במאמר אחד. יש לומר הוא מאמר בראשית שהוא נמי מאמר וכפירוש
> רש"י כי ביום הראשון נכללו כל הברואים והוא מאמר הראשון בראשית כו'
> השמים וכל צבאי'.
>
> אח"כ נתקן העולם ונאמר ויברך אלקים את נח כו' פרו ורבו כו' פירוש שבזמן
> המבול ניטל כח הבריאה והי' צריך אח"כ לתת מחדש חיות לכל הברואים . . .
> וע"ז הקשו חז"ל כי הי' יכול מקודם להיות הבריאה במאמר אחד.

Based on the above discussion, we propose that the מַאֲמָר אֶחָד, the *single statement*, that should have sufficed for creation, refers to בְּרֵאשִׁית. This is particularly true if we assume as *Rashi* (cf. *Rashi* 2:4 s.v. תולדות) does, that the root matter from which everything else was formed was created on the first day of Creation.

Alternatively, the expression מַאֲמָר אֶחָד does not refer to one of the statements utilized by Hashem during Creation but rather to the single statement, פְּרוּ וּרְבוּ שִׁרְצוּ בָאָרֶץ וּרְבוּ בָהּ, *Be fruitful and multiply; teem on the earth and multiply on it* (9:7), through which Hashem *recreated* the universe after the Flood. The Flood not only destroyed virtually all living beings but also was such a cataclysmic event that its few survivors (both Noach's family and the animals that were spared) had lost the capacity to reproduce. Through this Divine statement of פְּרוּ וּרְבוּ the remnants of the Flood were given renewed life. The *mishnah* wonders: If that single statement was sufficient to *recreate* a desolate universe, why wasn't it enough to create it originally?

■ אֶלָּא לְהִפָּרַע מִן הָרְשָׁעִים . . . וְלִתֵּן שָׂכָר טוֹב לַצַּדִּיקִים — *This was to exact punishment from the wicked . . . and to bestow goodly reward upon the righteous.*

◆§ Do the Wicked Really Destroy the World?

> בהרע"ב שכל המאבד נפש אחת מישראל כאילו אבד עולם מלא כו', וקשה דאדם
> נברא רק במאמר אחד נעשה אדם. ואולי כיון שנברא באחרונה וכולם שהיו
> מקודם היו הכנה אליו והאחרון כולל כל הקודמין וזה שכתוב (בראשית א,כו)
> נעשה אדם כו'.

punishment from the wicked who destroy the world that was created with ten statements, and to bestow goodly reward upon the righteous who sustain the world that was created with ten statements.

In response to this question, *Bartenura* suggests that by destroying even *one* Jewish soul (even their own), essentially the wicked are destroying the entire universe. However, it seems surprising that the act of corrupting people would be equivalent to destroying the entire universe, since man was created on the basis of merely *one* of ten Divine statements that were used to create the world.

It may be significant, however, that the statement which created man came at the end of Creation. This tells us that the rest of Hashem's Creation was merely preparatory to his arrival, indicating man's pivotal role in Hashem's blueprint for the universe. In fact, the Divine command נַעֲשֶׂה אָדָם, "let *us* create man" (*Bereishis* 1:26), may allude to Hashem's instruction to *all* of His previous creations, "Let us join together to form the apex of Creation, the one entity that deserves to be called a world in its own right — man."

◆§ Why Mention the Wicked First?

אומות העולם היו מקודם רעים כגון דור המבול דהם באמת איבדו את העולם, ואחר כך היה בהם טובים.

Though we generally discuss the reward due the righteous *before* the punishment inflicted on the wicked, in this instance the *mishnah* is following historical sequence. Only *after* the generation of the Flood (and the Tower of Bavel) were punished, could a smaller number of righteous gentiles emerge who would fulfill Hashem's will and be rewarded for doing so.

◆§ A Tzaddik "by Comparison"

אין צדיק בארץ אשר יעשה טוב ולא יחטא ויש כח ח״ו לקטרג עליהן אך בראות מעשה הצדיקים יסתם פי המקטרג נמצא עיקר שילום השכר להצדיקים בא על ידי ראיית ההפרש שבין הרשע לצדיק ומובן ממילא כל הנ״ל להפרע כו׳ כדי שעל ידו יותן שכר טוב לצדיקים.

Alternatively, the *mishnah*, mindful of the fact that even the most righteous often suffer flaws, nonetheless assures us that whatever their shortcomings, by comparison to the wicked, the *tzaddikim* certainly shine. Thus the unusual sequence — first the wicked are punished and then, merely by virtue of not deserving the condemnation of the wicked, the righteous reap reward (*Noam Elimelech, Maggidei HaEmes*).

◆§ Punishing Pharaoh, Rewarding the Jewish People

בוודאי להפרע מרשעים הוא פרעה דכתיב בי׳ ואני ועמי הרשעים ולתת שכר טוב לצדיקים היא התורה.

The *mishnah* may be alluding to a particular period during which Pharaoh, the Jewish people's archenemy, was punished while *Klal Yisrael* was richly rewarded. Pharaoh, who depicts himself as evil (cf. *Shemos* (9:27), וַאֲנִי וְעַמִּי הָרְשָׁעִים), was subjected to the ten plagues while *Klal Yisrael* was richly rewarded with the Ten Commandments and the Torah (*Sfas Emes Va'eira 5632*).

◆§ Finding the Shechinah . . . the World

אם הי׳ נברא העולם במאמר אחד שהוא האחדות כלל הראשון, לא הי׳ שכר ועונש, אבל בבחי׳ הריבוי והתחלקות המדרגות שברא הש״י להיות כמה רשעים המתנגדים לאמת וכופרין במלכות שמים ומצד זה לא הי׳ יכול להתגלות בחי׳ האחדות שע״ז נאמר וירא כו׳ האור כי טוב ויבדל כו׳ שגנזו לצדיקים . . . שיש לכל מאמר הסתר מיוחד.

While the *tzaddik* certainly deserves praise for upholding the universe, the relationship between the number of Divine statements and the amount of praise he receives seems difficult to understand.

Apparently, the *mishnah* is referring not only to the quantity of Divine statements that Hashem used in creating the universe but also to the perceived distance between us and Him that occurred as a result of those statements. Had the universe been created through one all-encompassing statement which would have directly led to the creation of all living beings, then the Divine imprint on the universe would have been potently visible. But instead, Hashem in His infinite wisdom preferred to create the universe sequentially in a multi-phased process known as the Six Days of Creation. As a result, man might be misled by the *yetzer hara* into believing that not only a time lapse of six days, but also an actual gap, existed between his own creation and the universe's origin at the beginning of Creation. He might be seduced into accepting the belief of many heretics that Hashem's Divine Providence only extended as far as those entities that He created in a comparative vacuum during the first days of Creation, but not to those implanted in a universe that was *already* thriving with many forms of life. By creating the universe with so many Divine statements — and, in the process, obscuring His Presence in the universe that He created — Hashem deliberately made it possible for the heretic to deny His existence, or at least His *management* of the universe.

Had man been created at the universe's inception — at a time when the primeval light of Creation, later hidden by Hashem, was still present, and the Divine Presence was still quite visible — it would have been comparatively easy to be a believer. To be a believer in a universe where His Presence is veiled in the ten statements is a great feat not to be minimized and merits reward (adapted from *Sfas Emes*).

■ שֶׁמְּקַיְּמִין אֶת הָעוֹלָם שֶׁנִּבְרָא בַּעֲשָׂרָה מַאֲמָרוֹת — *Who sustain the world that was created with ten statements.*

⧫§ Validating the Divine Imprint

פ׳ שמברכין ומעידין שחיות הכל מעשרה מאמרות.
מקיימים הוא כמו קיום שטר שמעיד ומאמת הדבר.

The term מְקַיְּמִין (*sustain*) may be related to the Talmudic concept of קיום שְׁטָרוֹת, validating a document's signature (cf. *Kesubos* 19a). *Tzaddikim*, through their pious lives and good deeds, confirm and endorse that Hashem created the entire universe through the ten statements.

⧫§ Parallels Between the Ten Statements and the Ten Commandments

אחר גאולת מצרים נעשה מעשרה מאמרות עשרת הדברות באמצעות עשר מכות . . .

עשרה מאמרות נעשו לעשרת הדברות ואיתא (שבת פח,ב) כל דיבור ודיבור שיצא מפי הקב״ה נתמלא כל העולם כולו בשמים וכיון שמדיבור ראשון נתמלא דיבור שני להיכן הלך הוציא הקב״ה הרוח מאוצרותיו והיה מעביר מעביר ראשון ראשון, וכמו כן בעשרה מאמרות נתגלה האור בכל מאמר שהרי בכל יום כתיב כי טוב. האור נגנז מיד ביום הראשון (בר״ר יא,ב) כדי להתגלות אחר כך ועל ידי שנגנז האור יש כח ליצר הרע להסתיר וכל ההסתר הוא כדי להתגבר עליו.

The *Chiddushei HaRim* commented, "The ten Divine statements (עֲשָׂרָה מַאֲמָרוֹת) were transmuted into the Ten Commandments (עֲשֶׂרֶת הַדִּבְּרוֹת) through the ten plagues (עֶשֶׂר מַכּוֹת)." It was only the ten plagues, which demonstrated Hashem's might in full public view, that convinced a skeptical mankind that indeed He had created the universe through ten statements. Fortified by its newly found faith in Hashem, the universe was now ready for Hashem Himself commanding them, אָנֹכִי ה׳ אֱלֹהֶיךָ, *I am Hashem, your God*, the first of the Ten Commandments, one of the most glorious manifestations of His *Shechinah*.

[ב] עֲשָׂרָה דוֹרוֹת מֵאָדָם וְעַד נֹחַ, לְהוֹדִיעַ כַּמָּה אֶרֶךְ
אַפַּיִם לְפָנָיו; שֶׁכָּל הַדּוֹרוֹת הָיוּ מַכְעִיסִין וּבָאִין, עַד
שֶׁהֵבִיא עֲלֵיהֶם אֶת מֵי הַמַּבּוּל.

An interesting parallel exists between the ten statements and the Ten Commandments. As the *Imrei Emes* pointed out, each instance of Divine Revelation
was followed by a retrenchment of His Presence. As is well known, one of the
first manifestations of the Divine Presence, the light of the first day of Creation, of which Hashem said, "Let there be light," was immediately hidden. So
too the Gemara (*Shabbos* 88b) relates that the world was filled with ethereal
spices when Hashem pronounced each commandment.[1] However, this heavenly fragrance was immediately removed to make way for the following
commandment (*Maggidei HaEmes*).

⊷§ Significance of the Number Ten — Unity Emerging From Diversity

וְהוּא הָעֲשִׂירִיּוֹת אֲשֶׁר הוּא ג׳׳כ אַחֲדוּת רַק חֶשְׁבּוֹן זֶה נַעֲשֶׂה אֶחָד מֵהִתְחַלְּקוּת
הַפְּרָטִים, וְזֶה עִנְיַן בַּעֲשָׂרָה מַאֲמָרוֹת כו׳. וּבֶאֱמֶת מִזֶּה נִתְרַבָּה כְּבוֹדוֹ ית׳ בְּיוֹתֵר מַה
שֶׁנָּתַן כֹּחַ לִהְיוֹת נִמְצָא סִיטְרָא דְשִׁקְרָא בָּעוֹלָם.

A n interesting relationship may be developed between the number one,
referred to in our *mishnah* as מַאֲמָר אֶחָד, *one statement*, and the number ten,
the number of edicts used by Hashem to create the world. Both numbers are a
form of *unity*. While it is obvious that the number one connotes unity — and
thus, had Hashem created the world with one statement there would have been
no opposition to His Sovereignty — the number ten also connotes a different
but equally valid form of unity. It combines disparate elements into a cohesive
whole. The challenge of the *tzaddik*, and the justification for his ample reward,
is to take the many apparently fragmented segments of the universe and find
the *One* Master Planner.

2.

■ עֲשָׂרָה דוֹרוֹת מֵאָדָם וְעַד נֹחַ – לְהוֹדִיעַ כַּמָּה אֶרֶךְ אַפַּיִם לְפָנָיו; שֶׁכָּל הַדּוֹרוֹת
הָיוּ מַכְעִיסִין וּבָאִין, עַד שֶׁהֵבִיא עֲלֵיהֶם אֶת מֵי הַמַּבּוּל — *There were ten
generations from Adam to Noach — to show the degree of His pa-
tience; for all those generations angered Him increasingly, until He
brought upon them the waters of the Flood.*

---

1. For further discussion of this concept see *The Three Festivals*, p. 281.

[2] *There were ten generations from Adam to Noach —*
to show the degree of His patience; for all those
generations angered Him increasingly, until He brought
upon them the waters of the Flood.

◆§ Reversal of the Ten Divine Statements

קאי אדלעיל שבכל דור דור קלקל מאמר א'.

This *mishnah*, discussing the ten generations from Adam to Noach, is not
only the historical sequel to the previous *mishnah*, but also describes the
complete reversal of the process of Creation initiated through the ten statements. Every generation, through its amoral behavior and its complete ignorance of the Divine will, had the effect of "reversing" (i.e. obscuring) one of the
Divine statements.

◆§ Even Noach

וגם בנח איתא במדרש אלא שמצא חן.

Noach himself is included among the ten increasingly wicked generations.
According to the Midrash (*Bereishis Rabbah* 29:1), Noach deserved the
same fate as his contemporaries but was saved as an act of Divine favor (חֵן)
whereby He spares the undeserving. As the Torah says, 'וְנֹחַ מָצָא חֵן בְּעֵינֵי ה, *But*
Noach found grace (favor) *in the eyes of Hashem* (*Bereishis* 6:8).

◆§ מֵאָדָם, From Adam — And Not Before Adam

תיבת מאדם מיותר ואפשר לאפוקי תתקע"ד דורות.

By stating the apparently superfluous word מֵאָדָם, *from Adam* (who, of course,
was the first man), the *mishnah* implies that we are not referring to any of
the 974 generations that may have existed in the "worlds" that Hashem created
(cf. *Chagigah* 13b) — and promptly destroyed — prior to creating our universe.

◆§ The Generation of Sheis

בדורו של שת לא מצינו חטאים ואולי כיון דבדור אנוש הוחל לקרוא כו' ושת חי
נמי בזמן אנוש שפיר נקרא שכל הדורות היו כו'.

> ‫[ג] עֲשָׂרָה דוֹרוֹת מִנֹּחַ וְעַד אַבְרָהָם, לְהוֹדִיעַ כַּמָּה‬
> ‫אֶרֶךְ אַפַּיִם לְפָנָיו; שֶׁכָּל הַדּוֹרוֹת הָיוּ מַכְעִיסִין‬
> ‫וּבָאִין, עַד שֶׁבָּא אַבְרָהָם אָבִינוּ וְקִבֵּל שְׂכַר כֻּלָּם.‬

We find no evidence that Sheis' generation had sinned. Perhaps, the *mishnah* is referring to the period of Sheis' life in which he witnessed the spiritual decline and flirtation with paganism of his son's (Enosh) generation.

◆§ Did Patience Prevail?

> ‫בהרע״ב אף אתה אל תתמה וכו' ולדבריו נראה שמדה זו הי' רק עד שלא‬
> ‫העונשים אבל אח״כ נשתנה מדה זאת, ונראה שאינו לגריעותא בלבד כי בב״מ‬
> ‫שנאמר ארך אפים לטובה וכן זה לחזק עצמו שלא יתייאש לדאוג שיבוא‬
> ‫פורעניות רק השי״ת ארך אפים וממתין.‬

According to the *Bartenura*, this *mishnah* is not merely recording historical events, but rather encouraging us to never become discouraged in face of the seemingly endless sovereignty of *Klal Yisrael's* oppressors. Just as those generations were eventually brought to judgment and punished, so too will the contemporary oppressors of the Jewish people. While patience is certainly a Divine Attribute, it does not apply to the permanent indulgence of evil.

It seems from the *Bartenura's* approach that the Attribute of Divine Patience was only in effect *prior* to the destruction of those ten generations. Their ultimate fate seems to have been a Divine act of retribution rather than patience. If, however, we consider the *lasting* effects of the entire sequence of events surrounding those ten generations, we realize that, in a sense, the Attribute of Patience remained even after the Flood had obliterated the Generation of the Flood. Whenever the Attribute of אֶרֶךְ אַפַּיִם is stated, it is intended to be a manifestation of Hashem's goodness. Clearly, Hashem's temporary (though prolonged) tolerance of the evildoers is evidence of His goodness. But a far more lasting manifestation of His goodness, known as אֶרֶךְ אַפַּיִם, is the constant encouragement given to Jews of all generations to never despair in the face of evil. This is the true and lasting patience.

3.

■ עֲשָׂרָה דוֹרוֹת מִנֹּחַ וְעַד אַבְרָהָם — לְהוֹדִיעַ כַּמָּה אֶרֶךְ אַפַּיִם לְפָנָיו; שֶׁכָּל הַדּוֹרוֹת הָיוּ מַכְעִיסִין וּבָאִין — *There were ten generations from Noach to Avraham — to show the degree of His patience; for all those generations angered Him increasingly.*

[3] *There were ten generations from Noach to Avraham — to show the degree of His patience; for all those generations angered Him increasingly, until our forefather Avraham came and received the reward of them all.*

◆§ To Whom Did Hashem Display Greater Tolerance?

קשה דכבר הודיענו כח ארך אפים לעשרה דורות הראשונים. וי״ל דכאן עדיפא דהו״ל להתייסר ממה שראו שהביא מבול לראשונים ומכל מקום האריך להם אפו.

Though the previous *mishnah* already taught us about Hashem's extraordinary patience, here we read of an even greater feat — displaying tolerance to those who should have known better than to anger Hashem. Unlike the first ten generations, who at least had no clear indication of the Divine wrath they were provoking and its eventual effect, the generation following Noach were well aware of the consequences of sinning — and yet they continued to sin. Tolerance in the face of recidivism (repeated evil behavior) — can there be a greater manifestation of אֶרֶךְ אַפַּיִם?

■ עַד שֶׁבָּא אַבְרָהָם אָבִינוּ וְקִבֵּל שְׂכַר כֻּלָּם — *Until our forefather Avraham came and received the reward of them all.*

◆§ Hashem Seeks a Worthy Recipient of His Bounty

קשה דכיון שהיו מכעיסין למה היה מגיע להם שכר. ויש לומר כי עיקר הכעס שגרמו אלו הרשעים היה ממה שלא היה מי מהם ראוי לקבל השכר והשפע שהיה מיוחד להם עד שבא אברהם וקבל שכר כולם ואז שקטה ונחה כביכול גרמת הכעס שלהם ויש להסביר זאת ע״פ משל מי שהכניס אורח לביתו ואין בידו לכבדו מפאת איזה סיבה ודאי זה כדי בזיון וקצף וכן הי׳ אז עד שבא אאע״ה ועשה תשובה עבור כולם ותיקן את כולם וע״יז קבל שכר כולם ומרומז כן בהפסוק (בראשית טו:א) אל תירא כו׳ שכרך הרבה מאד.

The *mishnah* tells us that Avraham received the reward due the unworthy generations which preceded him. It seems strange that they deserved any reward at all.

Upon further contemplation, we realize that Hashem avidly desires to bestow His munificent bounty upon *every* generation — if any worthy recipient exists. If not — as occurred with Noach's descendants — Hashem preserves the reward that would have been due those generations and bestows it upon the first deserving recipient, such as Avraham.

In fact, Hashem's anger may not have been directed merely at their sinful behavior but even more so, at the *result* of their incessant sinning — the absence of an appropriate recipient of His bounty. This somewhat esoteric concept can be better appreciated with a simple parable. Imagine a guest being invited to a notable's house and for some unanticipated reason the host is unable to demonstrate his usual generosity. Only Avraham Avinu — who not only adopted the lifestyle that his predecessors should have lived, but also repented on behalf of those generations (and according to the *Zohar* enabled them to receive *Olam Haba*) — could profit from Hashem's generous reward, reaping his own share of Divine reward as well as that of all previous generations. As Hashem assures Avraham, שְׂכָרְךָ הַרְבֵּה מְאֹד, *your reward is very great* (*Bereishis* 15:1), alluding to the "windfall" that Avraham reaped from past generations.

◆§ Avraham vs. Noach

בי נח אף על פי שהיה צדיק לא היה יכול לעמוד נגד רשעת הרשעים ומה שהיה
הוא מתקן, קלקלו אותן הרשעים עד שהיה צריך להסתר בתיבה ונאבדו הם
במבול, אבל אברהם היה מתחזק בצדקו וגבר על מעשי הרשעים ועל זה כתיב
(שה"ש ח:ז) מים רבים לא יוכלו לכבות האהבה, וידוע שכן דרך האש כשאין
המים יכולין לכבותו עוד הוא מתגבר על ידי המים וזה שקיבל עליו שכר כולן כי
עוד נתעלה ונתחזק בצדקתו על ידי רשעת הרשעים.

ומאברהם התחיל ב' אלפים תורה שהוא בח' שלמעלה מהטבע . . .

והנה אח"כ דור הפלגה קלקלו גם בחי' האחדות כמ"ש שפה א' ודברים אחדים
כו' וחטאו בזה ג"כ אבן חטאם הי' בחכמה כמ"ש בזוה"ק, לכן בעשרה דורות
ראשונים נאמר עד שהביא עליהם מי המבול כנ"ל שהי' כבהמות ונאמר ימותו
ולא בחכמה, אבל בדור הפלגה איתא שבא אברהם וקיבל שכר כולן נראה שהי'
בהם הכנות טובות בחכמה ונשאר זה לאברהם ולבנ"י דור הפלגה חטאו וניטל
מהם כח האחדות כמ"ש בי' דורות מנח עד שבא אברהם ונטל שכר כולן פי' שכח
האחדות נשאר אצלן

In stark contrast to Noach who only managed to escape with his immediate family, Avraham reaped the rich bounty of all his predecessors.

To appreciate the contrasting fates of Avraham and Noach, let us consider the effectiveness of their mission. Noach, though a great *tzaddik*, was unable to leave any impact on his contemporaries. All of his attempts at rectifying the immoral behavior of his contemporary society (either by persuading them to repent or even by personal example) were short lived. Whenever he thought that he had succeeded in ameliorating the horrible permissiveness and licentiousness of his society, he was presented with another round of moral backsliding. Noach's confrontations with the evildoers of his time were so patently unsuccessful (and dangerous) that he had to be spirited into the ark to ensure that he not be corrupted by their decadent ways.

Avraham, on the other hand, drew strength from his confrontations with evil. Just as fire upon coming in contact with a small amount of water (too little to extinguish it) burns brighter than ever, so too Avraham. When confronting *reshaim* — and whenever possible inducing them to do *teshuvah* — he became an even greater *tzaddik*. It is about Avraham Avinu that Shlomo Hamelech says (*Shir HaShirim* 8:7), מַיִם רַבִּים לֹא יוּכְלוּ לְכַבּוֹת אֶת הָאַהֲבָה, *mighty (many) waters* — the onrushing wave of evil practiced by his contemporaries — *could never extinguish the flame of love*, for Hashem nestled in Avraham's heart.

It is not surprising then that Avraham received *all* the Divine reward that could have been enjoyed by previous generations. By seeking to stifle the *tzaddik* — who, in turn, deflected their attempts and used it as a vehicle for his own growth — Avraham's contemporaries yielded whatever merit they had to their antagonist, Avraham Avinu.

Probing further, we can attribute some of Avraham's success in influencing his contemporaries (and avoiding their attempts to influence him) and Noach's inability to leave a lasting impact to the distinction between the observance of *mitzvos* and the commitment to Torah itself. Noach, described as אִישׁ צַדִּיק תָּמִים, *a righteous man, perfect* (*Bereishis* 6:9), certainly observed many of the specific *mitzvos*. However, living during the first two millennia of the universe's history, a period described by *Chazal* (*Avodah Zarah* 9a) as שְׁנֵי אַלְפִּים תֹּהוּ (two thousand years of desolation), it was virtually impossible for him to embrace a Torah lifestyle. On the basis of *mitzvos* alone, no matter how sincerely observed, it is difficult to deflect the attacks of the wicked. With Avraham's advent, the universe entered a new phase, the two millennia of Torah.[1]

The distinction between Noach's bare survival and Avraham's rich harvest of Divine reward may also be attributed to inherent distinctions between Noach's and Avraham's contemporaries. The lewd, promiscuous, amoral society of the generation prior to the Flood simply had no saving graces. They merited no reward to pass on to Noach. Just as Creation commenced with a primordial void (תֹּהוּ וָבֹהוּ), so too these first generations exemplified a wasted life, devoid of moral values. Of them, we learned above (4:28), הַקִּנְאָה, וְהַתַּאֲוָה, וְהַכָּבוֹד מוֹצִיאִין אֶת הָאָדָם מִן הָעוֹלָם, *jealousy lust*, and the pursuit of *glory* and crass materialism (a life devoted to hedonistic pleasures) contributed to their eventual doom, and *removed [them] from the world*.

By contrast, Avraham's contemporaries, known as the Generation of the Dispersal (דּוֹר הַפְּלָגָה), whatever their failings, possessed at least a kernel of goodness. In fact, they articulated and to an extent practiced their goal — a united mankind. To achieve their difficult objective, they vowed to build a common edifice, the Tower of Bavel, in which שָׂפָה אֶחָת וּדְבָרִים אֲחָדִים, *one language and common ideals*, would prevail (*Bereishis* 11:1).

Of course, a crucial ingredient was missing from their ideology — the true objective of unity, Divine service. Yet, the dream of Avraham's contemporaries, the unity of all mankind, flawed as it was, lived on through the person of

Avraham who united much of mankind behind the banner of Hashem. According to the *Chiddushei HaRim*, Avraham's role as the worthy successor to those misguided idealists was already predicted in the Divine reaction to their edifice, the Tower of Bavel: אֵ הֵן עַם אֶחָד וְשָׂפָה אַחַת לְכֻלָּם וְזֶה הַחִלָּם לַעֲשׂוֹת וְעַתָּה לֹא יִבָּצֵר מֵהֶם כֹּל אֲשֶׁר יָזְמוּ לַעֲשׂוֹת, *Behold, they are one nation with one language for all, and this they begin to do! And now, should it not be withheld from them all they propose to do* (ibid. v. 6)? Through the personality of Avraham, their nascent ideals would be realized.

As the successor to the dream of the builders of the Tower of Bavel, Avraham was entitled to reap their reward.

◆§ The Relevance of Those Generations to Us

ובאמת כל אלה המדריגות צריך כל אדם לעבור עליהם ולהשמר מכל זה כי מתחלה מעשה אדם כבהמה ואח״כ כשזוכה להשגת הדעת קצת צריך מאוד לזכור לבטל עצמו וכל הדעת שלו אל הבורא ית׳ ולידע כי מאתו הכל.

By discussing in *Avos* (a tractate devoted to ethics) the events that occurred millennia ago, the *mishnah* is implying that we can learn from the errors of early man. The lesson to be derived from the Generation of the Flood is quite clear — it is sheer folly pursuing a hedonistic, animalistic life devoted to the pursuit of material pleasures. However, the message conveyed by their successors, the builders of the Tower of Bavel, while less obvious, is equally vital: Ideals alone are not sufficient. Once you have ascended to the level where you are capable of rendering intellectual judgments — not of formulating objectives — dedicate your newly found sense of idealism, your wisdom and knowledge to the service of Hashem.

◆§ Additional Comments on the Ten Generations

והלא היו ביניהם טובים, אדם, שת שהיה גדול כל כך כדאיתא (סוכה נב:ב), מתושלח. אלא שהדור היה מושחת ולא הועיל מאומה. לא היה לזה קיום עם כל אלו העשרה.

מקשה בתוס׳ יו״ט שמונה ועד אברהם יש י״א דורות אם נח בכלל. ויתכן שנח אינו נמנה לפי שלא היה יכול למשוך אחריו את הדור.

אברהם אבינו תיקן את כולם. חסידים פירשו שקבל שכר כולם קאי גם על העשרה הקודמים, (שמאדם עד נח), שתיקן גם את הדורות שקודם המבול.

---

1. While the Giving of the Torah occurred centuries later, *Chazal* (*Kiddushin* 82a) relate that the *Avos* observed the entire Torah.

Before concluding our discussion of the universe's first 20 generations, a few short comments are in order.

Firstly, the *mishnah* emphasizes the *generations* of Noach and Avraham, rather than either of these great individuals themselves. Indeed, the major generalization of both of these *mishnahs* — the almost total moral vacuum and unbridled evil of those generations — is only true from a *generational* perspective. However, great *individuals*, such as Adam, Sheis and Mesushelach, did exist even in the worst of times. It is the *generations* that did not avail themselves of the *tzaddikim* residing in their midst that deserve condemnation (adapted from *Pnei Menachem, Maggidei HaEmes*).

In this light, we can resolve an interesting technical difficulty. The *mishnah* speaks of 10 generations from Noach to Avraham. Yet, upon close examination, the Torah cites 11 generations from Noach to Avraham.

However, in light of our previous remarks on the importance of leaving a lasting impact, we can appreciate that Noach, whose impact on his con- temporaries was limited, is not enumerated as a "generation" in his own right.

Finally, in the spirit of intergenerational lineage, the *Pnei Menachem* suggested that Avraham, through his sterling character, not only rectified the sin of the previous generations but also of the universe's first ten generations. As such, he was entitled to receive their reward as well as that of his more immediate predecessors (*Pnei Menachem, Maggidei HaEmes*).

⋖§ "Eating" for Seventy-Four Individuals

עַל פִּי מַתְנֵי' אֶפְשָׁר לְפָרֵשׁ מַה דְּאִיתָא (מֵס' סוֹפְרִים כא:כט) הָאָדָם הַגָּדוֹל בָּעֲנָקִים
זֶה אַבְרָהָם אָבִינוּ שֶׁאֲכִילָתוֹ וּשְׁתִיָּתוֹ הָיוּ כְּנֶגֶד שִׁבְעִים וְאַרְבָּעָה אֲנָשִׁים. פִּי' כִּי
הַתּוֹרָה מוֹנָה מִנֹּחַ וְעַד אַבְרָהָם שְׁמוֹתֵיהֶם שֶׁל שִׁבְעִים וְאַרְבָּעָה אִישׁ וְאַבְרָהָם אָבִינוּ
קִבֵּל שְׂכַר כֻּלָּם, וְזֶה הַפִּי' אֲכִילָתוֹ וּשְׁתִיָּתוֹ כְּנֶגֶד ע"ד אִישׁ כנ"ל.

With the insight derived from our *mishnah*, we can comprehend an otherwise inexplicable *Chazal* (cf. *Mesechtes Sofrim* 21:29) stating that Avraham Avinu's meal was equivalent to that of seventy-four people. It is highly unlikely that the surface reading of this *Chazal* (that the Patriarch ate such gluttonous meals) is its true intention. Instead, the seventy-four meals correspond to the seventy-four individuals cited in the Torah, beginning with Noach and culminating with Avraham who received the reward due all of them (*Imrei Emes, Maggidei HaEmes*).

4.

■ עֲשָׂרָה נִסְיוֹנוֹת נִתְנַסָּה אַבְרָהָם אָבִינוּ, וְעָמַד בְּכֻלָּם – לְהוֹדִיעַ כַּמָּה חִבָּתוֹ שֶׁל

אַבְרָהָם אָבִינוּ — *Our forefather Avraham was tested with ten trials, and he withstood them all — to show the degree of our forefather Avraham's love for God.*

◆§ The Uniqueness of Avraham's Tests

ומצינו נמי בשאר צדיקים כיעקב אע"ה וכן באהרן נסיתו במסה כו' אך באאע"ה הוי עשרה נסיונות.

Avraham was certainly not the only *tzaddik* to be tested. For example, we know that Aharon was tested at the waters of Merivah to determine whether he would accept Hashem's verdict (that he would perish in the Wilderness) without complaining. However, only Avraham was tested with as many as ten trials.

◆§ The Uniqueness of the Akeidah

ובתורה לא נזכר לשון נסיון רק בעקדה, וי"ל דבכל נסיון הי' גם רצון מיוחד בהדבר כגון מילה הי' הסתר ערלתו כו' ואינך היו צריכין להיות בלאו הכי רק ממילא הי' לו לנסיון למשל ירידתו למצרים כך הי' ראוי להיות במצרים אבל בעקדה הי' רצון הקב"ה שלא לשחטו רק לנסות אברהם שהוא יסבור כן בלבד.

It is also noteworthy that it is only with regard to the *Akeidah* that the Torah uses the term נִסָּיוֹן, *test* (cf. *Bereishis* 22:1). Whereas all the other trials experienced by Avraham (such as his circumcision at age 99 or his forced migration to Egypt almost immediately upon arriving in *Eretz Yisrael*) served a purpose other than testing his dedication, the *Akeidah* had no other purpose.

◆§ Growing Through Trials

כי על ידי נסיון מתעלה האדם למדריגה עליונה כי נסה הוא לשון הרמה כמו שאו נס (ישעיה יג:ב), וממילא על ידי עשרה נסיונות נתרוממו אברהם אבינו ע"ה בכל העשרה דרגין, ובצדיק כתיב (משלי כד:טז) שבע יפול צדיק וקם ואברהם שנקרא חסיד נתרומם ביותר.

The term נִתְנַסָּה, generally translated as "tested," may also connote being "elevated" (cf. *Shemos* 20:17, לְבַעֲבוּר נַסּוֹת אֶתְכֶם בָּא הָאֱלֹהִים, *in order to elevate you has God come*). Each trial, if successfully overcome, is a catalyst for great

and he withstood them all — to show the degree of our forefather Avraham's love for God.

personal growth. When describing the trials of the *tzaddik*, Shlomo Hamelech states (*Mishlei* 24:16): כִּי שֶׁבַע יִפּוֹל צַדִּיק וָקָם, *for though the righteous may fall* (are tested) *seven times* and even stumble at first, *he will arise* — he will be elevated as a result of those trials. Avraham, known as the חָסִיד, a spiritual level superior to that of the צַדִּיק, was subjected to even more trials and grew even greater as a result of those tests.

◆§ The Beneficial Impact of Avraham's Trial

אברהם אבינו ע״ה נתחזק בצדקו מאליו עד שהגיע למדריגה אשר אשר שום עבודה עבור השי״ת לא היתה קשה בעיניו וכמעט שנתבטלה אצלו הבחירה. לכן ניסה אותו השי״ת להודיע כמה חיבתו לפניו שיוכל לחזור על ידי הנסיון אל הבחירה ויעבוד את השי״ת כראוי.

ועל ידי זה זכו כל בני ישראל שיוכלו לעמוד בנסיונות ואם מתגברים על זה מגיעים לגאולת הנפש. והנה הקב״ה משלם מדה במדה ז״ש ומביא גואל לבני בניהם למען שמו באהבה כי שהקב״ה עושה חסדים לבני ישראל בזכות האבות אעפ״י שאינן ראויין מצד עצמם אעפ״כ עושה החסדים באהבה כאשר קיים אברהם אבינו את הנסיונות באהבה.

On a personal level, Avraham's trial of the *Akeidah* restored his level to that of having free will. Previously, the Patriarch had risen to such an exalted level of Divine service that he had virtually lost his capacity to defy Hashem's will. Now, confronted with a particularly difficult challenge, to sacrifice his beloved Yitzchak, Avraham's spiritual equilibrium and free will were restored (*Tiferes Shlomo, Maggidei HaEmes*).

However, the impact of Avraham's success was by no means confined to Avraham himself. As a result of Avraham's many trials, which he successfully withstood, *Klal Yisrael* attained the ability to withstand its many challenges. And just as Avraham grew spiritually as a result of overcoming impediments, so too *Klal Yisrael* grows from its many trials (*Beis Yisrael, Maggidei HaEmes*).

In the spirit of מִדָּה כְּנֶגֶד מִדָּה, *measure for measure* (cf. *Sotah* 8b), Avraham's love for Hashem (חִיבָּתוֹ שֶׁל אַבְרָהָם אָבִינוּ) was reciprocated through Hashem's ample and unyielding love for Avraham's descendants, the Jewish people. As we say in the *Shemoneh Esrei*, וּמֵבִיא גּוֹאֵל לִבְנֵי בְנֵיהֶם לְמַעַן שְׁמוֹ בְּאַהֲבָה, *Hashem brings the redeemer to their descendants* (of the *Avos*) *for the sake of His Name, with love* (*Sfas Emes, Vayeira* 5660).

■ וְעָמַד בְּכֻלָּם — *And he withstood them all.* ■

[ה] עֲשָׂרָה נִסִּים נַעֲשׂוּ לַאֲבוֹתֵינוּ בְּמִצְרַיִם וַעֲשָׂרָה עַל
הַיָּם. עֶשֶׂר מַכּוֹת הֵבִיא הַקָּדוֹשׁ בָּרוּךְ הוּא עַל
הַמִּצְרִיִּים בְּמִצְרַיִם וְעֶשֶׂר עַל הַיָּם.

◆§ Avraham Davened

אין עמידה אלא תפלה (ברכות ו:ב). בכל נסיון נתעטף אברהם אבינו לפני השי"ת
שיזכה להתגבר עליו.

ואברהם עודנו עומד לפני השם, עומד לכל הדורות ומתפלל שאנחנו גם כן נוכל
לעורר מדת הדין להפוך לרחמים.

The term וְעָמַד — which often connotes prayer — (cf. *Berachos* 26b, אֵין עֲמִידָה
אֶלָּא תְּפִילָה) may allude to the many prayers of Avraham Avinu.
Avraham always *davened* that he should be able to successfully withstand
each test (*R' Mordechai of Lechowitz, Maggidei HaEmes*).

Not only did Avraham *daven* but, in a sense, he *still davens*, praying to
Hashem that just as at the *Akeidah* he was able to transmute the Divine
Attribute of Justice into the Attribute of Mercy, leading to the sparing of
Yitzchak's life, so too Hashem should save His children, the Jewish people, from
any further misfortune. As the *pasuk* states (*Bereishis* 18:22), וְאַבְרָהָם עוֹדֶנּוּ עֹמֵד
לִפְנֵי ה', Avraham is still standing (עוֹמֵד) in Hashem's Presence (*Beis Yisrael,
Maggidei HaEmes*).

◆§ Ten Distinct Trials

י"ל בכולם, שבכל נסיון עמד בפני עצמו בלא שום קשר ושייכות לנסיונות שקדמו
לו.

The apparently superfluous term בְּכֻלָּם, *all of them*, suggests that each trial
was a separate event, completely unrelated to Avraham's previous trials.
Despite the Patriarch's success at overcoming previous challenges, each trial was
a totally distinct test (*Lev Simchah, Maggidei HaEmes*).

■ לְהוֹדִיעַ כַּמָּה חִבָּתוֹ שֶׁל אַבְרָהָם אָבִינוּ — *To show the degree of our
forefather Avraham's love for God.*

◆§ Hashem's Love for Avraham

ולא אמר צדקתו וכו', רק כדי להודיע חיבת הקב"ה את אברהם לכן כמו שכתוב
(תהלים יז:ה) ד' צדיק יבחן כו' . . . נתוודע כמה חיבב הקב"ה אותו.

[5] *Ten miracles were performed for our ancestors in Egypt and ten at the Sea. Ten plagues did the Holy One, Blessed is He, bring upon the Egyptians in Egypt and ten at the Sea.*

The term חִבָּתוֹ, usually translated as Avraham's love (for Hashem), may actually imply the reverse. It is well known that Hashem only tests the righteous (cf. *Tehillim* 11:5, ה׳ צַדִּיק יִבְחָן; also cf. *Ramban, Bereishis* 22:1). By subjecting Avraham to more trials than any other individual, Hashem demonstrated His profound love for Avraham.

⋑ The Relationship Between the Ten Statements
(עֲשָׂרָה נִסְיוֹנוֹת) and the Ten Trials (עֲשָׂרָה מַאֲמָרוֹת)

וכן חשבון המשנה עשרה מאמרות כו׳ עשרה נסיונות כו׳ עשרה ניסים כו׳ כי כמו
שעשרה מאמרות הם קיום עולם הטבע בכלל. כן עשרה נסיונות הכנה וקיום
הנהגת בני ישראל . . . ע״י אמצעות מעשה אבות מנהיג הבורא ית׳ בנ״י
במדריגת הנסים כנ״ל.

The sequence of these *mishnahs* — beginning with the ten statements, continuing with the ten trials, and concluding with the ten miracles — implies that just as the ten statements are essential for the continued existence of the natural world, so too the ten trials — and especially the greatest trial, the *Akeidah* — were crucial for the miraculous survival of Israel, through the ten miracles that our ancestors experienced in Egypt (*Sfas Emes, Vayeira* 5639).

5.

■ עֲשָׂרָה נִסִּים נַעֲשׂוּ לַאֲבוֹתֵינוּ בְּמִצְרַיִם וַעֲשָׂרָה עַל הַיָּם — *Ten miracles were performed for our ancestors in Egypt and ten at the Sea.*

⋑ "Twenty" Miracles at the Sea

ופירשו המפרשים דעשרה של מצרים כוונתו על שניצולו מעשר מכות של מצרים
ועשרה של הים עיין ברע״ב שמחשבם. והקשה אדמו״ר האמרי אמת ז״ל את
אביו השפ״א ז״ל דלמה לא מנה על הים גם כן מה שניצולו מעשרה מכות שהיו
למצרים בים, ואם כן על הים עשרים נסים. והשיבו דעשרה על הים היו רק
שלאחר הטביעה היה להם עוד צרות כמו שכתב הרע״ב, ואם כן כיון שישראל
לא נטבעו כלל לא שייך למיחשב שניצולו מאותן עשרה מכות.

According to the *Bartenura*, the ten miracles that our forefathers experienced in Egypt were not distinct miracles but rather their salvation from the ten

[ו] עֲשָׂרָה נִסְיוֹנוֹת נִסּוּ אֲבוֹתֵינוּ אֶת הַקָּדוֹשׁ בָּרוּךְ הוּא
בַּמִּדְבָּר, שֶׁנֶּאֱמַר: "וַיְנַסּוּ אֹתִי זֶה עֶשֶׂר פְּעָמִים, וְלֹא
שָׁמְעוּ בְּקוֹלִי."

[ז] עֲשָׂרָה נִסִּים נַעֲשׂוּ לַאֲבוֹתֵינוּ בְּבֵית הַמִּקְדָּשׁ: לֹא

plagues that afflicted the Egyptians.

The question occurs: If not suffering the same fate as the Egyptians is reckoned as a miracle, then, in the interest of consistency, it would appear that our forefathers experienced *twenty* (rather than ten) miracles at the Reed Sea: the ten miracles that *they* themselves experienced (refer to the *Bartenura* for their listing) and their salvation from the ten punishments inflicted on the *Egyptians*. In response to this question (which had been raised by his son, the future *Imrei Emes*), the *Sfas Emes* noted that being spared the Egyptians' fate is only miraculous when the Jewish people were together with the Egyptians as they were being punished, as they were at the ten plagues. At the Splitting of the Sea, however, the punishment experienced by the Egyptians occurred while they were drowning (refer to *Bartenura*). At that point, the Jewish people were no longer in danger, having already passed through the Sea.

◆§ The Fourth Miracle at the Sea

בהרע"ב ד' שקרקעית הים שדרכו בו המצריים שהיו רודפים אחרי ישראל
נתלחלחה ונעשה חומר וטיט. הקשה אדמו"ר האמרי אמת ז"ל את אביו השפ"א
ז"ל דזה היה של מצרים ולמה חשבו בהדי הני דלישראל והו"ל בסיפא י"א מכות.
והשיב לו דגם זה נמי של ישראל שיתעכבו ולא יוכלו לרדוף אחריהם.

R' *Ovadia Bartenura* considers the seabed's becoming muddy after the Jews' passing through as a miracle that occurred to the Jewish people. While it would seem that this event should be classified as a plague occurring to the Egyptians (resulting in a total of eleven, not ten plagues), in truth the primary purpose of this miracle was to assist the Jews, rather than to punish the Egyptians, because as a result of the seabed becoming virtually impassable, the Egyptian advance was delayed.

6.

■ עֲשָׂרָה נִסְיוֹנוֹת נִסּוּ אֲבוֹתֵינוּ אֶת הַקָּדוֹשׁ בָּרוּךְ הוּא בַּמִּדְבָּר, שֶׁנֶּאֱמַר: "וַיְנַסּוּ אֹתִי ■
זֶה עֶשֶׂר פְּעָמִים, וְלֹא שָׁמְעוּ בְּקוֹלִי." — [With] ten trials did our ancestors test the Holy One, Blessed is He, in the Wilderness, as it is said: "They have tested Me these ten times and did not heed My voice."

[6] *[With] ten trials did our ancestors test the Holy One, Blessed is He, in the Wilderness, as it is said (Bamidbar 14:22): "They have tested Me these ten times and did not heed my voice."*

[7] *Ten miracles were performed for our ancestors in the Holy Temple: No woman miscarried because*

⋖⋗ Diluting the Effect of Avraham's Trials

שלא להתפאר שאבינו עמד בעשרה נסיונות מפני שחטאנו נמי בעשרה נסיונות
כדכתיב זכור כו׳ הקצפתם.

By citing the ten occasions when the Jewish people tested Hashem in the Wilderness, the *mishnah* is cautioning us not to smugly assure ourselves that we will never be accountable for our misdeeds, since we may feel that we can rely on the merit of Avraham's ten trials. While the Patriarch's merit certainly benefits his children (refer to our remarks on *mishnah* 4), to a certain extent it was diluted by the ten trials through which our forefathers tested Hashem (adapted from *Sfas Emes*).

7.

■ עֲשָׂרָה נִסִים נַעֲשׂוּ לַאֲבוֹתֵינוּ בְּבֵית הַמִּקְדָּשׁ — *Ten miracles were performed for our ancestors in the Holy Temple.*

⋖⋗ The Impact of Miracles

כי בזמן שנעשה נסים ושינוי הטבע לבנ״י נתעלו נפשות בנ״י כמ״ש בפי׳ נתת כו׳
נס להתנוסס ומה הטבע נשתנה בעבור בנ״י מכ״ש שנשתנו המה בנפשותם
ובאמת מעין זה הי׳ תמיד בבית המקדש כשעלו בני ישראל לראות פני ה׳.

This *mishnah* is not merely enumerating the miracles that occurred in the *Beis HaMikdash*. Instead, as the words, נַעֲשׂוּ לַאֲבוֹתֵינוּ, *were performed for our ancestors*, imply, the *impact* of these miracles on our forefathers is being emphasized. Every Jew who made the thrice-annual pilgrimage to Yerushalayim, who merited the utterly sublime experience of "perceiving" Hashem (a concept far beyond our comprehension, refer to *The Three Festivals*, p. 34 for an elaboration of this theme), returned a changed person. As David Hamelech says, נָתַתָּה לִּירֵאֶיךָ נֵּס לְהִתְנוֹסֵס, *You gave to those who fear You a banner to be raised high* (Tehillim 60:6). The unusual form לְהִתְנוֹסֵס (using the reflexive verb, הִתְפָּעֵל) emphasizes the impact of miracles on those who fear Hashem (לִּירֵאֶיךָ).

הִפִּילָה אִשָּׁה מֵרֵיחַ בְּשַׂר הַקֹּדֶשׁ; וְלֹא הִסְרִיחַ בְּשַׂר
הַקֹּדֶשׁ מֵעוֹלָם; וְלֹא נִרְאָה זְבוּב בְּבֵית הַמִּטְבָּחַיִם; וְלֹא
אֵירַע קֶרִי לְכֹהֵן גָּדוֹל בְּיוֹם הַכִּפּוּרִים; וְלֹא כִבּוּ
הַגְּשָׁמִים אֵשׁ שֶׁל עֲצֵי הַמַּעֲרָכָה; וְלֹא נִצְּחָה הָרוּחַ אֶת
עַמּוּד הֶעָשָׁן; וְלֹא נִמְצָא פְסוּל בָּעֹמֶר, וּבִשְׁתֵּי הַלֶּחֶם,
וּבְלֶחֶם הַפָּנִים; עוֹמְדִים צְפוּפִים, וּמִשְׁתַּחֲוִים רְוָחִים;

The effect of miracles on those who witness them can be corroborated with a relatively simple *kal vachomer* (*a fortiori* reasoning). If the natural world can be transformed on behalf of the Jewish people (e.g., during the ten plagues) — despite the many barriers involved in transcending the laws of nature that Hashem enacted since Creation — then surely the hearts and souls of *Klal Yisrael* can be transformed as a result of changes in the natural world (see also *Days of Joy*, pp. 33,117 for further discussion of the impact of miracles).

■ וְלֹא הִסְרִיחַ בְּשַׂר הַקֹּדֶשׁ מֵעוֹלָם — *The sacrificial meat never became putrid.*

◆§ Even the Leftover Flesh (נוֹתָר) Did Not Rot

אפשר אף כשנעשה נותר מ"מ לא הסריח.

The apparently superfluous expression מֵעוֹלָם (*forever*) implies that even if the flesh of the sacrifices was not eaten within the halachically permissible time (never exceeding one day and one night), it still did not deteriorate and become spoiled.

■ וְלֹא נִרְאָה זְבוּב בְּבֵית הַמִּטְבָּחַיִם — *No fly was seen in the place where the [sanctified] meat was butchered.*

◆§ The ''Fly'' in the Beis HaMikdash

דרכה של טומאה לשרות דוקא במקום שחשיבותו נמשכת מהקדושה. על כן ציינו
כנס שלא נראה זבוב בבית המטבחיים של בית המקדש [זבוב הוא יצר הרע]. וגם
אצל אלישע היה בכלל נס שלא נראה זבוב על שולחנו.

According to the Kotzker Rebbe, the term *fly* alludes to the *yetzer hara*, depicted by *Chazal* as a ''fly'' (cf. *Berachos* 61a). Despite the propensity of the *yetzer hara* to tempt righteous people and to induce people in sacred places to sin, it lost all of its potency in the *Beis HaMikdash*. In a similar vein, *Chazal*

of the aroma of the sacrificial meat; the sacrificial meat never became putrid; no fly was seen in the place where the [sanctified] meat was butchered; no seminal emission occurred to the High Priest on Yom Kippur; the rains did not extinguish the fire on the Altar-pyre; the wind did not disperse the vertical column of smoke from the Altar; no disqualification was found in the Omer, or in the Two Loaves, or in the Showbread; the people stood crowded together, yet prostrated themselves in ample space;

(Berachos 10b) relate that no fly was seen on Elisha's table, alluding to the inability of the yetzer hara to seduce this great prophet.

■ וְלֹא אִירַע קֶרִי לְכֹהֵן גָּדוֹל בְּיוֹם הַכִּפּוּרִים — No seminal emission occurred to the High Priest on Yom Kippur.

⇜ Did the Kohen Gadol Require This Miracle?

במפרשים דקדקו וכי הכהן גדול היה נצרך לנס בזה. ואולי י״ל . . . בכהן גדול נצרך לנס מצד העם, שכאשר מוריד עצמו לעשות עם אחרים צריך להגיע להנס. גם יי״ל דאין הכוונה כהן גדול לעצמו, אלא שמכוחו היה הכח לכל בני ישראל שלא יארע להם מכשול.

While the High Priest, being on such an exalted level, would not have experienced a seminal emission on this most sacred of days, the mishnah is referring to the "transfer effect" of the Kohen Gadol's purity. Not only did he not have such an emission but in his merit, no Jew did. Alternatively, perhaps it is possible that this miracle was for the benefit of the Kohen Gadol. While ordinarily such a sainted individual would be shielded from so unbecoming an incident, as a consequence of his bonding on Yom Kippur with the entirety of the nation — which contained its fair share of sinners — his high spiritual level might have been compromised.

■ וְלֹא כָבוּ הַגְּשָׁמִים אֵשׁ שֶׁל עֲצֵי הַמַּעֲרָכָה — The rains did not extinguish the fire on the Altar-pyre.

⇜ Klal Yisrael's Own Fire

לכאורה הו״ל למימר אש המערכה. וי״ל דקמ״ל דאף האש שהביאו מהדיוט דהיינו של עצים גם כן לא נכבה דהאש משמים פשיטא שלא נכבה.

The fire on the Altar was of a Divine nature — it came from Heaven in response to the Jews bringing a fire to the Altar. If the *mishnah* merely meant to teach us that the fire was never extinguished, it should have said, וְלֹא כָּבוּ הַגְּשָׁמִים אֵשׁ הַמַּעֲרָכָה, *the rains did not extinguish the fire on the Altar-pyre.* By adding the word עֲצֵי, the *wood* (of the Altar-pyre), the *mishnah* is suggesting that even the fire that was provided by the Jewish nation through its offering of wood, despite its humble origins was also never extinguished.

■ וְלֹא נִמְצָא פְּסוּל בָּעֹמֶר, וּבִשְׁתֵּי הַלֶּחֶם, וּבְלֶחֶם הַפָּנִים ■ — *No disqualification was found in the Omer, or in the Two Loaves, or in the Show-bread.*

◆§ The Sequence of Miracles

> קצת קשה דלא הקדים לחם הפנים שהיה תמיד. וי"ל משום דעל ידי עומר ניתר במדינה ועל ידי שתי הלחם ניתרו המנחות של כל השנה לכן הקדימן. הא דמוזכר לחם הפנים רק בסוף אף שהיה תדיר בכל שבת ושבת, אולי כיון שבלחם הפנים כבר היה נס כדאיתא בגמ' לשום לחם חום ביום הלקחו, סילוקו כסידורו לכן אין זה רבותא כל כך.

Why did the *mishnah* list the Omer — which was offered on the second day of Pesach — and the Two loaves — brought on Shavuos — before the Showbread, which was brought each week?

Perhaps, these miracles are arranged in the order of the significance of the sacrifice with which they are associated. The Omer and the Two Loaves enjoyed significance beyond the actual offering itself. Upon offering the Omer sacrifice, *Klal Yisrael* was permitted to utilize "*chadash*" (grain which took root after the 16th of Nissan). After offering the Two Loaves on Shavuos, flour offerings were permitted from *chadash*. However, the Showbread enjoyed no such additional significance.

The *Lev Simchah* notes that the Showbread was already subject to a great miracle — remaining fresh and warm for the entire week even as it lay on the Temple's Table (cf. *Menachos* 96b). If so, we would anticipate that other miracles would occur to the Showbread. The Omer and the Two Loaves, on the other hand, were not otherwise miraculous, and it is thus more prominent that a miracle occurred in their regard.

■ עוֹמְדִים צְפוּפִים, וּמִשְׁתַּחֲוִים רְוָחִים — *The people stood crowded together, yet prostrated themselves in ample space.*

neither serpent nor scorpion ever caused injury in Jerusalem; nor did any man say to his fellow, "The space is insufficient for me to stay overnight in Jerusalem."

◆§ A Study in Contrasts

In this phrase, the *mishnah* is not only describing one of the greatest miracles that occurred in the *Beis HaMikdash* but is also alluding to a number of contrasting events, occurring almost simultaneously, as we will now discuss.

◆§ Heaven-Bound, Yet Down to Earth

שנתעלו ממש ויצאו מהתלבשות הגופים ונתרוממו ועד״ז י״ל פי׳ משתחוים רווחים כלומר אעפ״כ המשיכו ברכה לעוה״ז כידוע ענין השתחואה הוא המשכה מלמעלה למטה.

As we discussed previously, the thrice-annual pilgrimage to Yerushalayim left an enormous impact on the Jewish people. They "arose" (עוֹמְדִים) from the constraints of the material world, dominated by the physical needs of the human body, and entered the spiritual milieu of the soul. Even as they attained such a level of spiritual ecstasy, they left profound roots in *Olam Hazeh* as well. As the *mishnah* continues, וּמִשְׁתַּחֲוִים רְוָחִים (*yet prostrated themselves in ample space*) — by bowing down, one is, in effect, lowering oneself from an upright position to a lower position, kneeling on the earth itself. So too every *Yom Tov*, despite (or perhaps, as a result of) the lofty heights achieved (עוֹמְדִים), *Klal Yisrael* also lowered itself (מִשְׁתַּחֲוִים) so that the spiritual gains it acquired would lead to blessings in the material world that they returned to after *Yom Tov* (adapted from *Sfas Emes*).

◆§ Humility Leading to Self-Confidence

עומדים צפופים ומשתחוים רוחים רמז שע״י שפלות שמשתחוים בהכנעה נעשים רוחים.

Upon entering the *Beis HaMikdash*, the Jewish people felt exceedingly humble when presenting themselves before the awesome presence of the *Shechinah*. Not only were they physically confined to a narrow space (עוֹמְדִים צְפוּפִים), but when prostrating themselves in Hashem's Presence — always an indication of humility — they realized how infinitesimal they were. Yet, the Jewish people walked away from this humbling experience with a renewed sense of self-confidence and enthusiasm to fulfill Hashem's wishes (רְוָחִים).

A Disguised Miracle

עויי״ל הפי׳ עומדין צפופין פי׳ בנס, ומשתחוים רוחים כאלו הי׳ בזכותם, כדכתיב
תשלם לאיש כמעשהו שהקב״ה עוזר אל האדם באופן שיוכל לעשות טוב מעצמו
אם כי באמת הוא בעזר אלקי.

The term צְפוּפִים, *crowded*, and רְוָחִים, *spacious*, may refer not only to physical space but to the contrasting emotions of total dependence upon Hashem's miracle and a feeling of self-control. When the Jewish people stood, they felt compressed, totally dependent upon Hashem, yet, when they bowed — when they rendered homage to Him — Hashem gave *Klal Yisrael* a sense of spaciousness, a feeling of self-confidence. They felt that through their own merit, guided by Hashem's Torah and graced with His blessings, they could accomplish much. As David Hamelech says, כִּי אַתָּה תְשַׁלֵּם לְאִישׁ כְּמַעֲשֵׂהוּ, for *You reward every individual in accordance with his deeds* (*Tehillim* 62:13), so that he believes that his accomplishments are achieved through his own deeds.

The Humble Lack Nothing

כך היא גם הדרך בחיים, כאשר עומדים בזקיפות קומה יהירות וגאוה, דומה כי
צר המקום לאדם. ואילו כאשר משתחוים, מתכופפים בענוה ומסתפקים במועט,
אזי מרגישים במצב של רווחה שאינם חסרים מאומה.

The Kotzker Rebbe explained that only the haughty feel crowded. Those who stand proudly erect (עוֹמְדִים) often feel that they cannot coexist with others. They perceive the world as a very narrow place, lacking enough room for anyone besides themselves. On the other hand, the humble, who gladly bow (וּמִשְׁתַּחֲוִים) to other people's interests, will find that indeed there is ample space for all of Hashem's creations to coexist (*Maggidei HaEmes*).

Erect Body, Contrite Soul

עיקר השתחויה הוא כריעת המחשבה והלב, מפני שיחשוב בגדלות הבורא
יתב״ש, וכמו שכתב החכם ר׳ יחיאל ז״ל (חתנו של הבעש״ט) וכל קומה לפניך
תשתחוה, כי לפני מלך בשר ודם צריך להשתחות עם הגוף שיהא נראה כפוף. אבל
הבורא יתב״ש שהוא בוחן לבות לבות יכולים להשתחוות לפניו אף בקומה זקופה, רק
להשפיל ולהכניע לבבו. ועל זה רומז התנא עומדים צפופים ואף כן משתחוים
רוחים.

R' Yechiel, the Baal Shem Tov's son-in-law, offered a novel interpretation to a segment of the נִשְׁמַת prayer, וְכָל קוֹמָה לְפָנֶיךָ תִשְׁתַּחֲוֶה, *every erect spine shall prostrate itself before You.* Unlike all mortal rulers who insist that we prostrate ourselves when paying homage to them, Hashem is perfectly content with an erect *body* (קוֹמָה), as long as our *soul* is truly contrite. According to the Maggid of Koznitz, our *mishnah* conveys the same theme: Feel free to stand erect and proud in Hashem's Presence (עוֹמְדִים צְפוּפִים), but at the same time ensure that your soul will humble itself (מִשְׁתַּחֲוִים רְוָחִים) (adapted from *Maggidei HaEmes*).

■ וְלֹא הִזִּיק נָחָשׁ וְעַקְרָב בִּירוּשָׁלַיִם מֵעוֹלָם; וְלֹא אָמַר אָדָם לַחֲבֵרוֹ: ,,צַר לִי הַמָּקוֹם שֶׁאָלִין בִּירוּשָׁלָיִם.'' — *Neither serpent nor scorpion ever caused injury in Jerusalem; nor did any man say to his fellow, "The space is insufficient for me to stay overnight in Jerusalem."*

☙ In the Merit of Not Speaking Lashon Hara

דנחש הוא בענין לשון הרע. וזה כאשר לא הזיק כו' ולא היה לשון הרע, וממילא לא אמר אדם צר לי המקום כו', כענין שכתוב השם גבולך שלום חלב חטים ישביעך.

The Bendiner Rav explained the relationship between these two statements in the following manner. In the merit of not speaking *lashon hara*, an infraction which is compared to the behavior of a snake (cf. *Taanis 8a*), *Klal Yisrael* is blessed with the feeling of spaciousness. David alludes to the relationship between internal peace and contentment: הַשָּׂם גְּבוּלֵךְ שָׁלוֹם חֵלֶב חִטִּים יַשְׂבִּיעֵךְ, *He Who makes your borders peaceful, and with the cream of the wheat He sates you* (*Tehillim* 147:14). In the merit of peace within our borders, we will feel satiated as if we enjoyed abundant produce (*Maggidei HaEmes*).

☙ In the Merit of Not Complaining

אין הפירוש שנרחבה ירושלים, אלא מחמת אהבת ישראל והרצון לראות פני השכינה לא הרגיש אדם שצר לו המקום בירושלים אף בעת הרגלים שכל ישראל היו מגיעים לראות פני ה'.

In a famous comment, the Kotzker Rebbe explained that we need not assume that Yerushalayim expanded every *Yom Tov*. On the contrary, it retained its ordinary size and yet throngs of pilgrims, imbued with אַהֲבַת יִשְׂרָאֵל, love of their fellow Jew, and fueled with a burning desire to perceive the *Shechinah* to the greatest extent possible, never even realized how crowded their area was.

☙ Only Visitors Enjoyed This Miracle

ולא אמר א"י לי צר לי המקום קשה דכתיב עוד יאמרו וכו' צר לי וכו' גשה לי ואשבה

[ח] עֲשָׂרָה דְבָרִים נִבְרְאוּ בְּעֶרֶב שַׁבָּת בֵּין הַשְּׁמָשׁוֹת,
וְאֵלוּ הֵן: פִּי הָאָרֶץ, וּפִי הַבְּאֵר, פִּי הָאָתוֹן, וְהַקֶּשֶׁת,

The fire on the Altar was of a Divine nature — it came from Heaven in
response to the Jews bringing a fire to the Altar. If the *mishnah* merely meant
to teach us that the fire was never extinguished, it should have said, וְלֹא כָבּוּ
הַגְּשָׁמִים אֵשׁ הַמַּעֲרָכָה, *the rains did not extinguish the fire on the Altar-pyre.* By
adding the word עֲצֵי, the *wood* (of the Altar-pyre), the *mishnah* is suggesting
that even the fire that was provided by the Jewish nation through its offering
of wood, despite its humble origins was also never extinguished.

Perhaps we may distinguish between the denizens of the Holy City who
indeed will experience overcrowding and the pilgrims who benefited from the
miracle of always enjoying enough space.

8.

■ עֲשָׂרָה דְבָרִים נִבְרְאוּ בְּעֶרֶב שַׁבָּת בֵּין הַשְּׁמָשׁוֹת — *Ten things were created
on Sabbath eve, at twilight.*

◆§ Source of All Hashem's Creation

> ... יתכן לפרש כל אשר עשה לרבות עשרה דברים שנבראו בע"ש ביה"ש
> נראה מזה כי אלו עשרה דברים הם בכלל עשרה מאמרות שנמצא לכל הבריאה
> ענין פרט וכלל.

While the Torah does not explicitly mention these ten things, it alludes to
them when it discusses Hashem's reaction when He observed the com-
pleted universe — וַיַּרְא אֱלֹהִים אֶת כָּל אֲשֶׁר עָשָׂה וְהִנֵּה טוֹב מְאֹד, *And God saw all
that He had made, and behold it was very good* (Bereishis 1:31). The apparently
superfluous term כָּל, *all* (everything), refers to the ten creations, indicating that
they too met with Divine approval.

We generally assume (with some justification) that the ten creations were the
final acts of the Six Days of Creation. In a sense, however, they were the *source*
of all creation as well as its culmination. As was mentioned, the Torah alludes
to their creation with the phrase כָּל אֲשֶׁר עָשָׂה, "*all that He had made (created),*"
implying that these ten creations were the source of all else that Hashem
created.[1]

Just as the Torah is interpreted by explaining its כְּלָלוֹת, its *general* statements,
as well as its פְּרָטִים, its *specific* statements, so too the universe (created in

---

1. Refer to our commentary on בְּמַאֲמָר אֶחָד יָכוֹל לְהִבָּרְאוֹת (5:1) for a similar concept emphasizing
the role of certain core creations from which all of Hashem's other creations emanated.

[8] *Ten things were created on Sabbath eve, at twilight. They are: the mouth of the earth, the mouth of the well, the mouth of the donkey, the rainbow [which was*

---

consultation with the Torah, cf. *Yalkut Shimoni, Bereishis* 2) was created through ten highly spiritual general commands, referred to as the עֲשָׂרָה דְּבָרִים, leading to ten specific statements the עֲשָׂרָה מַאֲמָרוֹת (*Sfas Emes, Chukas 5659*).

◆§ The World of the Baal Teshuvah

נראה שהמה תיקונים גם על אחר החטא. שמכל אלה הדברים נשאר רמז גם אחר החטא. ואילו של אברהם יוכיח. וכמו שיש בזמן עשיי״ת כמו כן יש בעולם עשרה דברים.

The timing of these ten creations is of great significance. Man's first sin had just been committed as Adam partook of the forbidden fruit. It appeared as if the entire universe would founder on the basis of Adam's grave error. But instead, the first sinner also became the first *baal teshuvah*. During the waning hours of that first *Erev Shabbos*, Adam acknowledges his sin and repents. To celebrate the universe's renewal — this time as the world of the *baal teshuvah* — Hashem "enhances" His universe, creating ten additional entities. Many of these creations were of particular significance to the new *teshuvah*-dominated world. For example, the ram of Avraham Avinu, perpetuated through the *shofar*, is a powerful vehicle to convey *Klal Yisrael's* annual plea for forgiveness.

A parallel may also be drawn between the ten creations and the annual Ten Days of Repentance (עֲשֶׂרֶת יְמֵי תְּשׁוּבָה). Not only the timing of these ten creations, but also the amount of time involved in their creation, is significant. While it took a full week to create the entire universe, these ten creations were created within an incredibly short span, the brief period between sunset of the first Friday and nightfall, at the onset of the first Shabbos. This reminds us of the *Zohar's* (*Vayeira*) famous observation that a *baal teshuvah* can accomplish in a moment what others can only achieve over a long period (*Sfas Emes, Rosh Hashanah 5650*).

■ פִּי הָאָרֶץ, וּפִי הַבְּאֵר, פִּי הָאָתוֹן — *The mouth of the earth, the mouth of the well, the mouth of the donkey.*

◆§ The Three Openings and the Three Vices

הדברים האלו הם לפי סדר הפרשיות, פי הארץ קרח, פי הבאר חוקת ופי האתון בלק, קנאה תאוה וכבוד.

The *Pnei Menachem* noted that the three openings correspond to the three
character flaws that so often plague us (*jealousy, lust and glory;* cf. 4:21
above). Korach, motivated by jealousy of Moshe and Aharon, was thwarted by
the opening in the earth which engulfed him. The Jewish People's lust for water
was satisfied by Miriam's well. And Bilam, who despite his pretenses of humility eagerly sought honor and glory, was humiliated by his donkey.

He also noted that these "openings" are listed in the same sequence that they
are presented in the Torah — the story of Korach in *Parashas Korach,* followed
by the well in *Parashas Chukas,* and finally, Bilam's donkey in *Parashas Balak.*

■ פִּי הָאָרֶץ — *The mouth of the earth.* ■

◆§ Why the Earth's Opening Was Created on Erev Shabbos

איתא בזוה"ק שקרח חלק על השבת, על כן נברא עונשו בערב שבת בין השמשות
מדה כנגד מדה.

ובודאי הי' קרח ועדתו אנשים גדולים והיו נראין בהתגלות כאלו הם גדולים
מאהרן הכהן. אבל כח הפנימיות גובר וזה הי' הסימן פרח מטה אהרן שיש לו חלק
בנסתרות. ואיתא כהנים שומרים מבפנים ולוים מבחוץ שכן הי' משמרות הלוים
וכהם ועבודתם בבחי' חיצוניות וכהן בפנימיות . . . ולכן נקרא שבת שלום שיש
בו התגלות הפנימיות.

וזה בחי' מתנה כמ"ש עבודת מתנה אתן . . . והוא ג"כ בחי' השבת שכ' בזוה"ק
דקרח חלק על שבת דשבת הוא מתנה טובה.

Korach rebelled against the very institution of Shabbos, described as a Divine
gift (*Shemos* 16:29). While he could appreciate the מוֹעֲדִים (Festivals), and his
cohorts were known as קְרִיאֵי מוֹעֵד [*those summoned for meeting (Bamidbar* 16:2)]
— the מוֹעֲדִים are occasions which celebrated events that occurred to *Klal Yisrael*
— he disputed the notion that Hashem could grant us this day of rest, Shabbos.
Just as he spurned Hashem's gift of Shabbos, he also rejected the Divine gift of
performing the Temple service (cf. *Bamidbar* 18:7, עֲבֹדַת מַתָּנָה, *service that is a
gift*) granted to Aharon and his children (cf. *Sfas Emes, Korach* 5659).

Korach and his allies also challenged other aspects of Shabbos, especially the
sense of inner peace and serenity as well as the unity of *Klal Yisrael* that
permeates our life each Shabbos. Every Friday night, as we sense the enhanced
spirituality of Shabbos, we proclaim Hashem as One Who "spreads a canopy
of peace." Korach, who personified dissension, was the antithesis of the Shabbos
spirit of peace. Moreover, Korach was known for his lavish outer exhibition of
piety. According to *Chazal (Bamidbar Rabbah* 18:3), he encouraged his followers
to dress in garments made of *techeiles* (sky-blue wool) rather than merely wear
tzitzis dyed with that color. This exhibitionism is the antithesis of Shabbos, the
day of *inner* peace and serenity (cf. *Sfas Emes, Korach* 5652).

Above all, Korach's insurrection, and especially the venomous tone he used to pursue his cause, conflicted with the paramount theme of Shabbos, which is sanctity. [See *Shemos* 31:12: אַךְ אֶת שַׁבְּתֹתַי תִּשְׁמֹרוּ . . . לָדַעַת כִּי אֲנִי ה' מְקַדִּשְׁכֶם, *You must observe My Sabbaths . . . to know that I am Hashem, Who makes you holy.* Shabbos was given to *Klal Yisrael* to make us aware that Hashem sanctifies our lives] (*Sfas Emes, Korach* 5645).

Having defined Korach's revolt as a challenge to the venerable institution of Shabbos, we can appreciate why his ultimate end (*the mouth of the earth*) was created moments before the Shabbos began (*Maggidei HaEmes,* also cf. *Sfas Emes, Korach,* 5631, 5645, 5652).

๏§ A Plea for Teshuvah

פי הארץ נברא בערב שבת בין השמשות בכניסת השבת, שובו בני אדם. בני אדם הראשון שגם כן התיישב בשבת ואמר מזמור שיר ליום השבת

According to the *Beis Yisrael,* the open pit which engulfed Korach and his followers reminds us of the eventual fate of those who do not repent — the bottomless pit of *Gehinnom.* There is no more opportune time for *teshuvah* than *Erev Shabbos,* when Adam repented from mankind's first sin (*Yalkut Tehillim* 843) (adapted from *Maggidei HaEmes*).

๏§ The Opening to Gehinnom

והטעם כי העוה"ז אינו בשלימות וע"כ יש בו חסרון. ובכוונה ברא השי"ת כן שלא להיות הקיום בשלימות בלי עזר עליון. וכמו בגשמיות נברא צד צפון פרוץ כידוע שמג' רוחות העולם סתום ולצד צפון פתוח הכל להראות שאין לעולם קיום מצד עצמו. אך הקב"ה הוא שלימות העולם. וזה בחי' ש"ק שנק' שלום כידוע בזוה"ק בע"ש ביה"ש נבראו מזיקין ורצו לשלוט בעולם רק שהקב"ה השפיע קדושת ש"ק ונשבתו המזיקין. והיינו שסוף ימי המעשה הוא בחסרון שחסר השלמות. וע"ז אמרו מה הי' העולם חסר מנוחה פי' השלימות ובא שבת והשלים . . . וזה עצמו ענין פי הארץ לבלוע קרח שנברא בע"ש ביה"ש פ' כיון שרצה קרח להתנהג רק עפ"י דין קפץ עליו רוגז הגיהנם שהוא הצד הצפון . . . אבל קרח רצה לירד לעומק הדין וערער על הכהונה שהוא מדת החסד לומר שאינו צריך לחסד לכן לא הי' יכול להתקיים.

Korach desired that the universe be governed solely on the basis of Divine Justice. Korach's wish, however, was based upon a profound misconception that Hashem created a *complete,* self-contained universe, which could function on its own, based on the immutable laws of nature, without need of any further Divine intervention (see commentary on 5:20 for further elaboration).

In reality, Hashem deliberately designed the natural world to be *incomplete,* thereby compelling man to turn to Him and His Attribute of Mercy.

Chazal allude to the universe's "lack of completeness" by relating thatsealed three sides of the universe but deliberately left the fourth side — the northern flank — open (cf. *Bava Basra* 25a). This metaphor may refer to *Gehinnom* and other misfortunes which are associated with the northern direction (cf. *Yirmiyahu* 1:14, מִצָּפוֹן תִּפָּתַח הָרָעָה, *from the north the evil will be released*; also 4:6, 6:1). Appropriately enough, Korach, who envisioned the universe as being self-contained (complete), was swallowed up by the opening of the earth — its exposed flank and the passageway from This World to the purgatory of *Gehinnom*.

In this light, we can better appreciate why the earth's opening was created on *Erev Shabbos* at twilight. There was never a moment in which the universe's lack of completeness was more visible than the waning moments of *Erev Shabbos*. Everything physical had been consummated according to the strict regulations of the natural world, as Korach espoused. And yet, the completed universe still had a gaping hole — the opening through which Korach would eventually fall — that craved "closure." This could only come from the total spirituality of Shabbos. As *Chazal* state (Rashi, *Bereishis* 2:2 s.v. ויכל, .), מֶה הָיָה הָעוֹלָם חָסֵר? מְנוּחָה. בָּאת שַׁבָּת בָּאת מְנוּחָה, *What was the world lacking? Rest and tranquility. With Shabbos came rest and tranquility.*

The *mishnah* also relates that the demons were created at that time. According to the *Zohar*, their growth was stunted when Shabbos arrived (i.e. they remained as "disembodied souls" without the external casing of the body). There was no more propitious time than that first *Erev Shabbos* for the potential dominance of the demons and all other lethal forces — such as the פִּי הָאָרֶץ, the opening of the "incomplete" world — who were awaiting the Divine call. It was only during the period of Divine Mercy at the commencement of Shabbos, when the universe became spiritually complete, that the demons' development was finally curtailed (*Sfas Emes, Korach* 5636).

◄§ The Universe Seeks Completion

והכלל כי בעוה"ז חסר השלימות וסוף הכל צריכין לסייעתא דשמיא כמ"ש לאל
גומר עלי. לכן דרשו ז"ל מאוד זו מיתה. כלומר זה שסוף הכל צריכין אל הביטול
אליו ית' זה טוב מאוד כנ"ל. ולכן נברא פי הארץ בע"ש ביה"ש כי הזמן אז
להתקשר המעשים אל השורש שהוא השלימות כנ"ל.
וקרח מרד בזה השלימות כי רצה ליקח בעצמו ולא לבטל עצמו אל הכלל . . . לכן
החסרון הדבוק בעצם בעוה"ז והוא נקרא פי הארץ כלומר שמשתוקק הבריאה
לקבל השלימות והוא מנע השלימות לכן בלע אותם.

J ust as the human mouth craves nourishment, so too the earth (פִּי הָאָרֶץ) craved that sense of completion which could only come with the Divine Revelation on Shabbos. Korach thrived on factionalism and dissension, the antithesis of completion, and loathed the sense of serenity and closure that Shabbos brings.

Thus, he simply had no place.[1]

In this light, we can gain new insight into a cryptic comment of *Chazal* (*Bereishis Rabbah* 9:5), וְהִנֵּה "טוֹב מְאֹד" זוֹ מִיתָה, *the expression "very good" refers to death*. When Hashem pronounced the universe to be "very good" that first *Erev Shabbos*, He was reflecting upon a world whose sole desire was to be inexorably linked to Hashem (a status achieved with the advent of *Shabbos*). The same yearning for closure, for absolute self-negation to the Source of all life — Hashem — is eventually attained by all human beings upon their expiration (adapted from *Sfas Emes, Korach 5640*).

⋖§ The Attribute of Peace (שָׁלוֹם) Complains

ובאמת השלום אינו בעוה"ז רק בכח סייעתא דשמיא כמ"ש במד' בראשית אמת
ושלום אמרו אל יברא דכולא שקרים וכולא קטטה. ולכן האוחז במחלוקת יותר
מדאי אין לו קיום בעולם.

Korach's continued existence was harmful not only to *Klal Yisrael* but also to the very viability of the universe. *Chazal* (*Bereishis Rabbah* 8:5) relate that when Hashem contemplated creating man, the Attribute of Peace objected, arguing that mortals were simply too contentious for the universe. While Hashem overruled this objection and nonetheless created man, He also graced the universe with an extraordinary Divinely inspired "infusion" of peace. By stirring needless controversy, Korach upset the universe's delicate balance of peace. Rather than jeopardize the universe's equilibrium and endanger a peaceful haven for *Klal Yisrael*, the fomenter of controversy, Korach, had to fall by the wayside (*Sfas Emes, Korach 5651*).

■ וּפִי הַבְּאֵר — *The mouth of the well.*

⋖§ The Wellsprings of Shabbos

דכתיב שתה מים מבורך ונוזלים מתוך בארך. בור הוא מים מכונסין ובאר הוא
מעין נובע. ובכל איש ישראל יש נקודה חיות דכתי' ויפח באפיו כו'. רק האדם
צריך למצוא זאת הנקודה. והוא עבודת האדם להמשיך כל המעשים אחר זאת
הנקודה. וזה שתה מים מבורך והיא העבודה בימי המעשה. ובש"ק ונוזלים מתוך
בארך שנפתח המעין ובא אור חדש והיא נשמה יתירה.

While it is generally assumed that the term פִּי הַבְּאֵר refers to the opening of Miriam's well, it may also refer (allegorically) to the Shabbos day itself, as

1. The earth's longing for the spiritual completion of Shabbos is reflected in our own conduct every week as we eagerly await Shabbos' arrival, symbolized by our קַבָּלַת שַׁבָּת, *accepting the Shabbos.*

we shall now elucidate.

The inner spark, the relationship between the six weekdays and Shabbos is alluded to by Shlomo Hamelech in the verse, שְׁתֵה מַיִם מִבּוֹרֶךָ וְנֹזְלִים מִתּוֹךְ בְּאֵרֶךָ, *Drink water from your own cistern and flowing water from your own well* (*Mishlei* 5:15). Drink water from your "open pit" all week long; serve Hashem by observing those commandments stated explicitly in the Torah. And then on Shabbos luxuriate in the sparkling drops of spirituality emanating from the *inner* depths of your *neshamah*. By loyally fulfilling Hashem's will all week, we merit to reconnect with the Divine spark — our soul — created in His likeness, every Shabbos. "The mouth of the well" is the link between the surface "pit" (מִבּוֹרֶךָ) of the week and the bottomless depth of the Shabbos well (בְּאֵרֶךָ). It too was created during that transitional period of *Erev Shabbos* at twilight (*Sfas Emes, Chukas 5634*).

◆§ Becoming a Conduit for Hashem's Berachos

בענין פי הבאר שנברא בע״ש ביה״ש דכתיב אסף את העם ואתנה להם מים כי הקבה וב״ש לעולם מוכן כביכול להשפיע לתחתונים מטובו אך שיהיו התחתונים כלים לקבלו . . .

לכן בשבת קודש שמתעלין הברואים ומתאספין להיות מוכן לקבל השפע מהשי״ת וזה הוא בקבלת השבת שמניחין כל המעשים ומבטלים עצמם להשורש. וכפי מה שמבררין זאת שהכל לה׳ והכל מה׳. אז נאמר וירא אלהים כו׳ כל אשר עשה והנה טוב מאוד. ובודאי זה אמת לעולם כי הכלל היא טוב מאוד. רק לא בכל עת זוכין לאסוף כל הבריאה. וכשבאין לזה אז חל הברכה מן השמים. וזהו נעשה ע״ש ביה״ש והוא הנשמה יתירה שיורדת לתחתונים. ונמצא מפתיחת פי הבאר בכל שבת.

As stated previously (*mishnah* 3), Hashem is always seeking to shower His blessings upon *Klal Yisrael*. However, His blessings are only bestowed upon us if we are truly deserving of them.

There is no more auspicious time for Hashem's blessings to be absorbed than during the waning moments of *Erev Shabbos*, the very moment when Hashem "evaluated" His completed universe and expressed His great satisfaction with it — וַיַּרְא אֱלֹהִים אֶת כָּל אֲשֶׁר עָשָׂה וְהִנֵּה טוֹב מְאֹד, *And God saw all that He had made, and behold it was very good* (*Bereishis* 1:31).

While the individual components of the universe were described as being "good," it was only the completed universe that earned the distinction of being called "very good."

Every Shabbos, *Klal Yisrael* assumes its function of being a worthy recipient of Hashem's *berachos*. Just as Hashem viewed the universe in its *totality* at the inception of the very first Shabbos, so too by welcoming the Shabbos every week, *Klal Yisrael* is setting aside its weekday preoccupation with the mundane details of the material world (in which Hashem's Presence is often obscured) and instead focuses on the *entire* universe and its Creator. At such a moment Hashem is delighted to bestow His blessings upon *Klal Yisrael*.

Typically, a well serves as a receptacle for onrushing water. By creating the well *Erev Shabbos* at twilight, Hashem was restoring *Klal Yisrael* to its historic mission of being a truly worthy recipient of His blessings, just as a well retains water. However, an important prerequisite existed before *Klal Yisrael* could enjoy the waters of the well. As the Torah states, אֱסֹף אֶת הָעָם וְאֶתְּנָה לָהֶם מָיִם, *Assemble the people and I shall give them water (Bamidbar 21:16).*

Only by serving as a role model for all of mankind to forget its obsession with the petty details of the material world and instead to perceive the *Shechinah* as the universe's unifying factor — a role which we assume every *Erev Shabbos* — can the well's ample bounty be enjoyed (adapted from *Sfas Emes, Chukas 5645*).

◆§ Uniting Klal Yisrael

> וכ״כ אסוף את העם ואתנה להם מים שע״י התאספות בנ״י נפתח פי הבאר. וזה
> ג״כ מה שנברא פי באר בע״ש ביה״ש כי בשבת מתאספין בנ״י ומתאחדין ברזא
> דאחד.

Klal Yisrael puts aside its petty differences and hopefully unites every Shabbos (as we say in the כְּגַוְנָא prayer — רָזָא דְשַׁבָּת . . . דְּאִתְאַחֲדַת בְּרָזָא דְאֶחָד, *This is the secret of Shabbos . . . when she becomes united in the secret of Oneness.* There is a vital prerequisite for the well's water (see previous comment) and for all of Hashem's *berachos* — אֱסֹף אֶת הָעָם, *assemble the people*, our internal unity (*Sfas Emes, Chukas 5647*).

◆§ Ability to Sing Hashem's Praises

> ונדרך ה׳ תמיד כו׳ וזה עיקר המנוחה שבאין אל שורש הפנימיות, וז״ש והיית כגן
> רוה וכמוצא מים כו׳ ובשבת באין לזאת המנוחה ונעשין כמוצא מים אשר לא
> יכזבו מימיו.
> והאמת הוא כי כפי מה שמעידין על הבורא על הבורא ית׳ כך מתגבר כח הפה.

As explained previously, the well represents the wellsprings of the Jewish soul. On Shabbos, the day of spiritual respite, as well as physical rest, the Jew is able to get in touch with the innermost recesses of his soul. On Shabbos, the Jew realizes his full spiritual potential. He finds that spiritual core, that inner spark known as the "well." Upon doing so, the Jew also attains the ability to speak Hashem's praises. As the *mishnah* alludes, he has found the פִּי הַבְּאֵר, the *mouth* (פִּי) that sings the praises of Hashem emanating from the wellsprings of the Jewish heart.

Yeshayahu describes this state of spiritual bliss experienced every Shabbos in the following words: וְנָחֲךָ ה' תָּמִיד . . . וְהָיִיתָ כְּגַן רָוֶה וּכְמוֹצָא מָיִם, *Then Hashem will guide you always . . . and you will be like a well-watered garden and a spring of water* (58:11) (*Sfas Emes, Chukas 5650*).

✒ A Divine Gift

> אח"כ וממדבר מתנה שיש ג"כ דרך אפילו לאינם ראוים שיזכו במתנה לזו הבאר ע"י הביטול שנמשכים אחר הקב"ה באמונה. וזה פי' הבאר שנפתח בע"ש כי שבת נק' מתנה טובה ולכן בשבת הביטול כל מלאכות בחי' ממדבר מתנה.

In the same manner that the Shabbos is a Divine gift (cf. *Beitzah* 16a, מַתָּנָה טוֹבָה יֵשׁ לִי בְּבֵית גְּנָזַי וְשַׁבָּת שְׁמָהּ, *I have a goodly gift in My treasure-house and it is called Shabbos*), so too we can only comprehend the wellsprings of Torah through a gift of Divinely inspired wisdom. Just as the well was dug by *Klal Yisrael's* leaders (cf. *Bamidbar* 21:18, בְּאֵר חֲפָרוּהָ שָׂרִים כָּרוּהָ נְדִיבֵי הָעָם, *Well that the princes dug, that the nobles of the people excavated*), so too true comprehension of Torah requires much effort on our part. Yet, *our* efforts alone are hardly sufficient. *Klal Yisrael's* ability to always find water while in the Wilderness was truly a miracle. Similarly, our efforts to comprehend Torah are but a beginning and need to be consummated with Hashem's help (*Sfas Emes, Chukas 5652*).

✒ Transition From the Natural to Supernatural World

> כי שבת הוא עצם הבאר. אך לפתוח פי הבאר תליא בהכנת ימי המעשה זוכין בע"ש ביה"ש אל פי הבאר. וכן היא בהכנת האדם בעוה"ז זוכה לעוה"ב כמ"ש עוה"ז דומה לפרוזדור התקן עצמך בפרוזדור כדי שתכנוס לטרקלין שיפתח לך הפתח של עוה"ב שהוא יום שכולו [*שבת].

In our previous remarks, we distinguished between the *finite* limits symbolized by the pit and the *infinite* possibilities of the well. By extension, the pit represents the natural world and its finite laws — initiated by Hashem when He created the universe — which generally prevail during the six weekdays. The well, on the other hand, represents the supernatural world with its limitless potential; a world with which we connect every Shabbos. By abstaining from all work on Shabbos, we sever our ties with the "pit" and its natural limitations and enter the supernatural realm of Shabbos. Just as the waters of a deep well often overflow and fill an adjoining pit, so too Shabbos hopefully is not a mere isolated event, but rather a day that leaves an impact on the entire week.

This bridge from the natural to the supernatural is facilitated by the well's opening created by Hashem during the transition from the Six Days of Creation to Shabbos. By opening the well's mouth, *Klal Yisrael* demonstrates that it is not taking the spiritual treasures of the supernatural world that awaits it on Shabbos for granted, but instead it waits all week long for the veil of materialism that shrouds the beauty of the well to be lifted on Shabbos. Just as we prepare ourselves in the "hallway" of This World for entry to the "palace" of The World to Come, so too we open the well's cover all week, so we can tap the boundless spirituality of Shabbos (*Sfas Emes, Chukas* 5663).

◄§ Wellsprings of Torah

פי' הבאר שהוא תורה שבע"פ שצריכין למצוא מעצמו הארת התורה הגנוזה
בכל דבר כו'. שג"כ צריך האדם לידע כי אינו זוכה לשום דבר רק ע"י שבוטח
בהשי"ת כי הוא עוזר לכל דבר כמ"ש מתנה כו'.

The well symbolizes the profound thoughts of Torah. At times, the Jewish people actually had to dig for water; so too we must "dig" to achieve our goals in Torah study by investing considerable effort in studying Torah. However, despite our best efforts it is but a beginning, only reaching fruition when capped with the Divine gift of wisdom. The well too is described as a Divine gift (cf. *Bamidbar* 21:18). There is no better time to receive and immerse oneself in the Divine gift of Torah than the Shabbos day, which is also described by *Chazal* as a Divine gift (*Beitzah* 16a).

But one must be worthy of receiving such a gift. Just as *Klal Yisrael* merited the well because of their unstinting faith and loyalty to Hashem, so too we merit the gift of Shabbos and Torah because of our complete faith and trust in Hashem. The פִּי הַבְּאֵר mentioned in our *mishnah* may refer to the opening of the wellsprings of Torah attained through our unflinching *emunah* (*Sfas Emes, Chukas* 5632).

◄§ The Source of All Blessings

כי לעולם כל הנצרך לכל ברי' מוכן בכל מקום ובכל עת רק שנסתר מעין הגשמי
וכשהקב"ה מאיר עיניו רואה שהכל לפניו. וכמו כן הכא הי' רצונו ית' שיפקחו
עיני בני ישראל ויראו כי המים מוכן בסלע.

By using the phrase פִּי הַבְּאֵר, the "opening of the well," the *mishnah* is encouraging us to exploit that opening and look beyond the mouth of the well to seek its true treasures. On that first *Erev Shabbos*, the "well's mouth" was created and the ability to realize that a solution exists to most of our problems if we only shed the surface layer of materialism that pervades This World. Just as when she was in the desert Hagar's eyes were opened, leading to the realization that there was plentiful water in an already *existing* well

(Bereishis 21:19), so too the solutions to our own problems can be found if we would only penetrate beyond the surface and find the ample waters beneath (Sfas Emes, Chukas 5659).

■ פִּי הָאָתוֹן — The mouth of the donkey. ■

⇨ A Message to Bilam

וזה עצמו הרמז שפתח ה' פי האתון. לומר שהגם שנמצא בו הנבואה ידע בנפשו
כי אינו מוכן לזה בעצם. וכמו שנפתח פי האתון להיות מדבר לפי צורך השעה.
כמו כן בחי' הנבואה שהי' באותו רשע לאיזה צורך ולטובת בנ"י. אבל לא הי'
מוכן לזה בעצם כנ"ל.

By granting the gift of speech to a totally inarticulate being, the donkey, Hashem was also conveying a message to the donkey's master, the wicked prophet Bilam. The gift of prophecy was hardly an indication of his moral stature. On the contrary, just as the talking donkey was merely a vehicle to convey a Divine message to Bilam, so too, Bilam himself was nothing more than a human messenger of the Divine word (Sfas Emes, Balak 5645).

■ וְהַקֶּשֶׁת — The rainbow. ■

⇨ Curbing the Yetzer Hara

ברית הקשת הוא דבר חידוש כי תימה לומר שכל הדורות היו חייבין כלי' לולי
הברית. ואפשר כי ע"י הברית שהבטיח הקב"ה שלא יעשה כלי' לכן אין יצה"ר
מתעצם כל כך.

By displaying the rainbow, Hashem was assuring Noach — and through him, all of his descendants — that the universe would never again be totally destroyed by a flood — זֹאת אוֹת הַבְּרִית אֲשֶׁר אֲנִי נֹתֵן בֵּינִי וּבֵינֵיכֶם ... אֶת קַשְׁתִּי נָתַתִּי בֶּעָנָן ... וְהָיָה בְּעַנְנִי עָנָן עַל הָאָרֶץ וְנִרְאֲתָה הַקֶּשֶׁת בֶּעָנָן. וְזָכַרְתִּי אֶת בְּרִיתִי ... וְלֹא יִהְיֶה עוֹד הַמַּיִם לְמַבּוּל לְשַׁחֵת כָּל בָּשָׂר, This is the sign of the covenant that I give between Me and you ... I have set My rainbow in the cloud ... And it shall happen, when I place a cloud over the earth, and the bow will be seen in the cloud, I will remember My covenant ... and the water shall never again become a flood to destroy all flesh (Bereishis 9:12-16).

It seems difficult to comprehend that the mere display of a physical symbol, such as a rainbow, would be sufficient assurance of the universe's continued existence.

Apparently the sign of the rainbow contained an implied promise that the *yetzer hara* would never again tempt man to sin. The *yetzer hara*, knowing the limits on its ability to wreak havoc (since the world will never be destroyed again), does not even seek to tempt man again to the same extent that it had before the Flood (*Likutei Sfas Emes, Parashas Noach*).

■ וְהַקֶשֶׁת, וְהַמָּן, וְהַמַּטֶּה — *The rainbow, the manna, the staff.*

◄§ In the Order of Creation

> והקשת והמן והמטה לא נקיט כסדר דהא קשת קדים טובא וכן שאר הדברים וי״ל
> כי באמת נבראו באופן וסדר זה ולכך סדרם התנא כפי בריאתם.

The *mishnah* is likely following the order of the creation of these items on that first *Erev Shabbos*, not the sequence in which they appear in the Torah. Had we followed that sequence, of course, the rainbow would have been cited first, followed by the staff and then the manna.

■ וְהַמָּן — *The manna.*

◄§ Why the Manna Was Created Erev Shabbos

> פי׳ שכל המזון בצירוף הארה ממוצא פי ה׳ שמעורב בהלחם. ולכן כפי מה שנתעלו
> דור המדבר ניזונו ממאכל רוחני שהי׳ קרוב יותר לכח מוצא פי ה׳ קודם שהי׳ מתלבש
> בלבוש גשמיי ... והמן הי׳ מעשרה דברים שנבראו בע״ש בה״ש. והם היו בתכלית
> הדקות שהיו סמוכין להשבת.
> וכי׳ למען אנסנו הילך וכו׳, כי המן הי׳ נסיון שנתעלו נפשות בנ״י מהגשמיות לכן
> איתא לא ניתנה תורה אלא לאוכלי המן.

According to the *Ari HaKadosh*, all food contains spiritual elements nurturing our soul as well as nourishing our physical bodies. As the Torah says, כִּי לֹא עַל הַלֶּחֶם לְבַדּוֹ יִחְיֶה הָאָדָם כִּי עַל כָּל מוֹצָא פִי ה׳ יִחְיֶה הָאָדָם, *not by bread alone does man live, rather by everything that emanates from the mouth of Hashem does man live* (*Devarim* 8:3). However, the spiritual elements which emanate from the "mouth of Hashem" are often subsumed by the overtly physical qualities it may possess. The manna, however, created on *Erev Shabbos* at twilight, a period of transition from the physical creation of the Six Days of Creation to the spiritual ambiance of Shabbos, was completely spiritual. Apppriately enough, it nurtured the most spiritual of all generations, the

Generation of the Wilderness which was witness to so many of Hashem's miracles (*Sfas Emes, Beshalach 5647*).

Thus, the manna was an essential link in the chain of events which prepared *Klal Yisrael* to receive the Torah. Indeed, Hashem explained the objective of the manna — לְמַעַן אֲנַסֶּנּוּ הֲיֵלֵךְ בְּתוֹרָתִי אִם לֹא, *so that I can test them, whether they will follow My teaching or not* (*Shemos* 16:4) (*Sfas Emes 5639*).

◦§ A Link to Shabbos

> והנה בשבת מתגלה מתנה טובה שבבית גנזיו. ולכן יתכן לומר בעונג שבת שיש בו מעין טעמי המן. כי צנצנת המן נגנז היינו שנשאר ממנו משהו לדורות ואחז"ל לא ניתנה תורה אלא לאוכלי המן. וכי אין לדורות אלו חלק בתורה. ולכן נאמר שבש"ק זוכין בנ"י להיות בכלל אוכלי המן.
>
> וכן הוא בנוסח המעלות. אלו האכילנו את המן ולא נתן לנו את השבת דיינו .... וז"ש ראו. כי מקודם כ' שם לו חק ומשפט שידעו מצות השבת. אבל עתה ניתן להם בעין יפה. שהיי להם התקרבות להשיג ולראות בעין הארת השבת.

*C*hazal describe Shabbos as a Divine gift, emanating from Hashem's treasure-house (*Beitzah* 16a). This may be an allusion to the taste of the manna, of which a small sample was stored for generations — קַח צִנְצֶנֶת אַחַת וְתֶן שָׁמָּה מְלֹא הָעֹמֶר מָן וְהַנַּח אֹתוֹ לִפְנֵי ה' לְמִשְׁמֶרֶת לְדֹרֹתֵיכֶם, *Take one jar and put a full omer of manna into it; place it before Hashem for a safekeeping for your generations* (*Shemos* 16:33). Just as the manna was created at the inception of the first Shabbos, so too every Shabbos we enjoy a "taste" of the manna, through our עוֹנֶג שַׁבָּת, delighting in the Shabbos.

Likewise, the comment of *Chazal* (cf. *Yalkut Shemos* 258), לֹא נִתְּנָה תוֹרָה אֶלָּא לְאוֹכְלֵי הַמָּן, *the Torah was only given to those who eat the manna,* may refer not only to the Generation of the Wilderness but to *all,* throughout the generations, who partake of the manna's taste each Shabbos. Not only is the taste of the manna experienced every Shabbos, but also the entire ambiance of the Generation of the Wilderness — freedom from financial worries — is enjoyed by *Klal Yisrael* every Shabbos (*Sfas Emes, Beshalach 5647*).

The relationship between Shabbos and the manna is also reflected in the sequence of the *Dayeinu* hymn — אִלּוּ הֶאֱכִילָנוּ אֶת הַמָּן וְלֹא נָתַן לָנוּ אֶת הַשַּׁבָּת דַּיֵּנוּ, *Had He fed us the manna, but not given us the Shabbos, it would have sufficed us.* The effectiveness of the manna in preparing the Jewish People for the gift of Shabbos is demonstrated by Moshe's plea to the Jewish People: רְאוּ כִּי ה' נָתַן לָכֶם הַשַּׁבָּת, *See that Hashem has given you Shabbos* (*Shemos* 16:29). As a result of partaking of the manna, the Jewish People could actually see (not merely comprehend)[1] the spiritual heights to which the universe ascends on Shabbos (*Sfas Emes, Beshalach 5643*).

---

1. At Marah, prior to partaking of the manna, *Klal Yisrael* could only relate to Shabbos on an intellectual basis. As it says, שָׁם שָׂם לוֹ חֹק וּמִשְׁפָּט, *There he established for [the nation] a decree and an ordinance* (*Shemos* 15:25), which refers to their studying the laws of Shabbos.

๑ The Manna's Outstanding Characteristics

כי כל העולם ניזון מהשפעת השי"י. אך שנעשה התלבשות בטבע. ולכן הוא מצומצם
במדה וגבול. אבל קודם הצימצום נמצא הכל בנקודה אחת. לכן לא העדיף המרבה
כו'. ולכן נשתנה טעמים כמ"ש חז"ל לשד השמן מה שד מתהפך לכמה גוונים. כי
כשבא שבת לא נעשה להם גופים. והם רוחות בלי צימצום הגוף. לכן משתנים.

In light of our previous remarks about the pristine purity of the manna — it
was not modified in any manner from its heavenly origins — we can appreciate some of the outstanding characteristics of the manna.

It is well known that everyone received the exact same quantity of manna.
As the Torah states, וְלֹא הֶעְדִּיף הַמַּרְבֶּה וְהַמַּמְעִיט לֹא הֶחְסִיר, *and whoever took more
had nothing extra and whoever took less was not lacking* (Shemos 16:18). Only
material goods can be measured quantitatively. The manna, the epitome of
spirituality, the food of angels (cf. Yoma 75b), defied all attempts at being
measured. It remained the same single scintillating spark of spirituality, regardless of how much was amassed.

The manna was also known for its adaptability. According to *Chazal*,
the taste of the manna varied with individual preferences. While material
entities enjoy a standard, unchanging taste, the manna, not bound by physical laws and constraints, could assume any flavor and characteristic. *Chazal*
(*Yoma* 75b) comment on the *pasuk* in *Beha'aloscha* describing the מָן as follows:
וְהָיָה טַעְמוֹ כְּטַעַם לְשַׁד הַשָּׁמֶן, *and it tasted like the taste of dough kneaded with oil*
(*Bamidbar* 11:8). We may read the word לְשַׁד as לְשֵׁד (demons) — מַה שֵׁד מִתְהַפֵּךְ
לְכַמָּה גְוָונִים אַף הַמָּן, just as a demon takes on variegation and diversity, i.e.,
various missions, so too the מָן takes on many forms. The very spiritual nature
of מָן and שֵׁדִים (מַזִּיקִין) can be deduced from the fact that they were both created
on *Erev Shabbos* at twilight and are not bound by the physical parameters of
the natural world (*Sfas Emes, Beshalach* 5648).

๑ What Did the Angels Eat the First Days of Creation?

וקשה דהא מן מאכל מלאכים כדאיתא במס' יומא ומלאכים בשני נבראו. וי"ל
הפירוש מציאות מזון זה שירד לארץ וכח זה נברא בערב שבת בין השמשות.
ושמא י"ל שלא היו צריכים להמן עד ע"ש ביה"ש בשעה שנברא להם.
גם י"ל שהכוונה לירידת המן בער"ש לחם משנה.

Chazal state that the angels were created on the second day of Creation
(*Bereishis Rabbah* 3:11-12). The question then arises: If the angels were
created on Monday and the manna, which is the food of the angels, was not
created until Friday, what did they eat in the interim? This can be resolved
if we understand that the manna of the angels was a more rarefied, spiritual

form of sustenance than *Klal Yisrael's*.[1] This "primeval" form of manna was in fact created *prior* to its somewhat more physical counterpart for future generations of *Klal Yisrael*, which was created on *Erev Shabbos* at twilight (*Sfas Emes*).

Alternatively, the angels may not have required any form of nourishment, even the rarefied form of manna, until the universe's completion on *Erev Shabbos*.

It is also possible that our *mishnah* is not referring to the single portion of manna that was enjoyed by *Klal Yisrael* every day but rather to the double portion that would descend from heaven every Friday for Shabbos. It was this double portion of rarefied sustenance that was not created until the most sacred (and the final) moment of Creation, Friday, at twilight, and the angels subsisted on the regular manna, which had been created earlier, for the week of Creation (*Maggidei HaEmes*).

■ וְהַמַּטֶּה — *The staff.*

⋖§ Whose Staff?

בספר חזקוני הקשה אהא דאיתא שמטה נברא בערב שבת בין השמשות, והא בקרא משמע שפרח בימי אהרן, ובספר צדה לדרך תמה עליו שפירוש המשנה מטה משה, אכן לא ראה דבגמ' פסחים איתא ברייתא דחשיב דברים שנבראו בערב שבת ולא חשיב מטה ויש אומרים אף מקלו של אהרן שקדים ופרחים, רק מגמ' הנ"ל מוכח דפירוש מטה שבאבות גם כן על מטה אהרן דלמה נעשה מחלוקת בתנאים בכדי, אכן עיקר הקושיא לא קשה מידי לע"ד דכמו שפי הארץ נברא בערב שבת היינו שנגזר שיפתח בימי משה כן נגזר שיפרח מטה אהרן כנ"ל.

Many understand that the *mishnah* is referring to the staff of Aharon which blossomed to prove Aharon's legitimate rights to the priesthood (*Bamidbar* 17:19). *Chizkuni* notes, however, that Aharon's staff only blossomed in response to Korach's insurrection, not at twilight of the Friday of Creation.

In response, the *Tzeidah LaDerech* suggests that our *mishnah* is referring to the staff of Moshe which was used to perform many of the ten plagues and other miracles. However, a similar version of this *mishnah's* teaching is cited in *Pesachim* (54a) and there implies that the staff of Aharon, its almonds and blossoms, were created that first *Erev Shabbos*.

In truth, the *Chizkuni's* question may be answered by distinguishing between the Divine *decree* — that the staff of Aharon give forth blossoms —

---

1. Editor's Note: מַלְאָכִים are sustained by a rarefied form of manna, in contrast to מַזִּיקִים who are sustained by the vapor of blood (referring to oxygen transmitted to the tissues by hemoglobin, see *Sforno, Vayikra* 17:7). Both are nonsubstantive forms of sustenance. It is interesting to note that the מָן and מַזִּיקִין were created on *Erev Shabbos* at twilight.

which occurred during Creation's twilight, and the actual *blossoming* which occurred many generations later.

∽§ The Staff

In the following discussion, we will assume that the staff refers to Aharon's staff, which blossomed with almonds when placed beside the Tent of Testimony along with the staff of the Princes of all of Israel's tribes (*Bamidbar* 17:19). We will now elucidate how the blossoming of Aharon's staff established unequivocally that he had been chosen to serve Hashem and squelched any questions which remained after Korach's rebellion.

∽§ Divine Selection, Not Merit Alone

> והענין הוא להודיע לבנ"י כי לא מצד עבודת אהרן נבחר מכלל בנ"י. וכן הלוים אם
> כי היו צדיקים גדולים שזכו לזאת המעלה. אבל המעלה הזאת הוא מתנה מאת המקום
> ב"ה באהבתו לבני ישראל הוכן כלי מובחר והוא אהרן משרת עליון והשי"ת שלח
> מלמעלה כלי זו זה שמטהו יפרח הוא סימן. כי הוא כלי דבוק בשורשו ועושה פירות
> בדביקות.

By placing Korach's staff alongside the staff of *Klal Yisrael's* Princes and simply waiting for Hashem to indicate His choice, *Klal Yisrael* was leaving the decision as to who should be its leader to Hashem alone. Korach attempts to sway the masses by arguing his qualifications, and those of his adherents.[1] While certainly many of his followers were capable of assuming leadership positions [as the Torah (*Bamidbar* 16:2) describes them, נְשִׂיאֵי עֵדָה קְרִאֵי מוֹעֵד אַנְשֵׁי שֵׁם, *those summoned for meeting, men of renown*], the choice of true leadership is ultimately determined by Hashem — and Hashem alone. Only Aharon, whose staff blossomed when placed in *Klal Yisrael's* most sacred abode, enjoyed that intimate relationship with Hashem and could productively lead *Klal Yisrael*. The Torah signifies the importance of Divine selection by stating, וְהָיָה הָאִישׁ אֲשֶׁר אֶבְחַר בּוֹ מַטֵּהוּ יִפְרָח, *it shall be that the man whom I shall choose — his staff will blossom* (ibid. 17:20) (*Sfas Emes, Korach 5639*).

∽§ The Inside Not the Outside

> וקרח ועדתו נתדבקו בחיצוניות בלבד והי' נראה כל מעשיהם טובים מאוד. אבל אהרן
> הי' נראה איש פשוט ובאמת הי' לו הפנימיות ... וזה הי' סימן המטה להראות כי
> פנימיות שלו דבוק בשורש.

---

1. Korach may also have reasoned that as a *Levi*, not having participated in the Sin of the Golden Calf, he was better suited to lead *Klal Yisrael* than Aharon who was at least peripherally involved in that tragic episode.

In making his arguments against the leadership of Moshe and Aharon, Korach donned a garment of *techeiles* and certainly *looked* the part of a leader. Aharon, however, possessed the *inner* characteristics so necessary to lead *Klal Yisrael*. To demonstrate that Aharon's intrinsic qualifications were far superior to Korach's superficial qualities, Hashem commanded each of the Princes to place their staff alongside Aharon's in the Tent of Testimony. Each staff was simply a piece of lifeless wood and all were identical. Only Aharon's staff blossomed, its insides burst forth with life, and he was deemed worthy to lead *Klal Yisrael* (*Sfas Emes, Korach 5640*).

◈§ A Role for Everyone

 וע״י ששמאי ביטל עצמו להתורה מחלוקתן מתקיימת. וא״כ גם קרח הי׳ מוכן להיות
מחלוקת על אהרן ואם הי׳ ונבטל עצמו להתורה שהיא האמונה במשה רבינו ע״ה הי׳
מתקיים המחלוקת והי׳ נשלם ההלכה על ידי שניהם .... ומ״מ נאמר בתוך מטותם כי
ע״י הביטול שהם מבטלים עצמם לאהרן יש לו עלי׳ זו בשורש העליון מאוד נעלה.
לרמוז כי ע״י התכללות בנ״י אז עבודת הכהן העובד ה׳ עושה פירות וז״ש בתוך
מטותם שבאמת פעולת הצדיק אינו בכח עצמו רק שמאסף כל חלקי עבודת הפרטים
ומוציא אותם מכח אל הפעולה ... וז״ש אמרו צדיק כי טוב כי פרי מעלליהם יאכלו
ומדקדקין דהול״ל פרי מעלליו יאכל אך באמת כולם צריכין להחזיק טובה להצדיק
שהוא מוציא מעשיהם מכח אל הפועל שיזכו לאכול פרי מעלליהם ...
וכעין זה הגיד מו״ז ז״ל בשם הרב מפרשיסחא ז״ל שהרמז ויצץ ציץ ויגמול כו׳ כמו
שיש באילן פרחים וציצים ופירות כן יש לכל ישראל חלק. זה הפרח וזה הציצים.

The same test which confirmed Aharon's leadership role reserved a significant role for *Klal Yisrael's* Princes (and all other leaders) as well. Aharon's staff was not placed *above* their staffs but rather in their *midst* (בְּתוֹךְ מַטּוֹתָם). This indicated that if *Klal Yisrael's* leaders harmonized their efforts and, if necessary, subsumed their own identity to that of Aharon, they too would play a significant role (*Sfas Emes, Korach 5638, 5639*).

According to R' Simcha Bunim of Pesish'cha, this can be demonstrated from the Torah's painstaking description of every aspect of the blossoming of Aharon's staff — וַיֹּצֵא פֶרַח וַיָּצֵץ צִיץ וַיִּגְמֹל שְׁקֵדִים, *it brought forth a blossom, sprouted a bud and almonds ripened* (Bamidbar 17:23). Just as buds and flowers precede the fruit's arrival, so too every Jew, and certainly every potential leader, has a role to play. In fact, the role of *tzaddik* was never intended to be that of an individual who singlehandedly leads *Klal Yisrael*. Instead, the most notable feature of our leaders is their ability to elicit the numerous virtues and develop the many spiritual talents of *every* Jew. By consolidating *Klal Yisrael's* many sources of merit and assisting every individual Jew to exploit his potential for *avodas Hashem*, the *tzaddik* earns the gratitude of his peers. Yeshayahu describes the functions of a true *tzaddik* in the following words: אִמְרוּ צַדִּיק כִּי טוֹב, כִּי פְרִי מַעַלְלֵיהֶם יֹאכֵלוּ, *Tell [each] righteous man that it is good; for they shall eat the fruit of their deeds* (3:10). All of *Klal Yisrael*, not merely the *tzaddik*, will reap the fruit of his leadership. As it says, פְּרִי מַעַלְלֵיהֶם, *"their deeds,"* not פְּרִי מַעֲלָלָיו, *"his deeds" (Sfas Emes, Korach 5644).* [For further discussion of the *tzaddik's* role in developing *Klal Yisrael's* latent talent, please see *Days of Joy* and especially the essay entitled *Mordechai HaTzaddik, a Leader For All Generations*, pp. 261-264.]

◈§ Aharon: Soft and Vigorous
Korach: Hard and Rigid

הנה אות המטה של אהרן הי' להודיע כי כחות מרע"ה ואהרן הוא משמים דכתיב
וטח בעשרו יפול ובעלה צדיקים יפרחו וזה נתקיים במחלוקת קרח שהי' לו מפלה
פרח מטה אהרן. [וכן מצאתי ג'כ ברבינו בחיי וגם בילקוט] ... ופי' הפסוק כי הצדיקים
זם כעלה שהיא רכה ודקה וע"ז עצמו יש להם חיות וכח חדש בכל עת שהם דבוקים
שורש ע"י הביטול כדכתי' ואהרן מה הוא. אבל הבוטח בעשרו והוא קשה בעץ נופל.
שלא שינה מלשון השנות החלום שלא היו ב' ימים באופן אחד ובכל יום המשיך אור
זדש בהדלקות הנרות.

Wahile Aharon's staff blossomed with buds and fruit (almonds), the staffs of the Princes (whom Korach had purported to represent) remained hard and rigid wood. This represents the vast distinction between the rigid, unyielding refusal of Korach to change his ways and yield to the advice of his superiors, and the renewed vigor of Aharon, the *Kohen Gadol*, as he conducted the Divine service. It is significant that every day the *Kohen Gadol* brought the offering (¹⁄₁₀ of an *eiphah* of flour) that was contributed by an ordinary *Kohen* on his first day of that *Kohen's* service. The same vitality and freshness that an ordinary *Kohen* experiences upon commencing his sacred duties is experienced by the *Kohen Gadol* daily. The renowned *Chazal* praising Aharon, לְהַגִּיד שֶׁבְחוֹ שֶׁל אַהֲרֹן שֶׁלֹּא שִׁינָה (*Rashi, Bamidbar* 8:3 s.v. ויעש), may also be interpreted in this light: No matter how often he performed the Divine service, he never acted or felt that this was merely a repeat performance. For him, every day was the beginning of something new. As Shlomo *Hamelech* writes, בּוֹטֵחַ בְּעָשְׁרוֹ הוּא יִפֹּל וְכֶעָלֶה צַדִּיקִים יִפְרָחוּ, *He who trusts in his wealth — he will fall, but the righteous will sprout like foliage* (Mishlei 11:28). He who trusts in his wealth (such as Korach; cf. *Pesachim* 119a discussing Korach's affluence) will eventually fall. However, the righteous, known for their pliability and openness to spiritual growth, will blossom as a leaf (*Sfas Emes, Korach, 5647*) (adapted from *Sfas Emes, Korach, 5643*).

◈§ Leviim: Sanctifying the Earth
Kohanim: Bringing Heaven Down to Earth

איתא צדיי"ק כתמ"ר יפרי"ח ס"ת קרח. מדת הצדיק להפריח במעשים טובים

Korach, undoubtedly, enjoyed the potential to accomplish a great deal both
personally and on behalf of *Klal Yisrael*. In fact, the final letters of the words,
צַדִּיק כַּתָּמָר יִפְרָח, *a righteous man will flourish like a date palm* (*Tehillim* 92:13),
spell Korach, alluding to his capacity for righteousness. Like any
other *tzaddik*, Korach enjoyed the potential to grow, jut as a palm tree
eventually reaches its full towering height. However, Aharon, enjoying the
status of a חָסִיד (cf. *Devarim* 33:8, תֻּמֶּיךָ וְאוּרֶיךָ לְאִישׁ חֲסִידֶךָ, *Your Tumim and Your
Urim befit Your devout one*), is even more exalted than a *tzaddik*.
He enjoyed the unique capacity to bring the blessings of heaven down to earth.
As *Tehillim* Ch. 92 continues, שְׁתוּלִים בְּבֵית ה' בְּחַצְרוֹת אֱלֹהֵינוּ יַפְרִיחוּ, *planted in
the house of Hashem, in the courtyards of our God they will flourish* (v. 14),
those who are firmly planted in Hashem's House (such as Aharon) will
not only themselves flourish (יִפְרָח) but יַפְרִיחוּ, they will help bring down from
heaven Divine blessings. It was this capacity to evoke Divine assistance that
rendered Aharon suitable for Torah leadership. When confirming Aharon's
selection, the Torah states, עֲבֹדַת מַתָּנָה אֶתֵּן אֶת כְּהֻנַּתְכֶם, *I have presented
your priesthood as a service that is a gift* (*Bamidbar* 18:7) — his service is a Divine
gift.

The passage cited from *Tehillim* concludes, עוֹד יְנוּבוּן בְּשֵׂיבָה דְּשֵׁנִים וְרַעֲנַנִּים יִהְיוּ,
They will still be fruitful in old age, vigorous and fresh they will be (v. 15). Unlike
Leviim who face mandatory retirement because of advancing age, *Kohanim* —
and their unique capacity for invoking Divine blessings — always remain
vigorous and fresh (*Sfas Emes, Korach* 5657).

◆§ Aharon's Attribute of Kiruv

Perhaps Aharon's most enduring characteristic was his capacity for *kiruv*,
reaching out to his fellow Jews and bringing them closer to Torah. As we
learned in the first *perek*, Aharon was אוֹהֵב אֶת הַבְּרִיּוֹת וּמְקָרְבָן לַתּוֹרָה, *loving people
and bringing them closer to the Torah* (1:12). These attributes, which may be a

primary reason for his selection as the *Kohen Gadol,* is reflected in the blossoming of his staff. A seemingly lifeless piece of wood suddenly bursts forth with life, simply by virtue of its association with Aharon. Likewise, anything even tangentially linked to a *Kohen* radiates his sanctity. Not only the *Kohen,* but even the non-Jewish Canaanite slave and the animal who are members of the *Kohen's* household, may partake of the sacred portion of *terumah.*

If we reflect further, we realize that Aharon's dual characteristics — his gift for peacemaking and his outreach capacity — were closely related. It was precisely because of Aharon's penchant for peacemaking that he was able to embrace many of his brethren who had become alienated from Torah. As stated in *Mishlei,* וְכָל נְתִיבֹתֶיהָ שָׁלוֹם, *and all its paths* [of the Torah] *are peace* (3:17) (*Sfas Emes, Korach* 5660, 5663).

⋅§ Leviim: On the Outside
Kohanim: On the Inside

והלוים הם השומרים מבחוץ בחי׳ ריחוק. ואהרן כתיב בי׳ אוהב שלום כו׳ ומקרבן
לתורה.

Perhaps, all our previous discussions can be summarized by recalling (cf. *Midos* 1:5,9) that *Kohanim* guarded the *inner* chambers of the *Beis HaMikdash* while the *Leviim* stood sentry on the *outer* perimeters. While the *Leviim's* role is to vigorously and zealously guard *Klal Yisrael's* perimeter, searching relentlessly for the external foe, it is the *Kohen* who is on the inside, compassionately reacting to *Klal Yisrael's* most intimate concerns (*Sefas Emes, Korach* 5660).

■ הַכְּתָב, וְהַמִּכְתָּב וְהַלּוּחוֹת ■ — *The script, the inscription, and the Tablets.*

⋅§ Targum Yonasan's Reckoning

הכתב האותיות והמכתב הקולמוס והלוחות הניירות, ולפי זה דברים נפרדים הם
ושפיר יש מנין עשרה. אבל בתרגום יונתן חושב בתוך העשרה דברים מזיקין וענני
כבוד, דג׳ אלו חושב לדבר אחד.

Our *mishnah* enumerates three different creations pertaining to the *Luchos:* הַכְּתָב, the letters (*script*) of the *Luchos;* הַמִּכְתָּב, the stylus (*inscription*) by which Hashem engraved His sacred writing on the *Luchos;* and הַלּוּחוֹת, the *Luchos* themselves, the stone Tablets which served as the base for the Divine imprint. However, the *Targum* of Yonasan ben Uziel counts the destructive spirits and the Divine Clouds which protected the Jewish people in the Wilderness among the ten creations. This is based on the assumption that *all* aspects related to the *Luchos* are counted as *one* entity.

■ וְהַלּוּחוֹת — *And the Tablets.*

❧ Why the Tablets Were Created on Erev Shabbos

הענין הוא דאיתא כתב המכתב נברא בע״ש ביה״ש. כי יש להעשיי׳ מדריגות. לכן
נברא אדם באחרונה כדי שיכנוס לשבת מיד כו׳ ע״ש. פי׳ שהוא מובחר מכל
מעשה בראשית. ויש לו להתקשרות לשורש הבריאה. והוא השבת שיש בו עלי׳
לכל הברואים. והשורש נקרא מעשה אלקים שאינו גשמיי כבל העשיי׳ ... הכלל
כי זה הכח נקרא שורש העשיי׳. וע״ז רמוז שנברא בע״ש שיש בו תערובות ב׳
הכחות מהשבת ומהמעשה.

The Tablets are described as מַעֲשֵׂה אֱלֹהִים, which may be translated literally
as *Hashem's deed.* While lower forms of life were created during the Six
Days of Creation, culminating in the creation of man (created in Hashem's
image) on that first Friday, the Tablets, the most rarefied objects of all creation,
were appropriately created at the closing moments of the Six Days of Creation.
At twilight, on Friday, the physical world of the Six Days of Creation yielded
to the spirituality of Shabbos (adapted from *Sfas Emes, Ki Sisa 5640*).

❧ The First Luchos

שהיי׳ אור התורה שורה על בנ״י בהתגלות.
ונק׳ חירות שהיי׳ למעלה מהזמן והטבע. ולכן קודם החטא לא נצרך ארון ומקום
אל הלוחות.
כי רמז הלוחות והכתב הם בחי׳ גוף ונשמה.

The first set of Tablets, written by Hashem prior to the sin of the Golden Calf,
were supernatural. They required no Ark — they were not confined to any
physical space — since the light of Torah (and the Divine Presence) was
revealed everywhere (*Sfas Emes, Pekudei 5655*).

Not only the writing but also the stone itself was derived from Heaven. By
extension, we may say that the "body" as well as the "soul" of Those Tablets
came from Hashem (*Sfas Emes, Eikev 5651*).

ולוחות הראשונות היו בחי׳ עץ החיים.
כי בקבלת התורה נתעלו נפשות בנ״י ונדבקו בעץ החיים. והיו חירות ממיתה
כמ״ש אמרתי אלקים אתם כי הנשמה בכחה להפוך הגוף להיות חי.

These Tablets brought Israel back to the exalted level of the Tree of Life in
Gan Eden (*Sfas Emes, Parah 5634*).

At the time of their accepting the Torah through the First Tablets, bodies of the Jews joined their souls and they were transmuted into totally spiritual beings (*Sfas Emes, Parah* 5659).

⋘ Why Moshe Shattered the First Luchos

אבל הענין הוא שלא היה כתיבה זו על הלוחות בלבד. אבל הי' רשימה חקוקה
בלב כל איש ישראל בענין כתבם על לוח לבך.
וחבה יתירה נודעת לנו גלוי לכל העמים כי השי"ת שוכן בישראל והוא ענין
הקידושין לארוס וארוסתו כי בלי קידושין וכתובה נק' פילגש בצנעה ... וזאת
אמרו ישראל קודם קבלת התורה נעשה ונשמע ואחר החטא נסתלק ענין זה ונמצא
חסרון מצד המקבל ולזאת אמרו חז"ל כי היו אותיות פורחין באויר כי לא הי' יכול
להיות התדבקות ההעלם אל הגילוי כראוי ואם היו מקבלים ח"ו גם אחר החטא
העגל הי' מעוות שלא יוכל לתקן כי הי' נותן האות בהסתר גדול ...

The fate of the First Tablets was directly contingent upon *Klal Yisrael's* moral behavior. Its letters adhered securely to the Tablets only when the enlightened teachings of the Torah were engraved upon the hearts of the Jewish people. Once the writing no longer adhered to the stone because of Israel's sin, Moshe had no recourse other than to break the Tablets (*Sfas Emes, Ki Sisa* 5638).

In order to further appreciate why Moshe had to shatter the Tablets, let us consider why they were necessary in the first place. *Chazal* comment that following the sin of the Golden Calf Moshe was determined to annul the "marriage" between Hashem and *Klal Yisrael*. The "marriage" had been consummated when He gave us the Torah in full public view at Sinai. While Hashem always loved us, our relationship with Him before accepting the Torah was compared to that of a "concubine" who, lacking the proper confirmation of relationship, resides surreptitiously with her partner. Only at Sinai, after Israel proclaimed נַעֲשֶׂה וְנִשְׁמַע and Hashem reciprocated by giving us the Torah, was our intimate relationship with Him confirmed through the "marriage document" known as the Tablets. To deserve such an intimate, yet public relationship with Hashem, *Klal Yisrael* had to live up to its potential. After the sin of the Golden Calf, we no longer merited the public manifestation of Hashem's love — the Tablets. Moreover, we actually were far better off not having the Tablets anymore. Imagine the dichotomy of the letters of the Tablets if instead of floating into the atmosphere, as happened when *Klal Yisrael* sinned, they would have remained clinging to the Tablets. On one hand, our relationship with Hashem had reverted to its previous more private phase; yet, the public declaration of our relationship would have still been present to "haunt" us. The consequences of such a dichotomous situation would have been far worse than our present plight. There would have been confusion, disorientation, far less clarity in Torah and a more remote relationship with Hashem than we currently enjoyed (adapted from *Likutei Sfas Emes, Ki Sisa*).

⋙ The First Tablets Live On

> אך משה רע"ה זכה להשאר במעלה הראשונה וזיכה את כל בנ"י.

Although the First Tablets were shattered by Moshe, their aura and spirit still live on. For example, Moshe himself, untainted by the sin of the Golden Calf, always retained the exalted status of the First Tablets (*Sfas Emes, Vayakhel* 5646).

> לכן בש"ק מחזירן לישראל הכתרים.
> בשבת מתגלה מעין לוחות הראשונות.

Every Shabbos, the day imbued with a supernatural aura, the spiritual light once exuded by the First Tablets filters back to earth (*Sfas Emes, Ki Sisa* 5642, 5654).

⋙ Suspended Animation — Not Permanently Lost

> וכמו שהי' אדה"ר קודם החטא הי' עולה ויורד בעולם העליון והתחתון ... וזה עיקר
> החירות שלא יתקשר הנפש בגוף ויובל לעלות בכל עת ... וכן הי' הכתב שעל
> הלוחות עולה ויורד.

The First Tablets' writing is described as being חָרוּת, interpreted by *Chazal* as חֵרוּת, *free*. This may indicate that the letters themselves, though engraved on stone, were free "to leave" their physical casing (the stone Tablets) and return to Hashem at will, and then eventually come back to the Tablets (a status similar to Adam before sinning, whose body was firmly planted in *Gan Eden* on earth, but whose soul could ascend to Heaven at will). When Israel sinned, the writing — having ascended to heaven — was unable to adhere again to the stone, compelling Moshe to shatter them (*Sfas Emes, Ki Sisa* 5656).

⋙ The Luchos Will Return

> וגמירי משמיא מיהב יהבי משקל לא שקלי ולכן הארת לוחות הראשונות נשאר
> לעולם לגמרי אבל אותיות פורחות למעלה לפקדון לבנ"י וכפי מה שזוכין מאירין
> האותיות ... כי לעתיד לבוא יהי' י"ז בתמוז חג כשיתקנו בנ"י החטא יאירו הלוחות
> ראשונות.

A Divine gift is permanent. Thus, the First Tablets continued on earth (in the form of the shattered fragments placed in the *Aron*), enlightening the hearts of the Jewish People, and also in heaven, where Hashem is guarding them on behalf of Israel. If the Jewish People merit, the letters of the Tablets can still enlighten their lives. Once the sin of the Golden Calf will be fully expiated, the Tablets will reassert their previous impact on *Klal Yisrael*. Then the 17th of Tammuz, the date of the shattering of the Tablets, will become a Festival (*Sfas Emes, Balak 5660*).

✺ Retrieving the Fragments

וצריכין לתקן כל אלה השברים וזה היא באמת כמו פיזור וגלות בנ״י בכל
הארצות כדי ללקוט אותן השברים וכשיתוקן הכל נוכל לקבל הלוחות הראשונים.

While the shards of the First Tablets themselves came to rest in the *Aron*, alongside the Second Tablets, the letters of the Ten Commandments remained suspended in heaven. Perhaps, by using that metaphor *Chazal* are alluding to the cosmic impact of the Tablets: Instead of the letters adhering to the body of the Tablets which were in Israel's possession, they now were dispersed all over the universe, leaving a residual impact everywhere by conveying aspects of Torah to all of mankind. Perhaps the very purpose of *Klal Yisrael's* dispersal among mankind is to fulfill its sacred mission of somehow retrieving those sacred sparks — and elicit those souls that seek out Hashem — and return them to Torah. Once that mission has been accomplished, once all the *neshamos* influenced by the Tablets will have returned to the banner of Torah, we will be worthy of again receiving the First Tablets in their complete form (body as well as soul) (adapted from *Sfas Emes, Balak 5648*).

✺ The Second Luchos

כי רמז הלוחות והכתב הם בחי׳ גוף ונשמה ואח״כ היו הלוחות מלמטה והכתב
שהיא הנשמה מלמעלה.

The Second Tablets, whose writing was engraved by Hashem on stone excavated by Moshe, resembles our very temporary existence in This World. Like the Tablets, we too are a composite of heaven and earth — our souls emanating from Hashem implanted in our material bodies struggling with the challenges of This World (*Sfas Emes, Eikev 5651*).

ואחר החטא הי׳ התיקון ע״י בחי׳ טהרה טהור מטמא שע״י היגיעה בעוה״ז לברר
האמת ולהנצל מסט״א עי״ז יבוא כל אחד על מקומו.

Whereas the First Tablets elevated *Klal Yisrael* to the realm of the supernatural, the Second Tablets (consisting of Hashem's writing engraved on

וְיֵשׁ אוֹמְרִים: אַף הַמַּזִיקִין, וּקְבוּרָתוֹ שֶׁל מֹשֶׁה, וְאֵילוֹ
שֶׁל אַבְרָהָם אָבִינוּ. וְיֵשׁ אוֹמְרִים; אַף צְבַת בִּצְבַת
עֲשׂוּיָה.

Moshe's stone) also enjoyed a daunting mission — to sanctify the material world. We too, by leading a Torah-oriented life in a material and impure environment, are fulfilling the mission of the Second Tablets, consecrating the secular world (*Sfas Emes, Parah* 5634).

כענין שאמרו בלוחות אחרונות אין לך יפה מן הצניעות הוא זה הדרך המוסתר
תוך הטבע . . . לול' התלהבות הקודם בפירסום לא הי' אח''כ יכולת לילך בדרך
צניעות.

The Second Tablets testify eloquently to the power of modesty. They were given in quiet atmosphere and persevered, while the First Tablets, presented in full public view, with pomp and splendor, did not. However, the First Tablets served a critical function: The enthusiasm evoked by the exuberant giving of the First Tablets enabled the Second Tablets to *eternally* inspire Israel (*Sfas Emes, Vayakhel* 5646; *Ki Sisa* 5639).[1]

■ וּפִי הַבְּאֵר ... הַמַּזִיקִין, וּקְבוּרָתוֹ שֶׁל מֹשֶׁה — *The mouth of the well ... destructive spirits, Moshe's grave.*

פי הבאר נברא בערב שבת בין השמשות וקברו של משה פי הבאר להיות דורש
ומבקש מבקשים מים וקברו של משה מסייע לזה, וכן יש אומרים אף המזיקים
נבראו אז הרמז להתגבר על ההסתרות על ידי פי הבאר לבקש מהשי''ת וזכותו
של מרע''ה ובזה מתגבר על המזיקים.

The *Beis Yisrael* interprets פִּי הַבְּאֵר, *the mouth of the well*, to refer to the capacity of *Klal Yisrael* to *daven* for water. Based upon this we may conclude that by creating both demons and Moshe's grave on *Erev Shabbos*, Hashem is establishing a delicate balance of good and evil. The unknown final resting place of Moshe, the greatest intercessor on *Klal Yisrael's* behalf, who so often tapped the waters of the well with his own heartfelt prayers, can outweigh the demons, those negative forces — created by Hashem to chastise *Klal Yisrael* when necessary — which were also created at that time (adapted from *Maggidei HaEmes*).

1. For a more complete discussion of the Second Tablets and especially their value to *Klal Yisrael* and *baalei teshuvah* see *Days of Awe*, pp. 24-29.

inscription, and the Tablets. Some say also destructive spirits, Moshe's grave, and the ram of our forefather Avraham. And some say also tongs, which are made with tongs.

■ הַמַּזִּיקִין ■ — *Destructive spirits.*

ᴥ§ Stunting the Forces of Evil

> איתא במאור ושמש שנתעסק הקב"ה בבריאתן וכשבא לברוא הגופים קידש
> השבת. כיצד שייך לומר כן לגבי השי"ת, והרי הוא יודע הכל בדיוק, וכדאיתא
> בחצות כו'. אלא שכשנברא העולם היה אור גדול, ואילו היו רואים היקר
> והאור לא היה אפשרי בלל שיהיה חטא, לכן הוצרך להיות הסתרים, יצר
> הרע, עד שנעשה אפל יותר ויותר, קשה יותר ויותר, ונהיה צמצום יותר ויותר,
> העולם אחד מששים וכו' נמצא כל העולם כולו בכיסוי קדרה לגיהנם. ונהיה יותר
> אפל עד שהגיע שיהיה מוכרח החטא. יצרו של אדם מתגבר עליו בכל יום, ואמר
> הקב"ה עד כאן, אלמלא הקב"ה עוזרו אינו לו, אעשה לו עזר כנגדו, ונהיתה
> שבת.

There exists a well-known tradition (cited by *Ma'or VaShemesh, Parshas Mattos*) that Hashem commenced creating the *mazikin* on *Erev Shabbos* but was "unable" to consummate their creation because of the advent of Shabbos. Consequently, these demons remained unfinished, existing as nefarious souls without a body to match. What does *Chazal* mean by this intriguing statement? Surely, Hashem did not "run out of time," for it is He Who controls time.

The *Pnei Menachem* understood this esoteric *Chazal* to be an allusion to the process whereby Hashem's Presence was gradually obscured in the universe that He had created. At the beginning of Creation, Hashem created light. Had the light and its supernatural radiance remained in its original brilliance, mankind would never have enjoyed free will. Whenever one would have been tempted to sin, he would hesitate because of visualizing the awesome Presence of the *Shechinah*. In order to allow mankind to serve Him on their own initiative (with free will), Hashem progressively obscured His *Shechinah*. This process reached its climax with the creation of the מַזִּיקִין, a demonic negative force. Had this force been allowed to assume a body as well as a soul, Hashem's Presence would have been so greatly obscured that man's natural tendency would have been to sin rather than to do good. In His Infinite Mercy, at the very last moment of the Six Days of Creation, Hashem stunted this demonic force, leaving it in an unfinished form so that the forces of good would be able to eventually prevail in their battle against evil (*Maggidei HaEmes*).

[ט] שִׁבְעָה דְבָרִים בְּגֹלֶם, וְשִׁבְעָה בְּחָכָם. חָכָם אֵינוֹ מְדַבֵּר לִפְנֵי מִי שֶׁגָּדוֹל מִמֶּנּוּ בְּחָכְמָה וּבְמִנְיָן; וְאֵינוֹ נִכְנָס לְתוֹךְ דִּבְרֵי חֲבֵרוֹ; וְאֵינוֹ נִבְהָל לְהָשִׁיב; שׁוֹאֵל כָּעִנְיָן, וּמֵשִׁיב כַּהֲלָכָה; וְאוֹמֵר עַל רִאשׁוֹן רִאשׁוֹן, וְעַל אַחֲרוֹן אַחֲרוֹן; וְעַל מַה שֶּׁלֹּא שָׁמַע אוֹמֵר: ,,לֹא שָׁמַעְתִּי''; וּמוֹדֶה עַל הָאֱמֶת. וְחִלּוּפֵיהֶן בְּגֹלֶם.

■ וְאֵילוֹ שֶׁל אַבְרָהָם אָבִינוּ — *And the ram of our forefather Avraham.* ■

◆§ The Oldest Ram

קשה איך היה האיל כשר לקרבן ולא נפסל בשנים וי״ל על פי מה דאיתא במדרש דפרים שהביאו הנשיאים לא הזקינו ולא נשחטו אז אלא אחר כך בגלגל בימי יהושע, אם כן אף איל של עקידה יי״ל שנטמן לעתיד לשחוט ולא נזדקן.

If, indeed, Avraham's ram was created during twilight of the sixth day of Creation, it would have been far too old at the time of the *Akeidah* to be a valid sacrifice. Perhaps, miraculously, this ram never aged. It retained its youthful vibrancy — as if frozen in time — until the moment of its destiny at the *Akeidah*.

9.

■ שִׁבְעָה דְבָרִים בְּגֹלֶם וְשִׁבְעָה בְּחָכָם — *Seven traits characterize an uncultivated person and seven a learned one.* ■

◆§ The "Golem" Comes First

מה שמקדים דברים של הגולם מפני שכן הדרך גולמי כלי מקודם הגמר.

Although our *mishnah* focuses on the character traits of the wise, learned man, it commences with a general statement about the uncultivated person, because it is following the chronological order of a person's life. One's formative years always begin with a period of incomplete character development, which hopefully is followed by spiritual growth[1] (adapted from *Sfas Emes*).

---

1. The term גֹלֶם generally refers to an unfinished utensil. In this context, the *mishnah* applies this term to the formative stages of an individual's life (cf. *Chullin* 25a, גולמי כלי מתכות).

[9] *Seven traits characterize an uncultivated person and seven a learned one. A learned person does not begin speaking before one who is greater than he in wisdom or in years; he does not interrupt the words of his fellow; he does not answer impetuously; he asks relevant questions, and replies appropriately; he discusses first things first and last things last; about something he has not heard he says, "I have not heard"; and he acknowledges the truth. And the reverse of these [traits] characterizes an uncultivated person.*

■ חָכָם אֵינוֹ מְדַבֵּר לִפְנֵי מִי שֶׁגָּדוֹל מִמֶּנּוּ בְּחָכְמָה וּבְמִנְיָן ■ — *A learned person does not begin speaking before one who is greater than he in wisdom or in years.*

◄§ Show Deference Even When Aggressiveness Would Be Justified

אינו מדבר לפני מי שהוא גדול כו' בהרע"ב ראי' מאלעזר כו' פי' הגם שהיו צריכין להשיב תיכף כדי לתרץ את אביהם אך מ"מ זהו יותר עדיף שלא לדבר בפני שגדול ממנו.

The *Bartenura* cite the example of the deference displayed by Elazar and Issamar to Moshe (cf. *Vayikra* 10:17), when they refused to respond to his questioning Aharon's decision to burn — rather than eat — one of the three goats offered on the day of the *Mishkan's* dedication. Even though they could have responded, they correctly assumed that deferring to a greater scholar (Aharon) was more appropriate (see *Vayikra* 10:20, *Rashi* s.v. וידבר אהרן).

■ וְאוֹמֵר עַל רִאשׁוֹן רִאשׁוֹן ■ — *He discusses first things first.*

◄§ Take Nothing for Granted

אין הכוונה דוקא לענין תשובה על שאלה רק שמקדים בדבריו הקדמות שצריך להקדים כדי שיובנו דבריו.

The expression "first things first" does not only refer to the *Chacham's* ability to answer questions in the order in which they were posed. It also connotes his realization that his audience is often not as knowledgeable of the subject matter under discussion as he is. Thus, he presents a carefully structured intro-

[י] שִׁבְעָה מִינֵי פֻּרְעָנִיּוֹת בָּאִין לָעוֹלָם עַל שִׁבְעָה גּוּפֵי עֲבֵרָה: מִקְצָתָן מְעַשְּׂרִין וּמִקְצָתָן אֵינָן מְעַשְּׂרִין, רָעָב שֶׁל בַּצֹּרֶת בָּא, מִקְצָתָן רְעֵבִים וּמִקְצָתָן שְׂבֵעִים; גָּמְרוּ שֶׁלֹּא לְעַשֵּׂר, רָעָב שֶׁל מְהוּמָה וְשֶׁל בַּצֹּרֶת בָּא; וְשֶׁלֹּא לִטֹּל אֶת הַחַלָּה, רָעָב שֶׁל כְּלָיָה בָּא;

---

duction to his thoughts.[1]

■ וְעַל מַה שֶּׁלֹּא שָׁמַע אוֹמֵר: "לֹא שָׁמַעְתִּי" — *About something he has not heard he says: "I have not heard."*

◄§ Distinguishing Between His Ideas and Those of His Teachers

יש"ל שאינו אומר סתם כאילו זה הלכה פשוטה ושגורה בפיו מרבותיו רק אומר כך יראה לי כמו שכתב הרמב"ם כמה פעמים כדי שלא יסמכו על זה כל כך וכמו דמצינו (יומא סו: ב) ר"א שלא אמר מעולם דבר שלא שמע מפי רבו אם כן מדה טובה זה. וגם ראיה כי מימרא סתם הי המקובלת מרבותיו.

Perhaps, the *mishnah* is referring to the admirable trait of clearly distinguishing between one's own novella and the teachings transmitted to him by his *rebbi* (mentor). The *Rambam*, particularly in his classic *Yad Hachazakah*, practiced this by prefacing his own thoughts with the words נִרְאֶה לִי, *it appears to me*. This approach enjoys several advantages. Firstly, the reader is able to identify those halachic rulings not based on previous traditions. Of even greater importance, he may deduce that all other rulings of the *Rambam* are based on established tradition.

◄§ Acknowledging Even a Partial Debt

והקשו המפרשים אם אינו שקרן שאינו אומר שמעתי על שלא שמע האם חכם יתקרא. גם אם אינו רוצה להחניף ואומר האמת על מה ששמע שמעתי וכי יקרא בשם גולם. ויראה כי אם חבירו יגיד לו איזה חידוש הגם שתוכנו כבר ידוע לו אבל יש בו רק קצת חידוש, יקשיב וישמע ויהיה בעניניו כחדשות, וזה שאמר על מה שלא שמע. אם יש רק קצת מה ששמע שלא שמע אומר לא שמעתי וזה חכם יתקרא. ולהיפך בגולם שאפילו אם רק מה שמע, אומר על הכל שמעתי.

---

1. Author's note: In this same vein, we may interpret *"last things last,"* that he carefully summarizes his major points upon concluding his presentation.

PIRKEI AVOS / SFAS EMES / 360

[10] *Seven types of punishment come to the world for seven kinds of transgressions. (a) If some people tithe and others do not, a famine caused by lack of rain ensues; some go hungry and others are satisfied; (b) if all decided not to tithe, tumultuous famine caused by armed bands and drought ensues; and (c) and [if they also decided] not to separate the challah, a famine caused by destructive drought ensues;*

It seems strange that one is praiseworthy simply because he does not plagiarize his *rebbi's* comments and claim them as his own. According to *Pardes Yosef*, the *mishnah* is referring to the magnanimous individual who, when being told a Torah thought that largely replicates what he had already known (yet contains some novel element), nonetheless acknowledges his debt to his peer (*Maggidei HaEmes*).

10.

■ שִׁבְעָה מִינֵי פֻּרְעָנִיּוֹת בָּאִין לָעוֹלָם עַל שִׁבְעָה גוּפֵי עֲבֵרָה: מִקְצָתָן מְעַשְּׂרִין וּמִקְצָתָן אֵינָן מְעַשְּׂרִין — *Seven types of punishment come to the world for seven kinds of transgressions: If some people tithe and others do not.*

❧ Widespread Indifference

יי״ל הפי׳ שהרוב עושין כן לפעמים מעשרין ופעמים לא, ופירוש מקצתן מקצת זמנים.

The term מִקְצָתָן מְעַשְּׂרִין is usually interpreted as a segment of the population not tithing properly. However, it may actually refer to *Klal Yisrael's* inconsistent attitude towards this crucial *mitzvah*: At times (מִקְצָתָן) they are careful to take *maaser* and on other occasions they neglect to tithe. Such a haphazard and indifferent approach warrants drastic punishment.

■ וְשֶׁלֹּא לִטֹּל אֶת הַחַלָּה, רָעָב שֶׁל כְּלָיָה בָּא — *And [if they also decided] not to separate the challah, a famine caused by destructive drought ensues.*

❧ Neglecting the Mitzvah of Challah

זה חמור יותר משום דמקרבא הנייתה.

[יא] **דֶּבֶר בָּא לָעוֹלָם** — עַל מִיתוֹת הָאֲמוּרוֹת בַּתּוֹרָה שֶׁלֹּא נִמְסְרוּ לְבֵית דִּין, וְעַל פֵּרוֹת שְׁבִיעִית; **חֶרֶב בָּאָה לָעוֹלָם** — עַל עִנּוּי הַדִּין, וְעַל עִוּוּת הַדִּין, וְעַל הַמּוֹרִים בַּתּוֹרָה שֶׁלֹּא כַהֲלָכָה; **חַיָּה רָעָה בָּאָה לָעוֹלָם** — עַל שְׁבוּעַת שָׁוְא, וְעַל חִלּוּל הַשֵּׁם; **גָּלוּת בָּאָה לָעוֹלָם** עַל עוֹבְדֵי עֲבוֹדָה זָרָה, וְעַל גִּלּוּי עֲרָיוֹת, וְעַל שְׁפִיכוּת דָּמִים, וְעַל שְׁמִטַּת הָאָרֶץ.

[יב] **בְּאַרְבָּעָה פְּרָקִים הַדֶּבֶר מִתְרַבֶּה:** בָּרְבִיעִית,

It is significant that neglect of the *mitzvah* of separating *challah* (and, when appropriate, distributing it to a *Kohen*) is punished more harshly, in the form of a devastating hunger, whereas not tithing properly only engenders a more limited form of famine.

The severity — and the grave punishment — associated with neglect of the *mitzvah* of *challah* may be based on the *immediate* gratification that this sinner derives by eating bread from which *challah* had not been separated. On the other hand, much processing is still required before grain, which had not been properly tithed, could be consumed.

11.

■ **גָּלוּת בָּאָה לָעוֹלָם עַל עוֹבְדֵי עֲבוֹדָה זָרָה, וְעַל גִּלּוּי עֲרָיוֹת, וְעַל שְׁפִיכוּת דָּמִים** ■
. . . — *Exile comes to the world for idolatry, for immorality, for bloodshed . . .*

◄§ The Era of the Second Beis HaMikdash

והא דבית שני נחרב על שנאת חנם. יש לומר דהחרבן הבית הוא ענין אחר וגלות כבר התחיל מבית ראשון דבבית שני כבר היו רוב הזמן כפופים למלכות אחרת גם כן.

By only listing the sins which brought about the destruction of the first *Beis HaMikdash* and the subsequent exile of the Jewish People — omitting any reference to baseless hatred, the underlying cause of the second *Beis HaMikdash's* destruction — the *mishnah* is indicating that there has been only *one* true *galus* — following the destruction of the first *Beis HaMikdash*. While it is true that another *Beis HaMikdash* was built and that a small segment of the Jewish People returned eventually to *Eretz Yisrael*, the period of the Second *Beis*

[11] *(d) Pestilence comes to the world for the death penalties prescribed by the Torah that were not carried out by the court and for [not observing the laws of] the fruits of the Sabbatical year; (e) the sword [of war] comes to the world for the delay of justice, for the perversion of justice and for rendering decisions contrary to the halachah; (f) wild beasts come upon the world for vain oaths and for desecration of God's Name; (g) exile comes to the world for idolatry, for immorality, for bloodshed and for working the land during the Sabbatical year.*

[12] *At four periods [of the seven-year Sabbatical cycle] pestilence increases: in the fourth [year], in the*

HaMikdash was really nothing more than another phase of the same *galus*. It was still a time when the fragile Jewish nation was generally politically subservient to the other states, but this time, it was experienced on the sacred soil of *Eretz Yisrael*.[1]

12.

■ בְּאַרְבָּעָה פְּרָקִים הַדֶּבֶר מִתְרַבֶּה . . . בָּרְבִיעִית, מִפְּנֵי מַעְשַׂר עָנִי שֶׁבַּשְּׁלִישִׁית
— *At four periods [of the seven-year Sabbatical cycle] pestilence increases . . . In the fourth [year of the Shemittah cycle], for [neglecting] the tithe of the poor in the third [year].*

◆§ The Consequences of Not Tithing for the Poor

מעשר עני שבשלישית, הא דנענשו יותר על מעשר עני משאר מעשרות משום
דחמיר דכתיב וקבע את קובעיהם נפש. ושאר מעשרות די באם רק מפריש אף
אם עוד לא נתן אבל מעשר עני נענש אף אם כבר הפריש.

It is significant that neglecting the tithe of the poor carries far more serious consequences than that of any other tithe. Whereas the first tithe is given to a *Levi*, *Leviim* also benefit from other sources of income. The tithe of the poor, however, is given to the poor who are dependent upon this tithe for their sustenance. The significance of giving this tithe — and the consequences of not observing this tithe — can be deduced from Shlomo's warning about oppressing the poor: כִּי ה' יָרִיב רִיבָם וְקָבַע אֶת קֹבְעֵיהֶם נָפֶשׁ, *For Hashem will take up their grievance; He will steal the soul of those who would steal from them (Mishlei*

---

1. For a similar theme see R' Yehudah Nachshoni's *Studies in the Weekly Parashah*, pp. 883-886.

וּבַשְּׁבִיעִית, וּבְמוֹצָאֵי שְׁבִיעִית, וּבְמוֹצָאֵי הֶחָג שֶׁבְּכָל שָׁנָה וְשָׁנָה. בָּרְבִיעִית, מִפְּנֵי מַעְשַׂר עָנִי שֶׁבַּשְּׁלִישִׁית; בַּשְּׁבִיעִית, מִפְּנֵי מַעְשַׂר עָנִי שֶׁבַּשִּׁשִּׁית; בְּמוֹצָאֵי שְׁבִיעִית, מִפְּנֵי פֵּרוֹת שְׁבִיעִית; בְּמוֹצָאֵי הֶחָג שֶׁבְּכָל שָׁנָה וְשָׁנָה, מִפְּנֵי גֶּזֶל מַתְּנוֹת עֲנִיִּים.

[יג] אַרְבַּע מִדּוֹת בָּאָדָם. הָאוֹמֵר: „שֶׁלִּי שֶׁלִּי וְשֶׁלְּךָ שֶׁלָּךְ," זוֹ מִדָּה בֵּינוֹנִית, וְיֵשׁ אוֹמְרִים: זוֹ מִדַּת

22:23). This distinction between the tithes is reflected halachically, as well. Whereas it may be sufficient, under certain circumstances, to merely *designate* certain tithes (and retain possession until the recipient is available), the tithe of the poor must actually be *distributed* to the poor.

■ בְּמוֹצָאֵי הֶחָג שֶׁבְּכָל שָׁנָה וְשָׁנָה, מִפְּנֵי גֶּזֶל מַתְּנוֹת עֲנִיִּים — *Annually, at the conclusion of the festival [of Succos], for robbing the poor of their gifts.*

◆§ Why Every Year?

קשה איזה גזל מתנות עניים שייך בכל שנה ושנה, הלא מעשר עני אינו נוהג אלא בשלישי וששי. וי״ל שהכוונה לשאר מתנות עניים כגון לקט שכחה ופאה וכיוצא בהן.

It would seem appropriate that *Klal Yisrael* be punished only for not tithing for the poor during the third and sixth years of the seven-year *Shemittah* cycle, when the tithe of the poor is distributed. Nonetheless, if we are held accountable *every* Succos for neglecting the poor, this is in response to neglecting other forms of charity distributed to the poor during the harvest season which culminates on Succos (*Imrei Emes, Maggidei HaEmes*).

13.

■ אַרְבַּע מִדּוֹת בָּאָדָם: הָאוֹמֵר: "שֶׁלִּי שֶׁלִּי וְשֶׁלְּךָ שֶׁלָּךְ," זוֹ מִדָּה בֵּינוֹנִית, וְיֵשׁ אוֹמְרִים זוֹ מִדַּת סְדוֹם — *There are four character types among people: One who says, "My [property] is mine and yours is yours," is an average character type, but some say this is characteristic of Sodom.*

◆§ Insisting Upon Prior Permission

יי״ל הפירוש על שלא מדעתו כי הנהנה ממנו שלא בידיעתו הוא מקפיד על זה אבל

seventh [year], in the year following the Sabbatical year, and annually following the [Succos] festival. In the fourth [year of the Shemittah cycle], for [neglecting] the tithe of the poor in the third [year]; in the seventh [year], for [neglecting] the tithe of the poor in the sixth [year]; in the year following the Sabbatical year, for [violating the laws of] Sabbatical produce; annually at the conclusion of the festival [of Succos], for robbing the poor of their gifts.

[13] *There are four character types among people: (a) One who says, "My [property] is mine, and yours is yours," is an average character type, but some*

מרצונו הוא מהנה אחרים.
וי״א זו מדת סדום ואפשר דלדבריהם מדה בינונית היא מי שאינו מקפיד על משהו
ואנשי סדום היו מקפידין על כל שהוא.

It seems strange that the *mishnah* accepts — albeit reluctantly — such miserly behavior. Perhaps, the *mishnah* is referring to one who shares his material possessions, but only if he is informed in advance. A truly generous individual would allow other responsible people to use his possessions even without his express permission.

However, others argue, maintaining that there can be no excuse for such selfish behavior. Only the Sodomites would insist upon prior permission for the use of one's insignificant possessions (in such a manner that the *owner* would suffer no monetary loss).

⋐ I Will Support My Poor, You Will Support Yours

מי שאומר שלי שלי פי׳ אני אפרנס קרובים עניים שלי ואתה תפרנס את העניים
קרובים שלך זו מדה בינונית. אבל יש אומרים ר״ל יש שרק אומרים כן כדי לתרץ
עצמם אבל באמת אף העניים שלהם אינם מפרנסים, זו מדת סדום.

According to R' Yitzchak of Worka, our *mishnah* is referring to someone who refuses to give *tzedakah*, rationalizing, "I will support *my* poor relatives (שֶׁלִּי שֶׁלִּי), and you will support *yours* (שֶׁלָּךְ שֶׁלָּךְ)." While such behavior may be reluctantly condoned (מִדָּה בֵּינוֹנִית), if, in fact, the *tzedakah* is actually given, frequently such a response is nothing more than cheap rhetoric (וְיֵשׁ אוֹמְרִים, *some say*) disguising their true intention of *not* helping anyone — even their own relatives (*Maggidei HaEmes*).

Starving in Sodom

> כי כשהיה בא אורח לסדום ונכנס לחנות וביקש לקנות צרכי אוכל השיב לו בעל
> החנות, ,,שלי שלי – המאכל, ושלך שלך – הכסף.'' נמצא אותו אורח גוע ברעב,
> לכך הרי זו מדת סדום.

A visitor to Sodom seeking to purchase food would be told by merchants, "Keep your money (שֶׁלָּךְ שֶׁלָּךְ) and I will keep my food" (שֶׁלִּי שֶׁלִּי). Such a "hands-off" policy would ultimately lead to the visitor's starvation (R' Yechezkel of Kozmir, Maggidei HaEmes).

■ שֶׁלִּי שֶׁלָּךְ וְשֶׁלְּךָ שֶׁלִּי,'', עַם הָאָרֶץ — *"Mine is yours, and yours is mine,"* is an unlearned person.

"Negotiating" With Hashem

> דהנה מי שעובד ה' ועושה חסד כדי שיעשה הקב''ה גם כן חסדים עמו, וזהו האומר
> שלי שלך ושלך שלי, הוא עם הארץ.

An individual who "negotiates" with Hashem — reasoning that if he acts "charitably" towards Him by observing Torah and *mitzvos* (שֶׁלִּי שֶׁלָּךְ), then Hashem will reciprocate by acting with equal magnanimity (שֶׁלְּךָ שֶׁלִּי) — demonstrates a total misunderstanding of our relationship with Hashem. Such an inferior form of *avodas Hashem* only demonstrates that he is an ignorant person (Maggid of Koznitz, Maggidei HaEmes).

"My Money and Your Fear of Hashem"

> האומר שלי, כלומר מי שאומר על שלי פירוש על הדבר ששייך לי היינו יראת
> שמים, כאמרם ז''ל הכל בידי שמים חוץ מיראת שמים, על זה אומר שלך,
> שהקב''ה ימציא לו יראת שמים. ושלך היינו על שלך על העשירות שהיא מידי
> הקב''ה כמו שכתוב השלך על ה' יהבך כו', אומר שלי, שכוחי ועוצם ידי עשה לי
> את החיל הזה – עם הארץ, איש זה שאומר להיפר ממה שהוא באמת אינו אלא
> עם הארץ.

According to R' Simchah Bunim of Peshis'cha, this phrase refers to an individual whose understanding of responsibility is confused. This person is more

say this is characteristic of Sodom; (b) "Mine is yours, and yours is mine," is an unlearned person; (c) "Mine is yours, and yours is yours," is scrupulously pious; (d) "Yours is mine, and mine is mine," is wicked.

than willing to let Hashem instill in him a sense of fear of Heaven, which is actually *his* own obligation (שֶׁלִּי שֶׁלָּךְ) [cf. *Berachos* 33b, הַכֹּל בִּידֵי שָׁמַיִם חוּץ מִיִּרְאַת שָׁמַיִם]. On the other hand, he insists that his wealth, which is actually a blessing from Hashem, is derived through *his* own efforts (שֶׁלָּךְ שֶׁלִּי) (*Maggidei HaEmes*).

◆§ Clashing Perspectives

יתכן כי מהאי בבא נלמד הכלל דלא עם הארץ חסיד כי הגם שמה שאומר שלי שלך זהו מן מעשי החסיד מכל מקום הסיפא מקלקל גם מחצה הראשון של החסידות.

From this segment of the *mishnah* we may deduce the principle לֹא עַם הָאָרֶץ חָסִיד, *an unlearned person cannot be scrupulously pious* (2:6). The righteous sentiments of "mine is yours" emulating the behavior of a pious person are more than outweighed by the unlearned person's corollary of *"yours is mine."* While one may have imagined that this individual would be classified as a hybrid of a wicked person and a righteous one, in reality, the two sentiments are incompatible. A small dose of perverted reasoning classifies one as unlearned.

■ שֶׁלִּי שֶׁלָּךְ וְשֶׁלָּךְ שֶׁלָּךְ", חָסִיד — *"Mine is yours, and yours is yours,"* is scrupulously pious.

◆§ Doing Everything for Hashem's Sake

היינו יש מי שעובד במעלה יתירה רק כדי שיעשה נחת רוח להבורא ב״ה ושלא לשום תועלת וקיווי שכר, זהו האומר שלי שלך ושלך שלך הוא חסיד.

We can understand the term שֶׁלָּךְ, *for You*, refers to Hashem. Thus, this phrase defines the true *chassid's* desire for nothing for himself, but rather everything he does is for Hashem's sake. Such an enlightened individual seeks only to enhance Hashem's *nachas* by his own actions (*Maggid of Koznitz, Maggidei HaEmes*).

◆§ Acknowledging Others vs. Self-Attribution

והחסיד תולה מעשים טובים שלו בזכות אחרים, והרשע סובר שכל העולם ניזון

[יד] אַרְבַּע מִדּוֹת בְּדֵעוֹת: נוֹחַ לִכְעוֹס וְנוֹחַ לִרְצוֹת,
יָצָא שְׂכָרוֹ בְּהֶפְסֵדוֹ; קָשֶׁה לִכְעוֹס וְקָשֶׁה לִרְצוֹת,
יָצָא הֶפְסֵדוֹ בִשְׂכָרוֹ; קָשֶׁה לִכְעוֹס וְנוֹחַ לִרְצוֹת, חָסִיד;
נוֹחַ לִכְעוֹס וְקָשֶׁה לִרְצוֹת, רָשָׁע.

בשבילו וכאשר ראינו בגיאותן של עדת קרח ואהרן אדרבה לא ענה כלום
והאמין כי בכח הרבים עובד את עבודתו.

Unlike the wicked person who feels that the entire universe is sustained in *his*
merit (שֶׁלִּי — anything you have comes from me) — witness
the haughty, arrogant behavior of Korach and his associates — the righteous person attributes whatever good deeds he has performed to the merit
of other Jews (everything I have comes from you). During Korach's insurrection, Aharon simply remained silent, trusting that his stature and high
position were attained not in his own merit, but rather to act as *Klal
Yisrael's* agent. Thus, he would be vindicated even without any response on his
part.

■ „שֶׁלְּךָ שֶׁלִּי וְשֶׁלִּי שֶׁלִּי", רָשָׁע — *"Yours is mine and mine is mine,"* is
wicked.

◆§ Even the Mundane Is Sacred

היינו שלי הוא מה שיעשה האדם לצורך גופו כמו האכילה והשתיה והשינה,
והוא אומר שלי ר"ל אף הדברים שעושה לצורך גופו הוא גם כן לשם
שמים [שלך], ותמיד בכל מעשיו עושה הכל לכבוד הבורא יתברך, ומכל שכן
בתורה ותפלה. וזה שלך גם כן שלך, הוא חסיד. מה שאין כן האומר שלי שלי
כשעוסק בצרכי גופו כמו האכילה והשתיה, שוכח בה' וממלא כריסו לבד, וגם
שלך שלי שחומס הכל מאתו יתברך כביכול ואינו עושה שום דבר לשם שמים הוא
רשע.

The righteous and wicked characters portrayed here represent contrasting
perspectives on how a Jew relates to his physical needs. The righteous
perceives spirituality in *every* aspect of life. Even when he is taking care of his
mundane needs (שֶׁלִּי), it is merely as a means of serving Hashem with greater
vigor (שֶׁלְּךָ). As a result, the spiritual components of life — Torah and *tefillah*
— are imbued with even greater sanctity (שֶׁלְּךָ שֶׁלְּךָ).

On the other hand, the wicked person, who indulges in physical pleasures only for his own enjoyment (שֶׁלִּי שֶׁלִּי), will eventually lose touch even
with the spiritual aspects of his life, so that שֶׁלְּךָ, Hashem's "domain," will be

[14] *There are four types of temperament: (a) One who is angered easily and pacified easily, his gain is offset by his loss; (b) one who is hard to anger and hard to pacify, his loss is offset by his gain; (c) one who is hard to anger and pacified easily is pious; (d) one who is angered easily and hard to pacify is wicked.*

---

reduced to the *rasha's* material lifestyle (שֶׁלִּי) (*Maggid of Koznitz, Maggidei HaEmes*).

14.

■ אַרְבַּע מִדּוֹת בְּדֵעוֹת: נוֹחַ לִכְעוֹס וְנוֹחַ לִרְצוֹת, יָצָא שְׂכָרוֹ בְּהֶפְסֵדוֹ. קָשֶׁה לִכְעוֹס וְקָשֶׁה לִרְצוֹת, יָצָא הֶפְסֵדוֹ בִשְׂכָרוֹ — *There are four types of temperament: One who is angered easily and pacified easily, his gain is offset by his loss. One who is hard to anger and hard to pacify, his loss is offset by his gain.*

◆§ Cause and Effect

כלומר כי אלו תלוין זה בזה, מאי טעמא נוח לכעוס כיון שהוא נוח לרצות לכן יצא שכרו בהפסדו. ויש לכוון הלשון שהשכר מביא לו ההפסד כי כל ימיו מכאובים וכעס ולמה נכנס בדרך זה כיון שתלוי זה בזה. ומהאי טעמא נמי קשה לרצות כיון שקשה לכעוס. ויש לבאר יותר דהראשון אינו מתיישב להתחרט על מדה זו, דאינו רואה בגריעותה כיון דהוא נוח לרצות וסובר שהוא דבר קל כיון דתיכף מתרצה אבל השני כיון דהוא קשה לרצות רואה היאך גרועה המדה הזו ונותן לב ומתחרט לגמרי ממנה.

The *mishnah* is not merely juxtaposing two character traits — a predisposition to anger, as well as a tendency to be quickly appeased — but is actually stating a cause-and-effect relationship. Such an individual unfortunately rationalizes his tendency to anger by noting that he is also easily calmed. The unfortunate result of accepting anger as part of one's temperament is a wasted and truly miserable life, full of anger. As *Koheles* 2:23 states, כִּי כָל יָמָיו מַכְאוֹבִים וָכַעַס, *For all his days are anguish and vexation.* It follows then that such an individual will not be rewarded for his ability to be easily appeased, inasmuch as it was this trait that also served to rationalize his anger.

By contrast, the individual who rarely gets angry but is difficult to mollify once he is already upset enjoys a distinct advantage. Instead of using his redeeming trait as a justification for his other negative traits, he learns from his weak points: If I am so difficult to appease once aroused to anger, then it is best to avoid anger altogether.

[טו] אַרְבַּע מִדּוֹת בְּתַלְמִידִים: מָהִיר לִשְׁמֹעַ וּמָהִיר
לְאַבֵּד, יָצָא שְׂכָרוֹ בְּהֶפְסֵדוֹ; קָשֶׁה לִשְׁמֹעַ וְקָשֶׁה
לְאַבֵּד, יָצָא הֶפְסֵדוֹ בִּשְׂכָרוֹ; מָהִיר לִשְׁמֹעַ וְקָשֶׁה
לְאַבֵּד, זֶה חֵלֶק טוֹב; קָשֶׁה לִשְׁמֹעַ וּמָהִיר לְאַבֵּד, זֶה
חֵלֶק רָע.

[טז] אַרְבַּע מִדּוֹת בְּנוֹתְנֵי צְדָקָה: הָרוֹצֶה שֶׁיִּתֵּן וְלֹא

✦§ Anger Prevention, Not Rectification

דהבעס מדה מגונה מאוד ולכן נוח לכעוס קשה טפי ממי שאינו נוח לרצות כי נקל
לחפש עצה להעצר מלכעוס משכבר כועס ויתפרש ממנו.

It is apparent from our *mishnah* that it is far more meritorious to avoid anger altogether than to be appeased once one is already upset. This insight may be based on *Chazal's* perception that it is far easier to avoid situations which induce anger than to calm oneself after "exploding" in anger. If an individual, nonetheless, does not even attempt to avoid becoming angry, then he deserves condemnation.

■ קָשֶׁה לִכְעוֹס וְנוֹחַ לִרְצוֹת חָסִיד — *One who is hard to anger and pacified easily is pious.*

✦§ Easily Appeased — Even When Anger Is Justified

דכיון שהוא קשה לכעוס ומכל מקום בזה נתבעס ודאי הוצרך לכעוס ומכל מקום
גובר על עצמו ומתרצה, שמע מינה דיש בו מדת חסידות כנ"ל.

This individual, who rarely gets angry, may well be justified when he does display anger. Yet, acting as a true *chassid*, he relents and is easily appeased on those rare occasions.

■ נוֹחַ לִכְעוֹס וְקָשֶׁה לִרְצוֹת רָשָׁע — *One who is angered easily and hard to pacify is wicked.*

✦§ The Folly of Anger

נוח לכעוס וקל"ר רשע דהנה כתיב בח' כעס בחי' בסילים ינוח כי אין לך כסיל גדול מזה
כיון שכועס שהוא כעובד ע"ז הרי עושה לעצמו יותר רעה ממה שעשה לו חבירו

[15] *There are four types of students: (a) One who grasps quickly and forgets quickly, his gain is offset by his loss; (b) one who grasps slowly and forgets slowly, his loss is offset by his gain; (c) one who grasps quickly and forgets slowly, this is a good portion; (d) one who grasps slowly and forgets quickly, this is a bad portion.*

[16] *There are four types of donors to charity: (a) One*

המכעיסו ולכן קוראו רשע הגם שחבירו פשע בו.

One wonders: Should not the antagonist of this individual — the person who *caused* him to be angry — be identified as wicked rather than the person who *reacts* angrily?

Upon further contemplation, however, we realize that the *mishnah* is referring to the harm which one inflicts upon *oneself*. As *Koheles* states, כִּי כַעַס בְּחֵיק כְּסִילִים יָנוּחַ, *for anger lingers in the bosom of fools* (7:9). There is nothing more foolish and short sighted than becoming angry and remaining in such an emotional state. It is the antithesis of *Yiddishkeit* and is described by *Chazal* as tantamount to idolatry (cf. *Zohar* 3:179 a).

15.

■ — אַרְבַּע מִדּוֹת בְּתַלְמִידִים: מָהִיר לִשְׁמוֹעַ וּמָהִיר לְאַבֵּד, יָצָא שְׂכָרוֹ בְּהֶפְסֵדוֹ — *There are four types of students: One who grasps quickly and forgets quickly, his gain is offset by his loss.*

◆§ Quick Learning Leads to Forgetting

וקשה כיון שזה יש לו תפיסה יפה שמהיר לשמוע מה ענין לזה מה שהוא שכחן.
וי״ל דהכוונה שאילו היה מתייגע ולא מיהר לשמוע רק יותר במתינות לא היה
ממהר לאבד נמצא שהמהירות גרם לו האבידה לכן יוצא שכרו בהפסדו כי טוב
מעט כו'.

It seems surprising that someone would be faulted for his quick grasp of Torah. Apparently, the *mishnah* is premising a direct relationship between excessively quick (and superficial) learning and poor retention. Had the individual learned at a more deliberate pace, taking pains to truly comprehend what he learned, he would most likely not have forgotten at so rapid a pace.

יִתְּנוּ אֲחֵרִים, עֵינוֹ רָעָה בְּשֶׁל אֲחֵרִים; יִתְּנוּ אֲחֵרִים
וְהוּא לֹא יִתֵּן, עֵינוֹ רָעָה בְּשֶׁלּוֹ; יִתֵּן וְיִתְּנוּ אֲחֵרִים,
חָסִיד; לֹא יִתֵּן וְלֹא יִתְּנוּ אֲחֵרִים, רָשָׁע.

[יז] אַרְבַּע מִדּוֹת בְּהוֹלְכֵי בֵית הַמִּדְרָשׁ: הוֹלֵךְ וְאֵינוֹ
עוֹשֶׂה, שְׂכַר הֲלִיכָה בְּיָדוֹ; עוֹשֶׂה וְאֵינוֹ הוֹלֵךְ,

16.

■ **אַרְבַּע מִדּוֹת בְּנוֹתְנֵי צְדָקָה . . . יִתְּנוּ אֲחֵרִים וְהוּא לֹא יִתֵּן, עֵינוֹ רָעָה בְּשֶׁלּוֹ** —
*There are four types of donors to charity . . . that others should give
but that he should not give, he begrudges himself.*

ঌ Raising Funds From Others

שאינו משתדל שיתנו לכן ביתנו אחרים והוא לא יתן לא נקרא רשע שעל כל פנים
מתעסק בנתינת הצדקה ולולי זאת הו"ל רשע שאינו נותן צדקה.

Should not an individual who leaves the great *mitzvah* of charity to others be
deemed wicked? Why does the *mishnah* give merely the much milder appel-
lation of "he begrudges himself"?

If this individual is spared the designation of "wicked," it must be in the
merit of encouraging others to give *tzedakah*. It is only someone who has
totally disassociated himself from this *mitzvah* — by neither giving nor motivating others to give — who deserves the ignominious title of wicked.

■ **לֹא יִתֵּן וְלֹא יִתְּנוּ אֲחֵרִים, רָשָׁע** — *That he should not give and that
others should not give is wicked.* ■

ঌ Giving Under Duress

מקשין כי לא יתן ולא יתנו אחרים אינו בכלל נותני צדקה. וי"ל דהפי' אינו רוצה
היינו שאין ברצונו אבל באמת מוכרח ליתן על ידי כפיה או בושה. ועי' בתוס'
חולין.

It seems strange that an individual who neither gives nor wants anyone else
to give *tzedakah* is nonetheless included in the category of a "*a donor of
charity.*" Perhaps, the *mishnah* is referring to an individual who gives *tzedakah*
only under duress (coercion by *beis din* or public humiliation for acting so
miserly). Such a reluctant contributor, while technically speaking a donor, is

*who wishes to give himself but wants others not to give,
he begrudges others; (b) that others should give but that
he should not give, he begrudges himself; (c) that he
should give and that others should give is pious; (d) that
he should not give and that others should not give is
wicked.*

[17] *There are four types among those who go to the
house of study: (a) One who goes but does not
accomplish has the reward for going; (b) one who accomplishes [at home] but does not go (to the house of study)*

---

considered to be wicked because of his grudging attitude towards giving.[1]

17.

■ — אַרְבַּע מִדּוֹת בְּהוֹלְכֵי בֵית הַמִּדְרָשׁ: הוֹלֵךְ וְאֵינוֹ עוֹשֶׂה, שְׂכַר הֲלִיכָה בְּיָדוֹ ■
*There are four types among those who go to the house of study: One
who goes but does not accomplish has the reward for going.*

◄§ Just Leaving the Home

ומה שכר מגיע על הליכה בלבד, וכי מה פעל האדם בעצמו בהליכה גרידא. אלא
שמגיע לו שכר על עצם היציאה והפרישה מביתו. ויש להוסיף עפ"י מה שמביא
אימרה זו במדרש חכמים בשם הרבי מקאצק כי ע"י שמקושר בביתו מפריעו
בתורה ותפלה, ובזה שהולך אף שלא עשה מחמת שהיה עוד מקושר אף
בהליכתו, מ"מ ע"י עצם ההליכה והפרישה מביתו הריהו פועל בעצמו שיוכל
אח"כ להתנתק מביתו ויבוא לידי עשייה ג"כ, ולזה השכר על עצם ההליכה כיון
שמביא לידי עשיה וכנ"ל.

According to the Kotzker Rebbe, the *mishnah* is lauding someone who simply sets aside all the distractions of the home and goes to the *beis hamidrash*.
Future generations of Chassidic Rebbes expanded upon the Kotzker's terse
comment, each in his own inimitable fashion.

For example, the *Lev Simchah*, quoting his father the *Imrei Emes*, maintained
that simply leaving one's home — and all the ties that bind him there and
distract him from learning — is considered a form of admirable behavior.
Moreover, by leaving home he has set a process into motion. At first, he will
only leave his home — without accomplishing much learning in the *beis*

---

1. Cf. *Sefer HaChinuch* (Mitzvah 479) who defines the *mitzvah* of charity as giving joyously.

ה / יז   שְׂכַר מַעֲשֶׂה בְּיָדוֹ; הוֹלֵךְ וְעוֹשֶׂה, חָסִיד; לֹא הוֹלֵךְ וְלֹא
עוֹשֶׂה, רָשָׁע.

hamedrash. As he becomes more comfortable away from home, in the ambiance of Torah, he will begin learning as well, achieving the status of *one who goes and accomplishes.* This individual is rewarded not only for his eventual learning but also for going to the *beis hamidrash* since this was a necessary catalyst leading to his study of Torah (*Maggidei HaEmes*).

✑ Time to Meditate

אדמו״ר הבית ישראל ז״ל הזכיר אימרא זו כמה פעמים וכל פעם הוסיף נופך
מדיליה כדלהלן: דעל ידי זה שהולכים הרבה, אפשר ליישב עצמו שבשעת
ההליכה יכול להתיישב.

According to the *Beis Yisrael*, simply by walking alone, away from the distractions of home, the Jew enjoys the opportunity to reflect and, if necessary, to rectify his moral weaknesses (*Maggidei HaEmes*).

✑ Something Is Better Than Nothing

אם יוצאים והולכים בהכרח שיקלוט משהו . . . אם הוא הולך פעם ועוד פעם הוא
בוודאי יגיע לבסוף גם לידי עשיה, אם לא היום אז היום אז למחר, אבל זה ברור
שלידי עשיה הוא יגיע. עכלה״ק.

By going to the *beis hamedrash*, I am allowing for the distinct possibility that some modicum of Torah might be absorbed. By remaining at home, that possibility is forfeited.

Even if at first it appears as if nothing is accomplished by going to the study hall, eventually progress will be made (*Beis Yisrael, Maggidei HaEmes*).

✑ Going With the Intention of Learning

שהולך על דעת ללמוד והסוף היה שלא למד שנמנע עבור איזה סיבה אבל כשהלך
מיד על מנת שלא לעשות אינו בכלל הולכי לבית המדרש.

According to the *Sfas Emes*, the *mishnah* is referring to one who went to the *beis hamedrash* with the intention of learning Torah, but due to unexpected circumstances was unable to consummate his intention. On the other hand, someone who is simply walking to a *beis hamedrash* with no intention of doing

has the reward for accomplishment; (c) one who goes and accomplish is pious; (d) one who does not go and does not accomplish is wicked.

anything constructive there is not considered to be among those who go to the house of study.

◄§ Building a Beis Hamedrash

גם י״ל עושה שבונה בית המדרש.

The term עוֹשֶׂה (literally, *does, makes, accomplishes*) rather than לוֹמֵד, *learn*, may allude to the great *mitzvah* of building (or contributing funds to build) a *beis hamidrash*.

■ עוֹשֶׂה וְאֵינוֹ הוֹלֵךְ, שְׂכַר מַעֲשֶׂה בְּיָדוֹ — *One who accomplishes [at home] but does not go [to the house of study] has the reward for accomplishment.*

◄§ Doing Mitzvos — Yet Not

המשנה מתמיה מאין בא אדם שעושה מצוות תמיד ואינו הולך בזה ממדריגה למדריגה. ומתרץ המשנה שכר מעשה בידו, פירוש בוודאי כל עשיותיו אינם אלא לשם קבלת פרס.

R' Dov Ber of Mezeritch offered a beautiful allegorical explanation of this phrase: If an individual diligently performs *mitzvos* (עוֹשֶׂה), yet is not going (הוֹלֵךְ) from one spiritual level to another, we may attribute this to the fact that he is performing *mitzvos* for the sole purpose of receiving a reward. As this segment of the *mishnah* concludes, שְׂכַר מַעֲשֶׂה בְּיָדוֹ, *the reward* to be obtained from the *mitzvah* (rather than the *mitzvah* itself) *is in his hand* (i.e. uppermost in his mind) (*Maggidei HaEmes*).

■ הוֹלֵךְ וְעוֹשֶׂה חָסִיד — *One who goes and accomplishes is pious.*

◄§ Communal Affairs (צָרְכֵי צִבּוּר)

יל״פ הליכה נק׳ צורך אסיפת הקהל לפקח על עסקי רבים וכדומה והעשי׳ גוף הלימוד.

[יח] אַרְבַּע מִדּוֹת בְּיוֹשְׁבִים לִפְנֵי חֲכָמִים: סְפוֹג,
וּמַשְׁפֵּךְ, מְשַׁמֶּרֶת, וְנָפָה. סְפוֹג, שֶׁהוּא סוֹפֵג אֶת
הַכֹּל; וּמַשְׁפֵּךְ, שֶׁמַּכְנִיס בְּזוֹ וּמוֹצִיא בְזוֹ; מְשַׁמֶּרֶת,
שֶׁמּוֹצִיאָה אֶת הַיַּיִן וְקוֹלֶטֶת אֶת הַשְּׁמָרִים; וְנָפָה,
שֶׁמּוֹצִיאָה אֶת הַקֶּמַח וְקוֹלֶטֶת אֶת הַסֹּלֶת.

[יט] כָּל אַהֲבָה שֶׁהִיא תְלוּיָה בְדָבָר, בָּטֵל דָּבָר, בְּטֵלָה
אַהֲבָה; וְשֶׁאֵינָהּ תְלוּיָה בְדָבָר, אֵינָהּ בְּטֵלָה לְעוֹלָם.

We can understand the term הוֹלֵךְ to refer to those who attend a communal
gathering convened in the *beis hamidrash*, certainly a worthy undertaking. Whereas the one who goes and accomplishes comes to study Torah, the
one who just goes at least participates in a sacred undertaking while in the *beis
hamidrash*.

✧ Encouraging Others to Learn

יש לומר עושה כופה אחרים לעשות.

The term עוֹשֶׂה may also refer to the merit of those who motivate *other* people
to learn in a *beis hamidrash* (cf. *Bava Basra* 9a גדול המעשה. Also *Gittin* 88b
גט המעושה where the term עוֹשֶׂה is utilized in this fashion).

18.

■ — אַרְבַּע מִדּוֹת בְּיוֹשְׁבִים לִפְנֵי חֲכָמִים: סְפוֹג, וּמַשְׁפֵּךְ, מְשַׁמֶּרֶת, וְנָפָה *There
are four types [among students] who sit before the sages: a sponge, a
funnel, a strainer and a sieve.*

✧ All Good Attributes

מדות ביושבים לפני חכמים כנראה שבכל אלו המדרגות בתלמידי הרב יש מהם
שיקבל הפסולת ויש ללקוט הטוב כו' והם מיני מדרגות שצ"ל בכל רב.

Unlike previous *mishnahs* which enumerated undesirable as well as desirable attributes, *all* the traits mentioned in this *mishnah* are potentially
beneficial. The ideal *rebbi* is a composite of many different teaching styles. This
allows him to relate to *talmidim* with vastly different capabilities. Specifically,
he must be able to transmit copious quantities of knowledge to the willing and

[18] *There are four types [among students] who sit before the sages: a sponge, a funnel, a strainer and a sieve — (a) a sponge, which absorbs everything; (b) a funnel, which lets in from one [side] and lets out from the other; (c) a strainer, which lets the wine flow through and retains the sediment; (d) and a sieve, which lets the flour pass dust through and retains the fine flour.*

[19] *Any love that depends on a specific cause, when that cause is gone, the love is gone; but if it does not depend on a specific cause, it will never cease.*

able disciples. To those students who are only capable of assimilating *some* of his teachings, whether as a strainer or as a sieve, he must be prepared to help them reach their maximum potential. And even for the student whose capabilities are like a funnel, where the lesson "goes in one ear and out the other," he must be able to also stimulate and motivate him to achieve his fullest capability for learning Torah (adapted from *Sfas Emes*).

■ סְפוֹג, שֶׁהוּא סוֹפֵג אֶת הַכֹּל . . . וְנָפָה, שֶׁמוֹצִיאָה אֶת הַקֶּמַח וְקוֹלֶטֶת אֶת הַסֹּלֶת
— *A sponge, which absorbs everything . . . and a sieve, which lets the flour dust pass through and retains the fine flour.*

◄§ Complete or Partial Learning

שהוא סופג את הכל, הפשוט דספוג גרוע מנפה אבל בספרי פ׳ עקב משמע שספוג
הוא המובחר.

Initially, we might assume that a discriminating *talmid* who only absorbs the *best* of his *rebbi's* teachings — the sieve — would be valued more than the student who, spongelike, absorbs *everything* his *rebbi* taught him. However, the *Sifre* (*Parashas Eikev*) implies that the attribute of being a sponge and absorbing *everything* one is taught is superior to any *partial* retention of one's learning.

19.

■ כָּל אַהֲבָה שֶׁהִיא תְלוּיָה בְדָבָר, בָּטֵל דָּבָר, בְּטֵלָה אַהֲבָה; וְשֶׁאֵינָה תְלוּיָה בְדָבָר,
אֵינָה בְּטֵלָה לְעוֹלָם — *Any love that depends on a specific cause, when that cause is gone, the love is gone; but if it does not depend on a specific cause, it will never cease.*

אֵיזוֹ הִיא אַהֲבָה שֶׁהִיא תְלוּיָה בְדָבָר? זוֹ אַהֲבַת אַמְנוֹן
וְתָמָר. וְשֶׁאֵינָהּ תְלוּיָה בְדָבָר? זוֹ אַהֲבַת דָּוִד וִיהוֹנָתָן.

⊷§ Loving Hashem Altruistically

הענין רומז על אהבת הבורא ית', כשאדם אוהב את השי"ת מחמת רוב טוב
המשפיע לו, אין זה אהבה גמורה ונצחית, מחמת שאם יבוטל הדבר תתבטל
האהבה, אבל צריך האדם לאהוב את הבורא ית' בלתי שום סיבה המביאה לו
זאת האהבה, כמו שאמר הכתוב ואהבת את ה' אלקיך כו', ובכל מאדך, בכל מדה
ומדה שהוא מודד לך וכו', ואהבה כזו אין שום סיבה המונעת זאת האהבה,
רק תמיד דבוק בהשי"ת, והיא אהבה שאין לה סוף. וזה דקאמר אינה בטלה
לעולם.

According to the *Avodas Yisrael*, our *mishnah* is alluding to our love of Hashem which should not be contingent upon Him showering us with bountiful blessings. Such an inferior form of *Ahavas Hashem*, which is premised on material blessings, could lead to a serious weakening of our *emunah* in Him if our material expectations are not immediately realized. On the contrary, our love of Hashem should be unconditional and consequently will never cease — regardless of our current fortunes. This altruistic form of love of Hashem is reflected in the statement of *Chazal:* בְּכָל מִדָּה וּמִדָּה שֶׁהוּא מוֹדֵד לְךָ הֱוֵי מוֹדֶה לוֹ, *Whatever measure that He metes out to you, you are to thank Him* (*Berachos* 54a). True love is not, in any way, contingent upon gratification by the beloved of the whim of the suitor (*Maggidei HaEmes*).

⊷§ True Love Is Not Based on Verbal Skills

אי' בבית אהרן אם מזדמנים דיבורים הרי זה טוב, ואם לאו יושבים יחדיו באהבה
וחיבה.

The *Lev Simchah* interpreted the phrase אַהֲבָה שֶׁהִיא תְלוּיָה בְדָבָר (love that depends on a specified cause) as referring to love which is based upon the spoken word (דָבָר) [i.e. I love someone because I enjoy conversing with him]. In such a relationship, love ebbs when the conversation runs dry. On the other hand, true love exists regardless of the tenor of conversation. It is also possible to communicate without any words at all (*Maggidei HaEmes*).

■ אֵיזוֹ הִיא אַהֲבָה שֶׁהִיא תְלוּיָה בְדָבָר? . . . וְשֶׁאֵינָהּ תְלוּיָה בְדָבָר? — *What sort of love depended on a specific cause? . . . And what did not depend on a specific cause?*

The *mishnah* cites specific examples of both love for its own sake (David and Yonasan) and insincere love (Amnon and Tamar). We may expand upon this theme by considering examples of both forms of love.

◈ Love for Its Own Sake: Rivkah and Yaakov, Yitzchak and Esav

> הכתוב נותן טעם כי לא הי׳ אהבה אמיתית רק תלוי׳ בדבר לכן בטלה דבר בטלה אהבה ולכן כשהקדימו יעקב בצידה אבדה האהבה אבל רבקה אוהבת א״י בלי טעם ונתקיימה האהבה לעד.

Unlike Yitzchak's love for Esav which depended upon the latter's ability to provide him with game, Rivkah's love for Yaakov was purely altruistic. Since Yitzchak's love for Esav depended upon Esav's game, it could only endure as long as its source remained in existence. In contrast, Rivkah's love for Yaakov, which was based on his spiritual potential rather than any specific cause or benefit, is eternal and, in fact, increased over time. *Chazal* relate that Rivkah's love multiplied every time she heard Yaakov study Torah (*Bereishis Rabbah* 63:15) (*Sfas Emes, Toldos* 5637).

◈ Hashem's Love for Klal Yisrael

> וכן באהבת הקב״ה לישראל. שבאמת ע״י המצות ומעשים טובים נעשים אהובים להשי״ת. והיא תלוי׳ בדבר. לכן עבירה מכבה מצוה. אבל האהבה שיש בעצם בנ״י להקב״ה מצד חלק ה׳ עמו. זה אינה תלוי׳ בדבר. וע״ז כ׳ מים רבים לא יוכלו לכבות את האהבה הידועה שאינה תלוי׳ בדבר.

The *mishnah* is also alluding to two aspects of Hashem's love for His people. To a certain extent, His love for *Klal Yisrael* is based upon our performance of *mitzvos* and good deeds. That particular form of love may be diminished when *Klal Yisrael* does not heed its calling, when its spiritual conduct is not up to par. As *Chazal* (*Sotah* 21a) relate, עֲבֵרָה מְכַבֶּה מִצְוָה, *a sin extinguishes* the effects of *a mitzvah*.

On the other hand, Hashem's intrinsic love of *Klal Yisrael* remains steadfast regardless of our moral standing. This form of love is not contingent upon our behavior but simply upon our status as Hashem's chosen people (cf. *Devarim* 32:9, כִּי חֵלֶק ה׳ עַמּוֹ, *for Hashem's portion is His people*) and it is eternal. Nothing

— not even *Klal Yisrael's* deviating from its mission — can diminish that love. As Shlomo says, מַיִם רַבִּים לֹא יוּכְלוּ לְכַבּוֹת אֶת הָאַהֲבָה, *Many waters cannot extinguish the love* (*Shir HaShirim* 8:7). Even the mighty waters — the onrushing torrent of *aveiros* (ח"ו) — cannot extinguish *the* extraordinary love (emphasized by the definitive ה in הָאַהֲבָה) that Hashem demonstrates towards *Klal Yisrael* (*Sfas Emes, Rosh Hashanah* 5657).

◆§ Love for Its Own Sake: Shabbos
Love Based Upon Our Behavior: The Six Weekdays

בימי המעשה היא בחי' תלוי' בדבר. ובשבת שנק' מתנה טובה היא שאינה תלויה
בדבר. ונק' יום מנוחה.

Whereas our relationship with Hashem during the six weekdays is contingent upon our behavior, on Shabbos, the day described by *Chazal* (*Beitzah* 16a) as a Divine gift, His love for us is manifest regardless of our shortcomings. Shabbos is described as יוֹם מְנוּחָה, *a day of rest.* This refers not only to the physical cessation of work, but to a respite from the disruptions in our relationship to Hashem caused by our sins (ibid.).

◆§ Love for Its Own Sake: Hashem's Love for the Soul (נְשָׁמָה)
Love Based Upon Our Behavior: Hashem's Love for the Body (גוּף)

ובאמת אהבה זו היא בחי' נשמה.
ע"י החטא מסתלק כח הנשמה וע"י תשובה חוזר וניעור . . . אהבת נפש גוף תלוי
בדבר הנשמה אינה תלוי' בדבר שהיא חלק אלוקי ממעל.

Whereas Hashem's love for the body of every individual Jew is contingent upon how he utilizes it to perform *mitzvos* or *aveiros,* Hashem's love for the Divine soul, implanted by Him into man, knows no bounds. The soul, heavenly in origin, retains its purity despite man's transgressions. By sinning, we simply minimize the *neshamah's* power to influence our behavior. Upon doing *teshuvah,* we restore the Divine soul to its previous position of preeminence (ibid.).

20.

■ כָּל מַחֲלֹקֶת שֶׁהִיא לְשֵׁם שָׁמַיִם סוֹפָהּ לְהִתְקַיֵּם ■ — *Any dispute that is for the sake of Heaven will endure.*

◌§ Argument for Hashem's Sake

כל מחלוקת שהיא לש"ש סופה להתקיים זו מחלוקת שמאי והלל ושאינה לשם
שמים מחלוקת שמאי והלל ושאינה לשם שמים מחלוקת קרח כו' וכן הוא בזוה"ק
דפליג על שבת שנק' שלום ואחיד במחלוקת ע"ש, כי בודאי יש מקום לחילוקי
דעות שנמצא בבנ"י כמ"ש שאין פרצופיהם שוה כך אין דיעותיהם שוות, והענין
ע"פ מ"ש אא"ז מו"ר ז"ל על המשנה אם אין אני לי מי לי כי כל אדם נברא לתקן
דבר מיוחד שאין אחר יכול לתקן וכן בכל זמן וזמן מיוחד תיקון אחר, עכ"ז כשאני
לעצמי מה אני שצריך כל אחד לבטל חלק פרט שלו אל הכלל ע"כ דפ"ח, וענין
זה נוהג בעולם שנה נפש, כי בששת ימי בראשית נברא בכל יום ענין מיוחד לא
ראי זה כראי זה, אך השבת הוא הכלל כל הימים והוא כלי מחזיק ברכה ע"י שיש
בו האחדות לכן הוא קיום כל הימים כדאיתא באת שבת באת מנוחה ונגמרה
המלאכה כי אם אין שלום אין כלום, וכמו כן בנפשות כל נפש יש בו ענין מיוחד
ובנ"י הם הכלל, אעפ"כ בבנ"י עצמם יש ג"כ צדיק הכולל כל הפרטים כדאיתא
שיהי' יודע להלוך נגד רוחו של כל אחד וכמו כן בעולם ציון מכלל יופי שיש בכל
מקום ענין ויופי מיוחד, וארץ ישראל ובידהמ"ק הי' בו שורש כל מיני יופי של כל
המקומות, והנה כן עשה השי"ת שיהי' מקודם ששת ימי המעשה ואח"כ יהי' חיבור
אחד מכולם, וכמו כן הגם כי המחלוקת צריך להיות שכל אחד יאמר דעתו אבל
הכל כדי שיהי' אח"כ אחדות אחד.

The concept of arguing for Heaven's sake, which seems paradoxical at first
sight, in reality illustrates an important principle of Torah. Indeed, there is
ample room for differing opinions within the context of Torah, provided the
proponents of both positions advocate their viewpoint for Hashem's sake and
not for personal profit. This principle is reflected in the renowned saying כְּשֵׁם
שֶׁאֵין פַּרְצוּפֵיהֶם שָׁוֶה כָּךְ אֵין דֵעוֹתֵיהֶם שָׁווֹת, *Just as their faces inevitably vary, so too
their opinions (Yerushalmi, Berachos 5:9).* In fact, voicing one's own opinion on
an issue affecting Torah is a particularly effective means of achieving one's
potential. As we were taught in the first *perek* אִם אֵין אֲנִי לִי, מִי לִי, *If I am not
for myself, who will be for me (1:14),* which we interpreted as referring to the
unique contribution expected of every Jew (refer to our commentary there). In
fact, each of us was created for the purpose of accomplishing something distinctive and special. Often in the process of achieving our destiny, we are required
to formulate our own opinions which may put us at odds with other equally
well-intentioned individuals. This is truly *a dispute for the sake of Heaven,* in
which both sides are maintaining their positions for the greater good of *Klal*

וְשֶׁאֵינָהּ לְשֵׁם שָׁמַיִם אֵין סוֹפָהּ לְהִתְקַיֵּם. אֵיזוֹ הִיא
מַחֲלֹקֶת שֶׁהִיא לְשֵׁם שָׁמַיִם? זוֹ מַחֲלֹקֶת הִלֵּל וְשַׁמַאי.
וְשֶׁאֵינָהּ לְשֵׁם שָׁמַיִם? זוֹ מַחֲלֹקֶת קֹרַח וְכָל עֲדָתוֹ.

Yisrael. As this segment of the mishnah concludes, סוֹפָהּ לְהִתְקַיֵּם, [it] will endure. Both viewpoints are valid, and the proponents are properly motivated and sincerely intend to enhance Torah through their enthusiastic support of their own position.

However, participants in such a dispute must always bear in mind the following passage in the mishnah cited earlier, וּכְשֶׁאֲנִי לְעַצְמִי, מָה אֲנִי, and if I am for myself, what am I (1:14). My individual contribution is only truly significant if it benefits the community. By assiduously promoting my individual viewpoint, even to the extent of inviting some degree of dissension, I am fulfilling my unique mission. However, if after forcefully advocating my opinion, I am still unable to sway my peers, then I must clearly subordinate my interests to those of the community. This theme of legitimate individual differences subordinated to the communal interest is reflected in three distinct spheres (often discussed by Sfas Emes): (a) the realm of time; (b) the soul and (c) the universe itself. In the realm of time, the Six Days of Creation — during which Hashem created the individual components of His universe — yield to the Shabbos, the day known as כּוֹלֵל כָּל הַיָּמִים, the unifying force behind all of Creation. [Refer to our commentary on mishnah 8 for further discussion and, especially, the role of the ten creations in promoting unity among Hashem's diverse creations.] In the realm of the Divine soul, Klal Yisrael (ideally) plays the role of unifying the many diverse souls (and ideologies) of mankind into a cohesive whole, paying homage to the Creator of all souls. Within Klal Yisrael, the tzaddik plays a similar role, integrating within himself the many outstanding features of individual Jews. [See Days of Joy, pp. 261-264, for further discussion of the unifying role of the tzaddik, particularly Mordechai.] Finally, Eretz Yisrael, and especially Zion (described in Tehillim 50:2 as מִכְלַל יֹפִי, consummation of beauty), contains within its borders a sampling of all of the beauty found in the universe.

◆§ Antagonists Become "Mechutanim"

אָמַר פַּעַם ,,אִם הַמַּחֲלוֹקֶת לְשֵׁם שָׁמַיִם, מִתּוֹךְ אֱמֶת, סוֹפָהּ לְהִתְקַיֵּם, דְּהַיְנוּ
שֶׁבַּדּוֹרוֹת אַחֲרוֹנִים יִשְׁתַּדְּכוּ זֶה בָּזֶה.''

Perhaps the greatest indication that contending parties are arguing for Hashem's sake is that eventually the antagonists become close friends. In fact, the Kotzker Rebbe noted that eventually the descendants of the antagonists will marry into each other's families.

endure; but one that is not for the sake of Heaven will not endure. What sort of dispute was for the sake of Heaven? — The dispute between Hillel and Shammai. And which was not for the sake of Heaven? — The dispute of Korach and his entire company.

■ סוֹפָהּ לְהִתְקַיֵּם — *Will endure.*

◆§ The Litmus Test of Unity

הגם דגבי תורה ומצות אמרו מתוך שלא לשמים בא לשמה. אבל מחלוקת צריך
להיות רק לשם שמים.
ואז ניתקן לבוא לאחדות ... שאין סופה להתקיים פ׳ שאינו בא לאחדות ונשאר
במחלוקת.

While certain other spiritual ventures (such as Torah study) may be undertaken even for reasons which are not absolutely pure, dispute and controversy may be fomented only, solely, for Hashem's sake. Indeed, the litmus test of whether an argument was undertaken for the sake of Heaven is its eventual conclusion: Did it ultimately lead to a more harmonious relationship between the antagonists? As the *mishnah* reminds us, a dispute *for the sake of Heaven*, סוֹפָהּ לְהִתְקַיֵּם, *will endure* — i.e. it will lead to an enduring relationship and harmony (*Sfas Emes, Korach 5635*).

◆§ Even for Spiritual Growth

כי גם מי שרוצה לתקן עצמו לעלות למדריגה אינו מקרא לשם שמים. אף כי גם
זה טוב הוא. כן נראה לכאורה מ״מ כשהוא במחלוקת צריך להיות ממש לשם
שמים בלבד ואז ניתקן לבוא לאחדות. אבל ביש בו קצת נגיעה צריכין להיות רק
בשלום.

The apparently redundant term כָּל, *all*, includes even those controversies that are undertaken for the sake of spiritual growth. Korach cloaked his rebellion with the rhetoric of sanctity [כָּל הָעֵדָה כֻּלָּם קְדֹשִׁים, *for the entire assembly — all of them — are holy* (*Bamidbar* 16:3)]. Even if he was sincere in this regard, he was still not justified in fomenting controversy (ibid.)

◆§ Both Sides Are Correct

פירוש שלשניהם יש קיום כיון שהכוונה אחד, ומחלוקת קרח לא היה לשם שמים.

The term סוֹפָה לְהִתְקַיֵּם may be referring to the fact that *both* approaches will eventually play a role in the formulation of the final halachic ruling. Just as the opinions of Shammai are Torah even though they are not followed in practice, had Korach cooperated with Moshe and Aharon, he too would have played a role in the transmission of Torah.

Since Korach was not motivated for Hashem's sake, his opinions never became part of *Klal Yisrael's* heritage.

৵ Learn From Heaven!

שר של אש ושר של מים ע״י צווי הבורא ית׳ נעשה שלום ביניהם.

The term שָׁמַיִם, *heaven*, should be interpreted literally. Just as incompatible elements such as fire and water — and the heavenly angels which control these opposing forces — join together to form the firmament, performing the Divine will, so too, seemingly incompatible individuals can "fuse" their efforts to enhance the glory of Hashem (*Sfas Emes, Korach* 5640).

■ מַחֲלֹקֶת קֹרַח וְכָל עֲדָתוֹ — *The dispute of Korach and his entire company.*

৵ Korach's Dispute — Not Moshe's

ואמר מחלוקת קרח וכל עדתו ולא אמר קרח ומשה כמו שמאי והלל, אבן כיון
שמצד משה רבינו ע״ה נתקיים כי כוונתו לשם שמים לכן לא הזכירו.

With regard to the argument between Korach and Moshe the *mishnah* mentions only Korach, but in referring to the dispute between Hillel and Shammai it mentions both disputants. Why?

We suggest that the two situations were not identical. Only Korach's position of open defiance to Torah and its authorities was not intended for Hashem's sake. Moshe's staunch defense of *Klal Yisrael's* most cherished institutions and leaders, on the other hand, was undertaken for Heaven's sake. Similarly, it is only Korach's position in this dispute that has no future relevance. Moshe's resounding defense of all that we venerate is certainly of lasting significance. In regard to the dispute between Hillel and Shammai, however, both positions were for the sake of Heaven, and both opinions have lasting relevance.

◆§ The Internal Dispute Between Korach and His Followers

וזה שאמר התנא ואיזה מחלוקת שאינה לשם שמים זו מחלוקת קרח ועדתו
ר״ל שהם היו ר״ן איש והתאוו כל אחד כהונה גדולה כפי׳ רש״י ז״ל ונמצא גם
ביניהם היה לבם פרודות רק נגד משה רבינו היו כולם כאחד בעצה רעה לחלוק
עליו.

According to the *Noam Elimelech*,[1] our *mishnah* is referring to the internal dispute between Korach, who sought the High Priesthood for himself, and his 250 followers, who also sought the same position (cf. *Bamidbar* 16:6, *Rashi* s.v. זאת עשו). He reasoned that one of the most compelling indications that participants in a dispute are not motivated by concern for the glorification of Hashem's Name is the constant bickering among themselves, as occurred to Korach's group (*Maggidei HaEmes*).

◆§ Korach's Obstinance

המפרשים מדקדקים דה״ול למימר זו מחלוקת קרח עם משה כמו שאמר ברישא
מחלוקת הלל ושמאי. ויש ליישב על פי משא״כ באמרי אמת וז״ל מחלוקת קרח
היתה שלא לשמה שלא היתה לשם שמים, והיה עצה לתקן זה על ידי משה רבינו.
אבל קרח לא רצה בזה אלא שיהיה על ידי עצמו וזה לא היה יכול לעשות, ולכן לא
היה באפשרותו להישאר בחיים, שלא לשמה סמא דמותא.

Perhaps by referring to this as Korach's dispute rather than Korach's dispute with Moses, the *mishnah* is pinpointing the essence of Korach's problem — his refusal to engage in a true dialogue with Moshe. Had he discussed his concerns with Moshe, then his dispute would have been *with* Moshe rather than *against* him. It is only because the dispute was contained entirely *within* Korach's inner coterie that the dispute — and its protagonists — were relegated to oblivion (adapted from *Maggidei HaEmes*).

21.

■ בָּל הַמְזַכֶּה אֶת הָרַבִּים אֵין חֵטְא בָּא עַל יָדוֹ — *Whoever influences the masses to become meritorious shall not be the cause of sin.*

---

1. This thought is also widely attributed to the *Chasam Sofer*.

וְכָל הַמַּחֲטִיא אֶת הָרַבִּים, אֵין מַסְפִּיקִין בְּיָדוֹ לַעֲשׂוֹת תְּשׁוּבָה. מֹשֶׁה זָכָה וְזִכָּה אֶת הָרַבִּים, זְכוּת הָרַבִּים תָּלוּי בּוֹ, שֶׁנֶּאֱמַר: "צִדְקַת יהוה עָשָׂה, וּמִשְׁפָּטָיו עִם יִשְׂרָאֵל." יָרָבְעָם בֶּן נְבָט חָטָא וְהֶחֱטִיא אֶת הָרַבִּים, חֵטְא הָרַבִּים תָּלוּי בּוֹ, שֶׁנֶּאֱמַר: "עַל חַטֹּאות יָרָבְעָם אֲשֶׁר חָטָא, וַאֲשֶׁר הֶחֱטִיא אֶת יִשְׂרָאֵל."

[כב] כָּל מִי שֶׁיֵּשׁ בְּיָדוֹ שְׁלֹשָׁה דְבָרִים הַלָּלוּ, הוּא מִתַּלְמִידָיו שֶׁל אַבְרָהָם אָבִינוּ; וּשְׁלֹשָׁה דְבָרִים

◆§ How Many Constitutes the "Masses"?

צריך עיון שיעור רבים. ולמה שכתב הרע"ב שלא יהא הוא בגיהנם ותלמידיו בגן עדן, אף ביחיד כן.

The *mishnah* assures us that whoever benefits the public will never be a catalyst causing others to sin. The question occurs: What constitutes "the masses"? It is entirely possible that even leaving an impact on *one* Jew is sufficient to merit the *mishnah's* assurance. This contention is based on the Bartenura's explanation, כְּדֵי שֶׁלֹּא יְהֵא הוּא בְגֵיהִנֹּם וְתַלְמִידָיו בְּגַן עֵדֶן, *so that he not be consigned to Gehinnom while his disciples enjoy Gan Eden.* Based on this reason, even influencing one individual for good should be a sufficient basis to escape *Gehinnom.*

■ — וְכָל הַמַּחֲטִיא אֶת הָרַבִּים, אֵין מַסְפִּיקִין בְּיָדוֹ לַעֲשׂוֹת תְּשׁוּבָה — *But one who influences the masses to sin will not be given the means to repent.*

◆§ Why Did Yeravam Merit a Chance to Repent?

ק' דאחז"ל אחזו הקב"ה וא"ל חזור בך הרי דהספיק בידו לעשות תשובה, וי"ל ע"י שהי' צדיק גדול מעיקרא והי' מקודם מזכה את הרבים, עוד נראה כי אם הי' עושה תשובה הי' מחזיר גם כולם למוטב ול"ש הטעם שיהי' הוא בג"ע ותלמידיו בגיהנם וחזור בך פי' עם הסייעתא שלך.

It is surprising that Yeravam, who is cited in the *mishnah* as the paragon of one who causes others to sin, *did* receive an opportunity to repent (cf. *Sanhedrin* 101b). This seemingly contradicts our *mishnah's* assertion that such a villainous individual can never repent.

the masses to sin will not be given the means to repent. Moses was meritorious and influenced the masses to be meritorious, so the merit of the masses was to his credit, as it is said (Devarim 33:21): "Carrying out God's justice and His ordinances with Israel." Yeravam ben Nevat sinned and caused the masses to sin, so the sin of the masses is charged against him, as it is said (I Melachim 15:30): "For the sins of Yeravam that he committed and that he caused Israel to commit.".

[22] *Whoever has the following three traits is among the disciples of our forefather Avraham; and [whoever*

Perhaps, Yeravam was offered the opportunity to repent because he had previously been righteous and positively influenced others (ibid.). It is also possible that when Hashem asked Yeravam to repent, He meant for Yeravam to lead all of his followers in repentance. The leader who cannot repent is one who is unable to dissuade his followers from continuing on the path on which he had initially led them.

22.

■ עַיִן ... אָבִינוּ אַבְרָהָם שֶׁל מִתַּלְמִידָיו הוּא הַלָּלוּ, דְּבָרִים שְׁלֹשָׁה בְּיָדוֹ שֶׁיֵּשׁ מִי כָּל
שְׁפָלָה וְנֶפֶשׁ נְמוּכָה, וְרוּחַ טוֹבָה, — *Whoever has the following three traits is among the disciples of our forefather Avraham ... a good eye, a humble spirit and an undemanding soul.*

◄§ Avraham's Mission

דמאחר דכתיב אשר יצוה כו' ושמרו א"כ הוא מלמד לנו איך לעבוד את הקב"ה
וע"י ג' מדות הנ"ל זוכין לאהוב את ה' שהיא מדתו של אאע"ה כדמייתי קרא
להנחיל אוהבי יש שע"י ג' מדות הנ"ל שהם במחשבה דיבור ומעשה זוכין אל
אהבת הבורא וכתיב בפרשת ק"ש ואהבת את ה' כו' אשר אנכי מצוך היום וציווי
זו בכל יום הוא ע"י אברהם אבינו דכתיב בי' אשר יצוה את בניו.

As disciples of Avraham, we should study carefully the Torah's de-scription of his mission: ה' דֶּרֶךְ וְשָׁמְרוּ אַחֲרָיו בֵּיתוֹ וְאֶת בָּנָיו אֶת יְצַוֶּה אֲשֶׁר לְמַעַן וּמִשְׁפָּט צְדָקָה לַעֲשׂוֹת, *because he commands his children and his household after him that they keep the way of Hashem, doing charity and justice (Bereishis 18:19).*

It is by emulating Avraham's sterling traits of *a good eye, a humble spirit and a meek soul* that we are able to achieve his goal. Avraham served Hashem with every aspect of his personality — thought, speech and practical deeds. The three traits recommended in the *mishnah* correspond to those three realms. By not begrudging the success of others and by thinking of how we could enhance the fortunes of others, we are sanctifying our thought process. A humble spirit includes that we must always speak humbly. And, finally, the meek soul rejects material possessions, and will act in the spirit fostered by Avraham — doing charity and justice. Ultimately, those who emulate Avraham by practicing the traits recommended in the *mishnah* will merit the rare distinction that he achieved — to be known as Hashem's Beloved (cf. *Yeshayahu* 41:8, זֶרַע אַבְרָהָם אֹהֲבִי, *offspring of Avraham who loved Me*). Indeed, the *mishnah* continues, quoting from *Mishlei* 8:21, לְהַנְחִיל אֹהֲבַי יֵשׁ, *to cause those who love Me to inherit an everlasting possession.*

Though Avraham has departed to his eternal reward, his message lives on — to love Hashem, just as he loved his Creator. The Torah's command to love Hashem [וְאָהַבְתָּ אֵת ה' אֱלֹהֶיךָ, *you shall love Hashem, your God (Devarim* 6:5)] is really a plea to emulate Avraham Avinu. By modeling our behavior on that of Avraham, we can attain the same objective — love of Hashem. The critical importance of this commandment is signified by its recitation twice a day in the *Shema*; it is at the very heart of *Yiddishkeit.* It may also refer to Avraham's message of love which is transmitted to his descendants every day — to do charity and justice.

✂ Being a Talmid: Emulating Your Rebbi

פי' שהאבות הקדושים פעלו כל אלה המדות לדורות וכל מה שמתקן האדם עצמו ידע שהוא בכחם, רק כמו"ש הבוחר בדרכיהם ועי"ז עושה כמעשיהם, לכן כל מי שיש בו אלה המדות הוא מתלמידיו של אאע"ה שכשאמר אנכי עפר ואפר ביטל עצמו וכל זרעו אחריו להשי"ת.

The expression *"among the disciples of"* implies that we are following in the footsteps of these individuals generations later. In fact, all that we accomplish in contemporary times is because of the precedent set by the Patriarchs, beginning with Avraham. However, in order to earn the distinction of being a disciple of the Patriarchs, it is necessary to emulate their sterling character traits and especially the three traits specified in our *mishnah. Chazal* tell us (*Bereishis Rabbah* 76:3), that only one who carefully studies their path, in order to emulate their ways, can truly be considered a *talmid.* The *rebbi-talmid* relationship that spans generations of Jewish life is more than merely *following the teachings* of *Klal Yisrael's* founders. It also means *acting* as they did. While certainly a formidable challenge, the Patriarchs themselves, through their sterling behavior, made it so much easier for their children to follow in their ways. When, for instance, Avraham described himself as עָפָר וָאֵפֶר, *dust and ash (Bereishis* 18:27), he enabled us all to practice the virtue of רוּחַ נְמוּכָה, *a humble spirit.*

◄§ Evidence of Avraham's Traits

עיין הרע"ב, ועוד י"ל נפש שפלה מרכוש סדום ועין טובה מהכנסת אורחים.

Each of the traits enumerated in the *mishnah* as being attributed to Avraham is being supported by the Patriarch's behavior as related in the Torah. According to the *Bartenura*, Avraham's generosity was demonstrated by his decision to permit the king of Sodom to keep all the spoils that had been recovered from the Four Kings (cf. *Bereishis* 14:21-24). His humility was evident from his self-characterization as "dust and ash" (loc. cit. 18:27). Finally, his shunning of material pleasure[1] was indicated by many things, including his total unawareness of even his own wife's beauty (cf. *Rashi, Bereishis* 12:11).

Alternatively, we may suggest that his willingness to part with the spoils of Sodom is also evidence of his total disdain of material goods. However, Avraham's generosity is amply demonstrated by his royal treatment of all guests.

◄§ The Benefits of Being Avraham's Talmid

איתא במדרש לעתיד לבא אברהם אבינו יושב על פתח גיהנם ואינו מניח אדם
מהול מישראל לירד לתוכה, הרי כך איתא בגמרא שלא יהא הוא בגן עדן
ותלמידיו בגיהנם, על ידי השלשה דברים עין טובה רוח נמוכה ונפש שפילה נעשים
מתלמידיו של אברהם אבינו.
החסידים מתגעגים אחרי רבי ... למה לא יבקשו לקנות לעצמם את שלשת המצות
הטובות ... ואז יהיו מתלמידיו של אברהם אבינו ע"ה ואברהם אע"ה יהי להם
לרבי.

Chazal relate (*Bereishis Rabbah* 48:8) that Avraham Avinu sits beside the gateway to *Gehinnom* and prevents anyone who was circumcised from entering.

It follows that the Patriarch would similarly prevent any of his disciples (who emulate his traits) from being condemned to *Gehinnom*. It would be inappropriate that the leader enjoy *Gan Eden* while his disciples be consigned to the bottomless abyss of *Gehinnom* (*Imrei Emes, Maggidei HaEmes*).

In a similar vein, the great chassidic rebbe, R' Simchah Bunim, always urged his *chassidim* to not only content themselves with a contemporary rebbe but also emulate the three traits of Avraham and thereby acquire for themselves the greatest *rebbi*, Avraham Avinu (*Maggidei HaEmes*).

---

1. *Editor's Note:* This interpretation reflects the widely accepted approach of נֶפֶשׁ being interpreted as referring to the material side of man. This aspect was minimized in Avraham Avinu and his disciples.

אֲחֵרִים, הוּא מִתַּלְמִידָיו שֶׁל בִּלְעָם הָרָשָׁע. עַיִן טוֹבָה,
וְרוּחַ נְמוּכָה, וְנֶפֶשׁ שְׁפָלָה, תַּלְמִידָיו שֶׁל אַבְרָהָם אָבִינוּ.

■ **כָּל מִי שֶׁיֵּשׁ בְּיָדוֹ שְׁלֹשָׁה דְבָרִים הַלָּלוּ ... וּשְׁלֹשָׁה דְבָרִים אֲחֵרִים** — *Whoever has the following three traits ... and [whoever has] three different traits.*

◆§ Is There a Middle Way?

ולא נתבאר אם אין לו כל הג׳ מדות מהו. וי״ל כי אלו הג׳ מתנגדים זה לזה כי
מי שנפשו שפלה ודי לו במה שהוא, קשה להיות לו עין טובה לחבירו שיהיה לו
כל טוב ומי שנפשו רחבה על כל פנים יש לו עין טובה לחבירו גם כן, לכן מי שהוא
עין טובה אף שאין לו נפש שפלה הוא מתלמידיו של אברהם אבינו.
יש לדקדק האם אין דרך ממוצעת בין להיות מתלמידיו של א״א לבין להיות
מתלמידיו של בלעם הרשע. ואאז״ל תירץ כי עין טובה האמיתית היא שהאדם
רוצה שלחבירו יהיה כל טוב אף שלו בעצמו יש רק קב חרובין, אבל מי שיש לו
כל טוב ורוצה שגם לחבירו יהיה כל טוב זו מדה בינונית.
והתלמיד הרחוק ביותר של אאע״ה שמתקרב לתלמיד הרחוק ביותר מבלעם
הרשע ביניהם יש את שלשת החילוקים הללו של המשנה.

It is virtually impossible for any one individual to embody *all* of Avraham's sterling traits. For example, it is difficult to simultaneously personally subsist on very little (נֶפֶשׁ שְׁפָלָה) and yet be exceedingly magnanimous towards others (עַיִן טוֹבָה). On the other hand, someone who adopts a more comfortable lifestyle for himself (נֶפֶשׁ רְחָבָה) is less likely to begrudge others similar amenities. It follows, then, that those practicing *any* one of these traits (while not sufficient) deserve the distinction of being considered among Avraham's disciples (*Avos, Sfas Emes*).

Alternatively, we may argue that there is a middle road between being a disciple of Avraham or of Bilam. While the true disciple of Avraham subsists on very little (cf. *Taanis* 24b discussing how R' Chanina ben Dosa subsisted on a meager portion of carobs), yet wishes that his peer could live amidst splendor, not everyone can display so generous an attitude towards others. For most people, it is sufficient to live in comparative comfort oneself while wishing others the same amenities. This very common approach to life — while typical of Avraham Avinu — is certainly far removed from the contemptuous lifestyle of the wicked Bilam (*Imrei Emes, Maggidei HaEmes*).

On the other hand, the *Pnei Menachem* understood that these three traits serve as the "great divide" between *any* of Avraham's *talmidim* and *any* of Bilam's disciples. Certainly, many significant differences existed between Avraham and Bilam, well beyond the three traits enumerated in the *mishnah*. However, these three attributes serve as the defining factors. Any one of *has] three different traits is among the disciples of the wicked Bilam. Those who have a good eye, a humble spirit and an undemanding soul are the disciples of our forefather Avraham. Those who have an*

Avraham's *talmidim* — no matter how remote — and any one of Bilam's disciples — as estranged as they may be from their mentor — differ in respect to these three specific traits (*Maggidei HaEmes*).

■ עַיִן טוֹבָה, וְרוּחַ נְמוּכָה, וְנֶפֶשׁ שְׁפָלָה — *Those who have a good eye, a humble spirit and an undemanding soul.*

◆§ Is This the Entire "Gap" Between Avraham and Bilam?

ההיפך שכנגד אלו השלשה דברים הוא קנאה תאוה וכבוד ואל אלו הג' אין אזהרה אלא הם בכלל דרך ארץ שקדמה לתורה. אברהם אבינו המשיך דרך עוד קודם התורה בכדי שיוכלו ליישר את הגוף.

Please refer to our previous remarks in which we suggested that these three traits invariably distinguish between Avraham's and Bilam's disciples.

We may extend the point by suggesting that the character traits discussed here include *all* other traits. In particular, they correspond to the three base character traits denounced above (4:28): jealousy, lust and glory.

It is fitting that the distinction between Avraham's disciples and Bilam's is defined in terms of character traits rather than specific practices. This is significant all the more since Avraham Avinu's singular accomplishment was to instill in his followers a sense of decorum well before the Torah was given. As *Chazal* say, דֶּרֶךְ אֶרֶץ קָדְמָה לַתּוֹרָה, *respect and good manners are a prerequisite to Torah study* (cf. *Yalkut Bereishis* 3) (*Imrei Emes, Maggidei HaEmes*).

■ עַיִן טוֹבָה — *A good eye.*

◆§ Finding the Good in Every Aspect of Life

פירוש עין טובה שכל מה שהוא רואה מכיר בו חסד וטובת הבורא יתברך שמו והכל טוב בעיניו ובכח זה נעשה טוב וכדאיתא גבי נחום איש גם זו שאברהם ... אעפ"י שהוא דין חשבה לצדקה.

No one exemplified this trait better than the legendary Nachum (*Ish Gamzu*) who, in response to his many tribulations, would always react by saying גַּם זוּ לְטוֹבָה, "this is also for the good." This trait of always perceiving good was

עַיִן רָעָה, וְרוּחַ גְּבוֹהָה, וְנֶפֶשׁ רְחָבָה, תַּלְמִידָיו שֶׁל בִּלְעָם הָרָשָׁע. מַה בֵּין תַּלְמִידָיו שֶׁל אַבְרָהָם אָבִינוּ לְתַלְמִידָיו שֶׁל בִּלְעָם הָרָשָׁע? תַּלְמִידָיו שֶׁל אַבְרָהָם אָבִינוּ אוֹכְלִין בָּעוֹלָם הַזֶּה, וְנוֹחֲלִין הָעוֹלָם הַבָּא, שֶׁנֶּאֱמַר: ,,לְהַנְחִיל אֹהֲבַי יֵשׁ, וְאֹצְרֹתֵיהֶם אֲמַלֵּא.'' אֲבָל

initiated by Avraham of whom it says, וְהֶאֱמִן בַּה' וַיַּחְשְׁבֶהָ לּוֹ צְדָקָה, *he trusted Hashem, and He reckoned it to him as righteousness* (Bereishis 15:6), which we may interpret as follows: Avraham trusted Hashem and he considered everything that He did (even the apparent suffering) as a form of charity (adapted from *Sfas Emes*).

◆§ Shielding His Eyes From Evil

יש לפרש עינים טובות עינים שמורות בקדושה. אבל אם ח"ו אינו שומר את העינים עין רעה.

A true disciple of Avraham Avinu ensures that his eyes (his outlook) and perspective remain pure by shielding them from the lust and physical passions of This World. By contrast, Bilam and his followers are always seeking means of satiating their physical passions (*Lev Simchah, Maggidei HaEmes*).

◆§ Detecting a Good Eye

אפשר להכיר צר עין גם בין הממונים לחלק את המנות בסעודות גדולות. כי הטוב עין יברור תמיד המנה היותר יפה שנשאר לו במגש עד שלאחרון ישאר הקטנה יותר, ואילו הצר עין יברור תמיד המנה הקטנה קודם וישאר לאחרון המנה הי גדולה. ומזה ניכר ההפרש ביניהם, הגם ששניהם בהכרח יחלקו את כל המנות שהביאו אתם לחלקם.

The *Chiddushei HaRim* suggested that one can distinguish an individual's generosity by observing how he distributes portions to guests. The generous individual will always distribute the larger portions first while the parsimonious host, who experiences difficulty in sharing, will always distribute the smaller portions first (*Maggidei HaEmes*).

■ עַיִן רָעָה, וְרוּחַ גְּבוֹהָה, וְנֶפֶשׁ רְחָבָה, תַּלְמִידָיו שֶׁל בִּלְעָם הָרָשָׁע — *Those who have an evil eye, an arrogant spirit and a greedy soul are among the disciples of the wicked Bilam.*

evil eye, an arrogant spirit and a greedy soul are the disciples of the wicked Bilam. How are the disciples of our forefather Avraham different from the disciples of the wicked Bilam? The disciples of our forefather Avraham enjoy [the fruits of their good deeds] in This World and inherit the World to Come, as it is said (Mishlei 8:21): "To cause those who love Me to inherit an everlasting possession [the World to Come] and I will fill their storehouses [in

---

◆§ What Does Bilam Teach Us?

יש לדייק מה הלשון מתלמידיו, וכי בשביל זה צריך להיות תלמיד הלא כל שוטה מתנהג כן. אך כי גם הרשעים מכניעים עצמם והרי אמר אם יתן לי כו׳, מלא ביתו כו׳, לא אוכל לעבור כו׳, ומזה עצמו נלמד שהי׳ נפש רחבה להחטיאם. המשנה קורא תלמידיו של בלעם הרשע כנראה יש איזה לימוד והענין כי בלעם רצה להכניס בלבות בני ישראל שיכולין לעבוד את השי״ת גם עם הפסולת כעין עירוב טוב ורע אבל לבני ישראל דרך מיוחד מאברהם אבינו ע״ה כולו להשם. אולם באמת אפשר ללמוד הרבה מפרשה של בלעם ... בלעם קטרג בכל מקום שיכול, וכשראה שאינו יכול להרגם נתן לעמון ומואב עצה להחטיאם, כדאיתא קשה המחטיאו יותר מן ההורגו, מסר נפשו ונתן להם עזה רעה, בכאן מצא פינה להאחז בה. והלימוד מפרשה זו למדה טובה מרובה, אם על ידי מסירות נפש יכול היה בלעם להגיע לסוף כל סוף למשהו, בודאי שיהודי יכול להגיע על ידי מסירות נפש, ופנחס אבן היה להיפר, שמסר נפשו לקדושה והוציא ובלעו בלעו מפיו. א יוד האקט אדורך מיט קדושה. הוא נתן כח שיוכל יהודי למסור נפשו.

It is difficult to perceive Bilam as a mentor teaching disciples. In particular, the attributes that he espoused are traits that an ignoramus could practice, even without benefit of a teacher.

Apparently, Bilam sought to teach his followers how to simultaneously speak with humility and still act in a haughty fashion. Few individuals could match the pious rhetoric uttered by Bilam: אִם יִתֶּן לִי בָלָק מְלֹא בֵיתוֹ כֶּסֶף וְזָהָב לֹא אוּכַל לַעֲבֹר אֶת פִּי ה׳ אֱלֹהָי לַעֲשׂוֹת קְטַנָּה אוֹ גְדוֹלָה, *If Balak will give me his houseful of silver and gold, I cannot transgress the word of Hashem, my God, to do anything small or great (Bamidbar 22:18).* Yet, this lofty rhetoric was nothing more than a smokescreen for Bilam's lust for wealth and fame.

In a somewhat similar vein, Bilam sought to inculcate his disciples with a contradictory combination — Divine service coupled with wretched character traits, the antithesis of Hashem's service. We, the disciples of Avraham, realize that good *midos* are an integral part of Divine service (*Beis Yisrael, Maggidei HaEmes*).

On the other hand, the *Pnei Menachem* pointed out, Bilam unwittingly

תַּלְמִידָיו שֶׁל בִּלְעָם הָרָשָׁע יוֹרְשִׁין גֵּיהִנֹּם, וְיוֹרְדִין לִבְאֵר שַׁחַת, שֶׁנֶּאֱמַר: "וְאַתָּה אֱלֹהִים תּוֹרִדֵם לִבְאֵר שַׁחַת, אַנְשֵׁי דָמִים וּמִרְמָה לֹא יֶחֱצוּ יְמֵיהֶם, וַאֲנִי אֶבְטַח בָּךְ."

taught us a lesson that can be utilized to serve Hashem: the incredible effect of total dedication to a cause. The wicked seer was possessed with the objective of destroying the Jewish nation. After repeated unsuccessful efforts to curse the Jews, he entrusted Amon and Moab with the mission of bringing down the nation. They, in turn, carried out their assignment with uncanny (and unfortunate) success, culminating in the death of thousands at the plains of Moab. We thereby learn from Bilam the impact of dedication and perseverance.

Based on the premise that good deeds are more effective than evil ones (cf. *Makkos 5b, Rashi s.v. על*), we realize that our own dedicated efforts for Torah will certainly produce bountiful results. In fact it was Pinchas' selfless dedication that finally put an end to Bilam's objective of eliminating the Jewish nation (*Maggidei HaEmes*).

■ מַה בֵּין תַּלְמִידָיו שֶׁל אַבְרָהָם אָבִינוּ לְתַלְמִידָיו שֶׁל בִּלְעָם הָרָשָׁע — *How are the disciples of our forefather Avraham different from the disciples of the wicked Bilam?*

◆§ The Disciples — Not Themselves

קשה למה אמרו בין אברהם אבינו ע"ה לבלעם הרשע. אלא שהבדל בין אברהם אע"ה לבין בלעם לא יבין איש בקלות, משום שבלעם היה צבוע ומראה עצמו צדיק כאברהם אבינו ע"ה, והיה מרמה את הבריות. אבל בין התלמידים הכירו מיד.

The *mishnah* distinguishes between the *disciples* of Avraham and those of Bilam, rather than between Avraham and Bilam themselves, simply because it would be almost impossible to discern any difference between the great prophet and the wicked seer. On the surface, to the nondiscriminating observer the differences between Avraham and Bilam appear to be negligible. A highly gifted orator and manipulator, Bilam experienced no difficulty in convincing people that he was a righteous as Avraham. However, his disciples who were not quite as gifted in the art of deception, could not conceal how different they were from Avraham's disciples (*R' Yitzchak of Worka, Maggidei HaEmes*).

◆§ Are These the Only Distinctions?

ולא אמר החילוק שזה עושה מצוות וזה אינו עושה, אלא יש בני אדם שעושין

This world]." But the disciples of the wicked Bilam inherit Gehinnom and descend into the well of destruction, as it is said (Tehillim 55:24): "And You, O God, shall lower them into the well of destruction: men of bloodshed and deceit will not live out half their days; but as for me, I will trust in You."

מצוות ומתענין משבת לשבת ואף על פי כן יש בהם ג׳ מדות הללו, מתלמידיו של בלעם הרשע הם.

גילו לנו חז״ל כי אותו הרשע הי׳ היפוך מצדקת אברהם ע״ה ... כי הרשע הי׳ מכוין רגע זעמו של הקב״ה ... והרשע כל מגמתו למצוא אותו הזעם אבל הצדיקים מכוונים למצוא עת רצון . . .ולא עוד אלא שזוכין למצוא חוט של חסד בעוה״ז ... שע״י אותו הג׳ מדות טובות ... זוכין למצוא החסד בכל יום בעוה״ז כהצדיקים שזוכין למצוא חסד ה׳ בעולם אין כל הרשעים יכולין לבטל מהם כמ״ש מים רבים לא יוכלו לכבות את האהבה כו.

By *not* stating the obvious distinctions, that Avraham's disciples perform *mitzvos* and Bilam's commit *aveiros*, the *mishnah* is implying that some of Bilam's followers may also perform *mitzvos*. They may even appear to be very pious, to the extent of fasting every day. However, beneath this transparent piety there lies a very flawed inner personality, possessed with the same negative traits as their mentor, Bilam — *an evil eye, an arrogant spirit and a greedy soul*.

Upon further analysis, we may conclude that the traits specified here are not merely aspects of Avraham's and Bilam's personalities, but rather lie at the core of their very different natures.

Chazal note that Bilam possessed the uncanny knack of calculating the infinitesimal moment every day when Hashem is "angry." He would then exploit this talent for the purpose of invoking Hashem's wrath against His people. On the other hand, Avraham and his followers search for the moments of Divine goodwill and grace. In fact, not only do Avraham's and Bilam's disciples seek to evoke *preexisting* attributes of Hashem (i.e. anger, mercy), but through their behavior, they actually "reinforce" and augment those attributes. For example, Hashem's Attribute of Wrath would be totally "dormant," were it not for the evil behavior of Bilam and his disciples as reflected by their characteristics. Likewise, the righteous, deeds of Avraham and his disciples, exemplified by their characteristics actually *create* new dimensions of Divine kindness, a concept described by *Chazal* as חוּט שֶׁל חֶסֶד, a "thread" of Divine kindness spun by the deeds of the righteous. Fortunately, the goodwill evoked by the righteous good deeds far outweighs the Divine wrath evoked by the wicked (cf. *Makkos* 5b, *Rashi*, s.v. על). As Shlomo says (*Shir HaShirim* 8:7), מַיִם רַבִּים לֹא יוּכְלוּ לְכַבּוֹת אֶת הָאַהֲבָה, *the mighty waters* (i.e. the multitudes of evil deeds committed by the wicked) *can never extinguish the fiery* [eternal] *love* between Hashem and *Klal Yisrael* (*Sfas Emes, Balak 5645*).

⦿§ Inspiring Dedication (מְסִירוּת נֶפֶשׁ)

פי' שע"י מדות הללו יכולין לבוא למסירת הנפש שהוא עיקר שהניח אאע"ה ירושה לבנ"י כמ"ש אשר יצוה כו' ביתו אחריו. והוא בחי' ואהבת בכל לבבך נפשך מאודך. ובאמת יש הרבה מדריגות בג' דברים אלו. ומי שמתחיל בג' מדות אלו זוכה להיות מתלמידיו ובא לבחי' מס"נ ולאהוב ה' בכל לבבך נפשך מאודך. ואז נשרשים בו הג' מדות באמת בשלימות.

These traits are significant not only in their own right, but also because of their potent capacity to enable their adherents to selflessly dedicate themselves to Hashem. This sterling trait is identified as Avraham's life mission which he entrusted to his descendants. As the Torah says, לְמַעַן אֲשֶׁר יְצַוֶּה אֶת בָּנָיו וְאֶת בֵּיתוֹ אַחֲרָיו וְשָׁמְרוּ דֶּרֶךְ ה' לַעֲשׂוֹת צְדָקָה וּמִשְׁפָּט, *because he commands his children and his household after him that they keep the way of Hashem, doing charity and justice* (*Bereishis* 18:19).

Avraham, the epitome of dedication to Hashem, desired nothing more than that his children emulate his fealty to Hashem. While it is almost impossible for us to attain Avraham's degree of supreme self-sacrifice, we can in some small measure emulate him by practicing the three traits of *a good eye, humble spirit and an undemanding soul*, mentioned in the *mishnah*. As a result of emulating Avraham's three core traits — of following the example of dedication that he established — we too can develop love of Hashem which is also a three-fold process: וְאָהַבְתָּ אֵת ה' אֱלֹהֶיךָ בְּכָל לְבָבְךָ וּבְכָל נַפְשְׁךָ וּבְכָל מְאֹדֶךָ, *You shall love HASHEM, your God, with all your heart, with all your soul and with all your resources* (*Devarim* 6:5) (5656).

⦿§ Three Attributes, Three Festivals

כי פסח בחי' נפש שפלה לחם עוני. וזה עיקר החירות בנפש שלא יהי' מקושר לתאות בהמיות. והוא בחי' יציאת מצרים שבועות מתן תורה רוח נמוכה שהתורה כמו מים היורדין למקום נמוך והוא מתן תורתינו בחי' רוח. וסוכות הוא בחי' עין טובה היפוך מן הקנאה ולכן מקריבין ע' פרים ושמחים בברכה היורדת לכל האומות ...

וזה שרמזו בפסוק ג' רגלים שרצה לעקור אומה החוגגת ג' רגלים כו' מפני שזה הוא כח ג' דברים הנ"ל.

Bilam's donkey chastised its master for attempting to destroy the Jewish People who celebrate the Three Festivals (*Rashi, Bamidbar* 22:28). By singling out this particular vice (from Bilam's many *aveiros*), the donkey emphasized that the central purpose of Bilam's mission was to prevent the thrice-annual pilgrimage to Yerushalayim. He intended to accomplish this heinous goal not only by cursing *Klal Yisrael* but through his three traits of *an evil eye, an arrogant spirit and a greedy soul*. In fact, Avraham's and Bilam's core characteristics correspond to the Three Festivals. Specifically, the attribute of a humble spirit, limited material aspiration, is highlighted by eating matzah, every Pesach. On Shavuos, we celebrate the Giving of the Torah (compared to water) which always "resides" among those who are humble.[1] And every Succos, *Klal Yisrael* displays its generosity by offering lavish annual sacrifices on behalf of the 70 nations of the gentile world (*Sfas Emes, Balak* 5651).

‎ܝ§‎ Seeking Hashem or Evading Him

ומה זה הלימוד של אותו הרשע. אך הקב"ה ברא העולם בהנהגת הטבע. ויש הנהגה פנימיות. ולזה ניתן הברירה. כי מי שמבטל עצמו אל הנהגת ית' זוכה לחסות בצלו .... וזה הדרך של נחש וקוסם הוא למלאות תאוות הרשע וגבהות רוח שלו וכדאיתא כשפים שמכחישין כח פמליא של מעלה.... והלימוד של אאע"ה לבטל עצמו אל השורש להיות רוח נמוכה ונפש שפילה להמשיך אחר רצונו ית' כמ"ש תמים תהי' עם ה' לכן שמח בחלקו ויש לו עין טובה. והרשעים היפוך זה כל השביעה שלו למלאות תאות לבו ומבקש תחבולות לצאת מגזירת עליון בכח מכשפות וקסמים שהוא היפוך התמימות ... בנ"י לא נחש ביעקב כו' לכן מתגלה להם מה פעל אל בהתגלות הנהגה פנימיות.

Perhaps the clearest distinction between Bilam's and Avraham's disciples was stated by the evil seer himself: כִּי לֹא נַחַשׁ בְּיַעֲקֹב וְלֹא קֶסֶם בְּיִשְׂרָאֵל כָּעֵת יֵאָמֵר לְיַעֲקֹב וּלְיִשְׂרָאֵל מַה פָּעַל אֵל, *For there is no divination in Yaakov and no sorcery in Yisrael. Even now it is said to Yaakov and Yisrael what God has wrought* (Bamidbar 23:23).

Unlike Bilam's disciples who seek to evade Hashem's sovereignty by turning to the occult (cf. *Sanhedrin* 67b), Avraham's disciples turn towards Hashem. The defining character traits of Avraham and Bilam enumerated here similarly reflect their disparate approaches to life. Avraham's disciples, whose sole motive is to fulfill Hashem's will, are naturally humble. Their physical aspirations are modest. Consequently, they are blessed with the capacity to be satisfied with their portion, which, in turn, allows them to view graciously the success of others.

On the other hand, Bilam's evil disciples, whose sole goal is to satiate their passion, chose to evade Hashem's authority. Their core characteristics are not merely indicative of a seriously flawed personality but also signify their intention to live a lifestyle as far removed as possible from the *Shechinah* (*Sfas Emes, Balak* 5652).

---

1. Cf. *Taanis* 7a comparing Torah to water which originates in high places, but always descends.

~§ Allusions to Avraham's and Bilam's Characteristics

כתיב וישכם אברהם בבוקר וגו' ויקח את שני נעריו אתו, ואמר שאחז"ל שכאן
מרומזות הג' מדות הג"ל שכן נע"ר הוא ר"ת נפש עין ובתלמידיו של בלעם
איתא להיפך עין רעה ורוח גבוהה ונפש רחבה. וזה דכתיב ביה הנה אנכי יצאתי
לשטן, דשטן הוא ר"ת שפל טובה נמוכה היפך ממדות בלעם ... כל אדם להכניס
בנערותו, בבוקר.

The *Imrei Emes*, quoting his grandfather, the *Chiddushei HaRim*, noted that both the core characteristics of Avraham and Bilam are alluded to in the Torah. When discussing Avraham's supreme sacrifice, the *Akeidah*, the Torah writes, וַיִּקַּח אֶת שְׁנֵי נְעָרָיו אִתּוֹ, *he took his two young men* (נְעָרָיו) *with him* (*Bereishis* 22:3). The word נַעַר represents the first letters of נֶפֶשׁ, עַיִן, רוּחַ. Similarly, when discussing his determination to thwart Bilam's ill-suited mission, the angel says, הִנֵּה אָנֹכִי יָצָאתִי לְשָׂטָן, *Behold, I went out to impede* (*Bamidbar* 22:32). The word שָׂטָן is composed of the first letters of שְׁפָלָה, טוֹבָה, נְמוּכָה. The angel prevented Bilam from fulfilling his mission to curse *Klal Yisrael* because of his deeply flawed character traits which compared poorly with the sterling *middos* (alluded to in the term שָׂטָן) of *Klal Yisrael*. The words וַיַּשְׁכֵּם אַבְרָהָם בַּבֹּקֶר, *And Avraham awoke in the morning*, be gin the *pasuk* in *Bereishis* which alludes to these character traits; the Torah is suggesting that we cultivate these traits in the "morning" of our life, during our youth (*Maggidei HaEmes*).

~§ True Humility Vs. Feigned Modesty

אך כי גם הרשעים מכניעים עצמם והרי אמר אם יתן לי כו' מלא ביתו כו' מלא
ביתו כו' לא אוכל לעבור כו' ומזה עצמו נלמד שהי' נפש רחבה. כי זה נחשב אצלו
לחשיבות להקב"ה מה שהוא מכניע עצמו אף שהוא חשוב מאוד. וכל ההכנעה
שלו רק כדי לבוא למדריגה מה להתגאות אח"כ וז"ש נופל וגלוי עינים שע"י
ההכנעה בא למדריגתו.

As we noted above, Bilam's rhetoric, at least superficially, differs little from Avraham's. Just as the great prophet pronounced himself to be "dust and ash" (*Bereishis* 18:27), so too the wicked seer proclaims, אִם יִתֶּן לִי בָלָק מְלֹא בֵיתוֹ כֶּסֶף וְזָהָב לֹא אוּכַל לַעֲבֹר אֶת פִּי ה' אֱלֹהָי, *If Balak will give me his houseful of silver and gold, I cannot transgress the word of Hashem, my God* (*Bamidbar* 22:18). However, the crucial distinction lies not in their rhetoric but rather in their ultimate objective. Unlike Avraham whose modesty was genuine, Bilam (who constantly spoke about wealth) utilized humility as a means of achieving his material ambitions. No better description of the wicked seer's true intentions exist than his own words: נֹפֵל וּגְלוּי עֵינָיִם, *while fallen and with uncovered eyes* (ibid. 24:4, 16) — He was humble (נֹפֵל) for the purpose of attaining the status of גְלוּי עֵינָיִם, *open eyes* (i.e. eyes that can see all the secrets of the occult). For him, humility was a form of condescension. Bilam reasoned that if notable individuals such as he would nonetheless act humbly in Hashem's Presence, this would "enhance" Hashem's stature (*Sfas Emes, Balak* 5631).

■ אוֹכְלִין בָּעוֹלָם הַזֶּה וְנוֹחֲלִין הָעוֹלָם הַבָּא — *Enjoy [the fruits of their good deeds] in This World and inherit the World to Come.*

◁§ Learning in This World to Appreciate the Blessings of the World to Come

---

פי' שיכולין לקבל השפע גם בעודם בעוה"ז ועי"ז מתקנים הגוף שהוא כלי לקבל השכר כדאיתא המשל שיש לך כלי לקבל, כי בוודאי השכר בעוה"ב אין לו סוף והשי"ת בטובו חפץ ליתן לכל ברי', אבל כפי תיקון האדם בעולם הזה מכין לו כלים ואוצרות לקבל השכר ז"ש ואוצרותיהם אמלא, וז"ש שאוכלין בעולם הזה נוחלין לעזה"ב כמ"ש.

While this *mishnah* is usually understood to be referring to *two* distinct rewards enjoyed by Avraham's disciples, consuming the bounty of *Olam Hazeh and* inheriting the World to Come, in reality a direct relationship exists between the rewards of This World and the World to Come. By sampling Hashem's bountiful blessings in This World and appreciating that even material blessings come from Him, the body is enabled to receive the truly outstanding blessings of *Olam Haba*. As the *mishnah* continues, לְהַנְחִיל אֹהֲבַי יֵשׁ, *to cause those who love Me to inherit an everlasting possession (Mishlei* 8:21) — by bequeathing to those who love Me (i.e. Avraham's disciples) the material blessings of This World (known as "יֵשׁ," something of substance because of their material nature), וְאֹצְרֹתֵיהֶם אֲמַלֵּא, *I will [eventually be able to] fill their storehouses* (referring to the human body which is the receptacle for all Divine Reward), with the bounty of *Olam Haba*.

◁§ Infusing This World With the Spirit of Olam Haba

בי' אלו העולמות תלוין זה בזה עוה"ז נעלם הקדושה ע"י התאוות וקליפות. ועוה"ב נעלם ע"י שמאין תמצא ונעלמת מכל. אך מי שמוציא האמרה הגניזה בתוך ההעלם שבעוה"ז. זוכה שיתגלה לו ההעלם שבעוה"ב ג"כ. וז"ש להנחיל אוהבי יש שזוכה לראות בבחי' אין כאילו הי' ממשות.

The term נוֹחֲלִין may be related to נַחַל, *stream.* Just as a river originates in a higher location but meanders downstream, so too the true *talmid* of Avraham infuses This World with the lofty atmosphere of The World to Come. The rewards for consecrating This World are subsequently spelled out: לְהַנְחִיל אֹהֲבַי יֵשׁ, those who loved Me in This World will be able to enjoy the intensely spiritual treasures of the World to Come — treasures that are so sublime and lacking in physical substance that they are ordinarily described as אַיִן, *nothing* — with the same intensity and fervor that people reserve for material pleasures which are known as יֵשׁ.

The relationship between consecrating This World (עוֹלָם הַזֶּה) and partaking fully of the spiritual rewards of the World to Come (עוֹלָם הַבָּא) can be deduced from the term עוֹלָם itself, which is related to הֶעְלֵם, *hidden*. By penetrating the veil of materialism that shrouds This World in order to elicit the hidden spark of *kedushah* latent even in This World, we merit to enjoy the sublime treasures of the World to Come (*Sfas Emes, Balak 5631*).

⋙ The Ideal Eretz Yisrael

כי הנה בנ"י זכו לכנוס לארץ ישראל בזכותו של אברהם אע"ה דכתיב וכרות עמו
הברית. ומסתמא זכה לזה ע"י ג' דברים הנ"ל ומצאת את לבבו נאמן לפניך כולל
אלו הג'. והשכר הי' לזכות לנחלת ארץ ישראל שהיא הנאמר עלי' להנחיל אוהבי
יש כו' שא"י דבוק בשורש שלמעלה. ולכן כתיב וכרות כו' לתת. ב"פ לתת שהוא
להיות אוכלין בעוה"ז בדביקות נוחלין לעוה"ב.

Above, we discussed Bilam's plans to thwart *Klal Yisrael's* entry into *Eretz Yisrael*, especially the thrice-annual pilgrimage to Yerushalayim. In response to Bilam's evil designs, the *mishnah* assures us that *Klal Yisrael* will not only conquer *Eretz Yisrael* but will also be able to enjoy the ambiance of the World to Come while residing there (during their life span in This World). The expression "Enjoy in This World and inherit in the World to Come" does not refer to two distinct time periods but rather to the sublime and supreme privilege of living a spiritual, other-worldly existence in *Eretz Yisrael* while nominally residing in This World.

This "double" blessing — enjoying the World to Come while residing in This World — stems from the original covenant that Hashem established with Avraham, which we, as Avraham's disciples, are privileged to enjoy. As we recite in the daily *davening*, וְכָרוֹת עִמּוֹ הַבְּרִית לָתֵת אֶת אֶרֶץ הַכְּנַעֲנִי ... לָתֵת לְזַרְעוֹ, *and You established the covenant with him to give the land of the Canaanite ... to give it to his offspring* (Nechemiah 9:8).

The repetition of the word לָתֵת, *to give*, implies a double gift — the physical *Eretz Yisrael* and its spiritual roots in heaven. Avraham's outstanding traits enumerated in the *mishnah*, the true source of his inheritance of *Eretz Yisrael*, are alluded to in the first segment of this *pasuk* from *Nechemiah*, וּמָצָאתָ אֶת לְבָבוֹ נֶאֱמָן לְפָנֶיךָ, *You found his heart faithful before You*. The true נֶאֱמָן, the individual who places his trust in Hashem, acts humbly, curbs his passions and looks kindly upon everyone (*Sefas Emes, Balak 5651*).

◆§ A Spiritual Existence While in This World

פ׳ שיכולין לקבל השפע בעוה״ז להיות דבוק בשורש לכן לא יחצו ימיהם אפילו
החצי שלמטה בעוה״ז ניטל מהם.

As explained, the expression "eat in This World and Inherit in the World to Come" refers to the ability of Avraham's disciples to maintain a spiritual existence, a lifestyle permeated with the values of *Olam Haba*, while still residing in *Olam Hazeh*. Avraham's disciples, whose sole motive is to be guided by Hashem, merit this great blessing. On the other hand, Bilam's disciples, who seek to evade Hashem, do not truly enjoy even This World. As the *mishnah* concludes, לֹא יֶחֱצוּ יְמֵיהֶם, [they] *shall not live out half their days* (*Tehillim* 55:24). Even the physical half (יֶחֱצוּ) of their days — their existence in This World — is relatively shallow and meaningless since it is totally detached from the spiritual roots of *Olam Haba* (*Sfas Emes, Balak* 5652, 5650).

◆§ A Link Between Two Worlds

פירוש על פי מה דאיתא ר״ש בן יוחאי אומר אבן טובה היתה תלויה בצוארו של
אברהם אבינו שכל חולה הרואה אותו מיד מתרפא. וכתב בקול שמחה דהתואר
הוא שמחבר את הראש והגוף של אדם. והנה אברהם אבינו ע״ה היה רוצה
שיתגלה ממשלתו ית׳ בעולם הזה, והיה מחבר העולם העליון עם עולם התחתון
וכו׳ עיי״ש בדבריו הק׳. וזה שכתוב תלמידיו של אברהם אבינו אוכלין בעולם הזה
ונוחלין העוה״ב היינו ב׳ עולמות כהנ״ל.

Chazal (*Bava Basra* 16b) state that Avraham Avinu wore a precious stone around his neck. Anyone who was ill would be healed simply by gazing at the stone. According to R' Simcha Bunim of Peshis'cha, the neck, which joins the head to the body, represents the link between heaven and earth. Avraham enjoyed the singular ability to infuse the earth with the spirituality of heaven. In the merit of this great accomplishment, Avraham was able to heal the sick.

We, Avraham's disciples, by emulating our great teacher's character traits, also enjoy the unique gift of fusing the materialism of This World with the spirituality of the World to Come (*Maggidei HaEmes*).

◆§ Enjoying Both Worlds

עוד יי״ל דאיתא שישנם מצוות שאדם אוכל פירותיהן בעולם הזה והקרן קיימת
לו לעוה״ב וזה לא שייך בתלמידיו של בלעם הרשע.

[כג] יְהוּדָה בֶן תֵּימָא אוֹמֵר: הֱוֵי עַז כַּנָּמֵר, וְקַל כַּנֶּשֶׁר,
רָץ כַּצְּבִי, וְגִבּוֹר כָּאֲרִי לַעֲשׂוֹת רְצוֹן אָבִיךָ שֶׁבַּשָּׁמָיִם.

According to the *Pnei Menachem*, this "eating in This World and inheriting in The World to Come" refers to the capacity of *Klal Yisrael*, Avraham's disciples, to enjoy the blessings of This World without forfeiting the far more significant blessings of the World to Come. As the Gemara states, אֵלּוּ דְבָרִים שֶׁאָדָם אוֹכֵל פֵּרוֹתֵיהֶם בָּעוֹלָם הַזֶּה וְהַקֶּרֶן קַיֶּמֶת לוֹ לָעוֹלָם הַבָּא, *These are the precepts whose fruits a person enjoys in This World but whose principal remains intact for him in the World to Come (Shabbos 127a)*. This may be because the Jewish people is able to enjoy the physical pleasures of This World without becoming totally immersed in materialism. Bilam's disciples, on the other hand, totally caught up in the material pleasures of This World, forfeit their entire World to Come in favor of the relatively trivial pleasures of This World (*Maggidei HaEmes*).

23.

■ יְהוּדָה בֶן תֵּימָא אוֹמֵר: הֱוֵי עַז כַּנָּמֵר, וְקַל כַּנֶּשֶׁר, רָץ כַּצְּבִי וְגִבּוֹר כָּאֲרִי לַעֲשׂוֹת רְצוֹן אָבִיךָ שֶׁבַּשָּׁמָיִם — *Yehudah ben Teima said: Be bold as a leopard, light as an eagle, swift as a deer and strong as a lion, to carry out the will of your Father in Heaven.*

∼§ Versatility in Divine Service

כנראה שהם מדת מהופכות שאינם מתאחדין במדה אחת רק לעבודת הבורא צריך את כולם.

Each of these animals possesses a unique characteristic (not shared by any other). Moreover, these characteristics are often dichotomous. It is almost impossible to be simultaneously fleet as a deer and strong as a lion. However, the true servant of Hashem — one whose sole motive is to serve Hashem — combines *all* these attributes into his personality.

■ הֱוֵי עַז כַּנָּמֵר — *Be bold as a leopard.*

∼§ Courage Beyond Strength

הנמר אינו כה גבור רק יש בו מדת עזות. מתחילה כשמתחיל אדם לגשת לעבודת ה' צריך להתאמץ אף שאין בו כח מהקדושה ומכל שכן בעל תשובה צריך לאמץ לבו אף שהיצר מכביד לב, זכור מעשיך הראשונים.

[23] *Yehudah ben Teima says: Be bold as a leopard, light as an eagle, swift as a deer and strong as a lion, to carry out the will of your Father in Heaven.*

A leopard is not noted for its brute strength, but rather for its boldness and daring. So too, when serving Hashem, even if we lack the requisite strength to achieve our goals, we need to be bold in expressing our convictions. R' Yehudah ben Teima is especially exhorting the penitent to take a courageous stand in face of the *Yetzer Hara's* numerous attempts to diminish his self-confidence by reminding him of his previous behavior (*Chiddushei HaRim, Maggidei HaEmes*).

■ רָץ כַּצְבִי — *Swift as a deer.*

רץ כצבי זו מעלה גדולה וגם מציל מעבירה כדכתיב ביוסף הצדיק וינס ויצא החוצה.

Be as fleet footed as a deer to escape temptation. Yosef HaTzaddik did not merely walk away from the importunings of Potiphar's wife, he *ran* away — וַיָּנָס וַיֵּצֵא הַחוּצָה, *he fled, and went outside* (*Bereishis* 39:12).

◄§ The Soul's Irresistible Urge

פירוש על פי מה שכתוב ארץ צבי מה צבי עורו אינו מחזיק בשרו כו', כן הוא באדם אשר השי"ת נפח בו רוח חיים והנפש הם מצמצמים הרוח שלא יוכל להתפשט, כי אם לא כן היה עולה לשרשו מרוב תשוקת עלול להעילת כל העילות, אמנם אמת הדבר שעל ידי זה המאסר שהגוף אין מניח להרוח להתפשט כראוי על ידי זה עוד נתוסף כח להתשוקה עד שבכחו להמשיך מעט מעט גם את הלבוש עד שבסוף עולה לשרשו ומסתלק הצדיק בתשלום מעשיו, וזה רץ כצבי שעל ידי שעורו אינו מחזיק לכן רץ בכח יותר למרחוק.

The analogy to a deer may be interpreted homiletically. The Gemara (*Kesubos* 112a) observes that צְבִי עוֹרוֹ אֵינוֹ מַחֲזִיק בְּשָׂרוֹ, once a deer's hide is removed from the animal, it does not fit snugly over its skin. So too, the Jewish soul, emanating from Hashem, seeks to ascend to its Creator. For a while — during our life span — the body prevents the soul from fulfilling its aspirations. Eventually, upon the completion of its mission in This World, the body can no longer contain the soul (just as a deer's hide can no longer cover its skin). The soul, once liberated from its material constraints, is finally able to flee This World, as swiftly as a deer, and accomplish its goal — the inevitable rendezvous with Hashem, its Creator.

[כד] הוא הָיָה אוֹמֵר: עַז פָּנִים לְגֵיהִנֹּם, וּבְשֶׁת פָּנִים לְגַן עֵדֶן. יְהִי רָצוֹן מִלְּפָנֶיךָ יהוה אֱלֹהֵינוּ וֵאלֹהֵי אֲבוֹתֵינוּ שֶׁיִּבָּנֶה בֵּית הַמִּקְדָּשׁ בִּמְהֵרָה בְיָמֵינוּ וְתֵן חֶלְקֵנוּ בְּתוֹרָתֶךָ.

⋖§ Performing Mitzvos With Enthusiasm

לכן יסוד עבודת האדם הוא התשוקה כמו שאמרו חכמים עבודה שבלב זו תפלה היינו השתוקקות התלהבות הלב תמיד להתדבק בו יתברך הוא עיקר העבודה.

By urging us to be as fleet as a deer, the *mishnah* is emphasizing the importance of performing *mitzvos* with enthusiasm. Prayer, one of the essential pillars of Judaism, is described as עֲבוֹדָה שֶׁבַּלֵּב, *service of the heart* — serving Hashem with one's *heart* (i.e. heartfelt enthusiasm). *Avodas Hashem* consists not only of *acting* appropriately but of serving Hashem with heartfelt enthusiasm.

24.

■ עַז פָּנִים לְגֵיהִנֹּם, וּבְשֶׁת פָּנִים לְגַן עֵדֶן — *The brazen goes to Gehinnom, but the shamefaced goes to the Garden of Eden.*

⋖§ Some People Remain Defiant Even in Gehinnom

עז הפנים שאינו חת מפני כל אפילו בגיהנום ילך לבטח דרכו.

According to the Kotzker Rebbe, the *mishnah* is stating that some individuals never change. The rude, insolent individual remains defiant even in *Gehinnom*.

⋖§ So Similar, Yet So Different

ישנם שני דברים הדומים להם, נגד עז פנים יש עוז נפש, ונגד בושת פנים עצבות או מרה שחורה. וצריכים להיות מומחים גדולים להבדיל בין אלו כי היו כבר אנשים גדולים שטעו ועירבבו התחומין.

The *Chiddushei HaRim* noted that many character traits that appear to be similar are in reality radically different. For example, עַזּוּת פָּנִים, *brazenness,* is a character trait so repugnant that its practitioners are condemned to *Gehin-*

[24] *He [Yehudah ben Tema] used to say: The brazen goes to Gehinnom, but the shamefaced goes to the Garden of Eden. May it be Your will, Hashem, our God and the God of our forefathers, that the Holy Temple be rebuilt, speedily in our days, and grant us our share in Your Torah.*

---

nom. On the other hand, עַזּוּת הַנֶּפֶשׁ, the *courageous soul*, emulating the leopard, is a highly admirable trait.

Similarly, while בֹּשֶׁת פָּנִים, a natural sense of shame and restraint, is highly appropriate, it should not be carried to the extreme. The danger exists that one can easily lose oneself and veer from an appropriate sense of one's limitation to depression and melancholy.

It is only with the guidance of the recognized Torah leadership of every generation that we can distinguish between appropriate or improper application of these characteristics (*Maggidei HaEmes*).

■ יְהִי רָצוֹן . . . שֶׁיִּבָּנֶה בֵּית הַמִּקְדָּשׁ בִּמְהֵרָה בְיָמֵינוּ וְתֵן חֶלְקֵנוּ בְּתוֹרָתֶךְ — *May it be Your will. . . that the Holy Temple be rebuilt, speedily in our days, and grant us our share in Your Torah.*

⋖§ Why Is This Tefillah Inserted Here?

This seemingly totally unrelated prayer for the restoration of the *Beis HaMikdash* and for achievement in Torah study may actually flow from some of the earlier themes stated in the *mishnah*, as we will now elucidate.

⋖§ A ''Refined'' Nation Desperately Needs the Beis HaMikdash

יל״פ השייכות כי בנ״י הם בייישנים לכן מאוד נפל לבנו וראשנו ע״י שגלינו מעל
שלחן אבינו, כי אינו דומה ע״פ המתגרש יוכל למצוא לו פנים ומקום בכל אשר
ילך משא״כ בושת פנים כמונו לכן מבקשין במהרה ירחם עלינו הבורא ב״ה
עוויל״פ כי לאשר מדת בנ״י בייישנים והבהמ״ק מעין הג״ע לזאת מבקשין שבעוד
בחיינו נזכה לג״ע מקום בושת פנים היינו הבהמ״ק, ויתבן עוד כי אחז״ל מי שא״ל
בושת פנים בידוע שלא עמדו אבותיו על הר סיני כי בקבה״ת ב׳ למען תהי׳ יראתו
ע״פ כו׳ ואחז״ל זו הבושת וז״ש ותן חלקנו בתורתך, וי״ל עוד דקאי עמ״ש מקודם
הוי עז כנמר וקל כנשר כו׳ ובזמן שבהמ״ק קיים הי׳ בנקל להשיג אלה המדות קל
כנשר ר״ב כו׳ רק בגלות היא עבודה מרובה לכן מבקשין שיבנה כו׳, ולמ״ש
בתיו״ט דל״ג ב׳ משניות האחרונות יי״ל דמביא משנה ריב״ת וכן יה״ר כו׳ לסיים
בדבר טוב ובקשה.

[כה] **הוּא הָיָה אוֹמֵר:** בֶּן חָמֵשׁ שָׁנִים לַמִּקְרָא, בֶּן עֶשֶׂר שָׁנִים לַמִּשְׁנָה, בֶּן שְׁלֹשׁ עֶשְׂרֵה לַמִּצְוֹת, בֶּן חֲמֵשׁ עֶשְׂרֵה לַגְּמָרָא, בֶּן שְׁמוֹנֶה עֶשְׂרֵה לַחֻפָּה, בֶּן עֶשְׂרִים

W hereas a more belligerent people can successfully adapt to a foreign culture (as many expatriate ethnic groups have done so well), *Klal Yisrael*, possessed with a sense of בֹּשֶׁת פָּנִים, also translated as *modesty* and refinement, can never find a true home outside its natural environment, the *Beis HaMikdash* — may it be rebuilt speedily in our times.

In a similar vein, our natural sense of shame hopefully prevents our sinning and also defines *Klal Yisrael*. Thus, we pray to enjoy our just reward while still in This World in the form of the rebuilt *Beis HaMikdash*.

Perhaps, a direct link also exists between shame and study of Torah mentioned in the *mishnah's* conclusion. It is well known (cf. *Yevamos* 79a) that the "litmus test" of a true Jew is an inherent sense of modesty and shame. *Chazal* (*Nedarim* 20a) even remark that anyone lacking that requisite characteristic could not be a direct descendant of those who received the Torah at Sinai. We, however, guided by a sense of shame, do deserve to gain further insight into the teachings of the Torah.

It is even possible that this plea for the restoration of the *Beis HaMikdash* may refer to Ben Teima's first theme. Whereas it was reasonably easy to attain the traits recommended by the *mishnah* while the *Beis HaMikdash* existed, it is far more difficult to successfully practice these characteristics during *Klal Yisrael's* millennia of *galus*. In this spirit, we plead with Hashem to restore the *Beis HaMikdash* which will greatly facilitate the development of the true Torah personality.

Finally, if we assume as the *Tosafos Yom Tov* does, that this is the concluding *mishnah* of the *perek* [and actually of all of *Meseches Mishnayos Avos* since the sixth *perek* is a *Baraisa* rather than an integral part of *Maseches Avos*], it is entirely appropriate to close with a fervent prayer for the restoration of the *Beis HaMikdash* and growth in Torah study.

25.

■ בֶּן חָמֵשׁ שָׁנִים לַמִּקְרָא — *A five-year-old [begins] Scripture.* ■

◄§ Becoming Familiar With Chumash by the Age of Five

יש לדקדק למה היום מקדימין. ואולי הכוונה שבן חמש צריך כבר לדעת, ולכן מתחילים ללמדו קודם לכן.

[25] *He used to say: A five-year-old [begins] Scripture; a ten-year-old [begins] Mishnah; a thirteen-year-old [becomes obliged to observe] the commandments; a fifteen-year-old [begins the study of] Gemara; an eighteen-year-old [goes to] the marriage canopy; a twenty-year-old [begins] to pursue [a livelihood]; a thirty-*

Our practice of teaching *Chumash* to even younger children (such as the three-year-old children who are tuaght some *chumash* when brought to *cheder*) may be based on a somewhat revised interpretation of these words. It is not sufficient for a five-year-old to *commence* learning *Chumash*. On the contrary, he must be familiar with much of the *Chumash* by the age of five. This of course necessitates beginning several years earlier (*Pnei Menachem, Maggidei HaEmes*).

■ בֶּן שְׁמוֹנֶה עֶשְׂרֵה לַחֻפָּה, בֶּן עֶשְׂרִים לִרְדּוֹף — *An eighteen-year-old [goes to] the marriage canopy; a twenty-year-old [begins] [to pursue a livelihood].*

◌ᵍ Two Years of Financial Support ("Kest")

בשם החידושי הרי"ם דאותן ב' שנים שבינתיים לאכול "קעסט."

From the sequence of these two phases of the life cycle, we can deduce an important insight about whether parents (or parents-in-laws) ought to support their newly married children so that the young man can pursue in-depth Torah study. The *Chiddushei HaRim* suggests, based on this *mishnah*, that two years of support are generally appropriate. The *mishnah* recommends marriage at the age of 18, but delays pursuing a livelihood for another two years (*Pnei Menachem, Maggidei HaEmes*).

■ בֶּן עֶשְׂרִים לִרְדּוֹף — *A twenty-year-old [begins] to pursue [a livelihood].*

◌ᵍ Pursue the Yetzer Hara

היינו שכיוון שמגיע האדם לגיל עשרים ובבית דין של מעלה מענישים אותו על
חטאיו, עליו להתגבר ולרדוף את היצה"ר.
ולכן צריך אז להיות בן עשרים לרדוף, שנותנים לו כח מיוחד שיוכל לרדוף את
היצר הרע ולהתגבר עליו.

We previously assumed that "pursuit" refers to pursuit of a livelihood. However, it may also refer to the need to actively engage and even

לִרְדוֹף, בֶּן שְׁלֹשִׁים לַכֹּחַ, בֶּן אַרְבָּעִים לַבִּינָה, בֶּן
חֲמִשִּׁים לְעֵצָה, בֶּן שִׁשִּׁים לְזִקְנָה, בֶּן שִׁבְעִים לְשֵׂיבָה, בֶּן
שְׁמוֹנִים לִגְבוּרָה, בֶּן תִּשְׁעִים לָשׁוּחַ, בֶּן מֵאָה כְּאִלּוּ מֵת
וְעָבַר וּבָטֵל מִן הָעוֹלָם.

---

confront the *Yetzer Hara.* While certainly every individual over the age of *bar mitzvah* is obliged to remain steadfast in face of the *Yetzer Hara's* importuning, at the age of 20, we embark on a particularly critical juncture in our lives. From then on, we are subject to retribution by the Heavenly Court as well as to the terrestrial court of mortals. At so crucial a stage, it is imperative that we stage a renewed offensive against the *Yetzer Hara* (*Imrei Emes, Maggidei HaEmes*).

The *Beis Yisrael* added a reassuring note: We may assume that not only our obligation, but concomitantly, our ability to fulfill our obligation and successfully wrestle with the *Yetzer Hara* is enhanced at this stage (*Maggidei HaEmes*).

⇜ The Age to Pursue Mitzvos

אך יתכן גם הכוונה בן עשרים לרדוף על עשה טוב כדכתיב ונדעה נרדפה לדעת
את ה' כשחר נכון מוצאו.

The *Lev Simchah* extended his predecessor's analysis mentioned above by suggesting that at the age of 20, we are granted an increased capacity to perform positive commandments, as well as to deflect and defeat the *Yetzer Hara.* He noted that the *navi* uses the term רוֹדֵף in this manner — וְנֵדְעָה נִרְדְּפָה נִרְדְּפָה, *Let us know, let us strive to know Hashem, like the dawn whose emergence is certain* (*Hoshea* 6:3). Let us pursue our knowledge of Hashem which can be found in the morning (i.e. young adulthood) of our lives (*Maggidei HaEmes*).

■ בֶּן שְׁלֹשִׁים לַכֹּחַ — *A thirty-year-old [attains] full strength.*

⇜ Strength Acquired Through Torah

ענין הכוחות, כוחות טובים, על ידי תורה אפשר לתקן הכל.

Our *mishnah* is not only referring to physical strength, but also to the capacity to tackle and even rectify many of life's problems. This achievement is facilitated through the vast amounts of Torah knowledge which one has amassed at this point in one's life (*Lev Simchah, Maggidei HaEmes*).

year-old [attains] full strength; a forty-year-old [attains] understanding; a fifty-year-old [can offer] counsel; a sixty-year-old [attains] seniority; a seventy-year-old [attains] a ripe old age; an eighty-year-old [shows] strength; a ninety-year-old [becomes] stooped over; a hundred-year-old is as if he were dead, passed away and ceased from the world.

■ בֶּן אַרְבָּעִים לַבִּינָה — *A forty-year-old [attains] understanding.*

❧ Utilizing One's Knowledge Appropriately

> כשהאדם הוא בן ארבעים הרי הוא לעת זקנתו ואז הוא מוצא על ידי מה שיגע וזהו דאיתא בן ארבעים לבינה בענין דבר מבין דבר מתוך דבר.

At the age of 40, as one nears the mature phase of life, one gains the capacity to not only study Torah but also to derive new insights from existing Torah knowledge (*Imrei Emes, Maggidei HaEmes*).

■ בֶּן חֲמִשִּׁים לָעֵצָה — *A fifty-year-old [can offer] counsel.*

❧ The Road Not to Take

> מהו העצה שהיה נותן להם. מספרים מעשה שאיש אחד טעה ביער גדול ולא מצא את הדרך לצאת ממנו, לימים פגש בזקן אחד ושמח על זה מאד כי חשב שהוא יאמר לו היכן הדרך הנבונה. אמר לו הזקן אני תועה כאן כבר שבעים שנה, יכול אני רק לומר לך באיזה דרכים אל תלך, את הדרך הנבונה צריך אתה למצוא בעצמך וכמו כן כאן היה נותן להם עצה איך להשמר מרע. ובזה יובן מה שכתב רש"י אבל חוזר הוא לנעילת שערים ולא כתב לפתיחת שערים, הרמז שלפתוח צריך כל אחד בעצמו.

To explain the advice that can be offered by those who have reached the age of 50, the *Imrei Emes* offered the following parable: A young man, wandering aimlessly through a thick forest, finally meets an older person. He expects this individual to show him the way out of the forest. Much to his disappointment, the elderly man responds, "I've been wandering in this forest for 70 years. While I can tell you which paths *not* to take, only you can find your way out." So too, an older acquaintance can forewarn us of the pitfalls that lie ahead if we embark upon the wrong path. However, only we can determine our own unique path of life.

[כו] בֶּן בַּג בַּג אוֹמֵר: הֲפָךְ בָּה וַהֲפָךְ בָּה, דְּכֹלָּא בָה;
וּבָה תֶּחֱזֵי, וְסִיב וּבְלֵה בָּה, וּמִנָּה לָא תָזוּעַ, שֶׁאֵין
לְךָ מִדָּה טוֹבָה הֵימֶנָּה. בֶּן הֵא הֵא אוֹמֵר: לְפוּם צַעֲרָא
אַגְרָא.

❧ ❧ ❧

This insight can be deduced from the source of the statement that a fifty-
year-old can offer counsel. The Torah relates that the *Leviim*, upon reaching the
age of 50, would "retire" from much of their active duty (e.g. transporting the
Mishkan's utensils) in favor of serving in an advisory capacity; they mentored
younger *Leviim* (*Bamidbar* 8:25). At this stage, Rashi tells us, their responsibilities included נְעִילַת שְׁעָרִים, *closing the [Temple] gates*. This can be interpreted as
an allusion to their role as advisers: They "closed the gates," cautioning their
younger colleagues about where they should not go. "Opening the gates" —
deciding which path to take — however, is each person's own decision (*Maggidei HaEmes*).

■ בֶּן תִּשְׁעִים לָשׁוּחַ — *A ninety-year-old [becomes] stooped over.*

◁§ Not Conversing About Mundane Matters

כתב רבינו יונה ז"ל שיתחיל לפסוק שיחה מעולם הזה רק לקדש הפה בתורה
ותפלה.

The *Sfas Emes*, citing *Rabbeinu Yonah*, interpreted the term לָשׁוּחַ as referring to conversation (שִׂיחָה). Someone who has reached the venerable age of
90 should, in gratitude to Hashem, redirect his energies away from con- vers-
ing about material matters and instead focus only on Torah and prayer.

◁§ Self-Negation

אחר כל השלימות שחושב מקודם אחר כך בא הבריעה ולשחות בהודאה ממש
בנפילת אפים עד שנתבטל באמת ונעשה כעפר ממש כמו שכתוב הכל היה מן
העפר והכל שב אל העפר.

The term לָשׁוּחַ may also mean to prostrate oneself (שָׁחָה). The *mishnah* may
be referring to the need for ever increasing humility at that advanced age.
While it is tempting to sit back and take pride in the many achievements of our
long life, the *mishnah* is warning us not to adopt that approach. Instead,
acknowledge your indebtedness to Hashem, the guiding force behind all your

[26] *Ben Bag Bag says: Delve in it [the Torah] and [continue to] delve in it [the Torah] for everything is in it; look deeply into it; grow old and gray over it; do not stir from it, for you can have no better portion than. It. Ben Hei Hei says: The reward is in proportion to the exertion.*

❧ ❧ ❧

accomplishments. This thought may be alluded to by *Koheles*: הַכֹּל הָיָה מִן הֶעָפָר וְהַכֹּל שָׁב אֶל הֶעָפָר, *All originate from dust and all return to dust* (3:20). Since everything comes from dust and eventually returns to dust during the final phases of life, it is best to negate oneself — to be as dust — in the presence of the *Shechinah*.

26.

■ הֲפָךְ בָּהּ וְהֲפָךְ בָּהּ דְּכֹלָּא בָהּ; וּבָהּ תֶּחֱזֵי — *Delve in it [the Torah] and [continue to] delve in it [the Torah] for everything is in it; look deeply into it.*

❧ Everything Is Contained Within the Torah

פירוש שעל ידי רוב היגיעה ולפום צערא תחזי דכולא בה בהתורה ואין מחסור ליראיו.

By frequently reviewing the Torah (הֲפָךְ בָּהּ וְהֲפָךְ בָּהּ) and by experiencing some initial frustration in our efforts to understand Torah (לְפוּם צַעֲרָא אַגְרָא), we eventually realize that *everything* — the answer to all of life's baffling problems — lies in the Torah. According to this approach, the phrase וּבָהּ תֶּחֱזֵי means *through this you will realize*, and refers to the previous thought דְּכֹלָּא בָהּ, *that everything is contained in Torah*. We find that David Hamelech said, כִּי אֵין מַחְסוֹר לִירֵאָיו, *there is no deprivation for His reverent ones* (*Tehillim* 34:10). Nothing is lacking — there is nothing that cannot be resolved in the spirit of Torah — for those who fear Hashem.

❧ The Baal Shem Tov's Practices

כשהיו שואלין למרן העש״ט ז״ל איזה דבר היה פותח איזה ספר, זוהר או גמרא וכיוצא ולומד ואחר כך משיב לשואל, ואמר שאור שברא הקב״ה היה אדם צופה בו מסוף העולם ועד סופו והיכן גנזו לצדיקים בתורה; וכשהצדיק לומד תורה לשמה צופה מסוף העולם ועד סופו. וזה ובה תחזי מסוף העולם ועד סופו.

רַבִּי חֲנַנְיָא בֶּן עֲקַשְׁיָא אוֹמֵר: רָצָה הַקָּדוֹשׁ בָּרוּךְ הוּא לְזַכּוֹת אֶת יִשְׂרָאֵל, לְפִיכָךְ הִרְבָּה לָהֶם תּוֹרָה וּמִצְוֹת, שֶׁנֶּאֱמַר: "יהוה חָפֵץ לְמַעַן צִדְקוֹ יַגְדִּיל תּוֹרָה וְיַאְדִּיר."

Whenever the Baal Shem Tov was consulted on a matter, he would first occupy himself with studying a portion of the Torah. His practice was based on the tradition that the primeval light of Creation (cf. *Rashi, Bereishis* 1:4 s.v. וירא), too powerful for the naked eye of mortals, was subsumed in the Torah. The righteous man studying Torah could discern the rarefied light and thus grasp the arcane mysteries of the contemporary world. This practice is alluded to in our *mishnah*: Immerse yourself in the Torah, and through such study you will see the original light of Creation (*Knesses Yisrael, Maggidei HaEmes*).

◆§ Stronger Than Family Ties

אחרי נשואיו של אדמו"ר האמרי אמת ז"ל כשישב בבית חותנו רבי נח שחור ז"ל בביאלא, התגגע אל בית אביו הק' השפ"א ז"ל, כתב לו אביו השפ"א "ועתה אהובי בני שי' לא ידעתי מה יש לך כל כך געגועים לחזור לפה, ומה חסר לך שם, ואתה עוסק בתורת השם, והיא אב ואם, וכולא בה."

Immediately after his marriage, the *Imrei Emes* moved to his in-laws' residence. However, he found it difficult to suppress a natural longing for his father, the *Sfas Emes*. To overcome his son's homesickness, the *Sfas Emes* consoled him by quoting this *mishnah*: The Torah (in which you are now immersed) is everything — it is your father and your mother. You don't need me! (*Maggidei HaEmes*).

■ וּמִנָּה לָא תָזוּעַ, שֶׁאֵין לְךָ מִדָּה טוֹבָה הֵימֶנָּה — *Do not stir from it, for you can have no better portion than it.*

◆§ But a Beginner

פירוש לא תזוע מן התורה כי אין לך מדה טובה הימנה, פירוש שלא למדת שום מדה טובה מן התורה.

Rabbi Chanania ben Akashia says: The Holy One, Blessed is He, wished to confer merit upon Israel; therefore He gave them Torah and mitzvos in abundance, as it is said: "Hashem desired, for the sake of its [Israel's] righteousness, that the Torah be made great and glorious."

According to the Kotzker Rebbe, the *mishnah* is reminding us of something very important. Do not veer from the Torah; while you may think that you have learned everything that the Torah has to offer, the mere fact that you are contemplating going away from Torah indicates that you have not learned anything — not even a single exemplary character trait (שֶׁאֵין לְךָ מִדָּה טוֹבָה הֵימֶנָּה). Everyone who is influenced by Torah even peripherally would never seek to move away from it (*Maggidei HaEmes*).

■ בֶּן הֵא הֵא אוֹמֵר: לְפוּם צַעֲרָא אַגְרָא — *Ben Hei Hei says: The reward is in proportion to the exertion.*

⇜ R' Yochanan's Pseudonym

רמז למה דאיתא ברמב״ם שבן בג בג הוא ר׳ יוחנן. עוד איתא ברמב״ם שבן הא
הא הוא גם כן ר׳ יוחנן, ויש לרמז כי ״בן בג בג הא הא״ בגימט׳ ב ,יוחנ״ן.

According to the *Rambam*, both Ben Bag Bag (mentioned at the beginning of this *mishnah*) and Ben Hei Hei are, in fact, Rabbi Yochanan. This may be deduced from the fact that the numerical equivalent of בֶּן בַּג בַּג בֶּן הֵא הֵא *Ben Bag Bag Ben Hei Hei*, is equivalent to ב׳ יוֹחָנָן, *they are both Yochanan* (*Lev Simchah, Maggidei HaEmes*).

⇜ The Mouth Suffers and Is Rewarded

הפירוש לפומא יש צערא ואגרא, כי על לשון הרע וכדומה יש צערא עבור פיו,
ובשלומד תורה ומתפלל יש עבור פומא אגרא.

To conclude our commentary on the *perek*, we offer the interpretation of R' Baruch of Mezibozh: The mouth (פּום) suffers (צַעֲרָא) when it is abused by speaking *lashon hara* and is rewarded (אַגְרָא) when it is appropriately utilized to discuss Torah thoughts (*Maggidei HaEmes*).

פרק ששי

כָּל יִשְׂרָאֵל יֵשׁ לָהֶם חֵלֶק לָעוֹלָם הַבָּא, שֶׁנֶּאֱמַר: „וְעַמֵּךְ כֻּלָּם צַדִּיקִים; לְעוֹלָם יִירְשׁוּ אָרֶץ, נֵצֶר מַטָּעַי, מַעֲשֵׂה יָדַי לְהִתְפָּאֵר."

❦ ❦ ❦

ו

שָׁנוּ חֲכָמִים בִּלְשׁוֹן הַמִּשְׁנָה. בָּרוּךְ שֶׁבָּחַר בָּהֶם וּבְמִשְׁנָתָם.

■ שָׁנוּ חֲכָמִים בִּלְשׁוֹן הַמִּשְׁנָה. בָּרוּךְ שֶׁבָּחַר בָּהֶם וּבְמִשְׁנָתָם ■ — *The Sages taught [this chapter] in the language of the Mishnah. Blessed is He Who chose them and their teaching.*

◄§ Mishnah: Doubling the Impact of Torah

הנה תורה שבכ' היה התעוררות מלמעלה למטה ותורה שבע"פ מה שמבינים מצד עצמם . . . ולכן נק' משנה לשון כפול כמו משנה למלך, וכן כל לשון חכמים, כגון שניות מדברי סופרים, שנק' סופרים שהם מאירים האור הגנוז תוך התורה מלשון ספיר, וזה ענין תושבע"פ לברר ולזכך מה שהוא נסתר ונק' שניות כנ"ל, שנתן הש"י להם כח, להוסיף על התורה ע"י בינתם וזה שמברכין ונתן לנו את תורתו וחיי עולם נטע בתוכנו שנטע בתוך בנ"י להוסיף על התורה שזהו תורה שבע"פ, ונתן לנו תורתו היא תורה שבכתב וזה ברוך שבחר כו' שברוך השם שבחר בנו ובמשנתם שהוסיפו על התורה כנ"ל, וג"כ מלשון שינה שיכולין להפוך הפירוש מפשיטו ולשנות כפי חכמתם.

The term מִשְׁנָה may be related to שְׁנַיִם, *two*, and can be interpreted as the "doubling" of the impact of Torah. Whereas the Written Torah is a gift from Hashem to *Klal Yisrael*, the Oral Law — also given at Sinai — is enhanced by our own strenuous efforts to comprehend His Torah: The *combined* impact of Hashem's initial stimulus (in the form of the Written Torah) and our labors to understand it is far more effective than an unrequited gift from Hashem alone. In general, Rabbinic ordinances "intensify" the Torah's impact. Thus, those prohibited relationships that stem from a Rabbinic decree (e.g. marrying great-grandparents) are known as שְׁנִיּוֹת, not because they are secondary to the laws of the Torah, but because they "double" the impact of the Torah's regulations regarding illicit relationships. After receiving an *aliyah* to the Torah, we speak about *Klal Yisrael's* ability to "augment" the Written Law by reciting the *brachah* וְחַיֵּי עוֹלָם נָטַע בְּתוֹכֵנוּ, *and He implanted eternal life within us* — Hashem implanted into *Klal Yisrael* the ability to add to the eternal life of the Torah

Chapter Six

A*ll Israel has a share in the World to Come, as it is said (Yeshayahu 60:21): "And your people are all righteous; they shall inherit the land forever; a branch of My plantings, My handiwork, in which to take pride."*

❧ ❧ ❧

6

T*he Sages taught [this chapter] in the language of the Mishnah. Blessed is He Who chose them and their teaching.*

---

through its understanding of His Oral Law.

In this light, we can now comprehend the opening sentence of this *perek* in which the validity of *Chazal's* technique is emphasized: שָׁנוּ חֲכָמִים בִּלְשׁוֹן הַמִּשְׁנָה, *The Sages taught in the language of the Mishnah: Chazal* interpreted the Torah (שָׁנוּ חֲכָמִים) in such a manner leading to the "doubling" (i.e. maximization) (מִשְׁנָה) of the power of the Written Torah.

We then praise Hashem for granting validity to *Chazal* themselves (בָּהֶם) and to their ability to enhance the impact of the Torah through their interpretations (בָּרוּךְ שֶׁבָּחַר בָּהֶם וּבְמִשְׁנָתָם).

Alternatively, the term מִשְׁנָה may be related to שִׁינָה, *to revise. Chazal*, through their ability to use the Sinaitic principles of interpretation to understand the Oral Law, in effect, "revise" and infer new and additional insights from the surface meaning of the Written Law. Based on the *Mesorah, Chazal* deduce that the surface meaning of a *pasuk* is not always the true interpretation.[1] We bless Hashem for *Chazal* and their ability to elicit additional interpretations of the Written Law.

Nothing gives Hashem more satisfaction than the brilliant success of *Chazal* in uncovering the additional layers of meaning of the Torah itself. Perhaps, it is for this reason that our scholars are called סוֹפְרִים (traditionally interpreted as *scribes*), a term related to סַפִּיר, *sapphire*. Just as a sapphire stone sparkles brilliantly (even when there is minimal light), so too *Chazal*, through their skillful use of the Torah's principles, are able to illuminate the most mysterious passages of the Written Law.

❧ The Role of Baraisa (ברייתא)

והנה המשניות היא תורה שבע״פ ויש לה חיבור עם תורה שבכתב כמ״ש ששים

---

1. A classic example of this is the meaning of the words, וּסְפַרְתֶּם לָכֶם מִמָּחֳרַת הַשַּׁבָּת, *you shall count for yourselves from the morrow of the rest day* (Vayikra 23:15). They prove that it is not referring to Shabbos literally, but rather to the day after the first day of Pesach.

[א] רַבִּי מֵאִיר אוֹמֵר: כָּל הָעוֹסֵק בַּתּוֹרָה לִשְׁמָהּ זוֹכֶה
לִדְבָרִים הַרְבֵּה; וְלֹא עוֹד, אֶלָּא שֶׁכָּל הָעוֹלָם כֻּלּוֹ
כְּדַאי הוּא לוֹ. נִקְרָא רֵעַ, אָהוּב. אוֹהֵב אֶת הַמָּקוֹם,

המה מלכות דכ' בזוה''ק פינחס בר''מ דאינון כרוכין בה ע'''ש, ועלמות אין מספר
הם הלכות היוצאין ממנה שהיא התלמיד לכך נק' גמרא שהוא גמר העניו
והתלמיד הוא האור היוצא מתורה שבכתב ובע''פ, וכן ברייתות שאינם במשנה
הם במדרגה אחר המשנה שמתחיל להשפיע לחוץ לכך נק' ברייתא מלשון ברא
פי' חוץ כידוע, והנה יש חיבור לברייתות וגמ' אל המשניות.

Whereas the first five *perakim* (chapters) of *Pirkei Avos* consist of *mishnahs*, this final *perek* is comprised of a series of additional teachings of the *Tannaim*, not included in the Mishnah, and are known as *Baraisos*. The *Baraisos* supplement the Mishnah and were written in the same style.

In order to appreciate the relationship between the various components of the Oral Law, we cite the interpretation of the *Zohar* (*Pinchas* 216a) of a *pasuk* in *Shir HaShirim* שִׁשִּׁים הֵמָּה מְלָכוֹת ... וַעֲלָמוֹת אֵין מִסְפָּר, *There are sixty queens ... and all the countless nations* (6:8). The opening phrase, שִׁשִּׁים הֵמָּה מְלָכוֹת, refers to the 60 tractates of the Mishnah.[1] וַעֲלָמוֹת אֵין מִסְפָּר refers to the innumerable insights that *Chazal* derived from the Torah including the Talmud itself and the *Baraisa*. Whereas the *mishnah* is contained within the *finite* boundaries of the Torah — and therefore is fixed in number (60) — the *Baraisa*, related to the term בְּרָא, the Aramaic term for going outside, reflects the portion of the Oral Law which is beyond that stated in the Mishnah. So too, the Talmud represents the cumulative and final impact of all of the teachings of the Written and Oral Law. The Talmud's popular name גְּמָרָא also reflects that theme being derived from the word גָּמַר, *completion* — the final product of all the efforts of *Chazal* to comprehend Hashem's will. In fact, the Gemara may be compared to a great light that radiates from the teachings of the Oral and Written Law.

לְשׁוֹן הַמִּשְׁנָה: Tongue of the Mishnah

וזה נק' שנו בלשון המשנה שהתחלת החיבור הוא זה ששנו בלשון המשנה, שלשון
הוא המחבר חב''ד אל המידות שהוא פה ולב והבן, לכך הלשון נק' ע''ש החיבור
וזהו שנו בלשון המשנה.

Based on the foregoing assertion that the *Baraisa* represents the prolific impact of the Mishnah and the Torah into infinite areas, we may have a new understanding of the term לְשׁוֹן הַמִּשְׁנָה.

1. *Chazal* frequently refer to the 60 tractates of the Mishnah, though, in reality, there are 63.

[1] *Rabbi Meir says: Whoever engages in Torah study for its own sake merits many things; furthermore, [the creation of] the entire world is worthwhile for his sake alone. He is called, "Friend, Beloved." He loves the*

The tongue (לָשׁוֹן) serves as the bridge between the *intellect* associated with the *head* (and its qualities of חָכְמָה, בִּינָה וְדַעַת — *Knowledge, understanding and wisdom*) and the *emotions* (and personality traits of the individual) based in the *heart*. By articulating the innermost emotions of the heart, within the parameters set by the mind, the *Baraisos* of this *perek* — written in the style of the Mishnah and elaborating on themes discussed in the *mishnahs* — are the לְשׁוֹן הַמִּשְׁנָה. They are the "tongue" bridging the finite *mishnahs* with the infinite, boundless realm of *Baraisos*.

■ קִנְיַן הַתּוֹרָה — *Acquisition of Torah* ■

לכך קראו פ׳ זה קנין תורה שפרק זה הוא החיבור ממשנה לגמרא והוא הצירוף
להיות מחובר ומצורף לתורה שבע״פ ותורה שבע״פ לתורה שבכתב, וזה קנין
ע״י קן שנשרש במקומו וקנו.

This *perek* is popularly known as קִנְיַן הַתּוֹרָה, *Acquisition of Torah*, because it deals with acquiring Torah knowledge. We generally assume that this name is derived from the 48 qualities through which Torah is acquired as discussed in *mishnah* 6. In light of our assertion that this entire *perek* serves as the transition from the *mishnah* to the *Baraisa*, the term קִנְיַן may refer to another aspect of this chapter. Just as a bird's nest, a קַן צִפּוֹר, firmly roots the mother bird and her chicks, so too this chapter — by linking together the various components of Torah, especially the *mishnahs* and *Baraisos* — allows the Torah to become securely established within *Klal Yisrael* (adapted from *Sfas Emes*).

■ בָּהֶם וּבְמִשְׁנָתָם — *Them and their teaching.* ■

הגה״ק רבי מאיר שפירא מלובלין ז״ל דייק על לשון בהם ובמשנתם שלא מצינו
לשון כזה בכל הש״ס. אלא מכאן יש ללמוד שלא די להיות רק נאה דורש, אלא
צריך להיות נאה מקיים גם כן. וזה מה שדקדק לומר בהם ובמשנתם, שהייתה
תלמודם בידם והחכמים עצמם היו כמו משנתם.

The *Pnei Menachem*, citing Rav Meir Shapiro, noted that scholarship (מִשְׁנָתָם) alone is not a sufficient criterion for Torah greatness. Occasionally scholars behave in a manner that contradicts the very ideals that they espouse. It is only if their personal lifestyle (בָּהֶם) reflects their learning (מִשְׁנָתָם) that we value their scholarship (*Maggidei HaEmes*).

■ **Rabbi** — רַבִּי מֵאִיר אוֹמֵר: כָּל הָעוֹסֵק בַּתּוֹרָה לִשְׁמָהּ זוֹכֶה לִדְבָרִים הַרְבֵּה **Meir said: Whoever engages in Torah study for its own sake merits many things.**

⊷§ For Its Own Sake

The *mishnah* elaborates on the multiple rewards due to those who study Torah for its own sake. In the following remarks, we will attempt to elucidate this very difficult, often esoteric concept, citing from both the *Sfas Emes's* commentary on *Avos* as well as his commentary on the Torah.

⊷§ Infusing the Universe with the Light of Torah

פירוש כי התורה חיות הכל כמו שכתוב באורייתא ברא קוב"ה עלמא רק נתלבש אור התורה בכל הבריאה, ונמצא כל הבריאה שם של התורה כענין ה' אחד ושמו אחד, ולכך העוסק בתורה לשמה פי' להמשיך אור וחיות התורה לכל דבר, על ידי זה התורה מאירה לו בכל דבר ויכול לראות ולהכיר אור התורה שיש בכל דבר, וזוכה לדברים הרבה כי הקדושה אחד ודברי עולם הזה מרובים ועל ידי כח התורה יוכל אדם לחבר כל הדברים אל הכלל שהוא התורה כנ"ל.

Frequently, we distinguish between Hashem's Torah and the universe that He created. In reality, this distinction is entirely false. Hashem utilized the Torah for the purpose of creating the universe (cf. *Bereishis Rabbah* 1:2). It is true that if we perceive the universe superficially, we do not glimpse the Torah's imprint. However, if we penetrate beyond the surface that often obscures the universe's inner nature, we realize that Hashem infused the light of Torah into *all* of nature. What may appear to be strictly a natural phenomenon is really the Divine hand regulating the universe, according to the dictates of the Torah. The Torah is truly the inner mechanism that finely calibrates the natural world.

Based on the above discussion (regarding the Torah's impact on nature), we suggest that the universe is the name (שֵׁם) of the Torah. Just as one frequently refers to an individual by his name even though his true inner personality is often inscrutable, so too the universe is the outer casing of the Torah. By marveling at Hashem's stewardship of the universe, we are actually appreciating the Torah which was installed by Hashem as the inner mechanism to guide the universe. Rather than praise the inner, often hidden, nature of Torah itself, we marvel at its "name," its outer appearance, the universe.[1]

---

1. The *pasuk*, יִהְיֶה ה' אֶחָד וּשְׁמוֹ אֶחָד, *Hashem will be One and His Name will be One* (Zechariah 14:9), reflects a similar theme: While we cannot possibly appreciate Hashem's nature, we can perceive Him through His Name.

Rabbi Meir is extolling those who not only study Torah but do it in order that the entire universe, the Torah's name, is infused with the light of Torah (לִשְׁמָהּ). He praises those whose objective is that the Torah's impact should dominate the natural world.

It is entirely appropriate that one who studies Torah with the objective of consolidating the Torah's domination on the universe will eventually enjoy the ability to perceive clearly what he had only yearned for — he will sense the steady "hand" (the inner light) of the Torah guiding the entire universe. As the *mishnah* continues, such a person will merit to comprehend many things — he will understand how the universe, which appears to be a loose collection of many disparate entities, is really one totally unified entity guided by the Torah (adapted from *Sfas Emes*).

◆§ The Hidden Torah

כי התורה לא ידע אנוש ערכה כו', אך מי נתלבש אור התורה בדיבורים אלו שבתורה, ונמצא כי תורה זו היא רק לבוש לעיקר התורה וכמ"ש בזוה"ק בהעלותך, והוא להרבות כבוד ושם התורה ע"י המלבוש הזה כמ"ש ה' חפץ כו' יגדיל תורה ויאדיר, אך האמת תורה זו היא פתח להיות נפתח פנימיות התורה ע"י שמירת התורה ומצות, וכ"כ במדרש תנחומא ברחובות תתן קולה במקום שמרחיבין אותה, פי' כפי מה שמרבין כבוד התורה ומביאין כח התורה בכל הנבראים על ידי מצות התורה, שיש בכל מעשה גשמיי מצוה, ועי"ז מביאין הארת התורה בכל מקום, ועי"ז זוכין לקול התורה הפנימיות.

Iyov, when describing the wonders of Torah, exclaims, לֹא יָדַע אֱנוֹשׁ עֶרְכָּהּ, *Mankind does not know its worth (Iyov 28:13)*. And, indeed, the true nature of Torah is beyond human comprehension. However, Hashem granted us the Torah in its existing form so that *Klal Yisrael* can at least sample some of His wisdom by studying the Torah that they received. When we *practice* ever more assiduously the laws of the Torah, in addition to *studying* more Torah, we gradually come closer to the "inner" hidden components of Torah. As *Mishlei* (1:20) says, בָּרְחֹבוֹת תִּתֵּן קוֹלָהּ — by broadening (רְחֹבוֹת) the impact of Torah (in its external, viable form), we merit to hear the Torah's *inner* voice (קוֹלָהּ).

By studying Torah for its own sake we are doing everything possible to propagate the impact of the Torah in every aspect of the material world. In the merit of doing so, we are deemed worthy to receive many things. Foremost is the ability to understand the many aspects of Torah that are initially obscured from our view.

◆§ A Guide for Action

ה' הפשוט כדי לעשות .. והיינו שאדם מבטל עצמו שאין לו שום כח ופעולה בלי

חיות השי״ת . . . וכן עסק התורה להיות בטל אל הנהגת התורה . . . וע״י
שמכניע עצמו ומתבטל בכל מעשה אל חיות הפנימיות חיותו ית׳ ע״י אותיות
התורה שיש בכל מעשה וזה לשמה.

By studying Torah for its own sake, we are demonstrating that the Torah is
not only of theoretical interest but is our sole guide for every action that
we undertake. Just as everything is determined by Hashem, so too every
action of the Jew is dominated by the Torah. The very letters of the Torah
— its name (שְׁמָהּ) — are the guiding force behind everything that occurs.
By studying Torah for its "name," by negating oneself and subordinating
one's actions to the dictates of the Torah, we merit to perceive how the
Torah is the guiding force behind *all* human activity (*Sfas Emes, Bamidbar*
5631).

❧ To Be Completely Influenced by Torah

והאדם צריך לעסוק בתורה כדי שדברי תורה יכנסו בלבו וימשיכו כל מעשיו
אחרי׳ . . . והוא ענין שבע״פ כשהתורה נכנס, בעומק הלב וממילא נעשין כל
מעשיו עפ׳ התורה . . . ומצינו באבותינו הראשונם שכל מעשיהם הי׳ תורה שהרי
נכתב מעשיהם בתורה . . . וזה לשמה.

In our previous commentary, we focused on studying Torah with the objective of influencing the universe or in order to plumb its inner depths. However, this concept may also be appreciated on a more fundamental level —
simply studying Torah so that we *ourselves* are influenced by it. The extraordinary effort involved in studying the Oral Law inevitably leaves an impact
on its students. In rare instances, such as in the case of the *Avos* (Patriarchs), the
Torah leaves so profound an imprint on their lives that their every action is
chronicled in the Torah. Each of us — even those on a lesser spiritual level than
the *Avos* — who study Torah with the objective of being influenced by it will
disseminate the good name of Torah, because we reorient our entire lives to the
service of Hashem and His Torah (*Sfas Emes, Bamidbar* 5633).

❧ Never Forget the Torah's Origin

בתורה איתא בתחלה היא היא נקראת תורת ה׳ ומשעמל בה היא נקראת תורתו
כדכתיב ובתורתו יהגה, והלומד תורה לשמה היינו שיודע שהכל הוא מהשי״ת.

According to the *Pnei Menachem,* the "litmus test" and best indicator that a
particular individual is studying Torah for its own sake is that he never
forgets the Torah's Divine origins. While this may seem obvious — and especially to someone who is immersed in Torah — it is entirely possible that one

becomes so absorbed with his own original contributions to Torah[1] that he may momentarily forget the Torah's Divine origins (*Maggidei HaEmes*).

◆§ Are We Studying תּוֹרָה לִשְׁמָהּ?

כאן גלה לנו התנא רבי שאין אנחנו לומדים לשמה, דהיכן הם כל המידות הנמנות במשנה.

R' Yitzchak of Worka maintained that his generation (and probably ours, as well) did *not* merit to study for its own sake. He based his conclusion on the simple reasoning that if indeed we studied Torah as we should, why don't we and our scholars enjoy *all* the sterling character traits that the *mishnah* enumerates? (*Maggidei HaEmes*).

וכ״ק מרן אדמו״ר זצללה״ה הלב שמחה ביאר שבא התנא להורות שגם אחר שהאדם עוסק בתורה נצרך להגיע למדות טובות.

According to the *Lev Simchah*, our *mishnah* is telling us a *sequence* of events that follow from studying for its own sake; not the type of reward that automatically is granted to those who learn. Being concerned that one might assume that Torah study is the final phase in our spiritual development, the *Baraisa* emphasizes that, as great as pure Torah study is, it is only an *initial* phase leading to the gradual acquisition of perfected character traits (מדות טובות) (*Maggidei HaEmes*).

■ זוֹכֶה לִדְבָרִים הַרְבֵּה — *Merits many things.* ■

◆§ Vanquishing All of Torah's Opponents

שנותנת לו כח לנצח כל המתנגדים לתורה כמו שכתוב זכיתי פירוש נצחתי.

According to the *Chozeh* of Lublin, the term זוֹכֶה, usually translated here as *to merit*, may be similar to its use in the phrase, לֹא זָכִיתִי, *I did not succeed*, in the sense of "I did not prevail over my antagonists." Someone who studies Torah for its own sake will eventually succeed in vanquishing many of Torah's most relentless opponents (*Maggidei HaEmes*).

---

1. To some extent, a Torah student's preoccupation with *his* learning — rather than Hashem, the Source of the Torah — is appropriate. David speaks of the transition that occurs to the serious student of Torah. Prior to immersing himself, he is merely studying *Hashem's* Torah (cf. *Tehillim* 1:2). However, upon delving into Torah, he internalizes his learning, it becomes תּוֹרָתוֹ, his own Torah (cf. *Avodah Zarah* 19b).

דברים גדולים בענין שכתב בשפ"א ירא שמים בסתר ובגלוי פירוש על ידי
שיודע שהשי"ת משגיח על כל דבר ונופל עליו יראה, ובסתר הוא להיות נדבק
יראתו ית' בחיות האדם שלא יהיה שום פעולה ותנועה שישכח שהוא בכח
השי"ת. ע"כ צריכים לזכור ששום דבר אינו מעצמו אלא הכל מאתו יתברך.

The *Lev Simchah* interpreted the term דְּבָרִים הַרְבֵּה as referring to great accomplishments — in a *qualitative* sense — not necessarily *many* rewards (quantitative). Perhaps the greatest reward bestowed upon those who study Torah with no ulterior motive is an enhanced sense of clinging to Hashem. Such a fortunate individual does not initiate any action — does not take a single step in life — without total cognizance of Hashem's Presence. The selection from *Tanna D'Vei Eliyahu* (an ancient Midrash taught by Eliyahu HaNavi to the sage Rav Anan, cf. *Kesubos* 106a) cited in the daily *Tefillos:* לְעוֹלָם יְהֵא אָדָם יְרֵא שָׁמַיִם בְּסֵתֶר וּבַגָּלוּי, *Always let a person be God fearing privately and publicly,* may be interpreted in a similar fashion. As a result of my complete awareness of Hashem's Presence (a revelation which I perceive intensely, בַגָּלוּי), every action of mine, even if performed in complete seclusion, is based on only one criterion — which is the best course of action that will come closest to fulfilling the Divine will (*Maggidei HaEmes*).

⊲§ Being Accepted as the Authoritative Ruling

זוכה לדברים הרבה, מה שמלמדנו כן התנא היינו שיהי' כך פסק הלכה כעין
שמצינו מאיר בני אומר כו'.

Perhaps, "many things" refers to the ability of those who study Torah for its own sake to arrive at the correct halachic ruling in cases of dispute among scholars. In fact, Rabbi Meir, the author of this *Baraisa*, enjoyed this blessing to some extent. Despite having been a disciple of the controversial Elisha ben Avuyah (also known as *Acher*, who later became a heretic), Rabbi Meir's opinions were actually cited — even in Heaven — with great reverence (cf. *Chagigah* 15b).

■ נִקְרָא רֵעַ — *He is called, "Friend."*

⊲§ Hashem's "Friend"

כי אם האדם אינו לומד גורם צער כלפי מעלה, נמצא שעל ידי לימוד תורה לשמה
נקרא ריע ואהוב.

The justification for a person who studies being called a friend of Hashem, an accolade of great distinction, is actually quite simple. Since the *Shechinah* "suffers" grievously when a Jew does not realize his potential for Torah study, by learning to our utmost capacity, we spare Hashem any further grief. For that alone, we deserve the title רֵעַ, "a friend," of Hashem (*Maggidei HaEmes*).

תיבת נקרא היא רק על ריע דבזה הוי דרך כבוד לשמים שלא לומר הוא ריע רק נקרא ריע.

Yet, the *Baraisa* is careful not to state outright that such an individual *is a* friend of Hashem — but rather נִקְרָא רֵעַ, he is *considered* to be a friend of Hashem. Such deference is appropriate in view of the unbridgeable chasm that exists between even the greatest mortals — or angels, for that matter — and the *Shechinah*. In fact, according to the *Sfas Emes*, the term נִקְרָא refers only to the first of many attributes listed here, that of רֵעַ. Whereas all the other qualities mentioned here may be fully attained, no mortal can attain the distinction of *being* a "friend" of Hashem.

■ אָהוּב — *Beloved.*

◆§ Deserving to Be Loved

אהוב שזוכה לעשות מעשים שייטיב בעיני כל הברואים ויהי' אהוב.

The term אָהוּב, in the passive tense (נִפְעַל) "he is loved," implies that someone who studies Torah for its own sake will merit the love of his fellow man. As a reward for assiduous Torah study, he will *merit* to perform good deeds. This, in turn, will lead to public approval, and eventually love.

■ אוֹהֵב אֶת הַמָּקוֹם, אוֹהֵב אֶת הַבְּרִיּוֹת — *He loves the Omnipresent, he loves [His] creatures.*

◆§ The "By-Products" of Studying תּוֹרָה לִשְׁמָהּ

כי כאשר יש מחלוקת ובני אדם מריבים זה עם זה מתבטלין מן התורה, וכיון שהאדם לומד תורה לשמה בודאי אוהב הוא את המקום ואוהב את הבריות, ואחד תלוי בחבירו.
מי שאינו אוהב את הבריות בנפשו סימן שאינו לומד תורה לשמה.

These attributes are not necessarily the reward for studying Torah for its own sake, but rather the outcome — they occur *while* studying Torah: In an

אוֹהֵב אֶת הַבְּרִיּוֹת, מְשַׂמֵּחַ אֶת הַמָּקוֹם, מְשַׂמֵּחַ אֶת הַבְּרִיּוֹת. וּמַלְבַּשְׁתּוֹ עֲנָוָה וְיִרְאָה; וּמַכְשַׁרְתּוֹ לִהְיוֹת צַדִּיק, חָסִיד, יָשָׁר, וְנֶאֱמָן; וּמְרַחַקְתּוֹ מִן הַחֵטְא,

environment of dispute, controversy, the various antagonists are so preoccupied with their quarrel that they do not have sufficient time for Torah study. If, however, an individual devotes considerable time and effort to Torah study, this indicates that he is not engaged in controversy and thus will be beloved by all. It also follows that by being immersed in Torah, he earns Hashem's love as well (*Pnei Menachem, Maggidei HaEmes*).

R' Nachum of Chernobel would emphasize the reverse side of this relationship: If a Jew is unable to love his peers as much as himself, this is indicative that he most likely does not study Torah properly (*Maggidei HaEmes*).

■ **מְשַׂמֵּחַ אֶת הַמָּקוֹם, מְשַׂמֵּחַ אֶת הַבְּרִיּוֹת** — *He gladdens the Omnipresent, he gladdens [His] creatures.*

◄§ Making Hashem Happy

יבואר עפ"י מה דאיתא קוב"ה אורייתא וישראל חד, נמצא שבשעה שמשמח את המקום הרי הוא משמח את הבריות.

By making Hashem happy, one makes *Klal Yisrael* happy as well. This relationship is based on the *Zohar's* assertion that הקב"ה יִשְׂרָאֵל וְאוֹרַיְיתָא כּוּלָא חַד, *Hashem, Yisrael and the Torah are one* (cf. *Acharei Mos* 73a). Hashem, the Jewish People and the Torah are considered one unit. Thus, by enabling Hashem to rejoice, we allow *Klal Yisrael* to rejoice as well (*Pnei Menachem, Maggidei HaEmes*).

■ **וּמַלְבַּשְׁתּוֹ עֲנָוָה וְיִרְאָה** — *[The Torah] clothes him in humility and fear [of God].*

◄§ Learn Even Before Attaining Humility

ומלבשתו ענוה ויראה, כנראה שביכולות ללמוד תורה לשמה גם כשאין לו כל המדות הללו.

By stating that the study of Torah for its own sake *leads* to humility and fear of Hashem, the *mishnah* implies that one may, indeed must, begin to learn Torah despite his lack of fear of Heaven and modesty (*Sfas HaEmes*).

Omnipresent, he [His] creatures; he gladdens the Omnipresent, he gladdens [His] creatures. [The Torah] clothes
him in humility and fear [of God]; it makes him fit to be
righteous, pious, fair and faithful. It moves him away

◄§ The Relationship Between Humility and Yiras Shamayim

עונה ויראה מקדים עונה הגם שאחז״ל מה שעשתה חכמה עטרה לראשה עשתה
עונה עקב לסילותה דכ׳ עקב ענוה כו׳, אך יש שני מיני יראות, והרי כתיב
באברהם אע״ה ואנכי עפר ואפר ואין להשיג גודל ענוה כזו לומר כן וא״כ ודאי
כבר הי׳ ירא שמים ומ״מ כתיב אח״כ עתה ידעתי כי ירא״ אתה מכלל שנתהווה
רק עתה אבל מקודם הי׳ באופן אחר.

The sequence of the *mishnah* implies that humility is a prerequisite for fear
of Hashem. This does not necessarily contradict the assertion of the *Talmud
Yerushalmi* (*Shabbos Perek* 1 and cf. *Avodah Zarah* 20b) implying the opposite
relationship, since there are many levels of fear of Hashem. While a basic level
of fear of Heaven can be attained *prior* to achieving true humility, a more
advanced fear of Heaven can only be achieved *after* becoming truly humble.
This distinction may be deduced from Avraham Avinu who is described
as a יְרֵא אֱלֹהִים, a God-fearing individual, only *after* successfully completing
the test of the *Akeidah* (cf. *Bereishis* 22:12). This is despite his extraordinary
humility — Avraham described himself as nothing but עָפָר וָאֵפֶר
dust and ashes (*Bereishis* 18:27) — and his other sterling traits, which had been
demonstrated earlier.

◄§ How Can Anyone Be Assured of Fear of Heaven?

אף דאמרו חז״ל הכל בידי שמים חוץ מיראת שמים, אך הפירוש דעל ידי זה
שלומד תורה לשמה על ידי זה בא ליראה.

It is difficult to understand how the *mishnah* can assure us that fear of Heaven
is a reward for studying Torah for its own sake. Fear of Hashem is one of the
few realms *not* predetermined by Hashem, but rather is directly proportional to
our efforts (cf. *Berachos* 33b, הַכֹּל בִּידֵי שָׁמַיִם חוּץ מִיִּרְאַת שָׁמַיִם). Apparently, one
reward of sincere Torah study is spiritual *self-development* which leads to
enhanced fear of Hashem.

■ וּמַכְשַׁרְתּוֹ לִהְיוֹת צַדִּיק, חָסִיד, יָשָׁר וְנֶאֱמָן — *It makes him fit to be righteous, pious, fair and faithful.*

◄§ Learning Torah for Its Own Sake Before Attaining the Status of a *Tzaddik*

משמע שאפילו אינו צדיק ואינו חסיד ואינו ישר ואינו נאמן גם כן יכול ללמוד תורה
לשמה.

The *Chiddushei HaRim* deduced from the sequence of the *mishnah* — imply-ing that righteousness *results* from studying Torah for its own sake — that it is entirely possible to properly study Torah even *prior* to attaining the status of צַדִּיק, חָסִיד, יָשָׁר וְנֶאֱמָן, *righteous, pious, fair and faithful* (*Maggidei HaEmes*).

◄§ A Return to Our Previous Potential

ומכשרתו להיות צדיק, אף דאיתא צדיק ורשע לא קאמר וזה אינו ביד"ש, אך הפי'
דמתחלה אחר הלידה תלוי רק באדם, ואח"כ ע"י העוונת אובד הכשרתו להיות
צדיק וע"י התורה לשמה זוכה שוב לזה.

The expression וּמַכְשַׁרְתּוֹ לִהְיוֹת צַדִּיק, "it *prepares* him to be a *tzaddik*," may allude to every individual's innate potential to be a *tzaddik*. As *Chazal* emphasize (cf. *Berachos* 33b), spiritual development is one of the few aspects of life that is totally within our control. While it may be preordained whether we will be wise or ignorant, it is certainly not predetermined whether any individ-ual will be righteous or evil.

Although this innate purity and potential for good is present at birth, it often becomes dissipated as we grow older and commit *aveiros*. However, by study-ing תּוֹרָה לִשְׁמָהּ, we somehow elicit and reinvigorate this הַכְשָׁרָה, this innate potential for righteousness.

◄§ Becoming a "Kosher" Jew

קשה מהו לשון מכשרתו לכאן והלא כשרות שייך אצל בהמה. גם יש לדקדק
דבברייתא דרבי פנחס בן יאיר מהפך הסדר דירַאת חטא מביאה לידי חסידות.
אך הפי' הוא כך דכמו בבהמה כשיש לה סירכא ממשמש בה מעט מעט עד שיסיר
הסירכא והבהמה נשארת בכשרותה, כן על ידי תורה לשמה מסיר מעליו את
הזוהמה מעט מעט ונעשה ישר חסיד "א גלייכער חסיד."

R' Henoch of Alexsander interpreted the term וּמַכְשַׁרְתּוֹ as being related to *kashrus* (כָּשֵׁר). Just as the adhesions that may be found on an animal's lungs are gradually removed and thereby the animal remains kosher, so too by studying תּוֹרָה לִשְׁמָהּ we gradually remove the blemishes from our character that may have developed over time. This will permit us to attain the lofty objectives stated in the *mishnah* of being *righteous, pious, fair and faithful* (*Maggidei HaEmes*).

■ צַדִּיק, חָסִיד — *Righteous, pious.*

∞§ Not Even Fooling Himself

> שהצדיק הוא מקיים מה שכתוב ולא תונו איש את עמיתו שאינו מאנה אחרים
> נמצא שהחסיד עושה לפנים משורת הדין היינו מי שאינו מאנה אף את עצמו.

A *tzaddik* will never act unjustly to a peer (cf. *Vayikra* 25:17). A *chassid*, however, is one who goes לִפְנִים מִשּׁוּרַת הַדִּין, beyond the basic requirement of the law. He is even more demanding, and refuses to even act unjustly to himself (e.g. by harboring any delusions about himself) (adapted from R' Menachem Mendel of Worka, *Maggidei HaEmes*).

■ חָסִיד, יָשָׁר — *Pious, fair.* ■

∞§ A Rational Chassid

> פירוש להיות חסיד ישר ולא חסיד שוטה.

The terms חָסִיד יָשָׁר may be understood as a *single* concept. It refers to a rational-acting *chassid* who carefully considers his behavior. This is in contrast to a חָסִיד שׁוֹטֶה whose piety leads to foolish, albeit sincerely intentioned deeds (R' Henoch of Alexander, *Maggidei HaEmes*).

■ וּמְרַחַקְתּוֹ מִן הַחֵטְא — *It moves him away from sin.* ■

∞§ Expiating the Sins of Youth

> לכאורה קשה מאחר שקורא אותו צדיק וחסיד פשיטא שמרוחק מן החטא. אלא
> י"ל מן החטא היינו מן החטא שיש לו מנעוריו.

The phrase *from sin* may allude to the sins committed during his youth. An individual who studies Torah for its own sake not only attains the lofty levels of being righteous and pious but is even able to rectify his *past* sins (*Lev Simchah, Maggidei HaEmes*).

∞§ Protection Even in the Secular World

> די תורה מאבט א גדר סחור סחור מ'זאל אין גאנצען נישט צו קומען צו דעם חטא.

וּמְקָרַבְתּוֹ לִידֵי זְכוּת. וְנֶהֱנִין מִמֶּנּוּ עֵצָה וְתוּשִׁיָּה, בִּינָה וּגְבוּרָה, שֶׁנֶּאֱמַר: "לִי עֵצָה וְתוּשִׁיָּה, אֲנִי בִינָה, לִי גְבוּרָה." וְנוֹתֶנֶת לוֹ מַלְכוּת, וּמֶמְשָׁלָה, וְחִקּוּר דִּין;

בעידנא דלא עסיק בה טויג דאך נישט, אלא הכוונה אפילו אם קורה שהאדם צריך לצאת לפרנסתו, יגיעת שניהם משכחת עון.

The phrase "moves him away from sin" implies that the Torah acts as a protective cordon preventing those who study its teachings from coming close to sin — even when they are engaged in commerce (cf. *Sotah* 21a, בעידנא דלא עסיק בה אגוני מגנא, Torah protects its disciples even when they are not studying it). A similar thought is voiced in an earlier *perek* (2:2), שֶׁיְּגִיעַת שְׁנֵיהֶם מְשַׁכַּחַת עָוֹן, *for the exertion of them both makes sin forgotten* — The weariness (יְגִיעָה) often associated with being involved in *both* Torah and commerce prevents one from sinning.

⪧ Preventing Others From Sinning

לכאורה הרי גם תורה שלא לשמה מרחקת מן החטא כמו שאמרו רז״ל משכחו לביהמ״ד. אלא נראה דכשלומד לשמה נותנת לו כח להרחיק אחרים מן החטא, כענין ונהנין ממנו עצה ותושיה שהיא לגבי אחרים.

In truth, even Torah that is studied not for its own sake has the effect of stifling the *Yetzer Hara*. In fact, *Chazal* advise us: אִם פָּגַע בְּךָ מְנֻוָּל זֶה, מָשְׁכֵהוּ לְבֵית הַמִּדְרָשׁ, if the *Yetzer Hara* is bothering you, drag him to the study hall (*Succah* 52b). However, Torah study for its own sake is so potent that it gives its students the capacity to influence others not to sin (*Lev Simchah, Maggidei HaEmes*).

■ וּמְרַחֲקָתוֹ מִן הַחֵטְא וּמְקָרַבְתּוֹ לִידֵי זְכוּת — *It moves him away from sin and draws him near to merit.*

⪧ Meriting to Do Good Deeds

כמ״ש מגלגלין זכות ע״י זכאי לצאת מהרע ולכנוס בהטוב הגנוז.

The rather difficult expression וּמְקָרַבְתּוֹ לִידֵי זְכוּת, *and draws him near to merit;* may be understood by recalling that Hashem ensures that worthy people are the progenitors of good events and that evil people bring about tragic occurrences. As a result of studying Torah for its own sake, one will merit to be a

from sin and draws him near to merit. From him people enjoy counsel and wisdom, understanding and strength, as it is said (Mishlei 8:14): "Mine are counsel and wisdom, I am understanding, mine is strength." [The Torah] gives him kingship and dominion and analytical judgment;

catalyst for good deeds.

Alternatively, this phrase may be interpreted as the conclusion of the previous thought, *it moves him away from sin.* One who studies Torah for its own sake is not only shielded from sin but is also able to elicit much of the goodness that Hashem implanted in the universe. When Hashem created the universe, He concealed the primeval light of creation [described by the Torah (*Bereishis* 1:4) as being good] so that most mortals would not be able to benefit from its brilliant spiritual radiance. However, those who study Torah with the proper intentions not only are able to resist temptation but also merit to elicit and enjoy the sublime spiritual treasures that Hashem established — and concealed — in His universe.

■ וְנֶהֱנִין מִמֶּנּוּ עֵצָה וְתוּשִׁיָּה ■ — *From him people enjoy counsel and wisdom.*

⇜§ Both Sacred and Secular Advice

עצה בעניני עוה״ז ותושי׳ י״ל נמי עצה בעבדות ה׳ וו״ש לי עצה לי לשמי, ואפשר לומר פי׳ תושי׳ דהיינו גם בעומד במצודה ומצוקה והוא תש כח ומ״מ מוצא דרך זה נקרא תושי׳.

The repetition of the terms עֵצָה and תוּשִׁיָּה, *counsel and wisdom,* may indicate that an individual who studies Torah for its own sake is a resource for advice regarding *spiritual* concerns, known as תוּשִׁיָּה, as well as worldly matters, known as עֵצָה.

Alternatively, the term תוּשִׁיָּה may be related to תָּשׁ, to be weak. Even in troubled times when it appears that there are no solutions, the student who studies Torah for its own sake is able to cope.[1]

■ וְנוֹתֶנֶת לוֹ מַלְכוּת וּמֶמְשָׁלָה ■ — *[The Torah] gives him kingship and dominion.*

⇜§ Why Would a Talmid Chacham Desire to Reign?

אאז״ל פירש דמלכות היינו שיכול לקשר עצמו במלכות שמים וממשלה הוא

---

1. Cf. *Sanhedrin* 26b for a similar interpretation of the term תוּשִׁיָּה.

ומְגַלִּין לוֹ רָזֵי תוֹרָה; וְנַעֲשֶׂה כְּמַעְיָן הַמִּתְגַּבֵּר, וּכְנָהָר שֶׁאֵינוֹ פוֹסֵק; וְהֹוֶה צָנוּעַ, וְאֶרֶךְ רוּחַ, וּמוֹחֵל עַל עֶלְבּוֹנוֹ. וּמְגַדַּלְתּוֹ וּמְרוֹמַמְתּוֹ עַל כָּל הַמַּעֲשִׂים.
א / ו

על דרך שכתוב צדיק מושל יראת אלקים. ואיתא מי מושל בי צדיק. מלך הוא ברצון ומושל הוא בעל כרחו של הנמשל והצדיק יכול לבטל הגזירה שגזר הקב"ה.

It is unlikely that we are referring to becoming a monarch (in the traditional sense) or attaining political power. Why would a truly sincere student of Torah desire such material prerogatives? Perhaps, Rabbi Meir, the author of this passage, is alluding to a far more impressive power — the capacity to, on occasion, "influence" the Divine will. David describes this unusual "bonus" as צַדִּיק מוֹשֵׁל יִרְאַת אֱלֹהִים (II Shmuel 23:3), the tzaddik who truly fears Hashem can, in a sense, "reign," intervening on behalf of Klal Yisrael. He can prevail upon Hashem to reverse certain harsh decrees.

In fact, both the terms מַלְכוּת and מֶמְשָׁלָה can be understood in this light. Not only is the one who studies Torah for its own sake able to perceive a close link with the universe's Sovereignty (מֶלֶךְ), Hashem, but he is also able to leave an impact on His decrees to "reign" (מֶמְשָׁלָה), as it were — in conjunction with Him (Imrei Emes, Maggidei HaEmes).

✎§ Coronating the Yetzer Hatov

כלומר חירות גם י"ל כמ"ש ירא כו' ומלך ע"ש כל הפירושים במד"ר פ' בהעלותך.

The term מַלְכוּת may also refer to freedom from all constraints (both physical and spiritual) that so often restrict our growth. Just as a king does not fear his own subjects, so too the true talmid chacham is beyond fearing mortals.

Alternatively, we may be referring to the ability of the individual who studies Torah for its own sake to successfully "coronate" the Yetzer Hatov as the dominant force in his life.

■ וְחִקּוּר דִּין — And analytical judgment.

✎§ Mitigating Strict Justice

היינו שעושה מהדינים חסדים. כל הדינים הם כדי לעשות מהם חסדים, וזה הוא כח משה רבינו דאיתא שבמשנה תורה פוסק מאי טעמא וכו' ומשה מפי עצמו

the secrets of the Torah are revealed to him; he becomes like a steadily strengthening fountain and like an unceasing river. He becomes modest, patient, and forgiving of insult to himself. [The Torah] makes him great and exalts him above all things.

אמרן. פוסק היינו להמתיק.

The term חִקּוּר דִּין may refer to the *talmid chacham's* capacity to mitigate some of the harshest Divine decrees. Just as a thorough investigation of the ruling of a mortal judge often leads to a more profound understanding of his verdict, so too through proper Torah study the scholar often finds the underlying kindness which lies just beneath the superficial exterior of justice. Frequently, a verdict which appears on the surface to be harsh, is revealed upon closer investigation as a manifestation of Divine kindness (*Imrei Emes, Maggidei HaEmes*).

■ וּמְגַלִּין לוֹ רָזֵי תוֹרָה ■ — *The secrets of the Torah are revealed to him.*

◄§ The Angels Reveal Torah's Secrets

משמע לשון זה על המלאכים שאוהבין אותו ומגלין לו.

The expression וּמְגַלִּין לוֹ can be translated literally as *"they reveal"* the secrets of Torah to him. This may refer to the heavenly angels. Just as the angels at Sinai were fascinated by Moshe Rabbeinu and revealed to him many of the Torah's greatest secrets, so too in every generation those angels reveal the deepest secrets of the Torah to those who study it for its own sake.

■ וְנַעֲשֶׂה כְּמַעְיָן הַמִּתְגַּבֵּר וּכְנָהָר שֶׁאֵינוֹ פּוֹסֵק — *He becomes like a steadily strengthening fountain and like an unceasing river.*

◄§ An Extraordinary Fountain and River

כמעין המתגבר היינו במקום שנובע הוא קטן, ונהר שהוא גדול מכל מקום פוסק, מה שאין כן לזה בשניהם לשבח.

Unlike most wells whose sources are barely noticeable, the Torah scholar is compared to a fountain whose source visibly replenishes itself. Whereas most rivers eventually terminate, the student of Torah is described as a never-ceasing river.

■ וְהֹוֶה צָנוּעַ, וְאֶרֶךְ רוּחַ וּמוֹחֵל עַל עֶלְבּוֹנוֹ — *He becomes modest, patient, and forgiving of insult to himself.*

✑ Reward or Prerequisite

שהוא תנאי שכל זה יתקיים רק בהקדם מדת הצניעות דלא יתגלה מיד שלומד
תורה לשמה. גם יש לומר שהיא זכיה שיזכה להיות צנוע במעשיו כי אין לך יפה
מן הצניעות.

ומוחל על עלבונו קאי נמי על הדברים שזוכה דאם לא כן הו"ל למימר עלבונך
לשון נוכח כמו הוי צנוע.

ויל"פ דקאי אדלעיל מה שאמר ונעשה וכו', וכנהר שא"פ, ע"ז קאמר דלזה צריך
להיות אצלו אלו הדברים ג"כ להיות צנוע. דבאמת הלומד תורה לשמה אף שאין
בו אלו הדברים מ"מ מוכרח שיגיע לו כל המעלות הנ"ל אך אינם אצלו לעולם
ופוסקין ממנו אבל מי שיש אצלו גם אלו הדברים נעשה כנהר שאינו פוסק ונשאר
אצלו לעולם.

These traits may be understood as prerequisites for attaining all of the virtues mentioned in the *Baraisa*, or as a reward for their achievement. The *mishnah* may be telling a person: Remain modest — do not reveal to the public that you are studying Torah for its own sake. On the other hand, the trait of modesty may also be one of the significant rewards for such study. *Chazal* describe modesty as perhaps the greatest of all character traits (cf. *Rashi, Shemos* 34:3 אֵין לְךָ יָפָה מִן הַצְּנִיעוּת, ד"ה ואיש). This supreme reward — attaining true modesty — is reserved for the student of Torah for its own sake.

Similarly, this uncertainty arises regarding the trait of "forgiving of insult to himself." On one hand, it is stated in the third person ("*he forgives his* humiliation") rather than as a command in the second person, תִּמְחוֹל עַל עֶלְבּוֹנְךָ, "*you* should forgive *your* humiliation." Thus, it seems to be indicating that this is a *reward* for studying Torah. Alternatively, we may interpret this phrase to mean that this trait this is a *prerequisite* for attaining what is perhaps the greatest accolade of our *Baraisa*: enjoying the eternal life of Torah and never ceasing to find new meaning and insights from the Torah.

While anyone who studies Torah for its own sake is assured of most of the virtues enumerated here, not everyone can aspire to be a never-ceasing source of Torah insights. Only those individuals who embody the traits mentioned in the concluding passage — modesty, patience, and the ability to forgive any slights — deserve that exalted status.

■ וּמוֹחֵל עַל עֶלְבּוֹנוֹ וּמְגַדַּלְתּוֹ וּמְרוֹמַמְתּוֹ עַל כָּל הַמַּעֲשִׂים — *And forgiving of insult to himself. [The Torah] makes him great and exalts him above all things.*

פירוש שהגדולה והרוממות שיש לו לאדם על כל המעשים, הוא בזה שיכול

The *Pnei Menachem* emphasized the juxtaposition of the final two virtues described in the *Baraisa* to the preceding trait, the ability to forgive slights. A Torah scholar's greatness over all beings is demonstrated by his extraordinary capacity for forgiving others (*Maggidei HaEmes*).

⇜§ The Imrei Emes's Capacity for Forgiveness

פעם יצא הרה"ק רבי מאיר הי"ד בנו בכורו של אדמו"ר האמרי אמת ז"ל, מחדרו של אביו ז"ל וסיפר למקורבו "זה עתה גילה לי אבא שהיה כאן אדם נוכל שהתחזה כלפי חוץ לידיד ומקורב, אולם בלבו פנימה חרש מזימות נגד אבי. פעם ערך האיש מכתב הלשנה כנגדו לשלוח לפטרבורג, ומכתב שני ידידותי לשלוח אל אבי. אך בהשגחה פרטית נתחלפו האגרות וכתב ההלשנה בא לידו של אבא במקום לפטרבורג. תוך כדי סיפורו הראה לי אבי את המכתב והדברים שנכתבו מדברים בעדם, ברור שנס גדול התרחש לו אז. [והאמרי אמת ז"ל עצמו התבטא פעם אודות המכתב שאם היה מכתב זה מגיע לפטרבורג היו מוליכים אותו אסור באזיקים.] האיש ההוא ממשיך לנסוע לגור בתוך הבאים כאילו לא אירע דבר ואבא לא הזכיר לו אף פעם על אודות המכתב ולא עוד אלא שמראה לו אותות קירבה יתירה. תמיד התפלאתי, הפטיר רבי מאיר, מה פשר קירוב מופלג זה, באופן יוצא מן הכלל, אכן נודע הדבר."

The following incident — retold by R' Meir Alter, the oldest son of the *Imrei Emes*, a great *tzaddik* who was martyred in the Holocaust — illustrates the unusual capacity of the *Imrei Emes* to forgive even his most dangerous enemies.

A certain individual had prepared a letter to be sent to the Czar falsely accusing the *Imrei Emes* of heinous crimes against the Russian Empire. Simultaneously, this person wrote a friendly letter to the *Imrei Emes*, hoping to prevent the Rebbe from suspecting him of playing a role in the matter. Miraculously, the letters were switched, resulting in the Czar receiving a letter singing the Rebbe's praises and the *Imrei Emes* becoming fully aware of the gravity of the false accusations against him.

This particularly hypocritical individual continued to visit the Rebbe as if nothing untoward had ever occurred and the *Imrei Emes* received him graciously, never mentioning the incident.

■ עַל כָּל הַמַּעֲשִׂים — *Above all things.*

⇜§ The Torah Is a Guide, Even in the Secular World

הכוונה לא זה בלבד כשעוסק בתורה או בתפלה בזה עובד ה', אלא אפילו

[ב] אָמַר רַבִּי יְהוֹשֻׁעַ בֶּן לֵוִי: בְּכָל יוֹם וָיוֹם בַּת קוֹל יוֹצֵאת מֵהַר חוֹרֵב, וּמַכְרֶזֶת וְאוֹמֶרֶת: ,,אוֹי לָהֶם

כשעושה מעשיו גשמיות עושה הכל לשם שמים, שתורה הקדושה מורה לו הדרך
היאך לעשות הכל לשם שמים כשמה בלשון הוראה ומראה. וזה ומרוממתו על "כל
המעשים."

According to the Maggid of Koznitz, the expression עַל כָּל הַמַּעֲשִׂים, *above all things*, may refer to the guidance provided by Torah to those who study it for its own sake, even while they are engrossed in the material aspects of their life. In fact, the term תּוֹרָה is related to מַרְאֶה, *to show*, alluding to the Torah's capacity to guide us through the most treacherous paths of the secular world (*Maggidei HaEmes*).

2.

■ בְּכָל יוֹם וָיוֹם בַּת קוֹל יוֹצֵאת מֵהַר חוֹרֵב — *Every single day a heavenly voice emanates from Mount Horeb.*

⇜ The Voice of Sinai

זהו הבת קול הוא מכח קול התורה שכתיב קול גדול ולא יסף ולא פסיק שבכל יום
ויום יש התגלות מזה הקול, ועל זה כתיב אשר אנכי מצוך היום.

This heavenly voice is not a new sound that emanates from Sinai but simply the continuation of the Divine voice that we heard at Sinai when Hashem gave us the Ten Commandments. When describing the Revelation at Sinai we are told that the other sounds — the fire and lightning and thunder — eventually ceased. The Divine voice, however, never stopped, as it says in the Torah, קוֹל גָּדוֹל וְלֹא יָסָף, *a great voice that never ceased* (*Devarim* 5:19; cf. *Targum* on this *pasuk* ולא פסיק, "the sound never ceased"). Every day this eternal voice is heard again, pleading with us to study Torah.

⇜ Daily Repetition — Daily Renewal of the עֲשֶׂרֶת הַדִּבְּרוֹת

וע"ז כתיב אשר אנכי מצוך היום, אנכי דעשרת הדיברות, שהי' מוכן באלה
הדיברות קול מיוחד לכל יום ויום, וכמו שמעשיו בראשית מתחדש בכל יום, ומכח
הטבע נמצא ג"כ הסתר בכל יום שע"ז אמרו יצרו של אדם מתגבר עליו בכל יום
ולכן יש ג"כ גאולה וחירות בכל יום ויום וע"י העסק בתורה נעשה בן חורין כמ"ש
אנכי כו' אשר הוצאתיך מארץ מצרים.

[2] *Rabbi Yehoshua ben Levi said: Every single day a heavenly voice emanates from Mount Horeb, proclaiming and saying, "Woe to them, to the people, because*

Every day brings its own challenges, and sometimes even seemingly insurmountable obstacles, along the road to Divine service.

Likewise, the *Yetzer Hara* gains additional strength every day (cf. *Succah* 52b).

Anticipating those developments, Hashem provided the perfect antidote — the daily renewal of the Ten Commandments. In the *Shema* we remind ourselves of this renewal, saying: אֲשֶׁר אָנֹכִי מְצַוְּךָ הַיּוֹם, *that I command you today* (*Devarim* 6:6) — the "אָנֹכִי", the word "I" with which the Ten Commandments begins, is experienced anew every day.

Moreover, this heavenly voice is imploring us to regain our freedom by immersing ourselves in Torah study. Just as we were liberated from Pharaoh, so can we be extricated from the clutches of the *Yetzer Hara*.

The Lingering Sin of Bitul Torah

אין לך יום שנמסע הב״ק, אף שיש כמה וכמה ת״ח שלומדין כראוי . . . מ״מ אי אפשר להשלים כראוי דאין אדם ניצול בכ״י מביטול תורה שאין לו שיעור.

We are taught that the study of Torah is a *mitzvah* that is limitless and bears infinite reward: אֵלּוּ דְבָרִים שֶׁאֵין לָהֶם שִׁעוּר . . . אֵלּוּ דְבָרִים שֶׁאָדָם אוֹכֵל פֵּרוֹתֵיהֶם בָּעוֹלָם הַזֶּה וְהַקֶּרֶן קַיֶּמֶת לוֹ לָעוֹלָם הַבָּא . . . וְתַלְמוּד תּוֹרָה כְּנֶגֶד כֻּלָּם, *These are the precepts that have no prescribed measure . . . These are the precepts whose fruits a person enjoys in This World but whose principal remains intact for him in the World to Come . . . and the study of Torah is equivalent to them all* (*Peah* 1:1; *Shabbos* 127a)]. Conversely, neglecting Torah study is an eternal sin affecting almost everyone to some extent. The heavenly voice resonates every day with Hashem's plea to *Klal Yisrael* to beware of ignoring the study of Torah! Even if you have studied Torah your entire life, do not rest on your laurels; rather, continue performing this greatest of *mitzvos* daily.

Why Do We Not Hear This Voice?

ולמה אין אנו שומעים את הבת קול. ונראה שההתעוררות שמתעוררת בלב האדם באיזה רגע של חשבון נפשו, זאת היא הבת קול. הב״ק מתעורר בכ״א מה שמתעורר לפעמים הכל עי״ז הב״ק ממ״נ מי ששומע וודאי לומד כראוי וא״י לב״י ומי שאינו לומד אינו שומע וכ״כ בכש״ט. הר דומם ומ״מ הוא מדבר ומוציא קול ואנחנו מדברים ואין אנחנו שומעים עד מה. וכן יש בנו נשמה עליונה א״י מכ״ש שצריכים להתעורר.

W hile we may feel that we do not hear this heavenly voice, the Baal
Shem Tov suggests that, in a sense, we are all motivated and greatly
influenced by it. Those significant moments of inspiration in which we take
stock of ourselves, confront our deficiencies and as a result re-adjust our lifestyle
to more closely conform with Hashem's wishes are directly attributable to the
impact of this voice.

Perhaps the greatest source of inspiration is the very fact that an inanimate
mountain remains the vehicle for the Divine word simply because the Torah
was given there. This should encourage each Jew, who is gifted with a Divine
soul and who has the potential to be immersed in Torah, to exploit every
opportunity to study Torah.

Why isn't every Jew inspired by the Divine summons? We can understand
this based on the *Zohar's* assertion that the same call that Avraham received,
"Leave your homeland ...," is directed to every Jew — "Leave behind your
errant ways and return to Me." Unfortunately, we allow ourselves to be dis-
tracted by the temptations of This World and do not listen to the inner voice.
Avraham and the *tzaddikim* of every generation were sensitive enough to hear
Hashem's message clearly, and to heed its plea.

Similarly, the message of Sinai is directed towards *every* Jew — we have only
to be responsive and assimilate its contents. All too often, we unfortunately
drown out this heavenly voice with our infatuation with material matters
(based on *Sfas Emes, Lech Lecha* 5632; cf. Introduction to *Three Festivals*, pp.
23-24).

◆§ A Parent's Cry

והקשה הבעש"ט זצוק"ל ממה נפשך אם הקול יוצא לעורר לבבות בני ישראל
לתשובה אמיתית אזי כולם צריכים לשמוע הקול, ואם אי אפשר לשום איש
לשמוע הקול למה צריכין הקול. ונראה לתרץ על דרך משל לאחד שנסע לרגל
מסחרו לעיר אחת ואז היה בימות החמה והיה עמו עולם קטן. וכאשר נסעו דרך
יער בקש העולם שירשה לו אביו ללקוט דובדבניות. אמר לו אביו אבל בינתיים
אני אסע הלאה ותוכל לתעות ביער. ענה לו בנו אני אלך ללקוט ביער ואתה תסע
לדרכך ומדי פעם אקרא אותך וכאשר תשיב לי אזי אדע לילך אחר קריאת הקול.
הלך הבן ללקוט ואביו המשיך בדרכו, וכאשר לא שמע יותר את קול בנו צועק
אליו התחיל האב לצעוק בקול גדול בני היכן אתה, והבן לא שמע. והבן כאשר
רואה שהוא טועה בדרכו צריך להטות אזנו ולהשתדל לשמוע את קול אביו
בצעקתו כי אם יוכל ללכת אחרי הקול יהיה טוב, ואם ח"ו לא יטה אזנו ולא ילך
אחרי הקול אזי יכול לטעות מאד ח"ו.

R' Simchah Bunim of Peshis'cha explained the purpose of this heavenly voice through the following parable:

A father took along his young son on a business trip. As they were passing a forest, the son requested permission to pick cherries, promising to remain in close proximity to his father. In response to his father's concern that the boy would inevitably lose his way in the thick woods, the son assured his father that he would frequently call out to him. Upon hearing his father's voice in response, he would simply follow that voice and find his way back to his father.

So too in our relationship with Hashem. No matter how far we may have strayed into the thicket of sin, we are reassured, knowing that our father in Heaven hears our voice and will indeed call us back. It is this call — a father pleading with His children to return — that is the clarion call of Sinai voiced through this heavenly voice (adapted from *Maggidei HaEmes*).

✥ A Plea Against Excessive Materialism

היינו מה שהתרחק מהתורה, שהוא דבוק ב׳עם הארץ׳ שבו, בגופניות ובכל מיני
דברים, ואיתא מהאר״י הק׳ שהאדם שומע הבת קול ומזה מגיעים אליו הרהורי
תשובה, זהו הבת קול שמתעורר בנפש הישראלי, ואם האדם משוקע בגשמיות
אינו שומע, זהו עם הארץ אין מכריזין על אבידתו, שאצל תלמיד חכם איתא ודאי
עשה תשובה, אבל אצל עם הארץ יתכן שזה להיפך, אויב מ׳איז אפ געלאזט, און
מ׳איז אריין געטוהען אין די וועלט זאכען, מ׳איז אפ גערייסען, אזוי אין מכריזין על
אבידתו ס׳קומט נישט אפ די אבידה וואס דער מענטש פארלירט, די בעסטע
יאהר׳ן וכדאיתא על חיוו לא חס, ס׳קומט נישט אן צום מענטש די הרהורי תשובה.

According to the *Pnei Menachem*, a primary message of the heavenly voice is for us to forsake the petty pursuits of the material world which prevent us from assimilating Torah to our maximum capacity. In effect, the voice represents Hashem pleading with us, "Do not waste your best days, do not abuse your most precious asset — time!"

In this light, we can homiletically interpret the statement (*Pesachim* 49b), עַם הָאָרֶץ אֵין מַכְרִיזִין עַל אֲבֵידָתוֹ, to mean "An ignoramus does not cry out over his loss."[1] While a *talmid chacham* frets about every moment of wasted time, the ignoramus does not react to his lost time, and the amount of time and effort that he expends in pursuit of materialism (*Pnei Menachem*).

✥ The Most Opportune Time to Hear the Heavenly Voice

שבשבת קרוב עוד יותר לשמוע בת קול.

---

1. Literally, one must not announce that he found a lost object if it was lost by an ignorant person. This is contrary to the usual procedure that one must declare publicly that he has found a lost object. See the second chapter of *Bava Metzia* for the circumstances when this rule applies.

לַבְּרִיּוֹת, מֵעֶלְבּוֹנָהּ שֶׁל תּוֹרָה!" שֶׁכָּל מִי שֶׁאֵינוֹ עוֹסֵק
בַּתּוֹרָה נִקְרָא נָזוּף, שֶׁנֶּאֱמַר: "נֶזֶם זָהָב בְּאַף חֲזִיר, אִשָּׁה

Every Shabbos, when we put aside the material concerns that so often drown out the Heavenly voice, we are well disposed to hear its call (*Beis Yisrael, Maggidei HaEmes*).

■ מֵהַר חוֹרֵב — *From Mount Horeb.* ■

∽§ Mount Horeb

מהר חורב, מטורא דחורב, ולמה לא מסיני. אלא דאיתא בגמ' למה נקרא הר
חורב שירדה חורבה לגויים עליו, אבל בני ישראל שקבלו את התורה צריכים
לשמרה, שלא יהיה ח״ו חרב אל הבדים.

The term חוֹרֵב, related to חוּרְבָּן, *destruction*, is another name for Mount Sinai. This name alludes to the consequences that befell the gentile world as a result of rejecting the Torah. The *Baraisa* deliberately uses this name for the mountain to remind us of the dire consequences which befall those who abandon the Torah. Just as the gentile world suffered oblivion as a result of their mass rejection of Torah, so too *Klal Yisrael* should consider the consequences if they neglect the Torah (*Pnei Menachem, Maggidei HaEmes*).

■ אוֹי לָהֶם לַבְּרִיּוֹת — *Woe to them, to the people.* ■

∽§ Mankind's Loss

לכאורה הו״ל למימר אוי להם לישראל כו'. אלא לפי שהחזירה הקב״ה על כל
אומה ולשון ולא קבלוה כדאיתא.

It is significant that the *mishnah* does not say, אוֹי לָהֶם לְיִשְׂרָאֵל, "Woe to *Klal Yisrael*," for its neglect of Torah, but rather, אוֹי לָהֶם, לַבְּרִיּוֹת, "Woe to them, to the *people*."

While *Klal Yisrael* is culpable for its lack of *total* commitment to Torah, the gentile world was guilty of a far more serious offense — refusing Hashem's offer of the Torah (cf. *Rashi, Devarim* 33:2 s.v. זרח) (*Pnei Menachem, Maggidei HaEmes*).

■ מֵעֶלְבּוֹנָהּ שֶׁל תּוֹרָה — *Because of [their] insult to the Torah.* ■

of [their] insult to the Torah!" For whoever does not occupy himself with the Torah is called "Rebuked," as it is said (Mishlei 11:22): "Like a golden ring in a swine's snout is

---

◆§ Torah's "Shame" — Rejecting the Divine Gift

שהעלבון הגדול ביותר שאפשר לגרום לתורה הוא בזה שאין לומדים אותה.
ויובן על דרך משל למי ששלחו לו מתנה מבית המלך ולא קבלו, הלא אין לך בזיון
ועלבון גדול מזה. כן הוא בתורה כי הקב"ה נתן לנו את תורתו הנחמד מזהב ומפז,
נמצא דמי שעוזבה מונח בקרן זוית ואינו עוסק בה, אין לך בזיון ועלבון לתורה
גדול מזה.

To help us appreciate the concept of the Torah's "shame," the *Pnei Menachem* reminded us that Torah is a precious Divine gift — imagine rejecting a royal gift! Could anything be more insulting than rejecting a royal gift — even from a mortal monarch? How much greater the shame of the Jewish People if we discard the priceless, heavenly gift of the Torah. Perhaps, most simply stated, the greatest source of shame to the Torah is ignoring the Heavenly voice which continues to echo the Giving of the Torah (*Maggidei HaEmes*).

■ שֶׁכָּל מִי שֶׁאֵינוֹ עוֹסֵק בַּתּוֹרָה נִקְרָא נָזוּף — *For whoever does not occupy himself with the Torah is called "Rebuked."*

◆§ How Does Neglect Lead to Banishment

ולכן מי שאינו עוסק נקרא נזוף והואיל התורה מוכנת בכל יום לגלות טעמים
חדשים תמיד.
כי כפי החשיבות של דברי תורה אצל האדם כך הוא עושה פעולה בו, כמו שכתוב
גבי שאול ויאמרו מה יושיענו זה ויבזהו.
נזו'ף נוטריקון נזם זהב באף.

The Heavenly voice pleads with us to avail ourselves of the daily opportunity to develop Torah novellae, so that we may arrive at new insights in Torah. Failure to nurture oneself from the ever renewing wellsprings of Torah is tantamount to banishment from Hashem's "inner circle" (*Sfas Emes*).

The *Imrei Emes* also noted the relationship between involvement in Torah and its impact on the individual. By not studying Torah, this individual demonstrates that Torah is not significant and consequently the Torah will not have a meaningful impact on him, which in effect means that he is banished from Hashem. A precedent for such a deterioration of a relationship is that of the detractor's of Shaul (*I Shmuel* 10:27). Once they convinced themselves of Shaul's inability to help them (מַה יֹּשִׁעֵנוּ זֶה), they proceeded to degrade him as well (וַיִּבְזֻהוּ).

■ נֶזֶם זָהָב בְּאַף חֲזִיר — *Like a golden ring in a swine's snout.*

ᴈ The Torah Never Forsakes Us

וז"ש נזם זהב כו' שיש לנו התורה ואנו מניחין אותה ומתדבקין בגשמיות ועי"ז מגיע עלבון גם להתורה שהוא הנזם כתר תורה
ואף אין עוסקין בה אינה מתפרשת מהם כמ"ש חיי עולם נטע בתוכנו.

The analogy to a gold nose ring inserted in the nose of a pig, from one viewpoint, offers a message of hope. Just as the nose ring adheres to the pig even when the pig wallows in the mud, so too, despite the legitimate complaint, echoed by the Heavenly voice, that the Jewish nation has forsaken the Torah, the Torah never leaves us. As we recite after reading from the Torah, וְחַיֵּי עוֹלָם נָטַע בְּתוֹכֵנוּ, the Torah is eternally implanted in our midst.

On the other hand, the analogy of a gold ring inserted into a pig's nose hints at a great tragedy — how the Torah is forced to stand by and observe its own humiliation. Just as the nose ring remains implanted in the pig's nose even as it wallows in mud, so too the Torah, permanently wed to *Klal Yisrael*, is compelled to watch its potential students ignore it and indulge instead in the murky waters of the material world. The Heavenly voice reminds us of our abandonment and the Torah's "humiliation" at witnessing this.

ᴈ Waste of Our Potential

כי הקב"ה נתן באדם כלים יקרים מפז והם החושים החכמה והשכל שיש באדם וצריך להשתמש בהם לעבודתו ית' ולעסוק בתורה. וכשמניח הכלים הללו לדברים אחרים נאמר נזם זהב וכו'.

The analogy of a gold nose ring inserted in a pig's nose may allude not only to neglect of Torah, but also to the concomitant waste of one's G-d-given abilities when we forsake the Torah. Our senses, our wisdom, our intuition are all Divine gifts, the crown jewels of every Jew (נֶזֶם זָהָב), but are unfortunately being abused when they are primarily placed in the service of material pursuits.

a beautiful woman who turns away from good judgment."
And it says (Shemos 32:16): "The Tablets are God's hand-
iwork and the script was God's script charus (engraved)

In every sense, this misuse of our Divine gifts is as vain and futile as a pig wearing a gold nose ring and wallowing in mud.

■ נֶזֶם זָהָב ... אִשָּׁה יָפָה — *A golden ring . . . a beautiful woman.*

◆§ The Crown Jewels — Every Day of Jewish Life

אך דהענין הוא כי כל אדם מיום לידתו על האדמה יש לו שורש וחלק בתורת ה׳,
ונחלקת על כל ימי חייו הקצובים לו, ובכל יום ויום מאיר לו ניצוץ ושורש חלק אחד
מחלק אותו היום, וכל יום ויום משונה ומיוחד בענינו מחבירו, וכן כל שעה משונה
בענינה מחברתה, והן הן התכשיטים והקישוטין אשר נתנה אלקים להאשה יפה
היא הכנסת ישראל כדי להתקשט בהם בכל עת ורגע, ובכל יום ויום בקישוטים
שונים כדי להעלות נחת רוח לפניו ית׳ . . . לכן אם האדם אינו עוסק בתורה
ועזובה, נמצא שהיא אשה יפה בעבור שדבר זה מושרש בו ומחויב בדבר ועבורו
נברא, וסרת טעם, בהיותו מפסיד ועוזב כל זאת ואינו משגיח כלל בדבר.

According to the Maggid of Koznitz, the gold nose ring alludes to the enormous potential that every Jew possesses. Each Jew enjoys a distinct and unique role in the dissemination of Torah. This lifelong mission is divided into daily segments. Every day, *Klal Yisrael*, the beautiful woman referred to here, receives renewed inspiration in the form of the spiritual treasures (נֶזֶם זָהָב) given to us by Hashem.

By abandoning Torah and not utilizing our daily "ration" of spirituality, it is as if we are giving those treasures to a pig. By doing so, we are forfeiting our spiritual beauty in favor of an animal-like existence in a universe devoid of Torah (*Maggidei HaEmes*).

■ וְאוֹמֵר: וְהַלֻחֹת מַעֲשֵׂה אֱלֹהִים הֵמָּה . . . אַל תִּקְרָא "חָרוּת" אֶלָּא חֵרוּת —
And it says: The Tablets are God's handiwork . . . Do not read "charus" (engraved) but "cheirus" (freedom).

◆§ The Justification for Being Banished

ויל״פ דכיון שבכל כך טובה התורה עד שהוא בו חורין ואפי״ה אין עוסק בה נקרא
נזוף.

This *pasuk* is cited as a basis for the (seemingly extreme) designation of someone who does not study Torah as being banished. By forsaking the

Torah which brings freedom, one has earned this seemingly extreme designation.

■ וְהַלֻּחוֹת מַעֲשֵׂה אֱלֹהִים הֵמָּה — *Please refer to our commentary to 5:8 (וְהַלּוּחוֹת) for an extensive discussion of this concept.*

■ מִכְתַּב אֱלֹהִים הוּא — *Was God's script.*

אלקים נמצא בתורה ואדם המטוהר עצמו זוכה להשיג את האלקות מתוך התורה.

According to R' Simchah Bunim of Peshis'cha, this *pasuk* is not only stating that Hashem wrote the *Luchos* but also that by scrutinizing the *writing* on the *Luchos* (and all of Torah), the deserving Jew can find Hashem in the Torah itself.[1]

■ שֶׁאֵין לְךָ בֶן חוֹרִין אֶלָּא מִי שֶׁעוֹסֵק בְּתַלְמוּד תּוֹרָה — *For you can have no freer man than one who engages in the study of the Torah.*

◆§ No Excuses for Neglecting Torah

ואומר חרות כו' הוא להסיר התירוץ מטירדות עולם הזה מאחר שהעוסק בתורה
בדילין ממנו כל הטרדות ונעשה בן חורין כו'.

We frequently rationalize neglecting Torah study because of our obsession with the mundane concerns of daily life. The *mishnah* rejects this excuse and assures us that, on the contrary, by immersing ourselves in Torah we are better able to cope with all those concerns.

◆§ Body and Soul Reconciled

כי הנפש מלמעלה היפוך כל מעשה עוה"ז והגוף. לכן הנפש והגוף נלחמים זה עם
זה ואיתא במד' ויקרא וגם הנפש לא תמלא לעירוני משל לבת מלכים שנשא בת מלכים אפילו
מאכילה כל מעדנים אינו יוצא ידי חובתו כמו כן הנפש לא תשבע ממצות ומעש"ט
שהיא מלמעלה ע"ש. אכן התורה נותנת דרך שיתקיים הנפש בגוף לכן היא
משיבת נפש. וכ"כ נפשי ישובב כו' במעגלי צדק כו'. שהתורה מורה דרך איך
להשיב את הנפש בגוף לכן איתא אוי להם לבריות מעלבונה של תורה כו' אשה

---

1. Cf. *Tanya* for a similar theme that the *Shechinah* can be found between the lines of the Torah. Also see Rabbi Shamshon Raphael Hirsch's commentary on *Devarim* 30:10.

on the Tablets." Do not read "charus" (engraved) but
"cheirus" (freedom), for you can have no freer man than
one who engages in the study of the Torah. And anyone
who engages in the study of Torah becomes elevated,

יפה וסרת טעם כו'. פי' שבלי תורה אין הנפש מתיישב לעשות פעולות הראויות
לה. ולכן הקדושים שהיו קודם התורה הי' במס"נ שלא עפ"י הטבע כלל. אבל
בשניתנה תורה יכול כל איש ישראל למצוא לו קיום עפ"י מצות התורה
להתיישב הנפש בגוף. ולכן אמרו אין לך בן חורין אלא העוסק בתורה שמשבית
המלחמה שבין הנפש והגוף לכן הוא בן חורין.

Without Torah, the soul is unable to find its niche. Though implanted within
the human body, it feels like an alien in such a material environment. The
potential clash between body and soul can be compared to a princess who
marries a commoner. Despite her husband's affection and indulgence of her
previous life-style, the princess never feels comfortable away from the king's
palace. So too, the soul descending from Above can never reconcile itself to our
material world below. Only through Torah's impact on the body can a hos-
pitable environment for the soul be created. As David sings, נַפְשִׁי יְשׁוֹבֵב, *He
restores my soul* (*Tehillim* 23:3). The *pasuk* then continues, יַנְחֵנִי בְמַעְגְּלֵי צֶדֶק, *He
leads me on paths of justice* — through the righteous paths of the Torah. In
tribute to its vital function of balancing and unifying body and soul, the Torah
is given the distinctive title מְשִׁיבַת נָפֶשׁ, *it restores the soul* (ibid. 19:8). It is
precisely at the moment when the eternal battle between body and soul is
reconciled, through the efforts of the Torah, that true freedom is achieved —
אֵין לְךָ בֶן חוֹרִין אֶלָּא מִי שֶׁעוֹסֵק בְּתַלְמוּד תּוֹרָה, *for you can have no freer man than one
who engages in the study of the Torah.*

Consider an interesting corollary to our explanation of the freedom achieved
through Torah. It is much easier now to remain loyal to our heritage than it was
in the times of the Patriarchs who lived prior to the Giving of the Torah.
Whereas then, it took superhuman effort to impose the dictates of the soul on
an unwilling body, after Sinai the body was infused with spirituality and
became more of an equal partner with the soul in fulfilling the Divine will (*Sfas
Emes, Shavuos* 5651).

◆§ Freedom From the Yetzer Hara

היינו חירות מיצר הרע. כתיב ההופכי הצור אגם מים היינו כדאיתא בראתי יצר
הרע ובראתי לו תורה תבלין שהתורה מרככת את האבן.

Just as at the Giving of the Torah the Jewish People were freed from the evil
effects of the *Yetzer Hara* (cf. *Devarim* 5:26, מִי יִתֵּן וְהָיָה לְבָבָם זֶה לָהֶם, *who can*

תּוֹרָה הֲרֵי זֶה מִתְעַלֶּה, שֶׁנֶּאֱמַר: „וּמִמַּתָּנָה נַחֲלִיאֵל, וּמִנַּחֲלִיאֵל בָּמוֹת.‟

[ג] הַלּוֹמֵד מֵחֲבֵרוֹ פֶּרֶק אֶחָד, אוֹ הֲלָכָה אֶחָת, אוֹ פָּסוּק אֶחָד, אוֹ דִבּוּר אֶחָד, אוֹ אֲפִילוּ אוֹת אֶחָת — צָרִיךְ לִנְהָג בּוֹ כָּבוֹד. שֶׁכֵּן מָצִינוּ בְּדָוִד מֶלֶךְ יִשְׂרָאֵל, שֶׁלֹּא לָמַד מֵאֲחִיתֹפֶל אֶלָּא שְׁנֵי דְבָרִים בִּלְבָד, וּקְרָאוֹ רַבּוֹ, אַלּוּפוֹ, וּמְיֻדָּעוֹ, שֶׁנֶּאֱמַר: „וְאַתָּה אֱנוֹשׁ כְּעֶרְכִּי, אַלּוּפִי וּמְיֻדָּעִי.‟ וַהֲלֹא דְבָרִים קַל וָחֹמֶר: וּמַה דָּוִד מֶלֶךְ

---

assure that this heart should remain theirs. לְבָבָם literally means *hearts*, which implies that *both* hearts — the good and evil inclinations — were ready to serve Hashem), so too every time we are immersed in Torah we attain freedom from the *Yetzer Hara*. This concept is conveyed through the statement of *Chazal*, בָּרָאתִי יֵצֶר הָרָע וּבָרָאתִי תּוֹרָה תַּבְלִין, *I created the Yetzer Hara and I created the Torah as an antidote* (*Kiddushin* 30b).

Likewise the Gemara urges us to drag the *Yetzer Hara* to the *Beis Hamedrash*. There, in a Torah-saturated environment, this great tempter will become powerless (*Imrei Emes, Maggidei HaEmes*).

■ וּמִמַּתָּנָה נַחֲלִיאֵל וּמִנַּחֲלִיאֵל בָּמוֹת — *From Mattanah to Nachaliel, and from Nachaliel to Bamos.*

☙ The Gift of Torah

ואח״כ וממדבר מתנה שיש ג׳׳כ דרך אפילו לאינם ראויים שיזכו במתנה זו הבאה ע׳׳י הביטול שנמשכים אחר הקב׳׳ה באמונה.

The *mishnah* concludes by encouraging even those who lack the essential attributes necessary to acquire Torah (cf. *mishnah* 6 which lists 48 character traits which are vital for success in studying Torah) to nonetheless continue studying. Those who negate all their physical pleasures in favor of serving Hashem with complete *Emunah*, will eventually merit that the Torah will be granted to them as a gift (מַתָּנָה). Though they lack some of the essential prerequisites for Torah study, they will succeed on the basis of this unrequited Divine gift (*Sfas Emes, Chukas* 5652).

3.

■ הַלּוֹמֵד מֵחֲבֵרוֹ פֶּרֶק אֶחָד, אוֹ הֲלָכָה אֶחָת . . . אוֹ אֲפִילוּ אוֹת אֶחָת צָרִיךְ לִנְהָג

as it is said (Bamidbar 21:19): "From Mattanah to
Nachaliel, and from Nachaliel to Bamos."

[3] He who learns from his fellowman a single chapter,
a single halachah, a single verse, a single Torah statement, or even a single letter, must treat him with honor.
For thus we find in the case of David, King of Israel, who
learned nothing from Achitophel except for two things,
yet called him his teacher, his guide, his intimate, as it is
said (Tehillim 55:14): "You are a man of my measure, my
guide and my intimate." One can derive from this the
following: If David, King of Israel, who learned nothing

— בּוֹ כָּבוֹד. שֶׁכֵּן מָצִינוּ בְּדָוִד . . . שֶׁלֹּא לָמַד מֵאֲחִיתֹפֶל אֶלָּא שְׁנֵי דְבָרִים בִּלְבָד

*He who learns from his fellowman a single chapter, a single halachah
. . . or even a single letter, must treat him with honor. For thus we find
in the case of David . . . who learned nothing from Achitophel except
for two things.*

In the next section we consider the following renowned question: How can we
deduce from the respect paid to Achitophel by King David because he taught
him *two* concepts, that we must honor someone who taught us only *one* new
chapter, *halachah*, verse or letter?

⌛ Two Thoughts Only — a Fraction of David's Knowledge

פירוש דהקל וחומר הוא דמה דוד שהי יודע כל התורה ולא היה חסר לו רק אלו
השנים דברים.
לכאורה יקשה למיפרך דתינח דוד שידע כל התורה כולה ובזה שלימדו
אחיתופל אלו דברים אלו נעשה תורתו שלמה ומשום הכי קראו רבו אלופו ומיודעו
מה שאין כן בסתם בן אדם שרחוק מלהיות תורתו שלמה אפשר דאפילו אם
לימדו מאן דהוא כמה אותיות אינו צריך לנהוג בו כבוד ולקרותו רבי.
והנראה כי כל אות שבתורה אין לו שיעור ועל כל אות ניתן לדרוש תלי תילום
של הלכות ואם כן אף אצל דוד המע״ה לא נעשה שלם בתורתו כאשר למד
מאחיתופל ב׳ דברים אלו.

In regard to King David, the two things taught to him by Achitophel were but
a small fraction of his encyclopedic knowledge of Torah. Yet, he honored
Achitophel, calling him "his teacher, his guide, his intimate." Certainly we,

יִשְׂרָאֵל, שֶׁלֹּא לָמַד מֵאֲחִיתֹפֶל אֶלָּא שְׁנֵי דְבָרִים בִּלְבָד,
קְרָאוֹ רַבּוֹ אַלּוּפוֹ וּמְיֻדָּעוֹ – הַלּוֹמֵד מֵחֲבֵרוֹ פֶּרֶק אֶחָד,
אוֹ הֲלָכָה אֶחָת, אוֹ פָסוּק אֶחָד, אוֹ דִבּוּר אֶחָד, אוֹ
אֲפִילוּ אוֹת אֶחָת, עַל אַחַת כַּמָּה וְכַמָּה שֶׁצָּרִיךְ לִנְהֹג
בּוֹ כָּבוֹד! וְאֵין כָּבוֹד אֶלָּא תוֹרָה, שֶׁנֶּאֱמַר: „כָּבוֹד
חֲכָמִים יִנְחָלוּ"; „וּתְמִימִים יִנְחֲלוּ טוֹב" וְאֵין טוֹב אֶלָּא
תוֹרָה, שֶׁנֶּאֱמַר: „כִּי לֶקַח טוֹב נָתַתִּי לָכֶם, תּוֹרָתִי אַל
תַּעֲזֹבוּ."

lacking David's scope of Torah, should be grateful for every iota of knowledge (even one thought) shared with us by our fellow-man (adapted from *Sfas Emes*).

On the other hand, the very fact that the two concepts taught to David by Achitophel filled the gaps in his knowledge of Torah raises an interesting question. While it was certainly appropriate for David to honor Achitophel because, as a result of his teaching, David acquired mastery of the *entire* Torah, our situation is not necessarily analogous. Even after our exposure to teachings from teachers and friends, we remain far from knowing the *entire* Torah, therefore do we necessarily have to show the same respect?[1]

Apparently, no individual, not even the erudite King David, can ever truly master the *entire* Torah. Indeed, King David could always find additional layers of meaning in every letter of the Torah — how much more so does this apply to us (*Pnei Menachem, Maggidei HaEmes*).

⇜ The Creative Potential of One Letter

וְשָׁם הבעש״ט ז״ל איתא משום דד״ת פרין ורבין ונתוסף על אות א׳ הרבה,
משא״כ אחיתופל רשע הוה ודבריו לא נפרו ונרבו.

There is a crucial distinction between the two concepts taught by the wicked Achitophel (cf. *Sanhedrin* 90a stating that Achitophel does not merit a portion in the World to Come) and the single letter taught by a righteous Torah leader. The Torah taught by a *tzaddik*, though it may *quantitatively* be no more than one letter, has in a *qualitative* sense the potential to proliferate into much more. Creatively applied, one Torah thought taught by God-fearing teachers

---

1. This question, which was raised by the *Pnei Menachem*, can find a basis in the laws of Shabbos. While generally one only incurs the death penalty by writing *two* letters on Shabbos, if one completes a volume of the Torah by writing even *one* letter (*Shabbos* 104b), that individual is considered liable for *chilul* Shabbos.

from Achitophel except for two things, called him his teacher, his guide, his intimate — one who learns from his fellowman a single chapter, a single halachah, a single verse, a single Torah statement, or even a single letter, how much more must he treat him with honor! And honor is due only for Torah, as it is said (Mishlei 3:35, 28:10): "The wise shall inherit honor," "...and the perfect shall inherit good." And only Torah is truly good, as it is said (Mishlei 4:2): "I have given you a good teaching, do not forsake my Torah."

---

may be utilized in many different contexts. On the other hand, the teachings of Achitophel were in essence no more than שְׁנֵי דְבָרִים בִּלְבָד, *only* two things — sterile, unable to spur additional knowledge.

⇜ The Ramifications of One Letter

ואות א' הוה דבר א' כמו כיצד מאברין מעברין בגמ' למדתי דבר א' ע"ש
עירובין דף נ"ד.

At times the correct rendition of one letter can be more significant than the two concepts taught by Achitophel to David. The interpretation of a Talmudic text often is contingent upon the correct reading of merely one letter [cf. *Eruvin* 53b] (adapted from *Sfas Emes*).

⇜ One Letter Contains the Entire Torah

כתיב גל עיני ואביטה נפלאו מתורתך כשפותחים העינים רואים שבתורה יש כל
אות אחת מהתורה כוללת את כל התורה ... ואיתא בשם החוקרים שבכל
גרגיר דומם ישנים הרבה מיני ברואים, מכל שכן בתורה הקדושה יש בכל אות
ואות אלפים ורבבות עולמות כדכתיב ועלמות אין מספר.

The proper interpretation of one letter may affect the meaning of the entire Torah. As David pleads with Hashem, גַּל עֵינַי וְאַבִּיטָה נִפְלָאוֹת מִתּוֹרָתֶךָ, *Unveil my eyes that I may perceive wonders from Your Torah* (Tehillim 119:18). Even one word of the Torah contains many wondrous secrets. Scientists maintain that the entire natural world consists of small invisible organisms (e.g. molecules, atoms, microbes). We may deduce from this that behind every letter of the sacred and infinite Torah there lie many layers of spirituality. Likewise, the Torah is described as being תְּמִימָה, it is perfect and complete (*Tehillim* 19:8). Every word of the Torah is a microcosm of the entire Torah (*Imrei Emes, Maggidei HaEmes,* also cf. *The Three Festivals,* p. 277).

■ אוֹת אֶחָת — *A single letter.*

חשבתי שאפשר לתרץ הקושיא במשנה שהקשו המפרשים שהוא דוד למד מאחיתופל ב' דברים ומהי הראיה לדיבור אחד ואות אחת. שדיבור אחד שמירת הלשון ואות אחד שמירת האות.

The terms אוֹת and דִּבּוּר perhaps allude to the two covenants established between Hashem and *Klal Yisrael.* One is known as the בְּרִית הַלָּשׁוֹן, the covenant guarding *Klal Yisrael's* speech, and the other is the בְּרִית הַמָּעוֹר, the covenant of morality arranged between Hashem and Avraham's descendants at the time of the Patriarch's *bris milah.* Specifically, the term דִּבּוּר אֶחָד refers to שְׁמִירַת הַלָּשׁוֹן, the covenant regulating our speech (דִּבּוּר), and אוֹת אֶחָת refers to the sign (אוֹת) of the *bris milah* (cf. *Bereishis* 17:11, וְהָיָה לְאוֹת בְּרִית בֵּינִי וּבֵינֵיכֶם, *that shall be the sign of the covenant between Me and you*) (*Lev Simchah, Maggidei HaEmes*).

◄§ The "Sign" of Tefillin

וי"ל אות אחת הכוונה לאות של תפילין וכיוצא בו [שנכלל בי"ה דברים הרבה].

In a similar vein, the *Pnei Menachem* suggested that אוֹת אֶחָת refers to the *mitzvah* of *tefillin* which was described by the Torah as being an אוֹת — וּקְשַׁרְתָּם לְאוֹת עַל יָדֶךָ, *Bind them as a sign upon your arm* (*Devarim* 6:8).

◄§ Didn't David Learn Three Concepts From Achitophel?

והמפרשים הקשו דהלא דהע"ה למד מאחיתופל ג' דברים דלמד ממנו גם העצה לעשות לכבוש התהום ווי"ל לא למד ממנו רק אחיתופל בעצמו כתב שם ונתנו שם ועוד יי"ל דזה הי' מקודם בימי שאול קראו רבו.

According to *Kallah Rabbasi* 8, Achitophel taught David the importance of learning with a study partner and the propriety of acting humbly in a *beis hamedrash,* (particularly not to walk in with an erect posture).

It seems, however, that David sought Achitophel's advice in yet another situation: When David dug the foundations of the *Beis HaMikdash*), he authorized writing Hashem's Name on a shard and placing it on the deep waters, based on Achitophel's advice, in order to prevent the subterranean waters from engulfing the entire universe (cf. *Succah* 53b.)

One explanation may be that unlike the two instances alluded to in the *mishnah*, in the last case Achitophel not only gave David advice but actually implemented his own advice, writing out Hashem's Name on a piece of earth and casting it into the subterranean water.

Additionally, David may have bestowed the titles of respect on Achitophel even prior to assuming the monarchy. However, Achitophel's advice regarding the water was given at a much later date, when David had already been coronated.

◄§ Your Colleagues, Not Your Talmidim

הלומד מחבירו פ״א כו׳, אבל מתלמידו הגם דאחז״ל מתלמידי יותר מכולם מ״מ
ליכא בכלל זה רק בחבירו כמו שאמרו בת״ח שבבבל שנוהגין כבוד כו׳.

The term מֵחֲבֵרוֹ, one's colleague, is deliberately used to indicate that a *rebbi* need not demonstrate such respect to a *talmid*, even if he may have learned from him (cf. *Taanis* 7a וּמִתַּלְמִידַי יוֹתֵר מִכּוּלָן].

◄§ I Am Not Your Rebbi

פעם הלך השפת אמת ז״ל לאיזה מקום, ופגע בו אדם אחד ואמר לו שלום עליך
רבי, אמר לו השפ״א ז״ל ״כלום למדת ממני מה, עד שאתה קורא לי רבי״?

It is appropriate to mention here that the *Sfas Emes* applied this *mishnah* to himself. When the *Sfas Emes* visited a certain town, an individual approached him saying, "*Shalom Aleichem, Rebbi*," to which the *Sfas Emes* responded, "Did you ever learn anything from me that you refer to me as you *rebbi*?" (*Maggidei HaEmes*).

Years later, the *Sfas Emes*'s grandson, the *Beis Yisrael*, would remark that this was the only time that his grandfather had been in error. In fact, the *Sfas Emes* was the *rebbi* of the entire Jewish People!

◄§ Our Greatest Rebbi — the Torah

ומה נעשה לתורה בעצמה, אשר מלמדת אותנו תמיד איך לעבוד את ה׳. ומה
הכבוד אל התורה להגות בה יומם ולילה.

If we are obliged to honor any individual who taught us even one letter of the torah, certainly one should honor the Torah itself. How do we acknowledge

[ד] כַּךְ הִיא דַרְכָּה שֶׁל תּוֹרָה: פַּת בַּמֶּלַח תֹּאכֵל, וּמַיִם בַּמְּשׂוּרָה תִשְׁתֶּה, וְעַל הָאָרֶץ תִּישָׁן, וְחַיֵּי צַעַר תִּחְיֶה, וּבַתּוֹרָה אַתָּה עָמֵל; אִם אַתָּה עוֹשֶׂה כֵּן, "אַשְׁרֶיךָ וְטוֹב לָךְ": "אַשְׁרֶיךָ" — בָּעוֹלָם הַזֶּה, "וְטוֹב לָךְ" — לָעוֹלָם הַבָּא.

our indebtedness to the Torah? Simply by immersing ourselves in its teachings day and night — וְהָגִיתָ בּוֹ יוֹמָם וָלַיְלָה, *you should contemplate it day and night* (*Yehoshua* 1:8) (*Sfas Emes, Succos* 5664. For a more complete rendition of this piece refer to *The Three Festivals*, pp. 284-285).

4.

■ **כַּךְ הִיא דַרְכָּה שֶׁל תּוֹרָה: פַּת בַּמֶּלַח תֹּאכֵל, וּמַיִם בַּמְּשׂוּרָה תִשְׁתֶּה, וְעַל הָאָרֶץ תִּישָׁן, וְחַיֵּי צַעַר תִּחְיֶה – וּבַתּוֹרָה אַתָּה עָמֵל** — *This is the way of Torah: Eat bread with salt, drink water in small measure, sleep on the ground, live a life of deprivation — but toil in the Torah!*

While it would seem at first glance that the *mishnah* is advocating a program of strict austerity, upon closer examination we realize that is not necessarily the case. While one must be prepared to deprive himself at times of some physical amenities, the Torah by no means insists upon complete asceticism as a prerequisite for spiritual growth, as we will now demonstrate.

■ **כַּךְ הִיא דַרְכָּה שֶׁל תּוֹרָה** — *This is the way of Torah.*

◆§ This World Is Just a Road

משל לאחד שנסע ללייפציג ונסע דרך הקרעטשמעס לפעמים יש בה לאכול כל טוב ולפעמים אין בהם רק פת במלח. וקרה לו פעם אחת שעבר כל הקרעטשמעס ולא היה בהם כי אם פת במלח, וכי בשביל זה לא יסע ללייפציג כן הוא בלומד תורה אפילו אין לו לאכול כי אם פת במלח כו' וכי בשביל זה לא יהא עמלו בתורה. וזה לשון דרכה של תורה, שזה העולם הוא כמו דרך לעבור לעולם העליון.

According to R' Simchah Bunim of Peshis'cha the *mishnah* is emphasizing that This World is merely a road (דַרְכָּה), to the World to Come, and this road is best navigated through Torah (שֶׁל תּוֹרָה).

Our relationship to the amenities of This World could be compared to a business traveler to the Leipzig Fair. While he would certainly prefer to dine in

[4] *This is the way of Torah: Eat bread with salt,
drink water in small measure, sleep on the ground,
live a life of deprivation — but toil in the Torah! If you do
this, "You are praiseworthy, and all is well with you"
(Tehillim 128:2). "You are praiseworthy" — in this world;
"and all is well with you" — in the World to Come.*

---

the choicest restaurants and sleep at a place with the most comfortable accommodations as he traveled, he would be content to eat anything — even bread dipped in salt — in order to reach his destination promptly. While we may understandably desire some worldly comforts and pleasures, even in their absence we should never be deterred from our primary mission in This World — immersing ourselves in Torah (*Maggidei HaEmes*).

■ פַּת בַּמֶּלַח תֹּאכֵל — *Eat bread with salt.*

✌ A Plea Against Asceticism

> עכ״פ נשמע כי דרכה של תורה הוא לאכול ולשתות ולישן רק מוסיף גזירה
> לאכול פת במלח ולישן על הארץ אבל לא להתענות בכלל.
> עיקר הפירוש שלא לדקדק במה שיש לו לאכול אם רב אם מעט אם טוב או לא.
> ואא״ז זצ״ל סיפר כי היהודי הקדוש זצ״ל כשהיה רעב היה אוכל כל מה שבידו
> ולא הבחין מה שאכל ואחר כך התייגע בעבודתו לרוב עד שאכל שוב כי היה עובד
> גדול כנודע.

This *mishnah* can also be interpreted as an admonishment against asceticism: תֹּאכֵל — Eat, don't fast!

Do not allow yourself to be deterred from learning because of a lack of food. On the other hand, eat and drink whatever you are offered, bearing in mind that you are partaking of food for the sake of Heaven, and do not pay undue attention to its quantity or quality. By acting in this way, one emulates the behavior of the chassidic leader, the "Yid HaKadosh" who, when hungry, would eat whatever was placed in front of him. Immediately afterwards, he immersed himself in Torah and Divine service, not pausing until he realized that he was hungry again.

✌ The Beis Yisrael's "Ancient Vort"

> ושמעתי לפני ששים שנה מחסיד וזקן בן מאה שנה ששמע הרבי ר' בונם זי״ע
> שאמר פת במלח תאכל אפילו אם אין לך יותר מאשר פת במלח, בכל זאת
> תאכל גיגעסען זאל וערין ומים במשורה אפילו אין לך יותר מאשר מים במשורה

תשתה געטרינקען זאל ווערין וחיי צער, אפילו כל ימיך בצער תחי' גילעבט זאל
ווערין כי במה שיש לאדם צריך להיות בשמחה ובחיות.

The *Beis Yisrael* recalled an innovative *p'shat* that he had heard 60 years earlier from a 100-year-old *chassid* who had heard it from R' Simchah Bunim of Peshis'cha.

Even if your lot in life is to enjoy nothing more than bread and salt, do not perceive this regimen as being starvation but rather as appropriate nourishment (תֹּאכֵל). Similarly, even the most meager water rations should be considered an adequate drink (תִּשְׁתֶּה). Indeed, even sleeping on the ground (וְעַל הָאָרֶץ תִּישָׁן) and all the hardships associated with a life of deprivation (חַיֵּי צַעַר) should be accepted joyously and perceived as a form of vibrant life (תִחְיֶה) (*Maggidei HaEmes*).

◆§ Coping With Material Deprivation Through Torah

על ידי כח התורה מחליש כוחו של היצר בענין גשמיות וזה הפי' כך דרכה של
תורה על ידי דרך התורה תוכל להסתפק מפת במלח כו'.

While most people would be unable to cope with incessant poverty, *Klal Yisrael*, living on the basis of Torah (כָּךְ הִיא דַרְכָּה שֶׁל תּוֹרָה), is able to overcome any physical passions and the importuning of the *Yetzer Hara* and subsist on simple bread and rationed water alone if necessary (*Beis Yisrael, Maggidei HaEmes*).

◆§ A Lesson for the Affluent

ויש להוסיף דכל שכן מי שבאמת לא חסר לו מכל טוב ביותר צריך לעסוק
ולהתייגע בתורה.
יי״ל שגם כאשר תאכל לך המעדנים יהיה אצלך כמו פת במלח, וכן על הארץ
תישן שהיכן שתישן יהיה אצלך כאילו אתה ישן על הארץ. ואז אשריך וטוב לך
אשריך בעולם הזה וטוב לך בעולם הבא, שיש לך גם עולם הזה וגם עולם הבא.

If the poor, who are immersed in Torah, can subsist on very little, certainly, the affluent, blessed with abundant material wealth, must strive to be immersed in Torah (*Pnei Menachem, Maggidei HaEmes*).

In a similar vein, the *mishnah* is addressing the affluent Torah scholar and urging him that he should consider all his material comforts as nothing more than bread with salt. Similarly, when sleeping on his comfortable bed, he should not become obsessed with all his material comforts. Instead, he should view this experience as being no different than sleeping on the ground.

✥ Why Worry?

אולי כי אם אין לו לאדם כלום אינו דואג אלא לומד בשמחה כי הדאגה מטרידה
את כל הראש, וסופו ללמוד מתוך עושר.

Those who subsist on a simple diet of bread and water have comparatively little to worry about. It is only preoccupation with our material needs that leads us to worry. In the merit of studying Torah in this carefree, though impoverished environment, one will eventually merit to study Torah amidst material comfort (cf. *Perek 4, mishnah 11*).

■ מַיִם בַּמְשׂוּרָה תִּשְׁתֶּה — *Drink water in small measure.*

✥ Ration Your Water

פירוש גם אם יהיה מוכרח לשתות כמה פעמים לצמאו, טוב יותר לשתות
במשורה כמה פעמים מלשתות הרבה ביחד.

By telling us to drink water *in small measure*, the *mishnah* is teaching us that if we are faced with a limited supply of water, it is better to drink a small, carefully measured amount over a period of time rather than to consume one's total ration at once.

■ וְעַל הָאָרֶץ תִּישָׁן — *Sleep on the ground.*

✥ May One Sleep on the Ground?

הקשו לפני השפ"א ז"ל מהא דאיתא בגמ' על כל משכב שכב חוץ מן הקרקע.
והשיב שמשם ראיה דקרקע משכב הגרוע מכל, ומכל מקום כשאין לו רק זה גם
אז לא יתבטל מלימודו הגם שחי חיי צער.

The Gemara (*Berachos* 62b) recommends that one not sleep on the ground. To reconcile this seeming contradiction with our *mishnah*, we suggest that indeed one should strenuously avoid sleeping on the ground. If, however, no other alternative exists, it is certainly better to lie on the ground than to impede his Torah study (adapted from *Sfas Emes*).

✥ Emulate Yaakov

ועוד תי' דכאן הפי' שיניח תחת ראשו דבר מה שלא יהי' ממש שכיבה בקרקע
וכמו אבנים דמראשותיו של יעקב.

Perhaps, our *mishnah* is recommending that we emulate Yaakov Avinu who also slept on the ground while fleeing Esav. To avoid the prohibition against sleeping on the ground, he placed his head on a makeshift pillow of stones.

✥ Minimize the Material Side of Life

היינו בעסקי ארציות תהיה ישן כמו שנאמר אני ישנה ולבי ער, פירש״י שהם ישנים מן העבירות.

The term אֶרֶץ may refer not only to the ground in a literal sense but also to material matters which we associate with the earth (whereas spiritual matters are connoted as שָׁמַיִם, *heaven*). Be passive, quiescent, almost sleeping (תִּישָׁן), insofar as material matters are concerned (*Maggidei HaEmes*).

■ וְחַיֵּי צַעַר תִּחְיֶה — *Live a life of deprivation.*

✥ A Last Resort, Not an Ideal State

פירוש אף שיצטרך לכך דאם לא כן הרי אסור להביא עצמו לידי כך, ומינה נלמד לכל הדברים שהפירוש רק באם נצרך לכך וכן משמע קצת ממים במשורה תשתה.

It is unlikely that the *mishnah* advocates that we deliberately choose a life style replete with suffering. Rather, we are being encouraged to continue studying Torah, regardless of our material deprivations.

We may assume that the first segment of the *mishnah*, recommending austerity in food and drink (פַּת בַּמֶּלַח . . . מַיִם בַּמְשׂוּרָה), should also be interpreted in the same light — as a last resort, rather than as an ideal.

✥ Looking Down From Heaven

אמר לתלמידו הרה״ק רבי הערש בער מגרבוביץ ז״ל ״הנני מבטיח לך שכסף עבור לחם לא יהיה לך כל ימי חייך, אולם כשאגביה אותך למעלה מכיפת הרקיע אזי תראה שכל עניני העולם הזה אינם כדי להתאנח עליהם אפילו אנחה אחת.״

R' Simchah Bunim of Peshis'cha once guaranteed his stalwart disciple R' Hirsch Ber that he would rarely have enough money to buy bread. He also assured him that for individuals of his stature the mundane concerns, such as earning a livelihood, are insignificant. "If I could lift you above the clouds, permitting you to enter the World to Come in your lifetime, you would realize that from the perspective of Heaven, all the material matters of This World are not even worthy of a single sigh" (*Maggidei HaEmes*).

■ "אַשְׁרֶיךָ וְטוֹב לָךְ" . . . וּבַתּוֹרָה אַתָּה עָמֵל — *But toil in the Torah . . .* "*You are praiseworthy, and all is well with you.*"

✦§ Toiling Without Comprehending

הרמז על עמל ויגיעה אף שאינו מרגיש אחר כך מוצא טעם . . . וכן בעבדות השם אף שאין מוצא טעם . . . ואחר כך ירגיש וזה הרמז כך דרכה של תורה ובתורה אתה עמל, עמלים ואז לבסוף אשריך וטוב לך שיהיה הכל טוב.

The term עָמֵל is used regarding the toil and intense concentration associated with learning Torah. For example, *Chazal* interpret the *pasuk* אִם בְּחֻקֹּתַי תֵּלֵכוּ, *if you will follow My decrees* (*Vayikra* 26:3), as referring to עֲמָלָה שֶׁל תּוֹרָה, the strenuous effort involved in studying Torah. Despite our best efforts, however, we may sometimes fail to comprehend what we studied so intensely and our toil becomes frustrating. The *mishnah* thus assures us, אַשְׁרֶיךָ וְטוֹב לָךְ, eventually you will reap the benefit of your spiritual labor (*Beis Yisrael, Maggidei HaEmes*).

■ "אַשְׁרֶיךָ" — בָּעוֹלָם הַזֶּה, "וְטוֹב לָךְ" — לָעוֹלָם הַבָּא — "*You are praiseworthy*" — in This World; "*and all is well with you*" — in the World to Come.

✦§ This World: Road to Olam Haba

כי מה שטוב לצדיק בעניני העולם הזה הוא הכל כדי שיבא על ידם לעולם הבא כי הדברים הצריכים לעולם הבא המה התורה והמצות והם אינם יכולים להעשות ולהפעל אם לא שיש לו כל צורכי עולם הזה בריוח למשל הכנסת אורחים סוכה אתרוג ציצית מזוזה אשה ובנים וכדומה להם לזה צריך הכל שיהיה להצדיק מעות בריוח וזהו אשריך פירוש מה שיש לך טוב בעוה״ז אינה עיקר הכוונה כי אם וטוב לך לעוה״ב ולזה נאמר אשריך שפירושו דרך ונתיב לבא על ידו לעיקר טובת עוה״ב וק״ל.

The term אַשְׁרֶיךָ may be interpreted as a road (cf. *Mishlei* 4:14, 23:19 where אשר is used in a similar context).

All of the amenities of This World — money, material possessions — are merely the means enabling us to appropriately perform *mitzvos* and thus acquire the ultimate good of *Olam Haba* (*Noam Elimelech, Maggidei HaEmes*).

[ה] אַל תְּבַקֵּשׁ גְּדֻלָּה לְעַצְמְךָ, וְאַל תַּחְמֹד כָּבוֹד; יוֹתֵר מִלִּמּוּדְךָ עֲשֵׂה. וְאַל תִּתְאַוֶּה לְשֻׁלְחָנָם שֶׁל מְלָכִים, שֶׁשֻּׁלְחָנְךָ גָּדוֹל מִשֻּׁלְחָנָם, וְכִתְרְךָ גָּדוֹל מִכִּתְרָם; וְנֶאֱמָן הוּא בַּעַל מְלַאכְתְּךָ, שֶׁיְּשַׁלֶּם לְךָ שְׂכַר פְּעֻלָּתֶךָ.

5.

■ יוֹתֵר מִלִּמּוּדְךָ עֲשֵׂה — *Let your performance exceed your learning.*

◆§ A Difficult Mission

הפי' לעשות יותר מכפי הרגלו מכבר ולימודו של אדם ממש בכל פעם יותר ויותר.

How can anyone accomplish or perform more (i.e. perform *mitzvos*) than they have studied?

Perhaps, the term לִמּוּדְךָ should be interpreted as referring to one's accustomed pace, rather than the amount of one's Torah knowledge. Accomplish *more* than your own expectations. Achieve a greater level of Divine service than you think is possible for yourself. This, of course, is a call for ever increasing accomplishments, since each time we successfully perform a *mitzvah* or study Torah to an extent that we previously thought beyond our capacity, our confidence in our own potential increases. Correspondingly, the Torah's expectations for us grow as well (*Pnei Menachem, Maggidei HaEmes*).

◆§ If You Will It

ואיך יכולין לעשות יותר מהידיעה, רק ע"י החפץ והרצון בכל לב לעשות יותר מהשגות האדם, עי"ז נעשה מעצמו כל התקונים כמ"ש ויהי נועם כו' פי' בזוה"ק אף שא"י לעשות כראוי כו' וגם ע"י הרצון באמת עושה האדם שמזמנים לו מן השמים אף שא"י כמ"ש בדרך שאדם רוצה לילך מוליכין אותו שעל ידי קבלת עול תורה, נעשה ונשמע, מקבלים כוחות מהשמים. גם לאבות לא היה מתן תורה וקיימו כל התורה.

While it may seem impossible to accomplish more than one has learned, one should never underestimate the willpower of a Jew. By simply desiring to perform *mitzvos* to an even greater extent than the amount of Torah that I have studied, my dreams are realized and indeed I am able to accomplish far more than I ever thought possible. *Chazal* state (*Makkos* 10b) this succinctly: בְּדֶרֶךְ שֶׁאָדָם רוֹצֶה לֵילֵךְ מוֹלִיכִין אוֹתוֹ, Hashem ensures that a person will successfully traverse the spiritual road that he seeks to travel, and accomplish his objec-

[5] *Do not seek greatness for yourself, and do not crave honor; let your performance exceed your learning. Do not lust for the table of kings, for your table is greater than theirs, and your crown is greater than their crown; and your Employer is trustworthy to pay you remuneration for your deeds.*

---

tive — even if it appears that he is incapable of reaching his destination (*Sfas Emes*).

The *Pnei Menachem* supported this thesis by reminding us that the *Avos* were able to observe Torah despite not having formally received the Torah. We, their descendants, having also proclaimed at Sinai "We will do and we will hear" are assisted by Hashem to perform and observe far more than we have studied or understood (*Pnei Menachem, Maggidei HaEmes*).

■ וְאַל תִּתְאַוֶּה לְשֻׁלְחָנָם שֶׁל מְלָכִים, שֶׁשֻּׁלְחָנְךָ גָּדוֹל מִשֶּׁלָּחָנָם — *Do not lust for the table of kings, for your table is greater than theirs.*

◆§ Your Humble Table

פירוש שולחנך פת במלח ומים במשורה.

The term שֻׁלְחָנְךָ, *your table*, alludes to the simple table mentioned in the previous *mishnah*, one consisting of only bread and water. Even this very austere meal when accompanied by Torah learning is far more splendid than the regal banquets of kings.

■ וְכִתְרְךָ גָּדוֹל מִכִּתְרָם — *And your crown is greater than their crown.*

◆§ Through Torah One Can Experience כְּהוּנָה and מַלְכוּת

וזהו מה דאיתא כאן במתני׳ ואל תתאוה לשלחנם כו׳ היינו שלא צריך להיות כהן גדול ממש, אלא על ידי התורה אפשר להגיע לשלחנות יותר גבוהים כמו שלחן כהן גדול.

The kings referred to here are not only secular rulers but also, and perhaps particularly, the princes of the Jewish People including the *Kohen Gadol* and the king. As the *mishnah* continues, *your crown* — the crown of Torah — *is greater than their crown* — it is greater than the crown of priesthood and the crown of Jewish kingship.

Upon further analysis, we arrive at a more profound interpretation regarding the relationship of the crown of Torah to *Klal Yisrael's* other distinctions,

[ו] גְּדוֹלָה תוֹרָה יוֹתֵר מִן הַכְּהֻנָּה וּמִן הַמַּלְכוּת,
שֶׁהַמַּלְכוּת נִקְנֵית בִּשְׁלֹשִׁים מַעֲלוֹת, וְהַכְּהֻנָּה
נִקְנֵית בְּעֶשְׂרִים וְאַרְבָּעָה, וְהַתּוֹרָה נִקְנֵית בְּאַרְבָּעִים
וּשְׁמוֹנָה דְבָרִים, וְאֵלוּ הֵן: בְּתַלְמוּד, בִּשְׁמִיעַת הָאֹזֶן,
בַּעֲרִיכַת שְׂפָתָיִם, בְּבִינַת הַלֵּב, בְּשִׂכְלוּת הַלֵּב, בְּאֵימָה,

priesthood and monarchy. Torah is not only greater than any other honor achieved within Judaism, but through assiduous study of Torah one can almost experience the sense of being a *Kohen Gadol* and a monarch. By immersing oneself in those portions of Torah which deal with the priestly rites and the prerogatives of the Jewish king, one identifies with the *Kohen Gadol* or king and achieves a sense of their role.

Indeed, when a Gentile approached Shammai and agreed to convert if he could only be designated a *Kohen Gadol*, Shammai rebuffed him. Hillel, on the other hand, began teaching the man Torah. Hillel understood that through Torah study the non-Jew could experience for himself what it meant to be a *Kohen Gadol*. Indeed, upon reaching the *pasuk*, וְהַזָּר הַקָּרֵב יוּמָת, *and an alien who approaches shall die* (*Bamidbar* 1:51), the Gentile, comprehending the penalties associated with pretending to be a *Kohen Gadol*, withdrew his request (*Pnei Menachem, Maggidei HaEmes*).

6.

■ שֶׁהַמַּלְכוּת נִקְנֵית בִּשְׁלֹשִׁים מַעֲלוֹת — *For royalty is acquired along with thirty prerogatives.*

⊌§ The Association Between the Number Thirty and Royalty

והיינו דכתיב אצל יוסף כשזכה למלכות, ויוסף בן שלשים שנה בעמדו לפני פרעה
מלך מצרים וכתיב בפרשה זו שלשים פעם פרעה סתם קודם שכ׳ בו מלך מצרים.

The *Imrei Emes* pointed out that the association between the number 30 and royalty can be traced back to the period when Yosef HaTzaddik reigned over Egypt. Yosef assumed his office at the age of 30 (*Bereishis* 41:46), and the nominal ruler of Egypt, Pharaoh, is not described as the king of Egypt until the 30th time his name is mentioned (*Maggidei HaEmes*).

■ וְהַתּוֹרָה נִקְנֵית בְּאַרְבָּעִים וּשְׁמוֹנָה דְבָרִים — *But the Torah is acquired by means of forty-eight qualities.*

[6] *Torah is even greater than priesthood or royalty; for royalty is acquired along with thirty prerogatives, and the priesthood with twenty-four [gifts], but the Torah is acquired by means of forty-eight qualities, which are: Study, attentive listening, articulate speech, intuitive understanding, discernment, awe, reverence, modesty, joy,*

✑ Not an "All-or-Nothing" Proposition

נראה אם אחד מתוקן בקצת דברים אז קונה קצת מהתורה ולאו דוקא שיתוקן
בכולם כי בגוף מ״ח דברים יש שקדוש יותר בהם ויש שקדוש בפחות, וכמו בגוף
התורה איתא במשנה שתלמוד תורה אין לה שיעור כך בהכנת התורה לקנותה
אין לה שיעור.

These 48 methods of acquiring Torah should not be understood as an all-or-nothing proposition. An individual practicing *some* of the attributes listed in the *mishnah* will develop a relationship with Torah. As one adopts more of the qualities recommended by our *mishnah*, the relationship with Torah becomes more intimate. Just as the study of Torah is a lifelong pursuit, so too preparing for study has no limits.

✑ The Significance of the Number Forty-Eight

It is no coincidence that the Torah is acquired through 48 distinct methods. In the following remarks we elaborate on the significance of the number 48, both as a means of acquiring Torah and in other contexts throughout *Tanach*.

✑ Avraham Recognizes Hashem

בן מ״ח שנה הכיר אברהם את בוראו כנגד מ״ח דברים שהתורה נקנית בהם בן
ג׳ שנים ובודאי הכוונה להשלשה מדות . . . עין טובה, רוח נמוכה ונפש שפלה.

In the Midrash we find a dispute whether Avraham was 3 or 48 years old when he renounced Terach's idolatry and recognized Hashem (*Nedarim* 32a; *Pesikta Rabbasi* 21:18). These opinions may reflect various stages in Avraham's development and correspond to different character traits associated with Avraham Avinu. In particular, we may assume that at age 3 Avraham had already acquired the three attributes later associated with him and his disciples — the traits of *a good eye, a humble spirit and a meek soul* (see above, 5:22). By the age of 48, Avraham had already completed 48 prerequisites for Torah acquisition cited in this *mishnah*.

◄§ Forty-Eight Wells

איתא במדרש שה"ש באר נגד מ"ח דברים שהתורה נקנית בהם, כי הבארות הם
למצוא אור התורה אשר נטע השי"ת בתוכנו ממש, וזה פי' שהתורה נקנית בהם
הגם כי הכל עוסקין בתורה אך ע"י המ"ח דברים התורה נקנית.

According to the Midrash (*Shir HaShirim* 4:15), the 48 attributes mentioned
in the *mishnah* correspond to the 48 occasions that the Torah speaks about
wells using the term בְּאֵר. This association is not merely coincidental but helps
explain the role played by the 48 qualities in facilitating our acquisition of
Torah. Through the 48 attributes listed in our *mishnah*, we can penetrate
beyond the surface layer of Torah (which itself is sacred and profoundly
important) and plumb its inner depths, its wellsprings. By mastering the 48
steps through which Torah is acquired, we obtain not only a deeper understanding of Torah, but also a much greater appreciation of our *own* potential.
The human personality is comparable to a well; only a limited amount of water
is visible on the surface, but it is infinite in its bottomless subterranean assets.
By applying the 48 methods of acquiring Torah which correspond to the 48
"wells" mentioned in the Torah, we elicit the tremendous wellsprings of Torah
and the enormous potential to grow in Torah learning that lies embedded in
every Jew. Each time we are called up to read the Torah, we allude to our own
hidden reserves of spirituality, to these hidden wellsprings of Torah that we all
possess, by proclaiming, וְחַיֵּי עוֹלָם נָטַע בְּתוֹכֵנוּ, *and implanted eternal life* [of
Torah] *within us* — our connection to Torah lies within ourselves.

◄§ Forty-Eight Prophets

המ"ח נביאים הם מ"ח כחות לעורר התורה והם המ"ח דברים שהתורה נקנית
בהם.

The number 48 may also correspond to the 48 prophets of *Klal Yisrael* (cf.
Megillah 14a). These were individuals who practiced the virtues mentioned
in our *mishnah* and integrated the Torah in every fiber of their being, to the
extent that Hashem could actually implant His word into their mouth, so that
they served as His spokesman (cf. *Yeshayahu* 59:21). Moreover, the Prophets
were the most effective catalyst to remind *Klal Yisrael* of their potential to
implement the 48 attributes of our *mishnah*. In fact, the Prophets and their
teachings could be perceived as — the 48 potential means of acquiring Torah
(*Imrei Emes, Maggidei HaEmes*).

◄§ Forty-Eight Readings of the Torah

וכמו שיש בתורה שבכתב ג"ן סדרים וחמשה מהם הם בראש חמשה חומשי

While we generally assume that there are 53 Torah readings (counting *Mattos* and *Masei* as one, since with rare exceptions they are read together), in reality, we can segment the Torah readings into two components: the five opening portions of each Book of the Torah (*Bereishis*, *Shemos*, *Vayikra*, *Bamidbar*, *Devarim*) and the 48 following portions. The five opening portions of each Book correspond to the five organs that are used to articulate the sacred words of the Torah (tongue, lips, teeth, palate and throat) and which are an integral part of the head. The 48 following portions — each teaching us a unique approach of serving Hashem — correspond to the 48 prophets who also propounded their own approach to *Avodas Hashem*.

◄§ Gan Eden

ועיין בזוה״ק פרשת חיי שרה במדרש הנעלם כי מ״ח טיפות נוטפין בכל יום מגן עדן ומ״ח נביאים המשיכו מהם נבואותם ואלה ההארות מתחדשים תמיד כדכתיב ונהר יוצא מעדן יוצא לשון הווה . . . ובאלה הג״ן דרכים זוכים לג״ן סדרים דאורייתא.

According to the *Zohar*, the 48 Prophets are nurtured from 48 sacred "drops" (מ״ח טיפות) which are manifestations of *kedushah* emanating from the river that flows from Eden. The Torah states: וְנָהָר יֹצֵא מֵעֵדֶן לְהַשְׁקוֹת אֶת הַגָּן, *A river issues forth from Eden to water the garden* (*Bereishis* 2:10). A river is constantly flowing (as indicated by the present tense יֹצֵא), nurturing and inspiring *Klal Yisrael's* great ones. Returning to our previous theme, emphasizing the role of the 53 Torah Portions inspiring *Klal Yisrael* and its Prophets, we note that in the merit of heeding the lessons imparted by these 53 approaches to *Avodas Hashem*, we will enjoy the rarefied ambiance of the Garden (גַּן) of Eden whose numerical value is 53 (גַּן).

◄§ The First Forty-Eight Days of the Sefirah

כל יום הוא לתקן מדה אחת ממ״ח דברים שהתורה נקנית בהם, ויום האחרון כולל כל הימים לחזור ולשנות אותם.

There is no more opportune time to implement the 48 approaches to Torah than the first 48 days of the *Sefirah*. Each day provides an opportunity to integrate one of the *middos* enumerated in the *mishnah*. The 49th day (the day before Shavuos) provides an optimal occasion to review and integrate the lessons that we learned during this hallowed period in final preparation to accept the Torah.

בְּיִרְאָה, בַּעֲנָוָה, בְּשִׂמְחָה, בְּטָהֳרָה, בְּשִׁמּוּשׁ חֲכָמִים, בְּדִקְדּוּק חֲבֵרִים, בְּפִלְפּוּל הַתַּלְמִידִים, בְּיִשּׁוּב, בְּמִקְרָא, בְּמִשְׁנָה, בְּמִעוּט סְחוֹרָה, בְּמִעוּט דֶּרֶךְ אֶרֶץ, בְּמִעוּט תַּעֲנוּג, בְּמִעוּט שֵׁנָה, בְּמִעוּט שִׂיחָה, בְּמִעוּט שְׂחוֹק,

---

■ בִּשְׁמִיעַת הָאֹזֶן בַּעֲרִיכַת שְׂפָתָיִם — *Attentive listening, articulate speech.*

◄§ Listening and Articulating

הגם דכבר תני בשמיעת האוזן ובע״כ מעריך שפתיו י״ל שמיעת האוזן בלומד מאחרים גם י״ל עריכת שפתים לייגע את השפתים מרוב עבודה.

עֲרִיכַת שְׂפָתָיִם refers not only to the need to verbalize Torah but also to the intense — and constant — oral discussion of Torah, to the point where one's lips become weary.

■ בְּשִׁמּוּשׁ חֲכָמִים — *Ministering to the sages.*

◄§ Contemporary Application of "Serving Talmidei Chachamim"

יש לומר דבזמן הזה שלומדין מפי ספרים הוי שמוש חכמים.

Prior to the transcription of the Oral Law, one could only acquire hands-on experience by actually becoming personally acquainted with Torah scholars. In contemporary times, when not only the Talmud but also numerous commentaries have been written down, it is possible that one can achieve this attribute by studying their writings.

■ בְּמִעוּט סְחוֹרָה. . .דֶּרֶךְ אֶרֶץ. . .תַּעֲנוּג. . .שֵׁנָה. . .שִׂיחָה. . .שְׂחוֹק. — *Limited business activity . . . work . . . pleasure . . . sleep . . . conversation . . . laughter.*

◄§ The Reward for Self-Negation

וברש״י מביא לשון חז״ל כי אתם המעט שאתם ממעטין עצמכם. הכונה למיעוט שבארבעים ושמונה דברים, במיעוט דרך ארץ, במיעוט תענוג, במיעוט שיחה, במיעוט שחוק. זו הכונה בלשון חז״ל המובא ברש״י שאתם ממעטין עצמכם. שאין הכונה כי אתם המעט שאתם מועטים אלא שאתם ממעטין עצמכם.

mpurity inistering to the sages, closeness with colleagues, sharp discussion with students, deliberation, [knowledge of] Scripture, Mishnah, limited business activity, limited work, limited pleasure, limited sleep, limited conversation, limited laughter, slowness to anger, a good heart, faith

The various attributes listed in our *mishnah* which emphasize negation of the material aspects of life are not only conducive to the growth of the Torah scholar but also reflect the reasons for Hashem's ardent love for *Klal Yisrael*. As the *pasuk* says, כִּי אַתֶּם הַמְעַט מִכָּל הָעַמִּים, which our Sages interpret to mean, *for you "lessen yourselves" more than all the peoples* (Rashi, Devarim 7:7 s.v. אתם המעט). It is precisely because you are the nation that lessens its involvement in material matters — in favor of spirituality — that I have selected you (*Pnei Menachem, Maggidei HaEmes*).

■ בְּמִעוּט תַּעֲנוּג — *Limited pleasure.*

◄§ Minimizing Pleasure

מכאן משמע כהמפרשים לעיל פת במלח תאבל כו׳ היינו רק בשאין לו שלא יבטל עי״ז אבל לא שאינו רשאי לאכול יותר אף שיש לו דאל״כ כבר איתא לעיל דרכה של תורה לצער את עצמו.

This segment of the *mishnah* seems redundant in light of a previous *mishnah* (6:4) that had already said, כָּךְ הִיא דַרְכָּהּ שֶׁל תּוֹרָה: פַּת בַּמֶּלַח תֹּאכֵל, *This is the way of Torah: Eat bread with salt.* However, this question may be resolved by assuming (refer to our commentary there) that one should subsist only on bread and water as a last resort. Generally, it is entirely permissible for individuals to maintain a comfortable life style while studying Torah. However, in order to *acquire* Torah, one should refrain from partaking excessively in the amenities of This World.

■ בְּמִעוּט שִׂיחָה ... בְּמִעוּט שְׂחוֹק — *Limited conversation ... limited laughter.*

◄§ Limitation, Not Avoidance

מילתא דבדחותא.

The *mishnah* is not opposed to all forms of speech, but instead is recommending that an occasional, limited, moment of levity (cf. *Shabbos* 30b stating that Rabbi Akiva and subsequently Rabbah began their discourses on

בְּאֶרֶךְ אַפַּיִם, בְּלֵב טוֹב, בֶּאֱמוּנַת חֲכָמִים, בְּקַבָּלַת
הַיִּסּוּרִין, הַמַּכִּיר אֶת מְקוֹמוֹ, וְהַשָּׂמֵחַ בְּחֶלְקוֹ, וְהָעוֹשֶׂה

ו / ו

a light note) is conducive to retaining Torah.

■ בְּמֶעוּט שְׂחוֹק — *Limited laughter.*

◄§ Better Laughter Than Anger

ויי״ל הפי׳ שהוא מדבר עם חבירו, [ולא פירש יותר, אבל פעם אמר שאם אדם
מכעיסו אז הוא שוחק. ואולי זה הפי׳ כאן שכאשר מדבר עם חבירו והוא מכעיסו
אזי מותר לו לשחוק כדי שלא יכעס].

''Limited laughter'' implies that while laughter and frivolity are generally
inappropriate for a serious student of Torah, in certain circumstances such
behavior is acceptable. For example, when provoked by a peer's angry words,
rather than respond in kind, it would be best to simply laugh off the intended
insult (*Imrei Emes, Maggidei HaEmes*).

■ בְּאֶרֶךְ אַפַּיִם — *Slowness to anger [patience].*

◄§ The Benefit of Patience

יש לומר ב׳ פירושים, א׳ שעל ידי כך אין לו דבר המניעו מלימוד. ועוד שעל ידי
המדות טובות יזכה בתורה.

The benefits of this character trait and the association between patience and
growth in Torah are twofold. Firstly, the patient personality — who is
seldom aroused to anger — is rarely involved in needless acrimony. As a result,
he enjoys more time for Torah study. Furthermore, in the merit of this sterling
character trait he will merit increased understanding of Torah.

■ בְּלֵב טוֹב — *A good heart.*

◄§ A Good Heart

הגם שנזכר כבר בבינה בשכלות הלב, מ״מ לב טוב פי׳ כמו עין טוב כדאי׳ לעיל
בלב טוב בכלל דבריו דבריכם.

Whereas the *understanding heart*, cited previously, refers to the intellectual
qualities and wisdom required for learning, the attribute of ''a good heart''

is similar to "a good eye" discussed above (2:13).

In fact, Rabban Yochanan Ben Zakkai states explicitly that the attribute of a generous eye is subsumed within the category of a good heart. The *mishnah* here is emphasizing the importance of a generous approach to the learning of others as a prerequisite for one's growth.

■ בְּקַבָּלַת הַיִּסּוּרִין — *Acceptance of suffering.*

∞§ Accepting Suffering on Behalf of Others

נראה הפירוש כמו שאיתא ברבי ורבי אלעזר שקבלו עליהם יסורין ממש שבזה
ניצל כל העולם מיסורין.

The *acceptance of suffering* may allude to the sterling example set by the sages, such as Rebbi and Rabbi Eliezer (cf. *Bava Metzia* 85a), who agreed to suffer for a protracted period so that others may live in tranquility. In the merit of such altruistic suffering, one achieves great strides in the quest for spiritual growth.

∞§ Hashem Is Right

כאשר נפטרה בתו של הרה"ק רבי מנחם מענדיל ז"ל אב"ד זדונסקה-וואלה על
פניו באבה וימאן אביה להתנחם. אז בא לפני אדמו"ר זצ"ל מקאצק שבור ורצוץ.
השמיע הרבי קושיא על גמרא מסוימת והרב תירץ, הקשה על רש"י ותוס' והרב
תירץ. נענה הרבי מקאצק ואמר "אם הגמ' צודקת, רש"י ותוס' צודקים הרי שגם
הקב"ה צודק". נתנחם הרב מנחם מענדיל, ומאז נמנה על חסידיו הגדולים של
הרבי מקאצק.

When the daughter of R' Menachem Mendel of Zedonska-Wolla passed away in her prime, her broken-hearted father sought comfort from the Kotzker. Instead of directly addressing the subject, the Kotzker asked a question regarding a discussion in the Gemara to which his visitor responded appropriately. Subsequently, the Rebbe asked questions regarding discussions in *Rashi* and *Tosfos* commentaries, and his guest responded to those issues as well. The Kotzker concluded by saying that if the Gemara, *Rashi* and *Tosfos* were proven to be correct despite their surface difficulties, certainly Hashem's actions are just, despite our lack of appreciation or understanding of their merit. Comforted by this novel approach, R' Menachem Mendel became a devout follower of the Kotzker (*Maggidei HaEmes*).

סְיָג לִדְבָרָיו, וְאֵינוֹ מַחֲזִיק טוֹבָה לְעַצְמוֹ, אָהוּב, אוֹהֵב
אֶת הַמָּקוֹם, אוֹהֵב אֶת הַבְּרִיּוֹת, אוֹהֵב אֶת הַצְּדָקוֹת,
אוֹהֵב אֶת הַמֵּישָׁרִים, אוֹהֵב אֶת הַתּוֹכָחוֹת, וּמִתְרַחֵק מִן
הַכָּבוֹד, וְלֹא מֵגִיס לִבּוֹ בְּתַלְמוּדוֹ, וְאֵינוֹ שָׂמֵחַ בְּהוֹרָאָה,

---

■ הַמַּכִּיר אֶת מְקוֹמוֹ — *Knowing one's place.*

◆§ A Place in Hashem's Master Plan

והענין להיות כי כל הוה וכל שיש לצייר בעולם הכל כאשר לכל מחיות חי החיים
לזאת יכול כל אדם בכל זמן ובכל מעשיו ומחשבותיו אף בעמידתו לא טוב ר"ל
יוכל למצוא מקומו השייך לו והבכלל כי מעשה ה' בשלימות לכל וכל הוה רק
מחיות [חי החיים] נמצא יש תמיד מקום לכל דבר וזהו עיקר הפי' אין לך דבר
שאין לו מקום כו' וזהו עצמו נק' בחי' מקום שאחז"ל הוא מקומו של עולם ואין
עולמו מקומו כו'... איך זה תלוי בהאדם בבחי' ביטול להשורש יוכל למצוא הכל
גם ההיפוך, וזהו ענין כל המופתים מה שמגידים שהוציא יין מהכותל שע"י חיבור
אל השורש יש הכל ואין סתירה, וזה תלוי באדם שאם הוא דבוק בכולו בהש"י
יכול להתקשר הכל ג"כ.

E very individual enjoys a place (i.e., a unique role and function in this universe) in the master plan that Hashem has ordained for His universe. Each
of our undertakings, every one of our actions, has validity if it serves to
substantiate the realization of Hashem's Divine Plan for His world. Every
situation in life, the good as well as the bad, can be exploited to the maximum
if we but realize that all that occurs is part of Hashem's Master Plan for the
universe. Everything that happens is each individual's small contribution to the
fulfillment of that great objective. As we learned previously, אֵין לְךָ דָּבָר שֶׁאֵין לוֹ
מָקוֹם, there is no thing that does not enjoy a unique place in the Divine
Blueprint. The Divine Name הַמָּקוֹם, the Omnipresent, may be derived from the
same concept — Hashem's designation of a distinctive place and role for each
of us in His World. As *Chazal* state (*Bereishis Rabbah* 68:10) הקב"ה מְקוֹמוֹ שֶׁל
עוֹלָם, Hashem is the Place of the universe — He determines the appropriate
place and mission for everything in the world.

However, finding one's Divinely ordained niche is no simple feat. To accomplish this lofty objective, one must be capable of "connecting" to one's heavenly roots. (Refer to *Days of Awe*, pp. 49, 67, 145, 201 and 208, elaborating
upon the theme that even while we dwell on earth our spiritual roots lie in
heaven.) Only such a uniquely spiritual individual can find his precise place in
the Divine Blueprint.

The many traditional tales about miracles performed by *tzaddikim* may be
understood in this same context. All the natural limitations of this world may

fence around his words, claiming no credit for himself, being beloved, loving the Omnipresent, loving [His] creatures, loving righteous ways, loving proper character traits, loving reproof, keeping far from honor, not being arrogant with his learning, not enjoying halachic decision-

be transcended by those righteous individuals who, while sojourning on earth, actually cling to their spiritual roots in heaven.

■ וְהַשָּׂמֵחַ בְּחֶלְקוֹ — *Being happy with one's lot.*

✥ Being Satisfied With One's Spiritual Portion

> יש לומר בדברי תורה שמח במה שחננו ד'. הגם כי קנאת סופרים תרבה חכמה,
> מכל מקום בחלק שלו יש לו לשמוח גם כן.
> ויש לדחוק דעי"ז לא יוטרד וילמוד במנוחה

From the context of this *mishnah* which deals primarily with the spiritual attributes necessary to acquire Torah, it seems that the virtue of being happy with one's lot refers to being content with one's *spiritual* lot. While it is ce tainly true that a certain amount of rivalry among Torah scholars is conducive to the development of new Torah insights — קִנְאַת סוֹפְרִים תַּרְבֶּה חָכְמָה, *jealousy (vying) among scholars increases [Torah] wisdom;* (*Bava Basra* 21a) — such competition must be contained within acceptable limits.

Alternatively, the need to be happy may refer to being content with one's physical lot. Such an individual enjoys the piece of mind to immerse himself in Torah.

■ וְהָעוֹשֶׂה סְיָג לִדְבָרָיו — *Making a [protective] fence around his words.*

✥ Setting Limits to One's Speech

> יש לפרש שעל דבריו קאי ע"ד דאיתא סייג לחכמה שיתקה

The term עוֹשֶׂה סְיָג לִדְבָרָיו can be interpreted to mean "he sets limits to his speech." This approach corresponds to Rabbi Akiva's advice — סְיָג לַחָכְמָה שְׁתִיקָה, *a [protective] fence for wisdom is silence* (above, 3:17).

■ אָהוּב — *Being beloved.*

Prerequisite or Result?

ולמעלה אמר שזוכין לזה על ידי תורה לשמה ונראה שזה דבר גדול שאין משיגין זאת רק בהקדם הלימוד תורה לשמה, וכאן משמע שצריך להיות קודם התורה. וצריך לומר שהכל מדריגות ואין לו שיעור, ומעט יכול האדם לזכות בעצמו ובשלימות רק על ידי תורה לשמה.

Our *mishnah*, implying that to be beloved by Hashem is a prerequisite for advancement in Torah, seemingly contradicts the first *mishnah* in this *perek* which depicts this characteristic as a *result* of studying *Torah lishmah*. Apparently, the enviable attribute of being beloved by Hashem cannot be achieved all at once. While, to some extent, this must precede progress in Torah study, one can only be fully beloved by Hashem and by one's peers as a result of studying Torah for its own sake.

■ אוֹהֵב אֶת הַמֵּישָׁרִים — *Loving proper character traits.*

Appreciating the Right Middos

את המישרים מדות ישרות.

The term מֵישָׁרִים may be interpreted as "the straight path" and refers to the need for an aspiring Torah scholar to appreciate and follow the proper character traits.

■ אוֹהֵב אֶת הַתּוֹכָחוֹת — *Loving reproof.*

Remember — The One Who Gives Mussar Is Your Friend

וזה עיקר פי' אוהב את התוכחות להאמין כי הוא מאהבה כשיודעין שהמוכיח אוהב נאמן הוא. מקבלין התוכחה. ועי"ז נהפך באמת לאהבה. זע"ז כתי' על כל פשעים תכסה אהבה. ואיך יכולין לבא לאהבה כשיש רוב פשעים. רק שמקבלין התוכחה והעונשין והיסורין מתוך אהבה. ולכן כתי' לכו כו' ונוכחה כו' אם יהיו חטאיכם כשנים כו' פי' ע"י קבלת התוכחה יתלבנו החטאים כנ"ל. בנ"י מקבלין יסורי הגלות באהבה ומאמינים כי הוא חסד השי"י . . . יוכל להיות זאת מפתח של גאולה.

How can one love admonishment? If he recognizes and understands that the individual who is giving the admonishment is a true friend. The result is that one is able to accept and absorb those words.

With this approach, we gain new insight into Shlomo HaMelech's statement that וְעַל כָּל פְּשָׁעִים תְּכַסֶּה אַהֲבָה, *love covers* (i. e. atones) *all offenses* (*Mishlei* 10:12). By lovingly accepting the criticisms of others, which motivates us to repent — and, if necessary, submitting to the suffering to which we may be exposed — and recognizing that these are acts of loving kindness, we will merit Divine forgiveness. *Yeshayahu* (1:18) explicates the relationship between accepting criticism and meriting forgiveness by first stating, לְכוּ נָא וְנִוָּכְחָה, *Come, now, let us reason together* — let us accept rebuke; then, the proclamation of Divine forgiveness: אִם יִהְיוּ חֲטָאֵיכֶם כַּשָּׁנִים כַּשֶּׁלֶג יַלְבִּינוּ, *If your sins are like scarlet they will become white as snow.* Expanding upon this concept a bit further, we recall that the Jewish People "accused" Hashem of releasing them from Egypt because He hated them (cf. *Devarim* 1:27). This reckless and totally unjustified attribution of Hashem's goodness to His "hatred" of us was a a major factor in postponing our entry into *Eretz Yisrael*. By the same token, we may deduce that attributing what appears to be a harsh Divine decree to Hashem's loving kindness will be a source of merit leading to the Final Redemption (*Sfas Emes, Devarim* 5642, 5643).

◄§ Loving His Grandfather's Mussar

שפת אמת ז"ל בילדותו היה לומד כל הלילות בבית המדרש עם ידידו. פעם אחת למד במשך כל הלילה ולקראת הבוקר הלך לישון שינה חטופה, ונמשך השינה עד שאיחר לקום. כאשר נכנס מאוחר לתפילה, הוכיחו סבו החידושי הרי"ם ז"ל קשות, וקיבל את התוכחה ולא ענה מאומה. לאחר התפילה שאלו ידידו שלמד עמו כל הלילה, מדוע לא ענית שלמדת כל הלילה? אמר לו השפ"א מצינו אצל בני ראובן ובני גד כאשר הוכיחם משה רע"ה, לא ענו מאומה כל הזמן אלא הקשיבו לתוכחתו במשך שעה ארוכה ולא מצינו שענו לו אלא לאחר שגמר להוכיחם. והטעם לפי שהיה חביב עליהם תוכחתו של מרע"ה. אף אני חביבין עלי תוכחות מורי זקני על כן לא רציתי לתרץ עצמי.

The following incident illustrates how the *Sfas Emes* loved admonishment — and those who gave it — even as a very young man. As a young fellow, the *Sfas Emes* would often stay up all night learning Torah with his study partner. After one such session, he returned to his room for some much-needed rest. As a result of his short nap, the *Sfas Emes* arrived a little late for *davening*, and he was rebuked by his grandfather, the *Chiddushei HaRim*. Throughout this encounter, the *Sfas Emes* did not seek to defend himself by explaining that he had been awake all night studying Torah.

When his study partner expressed bewilderment that he had not defended himself, he responded, "I learned from the example of the children of Reuven and Gad who were roundly criticized by Moshe for apparently forsaking their brethren. Rather than interrupt Moshe to explain that they had no such intentions — and, would, in fact, serve heroically in the front lines of the Jewish armies conquering Canaan — they waited until Moshe had completed his criticisms. Just as they appreciated every word of Moshe's rebuke, so too every word of my grandfather's admonition is infinitely precious to me."

■ וְלֹא מֵגִיס לִבּוֹ בְּתַלְמוּדוֹ — *Not being arrogant with his learning.* ■

✥ The Unique Contribution of the Baal Shem Tov

בדורו של הבעש״ט ז״ל למדו הרבה תורה, אבל אם בדורו של רבי יהודה ברבי אלעאי למדו ששה בטלית אחת הרי בדורו של הבעש״ט ששה טליתים לא הספיקו ללמדן אחר, אנשים התפשטו לרוחב וכריסם גדל מלימודיהם כענין שכתוב וישמן ישורון ויבעט. בא הבעש״ט וגילה תורתו.

According to the *Chiddushei HaRim*, the Baal Shem Tov played a major role in the restoration of this character trait which emphasizes humility as a prerequisite to Torah study. Recalling the Gemara (*Sanhedrin* 20a) stating that during the time of Rabbi Yehuda ben Ela'i, six *talmidei chachamim* were forced to wrap themselves in the same cloak while studying Torah (due to their extreme poverty), the *Chiddushei HaRim* noted that at the time of the Baal Shem Tov, the ego and the obsession with materialism of some people had become so enormous that six cloaks would not have been sufficient for even one of them!

As a result of the revelation of the chassidic teachings of the Baal Shem Tov, the role of humility in acquiring Torah was restored to its former prominence.

✥ Not Becoming Too "Intimate" With the Torah

לא אמרו מגיס דעתו אלא מגיס לבו, חסידים פירשו אינו מגיס לבו עהר זאל נישט זיין צו היימיש מיט די תורה, שלא יהיה לבו גס בה, אלא באימה ביראה ברתת ובזיע.

The *Pnei Menachem* noted that it does not say וְלֹא מֵגִיס דַעְתּוֹ בְּתַלְמוּדוֹ, that his mind (דַעְתּוֹ) does not become haughty as a result of his learning, but rather וְלֹא מֵגִיס לִבּוֹ, his *heart* does not become too intimate. The *mishnah* is reminding the Torah student not to become too comfortable (cf. *Eruvin* 47a) where לִבּוֹ גַּס refers to an intimate relationship) with the Torah. Just as the Torah was given at Sinai in an atmosphere of awe and reverence, so too we should never become

making, sharing his fellow's yoke, judging him favorably, setting him on the truthful course, setting him on the peaceful course, thinking deliberately in his study, asking and answering, listening and contributing to the discussion,

---

overly relaxed while we study Torah (*Maggidei HaEmes*).

■ וּמִתְיַשֵּׁב לִבּוֹ בְּתַלְמוּדוֹ — *Thinking deliberately in his study.*

◢§ Overcoming All Distractions Through Torah

ואינו הך דבישוב לעיל, רק י״ל הכא הפירוש שמי שאין לבו מיושב מצער דברים אחרים וטרדות ועל ידי שלומד דברי תורה מתיישב ומתייישר לבו, הוא סימן שיש לו דביקות בדברי תורה.

Whereas the *mishnah* had previously underscored the importance of peace of mind as a prerequisite to Torah study, here the *mishnah* is addressing those individuals who are so beset by extraneous problems that it is virtually impossible for them to remove everything else from their mind prior to learning. In such a case, the only alternative is to continue learning despite one's numerous distractions (see above 2:5). By immersing oneself in Torah under such trying circumstances, one eventually gains peace of mind. As the precise translation of this phrase indicates, מִתְיַשֵּׁב לִבּוֹ, he achieves tranquility בְּתַלְמוּדוֹ, through his Torah study.

■ שׁוֹמֵעַ וּמוֹסִיף — *Listening and contributing to the discussion.*

◢§ ''Resurrecting'' Your Rebbi's Torah

כדאיתא במס׳ שבועות שלא יאמר התלמיד אמתין כו׳ ואסתרנו ואבננו משלי.

This concise phrase is alluding to a trait elucidated elsewhere (cf. *Shevuos* 31a), which states that a student who hears his *rebbi* making a gross error which would affect the verdict of a court case should listen carefully (שׁוֹמֵעַ) and then *immediately* suggest emendations and improvements to his *rebbi's* opinion (וּמוֹסִיף). He should proceed in this manner rather than wait for his *rebbi* to *conclude* his erroneous opinion and then refute him.

◢§ Always Contribute Something New

״וכאשר במ״ח דברים גם שומע ומוסיף . . . ותתרגל גם אתה, כשאתה שומע

וְהַלּוֹמֵד עַל מְנָת לַעֲשׂוֹת, הַמַּחְכִּים אֶת רַבּוֹ, וְהַמְכַוֵּן
אֶת שְׁמוּעָתוֹ, וְהָאוֹמֵר דָּבָר בְּשֵׁם אוֹמְרוֹ. הָא לָמַדְתָּ, כָּל
הָאוֹמֵר דָּבָר בְּשֵׁם אוֹמְרוֹ, מֵבִיא גְאֻלָּה לָעוֹלָם,
שֶׁנֶּאֱמַר: ,,וַתֹּאמֶר אֶסְתֵּר לַמֶּלֶךְ בְּשֵׁם מָרְדְּכָי.''

[ז] גְּדוֹלָה תוֹרָה, שֶׁהִיא נוֹתֶנֶת חַיִּים לְעוֹשֶׂיהָ בָּעוֹלָם

דבר, להוסיף מה על זה, ואולי מרומז ואלה תולדות יעקב – יוסף''.

In one of his letters, the *Lev Simchah* noted that this may refer to the fact that usually when a Torah scholar hears a novel Torah though, he is not content to merely repeat it; instead, he elaborates upon it. The importance of constantly being creative in the realm of Torah is alluded to by the phrase, אֵלֶּה תֹלְדוֹת יַעֲקֹב יוֹסֵף, *these are the children of Yaakov: Yosef (Bereishis 37:2)*. This may be interpreted homiletically — the contribution (i. e. the intellectual offspring, תֹלְדוֹת) of *Klal Yisrael*, Yaakov's descendants, add (יוֹסֵף) to the wellsprings of Torah.

■ וְהָאוֹמֵר דָּבָר בְּשֵׁם אוֹמְרוֹ — *And repeating a saying in the name of the one who said it.*

◆§ A Joint Effort

היינו שיש דבר שאין האדם יכול לאומרו בעצמו וצריך שיאמרו אחר.

This final attribute through which Torah is acquired involves much more than merely crediting a source. It implies that certain Torah thoughts are destined to be disseminated through a collaborative effort. The initiator of the thought, whose role is to develop this novel thought but not to teach it to a broader audience, is joined in his efforts by the disseminator, who is capable of relating this insight to others. It is through collaborative efforts such as these that the Final Redemption will be hastened (*Imrei Emes, Maggidei HaEmes*).

◆§ Even If It Is Your Own Thought as Well

ולכאורה מה השבח העצום הזה להביא גאולה אם אינו מתלבש בטליתו של חבירו

...

ולכן אפשר על פי המבואר בגמ' כי הנגלה לנביא ברוח הקודש נודע גם לנביאים
אחרים . . . ולכן כאן כשאמר ר''מ אסתר ברוה''ק נאמרה שנאמר ויודע הדבר
למרדכי, כן נודע מיד לאסתר שנחשבה משבע נביאות, ומרדכי הגיד לה כי כי לא

learning in order to teach, learning in order to practice, making his teacher wiser, pondering over what he has learned, and repeating a saying in the name of the one who said it. For this you have learned: Whoever repeats a thing in the name of the one who said it brings redemption to the world, as it is said (Esther 2:22): "And Esther said to the king in the name of Mordechai."

[7] Great is Torah, for it confers life upon its

ידע עוד שהיא נביאה, אם כן היתה יכולה לומר בשם עצמה למלך עם כל זה נהגה טובת עין במרדכי, וזה הטוב עין הביא גאולה לעולם שעל ידי זה וימצא כתוב וכו' וזה השבח הגדול.

While giving credit to the rightful source of a Torah thought is a matter of common decency, it does not seem to be something so virtuous that it would merit hastening the Final Redemption. However, if we examine closely the example of Esther, cited by our *mishnah*, we can appreciate why the *mishnah* so lavishly praises this particular attribute. The *Imrei Emes* points out that Esther, as a prophetess in her own right (cf. *Megillah* 14b), was well aware of the conspiracy to assassinate Achashveirosh, without being told by Mordechai. Yet, Esther took great pains to cite Mordechai — and not herself — as the source of the intelligence which saved Achashveirosh. Such altruism and self-efface-ment brought about *Klal Yisrael's* redemption at the time of the Purim miracle. Similarly, such devotion to a peer's Torah thoughts (even though you may have thought of it as well) is the final and ultimate prerequisite for acquiring Torah (*Maggidei HaEmes*).

◆§ It Is Really Hashem's Thought

בשם אומרו היינו שהוא דבוק בהשי"ת וזו היא גאולה.

Alternatively, the term אוֹמְרוֹ may refer to Hashem Who, of course, is the true progenitor of any Torah thought. A feeling of redemption is attained every time that an individual not only studies Torah but while learning senses an intimate attachment to Hashem. The individual recognizes that Hashem is the "Giver of the Torah," and is the true initiator of every Torah thought (*Imrei Emes, Maggidei HaEmes*).

7.

■ גְּדוֹלָה תוֹרָה שֶׁהִיא נוֹתֶנֶת חַיִּים לְעוֹשֶׂיהָ בָּעוֹלָם הַזֶּה וּבָעוֹלָם הַבָּא ■ — *Great is*

הַזֶּה וּבָעוֹלָם הַבָּא, שֶׁנֶּאֱמַר: „כִּי חַיִּים הֵם לְמֹצְאֵיהֶם,
וּלְכָל בְּשָׂרוֹ מַרְפֵּא." וְאוֹמֵר: „רִפְאוּת תְּהִי לְשָׁרֶּךָ,
וְשִׁקּוּי לְעַצְמוֹתֶיךָ." וְאוֹמֵר: „עֵץ חַיִּים הִיא לַמַּחֲזִיקִים
בָּהּ וְתֹמְכֶיהָ מְאֻשָּׁר." וְאוֹמֵר: „כִּי לִוְיַת חֵן הֵם לְרֹאשֶׁךָ,
וַעֲנָקִים לְגַרְגְּרֹתֶיךָ." וְאוֹמֵר: „תִּתֵּן לְרֹאשְׁךָ לִוְיַת חֵן,
עֲטֶרֶת תִּפְאֶרֶת תְּמַגְּנֶךָּ." וְאוֹמֵר: „כִּי בִי יִרְבּוּ יָמֶיךָ,
וְיוֹסִיפוּ לְךָ שְׁנוֹת חַיִּים." וְאוֹמֵר: „אֹרֶךְ יָמִים בִּימִינָהּ,
בִּשְׂמֹאולָהּ עֹשֶׁר וְכָבוֹד." וְאוֹמֵר: „כִּי אֹרֶךְ יָמִים וּשְׁנוֹת
חַיִּים, וְשָׁלוֹם יוֹסִיפוּ לָךְ."

---

*Torah, for it confers life upon its practitioners, both in This World and
in the World to Come.*

◀§ Renewal Through Torah

> נותנים חיים היינו כשכבר אבדו את החיות, כתיב אתהלך לפני ה' בארצות החיים
> וזה על ידי התורה. פירוש כי חיים הם, עולם הבא. ולכל בשרו מרפא, עולם הזה.

By using the expression נוֹתֶנֶת חַיִּים, *confers life* (implying renewal), the *mishnah* is emphasizing that even when physical life has ceased, the Jew lives on
in the spiritual ambiance of the World to Come. As David sings (*Tehillim*
116:9), אֶתְהַלֵּךְ לִפְנֵי ה' בְּאַרְצוֹת הַחַיִּים, *I shall walk before Hashem in the lands of
true life* (the World to Come), by remaining in Hashem's Presence through the
study of His Torah (*Imrei Emes, Maggidei HaEmes*).

The *pasuk* from *Mishlei* (4:22) cited by the *mishnah* also corroborates the
mishnah's theme that Torah enables us to persevere in the World to Come and
in This World. כִּי חַיִּים הֵם לְמֹצְאֵיהֶם וּלְכָל בְּשָׂרוֹ מַרְפֵּא, *For they* [the teachings of
the Torah] *are life to those who find them and a healing to his entire flesh* —
while Torah's teachings heal our flesh in This World (בְּשָׂרוֹ מַרְפֵּא), they also
revive us in the World to Come (חַיִּים הֵם).

◀§ A Torah-Based Olam Hazeh

> הגם כי שכר מצוה בהאי עלמא ליכא רק גדולה תורה שנותנת חיים לעושי'
> בעו"הז ובעוה"ב ופי' לעושי' כנ"ל שמביא הארת התורה בעשי' שהעושה ומקיים
> התורה זוכה שגם חיי עוה"ז יה' רק ע"י התורה.

This *mishnah* seems to contradict the renowned principle that we are not
rewarded in This World (*Chullin* 142a שְׂכַר מִצְוָה בְּהַאי עָלְמָא לֵיכָּא). While

practitioners, both in This World and in the World to Come, as it is said (Mishlei 4:22): "For they [the teachings of the Torah] are life to those who find them, and a healing to his entire flesh." And it says (Mishlei 3:8): "It shall be healing to your flesh, and marrow to your bones." And it says (Mishlei 3:18): "It is a tree of life to those who grasp it, and its supporters are praiseworthy." And it says (Mishlei 1:9): "They are a tiara of grace for your head and necklaces for your neck." And it says (Mishlei 4:9): "It will give to your head a tiara of grace, a crown of glory it will deliver to you." And it says (Mishlei 9:11): 'Indeed, through me [the Torah] your days shall be increased, and years of life shall be added to you." And it says (Mishlei 3:16): "Lengthy days are at its right, and at its left are wealth and honor." And it says (Mishlei 3:2): "For lengthy days and years of life, and peace shall they add to you."

---

ordinarily this is the case, someone who integrates Torah into the material world (עוֹשֵׂיהָ) *deserves* to be rewarded in This World.

Moreover, one whose existence is inseparable from Torah merits that even his fate in This World will be conducted on the basis of Torah and not defined solely by the natural laws of the universe (adapted from *Sfas Emes, Kedoshim 5636*).

■ בָּעוֹלָם הַזֶּה וּבָעוֹלָם הַבָּא — *Both in This World and in the World to Come.*

◄§ Life for the Great and for the Simple

בעולם הזה היינו לאנשים גדולים שהתורה נותנת להם כח שיוכלו להיות בעולם
הזה. ובעולם הבא היינו לאנשים פשוטים שיוכלו להאחז באנשים הגדולים ולזכות
לעולם הבא.

By stating explicitly that Torah provides life in both This World and the World to Come, the *mishnah* is offering assurances to two different types of Jews. To the learned Jew who is far more predisposed to the spiritual values of *Olam Haba* than to the material demands of This World, the Torah gives strength to cope with This World. On the other hand, the simple, unlearned

[ח] רַבִּי שִׁמְעוֹן בֶּן יְהוּדָה מִשּׁוּם רַבִּי שִׁמְעוֹן בֶּן יוֹחַאי
אוֹמֵר: הַנּוֹי, וְהַכֹּחַ, וְהָעֹשֶׁר, וְהַכָּבוֹד, וְהַחָכְמָה,
וְהַזִּקְנָה, וְהַשֵּׂיבָה, וְהַבָּנִים – נָאֶה לַצַּדִּיקִים וְנָאֶה
לָעוֹלָם, שֶׁנֶּאֱמַר: „עֲטֶרֶת תִּפְאֶרֶת שֵׂיבָה, בְּדֶרֶךְ צְדָקָה
תִּמָּצֵא." וְאוֹמֵר: „עֲטֶרֶת זְקֵנִים בְּנֵי בָנִים, וְתִפְאֶרֶת
בָּנִים אֲבוֹתָם." וְאוֹמֵר: „תִּפְאֶרֶת בַּחוּרִים כֹּחָם, וַהֲדַר
זְקֵנִים שֵׂיבָה." וְאוֹמֵר „וְחָפְרָה הַלְּבָנָה וּבוֹשָׁה הַחַמָּה,
כִּי מָלַךְ יהוה צְבָאוֹת בְּהַר צִיּוֹן וּבִירוּשָׁלַיִם, וְנֶגֶד זְקֵנָיו
כָּבוֹד." רַבִּי שִׁמְעוֹן בֶּן מְנַסְיָא אוֹמֵר: אֵלּוּ שֶׁבַע מִדּוֹת,
שֶׁמָּנוּ חֲכָמִים לַצַּדִּיקִים, כֻּלָּם נִתְקַיְּמוּ בְּרַבִּי וּבְבָנָיו.

[ט] אָמַר רַבִּי יוֹסֵי בֶּן קִסְמָא: פַּעַם אַחַת הָיִיתִי מְהַלֵּךְ

Jew may feel quite comfortable in This World but can only merit a portion in
the World to Come by developing a close relationship with Torah and its
teachers (*Imrei Emes, Maggidei HaEmes*).

■ עֵץ חַיִּים הִיא לַמַּחֲזִיקִים בָּהּ — *It is a tree of life to those who grasp it.*

✥ Negating Oneself in Favor of the Torah

כפי שהאדם מחזיק בתורה ויודע שמצד עצמו אין לו חיות כלל, כן התורה היא
בעבורו עץ חיים.

Torah supports those who cling to it — to the exclusion of anything else —
for life. To the extent one grasps Torah as his source of sustenance, in
general, the Torah *will* sustain him (*Chiddushei HaRim, Maggidei HaEmes*).

■ אֹרֶךְ יָמִים וּשְׁנוֹת חַיִּים — *Lengthy days and years of life.*

✥ Lengthy Days

ממה שכתוב אורך ימים ושנות חיים, נראה שהם ב' ענינים, שנות חיים הוא
הברכה כפשוטה ריבוי שנים לחיים, ואורך ימים היינו ימים ארוכים.
ועיי"ש שמביא מה שאמר האמרי אמת ז"ל לאחיו הרה"ק ר' משה בצלאל ז"ל
אחר הלוויית אביהם השפ"א ז"ל, "לאבא ז"ל היה אריכת ימים, ימים ארוכים
ימים גדולים, ופי' שאריכות ימים היינו שהימים ארוכים ומלאים, שניצל את הזמן
ואת הימים בשלמות.

[8] *Rabbi Shimon ben Yehudah says in the name of Rabbi Shimon ben Yochai: Beauty, strength, wealth, honor, wisdom, old age, hoary age, and children — these befit the righteous and befit the world, as it is said (Mishlei 16:31): "Ripe old age is a crown of splendor, it can be found in the path of righteousness." And it says (Mishlei 17:6): "The crown of the aged is grandchildren, and the splendor of children is their fathers." And it says (Mishlei 20:29): "The splendor of young men is their strength, and the glory of old men is hoary age." And it says (Yeshayahu 24:23): "The moon will grow pale and the sun be shamed, when Hashem, Master of Legions, will have reigned on Mount Zion and in Jerusalem, and honor shall be before His elders." Rabbi Shimon ben Menasya says: These seven qualities that the Sages attributed to the righteous were all realized in Rebbi and his sons.*

[9] *Rabbi Yose ben Kisma said: Once I was walking on the road, when a certain man met me. He greeted me*

Upon returning from the *Sfas Emes'* funeral, his son and successor R' Avraham Mordechai (later known as the *Imrei Emes*) remarked to his brother R' Moshe Betzalel that their father had enjoyed "lengthy days." Though he only lived to the age of 58, he was able to maximize the potential of each day.

The distinction between "lengthy days" and the more traditional concept of longevity is indicated in this *pasuk* from *Mishlei* (3:2) — כִּי אֹרֶךְ יָמִים וּשְׁנוֹת חַיִּים וְשָׁלוֹם יוֹסִיפוּ לָךְ, *For lengthy days and years of life, and peace shall they add to you.* The Torah grants its supporters not only many years (שְׁנוֹת חַיִּים) but also long *days* (אֹרֶךְ יָמִים), days that are effectively utilized.[1] (*Lev Simchah, Maggidei HaEmes*).

8.

■ וְנֶגֶד זְקֵנָיו כָּבוֹד ■ — *And honor shall be before His elders.*

◆§ The Desire for Kavod Never Ceases

לכאורה תיבת ונגד מיותר דהו״ל למימר ולזקניו כבוד. אבן יי״ל כי הנה בימי

---

1. Cf. *Sfas Emes Chayei Sarah* 5637 for a similar description in the *pasuk* stating that Avraham בָּא בַּיָּמִים, *came with his days* (24:1).

בַּדֶּרֶךְ, וּפָגַע בִּי אָדָם אֶחָד. וְנָתַן לִי שָׁלוֹם, וְהֶחֱזַרְתִּי לוֹ
שָׁלוֹם: אָמַר לִי: „רַבִּי, מֵאֵיזֶה מָקוֹם אָתָּה?" אָמַרְתִּי לוֹ:
„מֵעִיר גְּדוֹלָה שֶׁל חֲכָמִים וְשֶׁל סוֹפְרִים אָנִי." אָמַר לִי:
„רַבִּי, רְצוֹנְךָ שֶׁתָּדוּר עִמָּנוּ בִּמְקוֹמֵנוּ וַאֲנִי אֶתֵּן לְךָ אֶלֶף
אֲלָפִים דִּינְרֵי זָהָב וַאֲבָנִים טוֹבוֹת וּמַרְגָּלִיּוֹת?" אָמַרְתִּי
לוֹ: „אִם אַתָּה נוֹתֵן לִי כָּל כֶּסֶף וְזָהָב וַאֲבָנִים טוֹבוֹת
וּמַרְגָּלִיּוֹת שֶׁבָּעוֹלָם, אֵינִי דָר אֶלָּא בִּמְקוֹם תּוֹרָה." וְכֵן
כָּתוּב בְּסֵפֶר תְּהִלִּים עַל יְדֵי דָוִד מֶלֶךְ יִשְׂרָאֵל: „טוֹב לִי
תוֹרַת פִּיךָ מֵאַלְפֵי זָהָב וָכָסֶף." וְלֹא עוֹד אֶלָּא שֶׁבִּשְׁעַת
פְּטִירָתוֹ שֶׁל אָדָם אֵין מְלַוִּין לוֹ לְאָדָם לֹא כֶסֶף וְלֹא
זָהָב וְלֹא אֲבָנִים טוֹבוֹת וּמַרְגָּלִיּוֹת, אֶלָּא תוֹרָה וּמַעֲשִׂים
טוֹבִים בִּלְבָד, שֶׁנֶּאֱמַר, „בְּהִתְהַלֶּכְךָ תַּנְחֶה אֹתָךְ,
בְּשָׁכְבְּךָ תִּשְׁמֹר עָלֶיךָ, וַהֲקִיצוֹתָ הִיא תְשִׂיחֶךָ."
„בְּהִתְהַלֶּכְךָ תַּנְחֶה אֹתָךְ" — בָּעוֹלָם הַזֶּה; „בְּשָׁכְבְּךָ
תִּשְׁמֹר עָלֶיךָ" — בַּקֶּבֶר; „וַהֲקִיצוֹתָ הִיא תְשִׂיחֶךָ" —
לָעוֹלָם הַבָּא. וְאוֹמֵר: „לִי הַכֶּסֶף וְלִי הַזָּהָב, נְאֻם יהוה
צְבָאוֹת."

הבחרות של האדם ישנם הרבה דברים שהיצה"ר מתגבר אצלו, דהיינו קנאה
תאוה כבוד וכדומה, והם עומדים כנגדו. אבל בימי הזקנה בטלים אצלו רובם של
ענינים אלו, מלבד ענין הכבוד שנשאר אצלו עד זקנה ושיבה. וזהו ונגד זקניו כבוד,
כבוד הוא הכנגד של הזקנים.

R' Avraham of Slonim interprets this phrase homiletically. Reflecting upon one of the true (if unfortunate) realities of life, he noted that many of the passions of life subside with age. Certainly one's lust for material things tends to diminish with advancing years. However, the desire for honor may remain in full force. As this *pasuk* intimates, *and honor shall be before His elders* — the desire for honor always remains before the elderly (*Maggidei HaEmes*).

9.

■ וְנָתַן לִי שָׁלוֹם וְהֶחֱזַרְתִּי לוֹ שָׁלוֹם — *He greeted me and I returned his greeting.*

and I returned his greeting. He said to me, "Rabbi, from what place are you?" I said to him, "I am from a great city of scholars and sages." He said to me, "Rabbi, would you be willing to live with us in our place? I would give you thousands upon thousands of golden dinars, precious stones and pearls." I replied: "Even if you were to give me all the silver and gold, precious stones and pearls in the world, I would dwell nowhere but in a place of Torah." And so it is written in the Book of Psalms by David, King of Israel (Tehillim 119:72): "I prefer the Torah of Your mouth above thousands in gold and silver." Furthermore, when a man departs from this world, neither silver, nor gold, nor precious stones nor pearls escort him, but only Torah study and good deeds, as it is said (Mishlei 6:22): "When you walk, it shall guide you; when you lie down, it shall guard you; and when you awake, it shall speak on your behalf." "When you walk, it shall guide you" — in this world; "when you lie down, it shall guard you" — in the grave; "and when you awake, it shall speak on your behalf" — in the World to Come. And it says (Chaggai 2:8): "Mine is the silver, and Mine is the gold, says HaShem, Master of Legions."

◆§ Spurning a Friend's Offer

יש לדקדק למה צריך לספר זאת. וי״ל שהיה מכירו ואף על פי כן לא היה רוצה
ללכת עמו.

This individual who met Rabbi Yose ben Kisma was no stranger to him, as evidenced by the warm greeting that he extended to the sage. Yet, despite their previous relationship, Rabbi Yose spurned a financially lucrative offer that was clearly not in his best *spiritual* interests (*Imrei Emes, Maggidei HaEmes*).

■ שֶׁבָּעוֹלָם . . . אָם אַתָּה נוֹתֵן לִי כָּל כֶּסֶף וְזָהָב — *Even if you were to give me all the silver and gold . . . in the world.*

◆§ How Did Rabbi Yose Differ From Bilam?

בקטנותי הקשה לי מורי הרב ז״ל דפרשת בלק פירש״י על מה שכתוב אם יתן
לי בלק מלא ביתו וכו' למדנו שנפשו רחבה, ואם כן איך רבי יוסי אמר אם אתה
נותן לי כל כסף וזהב. ואני בעניי השבתי שבלעם אמר לא אוכל לעבור, אבל אם
היה יכול לעבור היה לוקח ממון הרבה. והכא רבי יוסי אמר אם אתה נותן לי כל
כסף וזהב איני דר וכו' ונמצא מחפצו ורצונו אינו פונה לכסף וזהב. ובנחלת יעקב
תירץ דבלעם שאל דבר שיוכל לקיימו ורבי יוסי בן קיסמא אמר דבר שאי אפשר
לקיימו ואין ספק שדרך גוזמא קאמר.

It appears that Rabbi Yose's refusal to sacrifice his principles for money differs
little (and is couched in very similar language) from the wicked seer Bilam's
statement that even if Balak offered him all the silver and gold in his possession, he would refuse to curse *Klal Yisrael* (see *Bamidbar* 22:18). Yet, Bilam's
declaration is interpreted as an indication of his enormous greed, while Rabbi
Yose Ben Kisma's refusal to accept this lucrative position is portrayed as a
model for others to follow.

When asked this question as a young child, the *Chida* pointed out a subtle
distinction between their language. Bilam said, לֹא אוּכַל, *I cannot transgress
Hashem's word* (ibid.) — which implies that if he were permitted to do so, he
would. Rabbi Yose, on the other hand, stated unequivocally, "I would dwell
nowhere but in a place of Torah." It was his *choice* to remain in a Torah
environment.

In response to this question, the *Nachalas Yaakov* noted that Balak offered
— and Bilam refused — a *finite* amount (all the gold and silver contained in
Balak's domain). His conspicuous mention of a specific amount of money while
rejecting Balak's overture is indicative of his desire for that sum. On the other
hand, Rabbi Yose rejects *all* the wealth in the universe, which should be interpreted as his reaffirmation of the primacy of Torah in his life rather than as
a rejection of an offer that could never be made realistically (*Maggidei HaEmes*).

■ מֵאַלְפֵי זָהָב וָכָסֶף — *Above thousands in gold and silver.* ■

⊰ The Lessons Derived From Torah — Not From Money

אלפי לשון לימוד שלא רצה ללמוד על ידי זהב וכסף רק תורת פיך.

The term אַלְפֵי, traditionally translated as "thousands," may also be interpreted as the "teachings" (as in the Gemara term יַלְפִינָן, *we learn*). The
lessons derived from Torah — whose insights pertain to every aspect of life —
are far better than the advice garnered from a lifetime of experience dealing

[10] *Five possessions did the Holy One, Blessed is He, acquire for Himself in His world, and they are:*

with gold and silver.

■ אֶלָּא תּוֹרָה וּמַעֲשִׂים טוֹבִים בִּלְבָד — *But only Torah study and good deeds.*

⋙ "Pure" Torah And Good Deeds (Maasim Tovim)

פירוש בלבד ר״ל אותה התורה ואותם המעשים טובים שהם בלבד, שעסק בהם רק לכבודו ית׳ בלבד, בלי שום השתתפות הנאת עצמו כלל, הם מלוין לו לאדם בשעת פטירתו.

The term בִּלְבָד, *only*, implies that *only* the Torah studied for its own sake — and not for personal profit — and *only* those good deeds performed in a similar fashion escort the soul upon its departure from this world (R' Yechiel of Mosh, *Maggidei HaEmes*).

10.

■ בֵּית . . . יִשְׂרָאֵל . . . אַבְרָהָם . . . שָׁמַיִם וָאָרֶץ . . . תּוֹרָה . . . חֲמִשָּׁה קְנָיָנִים הַמִּקְדָּשׁ — *Five acquisitions . . . Torah . . . heaven and earth . . . Avraham . . . Yisrael . . . the Beis HaMikdash.*

⋙ The Purpose of These Kinyanim (Acquisitions)

פירוש כי הקב״ה אין להשיגו ולדבוק בו מרוב עוצם קדושתו שהוא קדוש ונבדל ולכן הכין הקב״ה חמשה קנינים שעל ידיהם יכולין לדבוק בו יתברך על ידי התורה ובית המקדש וכו׳.

The purpose of these *acquisitions* is to enable mortals, who are so removed from Hashem's infinite sanctity, to develop a relationship with Him. By marveling at the infinite symmetry of heaven and earth, Hashem's handiwork; by following the sterling example of Avraham Avinu who brought many of his contemporaries closer to Hashem; by appreciating and benefiting from the unique role of the *Beis HaMikdash* and *Eretz Yisrael* — *Klal Yisrael* can acquire an intimate relationship with its Creator.

⋙ Fulfilling Adam's Mission

אילו היה אדם הראשון נשאר כמות שהיה היה לזה קיום לתמיד. ואחר כך שקלקל

וְאֵלּוּ הֵן: תּוֹרָה – קִנְיָן אֶחָד, שָׁמַיִם וָאָרֶץ – קִנְיָן אֶחָד,
אַבְרָהָם – קִנְיָן אֶחָד, יִשְׂרָאֵל – קִנְיָן אֶחָד, בֵּית

היה צריך להיות על ידי חמשה קנינים.

Had Adam not sinned, then he, himself created directly by Hashem and in His image, would have served as the perfect testament to Hashem's existence. Through his own righteous personality he would have been regarded as the best guarantor of the universe's continued existence. With Adam's tragic downfall, the universe's future now hinges upon the five acquisitions enumerated here (*Pnei Menachem, Maggidei HaEmes*).

⊷§ Testifying to Creation

כי אלו הקנינים צריכים אלה לאלה. ועל ידי שישראל מעידין עליו ית' נעשה שמים
וארץ קנינו ית' וכו', וכן כתוב באברהם שהקנה להקב"ה שמים וארץ.

According to the *Chiddushei HaRim*, these acquisitions are closely interrelated and share the common objective of teaching mankind that Hashem created the universe. *Klal Yisrael* fulfills its historic mission by testifying to Hashem's creation of heaven and earth, a mission that was fulfilled with distinction by Avraham Avinu. As *Chazal* note, שֶׁהִקְנָה לְהקב"ה שָׁמַיִם וָאָרֶץ, *Avraham "acquired" heaven and earth for Hashem* by teaching mankind that Hashem had created the universe (*Tanchuma, Acharei* 9:1).

■ תּוֹרָה קִנְיָן אֶחָד — *Torah, one acquisition.*

⊷§ Finding Hashem Through Torah Study

ובעת הגלות כ' ואמר כי אין אלקי בקרבי כו', הסתר אסתיר כו' אבל הש"י נמצא
לבנ"י באמצעיות התורה והקב"ה צוה למרע"ה לגנוז כל ההארות בתוך הספר
תורה. ולכן נקרא התורה עדות שהשכינה שורה בישראל.

Even during periods of exile, when the Divine Presence is not overtly revealed, Hashem can be "found" through Torah study. When Hashem commanded Moshe to write the Torah (*Devarim* 31:19), He in effect was telling him to subsume the light of His Presence in the Torah. By immersing himself in Torah study, the Jew can "find" the *Shechinah*. Thus, the Torah is called עֵדוּת, *testimony*, because it is the greatest evidence of Hashem's Presence (*Sfas Emes, Vayeilech* 5645).

◆§ Torah Is Perfect

שזה שלימות התורה למשוך בחי' התחתונות להראשית.

Torah is called perfect because of its ability to raise mortals, possessed by the values of the material world, to the lofty standards of Hashem. There can be no greater perfection than linking man to his creator (*adapted from Sfas Emes, Nasso 5636*).

◆§ Emunas Chachamim

אמונת חכמים היא יסוד התורה.

While by virtue of immersion in Torah an individual can accomplish much, there exists another element of Torah that can only be attained through trust in Torah sages. As stated in *Avos* 1:1, the Torah was transmitted from generation to generation. This heritage can only be appreciated by association with the Torah luminaries of every generation (*Sfas Emes, Nasso 5637*).

◆§ Achieving Greatness in Torah

והנה למה הי' צריך הבורא ית' לתת התורה באופן זה . . . והי' יכול לדבר עם
בנ"י באופן טבעי אבל רצה להראות לדורות שא"א להתקרב אל התורה רק ע"י
מסירת נפש.

Hashem gave Israel the Torah in a supernatural setting (e.g. fire, lightning, thunder) — even though He could have spoken to us in a perfectly natural context — to underscore that true Torah greatness can only be attained by renouncing the material pleasures of This World (*Sfas Emes, Va'eschanan 5638*).

◆§ Negating Oneself to Torah

מי שיכול לבטל עצמו אל התורה ולהיות קל ע"פ המים שממית עצמו על התורה
ואז יכול לרדת במים עמוקים אלו.

Just as anyone can wade in shallow water, so too one can appreciate the surface level of Torah. However, in order to swim in deeper, more turbulent water, an individual must be lighter than the Torah (lest he sink if he is heavier). So too, by negating oneself to Torah, one can plumb its inner depth (*Sfas Emes*, *Ki Savo* 5652).

■ שָׁמַיִם וָאָרֶץ מִנַּיִן — *From where do we know this about heaven and earth?*

⇜ Heaven and Earth

מנין שנאמר כו' מלאה הארץ קנינך, י״ל דמכ״ש שמים דהפי' קנין כאן היינו שהוא
דבר חשיבות לפני הקב״ה ומכיון שהארץ הדום רגליו הוא חשיבות וקנין מכש״כ
השמים שהוא כסאו, וקשה דהול״ל קונה שו״א על שמים וארץ קנין א'.

While the *pasuk* cited from *Tehillim* (104:24) only explicitly mentions that Hashem created the earth, we may draw the following logical conclusion. If the earth, identified in the previous citation (*Yeshayahu* 66:1) as being merely Hashem's "footstool," is considered a Divine acquisition, then certainly heaven itself, Hashem's throne, deserves similar status. However, it is somewhat surprising that the *mishnah* does not prove that heaven and earth are acquisitions from the *pasuk* that is used to prove Avraham's role, where heaven and earth are both explicitly mentioned.

■ אַבְרָהָם מִנַּיִן — *From where do we know this about Avraham?*

⇜ Avraham's Role

אברהם אבינו השריש מלכות שמים ולימד לעשות ברכה בשם ומלכות, ברוך
אברם לא-ל עליון, קודם לכן היה נקרא אלקי השמים ועכשיו אלקי הארץ.

Citing *Rashi* (*Bereishis* 24:6), the *Pnei Menachem* noted that prior to Avraham, Hashem was perceived as the God of heaven whose influence was confined to that sphere. With Avraham's advent as a messenger of monotheism, mankind came to appreciate that Hashem reigned on earth, as well. Moreover, Avraham influenced Shem to recite the first *berachah* acknowledging Hashem as the sole Creator of heaven and earth, as indicated by the *pasuk* cited here, בָּרוּךְ אַבְרָם לְאֵל עֶלְיוֹן קֹנֵה שָׁמַיִם וָאָרֶץ, *Blessed is Avram of God the Most High, Who acquired heaven and earth* (*Bereishis* 14:19) (*Pnei Menachem, Maggidei HaEmes*).

⇜ Avraham — "The Watchman"

שהאבות תקנו חטא האדם ונפתח להם שערי ג״ע ועץ החיים . . . ואברהם . . .
הוא עצמו השומר.

The *Avos's* great deeds helped rectify the sin of Adam. The gates of Eden, guarded closely by the Cherubs, were opened for them. In fact, they were assigned the same function as the Cherubs, to guard Eden (cf. *Bereishis* 18:19 in which Avraham is depicted as the watchman of the road to Hashem). As the guards of Eden's gates, the Patriarchs could enter Eden at will. Likewise, they could imbibe from the spiritual treasures of the Tree of Life (*Sfas Emes, Vayeira* 5662).

ᵴ Chessed Avraham

ולעתיד נאמר על יצחק אתה אבינו . . . אבל בעוה"ז חסד יבנה ונשענין בזכות אברהם אע"ה.

While in This World, based on kindness, the Jewish People cling to the merit of Avraham who personified *chessed*. In the World to Come, the time of the Final Judgment, they will rely upon the virtues of Yitzchak who demonstrated perfect trust in Hashem at the *Akeidah* (*Sfas Emes, Vayeira* 5656).

אבל אברהם אע"ה הוציא מכח אל הפועל בכלל התגלות החסד בעולם.

Although Hashem's kindness is inherent in the universe, Avraham, by virtue of his own kindness, brought this Divine virtue into the open (*Sfas Emes,* 5653).

ᵴ Overcoming Trials

אבל כשהוציא אאע"ה אלה הדברים מכח אל הפועל נעשה מזה הכנה לכל איש ישראל שיוכל לבטל את הטבע בשביל מצות המקום.

By remaining true to Hashem through ten trials (cf. above 5:3), Avraham enabled his descendants to overcome every natural force that might prevent them from serving Hashem (adapted from *Sfas Emes, Vayeira* 5659).

∎ יִשְׂרָאֵל קִנְיָן אֶחָד ∎ — *Israel, one acquisition.*

ᵴ Eretz Yisrael and Am Yisrael

ובנ"י צריכין לארץ ישראל וא"י צריכה לבנ"י לכן כשבאו בנ"י לא"י נגמר צורת א"י.

הַמִּקְדָּשׁ — קִנְיָן אֶחָד. תּוֹרָה מִנַּיִן? דִּכְתִיב: „יהוה קָנָנִי
רֵאשִׁית דַּרְכּוֹ, קֶדֶם מִפְעָלָיו מֵאָז.״ שָׁמַיִם וָאָרֶץ מִנַּיִן?
דִּכְתִיב: „כֹּה אָמַר יהוה, הַשָּׁמַיִם כִּסְאִי, וְהָאָרֶץ הֲדֹם
רַגְלַי, אֵי זֶה בַיִת אֲשֶׁר תִּבְנוּ לִי, וְאֵי זֶה מָקוֹם מְנוּחָתִי״;
וְאוֹמֵר: „מָה רַבּוּ מַעֲשֶׂיךָ יהוה, כֻּלָּם בְּחָכְמָה עָשִׂיתָ,
מָלְאָה הָאָרֶץ קִנְיָנֶךָ.״ אַבְרָהָם מִנַּיִן? דִּכְתִיב: „וַיְבָרְכֵהוּ
וַיֹּאמַר, בָּרוּךְ אַבְרָם לְאֵל עֶלְיוֹן, קֹנֵה שָׁמַיִם וָאָרֶץ.״
יִשְׂרָאֵל מִנַּיִן? דִּכְתִיב: „עַד יַעֲבֹר עַמְּךָ יהוה, עַד יַעֲבֹר
עַם זוּ קָנִיתָ״; וְאוֹמֵר: „לִקְדוֹשִׁים אֲשֶׁר בָּאָרֶץ הֵמָּה,
וְאַדִּירֵי כָּל חֶפְצִי בָם.״ בֵּית הַמִּקְדָּשׁ מִנַּיִן? דִּכְתִיב:
„מָכוֹן לְשִׁבְתְּךָ פָּעַלְתָּ יהוה, מִקְּדָשׁ אֲדֹנָי כּוֹנְנוּ יָדֶיךָ״;
וְאוֹמֵר: „וַיְבִיאֵם אֶל גְּבוּל קָדְשׁוֹ, הַר זֶה קָנְתָה יְמִינוֹ.״

The Land of Israel needs *Klal Yisrael*, it cannot tolerate any other nations and the Divine Presence cannot dwell there unless *Klal Yisrael* is there. Similarly, *Klal Yisrael* requires the Land. It can be said that the Land's true nature was only completed when the Jewish people entered (*Sfas Emes, Masei* 5647).

◆§ Eretz Yisrael's Kedushah

כמו שנתגלה הארה וקדושה בא״י בבוא בנ״י לשם כמו כן ירדה הארה וקדושה
לנפשות בנ״י בבואם לא״י . . . ולכן הזהיר הכתוב שלא להשאיר מרשעים כי הם
היו מעכבים התגלות הקדושה.

Upon entering the Land of Israel, the Jewish People received a Divine infusion of holiness similar to the additional soul we receive every Shabbos. Permitting the Canaanites to linger in the land blocked the full penetration of this newfound spirituality (ibid. 5646).

■ בֵּית הַמִּקְדָּשׁ קִנְיָן אֶחָד — *The Beis HaMikdash, one acquisition.*

◆§ Perceiving the Universe's Daily Renewal

בזמן הבמ״ק הי׳ מתעורר חיות והתחדשות . . . בכל יום יש דרך חדש . . . אבן
בזמן המקדש הי׳ בהתגלות.

Beis HaMikdash, one acquisition. From where do we know this about the Torah? Since it is written (Mishlei 8:22): "Hashem acquired me [the Torah] at the beginning of His way, before His works in times of yore." From where do we know this about heaven and earth? Since it is written (Yeshayahu 66:1): "So says Hashem: The heaven is My throne, and the earth is My footstool; what House can you build for Me, and where is the place of My rest?" And it says (Tehillim 104:24): "How abundant are Your works, Hashem, with wisdom You made them all, the earth is full of Your possessions." From where do we know this about Avraham? Since it is written (Bereishis 14:19): "And he blessed him and said: Blessed is Abram of God the Most High, Who acquired heaven and earth." From where do we know this about the people Israel? Since it is written (Shemos 15:16): "Until Your people passes through, Hashem, until it passes through — this people You acquired," and it [also] says (Tehillim 16:3): "But for the holy ones who are in the earth and for the mighty all my desires are due to them." From where do we know this about the Beis HaMikdash? Since it is written (Shemos 15:17): "Your dwelling place which You, Hashem, have made; the Sanctuary, my Lord, that Your hands established." And it says (Tehillim 78:54): "And He brought them to His sacred boundary, to this mountain which His right hand acquired."

While the *Beis HaMikdash* existed, the Jewish People could perceive Hashem's daily renewal of the universe.

While we know that Hashem renews the universe every day, only the person who is truly God-fearing can discern the subtle shifts in Hashem's management that occur daily. In particular, the Jew in the Diaspora has difficulty sensing this reality. In the *Beis HaMikdash*, however, Hashem's daily renewal and its subtle variations were readily apparent (*Sfas Emes, Korach 5643; Ki Savo 5641*).

◄§ Extra Spirituality

[יא] כָּל מַה שֶׁבָּרָא הַקָּדוֹשׁ בָּרוּךְ הוּא בְּעוֹלָמוֹ לֹא בְרָאוֹ אֶלָּא לִכְבוֹדוֹ, שֶׁנֶּאֱמַר: ,,כֹּל הַנִּקְרָא בִשְׁמִי וְלִכְבוֹדִי בְּרָאתִיו, יְצַרְתִּיו אַף עֲשִׂיתִיו"; וְאוֹמֵר: ,,יהוה יִמְלֹךְ לְעוֹלָם וָעֶד."

❧ ❧ ❧

רַבִּי חֲנַנְיָא בֶּן עֲקַשְׁיָא אוֹמֵר: רָצָה הַקָּדוֹשׁ בָּרוּךְ הוּא לְזַכּוֹת אֶת יִשְׂרָאֵל, לְפִיכָךְ הִרְבָּה לָהֶם תּוֹרָה וּמִצְוֹת, שֶׁנֶּאֱמַר: ,,יהוה חָפֵץ לְמַעַן צִדְקוֹ יַגְדִּיל תּוֹרָה וְיַאְדִּיר."

כמו שיורד נשמה יתירה לבנ״י בש״ק כן הי׳ הארה יתירה בירושלים.

Just as every Shabbos, the Jew enjoys the spiritual infusion provided by the extra soul, so too in the *Beis HaMikdash* every Jew would benefit from an extra dose of spirituality (*Sfas Emes, Devarim* 5642).

∾§ A Proper Atmosphere

מכח השלום שהי׳ בבנ״י שלא הי בהם קנאה ושנאה שהכיר כל אחד מקום הראוי לו זכו לבנין בהמ״ק.

Only by eradicating the root causes of the *Beis HaMikdash's* destruction can we hasten its rebuilding. Baseless hatred led to the destruction of the *Beis HaMikdash*. An atmosphere of love and an absence of jealousy were prerequisites for remaining in *Eretz Yisrael* and the *Beis HaMikdash's* continued existence. In fact, the Jewish People were counted and allotted their individual portions in *Eretz Yisrael* before entering there, to minimize possible jealousy (*Sfas Emes, Pinchas* 5648).

■ וַיְבִיאֵם אֶל גְּבוּל קָדְשׁוֹ הַר זֶה קָנְתָה יְמִינוֹ — *And He brought them to His sacred boundary, to this mountain which His right hand acquired.*

∾§ Two Batei Mikdashos

בהמ״ק כו׳ שנאמר מקדש כו׳ ואומר ויביאם א״ג קדשו כו׳ י״ל הכוונה על ב׳ בתי מקדשות.

[11] *All that the Holy One, Blessed is He, created in His world, He created solely for His glory, as it is said (Yeshayahu 43:7): "All that is called by My Name, indeed, it is for My glory that I have created it, and made it." And it says (Shemos 15:18): "Hashem shall reign for all eternity."*

❧ ❧ ❧

Rabbi Chanania ben Akashia says: The Holy One, Blessed is He, wished to confer merit upon Israel; therefore He gave them Torah and mitzvos in abundance, as it is said (Yeshayahu 42:21): "Hashem desired, for the sake of its [Israel's] righteousness, that the Torah be made great and glorious."

The apparent redundancy describing the *Beis HaMikdash* as "His sacred boundary" as well as "the mountain of His acquisition" indicates that both the First and Second *Beis HaMikdash* were Divine acquisitions.

11.

■ *All that* — כָּל מַה שֶּׁבָּרָא הַקָּדוֹשׁ בָּרוּךְ הוּא בְּעוֹלָמוֹ לֹא בְרָאוֹ אֶלָּא לִכְבוֹדוֹ *the Holy One, Blessed is He, created in His world, He created solely for His glory.*

◂§ Klal Yisrael's Unique Role

הגם שכל מה שברא הקב"ה לכבודו בראו, אולם בני ישראל מיוחדים לזה כמו שכתוב ברוך אלקינו שבראנו לכבודו.

The statement of our *mishnah* that everything was created for Hashem's glory was not meant in any fashion to denigrate *Klal Yisrael's* unique role as a perpetual, living testament to the honor of Heaven. Indeed, we say in our daily prayers, בָּרוּךְ אֱלֹקֵינוּ שֶׁבְּרָאָנוּ לִכְבוֹדוֹ, *Blessed be our G-d Who created us for His Glory* (*Imrei Emes, Maggidei HaEmes*).